Tenth
Edition

Critical Thinking

Brooke Noel Moore
Richard Parker
California State University, Chico

Chapter 12
by Nina Rosenstand and Anita Silvers

McGraw Hill

Connect
Learn
Succeed™

*Connect
Learn
Succeed*™

Published by McGraw-Hill, a business unit of The McGraw-Hill Companies, Inc., 1221 Avenue of the Americas, New York, NY 10020. Copyright © 2012, 2009, 2007, 2004, 2001, 1998, 1995, 1991 by The McGraw-Hill Companies, Inc. All rights reserved. No part of this publication may be reproduced or distributed in any form or by any means, or stored in a database or retrieval system, without the prior written consent of The McGraw-Hill Companies, Inc., including, but not limited to, any network or other electronic storage or transmission, or broadcast for distance learning. Some ancillaries, including electronic and print components, may not be available to customers outside the United States.

This book is printed on acid-free paper.

3 4 5 6 7 8 9 0 RJE/RJE 0 9 8 7 6 5 4 3

ISBN: 978-0-07-803828-0
MHID: 0-07-803828-6

Vice President, Editorial: *Michael Ryan*
Director, Editorial: *Beth Mejia*
Sponsoring Editor: *Mark Georgiev*
Development Editor: *Susan Messer*
Editorial Coordinator: *Amy Flauaus*
Marketing Director: *Allison Jones*
Marketing Manager: *Pamela Cooper*
Media Project Manager: *Shannon Gattens*
Production Editor: *Ruth Sakata Corley*
Cover Designer: *Laurie Entringer*
Manager, Photo Research: *Brian J. Pecko*
Buyer II: *Louis Swaim*
Production Service: *Matrix Productions, Inc.*
Composition: *10/12 Trump Medieval by Lachina Publishing Services*
Printing: *45# New Era Matte by R.R. Donnelley & Sons*

Cover image: ©Jose Luis Stephens/Radius Images/Getty Images; iPhone: © Kacper Kida / Alamy

Credits: The credits section for this book begins on page 535 and is considered an extension of the copyright page.

Library of Congress Cataloging-in-Publication Data

Moore, Brooke Noel.
    Critical thinking / Brooke Noel Moore, Richard Parker. — 10th ed.
        p. cm.
    Includes bibliographical references and index.
    ISBN-13: 978-0-07-803828-0 (alk. paper)
    ISBN-10: 0-07-803828-6 (alk. paper)
    1. Critical thinking.   I. Parker, Richard (Richard B.).   II. Title.
    B105.T54M66 2012
    160—dc22

                                                                    2010050768

The Internet addresses listed in the text were accurate at the time of publication. The inclusion of a website does not indicate an endorsement by the authors or McGraw-Hill, and McGraw-Hill does not guarantee the accuracy of the information presented at these sites.

www.mhhe.com

Brief Table of Contents

Table of Contents

Chapter 11 Causal Explanation 389

List of Boxes

Moore & Parker's *Critical Thinking*

More Engaging . . . More Relevant . . . More Student Success

Imagine a class where students are actively and personally engaged in thinking critically while also discovering how to apply those thinking skills in everyday life. Now imagine those same students confidently participating in class, working efficiently through the exercises outside class, and performing better in the course.

With *Connect Critical Thinking*, students can achieve this success. *Connect Critical Thinking* is a first: a learning program that integrates adaptive diagnostic instruction with pedagogical tools that are anchored in research on critical thinking.

Along with Moore & Parker's **engaging writing style** and the wealth of topical exercises and examples that are **relevant to students' lives**, *Connect Critical Thinking* helps ensure that students can come to class confident and prepared. What other course provides students with skills they can apply so broadly to **success in school and success in life?**

More Engaging

Moore & Parker are known for their fresh and lively writing style. They rely on their own classroom experience and on feedback from instructors in getting the correct balance between explication and example.

■ Examples and exercises are drawn from today's headlines.

■ Students learn to apply critical thinking skills to situations in a wide variety of areas: advertising, politics, the media, popular culture.

I love the sense of humor of the authors, the very clear and elegant way they make critical thinking come alive with visuals, exercises and stories.

—Gary John, *Richland College*

[Before reading this chapter] most students don't realize the extent of product placement and other similar attempts at subtle manipulation.

—Christian Blum, *Bryant & Stratton, Buffalo*

---

392   CHAPTER 11: CAUSAL EXPLANATION

Real Life

Behavioral Causal Explanations

Associated Press file, 2003

North Korea's march toward acquiring nuclear weapons could instigate an arms race in the Asia-Pacific region. Japan and South Korea have had the capability to enter the nuclear-weapons club but have not done so because they have had confidence in the U.S. nuclear umbrella.

This photo's caption is a behavioral causal explanation, explained in this chapter.

reference not to the past but to the future. Why did Peter leave class early? He wanted to get home in time to watch *American Idol*. Why did the union vote not to approve the contract? The contract contained provisions that members thought diminished benefits. Why is the governor asking the legislature to approve a state lottery? Because she thinks it will decrease the need for new taxes. Explanations in terms of reasons and motives are forward looking, not backward looking.

One mistake is peculiar to this type of explanation—namely, failing to see the difference between *a reason* for doing something and *a particular person's reason* for doing it. Let's take a simple example: There might be a reason for aiding homeless people, but that reason might not be any particular person's reason for helping them. We have to be clear about whether we are requesting (or giving) reasons for doing something, or whether we are requesting (or giving) some individual person's reasons for doing it. When we give a reason for doing something, we are presenting an *argument* for doing it. When we cite an individual person's reason for doing it, we are *explaining* why she or he did it.

More Relevant

Moore & Parker spark student interest in skills that will serve them throughout their lives, making the study of critical thinking a meaningful endeavor.

■ *Real Life* boxes show students how critical thinking skills are relevant to their day-to-day lives.

■ Striking visuals in every chapter show students how images affect our judgment and shape our thinking.

> *I particularly like the "real world" boxes and the "media" boxes, which will help students connect critical thinking to their everyday lives.*
>
> —Michelle Darnell, *Fayetteville State University*

> *The variety [in the exercises] was outstanding. [They] will provide ample opportunity for the students to put into practice the various logical principles being discussed.*
>
> —Ray Darr, *Southern Illinois University*

Real Life

Which Is It Going to Be, Springfield?

This   or   **THIS!**

This was the message on a flyer urging a "no" vote on a proposed zoning law change in a western city. Since the photos depict only two (fairly extreme) alternatives, and given that there are surely many other reasonable ones, the flyer presents an excellent example of a false dilemma.

winter. You also know that the only heating options available in their location are gas and electricity. Under these circumstances, if you find out that they do *not* have electric heat, it must indeed be true that they must use gas heat because that's the only alternative remaining. False dilemma occurs only when reasonable alternatives are ignored. In such cases, both X and Y may be false, and some other alternative may be true.

Therefore, before you accept X because some alternative, Y, is false, make certain that X and Y cannot *both* be false. Look especially for some third alternative, some way of rejecting Y without having to accept X. Example:

MOORE: Look, Parker, you've been worrying about whether you could afford that bigger house on the corner for over a year. You need to grit your teeth and just get used to staying where you are without the extra space.

Moore's alternatives (buying the house on the corner or making use of some obvious but unmentioned alternatives—another house to buy, bigger than his present one but smaller than the corner; or he might remodel his current house for less expense than buying the corner house.

Parker could point out that there is more than one alternative. Aside from the obvious "either X or Y" way of thinking, we can use the form "If not X, then Y."

In the Media

The Daschle Salute

This looks like a big-time "Oops!" moment for Tom Daschle, former majority leader in the U.S. Senate. In fact, as explained in the text, it is a clever attempt to influence opinion against Daschle through photo manipulation.

The photos in the box "Now You See Him—Now You Don't" on the previous page are from Hong Kong's newspaper, *The Standard*, from September 2, 2004. The original photo (lower right) showed China's then paramount leader Deng Xiaoping (in the gray jacket on the right) shaking hands with Hu Jintao (wearing the tie), who has been China's president since 2003. The person between them in the original photo is former President Jiang Zemin. We don't know what might have become of Jiang's reputation (he continued in high office for some years after the photo was made), but his image suffered a disappearing act.

In the next box, "The Daschle Salute," it looks as though Tom Daschle (the majority leader in the Senate at the time) doesn't know how to salute the flag or doesn't know his right hand from his left. In reality, he did it correctly, but someone reversed his image, flipping it right-to-left so that he appeared to be saluting with his left hand rather than his right. There are two clues to the doctoring that went on in this photo. It would take not just a critical thinker but a sharp eye to spot them. The first is that Daschle is married and wears a wedding ring. If this were really his left hand, one would see his ring. The second clue is more convincing. It's that his coat is buttoned backwards: Men's clothing always has buttons on the right side of the garment, so it's the left side that closes over the right. In the photo, the right side of Daschle's jacket closes over the left, indicating that it isn't just his hand that is on the wrong side, his clothing would have to be reversed, too!

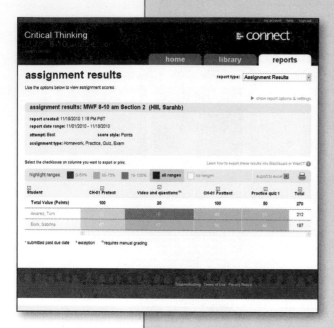

More Student Success

Moore & Parker provide a path to student success, making students active participants in their own learning while teaching skills they can apply in all their courses.

- Learning objectives link to chapter sections and in turn to print and online activities, so that students can immediately assess their mastery of the learning objective.

- Exercises are now dispersed throughout the chapters rather than grouped at the end, so that they link more tightly with the concepts as they are presented.

- Instructors can assess students' command of the material—online and at any time—so that they don't have to wait for a midterm to assess their own progress.

- Students can use the adaptive diagnostic program throughout the course to identify gaps in their understanding, and as a result can go into any test confident in their mastery of critical thinking skills.

- Students have access to over 2,000 exercises that provide practice in applying their skills.

Hands-on, practical, and one might say, even "patient" with the students' learning as it emphatically repeats concepts and slowly progresses them step by step through the process.

—Patricia Baldwin, *Pitt Community College*

There are a lot of exercises, which provides nice flexibility. The . . . mix of relatively easy and more challenging pieces . . . is useful in providing some flexibility for working in class.

—Dennis Weiss, *York College of Pennsylvania*

---

is too ugly to eat" translates into the I-claim "Some examples of boiled okra are things that are too ugly to eat."

As we noted, it's not possible to give rules or hints about every kind of problem you might run into when translating claims into standard-form categorical versions. Only practice and discussion can bring you to the point where you can handle this part of the material with confidence. The best thing to do now is to turn to some exercises.

Exercise 8-1

Translate each of the following into a standard-form claim. Make sure that each answer follows the exact form of an A-, E-, I-, or O-claim and that each term you use is a noun or noun phrase that refers to a class of things. Remember that you're trying to produce a claim that's equivalent to the one given; it doesn't matter whether the given claim is actually true.

1. Every salamander is a lizard.
2. Not every lizard is a salamander.
3. Only reptiles can be lizards.
4. Snakes are the only members of the suborder Ophidia.
5. The only members of the suborder Ophidia are snakes.
6. None of the burrowing snakes are poisonous.
7. Anything that's an alligator is a reptile.
8. Anything that qualifies as a frog qualifies as an amphibian.
9. There are frogs wherever there are snakes.
10. Wherever there are snakes, there are frogs.
11. Whenever the frog population decreases, the snake population decreases.
12. Nobody arrived except the cheerleaders.
13. Except for vice presidents, nobody got raises.
14. Unless people arrived early, they couldn't get seats.
15. Most home movies are as boring as dirt.
16. Socrates is a Greek.
17. The bank robber is not Jane's fiancé.
18. If an automobile was built before 1950, it's an antique.
19. Salt is a meat preservative.
20. Most corn does not make good popcorn.

Exercise 8-2

Follow the instructions given in the preceding exercise.

1. Students who wrote poor exams didn't get admitted to the program.
2. None of my students are failing.
3. If you live in the dorms, you can't own a car.
4. There are a few right-handed first basemen.
5. People make faces every time Joan sings.

Teaching with Moore & Parker's *Critical Thinking*

The complete content of Moore & Parker's *Critical Thinking* is available to instructors and students in traditional print format as well as online with integrated and time-saving tools.

McGraw-Hill's *Connect,* a new web-based assignment and assessment platform, connects students with their coursework and with their instructors. With *Connect Critical Thinking,* students no longer just read a textbook: they interact online with engaging activities and exercises. The result is a hands-on experience that deepens critical thinking skills.

Blackboard and McGraw-Hill Higher Education have teamed up! Now, all McGraw-Hill content (text, tools, and homework) can be accessed directly from within your Blackboard course—all with a single sign-on. Connect assignments within Blackboard automatically (and instantly) feed grades directly to your Blackboard grade center. No more keeping track of two grade books! Even if your institution is not currently using Blackboard, McGraw-Hill has a solution for you. Ask your sales representative for details.

Tegrity Campus is a service that makes class time available all the time by capturing audio and computer screen shots from your lectures in a searchable format for students to review when they study and complete assignments. With classroom resources available all the time, students can study more efficiently and learn more successfully.

CourseSmart, the largest provider of eTextbooks, offers students the option of receiving *Critical Thinking* as an eBook. At CourseSmart your students can take advantage of significant savings off the cost of a print textbook, reduce their impact on the environment, and gain access to powerful web tools for learning. CourseSmart eTextbooks can be viewed online or downloaded to a computer. Visit *www.CourseSmart.com* to learn more.

McGraw-Hill Create allows you to create a customized print book or eBook tailored to your course and syllabus. You can search through thousands of McGraw-Hill texts, rearrange chapters, combine material from other content sources, and include your own content or teaching notes. Create even allows you to personalize your book's appearance by selecting the cover and adding your name, school, and course information. To register and to get more information, go to *http://create.mcgraw-hill.com*.

Preface

CHANGES TO 10TH EDITION

Broad changes

- Learning objectives have been articulated and stated up front in each chapter.
- The text has been fully integrated with Connect, an online learning program with pedagogical tools anchored in research on critical thinking.
- Exercises have been interspersed within chapters, following each major section, so that students can more directly monitor their learning.
- Exercises have been updated to reflect current events and issues, and new exercise sets have been added to provide more practice for students.
- Examples of argument diagrams have been added to most chapters.

Chapter-specific changes

- Chapter 1, What *Is* Critical Thinking, Anyway?, has been completely rewritten in order to present a more direct, more clearly organized introduction. In addition, the chapter now includes new sections on important cognitive biases, fact and opinion, why one should bother to think critically, and what critical thinking can and cannot do.
- Chapter 2, Two Kinds of Reasoning, has new sections on pathos, ethos, and logos; what are NOT premises; balance-of-considerations arguments; and inference-to-best-explanation.
- Chapter 4, Credibility, has been reorganized to more accurately and logically present the topic.
- Chapter 5, Persuasion Through Rhetoric, has been reorganized to more logically group the multiple types of rhetorical devices.
- Chapter 9, Deductive Arguments II: Truth-Functional Logic, has a completely new section that provides a basic, introductory account of deductive arguments. Rather than proceed into the complications of deductions, this section deals at greater length with basic deductive argument forms—the sort of thing that was outlined previously on the inside back cover of the book.
- Chapter 10, Thinking Critically About Inductive Reasoning, has been completely rewritten for better coverage. In its new incarnation, the chapter includes sections on vague and glowing generalities, reasoning from general to general, the self-selection fallacy, and the principle of total evidence. In addition, the chapter has improved discussions of argument from analogy, scientific generalizing from samples, and everyday generalizing from samples. Illustrative evaluations of inductive reasoning have been added as well.

- Chapter 11, Causal Explanation, has an improved discussion of conditional probabilities in medical tests, and new exercises have been supplied.
- Can you guess the theme of the Chapter Openers?

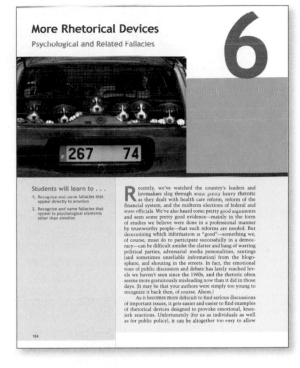

More Rhetorical Devices

Psychological and Related Fallacies

6

267 74

Students will learn to . . .

1. Recognize and name fallacies that appeal directly to emotion

2. Recognize and name fallacies that appeal to psychological elements other than emotion

184

Recently, we've watched the country's leaders and lawmakers slog through some pretty heavy rhetoric as they dealt with health care reform, reform of the financial system, and the midterm elections of federal and state officials. We've also heard some pretty good arguments and seen some pretty good evidence—mainly in the form of studies we believe were done in a professional manner by trustworthy people—that such reforms are needed. But determining which information is "good"—something we, of course, must do to participate successfully in a democracy—can be difficult amidst the clatter and bang of warring political parties, adversarial media personalities, rantings (and sometimes unreliable information) from the blogosphere, and shouting in the streets. In fact, the emotional tone of public discussion and debate has lately reached levels we haven't seen since the 1960s, and the rhetoric often seems more gratuitously misleading now than it did in those days. (It may be that your authors were simply too young to recognize it back then, of course. Ahem.)

As it becomes more difficult to find serious discussions of important issues, it gets easier and easier to find examples of rhetorical devices designed to provoke emotional, knee-jerk reactions. Unfortunately (for us as individuals as well as for public policy), it can be altogether too easy to allow

- Students rushing to register for Moore and Parker's course. *Inland Valley Daily Bulletin/*Thomas R. Cordova; appeared in the *Sacramento Bee*, 14 October 2006..

Acknowledgments

Despite the efforts of a lot of people, in a book this big and this complicated, errors slip by. Any you run across are the responsibility of either Moore or Parker, depending upon whom you happen not to be talking to. Certainly, errors are not the responsibility of the excellent people at McGraw-Hill who have helped us. These include Mark Georgiev, senior editor, whose insight and wisdom help in countless ways and who often returns telephone calls; Susan Messer, development editor, whose novel, *Grand River and Joy*, may move you at a deeper level than will this text, and who dragged us into making it clear, finally, what our learning objectives really are; Lisa Pinto, executive director of development; Amy Flauaus, editorial coordinator; Leslie Racanelli, lead production manager; Ruth Sakata Corley, production editor; Aaron Downey, production editor at Matrix Productions, Inc.; Barbara Hacha, copy editor; and Brian Pecko, photo researcher.

We have been fortunate to have the advice of the following reviewers of the current and previous editions as well as a number of others who have written to us about the book. Their guidance has been invaluable:

Keith Abney, California Polytechnic State University, San Luis Obispo
James Anderson, San Diego State University
Sheldon Bachus
Pat Baldwin, Pitt Community College
Tim Black, California State University, Northridge
Charles Blatz, University of Toledo
Christian Blum, Bryant & Stratton, Buffalo
Leah Blum
K. D. Borcoman, Coastline College/CSUDH
Keith Brown, California State University, East Bay
Melissa Brown
Lee Carter, Glendale Community College
David Connelly
Anne D'Arcy, California State University, Chico
Michelle Darnelle, Fayetteville State University
Ray Darr, Southern Illinois University, Edwardsville
Sandra Dwyer, Georgia State University
Aaron Edlin, University of California, Berkeley
Ellery Eells, University of Wisconsin-Madison
Ben Eggleston, University of Kansas
Geoffrey B. Frasz, Community College of Southern Nevada
Josh Fulcher
Rory Goggins
Geoffrey Gorham, University of Wisconsin-Eau Claire
Joseph Graves, North Carolina A&T University
Dabney Gray, Stillman College
Patricia Hammer, Delta College
Anthony Hanson, De Anza College
Judith M. Hill, Saginaw Valley State University
Steven Hoeltzel, James Madison University
J.F. Humphrey, North Carolina A&T University

Amro Jayousi
Gary John, Richland College
Sunghyun Jung
Allyn Kahn, Champlain College
David Keyt
William Krieger, California State University-Pomona
Michael LaBossiere, Florida A&M University
Marion Ledwig, University of Nevada-Las Vegas
Terrance MacMullon, Eastern Washington University
Eric Parkinson, Syracuse University
Steven Patterson, Marygrove College
Jamie L. Phillips, Clarion University
Scott Rappold, Our Lady of Holy Cross
Victor Reppert, Glendale Community College
Matt Roberts, Patrick Henry College
Greg Sadler, Fayetteville State University
Matt Schulte, Montgomery College
Richard Scott, Glendale Community College
Laurel Severino, Santa Fe Community College
Mehul Shah, Bergen Community College
Steven Silveria
Robert Skipper, St. Mary's University
Taggart Smith, Purdue University-Calumet
Richard Sneed, University of Central Oklahoma
Chris Soutter
Anne St. Germain
James Stump, Bethel College
Lou Suarez
Susan Vineberg, Wayne State University
Dennis Weiss, York College of Pennsylvania
Amy Goodman Wilson, Webster University
Christine Wolf
Marie G. Zaccaria, Georgia Perimeter College
Melinda Zerkle

Over the years, our Chico State colleague Anne Morrissey has given us more usable material than anybody else. She's also given us more unusable material, but never mind. We've also had fine suggestions and examples from Curtis Peldo of Chico State and Butte College; Dan Barnett, also of Butte College, has helped in many ways over the years.

We thank colleagues at Chico State, who are ever ready with a suggestion, idea, or constructive criticism; in particular, Marcel Daguerre, Randy Larsen, Becky White, Wai-hung Wong, Zanja Yudell, and Greg Tropea, whose recent death leaves us saddened beyond our ability to express. Greg was a dear friend whose deep wisdom and quiet insight contributed significantly to our thinking over the course of many years. We are also grateful to Bangs Tapscott, Linda Kaye Bomstad, Geoff Bartells, and Jeffrey Ridenour for contributions both archival and recent.

Lastly, and especially, we give thanks to the two people who put up with us with patience, encouragement, and grace, Alicia Alvarez *de* Parker and Marianne Moore.

A Note to Our Colleagues

Dear Colleagues,

Among the changes in this edition of *Critical Thinking* are several we'd like to bring to your attention here. If you are new to the book, don't let us talk past you. *Critical Thinking* is a guide to making wise decisions about what to think and do. It won't tell anyone whether God exists or who to vote for or when a recession will end. But it will help them spot bad reasons for having an opinion one way or the other, and recognize good reasons if they should run into them. It will also help them detect subtle, non-argumentative attempts at persuasion.

Possibly the most important change for this edition is that the book is now integrated with **Connect**, McGraw Hill's new online learning platform. Connect enables students to *personalize their learning* in ways that haven't heretofore been possible. With Connect, students can interact with each other and with their instructor online. Plus they can tackle real-life *simulations* that call on them to apply what they have learned. Connect also provides *self-assessments* keyed to *learning objectives* for each chapter of the text, which means students can proceed at their own pace. As an additional benefit, Connect can be integrated with **Blackboard** to simplify an instructor's course data management challenges.

Starting with this edition, the learning objectives we just mentioned are identified and listed at the beginning of each chapter. Even students who don't use Connect will benefit from knowing exactly what it is they are supposed to be getting from the material.

We also now for the first time *intersperse exercises* at the appropriate places within each chapter to help readers monitor their progress and reach learning objectives efficiently. Among these interspersed exercises as well as among those at the end of each chapter, you will find new ones here and there throughout the book.

Chapters 1 and 10 have been completely rewritten for this edition. Other chapters have been reorganized, especially Chapter 5 and, to a slightly lesser extent, Chapter 4. We especially like the new section in Chapter 1 on *cognitive biases*. Cognitive biases affect belief formation at an unconscious level and can interfere with clear thinking and sound reasoning. Moore thinks Parker has more cognitive biases than he does; Parker believes exactly the reverse. Thinking that you are less biased than others is itself a common cognitive bias.

Will learning about sources of bias help people think more clearly? At the very least it will underscore the importance of trying to think according to the standards of logic and good sense that are set forth in the book.

Another new section is *Ethos, Pathos, and Logos*. The section clarifies a distinction we regard as very important, the distinction between logic and persuasion. You may not agree with the distinction as we make it out, but at least you will see clearly what we think it is.

In this edition we also include in Chapter 9 an *introductory account of deductive argument forms*—for those who do not want to go into the complications of deductions. This account can stand alone as a basic treatment of categorical and truth-functional arguments. We have also revised the treatment of arguments from analogy and inductive arguments from samples, and we have added much-needed examples of inductive argument evaluations. Moreover, in response to comments from reviewers, we now discuss *Balance of Considerations* arguments as well as the *Principle of Total Evidence.*

Now, judging from parts of this preface we didn't write, you might think we two are clever devils whose refreshing and informal prose will make students stash their iPhones and work on critical thinking exercises. We can't promise any such thing, however. We are in fact two philosophy professors who have been teaching critical thinking so long we creak. We now have children of former students in our classes. Having spent so many years behind the podium, we have strong ideas about what critical thinking is, and we have devised ways of presenting material that engage students. What we have learned is reflected in this book.

These days you see much headshaking about the deplorable lack of critical thinking in the world. Everyone agrees that the need for critical thinking has never been greater. At the same time, the concept of critical thinking has become so marvelously inclusive that most educators are certain that *they* at any rate teach it in *their* courses—whatever their courses may be. This is exactly what you'd expect if the word *critical* had lost its power to differentiate critical thinking from other kinds of thinking. In this edition we emphasize that what distinguishes *critical thinking* from other kinds of thinking is precisely what the phrase originally conveyed: Critical thinking involves *thinking about thinking*. It's what happens, if it does, when you subject other thinking to a *critique*. This edition stresses that critical thinking is not just any old kind of mental grunting; it makes it clear you can be thinking hard or scientifically or creatively and so forth, and still fail to think critically.

About the Authors

Brooke Noel Moore and Richard Parker, not necessarily in the order pictured above.

Both Moore and Parker have taught philosophy at California State University, Chico, for more years than they care to count. Aside from courses in logic and critical thinking, Moore also tries to teach epistemology and analytic philosophy. He is also past chair of the department and once was selected as the university's Outstanding Professor. Parker's other teaching duties include courses in the history of modern philosophy and philosophy of law; he has chaired the academic senate and once upon a time was dean of undergraduate education.

Moore majored in music at Antioch College; his Ph.D. is from the University of Cincinnati. For a time he held the position of the world's most serious amateur volleyball player. He and Marianne currently share their house with three large dogs. Moore has never sold an automobile.

Parker's undergraduate career was committed at the University of Arkansas; his doctorate is from the University of Washington. He drives a '62 MG, rides a motorcycle, plays golf for fun, shoots pool for money, and is a serious amateur flamenco guitarist. He and Alicia live part of the year in southern Spain.

Moore and Parker have been steadfast friends through it all.

To Alexander, Bill, and Sherry,
and also to Sydney, Darby,
Peyton Elizabeth, and Griffin

This is not entirely a work of nonfiction.

WHAT *IS* CRITICAL THINKING, ANYWAY?

If you attend a university, we'd bet you hear a lot about critical thinking. Perhaps you will hear your professors telling you how important it is, or how dismayed they are there isn't more of it in today's world. Unfortunately, you may not be entirely sure what exactly it is they think is lacking. If you listen for a while you may get the idea that whatever it is, all your professors are certain *they* emphasize it in *their* courses. You may even get the idea that for many of them "critical thinking" is mainly just whatever it is they happen to teach—sociology, history, business, communications, or whatever.

Is there any common ground among educators about what critical thinking is? Yes! Most educators probably agree that a person who jumps to conclusions or makes ill-formed, indefensible, knee-jerk decisions has *not* thought critically. A while back we read about a teenager who was spotted shoplifting; the police were called and arrested the young man. While they were reading him his rights, he shook out of their grasp and made a run for it. Unfortunately, as he made his break his huge trousers tripped him, and that was the end of his getaway.* Everyone will agree that trying

---

*The lad had not been handcuffed, the police perhaps assuming his trousers would serve the same purpose.

Students will learn to . . .

1. Define critical thinking

2. Distinguish objective claims from subjective claims

3. Understand subjectivism as it relates to moral claims

4. Identify issues

5. Define and identify premises and conclusions

6. Recognize an argument

7. Define and identify twelve common cognitive biases

8. Understand the terms *truth* and *knowledge* as used in this book

to run from the police, especially when your pants are on the ground, is not thinking well, let alone thinking critically. This may seem like an unimportant or frivolous example, but it really is not much different in principle from signing on for mortgage payments that are more than you earn, or—if you are a mortgage broker or an insurance company—betting that people who do that will be able to manage the trick.

What, then, is critical thinking? Clearly it involves more than just blindly acting or reacting. Every educator will concede that critical thinking aims at making wise decisions and coming to correct conclusions, and not being waylaid by temptation, emotion, greed, irrelevant considerations, stupidity, bias, or other similar things.

To refine this a bit, on the one hand there is good, old-fashioned thinking. That's what we do when we form opinions or judgments, make decisions, arrive at conclusions, and the like. On the other hand, there's *critical* thinking. That's what we do when we *critique* the first kind of thinking—subject it to rational evaluation. You might say that *critical thinking involves thinking about thinking;* we engage in it when we consider whether our thinking (or someone else's) abides by the criteria of good sense and logic.

Possibly you've taken courses where all you have to do is remember stuff. But in other courses—and in the workplace or in the military—you will perhaps have been asked to do more—maybe to design or evaluate something, to make a proposal or diagnose a situation, to explain or comment on something, or to do any number of other things that involve coming to conclusions. Possibly it worked this way: your instructor or colleagues or friends or supervisors read or listened to your findings, then *they* offered critical commentary. *They* gave you feedback (usually, we hope, positive). *They* evaluated your reasoning. If you are brilliant, you may not have needed their feedback. If you are brilliant, perhaps you never err in your thinking or leave room for other criticism. But most of us do occasionally make mistakes in reasoning. We overlook important considerations and ignore viewpoints that conflict with our own, and in other ways we don't think as clearly as we might. Most of us can benefit from a little critical commentary—even when it comes from ourselves. Our chances of producing a good essay or offering a sound proposal or making a wise decision improve if we don't simply write or propose or decide willy-nilly, but reflect on our reasoning and try to make it better. Our chances of thinking well improve, in other words, if we think *critically:* if we critique our own thinking as a thinking coach might.

This is a book in *critical* thinking because it offers guidance about *critiquing* thinking. The book, and the course you are using it in, if you are, explain the minimum criteria of good reasoning—the requirements a piece of reasoning must meet, no matter what the context, if it is worth paying attention to. Along the way we will explore the most common and important impediments to good reasoning, as well as some of the most common mistakes people make when coming to conclusions. Other courses you take at the university offer refinements. In them you will learn what considerations are important from the perspective of individual disciplines. But in no course anywhere, at least in no course that involves arriving at conclusions, will thinking that violates the standards set forth in this book be accepted. If it does nothing else, what you read here and learn in your critical thinking course should help you avoid at least a few of the more egregious common errors people make when they reason. If you would have otherwise made these mistakes, you will

In Depth

Critical Thinking, the Long Version

In the text, we give a couple of brief characterizations of critical thinking, and as shorthand they will serve well enough. But the Collegiate Learning Assessment (CLA) Project of the Council for Aid to Education has come up with a list of skills that covers almost everything your authors believe is important in critical thinking. If you achieve mastery over all these or even a significant majority of them, you'll be well ahead of most of your peers—and your fellow citizens. In question form, here is what the council came up with:

How well does the student

- determine what information is or is not pertinent;
- distinguish between rational claims and emotional ones;
- separate fact from opinion;
- recognize the ways in which evidence might be limited or compromised;
- spot deception and holes in the arguments of others;
- present his/her own analysis of the data or information;
- recognize logical flaws in arguments;
- draw connections between discrete sources of data and information;
- attend to contradictory, inadequate, or ambiguous information;
- construct cogent arguments rooted in data rather than opinion;
- select the strongest set of supporting data;
- avoid overstated conclusions;
- identify holes in the evidence and suggest additional information to collect;
- recognize that a problem may have no clear answer or single solution;
- propose other options and weigh them in the decision;
- consider all stakeholders or affected parties in suggesting a course of action;
- articulate the argument and the context for that argument;
- correctly and precisely use evidence to defend the argument;
- logically and cohesively organize the argument;
- avoid extraneous elements in an argument's development;
- present evidence in an order that contributes to a persuasive argument?

<http://www.aacu.org/peerreview/pr_sp07_analysis1.cfm>

have become smarter. Not smarter in some particular subject, mind you, but smarter in general. The things you learn from this book (and from the course you may be reading it for) apply to nearly any subject people can talk or think or write about.

To a certain extent, questions we should ask when critiquing our own—or someone else's—thinking depend on what is at issue. Deciding whom to vote for, whether to buy a house, whether a mathematical proof is sound, which toothpaste to buy, or what kind of dog to get involve different considerations. In all cases, however, we should want to avoid making or accepting weak and invalid arguments. We should also avoid being distracted by irrelevancies or

■ The judges critique dancers on *Dancing With The Stars*, but that doesn't automatically qualify as thinking critically.

being ruled by emotion, succumbing to fallacies or bias, and being influenced by dubious authority or half-baked speculation. These are not the only criteria by which reasoning might be evaluated, but they are central and important, and they provide the main focus of this book.

BELIEFS AND CLAIMS

Why bother thinking critically? As we just said, the ultimate objective in thinking critically is to come to conclusions that are correct and to make decisions that are wise. Because our decisions reflect our conclusions, we can simplify things by saying that the purpose of thinking critically is to come to correct conclusions; the method used to achieve this objective is to evaluate our thinking by the standards of rationality. Of course, we can also evaluate someone else's thinking, though the objective there might simply be to help the person.

When we come to a conclusion, we have a belief. Concluding involves believing. If you *conclude* the battery is dead, you *believe* the battery is dead. Keeping this in mind, let's define a few key terms.

A belief is, obviously, something you believe. It is important to understand that a belief is *propositional*, which means it can be expressed in a declarative sentence—a sentence that is either true or false. A good bit of muddleheaded thinking can be avoided if you understand that beliefs are propositional entities, but more on this later.

As we use these words, *beliefs* are the same as *judgments* and *opinions*. When we express a belief (or judgment or opinion) in a declarative sentence, the result is a *statement* or *claim*, and for our purposes these are the same thing. Claims can be used for other purposes than to state beliefs, but this is the use we're primarily concerned with.

Objective Claims and Subjective Claims

Before we say something more about conclusions, we should make a distinction between claims that are objective and those that are subjective. An **objective claim** has this characteristic: whether it is true or false is independent of whether people think it is true or false. "There is life on Mars" is thus an objective claim, because whether or not life exists there doesn't depend on whether people think it does. If everyone suddenly believed there is life on Mars, that doesn't mean that suddenly there would be life on Mars. Likewise, "God exists" is an objective claim because whether it is true doesn't depend on whether people think it is true.

Although objective claims are either true or false, we may not know which a given claim is. "Portland, Oregon, is closer to the North Pole than to the Equator" is a true objective claim. "Portland, Oregon, is closer to the Equator than to the North Pole" is a false objective claim. "More stamp collectors live in Portland, Oregon, than in Portland, Maine" is an objective claim whose truth or falsity is not known, at least not by us.

Not every claim is objective, of course. "Barack Obama is one cool daddy" is not objective, for it lacks the characteristic mentioned previously. That is, whether or not someone is one cool daddy does depend on whether people think he is. If nobody thinks Barack Obama is one cool daddy, then he isn't. If Parker thinks Barack Obama is one cool daddy and Moore doesn't, you will say that Parker and Moore are each entitled to his opinion. That's because whether someone is one cool daddy is in the eyes of the beholder.

Claims of this variety are **subjective claims.** Whether a subjective claim is true or false is not independent of whether people think it is true or false. Examples of subjective claims would be judgments of taste, such as "Rice vinegar is too sweet." Is rice vinegar too sweet? It depends on what you think. Some kinds of comparisons also are subjective. Is snow boarding more fun than

A rescue team in action. Not thinking critically about your decision to ski in avalanche conditions can have grave consequences.

In Depth

Thinking About Thinking

A subjective statement is made true by someone's thinking it is true. Does this mean that statements about what someone is thinking are subjective? The answer is no, though it may take a second to see this. Take the statement "Joanie is thinking of moving." What makes that statement true, if it is, is *not* Joanie's thinking that the *statement* is true. What makes it true is that Joanie is thinking of *moving.* A statement about what someone is thinking is an objective statement about what is going on in the person's mind.

skiing? Again, it depends on what you think, and there is no further "truth" to consider. However, many statements contain both objective and non-objective elements, as in "Somebody stole our nifty concrete lawn duck." Whether the lawn duck is *concrete* is an objective question; whether it is *our* lawn duck is an objective question; and whether it was *stolen* is an objective question. But whether the stolen concrete lawn duck is *nifty* is a subjective question.

Fact and Opinion

Sometimes people talk about the difference between "fact" and "opinion," having in mind the notion that *all* opinions are subjective. But some opinions are not subjective, because their truth or falsity is independent of what people think. Again, in this book "opinion" is just another word for "belief." If you believe that Portland, Oregon, is closer to the North Pole than to the Equator, your opinion happens to be true, and would continue to be true even if you change your mind. You can refer to objective opinions as *factual* opinions or beliefs, if you want—*but that doesn't mean factual opinions are all true.* "Portland, Oregon, is closer to the Equator than to the North Pole" is a factual opinion that is false.

So: factual opinion/belief/claim = objective opinion/belief/claim = opinion/belief/claim whose truth/falsity is independent of what anyone thinks.

Moral Subjectivism

"There is nothing either good or bad, but that thinking makes it so," said Hamlet, nicely expressing a point of view known as **moral subjectivism.** Some beginning critical thinking students, like Hamlet, assume that when you ascribe a moral property to something, your claim is purely subjective: whether something is good or bad or right or wrong depends entirely on what you think. Is bullfighting wrong? Well, as moral subjectivists say, it's a matter of opinion, and one opinion is as correct as the next.

You should be wary of the notion that all moral opinions are subjective or that one moral opinion is as correct as the rest. Consider the following real-life event. (We must warn you the example is very unpleasant. Unfortunately, it often takes an example of this sort to get the point across.) In Kelsey

Creek Park in Bellevue, Washington,* three teenage boys sneaked into a corral where lived a twenty-one-year-old donkey, a favorite of local children. The boys attempted to ride the donkey, but the animal didn't cooperate. Annoyed, the boys picked up tree limbs and hit him. As the donkey weakened, the boys intensified their beating until he could no longer stand. They then found a piece of rope and used it to suspend the donkey from a tree so that he strangled to death.

Now ask yourself: If these boys didn't think their actions were wrong, would that make them right? Of course you wouldn't say that. If you could have stopped the beating simply by yelling at them, with no danger to yourself, would you have done it? Of course you would. A person who truly believed that any evaluation of the boys' behavior was as good as any other is someone we'd consider very peculiar indeed—and possibly defective in some way.

By now you should not be surprised to learn that most moral philosophers reject the notion that moral opinions are all purely subjective. Most would say that the rightness and wrongness of actions is independent of what people think. They would say that, regardless of what anyone might believe, it would be wrong to torture donkeys or execute orphans for kicks. They would say that, even if by some chain of events, *everyone* came to think it was okay to stone women to death when they are accused of adultery, it still wouldn't be okay to stone a woman to death for that or any other reason.

Now that you know what opinions and claims are, and understand the difference between objective opinions/claims and subjective opinions/claims, and see that some opinions/claims that at first blush seem to be subjective perhaps are not really so, we can talk about issues. Then we will get back to conclusions.

ISSUES

An issue, as we employ that concept in this book, is simply a question. Is Moore taller than Parker? When we ask that question, we raise the issue as to *whether* Moore is taller than Parker. To put it differently, we are considering whether the claim "Moore is taller than Parker" is true. Let us note in passing that as with claims, some questions or issues are **objective questions or issues.** Is Moore taller than Parker? Whether he is or isn't doesn't depend on whether we think he is, so this is an objective question.

Other issues, such as whether Simon Cowell dresses well, are subjective, in the sense explained previously.

The first order of business when it comes to thinking critically about an issue is to determine what, exactly, the issue *is*. Unfortunately, in many real-life situations, it is difficult to identify exactly what the issue is—meaning it is difficult to identify exactly what claim or belief is in question. This happens for lots of reasons, from purposeful obfuscation to ambiguous terminology to plain muddleheaded thinking. In his inaugural address President Warren G. Harding said,

> We have mistaken unpreparedness to embrace it to be a challenge of the reality and due concern for making all citizens fit for participation will give added strength of citizenship and magnify our achievement.

*April, 1992.

Do you understand what issue Harding is addressing? Neither does anyone else, because his statement is perfectly meaningless. (American satirist H. L. Mencken described it as a "sonorous nonsense driven home with gestures."*) Understanding what is meant by a claim has so many aspects that we'll devote a large part of Chapter 3 to the subject.

However, if you have absolutely no clue as to what an issue actually is, there isn't much point in considering it further—you don't know what "it" is. There also isn't much point in considering it further if you have no idea as to what would count toward settling it. For example, suppose someone asks, "Is there an identical you in a different dimension?" What sort of evidence would support saying either there is or isn't? Nobody has any idea. (Almost any question about different "dimensions" or "planes" or "universes" would be apt to suffer from the same problem unless, possibly, it were to be raised from someone well educated in physics who used those concepts in a technical way.) "Is everything really one?" would also qualify as something you couldn't begin to settle, as would wondering if "the entire universe was created instantly five minutes ago with all false memories and fictitious records."** And how about "Is there an invisible gremlin inside my watch that works the alarm?"

Obscure issues aren't always as metaphysical as the preceding examples. Listen carefully and you may hear more than one politician intone, "It is human nature to desire freedom." Oh, really? Well—saying so is a good sound bite—but when you look closely at the claim, it's hard to know exactly what sort of data would support it.

This isn't to imply that only issues that can be settled through scientific test or via the experimental method are worth considering. Moral issues cannot be settled in that way, for example. Mathematical and historical questions are not answered by experiment, and neither are important philosophical questions. Does God exist? Is there free will? What difference does it make if he does or doesn't or there is or isn't? Legal questions, questions of aesthetics—the list of important questions not subject to purely scientific resolution—is very long. The point here is merely that if a question is to be taken seriously, or if you want others to take it seriously, or if you want others who can think critically to take it seriously, you must have *some* idea as to what considerations bear on the answer.

ARGUMENTS

Jamela is trying to decide whether she should get a dog—specifically, a sweet little Shih Tzu puppy a friend wants to give her. Let's give the little dog a name and call him Priglet. Priglet, let's imagine, is rambunctious and adorable, and Jamela is sorely tempted.

After giving it careful thought, Jamela decides to get Priglet. She thinks, "I love little Priglet; I can take care of him, and I see no reason not to get him." When we set forth reasons for accepting a claim, we produce an **argument,** and that is exactly what Jamela has done. She has given herself reasons for accepting the claim "I should get Priglet."

---

*Reported on NBC News, *Meet the Press*, January 16, 2005.
**This famous example comes from philosopher Bertrand Russell.

Two concepts are traditionally used in talking about arguments. A reason for accepting a claim is expressed in something called a **premise;** the claim itself is called the **conclusion.**

So let's portray Jamela's argument this way:

Premises: I love Priglet; I can take care of him, and I can see no reason not to take him.

Conclusion: Therefore, I should get him.

Jamela's issue has been whether she should get Priglet. Notice that Jamela's conclusion represents her position on that issue. You should always think of the conclusion of an argument as stating a position on an issue, and of premises as giving reasons for taking that position.

What does this have to do with critical thinking? Jamela wants to make the best decision on an important question. She has concluded she should get Priglet. If she wants to think critically, she goes back over her reasoning and evaluates it.

Whether Jamela's reasoning is good depends on how much support her premises provide for accepting her conclusion. Later we'll examine the underlying principles of argument evaluation in depth, but for now we should point out two things so that you may get a general idea of the critical thinking process. First, a premise can offer support for a conclusion only if the premise is *true.* Second, it can offer support only if it is *relevant* to the conclusion. It must actually bear on the truth of the conclusion. Sometimes this is expressed by saying the premise must be *cogent.*

One of Jamela's premises stands out for especially careful consideration: "I can take care of him." This premise is relevant to Jamela's conclusion, but is it true? Can Jamela find the time to exercise Priglet? Does she have a place for doing it? What will she do with Priglet if she goes on a trip? What happens to Priglet in the summer, when Jamela lives at her parents' house?

The more carefully Jamela has thought about things originally, the less time she will need to spend reviewing her reasoning. Of course, she can't know how much her original thinking needs reviewing until she actually attempts to review it. Thinking critically is very much like writing an essay: When you write an essay, first you compose a draft; then you revise and improve your draft as often as it takes to make your essay as good as it can be. Likewise, when you think critically, you go over your original thinking several times to make it as airtight as it can be. Are you the kind of person who reasons well the first time? Some people are. Unfortunately, there is reason to believe that people who aren't very proficient at reasoning are the most likely to overestimate their reasoning ability. *

The analysis and evaluation of arguments will occupy us at length later, so for now let's make sure we understand the definition of "argument."

An **argument** consists of two parts; one part of which (the premise or premises) is intended to provide a reason for accepting the other part (the conclusion).

---

*See Justin Kruger and David Dunning, "Unskilled and Unaware of It: How Difficulties in Recognizing One's Own Incompetence Lead to Inflated Self-Assessments," *Psychology*, 2009, 1, 30–46.

Critical thinking happens, then, when we evaluate the thinking we or someone else has used in coming to a conclusion on an issue. Thus it will not surprise you to learn that we devote a great deal of time and space in this book to arguments and their proper analysis and evaluation.

Three minor points about arguments are worth noticing now:

1. Unfortunately, the word "argument" is sometimes used to refer to someone's reason for thinking something, as in "That's a good argument for not getting a dog." When "argument" is used this way, it refers to an argument's premise. In this book, to avoid confusion, when we speak of a person's argument, we will be referring to the person's premise *together with* his or her conclusion.

2. Jamela's argument was straightforward and easy to understand. Don't suppose all arguments are that way. Einstein's conclusion that $E = mc^2$ was proved by complex theoretical reasons requiring a lot of mathematics and physics to comprehend, and together they amounted to an argument that $E = mc^2$.

3. Not every issue requires an argument for resolution. Is your throat sore? There isn't room here for an argument; you can just tell directly and conclusively whether your throat is sore. Whether or not an issue requires an argument for resolution may itself be an issue, however.

Critical thinking, as we have explained it, happens when we submit our thinking, or the thinking of others, to the tribunal of logic and good sense. Unfortunately, there is no guarantee when we do this that we will always arrive at the truth. It is a rare individual who, even after painstaking deliberation, never acts unwisely or accepts contentions that turned out in hindsight to be false. We humans have an inborn taste for salt and fat and sugar and other things beyond what is good for us; likewise, we are wired to process information in ways that aren't necessarily in our best interest or that don't reflect reality accurately. In the next section we will look at psychological factors that impede clear thought.

Critical thinking won't immunize us against all errors in thinking—but the criteria set forth in this book are those that our thinking must adhere to, to qualify as rationally grounded.

The following exercises will test your understanding of the concepts of critical thinking, argument, premise, conclusion, and issue, and the difference between objective and subjective claims.

Exercise 1-1

Answer the questions based on your reading to this point, including the boxes.
▲—See answer key in back of book.

▲   1. What is an argument?
2. T or F: A claim is what you use to state an opinion or a belief.
3. T or F: Critical thinking consists in attacking other people's ideas.
▲   4. T or F: Whether a passage contains an argument depends on how long it is.

5. T or F: When a question has been asked, an issue has been raised.

6. T or F: All arguments have a premise.

▲ 7. T or F: All arguments have a conclusion.

8. T or F: You can reach a conclusion without believing it is true.

9. T or F: Beliefs, judgments, and opinions are the same thing.

▲ 10. T or F: All opinions are subjective.

11. T or F: All factual claims are true.

12. "There is nothing either good or bad but that thinking makes it so" expresses a doctrine known as _____.

▲ 13. The first order of business when it comes to thinking critically about an issue is (a) to determine whether the issue is subjective or objective (b) to determine whether the issue can be resolved (c) neither of these.

14. T or F: The conclusion of an argument states a position on an issue.

15. T or F: Issues can be resolved only through scientific testing.

▲ 16. T or F: Critical thinking is a foolproof way of avoiding errors in thinking.

17. T or F: The claim "Death Valley is an eyesore" is subjective.

18. T or F: Every issue requires an argument for a resolution.

▲ 19. Which one of these doesn't belong? (a) therefore (b) consequently (c) thus (d) since (e) so

20. T or F: It is not possible to reason correctly if you do not think critically.

On the basis of a distinction covered in this chapter, divide these items into two groups of five items each such that all the items in one group have a feature that none of the items in the second group have. Describe the feature on which you based your classifications. The items that belong in one group are listed in the back of the book.

Exercise 1-2

▲ 1. You shouldn't buy that car because it is ugly.

2. That car is ugly, and it costs more than $25,000, too. *therefore that's a complete waste of $*

3. Rainbows have seven colors, although it's not always easy to see them all. *2 connected things*

▲ 4. Walking is the best exercise. It places the least stress on your joints. *Reason with*

5. The ocean on the central coast is the most beautiful shade of sky blue, but it gets greener as you go north. *w/ Reason ≠ argument*

6. Her favorite color is yellow because it is the color of the sun. *w/o Reason is explanation*

▲ 7. Pooh is my favorite cartoon character because he has lots of personality. *w/o is explanation*

8. You must turn off the lights when you leave the room. They cost a lot of money to run, and you don't need them during the day. *Reason*

9. Television programs have too much violence and immoral behavior. Hundreds of killings are portrayed every month.

▲ 10. You'll be able to find a calendar on sale after the first of the year, so it is a good idea to wait until then to buy one.

■ Can bears and other animals think critically? Find out by checking the answer section in the back of the book.

Exercise 1-3

Which of the following claims are objective?

▲ 1. Bob Dylan's voice was perfect for the folk music of the sixties.
2. On a baseball field, the center of the pitcher's mound is 59 feet from home plate.
3. Staring at the sun will damage your eyes.
▲ 4. Green is the most pleasant color to look at.
5. Yellow is Jennifer's favorite color.
6. With enough experience, a person who doesn't like opera can come to appreciate it.
▲ 7. Opera would be easier to listen to if they'd leave out the singing.
8. Sailing is much more soothing than sputtering about in a motorboat.
9. Driving while drowsy is dangerous.
▲ 10. Pit vipers can strike a warm-blooded animal even when it is pitch dark.
11. Sarah Palin looks very presidential.
12. Sarah Palin looks very presidential to me.

Exercise 1-4

Which of the following are subjective?

▲ 1. Leno tells better jokes than Letterman.
2. Mays hit more home runs than McGwire.
3. Your teacher will complain if you wear a baseball cap in class.
▲ 4. Your teacher should complain if you wear a baseball cap in class.
5. There is life on Mars.

6. Golf is a waste of time.

▲ 7. *Halloween IV* scared the you-know-what out of my sister.

8. *Halloween IV* was lousy. A total letdown.

9. Movies like *Halloween IV* lack redeeming social value. [Hint: an assertion might have more than one subjective element.]

▲ 10. John Kerry has quite an unusual chin.

Exercise 1-5

Some of these items are arguments, and some are not. Can you divide them up correctly?

▲ 1. Federer is unlikely to win the U.S. Open this year. He has a nagging leg injury, plus he just doesn't seem to have the drive he once had.

2. Hey there, Marco! Don't go giving that cat top sirloin. What's the matter with you? You got no brains at all?

3. If you've ever met a pet bird, you know they are very busy creatures.

▲ 4. Everybody is saying the president earned the Nobel Prize. What a stupid idea! He hasn't earned it at all. There's not a lick of truth in that notion.

5. "Is the author really entitled to assert that there is a degree of unity among these essays which makes this a book rather than a congeries? I am inclined to say that he is justified in this claim, but articulating this justification is a somewhat complex task."

—From a book review by Stanley Bates

6. As a long-time customer, you're already taking advantage of our money management expertise and variety of investment choices. That's a good reason for consolidating your other eligible assets into an IRA with us.

▲ 7. PROFESSOR X: Well, I see where the new chancellor wants to increase class sizes.
PROFESSOR Y: Yeah, another of his bright ideas.
PROFESSOR X: Actually, I don't think it hurts to have one or two extra people in class.
PROFESSOR Y: What? Of course it hurts. Whatever are you thinking?
PROFESSOR X: Well, I just think there are good reasons for increasing the class size a bit.

8. Yes, I charge a little more than other dentists. But I feel I give better service. So I think my billing practices are justified.

9. Since you want to purchase the house, you should exercise your option before June 30, 2011. Otherwise, you will forfeit the option price.

▲ 10. John Montgomery has been the Eastern Baseball League's best closer this season. Unfortunately, when a closer fails, as Montgomery did last night, there's usually not much chance to recover. Draw your own conclusion.

Exercise 1-6

Determine which of the following passages contain arguments. For any that do, identify the argument's conclusion. Remember: an argument occurs when one or more claims (the premises) are offered as a reason for accepting the other claim (the conclusion). There aren't hard-and-fast rules for identifying arguments, so you'll have to read closely and think carefully about some of these.

▲ 1. The Directory of Intentional Communities lists more than 200 groups across the country organized around a variety of purposes, including environmentally aware living.

2. Carl would like to help out, but he won't be in town. We'll have to find someone else who owns a truck.

3. In 1976, Washington, D.C., passed an ordinance prohibiting private ownership of firearms. Since then, Washington's murder rate has shot up 121 percent. Bans on firearms are clearly counterproductive.

▲ 4. Computers will never be able to converse intelligently through speech. A simple example proves this. The sentences "How do you recognize speech?" and "How do you wreck a nice beach?" have different meanings, but they sound similar enough that a computer could not distinguish between the two.

5. Recent surveys for the National Science Foundation report that two of three adult Americans believe that alien spaceships account for UFO reports. It therefore seems likely that several million Americans may have been predisposed to accept the report on NBC's *Unsolved Mysteries* that the U.S. military recovered a UFO with alien markings.

6. "Like short-term memory, long-term memory retains information that is encoded in terms of sense modality and in terms of links with information that was learned earlier (that is, meaning)."

—*Neil R. Carlson*

▲ 7. Fears that chemicals in teething rings and soft plastic toys may cause cancer may be justified. Last week, the Consumer Product Safety Commission issued a report confirming that low amounts of DEHP, known to cause liver cancer in lab animals, may be absorbed from certain infant products.

■ Think you are welcome? Think again and think critically.

8. "It may be true that people, not guns, kill people. But people with guns kill more people than people without guns. As long as the number of lethal weapons in the hands of the American people continues to grow, so will the murder rate."

—*Susan Mish'alani*

9. June 1970: A Miami man gets thirty days in the stockade for wearing a flag patch on the seat of his trousers. March 2008: Miami department stores sell boxer trunks made up to look like an American flag. Times have changed.

▲ 10. Dockers are still in style, but pleats are out.

For each numbered passage, identify which lettered item best states the primary issue discussed in the passage. Be prepared to say why you think your choice is the correct one.

▲ 1. Let me tell you why Hank ought not to take that math course. First, it's too hard, and he'll probably flunk it. Second, he's going to spend the whole term in a state of frustration. Third, he'll probably get depressed and do poorly in all the rest of his courses.

    a. whether Hank ought to take the math course
    b. whether Hank would flunk the math course
    c. whether Hank will spend the whole term in a state of frustration
    d. whether Hank will get depressed and do poorly in all the rest of his courses

2. The county has cut the library budget for salaried library workers, and there will not be enough volunteers to make up for the lack of paid workers. Therefore, the library will have to be open fewer hours next year.

    a. whether the library will have to be open fewer hours next year
    b. whether there will be enough volunteers to make up for the lack of paid workers

3. Pollution of the waters of the Everglades and of Florida Bay is due to multiple causes. These include cattle farming, dairy farming, industry, tourism, and urban development. So it is simply not so that the sugar industry is completely responsible for the pollution of these waters.

    a. whether pollution of the waters of the Everglades and Florida Bay is due to multiple causes
    b. whether pollution is caused by cattle farming, dairy farming, industry, tourism, and urban development
    c. whether the sugar industry is partly responsible for the pollution of these waters
    d. whether the sugar industry is completely responsible for the pollution of these waters

▲ 4. It's clear that the mainstream media have lost interest in classical music. For example, the NBC network used to have its own classical orchestra conducted by Arturo Toscanini, but no such orchestra exists now. One newspaper, the no-longer-existent *Washington Star*, used to have thirteen classical music reviewers; that's more than twice as many as the *New York Times* has now. H. L. Mencken and other columnists used to devote considerable space to classical music; nowadays, you almost never see it mentioned in a major column.

    a. whether popular taste has turned away from classical music
    b. whether newspapers are employing fewer writers on classical music
    c. whether the mainstream media have lost interest in classical music

5. This year's National Football League draft lists a large number of quarterbacks among its highest-ranking candidates. Furthermore, quite a number of teams do not have first-class quarterbacks. It's therefore likely that an unusually large number of quarterbacks will be drafted early in this year's draft.

    a. whether teams without first-class quarterbacks will choose quarter-backs in the draft

    b. whether this year's NFL draft includes a large number of quarterbacks

    c. whether an unusually large number of quarterbacks will be drafted early in this year's draft

6. An animal that will walk out into a rainstorm and stare up at the clouds until water runs into its nostrils and it drowns—well, that's what I call the world's dumbest animal. And that's exactly what young domestic turkeys do.

    a. whether young domestic turkeys will drown themselves in the rain

    b. whether any animal is dumb enough to drown itself in the rain

    c. whether young domestic turkeys are the world's dumbest animal

▲ 7. The defeat of the school voucher initiative was a bad thing for the country because now public schools won't have any incentive to clean up their act. Furthermore, the defeat perpetuates the private-school-for-the-rich, public-school-for-the-poor syndrome.

    a. whether public schools now have any incentive to clean up their act

    b. whether the defeat of the school voucher initiative was bad for the country

    c. Two issues are equally stressed in the passage: whether public schools now have any incentive to clean up their act and whether the private-school-for-the-rich, public-school-for-the-poor syndrome will be perpetuated

8. From an editorial in a newspaper outside Southern California: "The people in Southern California who lost a fortune in the wildfires last year could have bought insurance that would have covered their houses and practically everything in them. And anybody with any foresight would have made sure there were no brush and no trees near the houses so that there would be a buffer zone between the house and any fire, as the Forest Service recommends. Finally, anybody living in a fire danger zone ought to know enough to have a fireproof or fire-resistant roof on the house. So, you see, most of the losses those people suffered were simply their own fault."

    a. whether fire victims could have done anything to prevent their losses

    b. whether insurance, fire buffer zones, and fire-resistant roofs could have prevented much of the loss

    c. whether the losses people suffered in the fires were their own fault

9. "Whatever we believe, we think agreeable to reason, and, on that account, yield our assent to it. Whatever we disbelieve, we think contrary to reason, and, on that account, dissent from it. Reason, therefore, is allowed to be the principle by which our belief and opinions ought to be regulated."

               —*Thomas Reid,* Essays on the Active Powers of Man

    a. whether reason is the principle by which our beliefs and opinions ought to be regulated

    b. whether what we believe is agreeable to reason

    c. whether what we disbelieve is contrary to reason

    d. both b and c

▲ 10. Most people you find on university faculties are people who are interested in ideas. And the most interesting ideas are usually new ideas. So
   most people you find on university faculties are interested in new ideas.
   Therefore, you are not going to find many conservatives on university
   faculties, because conservatives are not usually interested in new ideas.

   a. whether conservatives are interested in new ideas
   b. whether you'll find many conservatives on university faculties
   c. whether people on university faculties are interested more in new
      ideas than in other ideas
   d. whether most people are correct

COGNITIVE BIASES

Were we entirely rational, our conclusions would be grounded in logic and
based on evidence objectively weighed. Unfortunately, belief formation is
also affected by unconscious features of human psychology. Psychologists
refer to these features, some of which are unexpected and surprising, as cognitive biases. Cognitive biases skew our apprehension of reality and interfere
with our ability to think clearly, process information accurately, and reason
objectively.

■ When Glen Beck evaluates his and others' reasoning he is thinking critically, and when you evaluate his reasoning you are thinking critically.

   For example, we tend to evaluate an argument based on whether we agree
with it rather than on the criteria of logic. Is the following specimen good
reasoning?

> All dogs are animals.
> Some animals are German Shepherds.
> Therefore some dogs are German
> Shepherds.

   It isn't. You might as well conclude
some dogs are cats. After all, all dogs are
animals and some animals are cats. If it took
you a moment to see that the first argument
is illogical, it's because its conclusion is
something you know is true.

   The tendency to evaluate reasoning
by how believable its conclusion seems is
known as **belief bias.** Like other cognitive
biases, belief bias affects us unconsciously.
As you can see from the example, belief bias
may detract from our ability to think and
reason clearly. Unfortunately, this kind of
bias may be even more pronounced when
we evaluate extended pieces of persuasion,
in which underlying arguments are over-
laid with rhetorical flourishes. An editorial
favoring gun control, for example, or taking
a stand on illegal immigration may appear
especially well argued if its conclusion
accords with something we strongly believe.

Some cognitive biases involve **heuristics,** general rules we unconsciously follow in estimating probabilities.* An example is the **availability heuristic,** which involves unconsciously assigning a probability to a type of event on the basis of how often one thinks of events of that type. After watching multiple news reports of an earthquake or an airplane crash or a case of child abuse, thoughts of earthquakes and airplane crashes and child abuse will be in the front of one's mind. Accordingly, one may overestimate their probability. True, if the probability of airplane crashes were to increase, then one might well think about airplane crashes more often; but it does not follow that if one thinks about them more often, their probability has increased.

The availability heuristic may explain how easy it is to make the mistake known as generalizing from anecdote, a logical fallacy we discuss in Chapter 10. Generalizing from anecdote happens when one accepts a sweeping generalization based on a single vivid report. The availability heuristic is also probably related to the **false consensus effect,** which refers to the inclination we may have to assume that our attitudes and those held by people around us are shared by society at large.**

Another source of skewed belief is the **bandwagon effect,** which refers to an unconscious tendency to align one's thinking with that of other people. The bandwagon effect is potentially a powerful source of cognitive distortion. In famous experiments, psychologist Solomon Asch found that what other people say *they* see may actually alter what we think *we* see.† We—the authors—have students take tests and quizzes using smart phones and clickers, with software that instantly displays the opinion of the class in a bar graph projected on a screen. Not infrequently it happens that, if opinion begins to build for one answer, almost everyone switches to that option—even if it is incorrect or illogical.

If you have wondered why consumer products are routinely advertised as best sellers, you now know the answer. Marketers understand the bandwagon effect. They know that getting people to believe that a product is popular generates further sales.

Political propagandists also know we have an unconscious need to align our beliefs with the opinions of other people. Thus, they try to increase support for a measure by asserting that everyone likes it, or—and this is even more effective—by asserting that *nobody* likes whatever the opposition has proposed. "Nobody wants X!" is even more likely to generate support for alternative Y than is "Everyone wants Y!" This is because of **negativity bias,** the tendency people have to weight negative information more heavily than positive information when evaluating things. Negativity bias is hard-wired into us: the brain displays more neural activity in response to negative information than to positive information.†† A corollary to negativity bias from economics is that people generally are more strongly motivated to avoid a loss than to accrue a gain, a bias known as **loss aversion.**

---

*The field known as "heuristics and biases" was originated by Daniel Kahneman and Amos Tversky.

**See L. Ross, The "False Consensus Effect": An Egocentric Bias in Social Perception and Attribution Processes, *Journal of Experimental Social Psychology,* 13, 3, 279–301, May 1977.

†A copy of Asch's own summary of his experiments can be found at http://www.panarchy.org/asch/social.pressure .1955.html.

††See Tiffany A. Ito, and other authors, "Negative Information Weighs More Heavily on the Brain", *Journal of Personality and Social Psychology,* 1998, Vol. 75 No. 4, 887–900.

In Depth

Rational Choice?

Critical thinking is aimed at coming to correct conclusions and making wise choices or decisions. We know from everyday experience that desires, fears, personal objectives, and various emotions affect choices. As explained in the text, experimental psychologists have discovered other, more unexpected and surprising, influences on our thinking. Here are three additional examples:

- Social psychologist Dan Ariely found that when people are asked to write down the last two digits of their social security number and then submit mock bids for things like wine and chocolate, those with higher numbers submit higher bids. This is a phenomenon known as "anchoring," and it has been replicated in a variety of contexts.* When we are induced to think of a high numeral, for example, our thinking is "anchored" in the high-numeral range.

- In a recent experiment, researchers at Yale and Harvard Universities asked subjects to evaluate a job candidate by reading an applicant's resume, which had been attached to a clipboard. Some of the clipboards weighed ¾ pound; the others weighed 4½ pounds. Subjects holding the heavier clipboard rated the applicant as better overall. Evidently a "rational evaluation" of a person's qualifications is affected by irrelevant physical cues.**

- Amos Tversky and Daniel Kahneman famously found that people will go to more trouble to save money when buying a less expensive item than when buying a much costlier item, even when the savings would be the same.†

We might expect to see real-life manifestations of these phenomena. Paying to use a toilet on an airplane might be more upsetting than having to pay to use one in the terminal. If we were opening a restaurant, we'd not have too many items on our menu. Asking people to estimate whether the percentage of voters unhappy with the president is above or below 80% might yield a higher estimate than would asking them if it is above or below 40%.

---

*Reported by MIT psychologist Dan Ariely, *Predictably Irrational* (New York: HarperCollins Publishers, 2008).
**Reported by Randolph E. Schmid of the Associated Press, in *The Sacramento Bee*, June 23, 2010.
†See pages 19 and 20 of the book by Dan Ariely mentioned above.

It also should come as no surprise that we find it easier to form negative opinions of people who don't belong to our club, church, party, nationality, or other group. This is a part of **in-group bias,** another cognitive factor that may color perception and distort judgment. We may well perceive the members of our own group as exhibiting more variety and individuality than the members of this or that out-group, who we may view as indistinguishable from one another and as conforming to stereotypes. We may attribute the achievements of members of our own group to gumption and hard work and our failures to bad luck; whereas we may attribute *their* failures—those of the members of out-groups—to their personal shortcomings, while grudgingly discounting their achievements as mere good luck. The tendency to not appreciate that others' behavior is as much constrained by events and circumstances as our own would be if we were in their position is known as the **fundamental attribution error.**[*]

Experiments suggest that little common ground is required for people to forge a group identity. People assigned to a group on the basis of something as trivial as a coin flip will immediately begin exhibiting in-group and attribution biases.[**] In a famous experiment in social psychology, the Robber's Cave Experiment, twenty-two 12-year-old boys who previously hadn't known each other were divided arbitrarily into two groups. When the two groups were forced to compete, the members of each group promptly exhibited hostility and other indicators of in-group bias toward the members of the other group.[†]

People make snap judgments about who is and who is not a member of their group. Students transferring into a new high school are branded almost instantly. Once, one of the authors and his wife were walking their dogs, not necessarily the world's best-behaved pooches, along a street in Carmel, an affluent town on California's central coast. Stopping to tie his shoe, the author fell a few paces behind his wife, who continued on with the dogs. A well-dressed woman walking by glanced disapprovingly at the cavorting canines, perhaps because they were not pedigreed poodles, and thrust her chin in the air. An instant later she passed the author, with her chin still high. "Did you see that woman?" she asked indignantly, unaware that the woman in question was the wife of the man she was addressing. "You can tell she isn't from around here," she sniffed. She seemed to think the author, unlike his wife, was one of the in-group from her neck of the woods, though the only thing she had to base this on was that he didn't have a dog.

In a series of famous experiments in the 1960s regarding **obedience to authority,** psychologist Stanley Millgram discovered that a frightening percentage of ordinary men and women will administer apparently lethal electrical shocks to innocent people, when told to do so by an experimenter in a white coat.[††] The findings are subject to multiple interpretations and explanations, but the tendency of humans to obey authority simply for the sake of doing so hardly needs experimental confirmation. We read recently about a fake French TV game show that was much like the Millgram experiment. The host instructed contestants to deliver electrical shocks to an individual who was presented as another contestant, but who was really an actor. The contestants complied—right up to the point they had reason to think they might have killed the man. Whether they were simply blindly following the instructions of an authority or were responding to some other impulse isn't completely clear, but it is impossible to think that good judgment or rational thought would lead them to such excess.[§]

---

[*]E. E. Jones and V. A. Harris, "The Attribution of Attitudes," *Journal of Experimental Social Psychology,* 1967, *3,* 1–24. For in-group biases, see Henri Tajfel, *Human Groups and Social Categories,* (Cambridge, England: Cambridge University Press, 1981).

[**]See the work cited above by Henri Tajfel.

[†]A report of the Robber's Cave experiment is available online at http://psychclassics.yorku.ca/Sherif/.

[††]Millgram discusses his experiments in *Obedience to Authority: An Experimental View* (New York: Harpercollins, 1974).

[§]Jamey Keaton, Associated Press. Reported in *The Sacramento Bee,* Thursday, March 18, 2010. Did the subjects suspect the shocks weren't real? Their statements afterward don't rule out the possibility but certainly seem to suggest they believed they truly were administering painful electrical shocks to the actor.

Yet another possible source of psychological distortion is the **overconfidence effect**, one of several self-deception biases that may be found in a variety of contexts.* If a person estimates the percentage of his or her correct answers on a subject, the estimate will likely err on the high side—at least if the questions are difficult or the subject matter is unfamiliar.** Perhaps some manifestation of the overconfidence effect explains why, in the early stages of the *American Idol* competition, many contestants appear totally convinced they will be crowned the next American Idol—and are speechless when the judges inform them they cannot so much as carry a tune.[1]

Closely related to the overconfidence effect is the **better-than-average illusion.** The illusion crops up when most of a group rate themselves as better than most of the group relative to some desirable characteristic, such as resourcefulness or driving ability. The classic illustration is the 1976 survey of SAT takers, in which well over fifty percent of the respondents rated themselves as better than fifty percent of other SAT takers with respect to such qualities as leadership ability.†† The same effect has been observed when people estimate how their intelligence, memory, or job performance stacks up with the intelligence, memory, and job performances of other members of their profession or workplace. In our own informal surveys, more than eighty percent of our students rate themselves in the top ten percent of their class with respect to their ability to think critically.

Unfortunately, evidence indicates that even when they are informed about the better-than-average illusion, people may *still* rate themselves as better than most in their ability to not be subject to it.§

■ Does Simon Cowell dress well? The issue is *subjective*, or, as some people say, "a matter of opinion."

---

*However, a universal tendency among humans to irrationally exaggerate their own competencies hasn't been established. For an online quiz purportedly showing the overconfidence effect see: http://www.tim-richardson.net/joomla15/finance-articles-profmenu-70/73-over-confidence-test.html.

**See Sarah Lichtenstein and other authors, "Calibration of Probabilities: The State of the Art to 1980," in Daniel Kahneman, Paul Slovic, and Amos Iversky. *Judgment Under Uncertainty: Heuristics and Biases.* (Cambridge, England: Cambridge University Press, Cambridge, 1982), pp. 306–334.

†This possibility was proposed by Gad Saad, *Psychology Today,* http://www.psychologytoday.com/blog/homo-consumericus/200901/self-deception-american-idol-is-it-adaptive.

††See Mark D. Alicke and other authors in "The Better-Than-Average Effect," in Mark D. Alicke and others, *The Self in Social Judgment.* Studies in Self and Identity, Psychology Press, 2005, pp. 85–106. The better-than-average illusion is sometimes called the Lake Woebegone effect, in reference to Garrison Keillor's story about the fictitious Minnesota town "where all the children are above average."

§http://weblamp.princeton.edu/~psych/FACULTY/Articles/Pronin/The%20Bias%20Blind.PDF. The better-than-average bias has not been found to hold for all positive traits. In some things, people underestimate their abilities. The moral is that for many abilities, we are probably not the best judges of how we compare to others. And this includes our ability to avoid being subject to biasing influences.

That beliefs are generated as much by psychology and impulse as by evidence should come as no surprise. The new car that was well beyond our means yesterday seems entirely affordable today—though our finances haven't changed. If someone invited us to The Olive Garden we'd expect decent fare; but if they suggested we try dining at, say, The Lung Garden, we'd hesitate— even if we were told the food is identical. People will go out of their way to save $10 when buying a $25 pen, but won't do the same to save the same amount buying a $500 suit.* Programmed into our psyches are features that distort our perception, color our judgment, and impair our ability to think objectively.

The best defense? Making it a habit to think critically.

The following exercises may help you understand the cognitive biases discussed in the previous section.

Exercise 1-8

The following questions are for thought or discussion. Your instructor may ask you to write a brief essay addressing one or more of them.

▲ 1. Which of the cognitive biases discussed in this section do you think you might be most subject to? Why?

  2. Can you think of other psychological tendencies you have that might interfere with the objectivity of your thinking? For example, are you unusually generous or selfish?

  3. Read again about Jamela, on page 8. Is there a psychological factor discussed in this section that is especially likely to bias her thinking about getting Priglet? What could she do about it?

▲ 4. If you were in Jamela's position, is there anything that might especially bias your thinking about whether to get a dog? What could you do about it?

  5. What might you do to compensate for a bias factor you listed in questions 1 or 2 in this exercise?

Exercise 1-9

For each of the following attributes, rate yourself in comparison with other students in your class. Are you

a. in the top 10%?

b. in the top 50% to 89%?

c. in the lower 25% to 49%?

d. below the top 75%?

■ ability to think clearly

■ ability to think logically

■ ability to think critically

■ ability to be objective

■ ability to think creatively

*Daniel Ariely, *Predictably Irrational* (New York: HarperCollins Publishers, 2008), pp. 19–20.

■ ability to read with comprehension

■ ability to spot political bias in the evening news

■ IQ

If you answered (a) or (b) about one of the preceding abilities, would you change your mind if you learned that most of the class also answered (a) or (b) about that ability? Why or why not?

Exercise 1-10

Select one of the following claims you are inclined to strongly agree or disagree with. Then produce the best argument you can think of for the opposing side. When you are finished, ask someone to read your argument and tell you honestly whether he or she thinks you have been fair and objective.

■ "There is (is not) a God."

■ "Illegal immigrants should (should not) be eligible for health-care benefits."

■ "Handgun owners should (should not) be required to register each handgun they own."

■ "The words 'under God' should (should not) be removed from the Pledge of Allegiance."

■ "Sex education should (should not) be taught in public schools."

TRUTH AND KNOWLEDGE

At the end of the day, when we are ready to turn out the lights and go to bed, we want the conclusions we have reached through painstaking critical thinking to be *true*—and we want to *know* they are true. However, as simple as it may seem when we think of them casually, the concepts of truth and knowledge have a long and contentious history. Through the years, many competing theories have been offered to account for their real nature, but fortunately for you, we can tell you what you need to know for this discussion without getting too deeply into those controversies.

As for truth, all you really need to understand here is that a legitimate belief or claim—that is, one that makes sense—is either true or false in the normal, commonsense way. Truth and falsity are properties of propositional entities like beliefs, opinions, judgments, statements, claims, and the like. As mentioned previously, when any of those entities is objective, whether it is true or false does not depend on whether we think it is true or false.

You can assert a claim's truth in a number of ways. In normal conversation, we'd take each of the following as making the same statement:

■ A book is on the table.

■ It is true a book is on the table.

■ It is a fact a book is on the table.

■ Yes, a book is on the table.

The concept of knowledge is another that philosophers have contested at a deep, theoretical level despite a general agreement that in everyday life, we understand well enough what we mean when we say we know something.

Ordinarily, you are entitled to say you know a book is on the table, provided that (1) you believe a book is on the table, (2) you have justification for this belief in the form of an argument beyond a reasonable doubt that a book is on the table, and (3) you have no reason to suspect you are mistaken, such as that you haven't slept for several nights or have recently taken hallucinogenic drugs. Skeptics may say it is impossible to know anything, though one wonders how they know that. Presumably, they'd have to say they're just guessing.

Ideally we would always make claims to knowledge in accordance with the three criteria just listed, a habit that would be endorsed by the nineteenth-century mathematician W. K. Clifford, who famously said, "It is wrong always, everywhere, and for anyone, to believe anything upon insufficient evidence."

WHAT CRITICAL THINKING CAN AND CAN'T DO

As we use the term in this book, "critical thinking" is not synonymous with "good thinking," "hard thinking," "clear thinking," "constructing arguments," "problem solving," or "thinking outside the box." Critical thinking kicks in *after* you have done these and other kinds of thinking. It's what you do when you think about thinking, specifically, when you evaluate the thinking you or someone else uses in arriving at a conclusion about something. Unfortunately, critical thinking *won't* necessarily tell you whether you should get a dog or who to support for president, or whether there is global warming or why your car won't start. It can, however, help you spot a bad reason for getting a dog or voting for someone, or for thinking there is or isn't global warming or for this or that explanation of why your car won't start. Please notice we say it *can* do that, not that it *will*. In the end, reasoning may yield to self-interest, wishful thinking, desire for acceptance, or other temptations; and we may find it difficult to free our thinking from various cognitive biases, distortions, or blind spots. Just remember, reasoning that doesn't measure up to the standards set forth in this book is not worthy of acceptance. Reading the book thoughtfully, doing the exercises, and applying what you learn will be a good first step toward avoiding these problems.

A WORD ABOUT THE EXERCISES

To get good at tennis, golf, playing a musical instrument, or most other skills, you have to practice, practice, and practice some more. It's the same way with critical thinking, and that's why we provide so many exercises. For some exercises in this book, there is no such thing as only one correct answer, just as there is no such thing as only one correct way to serve a tennis ball. Some answers, however—just like tennis serves—are better than others, and that is where your instructor comes in. In many exercises, answers you give that are different from your instructor's are not necessarily incorrect. Still, your instructor's answers will be well thought out, reliable, and worth your attention. We recommend taking advantage of his or her experience to improve your ability to think critically.

By the way, if you did the exercises you've already come across, you will have noticed that the answers to the questions marked with a triangle are found in the answer section at the back of the book. You'll also find an occasional comment, tip, suggestion, joke, or buried treasure map back there.

Recap

We think critically when we evaluate the reasoning we (and others) use in coming to a conclusion about something. As human beings, we are an imperfect lot: we sometimes act impulsively, and even when we don't, we make important decisions when we are tired or angry or depressed or otherwise influenced by emotion or self-interest. A theme of this chapter has been that our thinking can also be contoured by unexpected psychological parameters, some of which are beyond consciousness. Should we then abandon critical thinking or view it as a futile exercise? On the contrary. Precisely because we are not purely rational beings who always think clearly and weigh considerations objectively, we should evaluate our reasoning against the criteria examined in this book.

Other ideas we explored in this chapter include the following:

- Claim: When a belief (judgment, opinion) is asserted in a declarative sentence, the result is a claim or statement.
- Objective claim vs. subjective claim: An objective claim is true or false regardless of whether people think it is true or false. Claims that lack this property are said to be subjective.
- "Fact vs. opinion": People sometimes refer to true objective claims as "facts," and use the word "opinion" to designate any claim that is subjective.
- "Factual claim": An objective claim. Saying that a claim is "factual" is not the same as saying it is true. A factual claim is simply a claim whose truth does not depend on our thinking it is true.
- Moral subjectivism: Moral subjectivism is the idea that all judgments and claims that ascribe a moral property to something are subjective. "There is nothing either good or bad but that thinking makes it so."
- Issue: A question.
- Argument: An argument consists of two parts—one part of which (the premise or premises) is intended to provide a reason for accepting the other part (the conclusion).
- "Argument": People sometimes use this word to refer to an argument's premise.
- Arguments and issues: The conclusion of an argument states a position on the issue under consideration.
- Cognitive bias: a feature of human psychology that skews belief formation. The ones discussed in this chapter include the following:
  - Belief bias: Evaluating reasoning by how believable its conclusion is.
  - Availability heuristic: Assigning a probability to an event based on how easily or frequently it is thought of.
  - False consensus effect: Assuming our opinions and those held by people around us are shared by society at large.
  - Bandwagon effect: The tendency to align our beliefs with those of other people.
  - Negativity bias: Attaching more weight to negative information than to positive information.

■ Loss aversion: Being more strongly motivated to avoid a loss than to accrue a gain.

■ In-group bias: A set of cognitive biases that make us view people who belong to our group differently from people who don't.

■ Fundamental attribution error: Understanding the behavior of others differently from how we understand our own behavior or that of other people in our group.

■ Obedience to authority: A tendency to comply with instructions from an authority.

■ Overconfidence effect: A cognitive bias that leads us to overestimate what percentage of our answers on a subject are correct.

■ Better-than-average illusion: A self-deception cognitive bias that leads us to overestimate our own abilities relative to those of others.

■ Truth: The question, What is Truth, has no universally accepted answer, and we don't try to answer it here. In this book we use the concept in a commonsense way: A claim is true if it is free from error.

■ Knowledge: For our purposes, if you believe something is so, have an argument that is beyond a reasonable doubt that it is so, and have no reason to think you are mistaken, you can claim you know it is so.

Additional Exercises

Here are more exercises to help you identify objective and subjective claims, recognize arguments, identify issues, and tell when two people are addressing the same issue. In addition, you will find writing exercises, as well as an exercise that will give you practice in identifying the purpose of a claim.

Exercise 1-11

Determine which of the following passages contain arguments. For any that do, identify the argument's conclusion. Remember: an argument occurs when one or more claims (the premises) are offered as a reason for accepting the other claim (the conclusion). There aren't hard-and-fast rules for identifying arguments, so you'll have to read closely and think carefully about some of these. We're not asking you to evaluate the argument—only to determine whether one is being made.

▲   1. There is trouble in the Middle East, there is a recession under way at home, and all economic indicators are trending downward. It seems likely, then, that the only way the stock market can go is down.

2. Lucy is too short to reach the bottom of the sign.

3. "Can it be established that genetic humanity is sufficient for moral humanity? I think there are very good reasons for not defining the moral community in this way."

—*Mary Anne Warren*

▲   4. Pornography often depicts women as servants or slaves or as otherwise inferior to men. In light of that, it seems reasonable to expect to find more women than men who are upset by pornography.

5. "My folks, who were Russian immigrants, loved the chance to vote. That's probably why I decided that I was going to vote whenever I got the chance. I'm not sure [whom I'll vote for], but I am going to vote. And I don't understand people who don't."

—*Mike Wallace*

6. "Dynamism is a function of change. On some campuses, change is effected through nonviolent or even violent means. Although we too have had our demonstrations, change here is usually a product of discussion in the decision-making process."

—*Hillary Clinton, while a student at Wellesley College in the 1960s*

▲ 7. What does it take to make a good soap opera? You need good guys and bad guys, sex, babies, passion, infidelity, jealousy, hatred, and suspense. And it must all be believable. Believability is the key.

8. We need to make clear that sexual preference, whether chosen or genetically determined, is a private matter. It has nothing to do with an individual's ability to make a positive contribution to society.

9. The report card on charter schools is mixed. Some show better results than public schools, others show worse. Charter schools have this advantage when it comes to test scores: the kids attending them are more apt to have involved parents.

▲ 10. *American Idol* may not be having its best season, but when you remember whose careers were launched by *AI*, you know it is the best talent show on TV.

Exercise 1-12

For each numbered passage in this exercise, identify which lettered item best states the primary issue discussed in the passage. Be prepared to say why you think your choice is the correct one.

▲ 1. In pre–civil war Spain, the influence of the Catholic Church must have been much stronger on women than on men. You can determine this by looking at the number of religious communities, such as monasteries, nunneries, and so forth. A total of about 5,000 such communities existed in 1931; 4,000 of them were female, whereas only 1,000 of them were male. This proves my point about the Church's influence on the sexes.
   a. whether the Catholic Church's influence was greater on women than on men in pre–civil war Spain
   b. whether the speaker's statistics really prove his point about the Church's influence
   c. whether the figures about religious communities really have anything to do with the overall influence of the Catholic Church in Spain

2. The TV show *The Sopranos* might have been a pretty good series without the profanity that occurred all the way through it. But without the profanity, it would not have been believable. Those people just talk that way. If you have them speaking Shakespearean English or middle-class suburban English, then nobody is going to pay any attention to the message because nobody will see it as realistic. It's true, of course, that like many

other programs with some offensive feature—whether it's bad language, sex, or whatever—it will never appeal to the squeamish.

a. whether movies with offensive features can appeal to the squeamish
b. whether *The Sopranos* would have been an entertaining series without the bad language
c. whether *The Sopranos* would have been believable without the bad language
d. whether believable programs must always have an offensive feature of one kind or another

3. "From information gathered recently, it has become clear that the single biggest environmental problem in Russia—many times bigger than anything we have to contend with in the United States—is radioactive pollution from nuclear energy plants and nuclear weapons testing and production. Soviet Communist leaders seemed to believe they could do anything to hasten the industrialization process and compete with Western countries and that the land and natural resources they controlled were vast enough to suffer any abuse without serious consequence. The arrogance of the Communist leaders produced a burden of misery and death that fell on the people of the region, and the scale of that burden only recently became clear. Nuclear waste was dumped into rivers from which downstream villages drew their drinking water; the landscape is dotted with nuclear dumps that now threaten to leak into the environment; and the seas around Russia are littered with decaying hulks of nuclear submarines and rusting metal containers with tens of millions of tons of nuclear waste. The result has been radiation poisoning and its awful effects on a grand scale.

"A science advisor to former Russian president Boris Yeltsin said, 'The way we have dealt with the whole issue of nuclear power, and particularly the problem of nuclear waste, was irresponsible and immoral.' "

—*Adapted from the Washington Post*

a. whether communism failed to protect people from nuclear contamination as well as capitalism did
b. whether nuclear waste problems in Russia are much worse than had been realized until just recently
c. whether Soviet leaders made large-scale sacrifice of the lives and health of their people in their nuclear competition with the West
d. whether communism, in the long run, is a much worse system than capitalism when it comes to protecting the population from harm

4. "The United States puts a greater percentage of its population in prison than any other developed country in the world. We persist in locking more and more people up despite the obvious fact that it doesn't work. Even as we build more prisons and stuff them ever more tightly, the crime rate goes up and up. But we respond, 'Since it isn't working, let's do more of it'! It's about time we learned that fighting criminals is not the same thing as fighting crime."

—*Richard Parker, radio commentary on CalNet, California Public Radio*

a. whether we build more prisons than any other country
b. whether we imprison more people than do other countries

    c. whether reliance on imprisonment is an effective method of reducing crime

    d. whether attacking the sources of crime (poverty, lack of education, and so on) will reduce crime more than just imprisoning people who commit crimes

    e. none of the above

5. In Miami–Dade County, Florida, schools superintendent Rudy Crew was inundated with complaints after a police officer used a stun gun on a six-year-old student. As a result, Crew asked the Miami–Dade police to ban the use of stun guns on elementary school children. Crew did the right thing. More than 100 deaths have been linked to tasers.

    a. whether a police officer used a stun gun on a six-year-old student

    b. whether the superintendent did the right thing by asking the police to ban the use of stun guns on elementary school children

    c. whether 100 deaths have been linked to tasers

    d. whether the fact that 100 deaths have been linked to tasers shows that the superintendent did the right thing when he asked the police not to use tasers on children

6. Letting your children surf the Net is like dropping them off downtown to spend the day doing whatever they want. They'll get in trouble.

    a. whether letting your children off downtown to spend the day doing whatever they want will lead them into trouble

    b. whether letting your children surf the Net will lead them into trouble

    c. whether restrictions should be placed on children's activities

▲ 7. The winner of this year's spelling bee is a straight-A student whose favorite subject is science, which isn't surprising, since students interested in science learn to pay attention to details.

    a. whether the winner of this year's spelling bee is a straight-A student

    b. whether science students learn to pay attention to detail

    c. whether learning science will improve a student's ability to spell

    d. whether learning science teaches a student to pay attention to details

    e. none of the above

8. Illinois state employees, both uniformed and non-uniformed, have been loyally, faithfully, honorably, and patiently serving the state without a contract or cost-of-living pay increase for years, despite the fact that legislators and the governor have accepted hefty pay increases. All public employee unions should launch a signature-gathering initiative to place on the ballot a proposition that the Illinois constitution be amended to provide for compulsory binding arbitration for all uniformed and non-uniformed public employees, under the supervision of the state supreme court.

    a. whether Illinois state employees have been loyally, faithfully, honorably, and patiently serving the state without a contract or cost-of-living pay increase for years

    b. whether public employee unions should launch a signature-gathering initiative to place on the ballot a proposition that the Illinois constitution be amended to provide for compulsory binding arbitration for all uniformed and non-uniformed public employees, under the supervision of the Illinois Supreme Court

    c. neither of the above

9. In 2007, the Dominican Republic banned the sale of two brands of Chinese toothpaste because they contained a toxic chemical responsible for dozens of poisoning deaths in Panama. The company that exported the toothpaste, the Danyang Household Chemical Company, defended its product. "Toothpaste is not something you'd swallow, but spit out, and so it's totally different from something you would eat," one company manager said. The company manager was taking a position on which issue?

   a. whether the Danyang Household Chemical Company included toxic chemicals in its toothpaste
   b. whether toothpaste should be eaten
   c. whether the Danyang Household Chemical Company did anything wrong by exporting its toothpaste
   d. whether China should have better product safety controls

▲ 10. YOU: So, what do you think of the governor?
   YOUR FRIEND: Not much, actually.
   YOU: What do you mean? Don't you think she's been pretty good?
   YOUR FRIEND: Are you serious?
   YOU: Well, yes. I think she's been doing a fine job.
   YOUR FRIEND: Oh, come on. Weren't you complaining about her just a few days ago?

   a. whether your friend thinks the governor has been a good governor
   b. whether you think the governor has been a good governor
   c. whether the governor has been a good governor
   d. whether you have a good argument for thinking the governor has been a good governor

Exercise 1-13

On what issue is the speaker taking a position in each of the following?

▲ 1. Police brutality does not happen very often. Otherwise, it would not make headlines when it does happen.

2. We have little choice but to concentrate our crime-fighting efforts on enforcement because we don't have any idea what to do about the underlying causes of crime.

3. A lot of people think the gender of a Supreme Court justice doesn't make any difference. But with three women on the bench, cases dealing with women's issues are being handled differently.

▲ 4. "The point is that the existence of an independent world explains our experiences better than any known alternative. We thus have good reason to believe that the world—which seems independent of our minds—really is essentially independent of our minds."

   —*Theodore W. Schick, Jr., and Lewis Vaughn,*
   How to Think About Weird Things

5. Sure, some of the hot-doggers get good grades in Professor Bubacz's class. But my guess is that, if Algernon takes it, all it'll get him is flunked out!

6. It is dumb to claim that sales taxes hit poor people harder than rich people. After all, the more money you have, the more you spend; and

the more you spend, the more sales taxes you pay. So people with more money are always going to be paying more in sales tax than poor people.

▲ 7. If you're going to buy a synthesizer, you might as well also sign up for lessons on how to use the thing. After all, no synthesizer ever worked for its owner until he or she learned how to make it work.

8. Intravenous drug use with nonsterile needles has become one of the leading causes of the spread of AIDS. Many states passed legislation allowing officials to distribute clean needles in an effort to combat this method of infection. But in eleven states, including some of the most populous, possession of hypodermic syringes without a prescription is illegal. The laws in these foot-dragging states have to be changed if we ever hope to bring this awful epidemic to an end.

9. The best way to avoid error—that is, belief in something false—is to suspend judgment about everything except what is absolutely certain. Because error usually leads to trouble, suspending judgment is usually the right thing to do.

▲ 10. "[Readers] may learn something about their own relationship to the earth from a people who were true conservationists. The Indians knew that life was equated with the earth and its resources, that America was a paradise, and they could not comprehend why the intruders from the East were determined to destroy all that was Indian as well as America itself."

—*Dee Brown* , Bury My Heart at Wounded Knee

Exercise 1-14

Is the second person addressing the issue raised by the first person?

Example

ELMOP: Toilet paper looks better unwinding from the back of the spool.

MARWOOF: Get real! That is so stupid! It should unwind the other way.

Analysis

Marwoof addresses the issue raised by Elmop.

▲ 1. MR.: Next weekend, we go on standard time again. We have to set the clocks ahead.
MRS.: It isn't next weekend; it's the weekend after. And you set the clocks back an hour.

2. MOORE: The administration's latest Afghanistan proposal may just make matters worse.
PARKER: Yeah, right. You're just saying that 'cause you don't like Obama.

3. SHE: You don't give me enough help around the house. Why, you hardly ever do anything!
HE: What??? I mowed the lawn on Saturday, and I washed both of the cars on Sunday. What's more, I clean up after dinner almost every night, and

I hauled all that garden stuff to the dump. How can you say I don't do anything?

SHE: Well, you sure don't want to hear about what I do! I do a lot more than that!

4. HEEDLESS: When people complain about what we're doing in Afghanistan, they just encourage terrorists to think Americans won't fight back. People who complain like that ought to just shut up.

CAUTIOUS: I disagree. Those people are reminding everyone that it isn't in our best interest to get involved in extended wars abroad.

5. MR. RJ: If you ask me, there are too many casinos around here already. We don't need more.

MR. JR: Yeah? Well that's a strange idea coming from you; you play the lottery all the time.

6. JOE FITNESS: Whoa, look at that! The chain on my bike is starting to jump around! If I don't fix it, it'll stop working.

COUCH POTATO: What you need is to stop worrying about it. You get too much exercise as it is.

7. YOUNG GUY: Baseball players are much better now than they were forty years ago. They eat better, have better coaching, you name it.

OLD GUY: They aren't better at all. They just seem better because they get more publicity and play with juiced equipment.

8. STUDENT ONE: Studying is a waste of time. Half the time, I get better grades if I don't study.

STUDENT TWO: I'd like to hear you say that in front of your parents. . . .

9. PHILATELIST: Did you know that U.S. postage stamps are now being printed in Canada?

PATRIOT: Gad, what an outrage! If there is one thing that ought to be made in the United States, it's U.S. postage stamps!

PHILATELIST: Oh, c'mon. If American printing companies can't do the work, let the Canadians have it.

10. FIRST NEIGHBOR: See here, you have no right to make so much noise at night. I have to get up early for work.

SECOND NEIGHBOR: Yeah? Well, you have no right to let your idiot dog run loose all day long.

11. STUDY PARTNER ONE: Let's knock off for a while and go get pizza. We'll function better if we eat something.

STUDY PARTNER TWO: Not one of those pizzas you like! I can't stand anchovies.

12. FEMALE STUDENT: The Internet is overrated. It takes forever to find something you can actually use in an assignment.

MALE STUDENT: Listen, it takes a lot longer to drive over to the library and find a place to park.

13. CITIZEN ONE: In 2012, it's going to be Mitt Romney for the Republicans and Barack Obama for the Democrats, what do you want to bet?

CITIZEN TWO: I doubt it. Romney has too many enemies. Besides, Republicans love Sarah Palin.

14. CULTURALLY CHALLENGED PERSON: A concert! You think I'm going to a concert when I can be home watching football?

CULTURALLY CHALLENGED PERSON'S SPOUSE: Yes, if you want dinner this week.

15. REPUBLICAN: I don't think Obama's budget requests make a lot of sense.
DEMOCRAT: You just can't stand more taxes, can you?

▲ 16. MOORE: I've seen the work of both Thomas Brothers and Vernon Construction, and I tell you, Thomas Brothers does a better job.
PARKER: Listen, Thomas Brothers is the highest-priced company in the whole state. If you hire them, you'll pay double for every part of the job.

17. URBANITE: The new requirements will force people off septic tanks and make them hook up to the city sewer. That's the only way we'll ever get the nitrates and other pollutants out of the groundwater.
SUBURBANITE: You call it a requirement, but I call it an outrage! They're going to charge us from five to fifteen thousand dollars each to make the hookups! That's more than anybody can afford!

18. CRITIC: I don't think it's morally proper to sell junk bonds to anybody without emphasizing the risk involved, but it's especially bad to sell them to older people who are investing their entire savings.
ENTREPRENEUR: Oh, come on. There's nothing the matter with making money.

▲ 19. ONE HAND: What with the number of handguns and armed robberies these days, it's hard to feel safe in your own home.
THE OTHER HAND: The reason you don't feel safe is you don't have a handgun yourself. Criminals would rather hit a house where there's no gun than a house where there is one.

20. ONE GUY: Would you look at the price they want for these DVD recording machines? They're making a fortune on every one of these things!
ANOTHER: Don't give me that. I know how big a raise you got last year—you can afford a truckload of those things!

21. FED UP: This city is too cold in the winter, too hot in the summer, and too dangerous all the time. I'll be happier if I exercise my early retirement option and move to my place in Arkansas.
FRIEND: You're nuts. You'll be miserable if you don't work, and if you move, you'll be back in six months.

▲ 22. KATIE: Hey, Jennifer, I hate to say this, but if you picked up your stuff once in a while, this place would look better.
JENNIFER: Hey, you leave things lying around, too. You and your stupid boyfriend.

23. DEZRA: What are you thinking, mowing the lawn in your bare feet? That's totally unsafe.
KEN: Like you never did anything you could get hurt doing?

24. YAO: Nice thing about an iMAC. It never gets viruses.
MAO: Of course you would say that; you own one.

▲ 25. INTERVIEWER: Secretary Clinton, how do you respond when your fellow Democrats criticize you for not trying to get us out of Afghanistan?
SENATOR CLINTON: You know, I think we Democrats have to stop talking about each other. This has never been our war, and we should not forget that.

Exercise 1-15

On the basis of a concept or distinction discussed in this chapter, divide the following claims into two groups, and identify the concept or distinction you used.

▲   1. Buttermilk tastes kind of funny, you know what I mean? Kind of like it's gone bad?

    2. It's more expensive to take a cruise than to lie around on the beach.

    3. You should bathe your dog more often.

▲   4. Paris Hilton lied to the judge, plain and simple.

    5. Hey, don't let your kids wear clothes like that!

    6. Carol can't hit a high C when she sings.

▲   7. Letterman tells sexist jokes, and he oughta be pulled off the air.

    8. Seeing that you drive a big, honking Hummer, you shouldn't complain about gas prices.

    9. The most economical car out this year? That would be the new Volt.

▲ 10. I've heard that stuff they put on popcorn can cause lung disease.

Exercise 1-16

Which of the following claims pertain to right/wrong, good/bad, or should/shouldn't?

▲   1. We did the right thing getting rid of Saddam. He was a sadistic tyrant.

    2. That guy is the smartest person I know.

    3. Contributing to the Humane Society is a good thing to do.

▲   4. It's high time you starting thinking about somebody other than yourself!

    5. Your first duty is to your family; after that, to God and country, in that order.

    6. You know what? I always tip 15%.

▲   7. The FBI and CIA don't share information all that often, at least that's what I've heard.

    8. You might find the parking less expensive outside.

    9. Help the guy! If the situation were reversed, he would help you.

▲ 10. Hip hop is better than country, any day.

  11. Rodin was a master sculptor.

  12. Whatever happened to Susan Boyle? You don't hear about her much any more.

▲ 13. If we want to stop the decline in enrollments here at Chaffee, we need to give students skills they can use.

Exercise 1-17

This exercise will give you an opportunity to work with the concepts of argument, conclusion, and critical thinking.

Decide which of the lettered options serve the same kind of purpose as the original remark. Then think critically about your conclusion. Do you have a reason for it? Be ready to state your reasoning in class if called on.

Example

> Be careful! This plate is hot.
>
> a. Watch out. The roads are icy.
> b. Say—why don't you get lost?

Conclusion: The purpose of (a) is most like the purpose of the original remark. Reason: Both are warnings.

▲ 1. I'd expect that zipper to last about a week; it's made of cheap plastic.

   a. The wrinkles on that dog make me think of an old man.
   b. Given Sydney's spending habits, I doubt Adolphus will stick with her for long.

2. If you recharge your battery, sir, it will be almost as good as new.

   a. Purchasing one CD at the regular price would entitle you to buy an unlimited number of CDs at only $4.99.
   b. I shall now serve dinner, after which you can play if you want.

3. To put out a really creative newsletter, you should get in touch with our technology people.

   a. Do unto others as you would have them do unto you.
   b. To put an end to this discussion, I'll concede your point.
   c. You'd better cut down on your smoking if you want to live longer.

▲ 4. GE's profits during the first quarter were short of GE's projections. Therefore, we can expect GE stock to fall sharply in the next day or so.

   a. Senator Craig apparently thought what he did in private was nobody's business but his own.
   b. The dog is very hot. Probably he would appreciate a drink of water.
   c. The dog's coat is unusually thick. No wonder he is hot.

5. How was my date with your brother? Well . . . he has a great personality.

   a. How do I like my steak? Well, not dripping blood like this thing you just served me.
   b. How do I like the dress? Say, did you know that black is more slimming than white?

6. The wind is coming up. We'd better head for shore.

   a. They finally arrived. I guess they will order soon.
   b. We shouldn't leave yet. We just got here.

▲ 7. Good ties are made out of silk. That's why they cost so much.

   a. Belts are like suspenders. They both keep your pants up.
   b. Rugby has lots of injuries because rugby players don't wear pads.

8. Daphne owns an expensive car. She must be rich.

   a. This dog has fleas. I'll bet it itches a lot.
   b. This dog has fleas. That explains why it scratches a lot.

9. Dennis's salary is going up. He just got a promotion.

   a. Dennis's salary went up after he got a promotion.
   b. Dennis's salary won't be going up; he didn't get a promotion.

▲ 10. Outlawing adult websites may hamper free speech, but pornography must be curbed.

   a. The grass must be mowed even though it is hot.
   b. The grass is getting long; time to mow.

Writing Exercises

1. Turn to the "Essays for Analysis" in Appendix 1. Identify and write in your own words the principal issues in the selections identified by your instructor.

2. Do people choose the sex they are attracted to? Write a one-page answer to this question, defending your answer with at least one supporting reason. Take about ten minutes to write your answer. Do not put your name on your paper. When everyone is finished, your instructor will collect the papers and redistribute them to the class. In groups of four or five, read the papers that have been given to your group. Divide the drafts into two batches, those that contain an argument and those that do not. Your instructor will ask each group to read to the class a paper that contains an argument and a paper that does not contain an argument (assuming that each group has at least one of each). The group should be prepared to explain why they feel each paper contains or fails to contain an argument.

3. Using the issues you identified in Exercise 1 for each of the selections, choose a side on one of the issues and write a short paper supporting it.

2

Two Kinds of Reasoning

ime to look more closely at arguments—the kind that actually show something (unlike the red herrings and emotional appeals and other fallacies we are going to be talking about in a moment).

ARGUMENTS: GENERAL FEATURES

To repeat, an argument consists of two parts. One part, the premise, is intended to provide a reason for accepting the second part, the conclusion. This statement is *not* an argument:

> God exists.

It's just a statement.

> Likewise, *this* is not an argument:

> God exists. That's as plain as the nose on your face.

It's just a slightly more emphatic statement.

> Nor is this an argument:

> God exists, and if you don't believe it, you will go to hell.

It just tries to scare us into believing God exists.

Students will learn to . . .

1. Recognize complications regarding premises and conclusions

2. Distinguish between deductive and inductive arguments

3. Understand the standards for validity, soundness, strength, and weakness in arguments

4. Assess an argument with an unstated premise

5. Distinguish between ethos, pathos, and logos

6. Identify a balance-of-considerations argument

7. Identify an inference to the best explanation (IBE)

8. Use techniques for understanding arguments

Also not an argument:

I think God exists, because I was raised a Baptist.

Yes, it looks a bit like an argument, but it isn't. It merely explains why I believe in God.

On the other hand, this *is* an argument:

God exists because something had to cause the universe.

The difference between this and the earlier examples? This example has a premise ("something had to cause the universe") and a conclusion ("God exists").

As we explained in Chapter 1 (see pages 8–10), an argument always has two parts: a premise part and a conclusion part. The premise part is intended to give a reason for accepting the conclusion part.

This probably seems fairly straightforward, but one or two complications are worth noting.

Conclusions Used as Premises

The same statement can be the conclusion of one argument and a premise in another argument:

Premise: The brakes aren't working, the engine burns oil, the transmission needs work, and the car is hard to start.
Conclusion 1: The car has outlived its usefulness.
Conclusion 2: We should get a new car.

In this example, the statement "The car has outlived its usefulness" is the conclusion of one argument, and it is also a premise in the argument that we should get a new car.

Clearly, if a premise in an argument is uncertain or controversial or has been challenged, you might want to defend it—that is, argue that it is true. When you do, the premise becomes the conclusion of a new argument. However, every chain of reasoning must begin somewhere. If we ask a speaker to defend each premise with a further argument, and each premise in that argument with a further argument, and so on and so on, we eventually find ourselves being unreasonable, much like four-year-olds who keep asking, "Why?" until they become exasperating. If we ask a speaker why he thinks the car has outlived its usefulness, he may mention that the car is hard to start. If we ask him why he thinks the car is hard to start, he probably won't know what to say.

Unstated Premises and Conclusions

Another complication is that arguments can contain unstated premises. For example,

Premise: You can't check out books from the library without an ID.
Conclusion: Bill won't be able to check out any books.

The unstated premise must be that Bill has no ID.

An argument can even have an unstated conclusion:

Example: The political party that best reflects mainstream opinion will win the presidency, and the Republican Party best reflects mainstream opinion.

If a person said this, he or she would be implying that the Republican Party will win the presidency; that would be the unstated conclusion of the argument.

In Depth

Conclusion Indicators

When the words in the following list are used in arguments, they usually indicate that a premise has just been offered and that a conclusion is about to be presented. (The three dots represent the claim that is the conclusion.)

Thus . . .	Consequently . . .
Therefore . . .	So . . .
Hence . . .	Accordingly . . .
This shows that . . .	This implies that . . .
This suggests that . . .	This proves that . . .

Example:

Stacy drives a Porsche. This suggests that either she is rich or her parents are.

The conclusion is

Either she is rich or her parents are.

The premise is

Stacy drives a Porsche.

Unstated premises are common in real life because sometimes they seem too obvious to need mentioning. The argument "the car is beyond fixing, so we should get rid of it" actually has an unstated premise to the effect that we should get rid of any car that is beyond fixing; but this may seem so obvious to us that we don't bother stating it.

Unstated conclusions also are not uncommon, though they are less common than unstated premises.

We'll return to this subject in a moment.

TWO KINDS OF ARGUMENTS

Good arguments come in two varieties: deductive demonstrations and inductive supporting arguments.

Deductive Arguments

The premise (or premises) of a good *deductive* argument, if true, *proves or demonstrates* (these being the same thing for our purposes) its conclusion. However, there is more to this than meets the eye, and we must begin with the fundamental concept of deductive logic, *validity*. An argument is **valid** *if it isn't possible for the premise to be true and the conclusion false.* This may sound complicated, but it really isn't. An example of a valid argument will help:

Premise: Jimmy Carter was president immediately before Bill Clinton, and George W. Bush was president immediately after Bill Clinton.
Conclusion: Jimmy Carter was president before George W. Bush.

In Depth

Premise Indicators

When the words in the following list are used in arguments, they generally introduce premises. They often occur just *after* a conclusion has been given. A premise would replace the three dots in an actual argument.

   Since . . .

   For . . .

   In view of . . .

   This is implied by . . .

Example:

   Either Stacy is rich or her parents are, since she drives a Porsche.

The premise is the claim that Stacy drives a Porsche; the conclusion is the claim that either Stacy is rich or her parents are.

As you can see, it's impossible for this premise to be true and this conclusion to be false. So the argument is valid.

However, you may have noticed that the premise contains a mistake. Jimmy Carter was not president immediately before Bill Clinton. George H. W. Bush was president immediately before Bill Clinton. Nevertheless, even though the premise of the preceding argument is not true, the argument is still valid, because it isn't possible for the premise to be true and the conclusion false. Another way to say this: If the premise *were* true, the conclusion *could not* be false—and that's what "valid" means.

Now, when the premise of a valid argument *is* true, there is a word for it. In that case, the argument is said to be **sound.** Here is an example of a sound argument:

> **Premise:** Bill Clinton is taller than George W. Bush, and Jimmy Carter is shorter than George W. Bush.
> **Conclusion:** Therefore, Bill Clinton is taller than Jimmy Carter.

This argument is sound because it is valid and the premise is true. As you can see, if an argument is sound, then its conclusion has been demonstrated.

Inductive Arguments

Again, the premise of a good deductive argument, if true, demonstrates that the conclusion is true. This brings us to the second kind of argument, the *inductive* argument. The premises of good inductive arguments don't demonstrate their conclusions; they *support* them. For example: A woman has been found murdered. The husband is known to have threatened her repeatedly.

That fact certainly does not demonstrate that the woman's husband murdered her. By itself, the fact barely even supports that conclusion. But it does support it slightly. It raises the probability slightly that the husband was the murderer. Certainly the investigators should question the husband closely if they learn he repeatedly threatened his wife before she died.

If you are thinking that support is a matter of degrees and that it can vary from just a little to a whole lot, you are right. If, say, the husband's fingerprints had been found on the murder weapon, that fact would offer much better support for the conclusion that the husband was the murderer. That is, it would make it likelier that the woman's murderer was her husband.

Inductive arguments are thus better or worse on a scale, depending on how much support their premises provide for the conclusion. Logicians have a technical word to describe this situation. The more support the premise of an inductive argument provides for the conclusion, the **stronger** the argument; the less support it provides, the **weaker** the argument. Put another way, the more likely the premise makes the conclusion, the stronger the argument; and the less likely, the weaker the argument. Discovering that the man repeatedly threatened his wife (that's the premise) raises the probability slightly that it is he who was the murderer (that's the conclusion). By comparison, discovering that his fingerprints are on the murder weapon raises the probability by a much larger jump: It is the stronger of the two arguments.

Real Life

Abe Lincoln Knew His Logic

Validity and Soundness in the Lincoln-Douglas Debates

Here's Abraham Lincoln speaking in the fifth Lincoln-Douglas debate:

> I state in syllogistic form the argument:
>
> Nothing in the Constitution . . . can destroy a right distinctly and expressly affirmed in the Constitution.
>
> The right of property in a slave is distinctly and expressly affirmed in the Constitution.
>
> Therefore, nothing in the Constitution can destroy the right of property in a slave.

Lincoln goes on to say:

> There is a fault [in the argument], but the fault is not in the reasoning; but the falsehood in fact is a fault of the premises. I believe that the right of property in a slave is *not* distinctly and expressly affirmed in the Constitution.

In other words, the argument is valid, Lincoln says, but unsound and thus not a good argument. Syllogisms, by the way, are covered in Chapter 8.

If ever, oh ever, a Wiz there was The Wizard of Oz is one because because because because because . . . Because of the wonderful things he does!

"Because" is sometimes followed by a premise, and sometimes by a phrase that refers to a cause. Which is it here?

ANSWER: ". . . the wonderful things he does" is *evidence* he is a wonderful wizard; it is a premise.

Many instructors use the word "strong" in an absolute sense to denote only those arguments whose premise gives the conclusion better than a 50-50 chance of being true. In this book, however, we use "strong" and "weak" in a comparative sense. Given two arguments for the same conclusion, the one whose premise makes the conclusion more likely is the stronger argument, and the other is the weaker.

These are a lot of concepts for you to remember, but you shouldn't be surprised if your instructor asks you to do so. To make this task easier, let's summarize everything to this point. Again, the two basic types of arguments are (1) deductive demonstrations and (2) inductive supporting arguments.

When we reason deductively, we try to *prove* or *demonstrate* a conclusion.

A deductive argument is said to be **valid** if it isn't possible for the premise to be true and the conclusion false. Further, if the premise of a valid argument is in fact true, the argument is said to be **sound.** The conclusion of a sound argument has been proved or demonstrated.

When we reason inductively, we try to *support* a conclusion.

Inductive arguments are "stronger" or "weaker" depending on how much support the premise provides for the conclusion; that is, depending on how likely the premise makes the conclusion.

Beyond a Reasonable Doubt

In common law, the highest standard of proof is proof "beyond a reasonable doubt." If you are a juror in a criminal trial, evidence will be presented to the court—facts that the interested parties consider relevant to the crime. Additionally, the prosecutor and counsel for the defense will offer arguments connecting the evidence to (or disconnecting it from) the guilt or innocence of the defendant. When the jury is asked to return a verdict, the judge will tell the jury that the defendant must be found not guilty unless the evidence proves guilt *beyond a reasonable doubt.*

Proof beyond a reasonable doubt actually is a somewhat lower standard than deductive demonstration. The latter corresponds more to what, in ordinary English, might be expressed by the phrase "beyond possible doubt." Recall that in logic, a proposition has been demonstrated when it has been shown to be the conclusion of a sound argument—an argument, that is, in which (1) all premises are true, and (2) it is impossible for the premises to be true and for the conclusion to be false. In this sense, many propositions people describe as having been demonstrated or proved, such as that smoking causes lung cancer or that the DNA found at a crime scene was the defendant's, have not actually been proved in our sense of the word. So, in real life, when people say something has been demonstrated, they may well be speaking "informally." They may not mean that something is the conclusion of a sound argument. However, when we—the authors—say that something has been demonstrated, that is *exactly* what we mean.

DEDUCTION, INDUCTION, AND UNSTATED PREMISES

Somebody announces, "Rain is on its way." Somebody else asks how he knows. He says, "There's a south wind." Is the speaker trying to demonstrate or prove rain is coming? Probably not. His thinking, spelled out, is probably something like this:

> **Stated premise:** The wind is from the south.
> **Unstated premise:** Around here, south winds are usually followed by rain.
> **Conclusion:** There will be rain.

In other words, the speaker was merely trying to show that rain was a good possibility.

Notice, though, that the unstated premise in the argument could have been a universal statement to the effect that a south wind *always* is followed by rain at this particular location, in which case the argument would be deductive:

> **Stated premise:** The wind is from the south.
> **Unstated premise:** Around here, a south wind is always followed by rain.
> **Conclusion:** Rain is coming.

Spelled out this way, the speaker's thinking is deductive: It isn't possible for the premises to be true and the conclusion to be false. So one might wonder abstractly what the speaker intended—an inductive argument that supports the belief that rain is coming, or a deductive demonstration.

There is, perhaps, no way to be certain short of asking the speaker something like, "Are you 100% positive?" But experience ("background knowledge") tells us that wind from a particular direction is not a surefire indicator of rain. So probably the speaker did have in mind merely the first argument. He wasn't trying to present a 100% certain, knock-down demonstration that it would rain; he was merely trying to establish there was a good chance of rain.

It isn't hard to turn an inductive argument with an unstated premise into a deductively valid argument by supplying a universal premise—a statement that something holds without exception or is true everywhere or in all cases. Is that what the speaker really has in mind, though? You have to use background knowledge and common sense to answer the question.

For example, you overhear someone saying,

Stacy and Justin are on the brink of divorce. They're always fighting.

One could turn this into a valid deductive argument by adding to it the universal statement "Every couple fighting is on the brink of divorce." But such an unqualified universal statement seems unlikely. Probably the speaker wasn't trying to demonstrate that Stacy and Justin are on the brink of divorce. He or she was merely trying to raise its likelihood.

Often it is clear that the speaker does have a *deductive* argument in mind and has left some appropriate premise unstated. You overhear Professor Greene saying to Professor Brown,

"Flunk her! This is the second time you've caught her cheating."

It would be very strange to think that Professor Greene is merely trying to make it more likely that Professor Brown should flunk the student. Indeed, it is hard even to make sense of that suggestion. Professor Greene's argument, spelled out, must be this:

Stated premise: This is the second time you've caught her cheating.
Unstated premise: Anyone who has been caught cheating two times should be flunked.
Conclusion: She should be flunked.

So context and content often make it clear what unstated premise a speaker has in mind and whether the argument is deductive or inductive.

Unfortunately, though, this isn't always the case. We might hear someone say,

The bars are closed; therefore it is later than 2 A.M.

If the unstated premise in the speaker's mind is something like "In this city, the bars all close at 2 A.M.," then presumably he or she is thinking deductively and is evidently proffering proof that it's after 2. But if the speaker's unstated premise is something like "Most bars in this city close at 2 A.M." or "Bars in this city usually close at 2 A.M.," then we have an inductive argument that merely supports the conclusion. So which is the unstated premise? We really can't say without knowing more about the situation or the speaker.

The bottom line is this. Real-life arguments often leave a premise unstated. One such unstated premise might make the argument inductive; another might make it deductive. Usually, context or content make reasonably clear what is intended; other times they may not. When they don't, the best practice is to attribute to a speaker an unstated premise that at least is believable, everything considered. We'll talk about believability in Chapter 4.

In the Media

Is an Ad Photo an Argument?

The short answer: No. The longer version: Still no. An advertising photograph can "give you a reason" for buying something only in the sense that it can *cause* you to think of a reason. A photo is not and cannot be an argument for anything.

"BALANCE OF CONSIDERATIONS" AND IBES

Should I get a dog? Cut class to attend my cousin's wedding? Vote for Obama? Get chemo? Much everyday reasoning involves weighing considerations for and against thinking or doing something. Indeed, a case can be made for **balance of considerations reasoning** as *the* most important kind of reasoning we do.

  Balance of considerations reasoning typically contains both deductive and inductive elements. When Jamela predicts she can take care of little Priglet (we hope you read Chapter 1), she has been reasoning inductively. On the other hand, when she concludes that one consideration outweighs another consideration, she has been reasoning deductively based on the relative values she has assigned the two considerations. Assigning values to considerations can be difficult, of course, but doing so is not hopelessly arbitrary, as perhaps we convinced you in Chapter 1. In Chapter 12 of this book we discuss the frameworks within which moral evaluations are made; you will see there that such reasoning involves deductions from one or more guiding moral principles.

Another exceptionally common type of reasoning is what philosophers refer to as "inference to the best explanation," or for short, **IBE**. Sometimes this type of reasoning is also referred to as "abduction." Why won't the car start? The best explanation is that the battery is dead. Why does my back hurt in the morning? The best explanation is that my mattress is too soft. Why is the dog scratching at the door? The best explanation is that it has to tend to business. Aficionados of the stories of Sir Arthur Conan Doyle will be aware that this is the type of reasoning Sherlock Holmes specializes in—and what his sidekick Dr. Watson inaccurately refers to as "deduction." An IBE is actually an inductive argument, which is to be evaluated as strong or weak in varying degrees.

Don't be deceived by the foregoing elementary examples. IBEs, like balance of consideration arguments, are utterly important. Darwin's theory of evolution is an IBE—and so is what many regard as the most compelling argument that God exists. This last is the famous "argument from design," the conclusion of which is that God, rather than evolution, best explains the appearance of life.

The criteria for appraising IBEs differ from those applied to other inductive arguments. In Chapter 11 we go into things in more detail, but the general idea is this: Given competing explanations of a phenomenon, the best explanation is the one that (a) explains the phenomenon most adequately, (b) leads to the most accurate predictions, (c) conflicts least with other well-established explanations, and (d) involves the fewest unnecessary assumptions. Proponents of the design argument believe the theory of evolution fails to adequately explain the origin of life; those on the other side of that debate say the God explanation involves unnecessary assumptions and, perhaps most important, has no predictive power.

WHAT ARE NOT PREMISES, CONCLUSIONS, OR ARGUMENTS

We hope you've noticed, when we use the word "argument," we are not talking about two people having a feud or fuss about something. That use of the word has nothing much to do with critical thinking, though many a heated exchange could use some critical thinking. Arguments in our sense do not even need two people; we make arguments for our own use all the time. And when we evaluate them, we think critically.

Speaking of what arguments are not, it's important to realize that not everything that might look like an argument, or like a premise or a conclusion, is one.

Pictures

Pictures are not premises, conclusions, or arguments. Neither are movies. Your iPhone can do lots of things, but it can't create a premise, a conclusion, or an argument. Sorry. Arguments have two parts, a premise part and a conclusion part, and both parts are propositional entities, which means (to repeat) that both parts must be expressible in a declarative, true-or-false sentence. Movies and pictures can be moving, compelling, beautiful, complex, realistic, and so forth—but they cannot be either true or false. Is that movie true? The question does not make literal sense. If it doesn't make sense to think of a thing as "true" or as "false," then that thing cannot be a premise or a conclusion. And if it doesn't make sense to think of it as valid, invalid, or sound, or as in varying degrees of strong or weak, it cannot be an argument. The things listed previously not only are not premises or conclusions, they are not arguments, either.

The list of things that aren't premises or conclusions or arguments therefore includes emotions, feelings, landscapes, faces, gestures, grunts, groans, bribes, threats, amusement parks, and hip hop. Since they may *cause* you to have an opinion or to form a judgment about something or produce an argument, you might be tempted to think of them as premises, but causes are not premises. A cause isn't a propositional entity: it is neither true nor false. So it cannot be a premise.

If . . . then . . . Sentences

"If you wash your car now, then it will get spots." This statement might be the premise of an argument whose conclusion is "Therefore you shouldn't wash your car now." It might also be the conclusion of an argument whose premise is "It is raining." But though it *could* be a premise or a conclusion, it is not *itself* an argument. An argument has a premise and a conclusion, and, though the preceding statement has two parts, neither part by itself is either a premise or a conclusion. If Jamela says to K.C., "If you wash your car now," Jamela has not said something that is either true or false; likewise, if she says, "Then it will get spots," she has not said something that is either true or false. In neither case has Jamela said something that could qualify either as a premise or a conclusion.

Lists of Facts

Though the following might look like an argument, it is nothing more than a list of facts:

> Identity theft is up at least tenfold over last year. More people have learned how easy it is to get hold of another's Social Security number, bank account numbers, and such. The local police department reminds everyone to keep close watch on who has access to such information.

Although they are related by being about the same subject, none of these claims is offered as a reason for believing another, and thus there is no argument here. But the following passage is different. See if you can spot why it makes an argument:

> The number of people who have learned how to steal identities has doubled in the past year. So you are now more likely to become a victim of identity theft than you were a year ago.

Here, the first claim offers a reason for accepting the second claim; we now have an argument.

"A because B"

Sometimes the word "because" refers to the cause of something. But other times it refers to a premise of an argument. Mike walks into the motel lobby, wearing a swim suit and dripping wet. Consider these two statements:

"Mike is in his swim suit because he was swimming."   "Mike was swimming because he's in his swim suit."

These two sentences have the same form, "X because Y." But the sentence on the left *explains why* Mike is wearing a swim suit. The sentence on the right offers an argument *that* Mike was swimming. Only the sentence on the right is an argument. Put it this way: What follows "because" in the sentence on the left is the *cause*. What follows "because" in the right-hand sentence is *evidence*.

Be sure you understand the difference between these two sentences. Arguments and cause/effect statements can both employ the phrase *"X because Y."* But there the similarity ends. When what follows "because" is a *reason* for accepting a contention, we have an argument; when what follows "because" states the *cause* of something, we have a cause/effect explanation. These are entirely different enterprises. Arguing *that* a dog has fleas is different from explaining what *gave* it fleas. Arguing *that* violent crime has increased is different from explaining what *caused* it to increase.

ETHOS, PATHOS, AND LOGOS

When he was a young man, Alexander the Great conquered the world. Alexander was enormously proud of his accomplishment and celebrated by renaming cities after himself. Alexander's teacher, the Greek philosopher Aristotle, had no cities named after him; nevertheless, his imprint on civilization turned out to be even more profound than Alexander's.

Aristotle, who now is regarded as the father of logic, biology, and psychology, made enduring contributions to virtually every subject. These include (in addition to those just mentioned) physics, astronomy, meteorology, zoology, metaphysics, political science, economics, ethics, and rhetoric.

Among Aristotle's contributions in the last field (rhetoric) was a theory of persuasion, which famously contained the idea that there are three modes by which a speaker may persuade an audience. Paraphrasing very loosely, Aristotle's idea was that we can be persuaded, first of all, by a speaker's personal attributes, including such things as his or her background, reputation, accomplishments, expertise, and similar things. Aristotle referred to this mode of persuasion as *ethos*. Second, a speaker can persuade us by connecting with us on a personal level, and by arousing and appealing to our emotions by a skillful use of rhetoric. This mode of persuasion Aristotle termed *pathos*. And third, the speaker may persuade us by using information and arguments—what he called *logos*.

Unfortunately, logos—rational argumentation—is one of the least effective ways of winning someone to your point of view. That's why advertisers rarely bother with it. When the sellers of the first home automatic breadmaker found that its new kitchen device didn't interest people, they advertised the availability of a second model of the same machine, which was only slightly larger but much more expensive. When consumers saw that the first model was a great buy, they suddenly discovered they wanted one, and began snapping it up. Why try to persuade people by rational argument that they need a breadmaker when you can get them to think they do simply by making them think they have sniffed out a bargain?*

---

*Dan Ariely, *Irrational Predictability* (New York: HarperCollins Publishers, 2008), pp. 14 and 15.

Still, despite the general inefficacy of logos as a tool of persuasion, people do frequently use arguments when they try to persuade others. This might lead you to *define* an argument as an attempt to persuade. But that won't do. Remember, there are two kinds of argument. Deductive arguments are either sound or unsound, and whether a deductive argument is one or the other doesn't depend in the least on whether anyone is persuaded by it. Likewise, inductive arguments are in varying degrees strong or weak; their strength depends on the degree to which their premises elevate the probability of the conclusion, and that, too, is independent of whether anyone finds them persuasive. The very same argument might be persuasive to Parker but not to Moore, which shows that the persuasiveness of an argument is a subjective question of psychology, not of logic. Indeed, the individual who does *not* think critically is precisely the person who is persuaded by specious reasoning. People notoriously are unfazed by good arguments while finding even the worst arguments compelling. If you want to persuade people of something, try propaganda. Flattery has been known to work, too.

We shall be looking at alternative modes of persuasion—what Aristotle called ethos and pathos—in considerable detail in Chapters 4, 5, 6, and 7. However, we do this not so you can persuade people, but so you can be alert to the influence of ethos and pathos on your own thinking.

Now, we aren't suggesting it is a bad thing to be a persuasive writer or speaker. Obviously it isn't; that's what rhetoric courses are for—to teach you to write persuasively. Let's just put it this way: Whenever you find yourself being persuaded by what someone says, find the "logos" in the "pathos," and be persuaded by it alone.

The following exercises will give you practice (1) identifying premises and conclusions as well as words that indicate premises and conclusions, (2) telling the difference between deductive demonstrations and inductive supporting arguments, and (3) identifying balance of considerations arguments and inferences to the best explanation.

Indicate which blanks would ordinarily contain premises and which would ordinarily contain conclusions.

Exercise 2-1

▲ 1. ___a___, and ___b___. Therefore, ___c___.

▲ 2. ___a___. So, since ___b___, ___c___.

▲ 3. ___a___, clearly. After all, ___b___.

▲ 4. Since ___a___ and ___b___, ___c___.

▲ 5. ___a___. Consequently, ___b___, since ___c___ and ___d___.

Identify the premises and conclusions in each of the following arguments.

Exercise 2-2

▲ 1. Since all Communists are Marxists, all Marxists are Communists.

2. The Lakers almost didn't beat the Kings. They'll never get past Dallas.

3. If the butler had done it, he could not have locked the screen door. Therefore, since the door was locked, we know the butler is in the clear.

▲ 4. That cat is used to dogs. Probably she won't be upset if you bring home a new dog for a pet.

5. Hey, he can't be older than his mother's daughter's brother. His mother's daughter has only one brother.

6. Mr. Stooler will never make it into the state police. They have a weight limit, and he's over it.

▲ 7. Presbyterians are not fundamentalists, but all born-again Christians are. So no born-again Christians are Presbyterians.

8. I guess Thork doesn't have a thing to do. Why else would he waste his time watching daytime TV?

9. "There are more injuries in professional football today than there were twenty years ago," he reasoned. "And if there are more injuries, then today's players suffer higher risks. And if they suffer higher risks, then they should be paid more. Consequently, I think today's players should be paid more," he concluded.

▲ 10. Let's see . . . since the clunk comes only when I pedal, the problem must be in the chain, the crank, or the pedals.

Exercise 2-3   Identify the premises and the conclusions in the following arguments.

▲ 1. The darned engine pings every time we use the regular unleaded gasoline, but it doesn't do it with super. I'd bet that there is a difference in the octane ratings between the two in spite of what my mechanic says.

2. Chances are I'll be carded at JJ's, since Kera, Sherry, and Bobby were all carded there, and they all look as though they're about thirty.

3. Seventy percent of freshmen at State College come from wealthy families; therefore, probably about the same percentage of all State College students come from wealthy families.

▲ 4. When blue jays are breeding, they become aggressive. Consequently, scrub jays, which are very similar to blue jays, can also be expected to be aggressive when they're breeding.

5. I am sure Marietta comes from a wealthy family. She told me her parents benefitted from the cut in the capital gains tax.

6. According to *Nature*, today's thoroughbred racehorses do not run any faster than their grandparents did. But human Olympic runners are at least 20 percent faster than their counterparts of fifty years ago. Most likely, racehorses have reached their physical limits but humans have not.

▲ 7. Dogs are smarter than cats, since it is easier to train them.

8. "Let me demonstrate the principle by means of logic," the teacher said, holding up a bucket. "If this bucket has a hole in it, then it will leak. But it doesn't leak. Therefore, obviously, it doesn't have a hole in it."

9. We shouldn't take a chance on this new candidate. She's from Alamo Polytech, and the last person we hired from there was rotten.

▲ 10. If she was still interested in me, she would have called, but she didn't.

Five of these items are intended to be deductive demonstrations, and five are intended to provide inductive support. Which are which?

Exercise 2-4

▲ 1. No mayten tree is deciduous, and all nondeciduous trees are evergreens. It follows that all mayten trees are evergreens.

2. Mike must belong to the Bartenders and Beverage Union Local 165, since almost every Las Vegas bartender does.

3. Either Colonel Mustard or Reverend Green killed Professor Plum. But whoever ran off with Mrs. White did not kill the professor. Since Reverend Green ran off with Mrs. White, Colonel Mustard killed Professor Plum.

▲ 4. I've never met a golden retriever with a nasty disposition. I bet there aren't any.

5. Since some grapes are purple, and all grapes are fruit, some fruit is purple.

6. Why is Shrilla so mean to Timeeda? The only thing I can think of is that she's jealous. Jealousy is what's making her mean.

▲ 7. Palin will make a fine president. After all, she made a fine governor.

8. The figure he drew has only three sides, so it isn't a square.

9. It was the pizza that made my stomach churn. What else could it be? I was fine until I ate it.

▲ 10. It's wrong to hurt someone's feelings, and that is exactly what you are doing when you speak to me like that.

Identify each of the following as either

Exercise 2-5

    a. IBE
    b. balance of considerations argument
    c. neither of the above

▲ 1. Let's go now. I know you wanted to work in the yard, but if we wait longer, we won't make the movie. Plus, it's gonna get cold if we don't make tracks.

2. He said he was for the bill when it was proposed, and now he vetoes it? The only thing I can see is, he must be trying to get the teachers' vote.

3. Yes, a card laid is a card played, but I kept my hand on it, so I didn't actually lay it.

▲ 4. All things considered, we'd be better off taking the Suburban. Plus, let's get AAA to help us make reservations.

5. Jackson will get an A in the course, since he aced the final.

6. "A gentleman goes forth on a showery and miry day. He returns immaculate in the evening with the gloss still on his hat and his boots. He has been a fixture therefore all day. He is not a man with intimate friends. Where, then, could he have been? Is it not obvious?"

—*Arthur Conan Doyle,* The Hound of the Baskervilles, Chapter 3

▲ 7. It's longer taking the 405, but you can drive faster—though who knows what the traffic's like at this hour. I would say if you want to play it safe, stay on San Pablo.

8. He made threats, plus he had the motive. Not only that, but who else had access to a gun? If Mitchell didn't do it, I don't know who did.

9. The question is, are you running a temperature? Because if you are, it can't be a cold. The runny nose and the sore throat could be a cold, but not the temperature. Only the flu would give you a temperature.

▲ 10. Sherry seems right for the job to me. She speaks French, knows biology, has people skills, and makes a great impression. The only down side is, she can't start until October. That pretty much eliminates her, unfortunately.

TECHNIQUES FOR UNDERSTANDING ARGUMENTS

If an argument has been offered to us, before we can evaluate it we must understand it. Many arguments are difficult to understand because they are spoken and go by so quickly we cannot be sure of the conclusion or the premises. Others are difficult to understand because they have a complicated structure. Still others are difficult to understand because they are embedded in nonargumentative material consisting of background information, prejudicial coloring, illustrations, parenthetical remarks, digressions, subsidiary points, and other window dressing. And some arguments are difficult to understand because they are confused or because the reasons they contain are so poor that we are not sure whether to regard them as reasons.

In understanding an argument that has been given to us, the first task is to find the conclusion—the main point or thesis of the passage. The next step is to locate the reasons that have been offered for accepting the conclusion—that is, to find the premises. Next, we look for the reasons, if any, offered for accepting these premises. To proceed through these steps, you have to learn both to spot premises and conclusions when they occur in spoken and written passages and to understand the interrelationships among these claims—that is, the structure of the argument.

Clarifying an Argument's Structure

Let's begin with how to understand the relationships among the argumentative claims, because this problem is sometimes easiest to solve. If you are dealing with written material that you can mark up, one useful technique is to number the premises and conclusions and then use the numbers to lay bare the structure of the argument. Let's start with this argument as an example:

> I don't think we should get Carlos his own car. As a matter of fact, he is not responsible because he doesn't care for his things. And anyway, we don't have enough money for a car, since even now we have trouble making ends meet. Last week you yourself complained about our financial situation, and you never complain without really good reason.

We want to display the structure of this argument clearly. First, circle all premise and conclusion indicators. Thus:

I don't think we should get Carlos his own car. He is not responsible (in view of the fact) that he doesn't care for his things. And anyway, we don't have enough money for a car, (since) even now we have trouble making ends meet. Last week you yourself complained about our financial situation, and you never complain without really good reason.

Next, bracket each premise and conclusion, and number them consecutively as they appear in the argument. So what we now have is this:

① [I don't think we should get Carlos his own car.] ② [He is not responsible] in view of the fact that ③ [he doesn't care for his things.] And anyway, ④ [we don't have enough money for a car], since ⑤ [even now we have trouble making ends meet.] ⑥ [Last week you yourself complained about our financial situation], and ⑦ [you never complain without really good reason.]

Then we diagram the argument. Using an arrow to mean "therefore" or "is intended as evidence [or as a reason or as a premise] for," we diagram the first three claims in the argument as follows:

Now, ⑥ and ⑦ together support ④; that is, they are part of the same argument for ④. To show that ⑥ and ⑦ go together, we simply draw a line under them, put a plus sign between them, and draw the arrow from the line to ④, like this:

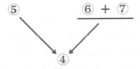

Because ⑤ and ⑥ + ⑦ are separate arguments for ④, we can represent the relationship between them and ④ as follows:

Finally, because ④ and ② are separate arguments for ①, the diagram of the entire passage is this:

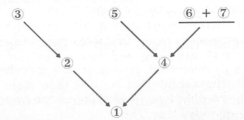

So the conventions governing this approach to revealing argument structure are very simple: First, circle all premise- and conclusion-indicating words. Then, assuming you can identify the claims that function in the argument (a big assumption, as you will see before long), number them consecutively. Then display the structure of the argument, using arrows for "therefore" and plus signs over a line to connect two or more premises that depend on one another.

Some claims, incidentally, may constitute reasons for more than one conclusion. For example:

① [Carlos continues to be irresponsible.] ② [He certainly should not have his own car], and, as far as I am concerned, ③ [he can forget about that trip to Hawaii this winter, too.]

Structure:

Frequently, too, we evaluate counterarguments to our positions. For example:

① We really should have more African Americans on the faculty. ② That is why the new diversity program ought to be approved. True, ③ it may involve an element of unfairness to whites, but ④ the benefits to society of having more black faculty outweigh the disadvantages.

Notice that claim ③ introduces a consideration that runs counter to the conclusion of the argument, which is stated in ②. We can indicate counterclaims by crossing the "therefore" arrow with lines, thus:

This diagram indicates that item ③ has been introduced by the writer as a consideration that runs counter to ②.

Of course, one might adopt other conventions for clarifying argument structure—for example, circling the main conclusion and drawing solid lines under supporting premises and wavy lines under the premises of subarguments. The technique we have described is simply one way of doing it; any of several others might work as well for you. However, *no* technique for revealing argument structure will work if you cannot spot the argumentative claims in the midst of a lot of background material.

Distinguishing Arguments from Window Dressing

It is not always easy to isolate the argument in a speech or a written piece. Often, speakers and writers think that because their main points are more or less clear to them, they will be equally apparent to listeners and readers. But it doesn't always work that way.

If you have trouble identifying a conclusion in what you hear or read, it *could* be the passage is not an argument at all. Make sure the passage in question is not a report, a description, an explanation, or something else altogether, rather than an argument. The key here is determining whether the speaker or writer is offering reasons intended to support or demonstrate one or more claims.

The problem could also be that the conclusion is left unstated. Sometimes it helps simply to put the argument aside and ask yourself, "What is this person trying to prove?" In any case, the first and essential step in understanding an argument is to spot the conclusion.

If you are having difficulty identifying the *premises*, consider the possibility that you have before you a case of rhetoric (see Chapter 5). (You can't find premises in a piece of pure rhetoric because there *are* no premises.) You will have an advantage over many students in having learned about rhetorical devices in Chapters 5, 6, and 7. By that time, you should be getting pretty good at recognizing them.

As you apply what you learn in this book to arguments you encounter in real life, you are apt to encounter arguments and argumentative essays whose organization is difficult to comprehend. When you do, you may find diagramming a useful technique. Also, as is obvious, what we have said in this section applies to arguments that others give us or that we otherwise encounter. You don't diagram what's in your head, though you need to be clear on your own conclusions, tentative or otherwise, and the reasons you have for accepting them. However, the diagramming technique does apply to material you write

On Language

Stupid Liberal!

The employer introduced himself to his new gardener.

"I am a professor of logic," the employer said.

"Oh. What's that?" the gardener asked.

"I shall give you a demonstration," announced the professor. "Do you own a wheelbarrow?"

"Yes," replied the gardener.

"Then I infer you are a hard worker," the professor continued. "And from that fact I infer you have a family. And from that I infer you are conscientious and responsible. And from that I infer you are a conservative. Am I right?"

"Wow!" exclaimed the gardener. "That's right! So that's logic?"

"That's logic," preened the professor.

Later the gardener met up with one of his buddies and told him he had a job with a professor of logic.

"Logic?" his friend asked. "What's that?"

"I'll show you," the gardener said. "Do you own a wheelbarrow?"

"No."

"Stupid liberal."

for others. If you find you have difficulty diagramming your arguments, it's a good indication you should reorganize your essay and make the structure of your reasoning clearer.

EVALUATING ARGUMENTS

Thinking critically requires us to evaluate arguments, and evaluating arguments has two parts. First, there is the *logic* part: Does the argument either demonstrate or support its conclusion? Is this argument either deductively valid or inductively relatively strong? You know now what these questions mean theoretically; over the course of this book, you will see what they involve in fact.

The other part, of course, is the *truth* part. Are the premises actually true? As we explain in Chapter 4, it is best to be suspicious of a premise that conflicts with our background information or other credible claims, as well as a premise that comes from a source that lacks credibility. And, as we develop at length in Chapters 5, 6, and 7, we want to avoid being tricked into accepting a claim by rhetoric or other psychological gimmickry. It also almost goes without saying that premises that are unclear require clarification before one accepts them—as we explain in Chapter 3. In general, determining the truth of premises requires knowledge, experience, a level head, and the inclination to look into things.

Recap

The main ideas of the chapter are these:

- Arguments consist of a premise (or premises) and a conclusion.
- The same claim can be a premise in one argument and a conclusion in a second argument.
- The two fundamental types of reasoning are deductive demonstration and inductive support.
- A deductive argument is used to demonstrate or prove a conclusion, which it does if it is sound.
- An argument is sound if it is valid and its premise (or premises) is true.
- An argument is valid if it is impossible for its premise (or premises) to be true and its conclusion to be false.
- An inductive argument is used to support rather than to demonstrate a conclusion.
- Support is a matter of degrees: An argument supports a conclusion to the extent its premise (or premises) makes the conclusion likely.
- An argument that offers more support for a conclusion is said to be stronger than one that offers less support; the latter is said to be weaker than the former.
- Some instructors use the word "strong" in an absolute sense to denote inductive arguments whose premise (or premises) makes the conclusion more likely than not.

- Inductive arguments and deductive arguments can have unstated premises.
- Whether an argument is deductive or inductive may depend on what the unstated premise is said to be.
- If the argument you are contemplating is one someone has offered you, and you are having trouble tracking the part of an argument that appears in a written passage, try diagramming the passage.
- Balance of considerations reasoning involves deductive and inductive elements. If considerations are compared quantitatively, weighing them involves deductive reasoning. Predictions as to outcomes involve inductive reasoning.
- Inference to best explanation is a common type of inductive reasoning in which one tries to determine the best explanation for a phenomenon by comparing alternative hypotheses in terms of their explanatory adequacy, predictive accuracy, compatibility with well-accepted explanations, and freedom from unnecessary assumptions.

Additional Exercises

These exercises will test your comprehension of the chapter. They will also give you additional practice (1) distinguishing between deductive demonstrations and inductive supporting arguments, (2) recognizing when a passage contains more than a single argument, (3) recognizing the difference between arguments and explanations, (4) identifying unstated assumptions, and (5) diagramming arguments.

Exercise 2-6

Fill in the blanks where called for, and answer true or false where appropriate.

1. Arguments that are relatively strong or weak are called _____ arguments.
2. All valid arguments are sound arguments.
3. All sound arguments are valid arguments.
4. If a valid argument has a false conclusion, then not all its premises can be true.
5. A sound argument cannot have a false conclusion.
6. "Strong" and "weak" are absolute terms.
7. If you try to demonstrate a conclusion, you are using _____ reasoning.
8. When a conclusion has been proved beyond a reasonable doubt, it has always been demonstrated.
9. An argument can never have an unstated conclusion.
10. When you try to support a conclusion, you are using _____ reasoning.

11. The most effective way to convince someone is through argument.

12. "If . . . then . . ." sentences may be arguments.

▲ 13. "If . . . then . . ." sentences may be premises.

14. Logic should be defined as the art of persuasion.

15. "A because B" is always an argument.

16. "A because B" is never an argument.

▲ 17. "IBE" refers to a type of deductive argument.

18. Inductive and deductive arguments both may occur in balance of considerations reasoning.

Exercise 2-7

Some of these passages are best viewed as attempted deductive demonstrations, and others are best viewed as offering inductive support. Which are which?

▲ 1. All mammals are warm-blooded creatures, and all whales are mammals. Therefore, all whales are warm-blooded creatures.

▲ 2. The brains of rats raised in enriched environments with a variety of toys and puzzles weigh more than the brains of rats raised in more barren environments. Therefore, the brains of humans will weigh more if humans are placed in intellectually stimulating environments.

3. Jones won't plead guilty to a misdemeanor, and if he won't plead guilty, then he will be tried on a felony charge. Therefore, he will be tried on a felony charge.

▲ 4. We've interviewed two hundred professional football players, and 60 percent of them favor expanding the season to twenty games. Therefore, 60 percent of all professional football players favor expanding the season to twenty games.

5. Jose is taller than Bill, and Bill is taller than Margaret. Therefore, Jose is taller than Margaret.

6. Exercise may help chronic male smokers kick the habit, says a study published today. The researchers, based at McDuff University, put thirty young male smokers on a three-month program of vigorous exercise. One year later, only 14 percent of them still smoked, according to the report. An equivalent number of young male smokers who did not go through the exercise program were also checked after a year, and it was found that 60 percent still smoked. Smokers in the exercise program began running three miles a day and gradually worked up to eight miles daily. They also spent five and a half hours each day in such moderately vigorous activities as soccer, basketball, biking, and swimming.

▲ 7. Believe in God? Yes, of course I do. The universe couldn't have arisen by chance, could it? Besides, I read the other day that more and more physicists believe in God, based on what they're finding out about the Big Bang and all that stuff.

▲   8. From an office memo: "I've got a good person for your opening in Accounting. Jesse Brown is his name, and he's as sharp as they come. Jesse has a solid background in bookkeeping, and he's good with computers. He's also reliable, and he'll project the right image. He will do a fine job for you."

Exercise 2-8

Some of these passages contain separate arguments for the main conclusion. Others contain a single argument (though it might have more than one premise). Which passages contain separate arguments for the main conclusion?

▲   1. North Korea is a great threat to its neighbors. It has a million-person army ready to be unleashed at a moment's notice, and it also has nuclear weapons.

2. Shaun is going to the party with Mary, so she won't be going alone.

3. Michael should just go ahead and get a new car. The one he's driving is junk; also, he has a new job and can afford a new car.

4. If Karper goes to Las Vegas, he'll wind up in a casino; and if he winds up in a casino, it's a sure thing he'll spend half the night at a craps table. So you can be sure: If Karper goes to Las Vegas, he'll spend half the night at a craps table.

5. It's going to be rainy tomorrow, and Serj doesn't like to play golf in the rain. It's going to be cold as well, and he *really* doesn't like to play when it's cold. So you can be sure Serj will be someplace other than the golf course tomorrow.

▲   6. Hey, you're overwatering your lawn. See? There are mushrooms growing around the base of that tree—a sure sign of overwatering. Also, look at all the worms on the ground. They come up when the earth is oversaturated.

7. "Will you drive me to the airport?" she asked. "Why should I do that?" he wanted to know. "Because I'll pay you twice what it takes for gas. Besides, didn't you say you were my friend?"

8. If you drive too fast, you're more likely to get a ticket, and the more likely you are to get a ticket, the more likely you are to have your insurance premiums raised. So, if you drive too fast, you are more likely to have your insurance premiums raised.

▲   9. If you drive too fast, you're more likely to get a ticket. You're also more likely to get into an accident. So you shouldn't drive too fast.

▲   10. There are several reasons why you should consider installing a solarium. First, you can still get a tax credit. Second, you can reduce your heating bill. Third, if you build it right, you can actually cool your house with it in the summer.

11. From a letter to the editor: "By trying to eliminate Charles Darwin from the curriculum, creationists are doing themselves a great disservice. When read carefully, Darwin's discoveries only support the thesis that species change, not that they evolve into new species. This is a thesis that most creationists can live with. When read carefully, Darwin actually supports the creationist point of view."

12. Editorial comment: "The Supreme Court's ruling, that schools may have a moment of silence but not if it's designated for prayer, is sound. Nothing stops someone from saying a silent prayer at school or anywhere else. Also, even though a moment of silence will encourage prayer, it will not favor any particular religion over any other. The ruling makes sense."

▲ 13. We must paint the house now! Here are three good reasons: (a) If we don't, then we'll have to paint it next summer; (b) if we have to paint it next summer, we'll have to cancel our trip; and (c) it's too late to cancel the trip.

Exercise 2-9

Which five of the following statements are probably intended to explain the cause of something, and which five are probably intended to argue that some claim is true?

▲ 1. The reason we've had so much hot weather recently is that the jet stream is unusually far north.

2. The reason Ms. Mossbarger looks so tired is that she hasn't been able to sleep for three nights.

3. The reason it's a bad idea to mow the lawn in your bare feet is that you could be seriously injured.

▲ 4. The reason Ken mows the lawn in his bare feet is that he doesn't realize how dangerous it is.

5. You can be sure that Ryan will marry Beth. After all, he told me he would.

6. If I were you, I'd change before going into town. Those clothes look like you slept in them.

▲ 7. Overeating can cause high blood pressure.

8. Eating so much salt can cause high blood pressure, so you'd better cut back a little.

▲ 9. It's a good bet Iran wants to build nuclear weapons, because the U.N. inspectors found devices for the enrichment of plutonium.

10. The reason Iran wants to build nuclear weapons is to gain control over neighboring Middle Eastern countries.

Exercise 2-10

Which of the following items are (a) true beyond any possible doubt, (b) true beyond a reasonable doubt, or (c) neither of the above? Expect disagreement on some items.

▲ 1. Squares have four sides.

2. You will not live to be 130 years old.

3. A cow cannot yodel.

▲ 4. A six-foot person is taller than a five-foot person.

5. If the sign on the parking meter says, "Out of Order," the meter won't work.

6. Nobody can be her own mother.

▲ 7. God exists or does not exist.

8. They will never get rid of all disease.

9. The ice caps couldn't melt entirely.

▲ 10. The day two days after the day before yesterday is today.

Exercise 2-11

For each of the following, supply a universal principle (a statement that says that something holds without exception) that turns it into a valid deductive argument.

Example

Tay is opinionated. She should be more open-minded.

One universal principle that makes it valid

Opinionated people should all be more open-minded. (Note: There are alternative ways of phrasing this.)

▲ 1. Jamal keeps his word, so he is a man of good character.

2. Betty got an A in the course, so she must have received an A on the final.

3. Iraq posed a threat to us, so we had a right to invade it.

▲ 4. Colonel Mustard could not have murdered Professor Plum, because the two men were in separate rooms when the professor was killed.

5. Avril is no liberal, since she voted against gun control.

6. Jimmi has a gentle soul; if there is a heaven, he should go to it when he dies.

▲ 7. Of course that guy should be executed; he committed murder, didn't he?

8. I don't think you could call the party a success; only eight people showed up.

9. Mzbrynski proved Goldbach's conjecture; that makes him the greatest mathematician ever.

▲ 10. The fan needs oil; after all, it's squeaking.

Exercise 2-12

For each of the following arguments, supply a principle that makes it inductive rather than deductive.

Example

Susan is sharp, so she will get a good grade in this course.

One claim that makes it inductive

Most sharp people get good grades in this course.

▲ 1. There are puddles everywhere; it must have rained recently.

2. The lights are dim; therefore, the battery is weak.

3. Simpson's blood matched the blood on the glove found at the victim's condo: He killed her.

▲ 4. Of course it will be cold tomorrow! It's been cold all week, hasn't it?

5. Ambramoff isn't very good with animals. I doubt he'd make a great parent.

6. The dog has either fleas or dry skin; it's scratching a lot.

▲ 7. Why do I say their party wasn't a success? Remember all the leftovers?

8. Cheston owns a rifle; he's sure to belong to the NRA.

9. The dessert contained caffeine, so you might have trouble sleeping tonight.

▲ 10. I took Zicam, and my cold disappeared like magic. Obviously, it works.

Exercise 2-13

Diagram the following "arguments," using the method explained in the text.

▲ 1. ①, in light of the fact that ② and ③. [Assume ② and ③ are part of the same argument for ①.]

2. ① and ②; therefore ③. [Assume ① and ② are separate arguments for ③.]

3. Since ①, ②; and since ③, ④. And since ② and ④, ⑤. [Assume ② and ④ are separate arguments for ⑤.]

▲ 4. ①; therefore ② and ③. But in light of the fact that ② and ③, ④. Consequently, ⑤. Therefore, ⑥. [Assume ② and ③ are separate arguments for ④.]

5. ①, ②, ③; therefore ④. ⑤, in view of ①. And ⑥, since ②. Therefore ⑦. [Assume ①, ②, and ③ are part of the same argument for ④.]

Exercise 2-14

Diagram the arguments contained in the following passages, using the method explained in the text.

▲ 1. Dear Jim,
    Your distributor is the problem. Here's why. There's no current at the spark plugs. And if there's no current at the plugs, then either your alternator is shot or your distributor is defective. But if the problem were in the alternator, then your dash warning light would be on. So, since the light isn't on, the problem must be in the distributor. Hope this helps.
    Yours,
    Benita Autocraft

2. The slide in the dollar must be stopped. It contributes to inflation and increases the cost of imports. True, it helps exports, but on balance it is bad for the economy.

3. It's high time professional boxing was outlawed. Boxing almost always leads to brain damage, and anything that does that ought to be done away with. Besides, it supports organized crime.

▲ 4. They really ought to build a new airport. It would attract more business to the area, not to mention the fact that the old airport is overcrowded and dangerous.

5. Vote for Kucinich? No way. He's too radical, and he's too inexperienced, and those two things make him dangerous. I do like his stand on trade, but I still don't think you should vote for him.

Exercise 2-15

Diagram the arguments contained in the following passages, using the method explained in the text. (Your instructor may have different instructions for you to follow.)

▲ 1. Cottage cheese will help you to be slender, youthful, and more beautiful. Enjoy it often.

2. If you want to listen to loud music, do it when we are not at home. It bothers us, and we're your parents.

3. If you want to see the best version of *The Three Musketeers*, try the 1948 version. Lana Turner is luscious; Vincent Price is dastardly; Angela Lansbury is exquisitely regal; and nobody ever has or ever will portray D'Artagnan with the grace, athleticism, or skill of Gene Kelly. Download it. It's a must.

▲ 4. From a letter to the editor: "The idea of a free press in America today is a joke. A small group of people, the nation's advertisers, control the media more effectively than if they owned it outright. Through fear of an advertising boycott, they can dictate everything from programming to news report content. Politicians as well as editors shiver in their boots at the thought of such a boycott. This situation is intolerable and ought to be changed. I suggest we all listen to National Public Radio and public television."

5. Too many seniors, disabled veterans, and families with children are paying far too much of their incomes for housing. Proposition 168 will help clear the way for affordable housing construction for these groups. Proposition 168 reforms the outdated requirement for an election before affordable housing can even be approved. Requiring elections for every publicly assisted housing venture, even when there is no local opposition, is a waste of taxpayers' money. No other state constitution puts such a roadblock in front of efforts to house senior citizens and others in need. Please support Proposition 168.

6. Fifty years after President John F. Kennedy's assassination, it's no easier to accept the idea that a loser like Lee Harvey Oswald committed the crime of the century all by himself with a $12.78 mail-order rifle and a $7.17 scope. Yet even though two-thousand-plus books and films about the episode have been made, there is no credible evidence to contradict the Warren Commission finding that "the shots which killed President Kennedy and wounded Governor Connally were fired by Lee Harvey Oswald" and that "Oswald acted alone."

After all these years, it's time to accept the conclusion. The nation pays a heavy price for chronic doubts and mistrust. Confidence in the government has declined. Participation in the voting process has steadily slid downward. The national appetite for wild theories encourages peddlers to persist. Evil is never easy to accept. In the case of JFK, the sooner we let it go, the better.

▲   7. "Consumers ought to be concerned about the Federal Trade Commission's dropping a rule that supermarkets must actually have in stock the items they advertise for sale. While a staff analysis suggests costs of the rule outweigh the benefits to consumers, few shoppers want to return to the practices that lured them into stores only to find the advertised products they sought were not there.

"The staff study said the rule causes shoppers to pay $200 million to receive $125 million in benefits. The cost is a low estimate and the benefits a high estimate, according to the study.

"However, even those enormously big figures boil down to a few cents per shopper over a year's time. And the rule does say that when a grocer advertises a sale, the grocer must have sufficient supply of sale items on hand to meet reasonable buyer demand."

—*The Oregonian*

8. "And we thought we'd heard it all. Now the National Rifle Association wants the U.S. Supreme Court to throw out the ban on private ownership of fully automatic machine guns.

"As the nation's cities reel under staggering murder totals, as kids use guns simply to get even after feuds, as children are gunned down by random bullets, the NRA thinks it is everybody's constitutional right to have their own personal machine gun.

"This is not exactly the weapon of choice for deer hunting or for a homeowner seeking protection. It is an ideal weapon for street gangs and drug thugs in their wars with each other and the police.

"To legalize fully automatic machine guns is to increase the mayhem that is turning this nation—particularly its large cities—into a continual war zone. Doesn't the NRA have something better to do?"

—Capital Times, *Madison, Wisconsin*

9. From a letter to the editor: "Recently the California Highway Patrol stopped me at a drunk-drive checkpoint. Now, I don't like drunk drivers any more than anyone else. I certainly see why the police find the checkpoint system effective. But I think our right to move about freely is much more important. If the checkpoint system continues, then next there will be checkpoints for drugs, seat belts, infant car seats, drivers' licenses. We will regret it later if we allow the system to continue."

▲ 10. "Well located, sound real estate is the safest investment in the world. It is not going to disappear, as can the value of dollars put into savings accounts. Neither will real estate values be lost because of inflation. In fact, property values tend to increase at a pace at least equal to the rate of inflation. Most homes have appreciated at a rate greater than the inflation rate (due mainly to strong buyer demand and insufficient supply of newly constructed homes)."

—*Robert Bruss*, The Smart Investor's Guide to Real Estate

11. "The constitutional guarantee of a speedy trial protects citizens from arbitrary government abuse, but it has at least one other benefit, too. It prevents crime.

"A recent Justice Department study found that more than a third of those with serious criminal records—meaning three or more felony convictions—are arrested for new offenses while free on bond awaiting federal court trial. You don't have to be a social scientist to suspect that the longer the delay, the greater the likelihood of further violations. In short, overburdened courts mean much more than justice delayed; they quite literally amount to the infliction of further injustice."

—*Scripps Howard Newspapers*

▲ 12. As we enter a new decade, about 200 million Americans are producing data on the Internet as rapidly as they consume it. Each of these users is tracked by technologies ever more able to collate essential facts about them—age, address, credit rating, marital status, etc.—in electronic form for use in commerce. One website, for example, promises, for the meager sum of seven dollars, to scan "over two billion records to create a single comprehensive report on an individual." It is not unreasonable, then, to believe that the combination of capitalism and technology poses a looming threat to what remains of our privacy.

—*Loosely adapted from* Harper's

13. Having your car washed at the car wash may be the best way to go, but there are some possible drawbacks. The International Carwashing Association (ICA) has fought back against charges that automatic car washes, in recycling wash water, actually dump the salt and dirt from one car onto the next. And that brushes and drag cloths hurt the finish. Perhaps there is some truth to these charges.

The ICA sponsored tests that supposedly demonstrated that the average home car wash is harder on a car than an automatic wash. Maybe. But what's "the average" home car wash? And you can bet that the automatic car washes in the test were in perfect working order.

There is no way you or I can tell for certain if the filtration system and washing equipment at the automatic car wash are properly maintained. And even if they are, what happens if you follow some mud-caked pickup through the wash? Road dirt might still be caught in the bristles of the brushes or strips of fabric that are dragged over your car.

Here's my recommendation: Wash your own car.

▲ 14.   **Argument in Favor of Measure A**

"Measure A is consistent with the City's General Plan and City policies directing growth to the City's non-agricultural lands. A 'yes' vote on Measure A will affirm the wisdom of well-planned, orderly growth in the City of Chico by approving an amendment to the 1982 Rancho Arroyo Specific Plan. Measure A substantially reduces the amount of housing previously approved for Rancho Arroyo, increases the number of parks and amount of open space, and significantly enlarges and enhances Bidwell Park.

"A 'yes' vote will accomplish the following: • Require the development to dedicate 130.8 acres of land to Bidwell Park • Require the developer to dedicate seven park sites • Create 53 acres of landscaped corridors and greenways • Preserve existing arroyos and protect sensitive plant habitats and other environmental features • Create junior high school and church sites • Plan a series of villages within which, eventually, a total of 2,927 residential dwelling units will be developed • Plan area which will provide onsite job opportunities and retail services. . . ."

—County of Butte sample ballot

15.   **Rebuttal to Argument in Favor of Measure A**

"Villages? Can a project with 3,000 houses and 7,000 new residents really be regarded as a 'village'? The Sacramento developers pushing the Rancho Arroyo project certainly have a way with words. We urge citizens of Chico to ignore their flowery language and vote no on Measure A.

"These out-of-town developers will have you believe that their project protects agricultural land. Hogwash! Chico's Greenline protects valuable farmland. With the Greenline, there is enough land in the Chico area available for development to build 62,000 new homes. . . .

"They claim that their park dedications will reduce use of our overcrowded Bidwell Park. Don't you believe it! They want to attract 7,000 new residents to Chico by using Rancho Arroyo's proximity to Bidwell Park to outsell other local housing projects.

"The developers imply that the Rancho Arroyo project will provide a much needed school site. In fact, the developers intend to sell the site to the school district, which will pay for the site with taxpayers' money.

"Chico doesn't need the Rancho Arroyo project. Vote no on Measure A."

—County of Butte sample ballot

16. Letter to the editor: "A relative of mine is a lawyer who recently represented a murderer who had already had a life sentence and broke out of prison and murdered someone else. I think this was a waste of the taxpayers' money to try this man again. It won't do any good. I think murderers should be executed.

"We are the most crime-ridden society in the world. Someone is murdered every 27 minutes in the U.S., and there is a rape every ten minutes and an armed robbery every 82 seconds. According to the FBI, there are 870,000 violent crimes a year, and you know the number is increasing.

"Also according to the FBI, only 10 percent of those arrested for the crimes committed are found guilty, and a large percentage are released on probation. These people are released so they can just go out and commit more crimes.

"Why are they released? In the end it is because there aren't enough prisons to house the guilty. The death sentence must be restored. This would create more room in prisons. It would also drastically reduce the number of murders. If a robber knew before he shot someone that if he was caught his own life would be taken, would he do it?

"These people deserve to die. They sacrificed their right to live when they murdered someone, maybe your mother. It's about time we stopped making it easy for criminals to kill people and get away with it."

—Cascade News

▲ 17. Letter to the editor: "In regard to your editorial, 'Crime bill wastes billions,' let me set you straight. Your paper opposes mandatory life sentences for criminals convicted of three violent crimes, and you whine about how criminals' rights might be violated. Yet you also want to infringe on a citizen's right to keep and bear arms. You say you oppose life sentences for three-time losers because judges couldn't show any leniency toward the criminals no matter how trivial the crime. What is your definition of trivial, busting an innocent child's skull with a hammer?"

—*North State Record*

▲ 18. Freedom means choice. This is a truth antiporn activists always forget when they argue for censorship. In their fervor to impose their morality, groups like Enough Is Enough cite extreme examples of pornography, such as child porn, suggesting that they are easily available in video stores.

This is not the way it is. Most of this material portrays not actions such as this but consensual sex between adults.

The logic used by Enough Is Enough is that, if something can somehow hurt someone, it must be banned. They don't apply this logic to more harmful substances, such as alcohol or tobacco. Women and children are more adversely affected by drunken driving and secondhand smoke than by pornography. Few Americans would want to ban alcohol or tobacco, even though these substances kill hundreds of thousands of people each year.

Writing Exercises

1. Write a one-page essay in which you determine whether and why it is better (you get to define "better") to look younger than your age, older than your age, or just your age. Then number the premises and conclusions in your essay and diagram it.

2. Should there be a death penalty for first-degree murder? On the top half of a sheet of paper, list considerations supporting the death penalty, and on the bottom half, list considerations opposing it. Take about ten minutes to compile your two lists.

After everyone is finished, your instructor will call on people to read their lists. He or she will then give everyone about twenty minutes to write a draft of an essay that addresses the issue "Should there be a death penalty for first-degree murder?" Put your name on the back of your paper. After everyone is finished, your instructor will collect the papers and redistribute them to the class. In groups of four or five, read the papers that have been given to your group. Do not look at the names of the authors. Select the best essay in each group. Your instructor will ask each group to read the essay it has selected as best.

As an alternative, your instructor may have each group rank-order the papers. He or she will have neighboring groups decide which of their top-ranked papers is the best. The instructor will read the papers that have been top-ranked by two (or more) groups, for discussion.

3. Is it possible to tell just by looking at someone whether he or she is telling the truth? Do a little Internet research and then take a position on the issue and defend it in a two-page essay. This assignment will help prepare you for Chapter 4.

4. Find an interesting issue broached in one of the essays in Appendix 1. Take a position on that issue and defend it in a two-page essay. Identify each argument you used as either inductive or deductive.

3

Clear Thinking, Critical Thinking, and Clear Writing

From August 1987 until January 2007, Alan Greenspan was chairman of the Federal Reserve Board ("the Fed"). Because any remark he made about U.S. monetary policy could cause markets all over the world to fluctuate wildly, he developed a complicated way of speaking that came to be known as "Fedspeak."

Here's an example:

> It is a tricky problem to find the particular calibration in timing that would be appropriate to stem the acceleration in risk premiums created by falling incomes without prematurely aborting the decline in the inflation-generated risk premiums.*

Greenspan has admitted that such remarks were not really intended to be understood.

Asked to give an example by commenting on the weather, Greenspan replied,

> I would generally expect that today in Washington, D.C., the probability of changes in the weather is

---

*<http://en.wikipedia.org/wiki/Fedspeak>.

Students will learn to . . .

1. Determine acceptable and unacceptable degrees of vagueness in language

2. Understand and identify types of ambiguity

3. Identify the problems generality causes in language

4. Use definitions to increase precision and clarity and to influence attitudes

5. Understand the types of definitions

6. Acquire skills for writing an effective argumentative essay

highly uncertain. But we are monitoring the data in such a manner that we will be able to update people on changes that are important.*

This tells us nothing about the weather, of course, and was not intended to. Many times, though, we run across similarly complicated examples of speech or writing that do seem to be intended to inform us.

For example, Allan Bloom, the famous American educator who authored *The Closing of the American Mind*, which was read (or at least purchased) by millions, wrote in that book:

> If openness means to "go with the flow," it is necessarily an accommodation to the present. That present is so closed to doubt about so many things impeding the progress of its principles that unqualified openness to it would mean forgetting the despised alternative to it, knowledge of which makes us aware of what is doubtful in it.

Is this true? Well—that's really hard to say. The problem is, you don't know exactly what Professor Bloom is asserting in this passage.

Any number of problems may make a statement unclear. Not infrequently, people just don't say what they mean. Consider this statement made by President George W. Bush:

> You know, when you give a man more money in his pocket—in this case, a woman more money in her pocket to expand a business, it—they build new buildings. And when somebody builds a new building somebody has got to come and build the building. And when the building expanded it prevented additional opportunities for people to work. (Lancaster, PA, October 3, 2007)**

We think he meant "presented" rather than "prevented," but even then, the point can surely be made more clearly. Here's an example from former Canadian prime minister Jean Chrétien, when asked in Parliament about old versus new money in the health care program:

> They say that the money we had promised three years ago to be new money this year is not new money. We have not paid it yet and it is old money versus new money. For me new money is new money if paying in $5 or $10, it's the same money.†

We have no clue what he had in mind.

One of your authors noticed this as a tease on the front page of a newspaper: "49ers are upset." This probably means that somebody who was not supposed to beat the San Francisco football team did manage to beat them. On the other hand, it *could* mean that the team is dismayed about something.

---

*Broadcast on *BBC World Service Interview*, October 25, 2007.
**From *The Complete Bushisms*, by Jacob Weisberg, <www.slate.com/id/76886/>.
†Reported in the *Globe and Mail*, February 7, 2003.

In the Media

Say What?? . . .

You don't have to be a national political figure to put your foot in your mouth. Ordinary folks can do it, too!

The president's energy tax won't even be noticed. Besides, it will discourage consumption.

[Hey, if it won't be noticed, it won't discourage consumption.]

Females score lower on the SAT than males, which right there proves the tests don't show anything. They also demonstrate that teachers do a better job of teaching male students, which is just what you'd expect given the sexual bias that exists in the classroom.

[If the SATs don't show anything, then they don't show that teachers do a better job teaching males.]

We have to liberate discussion on this campus and not be so restrained by the First Amendment.

[Right. And we can make people free by sticking them in jail.]

Once your body gets cold, the rest of you will get cold, too.

[On the other hand, if you can keep your body warm, the rest of you will stay warm, too.]

It's hard to support the president's invasion of Haiti when the American public is so strongly against it. And besides, he's just doing it to raise his standings in the polls.

[Hmmm. How's it going to raise his standings if the public is so strongly against it?]

Has anyone put anything in your baggage without your knowledge?

[Asked of our colleague Becky White by an airport security employee.]

Although obscurity can issue from various causes, four sources of confusion stand out as paramount: excessive vagueness, ambiguity, excessive generality, and undefined terms. In this chapter, we shall consider vagueness, ambiguity, and generality in some detail and then talk about definitions.

Also, from time to time situations arise in which we need to think critically about what we write, especially when we are trying to produce an argumentative essay. In this type of writing enterprise, one takes a position on an issue and supports it with argument. A good argumentative essay usually consists of four parts: a statement of the issue, a statement of one's position on that issue, arguments that support one's position, and rebuttals of arguments that support contrary positions. Obviously, an argumentative essay is weakened by statements that are obscure, and what we say in this chapter has direct application to writing clear argumentative essays. We shall return to this subject after we discuss vagueness, ambiguity, generality, and definitions.

Wabash College student newspaper headline: Carter Swears in Church

As it turned out, a Judge Carter gave the oath of office to a deputy attorney general whose last name is Church.

Was this an accident, or was a headline writer at Wabash College having a bit of fun?

VAGUENESS

Perhaps the most common form of unclear thinking or writing is excessive vagueness. Pursued to its depths, the concept of vagueness can be a knotty one, and it has been the focus of much philosophical attention in the past

Real Life

Vagueness at the Border

As the text explains, vagueness results when the scope of a concept is not clear—that is, when there are border-line cases. "Bald" is a typical example. Here, Ms. Hilton is clearly *not* bald, and Mr. Stewart clearly *is* bald. But whether Bruce Willis is bald or not is a good question. He has hair—although it seems to be on the wane—but these days, he keeps his head shaved and thus appears bald. How much hair would he have to lose to be bald whether or not he shaved his head? The fact that there is no good answer demonstrates that "baldness" is a vague concept.

■ Hilton   ■ Willis, with . . .   ■ . . . and without   ■ Stewart

Man is ready to die for an idea, provided that idea is not quite clear to him.

—PAUL ELDRIDGE

few decades.* Fortunately, at a practical level, the idea is not difficult to grasp. A word or phrase is **vague** if the group of things to which it applies has border-line cases. Consider the word "bald." It's clear that Paris Hilton is *not* bald. It's equally clear that Patrick Stewart *is* bald. But there are lots of people in between (including both your authors). Many of those between the two extremes are borderline cases: It is not at all clear whether the word "bald" should apply to them—it's the sort of thing about which reasonable people could disagree. For this reason, it is correct to say that baldness is a vague concept.

Vagueness plays a very important role in much that we do. In the law, for example, how we deal with vagueness is crucial. Whether the word "tor-ture" applies to various types of interrogation techniques, especially including "waterboarding," for example, has been a serious issue for several years. Many former officials have claimed that these techniques did not count as torture, but many others have disagreed. (Some, who subjected themseves to the pro-cedure, have disagreed rather violently.) Possibly more relevant to us and to you personally, whether a bit of driving is "reckless" or not may determine

*See, for example, *Vagueness: A Reader,* by R. Keefe and P. Smith, eds. (Cambridge, MA: MIT Press, 1996), and *Vagueness,* by T. Williamson (London and New York: Routledge, 1994).

whether you pay a small fine or a large one—or even go to jail. Consider, too, the speed limits we are asked to observe on the highways. Ideally, the offense in question would be something like "driving too fast for the circumstances" rather than driving faster than a particular speed. This is because what is safe at 80 miles per hour in one set of circumstances (midday, no traffic, clear weather, and dry roads) might be dangerously unsafe at 40 miles per hour in another (dark, heavy traffic, rain or fog, slick roads). But we have opted for set speed limits because "driving too fast" is a vague term, and we do not want to put our fate in the hands of patrol officers and judges who are in a position to make arbitrary decisions about whether it applies in our case. So, because we are afraid of the consequences of the vague concept, we sometimes get away with driving dangerously fast under bad circumstances, and we are sometimes ticketed for driving over the posted limit when it is quite safe to do so.

Sometimes vagueness is just annoying. Suppose that it's late and you're looking for someone's house and you're given the following directions: "Go on down this street a ways 'til you get to the first major intersection, make a sharp right, then, when the street starts to curve to the left, you'll be there." The vagueness in these directions is as likely to get your blood pressure up as it is to help you find your destination. (How do you decide that a particular intersection is "major," for example?)

Vagueness is often intentional, used as a means to avoid giving a clear, precise answer. Politicians often resort to vague statements if they don't want their audience to know exactly where they stand. A vague answer to the question "Do you love me?" may mean there's trouble ahead in the relationship.

Vagueness occurs to varying degrees, and it is difficult to the point of impossibility to get rid of it entirely. Fortunately, there is no need to get rid of it entirely. We live very comfortably with a certain amount of vagueness in most of what we say. "Butte City is a very small town" presents us with no problems under ordinary circumstances, despite the vagueness of "very small town." "Darren has no school loans because his parents are rich" doesn't tell us how much money the parents have, but it tells us enough to be useful. "Rich" and "small," like "bald," are vague concepts; there is no accepted clear line between the things to which they apply and those to which they don't. Nonetheless, they are valuable notions; we get a lot of good use out of them.

Problems arise with vagueness when there is too much of it, as in our direction-giving example above. Similarly, if a politician claims he will "raise taxes on the wealthy," what should we take that to mean? Unlike with the earlier example of Darren's rich parents, in this case it would be worthwhile to spend some effort trying to pin down just what our speaker means by "wealthy," since where the borders fall here really *do* make a difference.

So, when is a level of vagueness acceptable and when is it not? It's difficult to give a general rule, aside from urging due care and common sense, but we might say this: When a claim is not too vague to convey appropriately useful information, its level of vagueness is acceptable. For example, if the directions we're given are not too vague to help us find our destination, they pass the test. If the politician specifies enough about his tax plan to assure us that we understand how it would apply, then we should not complain of vagueness. But when a speaker or writer does indulge in excessive vagueness, thereby making it difficult or impossible for us to fairly assess his or her claim, it is our job to hold that person accountable.

Everything is vague to a degree you do not realize until you have tried to make it precise.

—BERTRAND RUSSELL

Ask a man which way he is going to vote, and he will probably tell you. Ask him, however, why, and vagueness is all.

—BARNARD LEVIN

AMBIGUITY

Asked why the desertion rate in the army had risen so much, director of plans and resources for Army personnel Roy Wallace replied, "We're asking a lot of soldiers these days."

You might at first want to know *what* they're asking the soldiers, until you see the ambiguity in Wallace's remark.

A word, phrase, or sentence is said to be **ambiguous** when it has more than one meaning. Does "Paul cashed a check" mean that Paul gave somebody cash, or that somebody gave cash to him? It could mean either. "Jessica is renting her house" could mean that she's renting it *to* someone or *from* someone. Jennifer gets up from her desk on Friday afternoon and says, "My work here is finished." She might mean that she has finished the account she was working on, or that her whole week's work is done and she's leaving for the weekend, or that she's fed up with her job and is leaving the company. If you look online, you can find several collections of amusing headlines that are funny because of their ambiguity: "Kids make nutritious snacks," for example, or "Miners refuse to work after death."

Most of the time the interpretation that a speaker or writer intends for a claim is obvious, as in the case of these headlines. But ambiguity can have

In the Media

A Subtle Ambiguity

A while back, when John Edwards was still a viable presidential candidate, he was asked the following question on *Meet the Press:*

> **TIM RUSSERT:** Why don't you support gay marriage?

> **JOHN EDWARDS:** Well, I guess it was the way I was brought up.

Do you see the ambiguity here, and how it works to Edwards's advantage? You'll find an explanation in the text.

consequences beyond making us smile. Take a look at the box "A Subtle Ambiguity." The question Russert asks is ambiguous, although you might not notice it at first. It could be a question about the cause—that is, the *explanation*—for one's not supporting gay marriage, or it might be about his reasons—that is, his *argument*—for not supporting it. Presidential candidate Edwards took advantage of the ambiguity to duck the question Russert really wanted him to answer, which was the second version. The way Edwards was brought up is something he is not responsible for and which he does not have to defend. On the other hand if he were asked to give arguments for his side of the issue, he could then be asked to defend those arguments.

In discussions of gay rights, we've seen an ambiguity in the term "rights" that often stymies rational debate. The issue is whether laws should be passed to prevent discrimination against gays in housing, in the workplace, and so forth. One side claims that such laws would themselves be discriminatory because they would specifically grant to gay people rights that are not specifically guaranteed to others—they would be "special" rights. The other side claims that the laws are only to guarantee for gays the right to be treated the same as others under the law. When the two sides fail to sort out just what they mean by their key terms, the result is at best a great waste of breath and at worst angry misunderstanding.

Brad and Angelina are not pleased with this book. *Of course, they aren't displeased, either, since it's almost certain they've never heard of it. Note the ambiguity in the original statement.*

Semantic Ambiguity

A claim can be ambiguous in any of several ways. The most obvious way is probably by containing an ambiguous word or phrase, which produces a case of **semantic ambiguity.** See if you can explain the ambiguity in each of the following claims:

1. Wingo, the running back, always lines up on the right side.
2. Jessica is cold.
3. Aunt Delia never used glasses.

In the first case, it may be that it's the right and not the left side where Wingo lines up, *or* it may be that he always lines up on the correct side. The second example may be saying something about Jessica's temperature or something about her personality. In the third case, it may be that Aunt Delia always had good eyes, but it also might mean that she drank her beer directly from the bottle (which was true of one of your authors' Aunt Delia). Semantically ambiguous claims can be made unambiguous ("disambiguated") by substituting a word or phrase that is not ambiguous for the one making the trouble. "Correct" for "right," for example, in #1; "eyeglasses" for "glasses" in #3.

Grouping Ambiguity

There is a special kind of semantic ambiguity, called **grouping ambiguity,** that results when it is not clear whether a word is being used to refer to a group collectively or to members of the group individually. Consider:

Secretaries make more money than physicians do.

The example is true if the speaker refers to secretaries and physicians collectively, since there are many more secretaries than there are physicians. But it is obviously false if the two words refer to individual secretaries and physicians.

"Lawn mowers create more air pollution than dirt bikes do" is something a dirt biker might say in defense of his hobby. And, because it is ambiguous, there is an interpretation under which his claim is probably true as well as one under which it is probably false. Taken collectively, lawn mowers doubtless create more pollution because there are so many more of them. Individually, we'd bet it's the dirt bike that does more damage.

Like other types of ambiguity, grouping ambiguity can be used intentionally to interfere with clear thinking. A few years ago, federal taxes were increased, and opponents of the change referred to it as "the biggest tax increase in history." If true, that makes the increase sound pretty radical, doesn't it? And it was true, if you looked at the total tax revenue that was brought in by the increase. But this result was largely due to the numbers of people and the circumstances to which the increase applied. If we look at the percentage increase paid by individual taxpayers, this was *not* the biggest increase in history. Since most of us are mainly interested in how much more we as individuals have to pay, it is the latter interpretation that is usually more important. But the grouping ambiguity underlying the phrase "the biggest tax increase in history" allows one to give another interpretation under which the claim is true; although the individual tax increases were not the biggest, the collective tax increase was.

There are two venerable fallacies based on the grouping type of ambiguity. Each involves taking the ambiguity one step further than we've done so far.

■ This package of doggie diapers (we're not kidding) must never have been given a critical look. A well-placed hyphen would make clear what the advertisers meant to say. (Thanks to *Consumer Reports* for the example.)

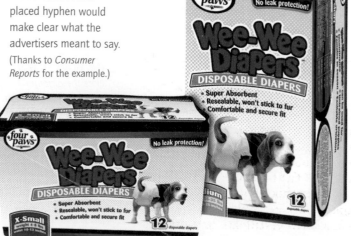

In Depth

Composition and the First Cause Argument

Here is a brief version of an old and famous argument for the existence of God. It is known as the first cause argument.

Premise: Everything had to have been caused.

Therefore: The universe, too, had to have been caused.

And therefore: God, the cause of the universe, exists.

This argument, at least this version of it, can be analyzed as an example of the fallacy of composition. Do you see how to analyze it this way?

A person commits the **fallacy of division** when he or she reasons from the fact that a claim about a group taken collectively is true to the conclusion that the same claim about members of the group taken individually is also true. In 1973, the Miami Dolphins were undefeated for the entire NFL football season and went on to win the Super Bowl in early 1974. Nobody disputes the fact that the team was the best in the league that year. Does it follow that the individual players on that team were the best players in the league? That is, that Bob Griese was the best quarterback, Larry Csonka the best running back, Mercury Morris the best receiver? No, of course not. What is true of the whole may not be true of each individual part. A round building, remember, does not have to be built of round bricks.

Going the other direction, a person commits the **fallacy of composition** when he or she reasons from the fact that each member of a group has a certain property to the conclusion that the group as a whole must have that property. An example: At the current moment (and it is true most of the time, in fact) in their various states and districts, individual members of Congress receive fairly high marks in opinion polls. One might therefore think that opinion polls would give Congress as a whole fairly high marks. But this would be a mistake, since Congress in general gets very low marks in these same polls. The way people feel about the parts is not necessarily what they feel about the whole. To turn our earlier example around: You can use rectangular bricks to build a building that is not rectangular.

You'll find other examples of these two fallacies in the following "In Depth" box.

Syntactic Ambiguity

Syntactic ambiguity occurs when a claim is open to two or more interpretations because of its *structure*—that is, its syntax. Not long ago, one of us received information from the American Automobile Association prior to driving to British Columbia. "To travel in Canada," the brochure stated, "you will need a birth certificate or a driver's license and other photo ID."

Just what is the requirement for crossing the border? Under one interpretation, you have to take a photo ID other than a birth certificate or a driver's

In Depth

More Examples of the Composition and Division Fallacies

Division: "A balanced diet consists of the right proportion of protein, carbohydrates, and fat. Therefore, each meal should consist of the same proportion of protein, carbohydrates, and fat."

—DR. NICHOLAS PERRICONE, author of the best-selling book *The Wrinkle Cure*

Mistake: The balance necessary for a daily intake is not necessary for each *part* of one's daily intake—that is, each meal.

Division: After the 2008 elections, the Democrats took over both the U.S. Senate and the House of Representatives. A number of pundits characterized the election by saying "the voters have overwhelmingly voted for a Democratic Congress."

Mistake: It's true that voters *collectively* voted for a Democratic Congress, but voters *individually* did no such thing. No person *anywhere* voted for a Democratic Congress, since the issue did not appear on any ballot anywhere.

Composition: "The Kings don't have a chance against the Lakers. The Lakers are better at every position except power forward."

—CHARLES BARKLEY

Mistake: Individual players, however talented, may not play that well together.

Neurosis is the inability to tolerate ambiguity.

—SIGMUND FREUD

Okay. But it's still true that we should not have to live with too much of it!

---

license, and under another, you don't. If we group by brackets, we can make the two interpretations clear, we hope:

1. [You will need a birth certificate or a driver's license] *and* [other photo ID]
2. [You will need a birth certificate] *or* [a driver's license and other photo ID]

The problem with the original version of the claim is that, because of its poor construction, we don't know whether to associate the driver's license requirement with the birth certificate (as in interpretation 1) or with the "other photo ID" (as in interpretation 2). Rewriting is the key to eliminating syntactic ambiguity. Depending on the intended interpretation, the original could have been written:

1. You will need either a birth certificate or a driver's license *and you will also need* an additional photo ID.

   Or

2. You will need either a birth certificate or *both* a driver's license and an additional photo ID.

Neither of these is ambiguous.

In the previous example, the problem was produced by a failure to make clear how the logical words "or" and "and" were to apply.* Here are some

---

*This particular kind of syntactic ambiguity is analyzed further in Chapter 9, which deals with truth-functional logic.

other examples of syntactic ambiguity, along with various possible interpretations, to help you get the idea.

Players with beginners' skills only may use Court 1.

In this case, we don't know what the word "only" applies to. This word, as we'll see in later chapters, is both very useful and very easy to use incorrectly. Here, it might mean that beginners may use *only Court 1*. Or it might mean that players with *only beginners' skills* may use Court 1. Finally, it might mean that *only players with beginners' skills* may use Court 1. Obviously, whoever puts up such a sign needs to be more careful. (And so does the person who put up a sign in our university's student union that said, "Cash only this line." Do you see the ambiguity?)

Susan saw the farmer with binoculars.

This ambiguity results from a modifying phrase ("with binoculars") that is not clear in its application. Who had the binoculars in this case? Presumably Susan, but it looks as though it was the farmer. "Looking through her binoculars, Susan saw the farmer" clears it up.

People who protest often get arrested.

This is similar to the previous example: Does "often" apply to protesting or to getting arrested?

There's somebody in the bed next to me.

Does "next to me" apply to a person or to a bed? One might rewrite this either as "There's somebody next to me in the bed" or as "There's somebody in the bed next to mine."

Ambiguous pronoun references occur when it is not clear to what or whom a pronoun is supposed to refer. "The boys chased the girls and they giggled a lot" does not make clear who did the giggling. "They" could be either the boys or the girls. A similar example: "After their father removed the trash

On Language

Making Ambiguity Work for You

Have you ever been asked to write a letter of recommendation for a friend who was, well, incompetent? To avoid either hurting your friend's feelings or lying, Robert Thornton of Lehigh University has some ambiguous statements you can use. Here are some examples:

I most enthusiastically recommend this candidate with no qualifications whatsoever.

I am pleased to say that this candidate is a former colleague of mine.

I can assure you that no person would be better for the job.

I would urge you to waste no time in making this candidate an offer of employment.

All in all, I cannot say enough good things about this candidate or recommend the candidate too highly.

In my opinion, you will be very fortunate to get this person to work for you.

from the pool, the kids played in it." A less amusing and possibly more trouble-making example: "Paul agreed that, once Gary removed the motor from the car, he could have it." What does Gary have permission to take, the motor or the car? (Just imagine a written agreement containing this sentence. We'd predict a lawsuit.) It pays to be careful; a speaker or writer who is thinking critically will make clear exactly what he or she means to say.

There are other examples of ambiguity that are difficult to classify. For example, one of us was at lunch with the dean of a college at our university, and the dean said to the waiter, "You can bring the sauce separately, and I'll put it on myself." The ambiguity, obviously, is in *how* he'll put the sauce on versus *where* he'll put it. As in all cases of ambiguity, it is important to *see that* the claim is ambiguous rather than to be able to classify the type of ambiguity. (This one could be called either semantic or syntactic, by our lights.) By improving your ability to notice when claims are ambiguous, you will be less likely to be misled by them and less likely to mislead others by using them—unless, of course, you mean to mislead them!

GENERALITY

The traveler must, of course, always be cautious of the overly broad generalization. But I am an American, and a paucity of data does not stop me from making sweeping, vague, conceptual statements, and, if necessary, following these statements up with troops.

—GEORGE SAUNDERS, *The Guardian*, July 22, 2006

We turn now to the notion of generality, which is closely related to both vagueness and ambiguity and which can cause trouble in the same way they do.

From what we learned of vagueness, we realize that the word "child" is vague, since it is not clear where the line is drawn between children and non-children. It can also be ambiguous, because it can refer not only to a person of immature years but also to a person's offspring. As if this weren't enough, it is also general because it applies to both boys and girls. Roughly speaking, the less detail a claim provides, the more **general** it is. Regarding specific words and phrases, the more different kinds of Xs to which a word applies, the more general the word "X" is. "Moore has a dog" is more general than "Moore has an otterhound." "Moore has a pet" is still more general.

If you learn that Clarence has an arrest record, it may well lower your estimate of him and may prevent you from hiring him to do work around your house, for example. But if some more detail were supplied—for instance, that he had been arrested during a protest against a company that was polluting the local river—it might well make a difference in your opinion of him. The difference between a very general description and one with sufficient detail can be crucial to nearly any decision.

There has been a lot of discussion about whether the War on Terror should really be called a "war" at all. The phrase has continued to be used because "war" is both vague and general. Some believe that the word as traditionally used requires an enemy that is organized and identifiable, such as a country or province, and those are difficult to identify in the War on Terror. Still less-clearly a war is the so-called "War on Drugs." This seems to be a purely metaphorical use of the word "war," meant to show that somebody is serious about the issue.

We don't mean to confuse you with these closely related and overlapping pitfalls—vagueness, ambiguity, and generality. In practical fact, it is less important that you classify the problem that infects a claim or idea than that you see what's going on and can explain it. For example, "Just what do you mean by 'war'?" is a good response to someone who is using the word too loosely. In some of the exercises that follow, we'll ask you to identify problems in different passages in order to help you become familiar with the ideas. In others, we'll simply ask you to explain what is needed for clarification.

Anyhow, with all these potential pitfalls to clear thinking and clear communication, what is a critically thinking person to do? To start, we can do the best we can to be clear in what our words mean. So after the following exercises we will turn our attention to the definition of terms.

Here are several exercises to give you practice identifying precision (or lack thereof) in sentences.

The lettered words and phrases that follow each of the following fragments vary in their vagueness and/or generality. In each instance, determine which is the most precise and which is the least precise; then rank the remainder in order of precision, to the extent possible. If these exercises are discussed in class, you'll discover that many of them leave room for disagreement. Discussion with input from your instructor will help you and your classmates reach closer agreement about items that prove especially difficult to rank.

Exercise 3-1

Example

Over the past ten years, the median income of wage earners in St. Paul
a. nearly doubled
b. increased substantially
c. increased by 85.5 percent
d. increased by more than 85 percent

Answer

Choice (b) is the most general (vague is okay, too) because it provides the least information; (c) is the most precise because it provides the most detailed figure. In between, (d) is the second most precise, followed by (a).

▲ 1. Eli and Sarah
  a. decided to sell their house and move 1
  b. made plans for the future 5
  c. considered moving 4
  d. talked 6
  e. discussed their future 3
  f. discussed selling their house 2

2. Manuel
  a. worked in the yard all afternoon 3
  b. spent the afternoon planting flowers in the yard 2
  c. was outside all afternoon 5
  d. spent the afternoon planting salvia alongside his front sidewalk 1
  e. spent the afternoon in the yard 4

3. The hurricane that struck South Carolina
  a. caused more than $20 million in property damage 2
  b. destroyed dozens of structures 3
  c. was severe and unfortunate 4
  d. produced no fatalities but caused $25 million in property damage 1

▲ 4. The recent changes in the tax code
  a. will substantially increase taxes paid by those making more than $200,000 per year
  b. will increase by 4 percent the tax rate for those making more than $200,000 per year; will leave unchanged the tax rate for people making between $40,000 and $200,000; and will decrease by 2 percent the tax rate for those making less than $40,000
  c. will make some important changes in who pays what in taxes
  d. are tougher on the rich than the provisions in the previous tax law
  e. raise rates for the wealthy and reduce them for those in the lowest brackets

5. Smedley is absent because
  a. he's not feeling well
  b. he's under the weather
  c. he has an upset stomach and a fever
  d. he's nauseated and has a fever of more than 103°
  e. he has flulike symptoms

Exercise 3-2

Which of each set of claims is more precise (i.e., suffers least from vagueness, ambiguity, or generality)?

Example

  a. The trees served to make shade for the patio.
  b. He served his country proudly.

Answer

  The use of "served" in (b) is more vague than that in (a). We know exactly what the trees did; we don't know what he did.

▲ 1. a. Rooney served the church his entire life.
     b. Rooney's tennis serve is impossible to return.
   2. a. The window served its purpose.
     b. The window served as an escape hatch.
   3. a. Throughout their marriage, Alfredo served her dinner.
     b. Throughout their marriage, Alfredo served her well.
▲ 4. a. Minta turned her ankle.
     b. Minta turned to religion.
   5. a. These scales will turn on the weight of a hair.
     b. This car will turn on a dime.
   6. a. Fenner's boss turned vicious.
     b. Fenner's boss turned out to be forty-seven.
▲ 7. a. Time to turn the garden.
     b. Time to turn off the sprinkler.
   8. a. The wine turned to vinegar.
     b. The wine turned out to be vinegar.
   9. a. Harper flew around the world.
     b. Harper departed around 3:00 A.M.

▲ 10. (a.) Clifton turned out the light.
       b. Clifton turned out the vote.

   11. a. The glass is full to the brim.
       (b.) Mrs. Couch has a rather full figure.

   12. a. Kathy gave him a full report.
       (b.) "Oh, no, thank you! I am full."

   13. a. Oswald was dealt a full house.
       (b.) Oswald is not playing with a full deck.

   14. a. Money is not the key to happiness.
       (b.) This is not the key to the garage.

▲ 15. a. Porker set a good example.
       (b.) Porker set the world record for the 100-meter dash.

DEFINING TERMS

When today's typical student hears the word "definition," we wouldn't be surprised if the first thing to come to mind is television. "High definition" is the new standard of clarity in what we see on the home screen. This is directly analogous to the clarity and distinctness we're looking for as critical thinkers, and the careful definition of terms is one of our most useful tools in pursuing this goal. While the business of definitions may seem straightforward ("'carrot' refers to a tapering, orange-colored root eaten as a vegetable"), you'll soon see that there's more to it than you might have thought. For example, a multitude of attempts have been made to construct a definition of "person" (or, if you like, "human being"). Everything from "rational animal" to "featherless biped" has been suggested. But such important issues as whether abortion is morally permissible, whether fetuses have rights, whether a fetus is correctly referred to as an "unborn child," and doubtless many others—all turn on how we define "person" and some of these other basic concepts. Indeed, if we define "abortion" as "the murder of an unborn child," the debate on abortion is over before it begins.

> A definition is the start of an argument, not the end of one
>
> —NEIL POSTMAN, author of
> *Amusing Ourselves to Death:
> Public Discourse in the Age of
> Show Business*

Some arguments against the acceptance of rights for homosexuals depend on the claim that their orientation is "unnatural."* But to arrive at a definition of "natural" (or "unnatural") is no easy task. If you spend a few minutes thinking about this difficulty—even better, if you discuss it with others—we think you'll see what we mean. What is "natural," depending on who is defining the term, can mean anything from "occurs in nature" to "correct in the eyes of God."

The definition of the word "use" by the U.S. Supreme Court made a difference of thirty years in the sentence of John Angus Smith in a criminal case a few years ago.** We hope you are convinced of the importance of the subject. Now, let's have a look at how to deal with definitions.

Purposes of Definitions

We'll start by indicating some of the purposes that definitions serve, then go on to describe several different types of definitions. After that, we'll give some rough and ready ideas on giving good definitions.

Definitions can serve several purposes, but we want to call your attention to four.

1. The first and main purpose served by definitions is to tell us what a word means. When we don't know a word's meaning, we often look it up in a dictionary. The definitions given there are **lexical definitions;** they tell us what the word ordinarily means ("**tamarin.** *noun*: a small, forest-dwelling South American monkey of the marmoset family, typically brightly colored and with tufts and crests of hair around the face and neck."). You might well ask, Isn't this what all definitions do? A good question, and the answer is *no*. Check these next two items.

2. Sometimes a word needs to take on a special meaning in a given context. For this, we need a **stipulative definition.** An example: "In this environment, 'desktop' means the basic opening screen of the operating system—the one with the trash can." We also assign stipulative definitions to words we invent. Stephen Colbert invented the word "truthiness" on his inaugural *Colbert Report* in 2005. Its assigned meaning (its stipulative definition) can be stated as "[the quality possessed by] those things a person claims to know intuitively or 'from the gut' without regard to evidence, logic, intellectual examination, or facts."†

3. A third important purpose of definitions is to reduce vagueness or generality or to eliminate ambiguity. "In this contract, the word 'dollars' will refer only to Canadian dollars, even if one party normally deals in U.S. dollars or Australian dollars." Definitions that serve this purpose are said to be **precising definitions.**

---

*"[W]e're talking about a particular behavior that most American's [*sic*] consider strange and unnatural, and many Americans consider deeply immoral." "Equal Rights for Homosexuals," by Gregory Kouki, <http://www.str.org/site/News2?page=NewsArticle&id=5226>.
**See Exercise 12–13, p. 463, for details.
†This version is due to Dick Meyer, *CBS News*, December 12, 2006. Actually, the word "truthiness" had been around for a very long time before Colbert *re*invented it. It was mentioned in the *Oxford English Dictionary* as a variant of "truth."

4. Finally, definitions can be used to persuade. These troublesome items are known as **persuasive** or **rhetorical definitions.** It isn't clear that we should think of them as *real* definitions, since they are not intended to provide either ordinary or agreed-upon meanings for terms. Nonetheless, they are often listed with the others we've mentioned. But be warned, these "definitions" are designed to influence beliefs or attitudes, not simply to convey linguistic information. If a liberal friend tries to "define" a conservative as "a hidebound, narrow-minded hypocrite who thinks the point to life is making money and ripping off poor people," you know the point here is not the clarification of the meaning of the word "conservative." It is a way of trashing conservatives. Such rhetorical definitions frequently make use of the **emotive meaning** (or, if you prefer, the **rhetorical force**) of words. This meaning consists of the positive or negative associations of a word. Consider the difference between "government-guaranteed health care" and a "government takeover of health care." These terms might reasonably be used to refer to the same thing, but they clearly have different emotional associations—one positive and one negative. The word "connotation" is the traditional term for these associations.

Our definition of "abortion" as "the murder of an unborn child" at the beginning of this section is another much-quoted example of this type of definition.*

Kinds of Definitions

We've looked at some important purposes to which definitions can be put, and we must now distinguish between those purposes and the *types* of definitions that are used to serve them. Remember that the purpose of a definition and the type of definition it is are different things. (Compare: The *purpose* of food is to nourish our bodies and please our palettes, whereas *types* of food are vegetables, meat, Pringles, etc.)

Regardless of what purpose is served by defining a term, most definitions are of one of the three following types:

1. **Definition by example** (also called **ostensive definition**): Pointing to, naming, or otherwise identifying one or more examples of the sort of thing to which the term applies: "By 'scripture,' I mean writings like the Bible and the Koran." "A mouse is this thing here, the one with the buttons."

2. **Definition by synonym:** Giving another word or phrase that means the same as the term being defined. "'Fastidious' means the same as 'fussy.'" "'Pulsatile' means 'throbbing.'" "To be 'lubricious' is the same as to be 'slippery.'"

3. **Analytical definition:** Specifying the features that a thing must possess in order for the term being defined to apply to it. These definitions often take the form of a genus-and-species classification. For example, "A samovar is an urn that has a spigot and is used especially in Russia to boil water for tea." "A mongoose is a ferret-sized mammal native to India that eats snakes and is related to civets."

Almost all dictionary definitions are of the analytical variety.

*How this particular definition *begs the question* is noted in Chapter 7.

It's bad poetry executed by people who can't sing. That's my definition of Rap.

—PETER STEELE

We're guessing he doesn't like it.

Some Tips on Definitions

So far, we've seen that definitions serve a variety of purposes and take several different forms. Combinations can be of many sorts: a definition by synonym that is precising ("minor" means under eighteen); an analytical definition designed just to persuade (a liberal is somebody who wants the able and willing to take care of both the unable and the unwilling). But what makes a definition a good one?

First, definitions should not prejudice the case against one side of a debate or the other. This is one form of *begging the question*, which will be discussed in some detail in Chapter 7. For now, just recall that one cannot usually win a debate simply by insisting on one's own favored definition of key terms, since those who disagree with your position will also disagree with your definitions. Definitions are instances in which people have to try to achieve a kind of neutral ground.

Second, definitions should be clear. They are designed to clear the air, not muddy the water. This means they should be expressed in language that is as clear and simple as the subject will allow. If we define a word in language that is more obscure than the original word, we accomplish nothing. This includes avoiding emotively charged language whenever possible.

Realize that sometimes you must get along with incomplete definitions. In real life, we sometimes have to deal with claims that include such big-league abstractions as friendship, loyalty, fair play, freedom, rights, and so forth. If you have to give a *complete* definition of "freedom" or "fair play," you'd best not plan on getting home early. Such concepts have subtle and complex parameters that might take a lifetime to pin down. For practical purposes, what is usually needed for words like these is not a complete definition but a precising definition that focuses on one aspect of the concept and provides sufficient guidance

In Depth

Are We Innately Selfish?

You sometimes hear beginning students in philosophy maintaining that every voluntary action is a selfish one, done only to benefit oneself. This is a striking idea, and the student typically is quite impressed by the finding. The argument for the idea normally proceeds something like this: All voluntary acts are done to satisfy one's own desire to do them; thus, all voluntary acts are done for self-benefit; thus, all voluntary acts are selfish acts.*

The problem, if it isn't obvious, is that this argument does not make use of our ordinary notion of selfishness. Ordinarily, if we're told that someone is a selfish person, we think we've learned something important about them, not simply that they perform voluntary actions. This indicates that the argument above makes use of a new and different meaning for "selfish." If we had only the new meaning for the word, we'd probably stop using it, since it conveys nothing interesting about a person.

The key to spotting mistakes like this is to have a clear definition of key terms and to keep it in mind throughout the discussion.

*A diagram for this simple argument is provided in the answer section, p. 509.

for the purposes at hand: "To me, the word 'justice' does not include referring to a person's private life when evaluating his or her work performance."

The following exercise will give you practice with definitions.

In groups (or individually if your instructor prefers), determine what term in each of the following is being defined and whether the definition is by example or by synonym or an analytical definition. If it is difficult to tell which kind of definition is present, describe the difficulty.

Exercise 3-3

▲ 1. A piano is a stringed instrument in which felt hammers are made to strike the strings by an arrangement of keys and levers. *Analytical*

2. "Decaffeinated" means without caffeine.

3. Steve Martin is my idea of a successful philosophy major.

▲ 4. The red planet is Mars.

5. "UV" refers to ultraviolet light.

6. The Cheyenne perfectly illustrate the sort of Native Americans who were Plains Indians.

7. Data, in our case, is raw information collected from survey forms, which is then put in tabular form and analyzed. *EX*

▲ 8. "Chiaroscuro" is just a fancy word for shading.

9. Bifocals are glasses with two different prescriptions ground into each lens, making it possible to focus at two different distances from the wearer.

10. Red is the color that we perceive when our eyes are struck by light waves of approximately seven angstroms.

▲ 11. A significant other can be taken to be a person's spouse, lover, long-term companion, or just girlfriend or boyfriend.

12. "Assessment" means evaluation.

13. A blackout is "a period of total memory loss, as one induced by an accident or prolonged alcoholic drinking." When your buddies tell you they loved your rendition of the Lambada on Madison's pool table the other night and you don't even remember being at Madison's, that is a blackout.

—*Adapted from the CalPoly, San Luis Obispo,* Mustang Daily

14. A pearl, which is the only animal-produced gem, begins as an irritant inside an oyster. The oyster then secretes a coating of nacre around the irritating object. The result is a pearl, the size of which is determined by the number of layers with which the oyster coats the object.

15. According to my cousin, who lives in Tulsa, the phrase "bored person" refers to anybody who is between the ages of sixteen and twenty-five and lives in eastern Oklahoma.

example
synonym
definition

WRITING ARGUMENTATIVE ESSAYS

Recently, the Educational Testing Service revamped the infamous Scholastic Aptitude Test (SAT), which many universities use when determining whether to admit an applicant. The most significant change was to have test takers write an argumentative essay. This change in the SAT shows the importance the educators place on the ability to write this type of essay. That's because writing an argumentative essay is doing nothing other than thinking critically—and leaving a paper trail for others to follow. This isn't a book on writing, but writing an argumentative essay is so closely related to thinking critically that we would like to take the opportunity to offer our recommendations. We know professors who have retired because they could not bear to read another student essay. As a result, we offer our two bits' worth here in hopes of continuing to see familiar faces.

As we said back on p. 71, an argumentative essay generally has four components:

1. **A statement of the issue**
2. **A statement of one's position on that issue**
3. **Arguments that support one's position**
4. **Rebuttals of arguments that support contrary positions**

Ideally, your essay should begin with an introduction to the issue that demonstrates that the issue is important or interesting. This is not always easy, but even when you are not excited about the subject yourself, it is still good practice to try to make your reader interested. Your statement of the issue should be fair; that is, don't try to state the issue in such a way that your position on it is obviously the only correct one. This can make your reader suspicious; the burden of convincing him or her will come later, when you give your arguments.

Your position on the issue should be clear. Try to be brief. If you have stated the issue clearly, it should be a simple matter to identify your position.

Your arguments in support of your position also should be as succinct as you can make them, but it is much more important to be clear than to be brief. After all, this is the heart of your essay. The reasons you cite should be clearly relevant, and they should be either clearly reliable or backed up by further arguments. Much of the rest of this book is devoted to how this is done; hang in there.

If there are well-known arguments for the other side of the issue, you should acknowledge them and offer some reason to believe that they are unconvincing. You can do this either by attacking the premises that are commonly given or by trying to show that those premises do not actually support the opposing conclusion. More on these topics later, too.

Following are some more detailed hints that might be helpful in planning and writing your argumentative essay.

1. *Focus.* Make clear at the outset what issue you intend to address and what your position on the issue will be. However, nothing is quite so boring as starting off with the words "In this essay, I shall argue that X, Y, and Z," and then going on to itemize everything you are about to say, and at the end concluding with the words "In this essay, I argued that X, Y, and Z." As a matter of style, you should let the reader know what to expect without using trite phrases and without going on at length. However, you should try to find

an engaging way to state your position. For example, instead of "In this essay, I shall discuss the rights of animals to inherit property from their masters," you might begin, "Could your inheritance wind up belonging to your mother's cat?"

2. *Stick to the issue.* All points you make in an essay should be connected to the issue under discussion and should always either (a) support, illustrate, explain, clarify, elaborate on, or emphasize your position on the issue, or (b) serve as responses to anticipated objections. Rid the essay of irrelevancies and dangling thoughts.

3. *Arrange the components of the essay in a logical sequence.* This is just common sense. Make a point before you clarify it, for example, not the other way around.

When supporting your points, bring in examples, clarification, and the like in such a way that a reader knows what in the world you are doing. A reader should be able to discern the relationship between any given sentence and your ultimate objective, and he or she should be able to move from sentence to sentence and from paragraph to paragraph without getting lost or confused. If a reader cannot outline your essay with ease, you have not properly sequenced your material. Your essay might be fine as a piece of French philosophy, but it would not pass as an argumentative essay.

4. *Be complete.* Accomplish what you set out to accomplish, support your position adequately, and anticipate and respond to possible objections. Keep in mind that many issues are too large to be treated exhaustively in a single essay. The key to being complete is to define the issue sharply enough that you can be complete. Thus, the more limited your topic, the easier it is to be complete in covering it.

Also, be sure there is closure at every level. Sentences should be complete, paragraphs should be unified as wholes (and usually each should stick to a single point), and the essay should reach a conclusion. Incidentally, reaching a conclusion and summarizing are not the same thing. Short essays do not require summaries.

Good Writing Practices

Understanding the four principles just mentioned is one thing, but actually employing them may be more difficult. Fortunately, there are five practices that a writer can follow to improve the organization of an essay and to help avoid other problems. We offer the following merely as a set of recommendations within the broader scope of thinking critically in writing.

1. At some stage *after* the first draft, outline what you have written. Then, make certain the outline is logical and that every sentence in the essay fits into the outline as it should. Some writers create an informal outline before they begin, but many do not. Our advice: Just identify the issue and your position on it, and start writing by stating them both.

2. Revise your work. Revising is the secret to good writing. Even major-league writers revise what they write, and they revise continuously. Unless you are more gifted than the very best professional writers, revise,

I'm for abolishing and doing away with redundancy.

—J. Curtis McKay, of the Wisconsin State Elections Board (reported by Ross and Petras)

We ourselves are also for that too.

revise, revise. Don't think in terms of two or three drafts. Think in terms of *innumerable* drafts.

3. Have someone else read your essay and offer criticisms of it. Revise as required.

4. If you have trouble with grammar or punctuation, reading your essay out loud may help you detect problems your eyes have missed.

5. After you are completely satisfied with the essay, put it aside. Then, come back to it later for still further revisions.

Essay Types to Avoid

Seasoned instructors know that the first batch of essays they get from a class will include samples of each of the following types. We recommend avoiding these mistakes:

■ **The Windy Preamble.** Writers of this type of essay avoid getting to the issue and instead go on at length with introductory remarks, often about how important the issue is, how it has troubled thinkers for centuries, how opinions on the issue are many and various, and so on, and so on. Anything you write that smacks of "When in the course of human events . . ." should go into the trash can immediately.

On Language

And While We're on the Subject of Writing

Don't forget these rules of good style:

1. Avoid clichés like the plague.
2. Be more or less specific.
3. NEVER generalize.
4. The passive voice is to be ignored.
5. Never, ever be redundant.
6. Exaggeration is a billion times worse than understatement.
7. Make sure verbs agrees with their subjects.
8. Why use rhetorical questions?
9. Parenthetical remarks (however relevant) are (usually) unnecessary.
10. Proofread carefully to see if you any words out.
11. And it's usually a bad idea to start a sentence with a conjunction.

This list has been making the rounds on the Internet.

- **The Stream-of-Consciousness Ramble.** This type of essay results when writers make no attempt to organize their thoughts and simply spew them out in the order in which they come to mind.

- **The Knee-Jerk Reaction.** In this type of essay, writers record their first reaction to an issue without considering the issue in any depth or detail. It always shows.

- **The Glancing Blow.** In this type of essay, writers address an issue obliquely. If they are supposed to evaluate the health benefits of bicycling, they will bury the topic in an essay on the history of cycling; if they are supposed to address the history of cycling, they will talk about the benefits of riding bicycles throughout history.

- **Let the Reader Do the Work.** Writers of this type of essay expect the reader to follow them through non sequiturs, abrupt shifts in direction, and irrelevant sidetracks.

Persuasive Writing

The primary aim of argumentation and the argumentative essay is to support a position on an issue. Good writers, however, write for an audience and hope their audience will find what they write persuasive. If you are writing for an audience of people who think critically, it is helpful to adhere to these principles:

1. Confine your discussion of an opponent's point of view to issues rather than personal considerations.
2. When rebutting an opposing viewpoint, avoid being strident or insulting. Don't call opposing arguments absurd or ridiculous.
3. If an opponent's argument is good, concede that it is good.
4. If space or time is limited, be sure to concentrate on the most important considerations. Don't become obsessive about refuting every last criticism of your position.
5. Present your strongest arguments first.

There is nothing wrong with trying to make a persuasive case for your position. However, in this book, we place more emphasis on making and recognizing good arguments than on simply devising effective techniques of persuasion. Some people can be persuaded by poor arguments and doubtful claims, and an argumentative essay can be effective as a piece of propaganda even when it is a rational and critical failure. One of the most difficult things you are called upon to do as a critical thinker is to construct and evaluate claims and arguments independently of their power to win a following. The remainder of this book—after a section on writing and diversity—is devoted to this task.

Writing in a Diverse Society

In closing, it seems appropriate to mention how important it is to avoid writing in a manner that reinforces questionable assumptions and attitudes about people's gender, ethnic background, religion, sexual orientation, physical ability or disability, or other characteristics. This isn't just a matter of ethics; it is a matter of clarity and good sense. Careless word choices relative to such characteristics not only are imprecise and inaccurate but also may be viewed as biased even if they were not intended to be, and thus they may diminish the writer's credibility. Worse, using sexist or racist language may distort the writer's own perspective and keep him or her from viewing social issues clearly and objectively.

But language isn't entirely *not* a matter of ethics, either. We are a society that aspires to be just, a society that strives not to withhold its benefits from individuals on the basis of their ethnic or racial background, skin color, religion, gender, or disability. As a people, we try to end practices and change or remove institutions that are unjustly discriminatory. Some of these unfair practices and institutions are, unfortunately, embedded in our language.

Some common ways of speaking and writing, for example, assume that "normal" people are all white males. It is still not uncommon, for instance, to mention a person's race, gender, or ethnic background if the person is *not* a white male, and *not* to do so if the person *is*. Of course, it may be relevant to whatever you are writing about to state that this particular individual is a male of Irish descent, or whatever; if so, there is absolutely nothing wrong with saying so.

Some language practices are particularly unfair to women. Imagine a conversation among three people, you being one of them. Imagine that the other two talk only to each other. When you speak, they listen politely; but when you are finished, they continue as though you had never spoken. Even though what you say is true and relevant to the discussion, the other two proceed as though you were invisible. Because you are not being taken seriously, you are at a considerable disadvantage. You have reason to be unhappy.

In an analogous way, women have been far less visible in language than men and have thus been at a disadvantage. Another word for the human race is not "woman," but "man" or "mankind." The generic human has often been referred to as "he." How do you run a project? You *man* it. Who supervises the department or runs the meeting? The chair*man*. Who heads the crew? The fore*man*. Picture a research scientist to yourself. Got the picture? Is it a picture of a *woman*? No? That's because the standard picture, or stereotype, of a research scientist is a picture of a man. Or, read this sentence: "Research scientists often put their work before their personal lives and neglect their husbands." Were you surprised by the last word? Again, the stereotypical picture of a research scientist is a picture of a man.

A careful and precise writer finds little need to converse in the lazy language of stereotypes, especially those that perpetuate prejudice. As long as the idea prevails that the "normal" research scientist is a man, women who are or who wish to become research scientists will tend to be thought of as out of place. So they must carry an *extra* burden, the burden of showing that they are *not* out of place. That's unfair. If you unthinkingly always write, "The research scientist . . . he," you are perpetuating an image that places women at a disadvantage. Some research scientists are men, and some are women. If you wish to make a claim about male research scientists, do so. But if you wish to make a claim about research scientists in general, don't write as though they were all males.

"Always" and "never" are two words you should always remember never to use.

—Wendell Johnson

Another tip on writing.

What day is the day after three days before the day after tomorrow?

Complicated, but neither vague nor ambiguous.

The rule to follow in all cases is this: Keep your writing free of *irrelevant implied evaluation* of gender, race, ethnic background, religion, or any other human attribute.

Recap

This list summarizes the topics covered in this chapter:

- Clarity of language is extremely important to the ability to think critically.
- Clarity of language can often be lost as a result of multiple causes, including, importantly, vagueness, ambiguity, and generality.
- Vagueness is a matter of degree; what matters is not being too vague for the purposes at hand.
- A statement is ambiguous when it is subject to more than one interpretation and it isn't clear which interpretation is the correct one.
- Some main types of ambiguity are semantic ambiguity, syntactic ambiguity, grouping ambiguity, and ambiguous pronoun reference.
- A claim is overly general when it lacks sufficient detail to restrict its application to the immediate subject.
- To reduce vagueness or eliminate ambiguity, or when new or unfamiliar words are brought into play, or familiar words are used in an unusual way, definitions are our best tool.
- The most common types of definitions are definition by synonym, definition by example, and analytical definition.
- Some "definitions" are intended not to clarify meaning but to express or influence attitude. These are known as rhetorical definitions.
- Rhetorical definitions accomplish their ends by means of the rhetorical force (emotive meaning) of terms.
- Critical thinking done on paper is known as an argumentative essay, a type of writing worth mastering, perhaps by following our suggestions.

Additional Exercises

Exercise 3-4

Are the italicized words or phrases in each of the following too imprecise given the implied context? Explain.

▲ 1. Please cook this steak *longer*. It's too rare.
2. If you get ready for bed quickly, Mommy has a *surprise* for you.
3. This program contains language that some viewers may find offensive. It is recommended for *mature* audiences only.
▲ 4. *Turn down the damned noise!* Some people around here want to sleep!

5. Based on our analysis of your eating habits, we recommend that you *lower* your consumption of saturated fat.

6. NOTICE: Hazard Zone. *Small* children not permitted beyond this sign.

▲ 7. SOFAS CLEANED: $48 & *up*. MUST SEE TO GIVE *EXACT* PRICES.

8. And remember, all our mufflers come with a *lifetime guarantee.*

9. CAUTION: *To avoid* unsafe levels of carbon monoxide, do not set the wick on your kerosene stove *too high.*

▲ 10. Uncooked Frosting: Combine 1 unbeaten egg white, ½ cup corn syrup, ½ teaspoon vanilla, and dash salt. Beat with electric mixer until of fluffy spreading consistency. Frost cake. Serve *within a few hours* or refrigerate.

Exercise 3-5

Read the following passage, paying particular attention to the italicized words and phrases. Determine whether any of these expressions are too vague in the context in which you find them here.

> Term paper assignment: Your paper *should be* typed, *between eight and twelve pages in length*, and double-spaced. You should *make use of* at least three *sources*. Grading will be based on *organization, use of sources, clarity of expression, quality of reasoning*, and *grammar*.
>
> A *rough draft* is due *before Thanksgiving*. The final version is due *at the end of the semester.*

Exercise 3-6

▲ Read the following passage, paying particular attention to the italicized words and phrases. All of these expressions would be too imprecise for use in *some* contexts; determine which are and which are not too imprecise in *this* context.

> In view of what can happen in twelve months to the fertilizer you apply at any one time, you can see why just one annual application may not be adequate. Here is a guide to timing the *feeding* of some of the more common types of garden flowers.
>
> Feed begonias and fuchsias *frequently* with label-recommended amounts or less frequently with *no more than half* the recommended amount. Feed roses with *label-recommended amounts* as a *new year's growth begins* and as *each bloom period ends.* Feed azaleas, camellias, rhododendrons, and *similar* plants *immediately after bloom* and again *when the nights begin cooling off.* Following these simple instructions can help your flower garden to be as attractive as it can be.

Exercise 3-7

Rewrite the following claims to remedy problems of ambiguity. Do *not* assume that common sense by itself solves the problem. If the ambiguity is intentional, note this fact, and do not rewrite.

Example

Former professional football player Jim Brown was accused of assaulting a thirty-three-year-old woman with a female accomplice.

Answer

This claim is syntactically ambiguous because it isn't clear what the phrase "with a female accomplice" modifies—Brown, the woman who was attacked, or, however bizarre it might be, the attack itself (he might have thrown the accomplice at the woman). To make it clear that Brown had the accomplice, the phrase "with a female accomplice" should have come right after the word "Brown" in the original claim.

▲ 1. The Raider tackle threw a block at the Giants linebacker.

2. Please close the door behind you.

3. We heard that he informed you of what he said in his letter.

▲ 4. "How Therapy Can Help Torture Victims"

—Headline in newspaper

5. Charles drew his gun.

6. They were both exposed to someone who was ill a week ago.

▲ 7. Chelsea has Hillary Clinton's nose.

8. I flush the cooling system regularly and just put in new thermostats.

9. "Tuxedos Cut Ridiculously!"

—An ad for formal wear, quoted by Herb Caen

▲ 10. "Police Kill 6 Coyotes After Mauling of Girl"

—Headline in newspaper

11. "We promise nothing"

—Aquafina advertisement

12. A former governor of California, Pat Brown, viewing an area struck by a flood, is said to have remarked, "This is the greatest disaster since I was elected governor."

—Quoted by Lou Cannon in the Washington Post

▲ 13. "Besides Lyme disease, two other tick-borne diseases, babesiosis and HGE, are infecting Americans in 30 states, according to recent studies. A single tick can infect people with more than one disease."

—Self magazine

14. "Don't freeze your can at the game."

—Commercial for Miller beer

15. Volunteer help requested: Come prepared to lift heavy equipment with construction helmet and work overalls.

▲ 16. "GE: We bring good things to life."

—Television commercial

17. "Tropicana 100% Pure Florida Squeezed Orange Juice. You can't pick a better juice."

—Magazine advertisement

18. "It's biodegradable! So remember, Arm and Hammer laundry detergent gets your wash as clean as can be [pause] without polluting our waters."

—Television commercial

▲ 19. If you crave the taste of a real German beer, nothing is better than Dunkelbrau.

20. Independent laboratory tests prove that Houndstooth cleanser gets your bathroom cleaner than any other product.

21. We're going to look at lots this afternoon.

▲ 22. Jordan could write more profound essays.

23. "Two million times a day Americans love to eat, Rice-a-Roni—the San Francisco treat."

—Advertisement

24. "New York's first commercial human sperm-bank opened Friday with semen samples from 18 men frozen in a stainless steel tank."

—Strunk and White, The Elements of Style

▲ 25. She was disturbed when she lay down to nap by a noisy cow.

26. "More than half of expectant mothers suffer heartburn. To minimize symptoms, suggests Donald O. Castell, M.D., of the Graduate Hospital in Philadelphia, avoid big, high-fat meals and don't lie down for three hours after eating."

—Self magazine

27. "Abraham Lincoln wrote the Gettysburg address while traveling from Washington to Gettysburg on the back of an envelope."

—Richard Lederer

▲ 28. "When Queen Elizabeth exposed herself before her troops, they all shouted 'harrah.'"

—Richard Lederer

29. "In one of Shakespeare's famous plays, Hamlet relieves himself in a long soliloquy."

—Richard Lederer

30. The two suspects fled the area before the officers' arrival in a white Ford Mustang, being driven by a third male.

▲ 31. "AT&T, for the life of your business."

▲ 32. The teacher of this class might have been a member of the opposite sex.

▲ 33. "Woman gets 9 years for killing 11th husband."

—Headline in newspaper

34. "Average hospital costs are now an unprecedented $2,063.04 per day in California. Many primary plans don't pay 20% of that amount."

—AARP Group Health Insurance Program advertisement

35. "I am a huge Mustang fan."

   —*Ford Mustang advertisement*

36. "Visitors are expected to complain at the office between the hours of 9:00 and 11:00 A.M. daily."

   —*Sign in an Athens, Greece, hotel*

37. "Order your summers suit. Because is big rush we will execute customers in strict rotation."

   —*Sign in a Rhodes tailor shop*

38. "Please do not feed the animals. If you have any suitable food, give it to the guard on duty."

   —*Sign at a Budapest zoo*

39. "Our wines leave you with nothing to hope for."

   —*From a Swiss menu*

40. "Our Promise—Good for life."

   —*Cheerios*

41. Thinking clearly involves hard work.
42. "Cadillac—Break Through"

Exercise 3-8

Determine which of the italicized expressions are ambiguous, which are more likely to refer to the members of the class taken as a group, and which are more likely to refer to the members of the class taken individually.

Example

   Narcotics are habit forming.

Answer

   In this claim, *narcotics* refers to individual members of the class because it is specific narcotics that are habit forming. (One does not ordinarily become addicted to the entire class of narcotics.)

▲   1. *Swedes* eat millions of quarts of yogurt every day.
  2. *Professors at the university* make millions of dollars a year.
  3. *Our amplifiers* can be heard all across the country.
▲   4. *Students at Pleasant Valley High School* enroll in hundreds of courses each year.
  5. *Cowboys* die with their boots on.
  6. The *angles of a triangle* add up to 180 degrees.
▲   7. *The New York Giants* played mediocre football last year.
  8. On our airline, *passengers* have their choice of three different meals.
  9. On our airline, *passengers* flew fourteen million miles last month without incident.

▲ 10. *Hundreds of people* have ridden in that taxi.

11. *All our cars* are on sale for two hundred dollars over factory invoice.

▲ 12. *Chicagoans* drink more beer than *New Yorkers*.

13. *Power lawn mowers* produce more pollution than *motorcycles*.

14. *The Baltimore Orioles* may make it to the World Series in another six or seven years.

▲ 15. *People* are getting older.

Exercise 3-9

From your reading of this chapter, it should be fairly easy to identify the two kinds of mistakes present in the following ten examples. Identify which of the mistakes is present in each.

1. Irish wolfhounds are becoming increasingly popular these days. My dog is an Irish wolfhound. Therefore, my dog is becoming increasingly popular these days.

2. Humans are made of atoms and molecules. But neither atoms nor molecules are visible to the unaided eye. Therefore, humans should not be visible to the naked eye.

3. Salmon are disappearing from this river. Hey! There's a salmon now! Let's watch and see if it disappears!

4. During the nineteenth century, the English ruled the world. Harold Bingham was a nineteenth-century Englishman. Therefore, during the nineteenth century, Harold Bingham ruled the world.

5. A Humvee uses much more gasoline than a Honda automobile. So, clearly, more of the gasoline pumped these days is used by Humvees than by Hondas.

6. Humans give live birth to their children. Arnold Schwarzenegger is a human. Therefore, Arnold Schwarzenegger gives live birth to his children.

7. Every actor in the movie, as well as the director and the screenwriter, is Oscar-winner quality. So, the movie is surely Oscar-winner quality.

8. Sodium is dangerous if ingested in even modest quantities. The same is true of chloride. So, a combination of sodium and chloride will surely be very dangerous if ingested.

9. Students at the University of South Carolina consume more than 1,000 kilos of grits every semester. Susan is a student at South Carolina. Hard to see how anyone could eat that much of anything, but I guess she does.

10. If people are thrifty and save a large percentage of their money, then their personal economy is better off in the long run. Therefore, if a society is thrifty and saves a large percentage of its money, the society will be better off in the long run.

Exercise 3-10

"How's everything?"

What is the ambiguity behind the joke?

Exercise 3-11

Determine which of the following definitions are more likely designed to persuade and which are not.

1. Punk is musical freedom. It's saying, doing and playing what you want. In Webster's terms, 'nirvana' means freedom from pain, suffering and the external world, and that's pretty close to my definition of Punk Rock.

   —*Kurt Cobain*

2. Congress's definition of torture . . . [is] the infliction of severe mental or physical pain.

   —*John Yoo*

3. Democrats' definition of "rich"—always seems to be set just above whatever the salary happens to be for a member of Congress. Perhaps that says it all.

   —*Steve Steckler*

4. That is the definition of faith—acceptance of that which we imagine to be true, that which we cannot prove.

   —*Dan Brown*

5. Sin: That's anything that's so much fun it's difficult not to do it.

   —*Dave Kilbourne*

Exercise 3-12

Make up six definitions, two of which are designed to make the thing defined look good, two of which are designed to make it look bad, and two of which are neutral.

Exercise 3-13

The sentences in this Associated Press health report have been scrambled. Rearrange them so that the report makes sense.

1. The men, usually strong with no known vices or ailments, die suddenly, uttering an agonizing groan, writhing and gasping before succumbing to the mysterious affliction.

2. Scores of cases have been reported in the United States during the past decade.

3. In the United States, health authorities call it "Sudden Unexplained Death Syndrome," or "SUDS."

4. Hundreds of similar deaths have been noted worldwide.

5. The phenomenon is known as "lai tai," or "nightmare death," in Thailand.

6. In the Philippines, it is called "bangungut," meaning "to rise and moan in sleep."

7. Health officials are baffled by a syndrome that typically strikes Asian men in their thirties while they sleep.

8. Researchers cannot say what is killing SUDS victims.

Exercise 3-14

▲ The sentences in the following passage have been scrambled. Rearrange them so that the passage makes sense. You'll find an answer in the answer section.

1. Weintraub's findings were based on a computer test of 1,101 doctors twenty-eight to ninety-two years old.

2. She and her colleagues found that the top ten scorers aged seventy-five to ninety-two did as well as the average of men under thirty-five.

3. "The test measures memory, attention, visual perception, calculation, and reasoning," she said.

4. "The studies also provide intriguing clues to how that happens," said Sandra Weintraub, a neuropsychologist at Harvard Medical School in Boston.

5. "The ability of some men to retain mental function might be related to their ability to produce a certain type of brain cell not present at birth," she said.

6. The studies show that some men manage to escape the trend of declining mental ability with age.

7. Many elderly men are at least as mentally able as the average young adult, according to recent studies.

Exercise 3-15

Rewrite each of the following claims in gender-neutral language.

Example

   We have insufficient manpower to complete the task.

Answer

   We have insufficient personnel to complete the task.

▲ 1. A student should choose his major with considerable care.

   2. When a student chooses his major, he must do so carefully.

   3. The true citizen understands his debt to his country.

▲ 4. If a nurse can find nothing wrong with you in her preliminary examination, she will recommend a physician to you. However, in this city the physician will wish to protect himself by having you sign a waiver.

   5. You should expect to be interviewed by a personnel director. You should be cautious when talking to him.

   6. The entrant must indicate that he has read the rules, that he understands them, and that he is willing to abide by them. If he has questions, then he should bring them to the attention of an official, and he will answer them.

▲ 7. A soldier should be prepared to sacrifice his life for his comrades.

   8. If anyone wants a refund, he should apply at the main office and have his identification with him.

   9. The person who has tried our tea knows that it will neither keep him awake nor make him jittery.

▲ 10. If any petitioner is over sixty, he (she) should have completed form E-7.

   11. Not everyone has the same beliefs. One person may not wish to put himself on the line, whereas another may welcome the chance to make his view known to his friends.

   12. God created man in his own image.

▲ 13. Language is nature's greatest gift to mankind.

   14. Of all the animals, the most intelligent is man.

   15. The common man prefers peace to war.

▲ 16. The proof must be acceptable to the rational man.

▲ 17. The Founding Fathers believed that all men are created equal.

   18. Man's pursuit of happiness has led him to prefer leisure to work.

   19. When the individual reaches manhood, he is able to make such decisions for himself.

▲ 20. If an athlete wants to play for the National Football League, he should have a good work ethic.

   21. The new city bus service has hired several women drivers.

22. The city is also hiring firemen, policemen, and mailmen; and the city council is planning to elect a new chairman.

23. Harold Vasquez worked for City Hospital as a male nurse.

▲ 24. Most U.S. senators are men.

25. Mr. and Mrs. Macleod joined a club for men and their wives.

26. Mr. Macleod lets his wife work for the city.

▲ 27. Macleod doesn't know it, but Mrs. Macleod is a women's libber.

28. Several coeds have signed up for the seminar.

29. A judge must be sensitive to the atmosphere in his courtroom.

▲ 30. To be a good politician, you have to be a good salesman.

Exercise 3-16

▲ A riddle: A man is walking down the street one day when he suddenly recognizes an old friend whom he has not seen in years walking in his direction with a little girl. They greet each other warmly, and the friend says, "I married since I last saw you, to someone you never met, and this is my daughter, Ellen." The man says to Ellen, "You look just like your mother." How did he know that?

This riddle comes from Janice Moulton's article "The Myth of the Neutral Man." Discuss why so many people don't get the answer to this riddle straight off.

Classroom/Writing Exercise

This exercise is designed for use in the classroom, although your instructor may make a different kind of assignment. Consider the often heard claim, "Homosexuality is not natural." Many people agree or disagree with this statement even though they have only the most rudimentary idea of what it might mean. Discuss what you think might be meant by the claim, taking note of any vagueness or ambiguity that might be involved.

Writing Exercises

Everyone, no matter how well he or she writes, can improve. And the best way to improve is to practice. Since finding a topic to write about is often the hardest part of a writing assignment, we're supplying three subjects for you to write about. For each—or whichever your instructor might assign—write a one- to two-page essay in which you clearly identify the issue (or issues), state your position on the issue (a hypothetical position if you don't have one), and give at least one good reason in support of your position. Try also to give at least one reason why the opposing position is wrong.

1. The exchange of dirty hypodermic needles for clean ones, or the sale of clean ones, is legal in many states. In such states, the transmission of HIV and hepatitis from dirty needles is down dramatically. But bills [in

the California legislature] to legalize clean-needle exchanges have been stymied by the last two governors, who earnestly but incorrectly believed that the availability of clean needles would increase drug abuse. Our state, like every other state that has not yet done it, should immediately approve legislation to make clean needles available.

—Adapted from an editorial by Marsha N. Cohen,
professor of law at Hastings College of Law

2. On February 11, 2003, the Eighth Circuit Court of Appeals ruled that the state of Arkansas could force death-row prisoner Charles Laverne Singleton to take antipsychotic drugs to make him sane enough to execute. Singleton was to be executed for felony capital murder but became insane while in prison. "Medicine is supposed to heal people, not prepare them for execution. A law that asks doctors to make people well so that the government can kill them is an absurd law," said David Kaczynski, the executive director of New Yorkers Against the Death Penalty.

3. Some politicians make a lot of noise about how Canadians and others pay much less for prescription drugs than Americans do. Those who are constantly pointing to the prices and the practices of other nations when it comes to pharmaceutical drugs ignore the fact that those other nations lag far behind the United States when it comes to creating new medicines. Canada, Germany, and other countries get the benefits of American research but contribute much less than the United States does to the creation of drugs. On the surface, these countries have a good deal, but in reality everyone is worse off, because the development of new medicines is slower than it would be if worldwide prices were high enough to cover research costs.

—Adapted from an editorial by Thomas Sowell,
senior fellow at the Hoover Institution

Credibility

Students will learn to . . .

1. Evaluate degrees of credibility

2. Assess whether a source is an interested versus a disinterested party

3. Assess claims in relation to their own observations, experiences, or background information

4. Evaluate a source based on veracity, objectivity, and accuracy

5. Evaluate a source based on knowledge or expertise

6. Understand the influences and biases behind the news

7. Become better (and perhaps more skeptical) evaluators of media messages

8. Limit the influence of advertising on their consumer behavior

R aymond James Merrill was the brother of an acquaintance of one of your authors. In his mid-fifties, Merrill still cut a striking figure—tall and lean, with chiseled features, a bushy mustache, and a mane of blond hair. But he had been in a funk. He had broken up with his girlfriend, and he did not want to be alone. Then a website that featured "Latin singles" led him to Regina Rachid, an attractive woman with a seductive smile who lived in San Jose dos Campos, a city in southern Brazil, and suddenly Merrill was in love. Desperately so, it seems. He believed everything Rachid told him and was credulous enough to make three trips to Brazil to be with her, to give her thousands of dollars in cash, and to buy her a $20,000 automobile. He even refused to blame her when thousands of dollars in unexplained charges turned up on his credit card account. Sadly, Rachid was more interested in Merrill's money than in his affection, and when he went to Brazil the third time, to get married and, he believed, begin a new life, he disappeared. The story ended tragically: Merrill's strangled and burned body was found in an isolated spot several miles out of town. Rachid and two accomplices are now in jail for the crime, and two accessories are under investigation as we write this.* The moral of the story: It can be a horrible mistake to let our needs and desires overwhelm our critical abilities when we are not sure with whom or with what we're dealing. Our focus in this chapter is on how to determine when a claim or a source of a claim is credible enough to warrant belief.

A second story, less dramatic but much more common, is about a friend of ours named Dave, who not long ago received an email from Citibank. It notified him that there might be a problem with his credit card account and asked him to visit the bank's website to straighten things out. (These notices often include a threat that if you fail to respond, your account may be closed.) A link was provided to the website. When he visited the site, he was asked to confirm details of his personal information, including account numbers, Social Security number, and his mother's maiden name. The website looked exactly like the Citibank website he had visited before, with the bank's logo and other authentic-appearing details. But very shortly after this episode, he discovered that his card had paid for a plasma television, a home theater set, and a couple of expensive car stereos, none of which he had ordered or received.

Dave was a victim of "phishing," a ploy to identify victims for identity theft and credit card fraud. As this edition goes to press, the number of phishing

Real Life

The Nigerian Advance Fee 4-1-9 Fraud: The Internet's Longest-Running Scam Is Still Running Strong

If you have an email account, chances are you've received an offer from someone in Nigeria, probably claiming to be a Nigerian civil servant, who is looking for someone just like you who has a bank account to which several millions of dollars can be sent—money that results from "overinvoicing" or "double invoicing" oil purchases or otherwise needs laundering outside the country. You will receive a generous percentage of the money for your assistance, but you will have to help a bit at the outset by sending some amount of money to facilitate the transactions, or to show *your* good faith!

This scam, sometimes called "4-1-9 Fraud," after the relevant section of Nigeria's criminal code, is now celebrating more than a quarter century of existence. (It operated by telephone and FAX before the web was up and running.) Its variations are creative and numerous. Critical thinkers immediately recognize the failure of credibility such offers have, but thousands of people have not, and from a lack of critical thinking skills or from simple greed, hundreds of millions of dollars have been lost to the perpetrators of this fraud.

To read more about this scam, check out these websites: <http://www.secretservice.gov/alert419.shtml> and <http://home.rica.net/alphae/419coal/>.

---

*The whole story can be found at www.justice4raymond.org.

scams continues to rise, with millions of people receiving phony emails alleging to be from eBay, PayPal, and other Internet companies as well as an assortment of banks and credit card companies. Some of these phishing expeditions threaten to suspend or close the individual's account if no response is made. Needless to say, a person should give *no credibility* to an email that purports to be from a bank or other company and asks for personal identifying information via email or a website.

There are two grounds for suspicion in cases where credibility is the issue. The first ground is the claim itself. Dave should have asked himself just how likely it is that Citibank would notify him of a problem with his account by email and would ask him for his personal, identifying information. (Hint: *No* bank will approach its customers for such information by email or telephone.) The second ground for suspicion is the source of the claim. In this case, Dave believed the source was legitimate. But here's the point, one that critical thinkers are well aware of these days: *On the Internet, whether by website or email, the average person has no idea where the stuff on the computer screen comes from.* Computer experts have methods that can sometimes identify the source of an email, but most of us are very easy to mislead.

Dave is no dummy; being fooled by such scams is not a sign of a lack of intelligence. His concern that his account might be suspended caused him to overlook the ominous possibility that the original request might be a fake. In other cases, such as the one described in the "4-1-9 Fraud" box, it may be wishful thinking or a touch of simple greed that causes a person to lower his or her credibility guard.

Every time we revise and update this book, we feel obliged to make our warnings about Internet fraud more severe. And every year we seem to be borne out by events. The level of theft, fraud, duplicity, and plain old vandalism seems to rise like a constant tide. We'll have some suggestions for keeping yourself, your records, and your money safe later in the chapter. For now, just remember that you need your critical thinking lights on whenever you open your browser.

THE CLAIM AND ITS SOURCE

As indicated in the phishing story, there are two arenas in which we assess credibility: the first is that of *claims* themselves; the second is the claims' *sources.* If we're told that ducks can communicate by quacking in Morse code, we dismiss the claim immediately. Such claims lack credibility no matter where they come from. (They have no initial plausibility, a notion that will be explained later.) But the claim that ducks mate for life is not at all outrageous; it might be true: it's a credible claim. Whether we should believe it depends on its source; if we read it in a bird book or hear it from a bird expert, we are much more likely to believe it than if we hear it from our editor, for example.

There are degrees of credibility and incredibility; they are not all-or-nothing kinds of things, whether we're talking about claims or sources. Consider the claim that the president of the United States has been hypnotized and is acting completely under the spell of wizards who are hiding in warehouses in suburban Washington, D.C. This truly requires a stretch of the imagination; it is very unlikely. But, however unlikely, it is still more credible than the claim that the president is not human at all but a robot constructed and controlled by aliens from another galaxy. Sources (i.e., people) vary in their credibility just as do the claims they offer. If the next-door neighbor you've always liked is arrested for bank robbery, his denials will probably seem credible to you. But he loses credibility if it turns out he owns a silencer and a .45 automatic with the serial numbers removed. Similarly, a knowledgeable friend who tells us about an investment opportunity has a bit more credibility if we learn he has invested his own money in the idea. (At least we could be assured he believed the information himself.) On the other hand, he has less credibility if we learn he will make a substantial commission from our investment in it.

So, there are always two questions to be asked about a claim with which we're presented. First, when does a *claim itself* lack credibility—that is, when does its *content* present a credibility problem? Second, when does the *source* of a claim lack credibility?

We'll turn next to the first of these questions, which deals with what a claim actually says. The general answer is

> A claim lacks inherent credibility to the extent that it conflicts with what we have observed or what we think we know—our background information—or with other credible claims.

In the Media

Guaranteeing an Interested Party, or the Fox Audits the Henhouse

In 2005, an audit program was established by the federal government to root out fraud and waste in the Medicare program. An Atlanta-based auditing firm, PRG-Schultz, was given the job of reviewing Medicare records and searching for mistakes and overcharges in three states. So far, so good.

But the way the program was set up, the auditors were paid only when they found such mistakes and overcharges—they kept a commission of 25 to 30 cents for every dollar determined to be in error. Naturally, this makes the firm a very interested party, since the more fraud and waste it finds, the more money it makes.

As a critical thinker might expect, PRG-Schultz found lots of fraud and waste; they had rejected more than $105 million in Medicare claims by September 2006 and millions more by the time the program came under review by an administrative law judge. As a critical thinker might expect, many of the rejected charges were reversed on appeal; they were found to be legitimate after all.

Remember, putting an interested party in charge of making decisions is an invitation to error—or worse. That's why the expression "Don't put the fox in charge of the henhouse" is an important warning.

P.S. Because of the way the law was originally implemented, PRG-Schultz will be allowed to keep the money it received in commissions even though its decisions in many cases were reversed. The fox got away with this one.

Seattle Times online (seattletimes.nwsource.com), May 19, 2007, and the *Sacramento Bee*, September 16, 2007.

Just what this answer means will be explained in the section that follows. After that, we'll turn our attention to the second question we asked earlier, about the credibility of sources.

ASSESSING THE CONTENT OF THE CLAIM

So, some claims stand up on their own; they tend to be acceptable regardless of from whom we hear them. But when they fail on their own, as we've said, it's because they come into conflict either with our own observations or with what we call our "background knowledge." We'll discuss each of these in turn.

Does the Claim Conflict with Our Personal Observations?

Our own observations provide our most reliable source of information about the world. It is therefore only reasonable to be suspicious of any claim that comes into conflict with what we've observed. Imagine that Moore has just come from the home of Mr. Marquis, a mutual friend of his and Parker's, and has seen his new red Mini Cooper automobile. He meets Parker, who tells him, "I heard that Marquis has bought a new Mini Cooper, a bright blue one." Moore does not need critical thinking training to reject Parker's claim about the color of the car, because of the obvious conflict with his earlier observation.

In the Media

Incredible Claims!

We've had a lot of fun with lunatic headlines from supermarket tabloids in past editions. Here is this edition of "Run for Your Life" headlines:

> ### Demons Made Jessee Cheat on Sandra!
> "Possibly the same ones that got hold of Tiger Woods," says seer.
>
> ### How to Tell if You've Been Abducted by Aliens
> Memory loss, other symptoms can tell for sure, according to Dr. Brad Steiger.
>
> ### Elvis Alive and Working in Vegas as Elvis Impersonator
> He's better at it than most of them, reviews say.
>
> ### Beer Can Prevent Prostate Cancer
> Very few career drinkers die of it, say medicos.
>
> ### Nebraska Doesn't Exist, Says Author
> Admission process was botched, according to historian.

We don't have to make these up.

Real Life

When Personal Observation Fails . . .

According to the Innocence Project, a group in New York that investigates wrongful convictions, eyewitness misidentification is the single greatest cause of conviction of innocent persons. Of all the convictions overturned by DNA analysis, witness misidentification played a role in over 75 percent. Of the first 239 DNA exonerations, 62 percent of the defendants were misidentified by one witness; in 25 percent of the cases, the defendant was misidentified by two witnesses; and *in 13 percent of the cases the same innocent defendant was misidentified by three or more separate eyewitnesses.* Even though eyewitness testimony can be persuasive before a judge and jury, it is *much* more unreliable than we generally give it credit for being.

But observations and short-term memory are far from infallible, or professional dancer Douglas Hall would not have been awarded $450,000 in damages by a New York jury in January 2005.* It seems Dr. Vincent Feldman, twenty minutes after having placed a large "X" on the dancer's right knee, where the latter had complained of pain, sliced open the patient's *left* knee, which had been perfectly healthy up until that moment, and effectively ended his dancing career in the process. Although he had just *seen* where he was to operate and had marked the spot, he nonetheless managed to confuse the location and the result may have put a serious wrinkle in his own career as well as that of the dancer.

---

*New York Post, January 29, 2005.

All kinds of factors influence our observations and our recollections of them, and Dr. Feldman may have been affected by one or more of them: tiredness, distraction, worry about an unrelated matter, or emotional upset could easily account for such mistakes. There are also physical conditions that often affect our observations: bad lighting, lots of noise, the speed of events, and more. We are also sometimes prey to measuring instruments that are inexact, temperamental, or inaccurate. Parker once blew out a tire at high speed as a result of a faulty tire-pressure gauge.

It's also important to remember that people are not all created equal when it comes to making observations. We hate to say it, dear reader, but there are lots of people who see better, hear better, and remember better than you. Of course, that goes for us as well.

Our beliefs, hopes, fears, and expectations affect our observations. Tell someone that a house is infested with rats, and he is likely to believe he sees evidence of rats. Inform someone who believes in ghosts that a house is haunted, and she may well believe she sees evidence of ghosts. At séances staged by the Society for Psychical Research to test the observational powers of people under séance conditions, some observers insist that they see numerous phenomena that simply do not exist. Teachers who are told that the students in a particular class are brighter than usual are very likely to believe that the work those students produce is better than average, even when it is not.

In Chapter 6, we cover a fallacy (a fallacy is a mistake in reasoning) called *wishful thinking,* which occurs when we allow hopes and desires to influence our judgment and color our beliefs. Most of the people who fall for the 4-1-9 Fraud Internet scam (see box, p. 105) are almost surely victims of wishful thinking. It is very unlikely that somebody, somewhere, wants to send you millions of dollars just because you have a bank account and that the money they ask for really is just to facilitate the transaction. The most gullible victim, with no stake in the matter, would probably realize this. But the idea of getting one's hands on a great pile of money can blind a person to even the most obvious facts.

Our personal interests and biases affect our perceptions and the judgments we base on them. We overlook many of the mean and selfish actions of the people we like or love—and when we are infatuated with someone, everything that person does seems wonderful. By contrast, people we detest can hardly do anything that we don't perceive as mean and selfish. If we desperately wish for the success of a project, we are apt to see more evidence for that success than is actually present. On the other hand, if we wish for a project to fail, we are apt to exaggerate flaws that we see in it or imagine flaws that are not there at all. If a job, chore, or decision is one that we wish to avoid, we tend to draw worst-case implications from it and thus come up with reasons for not doing it. However, if we are predisposed to want to do the job or make the decision, we are more likely to focus on whatever positive consequences it might have.

Finally, as we hinted above, the reliability of our observations is no better than the reliability of our memories, except in those cases where we have the means at our disposal to record our observations. And memory, as most of us know, can be deceptive. Critical thinkers are always alert to the possibility that what they remember having observed may not be what they did observe.

But even though firsthand observations are not infallible, they are still the best source of information we have. Any report that conflicts with our own direct observations is subject to serious doubt.

In Depth

Incredible but True

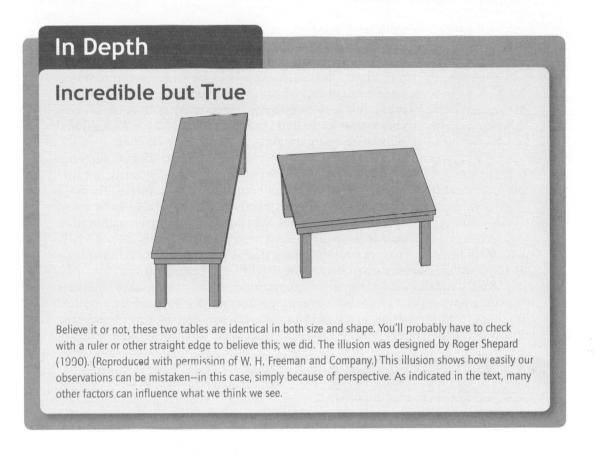

Believe it or not, these two tables are identical in both size and shape. You'll probably have to check with a ruler or other straight edge to believe this; we did. The illusion was designed by Roger Shepard (1990). (Reproduced with permission of W. H. Freeman and Company.) This illusion shows how easily our observations can be mistaken—in this case, simply because of perspective. As indicated in the text, many other factors can influence what we think we see.

Does the Claim Conflict with Our Background Information?

Reports must always be evaluated against our **background information**—that immense body of justified beliefs that consists of facts we learn from our own direct observations and facts we learn from others. Such information is "background" because we may not be able to specify where we learned it, unlike something we know because we witnessed it this morning. Much of our background information is well confirmed by a variety of sources. Reports that conflict with this store of information are usually quite properly dismissed, even if we cannot disprove them through direct observation. We immediately reject the claim "Palm trees grow in abundance near the North Pole," even though we are not in a position to confirm or disprove the statement by direct observation.

Indeed, this is an example of how we usually treat claims when we first encounter them: We begin by assigning them a certain **initial plausibility,** a rough assessment of how credible a claim seems to us. This assessment depends on how consistent the claim is with our background information— how well it "fits" with that information. If it fits very well, we give the claim some reasonable degree of initial plausibility—there is a reasonable expectation of its being true. If, however, the claim conflicts with our background information, we give it low initial plausibility and lean toward rejecting it unless very strong evidence can be produced on its behalf. The claim "More guitars were sold in the United States last year than saxophones" fits very well with the background information most of us share, and we would hardly require detailed evidence before accepting it. However, the claim "Charlie's eighty-seven-year-old grandmother swam across Lake Michigan in the

There are three types of men in the world. One type learns from books. One type learns from observation. And one type just has to urinate on the electric fence.

—DR. LAURA SCHLESSINGER
(reported by Larry Englemann)

The authority of experience.

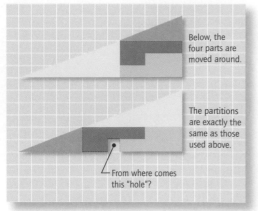

Below, the four parts are moved around.

The partitions are exactly the same as those used above.

From where comes this "hole"?

■ This optical illusion has made the rounds on the web. It takes a very close look to identify how the illusion works, although it's *certain* that *something* sneaky is going on here. The problem is solved back in the Answer Section.

middle of winter" cannot command much initial plausibility because of the obvious way it conflicts with our background information about eighty-seven-year-old people, about Lake Michigan, about swimming in cold water, and so on. In fact, short of observing the swim ourselves, it isn't clear just what *could* persuade us to accept such a claim. And even then, we should consider the likelihood that we're being tricked or fooled by an illusion.

Obviously, not every oddball claim is as outrageous as the one about Charlie's grandmother. Recently, we read a report about a house being stolen in Lindale, Texas—a brick house. This certainly is implausible—how could anyone steal a home? Yet there is credible documentation that it happened,* and even stranger things occasionally turn out to be true. That, of course, means that it can be worthwhile to check out implausible claims if their being true might be of benefit to you.

Unfortunately, there are no neat formulas that can resolve conflicts between what you already believe and new information. Your job as a critical thinker is to trust your background information when considering claims that conflict with that information—that is, claims with low initial plausibility—

Real Life

Do Your Ears Stick Straight Out?

According to Bill Cordingley, an expert in psychographicology—that's face-reading, in case you didn't know (and we certainly didn't)—a person's facial features reveal "the whole rainbow collection" of a person's needs and abilities. Mr. Cordingley (*In Your Face: What Facial Features Reveal About People You Know and Love*) doesn't mean merely that you can infer moods from smiles and frowns. No, he means that your basic personality traits are readable from facial structures you were born with.

Do your ears stick out? That means you have a need to perform in public. The more they stick out, the greater the need. Other features are said to reliably predict features of your personality. It appears that President Obama is fortunate in that he (and his ears) have lots of opportunities to appear in public.

Is there any reason to believe facial features can tell us such things about people? We think not. The fact that Cordingley was once mayor of San Anselmo, California, adds no credibility to the claim.

*Associated Press report, March 25, 2005.

Real Life

Fib Wizards

In *The Sleeping Doll*, novelist Jeffery Deaver invents a character who is incredibly adept at reading what people are thinking from watching and listening to them. This is fiction, but there seems to be at least a bit of substance to the claim that such talents exist.

> After testing 13,000 people for their ability to detect deception, Professor Maureen O'Sullivan of the University of San Francisco identified 31 who have an unusual ability to tell when someone is lying to them. These "wizards," as she calls them, are especially sensitive to body language, facial expressions, hesitations in speech, slips of the tongue, and similar clues that a person may not be telling the truth. The wizards are much better than the average person at noticing these clues and inferring the presence of a fib from them.
>
> Professor O'Sullivan presented her findings to the American Medical Association's 23rd Annual Science Reporters Conference.
>
> Maybe a few people can reliably tell when someone is lying. But we'd bet there are many more who merely *think* they can do this—these are the ones we want to play poker with.

From an Associated Press report.

but at the same time to keep an open mind and realize that further information may cause you to give up a claim you had thought was true. It's a difficult balance, but it's worth getting right. For example, let's say you've been suffering from headaches and have tried all the usual methods of relief: aspirin, antihistamines, whatever your physician has recommended, and so on. Finally, a friend tells you that she had headaches that were very similar to yours, and nothing worked for her, either, until she had an aromatherapy treatment. Then, just a few minutes into her aromatherapy session, her headaches went away. Now, we (Moore and Parker) are not much inclined to believe that smelling oils will make your headache disappear, but we think there is little to lose and at least a small possibility of something substantial to be gained by giving the treatment a try. It may be, for example, that the treatment relaxes a person and relieves tension, which can cause headaches. We wouldn't go into it with great expectations, however.

The point is that there is a scale of initial plausibility ranging from quite plausible to only slightly so. Our aromatherapy example would fall somewhere between the plausible (and in fact true) claim that Parker went to high school with Bill Clinton and the rather implausible claim that Paris Hilton has a Ph.D. in physics.

As mentioned, background information is essential to adequately assess a claim. It is pretty difficult to evaluate a report if you have no background information relating to the topic. This means the broader your background information, the more likely you are to be able to evaluate any given report effectively. You'd have to know a little economics to evaluate assertions about the dangers of a large federal deficit, and knowing how Social Security works can help you know what's misleading about calling it a savings account. Read widely, converse freely, and develop an inquiring attitude; there's no substitute for broad, general knowledge.

Exercise 4-1

1. The text points out that physical conditions around us can affect our observations. List at least four such conditions.

2. Our own mental state can affect our observations as well. Describe at least three of the ways this can happen, as mentioned in the text.

3. According to the text, there are two ways credibility should enter into our evaluation of a claim. What are they?

4. A claim lacks inherent credibility, according to the text, when it conflicts with what?

5. Our most reliable source of information about the world is _____.

6. The reliability of our observations is not better than the reliability of _____.

Exercise 4-2 ▲ In your judgment, are any of these claims less credible than others? Discuss your opinions with others in the class to see if any interesting differences in background information emerge.

1. They've taught crows how to play poker.

2. The center of Earth consists of water.

3. Ray Charles was just faking his blindness.

4. The car manufacturers already can build cars that get more than 100 miles per gallon; they just won't do it because they're in cahoots with the oil industry.

5. If you force yourself to go for five days and nights without any sleep, you'll be able to get by on less than five hours of sleep a night for the rest of your life.

6. It is possible to read other people's minds through mental telepathy.

7. A diet of mushrooms and pecans supplies all necessary nutrients and will help you lose weight. Scientists don't understand why.

8. Somewhere on the planet is a person who looks exactly like you.

9. The combined wealth of the world's 225 richest people equals the total annual income of the poorest 2.5 billion people, which is nearly half the world's total population.

10. George W. Bush arranged to have the World Trade Center attacked so he could invade Afghanistan. He wanted to build an oil pipeline across Afghanistan.

11. Daddy longlegs are the world's most poisonous spider, but their mouths are too small to bite.

12. Static electricity from your body can cause your gas tank to explode if you slide across your seat while fueling and then touch the gas nozzle.

13. Japanese scientists have created a device that measures the tone of a dog's bark to determine what the dog's mood is.

14. Barack Obama (a) is a socialist, (b) is a Muslim, (c) was not born in the United States.

THE CREDIBILITY OF SOURCES

We turn now from the credibility of claims themselves to the credibility of the sources from which we get them. We are automatically suspicious of certain sources of information. (If you were getting a divorce, you wouldn't ordinarily turn to your spouse's attorney for advice.) We'll look at several factors that should influence how much credence we give to a source.

Interested Parties

We'll begin with a very important general rule for deciding whom to trust. Our rule makes use of two correlative concepts, interested parties and disinterested parties:

> A person who stands to gain from our belief in a claim is known as an **interested party,** and interested parties must be viewed with much more suspicion than **disinterested parties,** who have no stake in our belief one way or another.

Real Life

Not All That Glitters

Since the U.S. dollar began to decline seriously in about 2004, quite a few financial "experts" have claimed that gold is one of the few ways to protect one's wealth and provide a hedge against inflation. Some of the arguments they make contain some good sense, but it's worth pointing out that many of the people advocating the purchase of gold turn out to be brokers of precious metals themselves, or are hired by such brokers to sell their product. As we emphasize in the text: Always beware of interested parties!

It would be hard to overestimate the importance of this rule—in fact, if you were to learn only one thing from this book, this might be the best candidate. Of course, not all interested parties are out to hoodwink us, and certainly not all disinterested parties have good information. But, all things considered, the rule of trusting the latter before the former is a crucially important weapon in the critical thinking armory.

We'll return to this topic later, both in the text and in some exercises.

Physical and Other Characteristics

The feature of being an interested or disinterested party is highly relevant to whether he, she, it, or they should be trusted. Unfortunately, we often base our judgments on irrelevant considerations. Physical characteristics, for example, tell us little about a person's credibility or its lack. Does a person look you in the eye? Does he perspire a lot? Does he have a nervous laugh? Despite being generally worthless in this regard, such characteristics are widely used in siz-

Real Life

Whom Do You Trust?

As mentioned in the text, we often make too much of outward appearances when it comes to believing what someone tells us. Would you be more inclined to believe one of these individuals than the other? As a matter of fact, we can think of at least as many reasons for the man on the left telling us something that isn't true as for the man on the right.

ing up a person's credibility. Simply being taller, louder, and more assertive can enhance a person's credibility, according to a recent study.* A practiced con artist can imitate a confident teller of the truth, just as an experienced hacker can cobble up a genuine-appearing website. ("Con," after all, is short for "confidence.")

Other irrelevant features we sometimes use to judge a person's credibility include gender, age, ethnicity, accent, and mannerisms. People also make credibility judgments on the basis of the clothes a person wears. A friend told one of us that one's sunglasses "make a statement"; maybe so, but that statement doesn't say much about credibility. A person's occupation certainly bears a relationship to his or her knowledge or abilities, but as a guide to moral character or truthfulness, it is less reliable.

Which considerations are relevant to judging someone's credibility? We shall get to these in a moment, but appearance isn't one of them. You may have the idea that you can size up a person just by looking into his or her eyes. This is a mistake. Just by looking at someone, we cannot ascertain that person's truthfulness, knowledge, or character. (Although this is generally true, there are exceptions. See the "Fib Wizards" box on page 113.)

Of course, we sometimes get in trouble even when we accept credible claims from credible sources. Many of us rely, for example, on credible advice from qualified and honest professionals in preparing our tax returns. But qualified and honest professionals can make honest mistakes, and we can suffer the consequences. In general, however, trouble is much more likely if we accept either doubtful claims from credible sources or credible claims from doubtful sources (not to mention doubtful claims from doubtful sources). If a mechanic says we need a new transmission, the claim itself may not be suspicious—maybe the car we drive has many miles on it; maybe we neglected routine maintenance; maybe it isn't shifting smoothly. But remember that the mechanic is an interested party; if there's any reason to suspect he would exaggerate the problem to get work for himself, we'd get a second opinion about our transmission.

One of your authors currently has an automobile that the local dealership once diagnosed as having an oil leak. Because of the complexity of the repair, the cost was almost a thousand dollars. Because he'd not seen any oil on his garage floor, your cautious author decided to wait and see how serious the problem was. Well, a year after the "problem" was diagnosed, there was still no oil on the garage floor, and the car used less than half a quart of oil, about what one would have expected to add during the course of a year. What to conclude? The service department at the dealership is an interested party. If they convince your author that the oil leak is serious, they make almost a thousand dollars. This makes it worth a second opinion, or, in this case, one's own investigation. We now believe his car will never need this thousand-dollar repair.

Remember: Interested parties are less credible than other sources of claims.

I looked the man in the eye. I found him to be very straightforward and trustworthy. We had a very good dialogue. I was able to sense his soul.

—GEORGE W. BUSH, commenting on his first meeting with Russian president Vladimir Putin

By the end of 2007, Bush had changed his mind about Putin, seeing him as a threat to democracy. So much for the "blink" method of judging credibility.

---

*The study, conducted by Professor Lara Tiedens of the Stanford University Graduate School of Business, was reported in *USA Today*, July 18, 2007.

Expertise

Much of our information comes from people about whom we have no reason to suspect prejudice, bias, or any of the other features that make interested parties such bad sources. However, we might still doubt a source's actual knowledge of an issue in question. The state of a person's knowledge depends on a number of factors, especially that person's level of expertise and experience, either direct (through personal observation) or indirect (through study), with the subject at hand.

Just as you generally cannot tell merely by looking at someone whether he or she is speaking truthfully, objectively, and accurately, you can't judge his or her knowledge or expertise by looking at surface features. A British-sounding scientist may appear more knowledgeable than a scientist who speaks, say, with a Texas drawl, but his or her accent, height, gender, ethnicity, or clothing doesn't have much to do with a person's knowledge. In the municipal park in our town, it can be difficult to distinguish the people who teach at the university from the people who live in the park, based on physical appearance.

So, then, how do you judge a person's **expertise?** Education and experience are often the most important factors, followed by accomplishments, reputation, and position, in no particular order. It is not always easy to evaluate the credentials of an expert, and credentials vary considerably from one field to another. Still, there are some useful guidelines worth mentioning.

Education includes, but is not strictly limited to, formal education—the possession of degrees from established institutions of learning. (Some "doctors" of this and that received their diplomas from mail-order houses that advertise on matchbook covers. The title "doctor" is not automatically a qualification.)

Experience—both the kind and the amount—is an important factor in expertise. Experience is important if it is relevant to the issue at hand, but the mere fact that someone has been on the job for a long time does not automatically make him or her good at it.

Real Life

War-Making Policies and Interested Parties

In the 1960s, the secretary of defense supplied carefully selected information to President Lyndon Johnson and to the Congress. Would the Congress have passed the Gulf of Tonkin Resolution, which authorized the beginning of the Vietnam War, if its members had known that the secretary of defense was determined to begin hostilities there? We don't know, but certainly they and the president should have been more suspicious if they had known this fact. Would President Bush and his administration have been so anxious to make war on Iraq if they had known that Ahmad Chalabi, one of their main sources of information about that country and its ruler, Saddam Hussein, was a very interested party? (He hoped to be the next ruler of Iraq if Hussein were overthrown, and much of his information turned out to be false or exaggerated.) We don't know that either, of course. But it's possible that more suspicion of interested parties may have slowed our commencement of two costly wars.

Accomplishments are an important indicator of someone's expertise but, once again, only when those accomplishments are directly related to the question at hand. A Nobel Prize winner in physics is not necessarily qualified to speak publicly about toy safety, public school education (even in science), or nuclear proliferation. The last issue may involve physics, it's true, but the political issues are the crucial ones, and they are not taught in physics labs.

A person's reputation is obviously very important as a criterion of his or her expertise. But reputations must be seen in a context; how much importance we should attach to somebody's reputation depends on the people among whom the person has that reputation. You may have a strong reputation as a pool player among the denizens of your local pool hall, but that doesn't necessarily put you in the same league with Allison Fisher. Among a group of people who know nothing about investments, someone who knows the difference between a 401(k) plan and a Roth IRA may seem like quite an expert. But you certainly wouldn't want to take investment advice from somebody simply on that basis.

Most of us have met people who were recommended as experts in some field but who turned out to know little more about that field than we ourselves knew. (Presumably, in such cases those doing the recommending knew even less about the subject, or they would not have been so quickly impressed.) By and large, the kind of reputation that counts most is the one a person has among other experts in his or her field of endeavor.

The positions people hold provide an indication of how well *somebody* thinks of them. The director of an important scientific laboratory, the head of an academic department at Harvard, the author of a work consulted by other experts—in each case the position itself is substantial evidence that the individual's opinion on a relevant subject warrants serious attention.

But expertise can be bought. Our earlier discussion of interested parties applies to people who possess real expertise on a topic as well as to the rest of us. Sometimes a person's position is an indication of what his or her opinion, expert or not, is likely to be. The opinion of a lawyer retained by the National Rifle Association, offered at a hearing on firearms and urban violence, should be scrutinized much more carefully (or at least viewed with more skepticism) than that of a witness from an independent firm or agency that has no stake in the outcome of the hearings. The former can be assumed to be an interested party, the latter not. It is too easy to lose objectivity where one's interests and concerns are at stake, even if one is *trying* to be objective.

Experts sometimes disagree, especially when the issue is complicated and many different interests are at stake. In these cases, a critical thinker is obliged to suspend judgment about which expert to endorse, unless one expert clearly represents a majority viewpoint among experts in the field or unless one expert can be established as more authoritative or less biased than the others.

Of course, majority opinions sometimes turn out to be incorrect, and even the most authoritative experts occasionally make mistakes. For example, various economics experts predicted good times ahead just before the Great Depression. The same was true for many advisors right up until the 2008 financial meltdown. Jim Denny, the manager of the Grand Ole Opry, fired Elvis Presley after one performance, stating that Presley wasn't going anywhere and ought to go back to driving a truck. A claim you accept because it represents the majority viewpoint or comes from the most authoritative expert may turn out to be thoroughly wrong. Nevertheless, take heart: At the time, you were

Real Life

Smoking and Not Paying Attention Can Be Deadly

David Pawlik called the fire department in Cleburne, Texas, in July to ask if the "blue flames" he and his wife were seeing every time she lit a cigarette were dangerous, and an inspector said he would be right over and for Mrs. Pawlik not to light another cigarette. However, anxious about the imminent inspection, she lit up and was killed in the subsequent explosion. (The home was all electric, but there had been a natural gas leak underneath the yard.)

—*Fort Worth Star Telegram*, July 11, 2007
News of the Weird <http://groups.google.com/group/NewsoftheWeird/>

Sometimes it is *crucial* that you take the word of an expert.

rationally justified in accepting the majority viewpoint as the most authoritative claim. The reasonable position is the one that agrees with the most authoritative opinion but allows for enough open-mindedness to change if the evidence changes.

Finally, we sometimes make the mistake of thinking that whatever qualifies someone as an expert in one field automatically qualifies that person in other areas. Being a top-notch programmer, for example, surely would not be an indication of top-notch management skills. Indeed, many programmers get good at what they do by shying away from dealing with other people—or so the stereotype runs. Being a good campaigner does not always translate into being a good office-holder, as anyone who observes politics knows. Even if the intelligence and skill required to become an expert in one field could enable someone to become an expert in any field—which is doubtful—having the ability to become an expert is not the same as actually being an expert. Claims put forth by experts about subjects outside their fields are not automatically more acceptable than claims put forth by nonexperts.

List as many irrelevant factors as you can think of that people often mistake for signs of a person's truthfulness (for example, the firmness of a handshake).

Exercise 4-3

List as many irrelevant factors as you can think of that people often mistake for signs of expertise on the part of an individual (for example, appearing self-confident).

Exercise 4-4

Expertise doesn't transfer automatically from one field to another: Being an expert in one area does not automatically qualify a person as an expert (or even as competent) in other areas. Is it the same with dishonesty? Many people think dishonesty does transfer, that being dishonest in one area automatically discredits that person in all areas. For example, when Bill Clinton lied about having sexual encounters with his intern, some said he couldn't be trusted about anything.

Exercise 4-5

If someone is known to have been dishonest about one thing, should we automatically be suspicious of his or her honesty regarding other things? Discuss.

1. In a sentence, describe the crucial difference between an interested party and a disinterested party.
2. Which of the two parties mentioned in item 1 should generally be considered more trustworthy? Why?

Exercise 4-6

▲ Suppose you're in the market for a new television set, and you're looking for advice as to what to buy. Identify which of the following persons/subjects is likely to be an interested party and which is not.

Exercise 4-7

1. a flyer from a local store that sells televisions
2. the *Consumer Reports* website
3. a salesman at a local electronics store
4. the Sony website
5. an article in a major newspaper about television sets, including some rankings of brands

Now let's say you've narrowed your search to two brands: LG and Panasonic. Which of the following are more likely interested parties?

6. a friend who owns an LG set

7. a friend who used to own a Panasonic and now owns an LG
8. a salesperson at a store that sells both Panasonic and LG

CREDIBILITY AND THE NEWS MEDIA

You may have heard that newspapers and the print media in general have fallen on hard times in recent years. It's true: many newspapers are in bankruptcy, with advertising revenue falling 23 percent between 2006 and 2009 and one out of five newspaper journalists losing their jobs between 2001 and 2009.* Much of the losses in both the print media and in broadcast television have been the result of more and more people turning to the Internet for their news and information. During 2008, consumption of news on the Internet increased by some 19 percent, and it has no doubt expanded hugely since. Strangely enough, though, as more and more people turn to the web for news, they give it very low marks for credibility. On the other hand, according to the Pew Project report for 2009, leading newspapers and television news operations had stable credibility ratings during the past presidential election year. However, the ratings held stable at a level that was already pretty low. When evaluating seven print media sources, an average of only 19 percent of those polled said they "believe all or most" of what they read. CNN, which topped the list in believability among television sources, came in at only 30 percent. Why is the level of confidence in our media so low? Let's look at some likely factors.

Consolidation of Media Ownership

Although it is not well known to most citizens, one reason the quality of news available has decreased is that the media have become controlled by fewer and fewer corporations, the result of many mergers and buyouts over the past three or so decades. Since 2001, when the Federal Communications Commission loosened the regulations regarding ownership of newspapers, radio stations, and television stations, the concentration of media in fewer and fewer hands has been accelerating. From thousands of independent media outlets in the mid-twentieth century, media ownership dropped to only fifty companies by 1983. By late 2004, approximately 90 percent of all media companies in the United States were controlled by just five companies: Time Warner (Warner Bros., Time, Inc., HBO, CNN, etc.), Disney (ABC, ESPN, Miramax Films, etc.), News Corp. (Fox Television, Wall Street Journal, New York Post, etc.), General Electric (NBC, Universal Studios, A & E Television, etc.), and Viacom (Paramount Pictures, MTV, Comedy Central, etc.). The subsidiaries listed in parentheses are only a tiny portion of these companies' holdings. No matter what you see on television, the great likelihood is that one or more of these companies had a hand in producing it or getting it onto your screen. The fewer hands that control the media, the easier it is for the news we get to be "managed"—either by the owners themselves or by their commercial advertisers or even, as we'll next see, by the government.

*The State of the News Media, the Pew Project for Excellence in Journalism, 2009, a biennial report, from which we draw heavily in this section.

"Those are the headlines, and we'll be back in a moment to blow them out of proportion."

Government Management of the News

For a while there, our only known source of *fake* news was Jon Stewart on *The Daily Show*. But the federal government got into the fake news business as well. In recent years, a number of fake news reports, paid for by the government, have appeared on television touting the virtues of government schemes from the prescription drug program to airport safety to education programs. No criticism of the programs was included, and no mention was made that these were not legitimate independent news reports but rather were produced by the very same governmental departments that produced the policies in question.

These practices provide material for stations that cannot afford to produce a full plate of news themselves, which includes many, many stations across the country. Unfortunately, many viewers accept as news what is essentially official propaganda.

Leaving aside news reporting, problems also crop up on the op-ed page. Opinion and editorial pages and television commentaries are usually presumed to present the opinions of the writers or speakers who write or speak in them. But, as it turned out, some of those are bought and paid for as well. Our favorite example turned up in 2005: Syndicated columnist Michael McManus was paid $10,000 by the Department of Health and Human Services for writing positively about one of its programs. Ironically enough, his column is entitled "Ethics and Religion."

The military has its own methods for managing the media, from not allowing photographs to be taken of the coffins of slain American soldiers when they are sent home from Iraq to the more elaborately produced example seen in the box on p. 125, "Saving Private Lynch." Sometimes management takes the form of simple suppression of news, as when it took a whistle-blower to finally make public the video of a 2007 helicopter attack that killed a news photographer, his driver, and several others.

Bias Within the Media

It is commonly said that the media is biased politically. Conservatives are convinced that it has a liberal bias and liberals are convinced the bias favors conservatives.

The usual basis for the conservative assessment is that, generally speaking, reporters and editors are more liberal than the general population. Indeed, several polls have indicated that this is the case. On the other hand, the publishers and owners of media outlets tend to be conservative—not surprisingly, since they have an orientation that places a higher value on the bottom line: They are in business to make a profit. A book by Eric Alterman* argues

In the Media

Jumping to Conclusions in the News

On March 29, 2010, Fox Nation, the Fox News website, put up a story about a tragedy in Antarctica:

> Famed global warming activist James Schneider and a journalist friend were both found frozen to death on Saturday, about 90 miles from the South Pole Station, by the pilot of a ski plane practicing emergency evacuation procedures.

Well, Fox Nation was a bit too quick to jump on a story that fairly dripped with irony—a frozen global warming activist, indeed. However, the joke turned out to be on Fox: they had gotten the story from ecoEnquirer.com, a satirical website featuring spoof articles—James Schneider was a made-up name, not a real person. (Other headlines at the site: "Court Orders Fisherman to Apologize to Eagle," "Penguins Fed Up with Media Attention.")

---

*What Liberal Bias? (New York: Basic Books, 2003).

In the Media

Saving Private Lynch

Just after midnight on April 2, 2003, a battle group of Marine Rangers and Navy SEALs descended in helicopters on the Iraqi town of Nasiriyah. With shouts of "Go, go, go!" and rifle fire, they charged the hospital where Private Jessica Lynch was being held. The 19-year-old supply clerk was put on a stretcher and carried from the hospital to the choppers, and the unit was up and away as quickly as it had come. The entire scene was captured by military cameramen using night-vision cameras.

Eight days earlier, when Private Lynch's unit had taken a wrong turn and become separated from its convoy, it was apparently attacked by Iraqi fighters. According to the story in the *Washington Post,* Lynch put up a defiant stand against the attackers and "sustained multiple gunshot wounds" and was stabbed while she "fought fiercely and shot several enemy soldiers . . . firing her weapon until she ran out of ammunition." The paper cited a U.S. military official as saying "she was fighting to the death." This story was picked up by news outlets all over the world.

The ambush and the rescue sound like something out of *Black Hawk Down* or maybe a Bruce Willis movie. It also came at a time when the military was looking for some good press out of the Iraq invasion. Like many stories that seem too good to be true, this one was too good to be true.

At the hospital in Germany to which Private Lynch was flown, a doctor said her injuries included a head wound, a spinal injury, fractures in both legs and one arm, and an ankle injury. Apparently, none of her injuries were caused by bullets or shrapnel, according to the medical reports. A doctor at the Nasiriyah hospital where she was initially treated said Lynch suffered injuries consistent with an automobile wreck.

The rescue itself may have been rather seriously overdone. Quoted in the BBC News World Edition, Dr. Anmar Uday, who worked at the hospital, said, "We were surprised. Why do this? There was no military, there were no soldiers in the hospital. It was like a Hollywood film. They made a show for the American attack on the hospital—action movies like Sylvester Stallone or Jackie Chan."

The BBC referred to the "Saving Private Lynch" story as "one of the most stunning pieces of news management ever conceived." We shall probably never know the truth of the details, but it seems clear that the episode was stage-managed to some extent: It isn't likely an accident that the Special Forces just "happened to have" an American flag to drape over Ms. Lynch as she was carried to the helicopter on her stretcher.

that the "liberal media" has always been a myth and that, at least in private, well-known conservatives like Patrick Buchanan and William Kristol are willing to admit it. On the other hand, Bernard Goldberg, formerly of CBS, argues that the liberal bias of the press is a fact. *

Making an assessment on this score is several miles beyond our scope here. But it is important to be aware that a reporter or a columnist or a broadcaster who draws conclusions without presenting sufficient evidence

---

*Bias, (Washington, D.C.: Regnery Publishing, 2001).

is no more to be believed than some guy from down the street, even if the conclusions happen to correspond nicely to your own bias—indeed, *especially* if they correspond to your own bias!

What is important to remember is that there are many forces at work in the preparation of news besides a desire to publish or broadcast the whole truth. That said, our view is that the major network news organizations are generally credible, exceptions like those noted above notwithstanding. ABC, CBS, and NBC do a generally credible job, as does CNN, and the Public Broadcasting System and National Public Radio are generally excellent. Also in our view, the printed media, the *New York Times,* the *Washington Post,* the *Los Angeles Times,* and other major newspapers are generally credible, even though mistakes are sometimes made here as well. News magazines fall in the same category: usually credible but with occasional flaws.

The rise of the cable news networks has been an influence on what gets broadcast as news. CNN (which stands, unsurprisingly, for "Cable News Network") began the trend in 1980 as the first twenty-four-hours-a-day news broadcaster. Fox News and MSNBC now also compete for viewers' attention both day and night. While spreading across the hours of the day, these networks have also spread across the political spectrum. You can now find "news" that satisfies nearly any political bias. What's more, with the need to fill screens for so many hours, the notion of what actually counts as news has had to be expanded. The result has affected not just the cable networks but traditional news programs as well: "Feature stories" from prison life to restaurant kitchen tours take up more and more space that used to be devoted to so-called hard news. One of our northern California newspapers, the *Sacramento Bee,* recently did a story on how "silly news" was taking up more and more space in local news programs. Ben Bagdikian, author and former dean of the Graduate School of Journalism at the University of California, Berkeley, has pointed out that a commercial for Pepsi Cola seems to connect better after a fluff piece or a sitcom than after a serious piece on, say, massacres in Rwanda or an ambush in Afghanistan.

It would be difficult to boil down our advice regarding accepting claims from the news media, but it would certainly include keeping the following points in mind:

1. Like the rest of us, people in the news media sometimes make mistakes; they sometimes accept claims with insufficient evidence or without confirming the credibility of a source.

2. The media are subject to pressure and sometimes to manipulation from government and other news sources.

3. The media, with few exceptions, are driven in part by the necessity to make a profit, and this can bring pressure from advertisers, owners, and managers.

Finally, we might remember that the news media are to a great extent a reflection of the society at large. If we the public are willing to get by with superficial, sensationalist, or manipulated news, then we can rest assured that, eventually, that's all the news we'll get.

Bias in the universities? According to CNN news anchor Lou Dobbs, citing a *Washington Post* survey, 72 percent of collegiate faculty across the country say they are liberal; 15 percent say they are conservative. At elite universities, 87 percent say they are liberal, and 3 percent say they are conservative.

Talk Radio

On the surface, talk radio seems to offer a wealth of information not available in news reports from conventional sources. And many talk radio hosts scour traditional legitimate news sources for information relevant to their political agenda, and to the extent that they document the source, which they often do, they provide listeners with many interesting and important facts. But radio hosts from all sides are given to distortion, misplaced emphasis, and bias with regard to selection of which facts to report. And, really, the shouting gives us a headache.

Advocacy Television

We mentioned earlier that some cable networks have moved left while others have moved right on the political spectrum, so the news you can expect from them comes with a predictable slant. This is good insofar as it exposes people to opinions different from their own; it is not so good insofar as it simply reinforces what the viewer already believes, especially if there is no evidence offered in support of the opinions.

The Comedy Central channel features *The Daily Show with Jon Stewart*, which generally approaches the news from a leftish (and completely zany) viewpoint, and *The Colbert Report*, in which Steve Colbert, in reality a liberal, plays the part of a right-wing host. (Before the show, Colbert reminds his guests that "My on-air character is an idiot.") It is ironic, because he appears on the Comedy Central channel, but when Jon Stewart isn't going for the laughs, we think he may be the best, and the toughest, interviewer currently on television. He's doubtless tougher on guests from the right than the left, but he takes no guff from either.

MSNBC offers *The Ed Show*, *Countdown with Keith Olbermann*, and *The Rachel Maddow Show*, all of which offer a liberal perspective on the news of the day, and all of which editorialize from that perspective.

Fox News features Bill O'Reilly, Sean Hannity, and Glenn Beck, who represent various conservative constituencies and do something similar from the other side.

We could write an entire chapter on this subject, and maybe, given the influence the media have on American public opinion these days, we should. We could discuss other channels and other organizations (e.g., Accuracy in Media on the right and MoveOn.org on the left, to name just two of a thousand), but we think you get the idea: We remind you to always listen with a skeptical ear (and maybe a jaundiced eye) to political news and commentary. We know it's difficult, but it's important to be especially careful about accepting claims (without good evidence), and in particular, those with which you sympathize.

The Internet, Generally

It is getting to be difficult to overestimate the importance of the Internet—that amalgamation of electronic lines and connections that allows nearly anyone with a computer and a modem to link up with nearly any other similarly equipped person on the planet. Although the Internet offers great benefits,

In the Media

Evaluating Website Credibility: A Tip from the Professionals

In a study done a few years ago,* it was determined that when it comes to evaluating the credibility of a website, experts in a field go about it much differently than do ordinary consumers. Since, as we've indicated, credibility varies hugely on the web, we must do the best job we can in assessing this feature of any website we consider important. Unfortunately, as was shown in the study just mentioned, most ordinary visitors do a much less effective job of evaluating credibility than do people knowledgeable about the field. In particular, while professionals attend most carefully to the information given at a website, most of the rest of us pay more attention to its visual appeal. Layout, typography, color schemes, and animation affect the general public's estimate of a site's credibility—54 percent of comments are about these features—whereas the professionals' interest is more in the quality of the site's references, the credentials of individuals mentioned, and so on. Only 16 percent of professional evaluators' comments had to do with a website's visual design.

What should we take from this? A general rule: Don't be taken in by how visually attractive a website might be. A flashy design with attractive colors and design features is no substitute for information that is backed up by references and put forward by people with appropriate credentials.

*Experts vs. Online Consumers, a Consumer Reports WebWatch research report, October, 2009. (www.consumerwebwatch.org).

the information it provides must be evaluated with even *more* caution than information from the print media, radio, or television. We presented two stories at the beginning of the chapter that show just how wrong things can go.

There are basically two kinds of information sources on the Internet. The first consists of commercial and institutional sources; the second, of individual and group sites on the World Wide Web. In the first category, we include sources like the Lexis-Nexis facility, as well as the online services provided by newsmagazines, large electronic news organizations, and government institutions. The second category includes everything else you'll find on the web—an amazing assortment of good information, entertainment of widely varying quality, hot tips, advertisements, come-ons, fraudulent offers, and outright lies.

Just as the fact that a claim appears in print or on television doesn't make it true, so it is for claims you run across online. Keep in mind that the information you get from a source is only as good as that source. The Lexis-Nexis information collection is an excellent asset for medium-depth investigation of a topic; it includes information gathered from a wide range of print sources, especially newspapers and magazines, with special collections in areas like the law. But the editorials you turn up there are no more likely to be accurate, fair-minded, or objective than the ones you read in the newspapers—which is where they first appeared anyhow.

Possibly the fastest-growing source of information in terms of both its size and its influence is the online encyclopedia Wikipedia. "Wiki" refers to a collaborative voluntary association (although the word seems to have been coined by a programmer named Ward Cunningham from the Hawaiian term "wiki-wiki"—"quick-quick"). Begun in 2001 by Larry Sanger and Jimmy Wales, the encyclopedia's content and structure are determined by its users. This accounts for its major strengths as well as its major weaknesses. Because there are many thousands of contributors, the coverage is immense. There are well over three million articles in English alone, and more than two hundred other languages and dialects are also employed. Because access is available to virtually everybody who has a computer and modem, coverage is often very fast; articles often appear within hours of breaking events.

But also because of this wide access, the quality of the articles varies tremendously. You should be especially wary of recent articles; they are more likely to contain uncorrected errors that will eventually disappear as knowledgeable people visit the page and put right whatever mistakes are present. Not just factual errors, but bias and omission can affect the quality of material found on Wikipedia's pages. Occasionally, a writer will do a thorough job of reporting the side of an issue that he favors (or knows more about, or both), and the other side will go underreported or even unmentioned. Over time, these types of errors tend to get corrected after visits by individuals who favor the other side of the issue. But at any given moment, in any given Wikipedia entry, there is the possibility of mistakes, omissions, citation errors, and plain old vandalism.

Our advice: We think Wikipedia is an excellent starting point in a search for knowledge about a topic. We use it frequently. But you should always check the sources provided in what you find there; it should never be your sole source of information if the topic is important to you or is to become part of an assignment to be turned in for a class. That said, we add that articles dealing with technical or scientific subjects tend to be more reliable (although errors are often more difficult to spot), with an error rate about the same as that found in the *Encyclopedia Britannica.*[*] Such articles and, as mentioned, articles that have been around for a while can be extremely helpful in whatever project you are engaged in.

Now we come to blogs. Blogs are simply journals, the vast majority of them put up by individuals, that are left open to the public on an Internet site. Originally more like public diaries dealing with personal matters, they now encompass specialties of almost every imaginable sort. Up to three million blogs were believed to be up and running by the end of 2004, with a new one added every 5.8 seconds (ClickZ.com, "The Blogosphere by the Numbers"). Nobody knows how many there are now.

You can find blogs that specialize in satire, parody, and outright fabrication. They represent all sides of the political spectrum, including some sides that we wouldn't have thought existed at all. The Drudge Report is a standard on the right; the Huffington Post is equally well known on the left. On a blog site, like any other website that isn't run by a responsible organization such as

Wikipedia

Blogs

---

[*]"Internet Encyclopedias Go Head to Head," by Jim Giles, *Nature*, December 12, 2005.

In the Media

Webcheckers

Along with other sites we've already mentioned, here are some other places where you can go to get to the bottom of an issue you've seen brought up on the web. We believe these to be among the most reliable sources currently available; we use them all ourselves.

Snopes.com. The original, and still the best site, for checking out rumors, stories, urban legends, and any other type of strange claim that turns up on the web. Run by Daniel and Barbara Mikkelson since 1996, it classifies as true or false a host of claims that circulate on the Internet. Analysis of the history and nature of the claims under investigation is usually provided.

TruthorFiction.com. A general fact-finding, debunking site. Generally up-to-date findings by owner Rich Buhler. Analyses tend to be less thorough than those found on Snopes, but a generally trustworthy site.

Factcheck.org. Run by Brooks Jackson, a former CNN and *Wall Street Journal* reporter out of the University of Pennsylvania's Annenberg Public Policy Center. Completely neutral politically, the site attacks anybody who stretches the truth concerning any topic in politics.

PolitiFact.com. Operated by the *St. Petersburg* (Florida) *Times* newspaper. Reporters and editors fact-check claims made by politicians, lobbyists, and interest groups. The website won a Pulitzer Prize in 2009 for its work during the presidential election of 2008.

Consumerreports.com. Evaluates consumer issues (including health care and financial planning) and products. Not to be confused with other organizations with similar names, this site, like the magazine of the same name that sponsors it, accepts no advertising and bends over backwards to avoid bias. Careful evaluation and analysis can be expected. The organization buys products to be evaluated from stores, just like we do, rather than being given them by manufacturers.

For the general evaluation of websites, several checklists are available. You will find Cornell University's and the University of Maryland's checklists at www.library.cornell.edu/olinuris/ref/research/skill26.htm and www.lib.umd.edu/guides/evaluate.html.

most of those previously indicated, you can find *anything that a person wants to put there*, including all kinds of bad information. You can take advantage of these sources, but you should always exercise caution, and if you're looking for information, always consult another source, but be especially careful about any that are linked to your first source!

Before we leave the topic of web worthiness, we want to pass along a warning that comes from Barbara Mikkelson, co-founder of Snopes.com. She reminds us that rumors often give people a great sense of comfort; people are quick to reject nuance and facts that are contrary to their own point of view, but quickly accept them when they are agreeable to the hearer. "When you're looking at truth versus gossip," Mikkelson says, "truth doesn't stand a chance." We hope she's being unduly pessimistic.

So remember, when you take keyboard and mouse in hand, be on guard. You have about as much reason to believe the claims you find on most sites as you would if they came from any other stranger, except you can't look this one in the eye.

Exercise 4-8

See who in the class can find the strangest news report from a credible source. Send it to us at McGraw-Hill. If your entry is selected for printing in our next edition, Moore might send you $100. (In the next chapter you'll see why we call the word "might" a weaseler in this context.)

Exercise 4-9

Identify at least three factors that can cause inaccuracies or a distortion of reports in the news media.

ADVERTISING

> Advertising [is] the science of arresting the human intelligence long enough to get money from it.
>
> —*Stephen Leacock*

If there is anything in modern society besides politics that truly puts our sense of what is credible to the test, it's advertising. As we hope you'll agree after reading this section, skepticism is always the best policy when considering any kind of advertising or promotion.

Ads are used to sell many products other than toasters, television sets, and toilet tissue. They can encourage us to vote for a candidate, agree with a political proposal, take a tour, give up a bad habit, or join a Tea Party or the army. They can also be used to make announcements (for instance, about job openings, lectures, concerts, or the recall of defective automobiles) or to create favorable climates of opinion (for example, toward labor unions or offshore oil drilling).

Advertising firms understand our fears and desires at least as well as we understand them ourselves, and they have at their disposal the expertise to exploit them.* Such firms employ trained psychologists and some of the world's most creative artists and use the most sophisticated and well-researched theories about the motivation of human behavior. Maybe most important, they can afford to spend whatever is necessary to get each detail of an advertisement exactly right. (On a per-minute basis, television ads are the most expensively produced pieces that appear on your tube.) A good ad is a work of art, a masterful blend of word and image often composed in accordance with the exacting standards of artistic and scientific genius (other ads, of course, are just plain silly). Can untrained laypeople even hope to evaluate such psychological and artistic masterpieces intelligently?

Fortunately, it is not necessary to understand the deep psychology of an advertisement to evaluate it in the way that's most important to us. When confronted with an ad, we should ask simply: Does this ad give us a good reason to buy this product? And the answer, in general terms, can be simply put:

According to zFacts.com, $412 *billion* dollars were spent on advertising in America during 2008. Somebody really wants to sell us something!

People watching a sexual program are thinking about sex, not soda pop. Violence and sex elicit very strong emotions and can interfere with memory for other things.

—BRAD BUSHMAN of Iowa State University, whose research indicated that people tend to forget the names of sponsors of violent or sexual TV shows (reported by Ellen Goodman)

---

*For an excellent treatment of this and related subjects, we recommend *Age of Propaganda: The Everyday Use and Abuse of Persuasion*, rev. ed., by Anthony R. Pratkanis and Elliot Aronson (New York: W. H. Freeman and Co., 1998).

Because the only good reason to buy anything in the first place is to improve our lives, the ad justifies a purchase only if it establishes that we'd be better off with the product than without it (or that we'd be better off with the product than with the money we would trade for it).

However, do we always know when we'll be better off with a product than without it? Do we really want, or need, a bagel splitter or an exercise bike? Do people even recognize "better taste" in a cigarette? Do we *need* Viagra or are we just curious? Advertisers spend vast sums creating within us new desires and fears—and hence a need to improve our lives by satisfying those desires or eliminating those fears through the purchase of advertised products. They are often successful, and we find ourselves needing something we might not have known existed before. That others can instill in us, through word and image, a desire for something we did not previously desire may be a lamentable fact, but it *is* clearly a fact. Still, *we* decide what would make us better off, and *we* decide to part with our money. So, it is only with reference to what in *our* view would make life better for us that we properly evaluate advertisements.

There are basically two kinds of ads: those that offer reasons and those that do not. Those that offer reasons for buying the advertised product always promise that certain hopes will be satisfied, certain needs met, or certain fears eliminated. (You'll be more accepted, have a better image, be a better parent, and so on.)

Those ads that do not rely on reasons fall mainly into three categories: (1) those that bring out *feelings* in us (e.g., through humor, pretty images, scary images, beautiful music, heartwarming scenes); (2) those that depict the product being used or endorsed by *people* we admire or think of ourselves as being like (sometimes these people are depicted by actors, sometimes not); and (3) those that depict the product being used in *situations* in which we would like to find ourselves. Of course, some ads go all out and incorporate elements from all three categories—and for good measure also state a reason or two why we should buy the advertised product.

Buying a product (which includes joining a group, deciding how to vote, and so forth) on the basis of reasonless ads is, with one minor exception that we'll explain shortly, never justified. Such ads tell you only that the product exists and what it looks like (and sometimes where it is available and how much it costs); if an ad tells you much more than this, then it begins to qualify as an ad that gives reasons for buying the product. Reasonless ads do tell us what the advertisers think of our values and sense of humor (not always a pleasant thing to notice, given that they have us pegged so well), but

"Doctor recommended."

This ambiguous ad slogan creates an illusion that many doctors, or doctors in general, recommend the product. However, a recommendation from a single doctor is all it takes to make the statement true.

this information is irrelevant to the question of whether we should buy the product.

Ads that submit reasons for buying the product, or "promise ads," as they have been called, usually tell us more than that a certain product exists—but not much more. The promise, with rare exception, comes with no guarantees and is usually extremely vague (Gilbey's gin promises "more gin taste," Kleenex is "softer"). In other words, the reasons given are almost never *good* reasons.

Such ads are a source of information about what the *sellers* of the product are willing to claim about what the product will do, how well it will do it, how it works, what it contains, how well it compares with similar products, and how much more wonderful your life will be once you've got one. However, to make an informed decision on a purchase, you almost always need to know more than the seller is willing to claim, particularly because no sellers will tell you what's wrong with their products or what's right with those of their competitors. Remember that they are perfect examples of *interested parties*.

Further, the claims of advertisers are notorious not only for being vague but also for being ambiguous, misleading, exaggerated, and sometimes just plain false. Even if a product existed that was so good that an honest,

We are professional grade.

Meaningless but catchy slogan for GMC trucks. (We are professional grade, too.)

Real Life

When Is an Ad Not an Ad? When It's a Product Placement!

When Katharine Hepburn threw all of Humphrey Bogart's Gordon's gin overboard in *The African Queen*, it was an early example of product placement, since the makers of Gordon's paid to have their product tossed in the drink, as it were. Readers of a certain age may remember the 1960s television show *Route 66*, which starred not just Martin Milner and George Maharis but also a new Chevrolet Corvette and probably contributed to more than a few Corvette sales. Reese's Pieces were centrally placed in the movie *E.T.* and the sales of Red Stripe beer jumped 50 percent after it appeared prominently in the movie *The Firm*.

These days, the paid placement of products in both movies and television (and possibly even in novels) is a serious alternative

■ We suspect the Coke can is there because Pepsi wouldn't pay enough.

to traditional commercials, and it has the advantage of overcoming the Tivo effect: the viewer records programs and watches them while skipping over the commercials.

unexaggerated, and fair description of it would justify our buying it without considering competing items (or other reports on the same item), and even if an advertisement for this product consisted of just such a description, we would still not be justified in purchasing the product on the basis of that advertisement alone. For we would be unable to tell, simply by looking at the advertisement, that it was uninflated, honest, fair, and not misleading. Our suspicions about advertising in general should undercut our willingness to believe in the honesty of any particular advertisement.

Thus, even advertisements that present reasons for buying an item do not by themselves justify our purchase of the item. This is worth repeating, in stronger language: An advertisement *never justifies* purchasing something. Advertisements are written to *sell something;* they are not designed to be informative except insofar as it will help with the sales job. Sometimes, of course, an advertisement can provide you with information that can clinch your decision to make a purchase. Sometimes the mere existence, availability, or affordability of a product—all information that an ad can convey—is all you need to make a decision to buy. But if the purchase is justifiable, you must have some reasons, apart from those offered in the ad, for making it. If, for some reason, you already know that you want or need and can afford a car with an electric motor, then an ad that informs you that a firm has begun marketing such a thing would supply you with the information you need to buy one. If you can already justify purchasing a particular brand of microwave oven but cannot find one anywhere in town, then an advertisement informing you that the local department store stocks them can clinch your decision to make the purchase.

For people on whom good fortune has smiled, those who don't care what kind of whatsit they buy, or those to whom mistaken purchases simply don't matter, all that is important is knowing that a product is available. Most of us, however, need more information than ads provide to make reasoned purchasing decisions. Of course, we all occasionally make purchases solely on the basis of advertisements, and sometimes we don't come to regret them. In such cases, though, the happy result is due as much to good luck as to the ad.

On Language

WAY Too Good to Be True!

Since the country fell into a serious recession in 2008, many people have found themselves unable to meet their mortgage payments, and many find themselves saddled with more credit card debt than they can manage. Easy debt-relief schemers to the rescue! Some cable TV and radio ads promise to help get your mortgage paid off, make your credit card debt shrink or disappear altogether, or make you rich by teaching you to make quick killings in real estate.

According to a *Consumer Reports Money Adviser* article (April 2010), these schemes tend more toward guaranteeing fees for the operators than for debt relief or riches, quick or otherwise, for the client. Many clients wind up worse off than they started after signing up for these plans. Remember: advertising is always designed to help the folks who pay for the ads. If it looks too good to be true, you can bet it *is.*

A final suggestion on this subject. We know of only one source that maintains a fierce independence and still does a good job of testing and reporting on products. That's Consumers Union, the publishers of *Consumer Reports*, a magazine (mentioned in the box on p. 130) that accepts no advertising and that buys all the objects it tests and reports on (rather than accepting them for free from the manufacturers, as do several other "consumer" magazines). For reliable information and fair-mindedness, we recommend them. They're also on the web at <http://www.consumersunion.org>.

Recap

This list summarizes the topics covered in this chapter.

- Claims lack credibility to the extent they conflict with our observations, experience, or background information, or come from sources that lack credibility.

- The less initial plausibility a claim has, the more extraordinary it seems; and the less it fits with our background information, the more suspicious we should be.

- Interested parties should always be viewed with more suspicion than disinterested parties.

- Doubts about sources generally fall into two categories: doubts about the source's knowledge or expertise and doubts about the source's veracity, objectivity, and accuracy.

- We can form reasonably reliable judgments about a person's knowledge by considering his or her education, experience, accomplishments, reputation, and position.

- Claims made by experts, those with special knowledge in a subject, are the most reliable, but the claims must pertain to the area of expertise and must not conflict with claims made by other experts in the same area.

- Major metropolitan newspapers, national newsmagazines, and network news shows are generally credible sources of news, but it is necessary to keep an open mind about what we learn from them.

- Governments have been known to influence and even to manipulate the news.

- Sources like Wikipedia, institutional websites, and news organizations can be helpful, but skepticism is the order of the day when we obtain information from unknown Internet sources or talk radio.

- Advertising assaults us at every turn, attempting to sell us goods, services, beliefs, and attitudes. Because substantial talent and resources are employed in this effort, we need to ask ourselves constantly whether the products in question will really make the differences in our lives that their advertising claims or hints they will make. Advertisers are always more concerned with selling you something than with improving your life. They are concerned with improving their own lives.

- What goes for talk radio, above, also goes for advocacy television.

Additional Exercises

Exercise 4-10

In groups, decide which is the best answer to each question. Compare your answers with those of other groups and your instructor.

1. "SPACE ALIEN GRAVEYARD FOUND! Scientists who found an extra-terrestrial cemetery in central Africa say the graveyard is at least 500 years old! 'There must be 200 bodies buried there and not a single one of them is human,' Dr. Hugo Schild, the Swiss anthropologist, told reporters." What is the appropriate reaction to this report in the *Weekly World News*?

   a. It's probably true.
   b. It almost certainly is true.
   c. We really need more information to form any judgment at all.
   d. None of these.

2. Is Elvis really dead? Howie thinks not. Reason: He knows three people who claim to have seen Elvis recently. They are certain that it is not a mere Elvis look-alike they have seen. Howie reasons that, since he has absolutely no reason to think the three would lie to him, they must be telling the truth. Elvis must really be alive, he concludes!

   Is Howie's reasoning sound? Explain.

3. VOICE ON TELEPHONE: Mr. Roberts, this is SBC calling. Have you recently placed several long-distance calls to Lisbon, Portugal?
   MR. ROBERTS: Why, no . . .
   VOICE: This is what we expected. Mr. Roberts, I'm sorry to report that apparently someone has been using your calling card number. However, we are prepared to give you a new number, effective immediately, at no charge to you.
   MR. ROBERTS: Well, fine, I guess . . .
   VOICE: Again let me emphasize that there will be no charge for this service. Now, for authorization, just to make sure that we are calling Mr. Roberts, Mr. Roberts, please state the last four digits of your calling card number, and your PIN number, please.
   Question: What should Mr. Roberts, as a critical thinker, do?

4. On Thanksgiving Day 1990, an image said by some to resemble the Virgin Mary was observed in a stained glass window of St. Dominic's Church in Colfax, California. A physicist asked to investigate said the image was caused by sunlight shining through the window and reflecting from a newly installed hanging light fixture. Others said the image was a miracle. Whose explanation is more likely true?

   a. The physicist's
   b. The others'
   c. More information is needed before we can decide which explanation is more likely.

5. It is late at night around the campfire when the campers hear awful grunting noises in the woods around them. They run for their lives! Two

campers, after returning the next day, tell others they found huge footprints around the campfire. They are convinced they were attacked by Bigfoot. Which explanation is more likely true?

a. The campers heard Bigfoot.

b. The campers heard some animal and are pushing the Bigfoot explanation to avoid being thought of as chickens, or are just making the story up for unknown reasons.

c. Given this information, we can't tell which explanation is more likely.

6. Megan's aunt says she saw a flying saucer. "I don't tell people about this," Auntie says, "because they'll think I'm making it up. But this really happened. I saw this strange light, and this, well, it wasn't a saucer, exactly, but it was round and big, and it came down and hovered just over my back fence, and my two dogs began whimpering. And then it just, whoosh! It just vanished."

   Megan knows her aunt, and Megan knows she doesn't make up stories.

a. She should believe her aunt saw a flying saucer.

b. She should believe her aunt was making the story up.

c. She should believe that her aunt may well have had some unusual experience, but it was probably not a visitation by extraterrestrial beings.

7. According to Dr. Edith Fiore, author of *The Unquiet Dead,* many of your personal problems are really the miseries of a dead soul who has possessed you sometime during your life. "Many people are possessed by earthbound spirits. These are people who have lived and died, but did not go into the afterworld at death. Instead they stayed on Earth and remained just like they were before death, with the fears, pains, weaknesses and other problems that they had when they were alive." She estimates that about 80 percent of her more than 1,000 patients are suffering from the problems brought on by being possessed by spirits of the dead. To tell if you are among the possessed, she advises that you look for such telltale symptoms as low energy levels, character shifts or mood swings, memory problems, poor concentration, weight gain with no obvious cause, and bouts of depression (especially after hospitalization). Which of these reactions is best?

a. Wow! I bet I'm possessed!

b. Well, if a doctor says it's so, it must be so.

c. If these are signs of being possessed, how come she thinks that only 80 percent of her patients are?

d. Too bad there isn't more information available, so we could form a reasonable judgment.

8.   **EOC—Engine Overhaul in a Can**

Developed by skilled automotive scientists after years of research and laboratory and road tests! Simply pour one can of EOC into the oil in your crankcase. EOC contains long-chain molecules and special thermoactive metallic alloys that bond with worn engine parts. NO tools needed! NO need to disassemble engine.

   Question: Reading this ad, what should you believe?

9. ANCHORAGE, Alaska (AP)—Roped to her twin sons for safety, Joni Phelps inched her way to the top of Mount McKinley. The National Park Service says Phelps, 54, apparently is the first blind woman to scale the 20,300-foot peak.

This report is

a. Probably true
b. Probably false
c. Too sketchy; more information is needed before we can judge

Exercise 4-11

Within each group of observers, are some especially credible or especially not so?

 1. Judging the relative performances of the fighters in a heavyweight boxing match

a. the father of one of the fighters
b. a sportswriter for *Sports Illustrated* magazine
c. the coach of the American Olympic boxing team
d. the referee of the fight
e. a professor of physical education

2. You (or your family or your class) are trying to decide whether you should buy an Apple Macintosh computer or a Windows model. You might consult

a. a friend who owns either a Macintosh or a Windows machine
b. a friend who now owns one of the machines but used to own the other
c. a dealer for either Macintosh or Windows computers
d. a computer column in a big-city newspaper
e. reviews in computer magazines

3. The Surgical Practices Committee of Grantville Hospital has documented an unusually high number of problems in connection with tonsillectomies performed by a Dr. Choker. The committee is reviewing her surgical practices. Those present during a tonsillectomy are

a. Dr. Choker
b. the surgical proctor from the Surgical Practices Committee
c. an anesthesiologist
d. a nurse
e. a technician

4. The mechanical condition of the used car you are thinking of buying

a. the used-car salesperson
b. the former owner (who we assume is different from the salesperson)
c. the former owner's mechanic
d. you
e. a mechanic from an independent garage

5. A demonstration of psychokinesis (the ability to move objects at a distance by nonphysical means)

a. a newspaper reporter
b. a psychologist

c. a police detective
d. another psychic
e. a physicist
f. a customs agent
g. a magician

Exercise 4-12

For each of the items below, discuss the credibility and authority of each source relative to the issue in question. Whom would you trust as most reliable on the subject?

▲   1. Issue: Is Crixivan an effective HIV/AIDS medication?

a. *Consumer Reports*
b. Stadtlander Drug Company (the company that makes Crixivan)
c. the owner of your local health food store
d. the U.S. Food and Drug Administration
e. your local pharmacist

▲   2. Issue: Should possession of handguns be outlawed?

a. a police chief
b. a representative of the National Rifle Association
c. a U.S. senator
d. the father of a murder victim

▲   3. Issue: What was the original intent of the Second Amendment to the U.S. Constitution, and does it include permission for every citizen to possess handguns?

a. a representative of the National Rifle Association
b. a justice of the U.S. Supreme Court
c. a Constitutional historian
d. a U.S. senator
e. the president of the United States

4. Issue: Is decreasing your intake of dietary fat and cholesterol likely to reduce the level of cholesterol in your blood?

a. *Time* magazine
b. *Runner's World* magazine
c. your physician
d. the National Institutes of Health
e. the *New England Journal of Medicine*

5. Issue: When does a human life begin?

a. a lawyer
b. a physician
c. a philosopher
d. a minister
e. you

Exercise 4-13

Each of these items consists of a brief biography of a real or imagined person, followed by a list of topics. On the basis of the information in the biography, discuss the credibility and authority of the person described on each of the topics listed.

▲   1. Anne St. Germain teaches sociology at the University of Illinois and is the director of its Population Studies Center. She is a graduate of Harvard College, where she received a B.A. in 1975, and of Harvard University, which granted her a Ph.D. in economics in 1978. She taught courses in demography as an assistant professor at UCLA until 1982; then she moved to the sociology department of the University of Nebraska, where she was associate professor and then professor. From 1987 through 1989, she served as acting chief of the Population Trends and Structure Section of the United Nations Population Division. She joined the faculty at the University of Illinois in 1989. She has written books on patterns of world urbanization, the effects of cigarette smoking on international mortality, and demographic trends in India. She is president of the Population Association of America.

Topics

   a. The effects of acid rain on humans
   b. The possible beneficial effects of requiring sociology courses for all students at the University of Illinois
   c. The possible effects of nuclear war on global climate patterns
   d. The incidence of poverty among various ethnic groups in the United States
   e. The effects of the melting of glaciers on global sea levels
   f. The change in death rate for various age groups in all Third World countries between 1970 and 1990
   g. The feasibility of a laser-based nuclear defense system
   h. Voter participation among religious sects in India
   i. Whether the winters are worse in Illinois than in Nebraska

   2. Tom Pierce graduated cum laude from Cornell University with a B.S. in biology in 1973. After two years in the Peace Corps, during which he worked on public health projects in Venezuela, he joined Jeffrey Ridenour, a mechanical engineer, and the pair developed a water pump and purification system that is now used in many parts of the world for both regular water supplies and emergency use in disaster-struck areas. Pierce and Ridenour formed a company to manufacture the water systems, and it prospered as they developed smaller versions of the system for private use on boats and motor homes. In 1981, Pierce bought out his partner and expanded research and development in hydraulic systems for forcing oil out of old wells. Under contract with the federal government and several oil firms, Pierce's company was a principal designer and contractor for the Alaskan oil pipeline. He is now a consultant in numerous developing countries as well as chief executive officer and chairman of the board of his own company, and he sits on the boards of directors of several other companies.

Topics

   a. The image of the United States in Latin America
   b. The long-range effects of the Cuban revolution on South America
   c. Fixing a leaky faucet

    d. Technology in Third World countries
    e. The ecological effects of the Alaskan pipeline
    f. Negotiating a contract with the federal government
    g. Careers in biology

Exercise 4-14

According to certain pollsters, quite a number of people vote for candidates for president not because they especially like those candidates' policies and programs or their idea of where the country should be going, but because they like the candidates personally. Discuss what features a candidate from the recent past (e.g., George W. Bush, Hillary Clinton, Barack Obama, John McCain, Sarah Palin) may have that might cause such people to vote for him or her. Which of these features, if any, might be relevant to how good a job the candidate would do as president?

Exercise 4-15

From what you know about the nature of each of the following claims and its source, and given your general knowledge, assess whether the claim is one you should accept, reject, or suspend judgment on due to ambiguity, insufficient documentation, vagueness, or subjectivity (e.g., "Tom Cruise is cute"). Compare your judgment with that of your instructor.

▲   1. "Campbell Soup is hot—and some are getting burned. Just one day after the behemoth of broth reported record profits, Campbell said it would lay off 650 U.S. workers, including 175—or 11% of the workforce—at its headquarters in Camden, New Jersey."

                                          —Time

  2. [The claim to evaluate is the first one in this passage.] Jackie Haskew taught paganism and devil worship in her fourth-grade classroom in Grand Saline, Texas, at least until she was pressured into resigning by parents of her students. (According to syndicated columnist Nat Hentoff, "At the town meeting on her case, a parent said firmly that she did not want her daughter to read anything that dealt with 'death, abuse, divorce, religion, or any other issue.'")

  3. "By 1893 there were only between 300 and 1,000 buffaloes remaining in the entire country. A few years later, President Theodore Roosevelt persuaded Congress to establish a number of wildlife preserves in which the remaining buffaloes could live without danger. The numbers have increased since, nearly doubling over the past 10 years to 130,000."

           —*Clifford May, in the* New York Times Magazine

  4. Lee Harvey Oswald, acting alone, was responsible for the death of President John F. Kennedy.

            —*Conclusion of the Warren Commission on the assassination of President Kennedy*

  5. "[N]ewly released documents, including the transcripts of telephone conversations recorded by President Lyndon B. Johnson in November and December 1963, provide for the first time a detailed . . . look at why and

how the seven-member Warren [Commission] was put together. Those documents, along with a review of previously released material . . . describe a process designed more to control information than to elicit and expose it."

—*"The Truth Was Secondary,"* Washington Post National Weekly Edition

6. "Short-sighted developers are determined to transform Choco [a large region of northwestern Colombia] from an undisturbed natural treasure to a polluted, industrialized growth center."

—*Solicitation letter from the World Wildlife Fund*

7. "Frantic parents tell shocked TV audience: space aliens stole our son."

—Weekly World News

▲ 8. "The manufacturer of Sudafed 12-hour capsules issued a nationwide recall of the product Sunday after two people in the state of Washington who had taken the medication died of cyanide poisoning and a third became seriously ill."

—Los Angeles Times

9. "In Canada, smoking in public places, trains, planes or even automobiles is now prohibited by law or by convention. The federal government has banned smoking in all its buildings."

—*Reuters*

10. "The list of vanishing commodities in Moscow now includes not only sausage and vodka, long rationed, but also potatoes, eggs, bread, and cigarettes."

—National Geographic

11. "Maps, files and compasses were hidden in Monopoly sets and smuggled into World War II German prison camps by MI-5, Britain's counter-intelligence agency, to help British prisoners escape, according to the British manufacturer of the game."

—*Associated Press*

▲ 12. "Cats that live indoors and use a litter box can live four to five years longer."

—*From an advertisement for Jonny Cat litter*

13. "A case reported by Borderland Sciences Research Foundation, Vista, California, tells of a man who had attended many of the meetings where a great variety of 'dead' people came and spoke through the body mechanism of Mark Probert to the group of interested persons on a great variety of subjects with questions and answers from 'both sides.' Then this man who had attended meetings while he was in a body, did what is called 'die.' Presumably he had learned 'while in the body' what he might expect at the change of awareness called death, about which organized religion seems to know little or nothing."

—*George Robinson,* Exploring the Riddle of Reincarnation,
undated, no publisher cited

14. "Because of cartilage that begins to accumulate after age thirty, by the time . . . [a] man is seventy his nose has grown a half inch wider and

another half inch longer, his earlobes have fattened, and his ears themselves have grown a quarter inch longer. Overall, his head's circumference increases a quarter inch every decade, and not because of his brain, which is shrinking. His head is fatter apparently because, unlike most other bones in the body, the skull seems to thicken with age."

—*John Tierney (a staff writer for* Esquire)

15. "Gardenias . . . need ample warmth, ample water, and steady feeding. Though hardy to 20°F or even lower, plants fail to grow and bloom well without summer heat."

—The Sunset New Western Garden Book
(a best-selling gardening reference in the West)

16. "Exercise will make you feel fitter, but there's no good evidence that it will make you live longer."

—*Dr. Jordan Tobin, National Institute on Aging*

17. "Your bones are still growing until you're 35."

—*From a national milk ad by the National Fluid Milk
Processor Promotion Board*

18. "*E. coli* 0157:H7 has become common enough to be the current major cause of acute kidney failure in children." [*E. coli* is a food-borne toxin originally found in the intestines of cows.]

—*Robin Cook, a physician-turned-novelist. This claim was made by
a fictional expert on food-borne illnesses in the novel* Toxin.

19. "A woman employed as a Santa Claus at a Walmart in Kentucky was fired by Walmart when a child pinched her breast and complained to his mother that Santa was a woman. The woman complained to store managers."

—*Associated Press*

▲ 20. Paris Hilton requested a trademark for the phrase "That's hot" from the U.S. Office of Trademarks and Patents.

—*Defamer blog*

Exercise 4-16

The following appeared in a local newspaper, criticizing the position on global warming taken by local television weatherman and political activist Anthony Watts. Read it carefully and decide whether anything the author says should affect the credibility of Watts or the project he endorsed. Compare your judgment with those of your classmates.

"[Anthony] Watts endorsed the 'Petition Project,' which refutes manmade global warming. Besides many fictitious names submitted, only about one percent of the petition signers had done any climate research.

"The petition was prepared by Frederick Seitz, a scientist who, from 1975 to 1989, was paid $585,000 by the tobacco industry to direct a $45 million scientific effort to hide the health impact of smoking. Does Watts agree that cigarettes are not harmful, as Seitz's studies showed?"

—Chico News & Review

Exercise 4-17

Find five advertisements that give no reasons for purchasing the products they are selling. Explain how each ad attempts to make the product seem attractive.

Exercise 4-18

Find five advertisements that give reasons for purchasing the products they are selling. Which of the reasons are promises to the purchaser? Exactly what is being promised? What is the likelihood that the product will fulfill that promise?

Exercise 4-19

Watch Fox News, MSNBC, and CNN news programs on the same day. Compare the three on the basis of (1) the news stories covered, (2) the amount of air time given to two or three of the major stories, and (3) any difference in the slant of the presentations of a controversial story. Make notes. Be prepared to discuss in class the differences in coverage on the basis of the three criteria just mentioned.

Writing Exercises

1. Although millions of people have seen professional magicians like David Copperfield and Siegfried and Roy perform in person or on television, it's probably a safe assumption that almost nobody believes they accomplish their feats by means of real magical or supernatural powers—that is, that they somehow "defy" the laws of nature. But even though they've never had a personal demonstration, a significant portion of the population believes that certain psychics are able to accomplish apparent miracles by exactly such means. How might you explain this difference in belief?

2. In the text, you were asked to consider the claim "Charlie's eighty-seven-year-old grandmother swam across Lake Michigan in the middle of winter." Because of the implausibility of such a claim—that is, because it conflicts with our background information—it is reasonable to reject it. Suppose, however, that instead of just telling us about his grandmother, Charlie brings us a photocopy of a page of a Chicago newspaper with a photograph of a person in a wet suit walking up onto a beach. The caption underneath reads, "Eighty-Seven-Year-Old Grandmother Swims Lake Michigan in January!" Based on this piece of evidence, should a critical thinker decide that the original claim is significantly more likely to be true than if it were backed up only by Charlie's word? Defend your answer.

3. Turn to the "Essays for Analysis" in Appendix 1, and assess the credibility of an author in a selection identified by your instructor. Based on the blurb about the author, say what you can about the author's likely expertise and susceptibility to bias on the subject of the essay.

4. Are our schools doing a bad job educating our kids? Do research in the library or on the Internet to answer this question. Make a list (no more than one page long) of facts that support the claim that our schools are not doing as good a job as they should. Then list facts that support the

opposite view (or that rebut the claims of those who say our schools aren't doing a good job). Again, limit yourself to one page. Cite your sources.

Now, think critically about your sources. Are any stronger or weaker than the others? Explain why on a single sheet of paper. Come prepared to read your explanation, along with your list of facts and sources, to the class.

5. Jackson says you should be skeptical of the opinion of someone who stands to profit from your accepting that opinion. Smith disagrees, pointing out that salespeople are apt to know a lot more about products of the type they sell than do most people.

"Most salespeople are honest, and you can trust them," Smith argues. "Those who aren't don't stay in business long."

Take about fifteen minutes to defend either Smith or Jackson in a short essay. When everyone is finished, your instructor will collect the essays and read three or more to the class to stimulate a brief discussion. After discussion, can the class come to any agreement about who is correct, Jackson or Smith?

6. Your instructor will survey the class to see how many agree with this claim: The media are biased. Then he or she will ask you to list your reasons for thinking that this claim is true. (If you do not think it is true, list reasons people might have for believing it.) After ten minutes, your instructor will collect the lists of reasons and read from several of the lists. Then he or she will give you twenty minutes to defend one of these claims:

a. The media are biased.
b. Some of the reasons people have for believing that the media are biased are not very good reasons.
c. It is difficult to say whether the media are biased.

At the end of the period, your instructor may survey the class again to see if anyone's mind has changed and why.

Persuasion Through Rhetoric

Common Devices and Techniques

When the military uses the phrase "self-injurious behavior incidents" regarding detainees at Guantánamo Bay, it means what most of us call "attempted suicides." In fact, when the word "detainees" is used, it means what most of us call "prisoners." "Waterboarding" sounds at first like something you'd expect to see young people doing on a California beach, not a torture technique that involves forced simulated drowning. Less remarkable, perhaps, but possibly more relevant for most of us, we've heard the term "downsized" used when someone is fired or laid off. "Ethnic cleansing" covers everything from deportation to genocide.

What we have to say may be important, but the words we choose to say it with can be equally important. The examples just given are cases of a certain type of linguistic coercion—an attempt to get us to adopt a particular attitude toward a subject that, if described differently, would seem less attractive to us. Words have tremendous persuasive power, or what we have called their **rhetorical force** or **emotive meaning**—their power to express and elicit images, feelings, and emotional associations. In the next few chapters, we examine some of the most common rhetorical techniques used to affect people's attitudes, opinions, and behavior.

Rhetoric refers to the study of persuasive writing. As we use the term, it denotes a broad category of linguistic techniques people use when their primary objective is to influence beliefs and attitudes and behavior. Is Hezbollah, the Shia paramilitary organization based in Lebanon, a resistance movement of freedom fighters or a dangerous terrorist organization? The different impressions these two descriptions create is largely due to their differing rhetorical meaning. Does Juanita "still owe over $1,000 on her credit card"? Or does Juanita "owe only a little over $1,000 on her credit card"? There's no factual difference between the two questions—only a difference in their rhetorical force. The thing to remember through these next few chapters is that rhetorical force may be psychologically effective, but by itself it establishes nothing. If we allow our attitudes and beliefs to be affected by sheer rhetoric, we fall short as critical thinkers.

Now, before we get in trouble with your English teacher, let's make it clear that there is nothing wrong with trying to make your case as persuasive as possible by using well-chosen, rhetorically effective words and phrases. Good writers always do this. But we, as critical thinkers, must be able to distinguish the *argument* (if any) contained in what someone says or writes from the *rhetoric*; we must be able to distinguish the *logical* force of a set of remarks from their *psychological* force.

One of the things you will become aware of—as you read these pages, do the exercises, apply what you have learned to what you read and write—is that rhetoric is often mixed right in with argument. The message isn't that you should *deduct* points from an argument if it is presented in rhetorically charged language, and it isn't that you should try to take all the rhetoric out of your own writing. The message is simply that you shouldn't *add* points for rhetoric. You don't make an argument stronger by screaming it at the top of your lungs. Likewise, you don't make it stronger by adding **rhetorical devices.**

Many of these rhetorical bells and whistles have names because they are so common and so well understood. Because they are used primarily to give a statement a positive or negative slant regarding a subject, they are sometimes called **slanters.** We'll describe some of the more widely used specimens.

Such images as this add to the negative impact of the "death tax," described in the box on the next page.

RHETORICAL DEVICES I

Our first group of slanters consists of what are usually single words or short phrases designed to accomplish one of four specific rhetorical tasks.

Euphemisms and Dysphemisms

Language usually offers us a choice of words when we want to say something. Until recently, the term "used car" referred to an automobile that wasn't new, but the trend nowadays is to refer to such a car as "pre-owned." The people who sell such cars, of course, hope that the different terminology will keep

Real Life

The Death Tax

Here is Grover Norquist, who is the head of Americans for Tax Reform in Washington, D.C., in a press release from that organization:

> Over seventy percent of Americans oppose the Death Tax, and with good reason. It is the worst form of double-taxation, where, after taxing you all your life, the government decides to take even more when you die.

"Death Tax" is a dysphemism, of course. The estate tax is a tax not on death but on inherited wealth, imposed on the occasion of a person's death. And the person paying the tax is not the deceased, but the inheritors, who have never paid tax on the money.

"Wardrobe malfunction"

Justin Timberlake's phrase for his tearing of Janet Jackson's costume during the half-time performance at Super Bowl XXXVIII.

potential buyers from thinking about *how* "used" the car might be—maybe it's *used up*! The car dealer's replacement term, "pre-owned," is a **euphemism**—a neutral or positive expression instead of one that carries negative associations. Euphemisms play an important role in affecting our attitudes. People may be less likely to disapprove of an assassination attempt on a foreign leader, for example, if it is referred to as "neutralization." People fighting against the government of a country can be referred to neutrally as "rebels" or "guerrillas," but a person who wants to build support for them may refer to them by the euphemism "freedom fighters." A government is likely to pay a price for initiating a "revenue enhancement," but voters will be even quicker to respond negatively to a "tax hike." The U.S. Department of Defense performs the same function it did when it was called the Department of War, but the current name makes for much better public relations.

The opposite of a euphemism is a **dysphemism.** Dysphemisms are used to produce a negative effect on a listener's or reader's attitude toward something or to tone down the positive associations it may have. Whereas "freedom fighter" is a euphemism for "guerrilla" or "rebel," "terrorist" is a dysphemism.

Euphemisms and dysphemisms are often used in deceptive ways or ways that at least hint at deception. All the examples in the preceding paragraphs are examples of such uses. But euphemisms can at times be helpful and constructive. By allowing us to approach a sensitive subject indirectly—or by skirting it entirely—euphemisms can sometimes prevent hostility from bringing rational discussion to a halt. They can also be a matter of good manners: "Passed on" may be much more appropriate than "dead" if the person to whom you're speaking is recently widowed. Hence, our *purpose* for using euphemisms and dysphemisms determines whether or not those uses are legitimate.

It bears mentioning that some facts just are repellent, and for that reason even neutral reports of them sound horrible. "Lizzie killed her father with an ax" reports a horrible fact about Lizzie, but it does so using neutral language. Neutral reports of unpleasant, evil, or repellent facts do not automatically count as dysphemistic rhetoric.

Weaselers

Weaselers are linguistic methods of hedging a bet. When inserted into a claim, they help protect it from criticism by watering it down somewhat, weakening it, and giving the claim's author a way out in case the claim is challenged. So, what a claim asserts, a weaseler either minimizes or takes away entirely.

Without doubt you've heard the words "up to" used as a weaseler a thousand times, especially in advertising. "Up to five more miles per gallon." "Up to twenty more yards off the tee." "Lose up to ten pounds a week." None of these guarantee anything. Sure, you might lose ten pounds, but you might lose nothing. The statement still stands, thanks to "up to."

Let's make up a statistic. Let's say that 98 percent of American doctors believe that aspirin is a contributing cause of Reye's syndrome in children, and that the other 2 percent are unconvinced. If we then claim that "some doctors are unconvinced that aspirin is related to Reye's syndrome," we cannot be held accountable for having said something false, even though our claim might be misleading to someone who did not know the complete story. The word "some" has allowed us to weasel the point.

Words that sometimes weasel—such as "perhaps," "possibly," "maybe," and "may be," among others—can be used to produce innuendo, to plant a *suggestion* without actually making a claim that a person can be held to. We can suggest that Berriault is a liar without actually saying so (and thus without making a claim that might be hard to defend) by saying that Berriault *may be* a liar. Or we can say it is *possible* that Berriault is a liar (which is true of all of us, after all). "*Perhaps* Berriault is a liar" works nicely, too. All of these are examples of weaselers used to create innuendo (to be explained below).

Not every use of words and phrases like these is a weaseling one, of course. Words that can weasel can also bring very important qualifications to bear on a claim. The very same word that weasels in one context may not weasel at all in another. For example, a detective who is considering all the

> Great Western pays up to 12 percent *more interest on checking accounts.*
>
> —Radio advertisement

Even aside from the "up to" weaseler, this ad can be deceptive about what interest rate it's promising. Unless you listen carefully, you might think Great Western is paying 12 percent on checking accounts. The presence of the word "more" changes all that, of course. If you're getting 3 percent now, and Great Western gives you "up to 12 percent more" than that, they'll be giving you about 3⅓ percent—hardly the fortune the ad seems to promise.

In the Media

Innuendo with Statistics

Taxpayers with incomes over $200,000 could expect on average to pay about $99,000 in taxes under [the proposed] plan.

—*Wall Street Journal*

Wow! Pity the poor taxpayer who makes over $200,000! Apparently, he or she will pay almost half of that amount in taxes.

But think again: In the words of the *New Republic* (February 3, 2003), "The *Journal's* statistic is about as meaningful as asserting that males over the age of six have had an average of three sexual partners." Bill Gates and many billionaires like him are among those who make over $200,000.

possible angles on a crime and who has just heard Smith's account of events may say to an associate, "Of course, it is *possible* that Smith is lying." This need not be a case of weaseling. The detective may simply be exercising due care. Other words and phrases that are sometimes used to weasel can also be used legitimately. Qualifying phrases such as "it is arguable that," "it may well be that," and so on have at least as many appropriate uses as weaseling ones. Others, such as "some would say that," are likely to be weaseling more often than not, but even they can serve an honest purpose in the right context. Our warning, then, is to be watchful when qualifying phrases turn up. Is the speaker or writer adding a reasonable qualification, insinuating a bit of innuendo, or preparing a way out? We can only warn; you need to assess the speaker, the context, and the subject to establish the grounds for the right judgment.

Downplayers

Downplaying is an attempt to make someone or something look less important or less significant. Stereotypes, rhetorical comparisons, rhetorical explanations, and innuendo (all discussed later) can all be used to downplay something. Consider this statement, for example: "Don't mind what Mr. Pierce says in class; he's a liberal." This attempt to downplay Mr. Pierce and whatever views he expresses in class makes use of a stereotype. We can also downplay by careful insertion of certain words or other devices. Let's amend the preceding example like this: "Don't mind what Mr. Pierce says in class; he's just another liberal." Notice how the phrase "just another" denigrates Mr. Pierce's status still further. Words and other devices that serve this function are known as **downplayers.**

Perhaps the words most often used as downplayers are "mere" and "merely." If Kim tells you that she has a yellow belt in the Tibetan martial art of Pujo and that her sister has a mere green belt, you would quite naturally make the assumption that a yellow belt ranks higher than a green belt. We'd probably say that Kim's use of the word "mere" gives you the *right* to make that assumption. Kim has used the word to downplay the significance of her sister's accomplishment. But notice this: It could still be that Kim's sister's belt signifies the higher rank. If called on the matter, Kim might claim that she said "mere" simply because her sister has been practicing the art for much longer and is, after all, not *that* far ahead. Whether Kim has such an out or not, she has used a downplayer to try to diminish her sister's accomplishment.

The term "so-called" is another standard downplayer. We might say, for example, that the woman who made the diagnosis is a "so-called doctor," which downplays her credentials as a physician. Quotation marks can be used to accomplish the same thing:

She got her "degree" from a correspondence school.

Use of quotation marks as a downplayer is somewhat different from their use to indicate irony, as in this remark:

John "borrowed" Hank's umbrella, and Hank hasn't seen it since.

The idea in the latter example isn't to downplay John's borrowing the umbrella; it's to indicate that it wasn't really a case of borrowing at all. But the use of quotation marks around the word "degree" and the use of "so-called" in the earlier examples are designed to play down the importance of their subjects. And, like "mere" and "merely," they do it in a fairly unsubtle way.

Many conjunctions—such as "nevertheless," "however," "still," and "but"—can be used to downplay claims that precede them. Such uses are more subtle than the first group of downplayers. Compare the following two versions of what is essentially the same pair of claims:

> (1) The leak at the plant was a terrible tragedy, all right; however, we must remember that such pesticide plants are an integral part of the "green revolution" that has helped to feed millions of people.

> (2) Although it's true that pesticide plants are an integral part of the "green revolution" that has helped to feed millions of people, it was just such a plant that developed a leak and produced a terrible tragedy.

The differences may not be as obvious as those in the cases of "mere" and "so-called," but the two versions give an indication of where their authors' sympathies lie.

The context of a claim can determine whether it downplays or not. Consider the remark "Chavez won by only six votes." The word "only" may or may not downplay Chavez's victory, depending on how thin a six-vote margin is. If ten thousand people voted and Chavez won by six, then the word "only" seems perfectly appropriate: Chavez won by just the skin of his teeth. But if the vote was in a committee of, say, twenty, then six is quite a substantial margin (it would be thirteen votes to seven, if everybody voted— almost two to one), and applying the word "only" to the result is clearly a slanting device designed to give Chavez's margin of victory less importance than it deserves.

As mentioned earlier, slanters really can't—and shouldn't—be avoided altogether. They can give our writing flair and interest. What *can* be avoided is being unduly swayed by slanters. Learn to appreciate the effects that subtle and not-so-subtle manipulations of language can have on you. By being aware, you decrease your chances of being taken in unwittingly by a clever writer or speaker.

Identify any of the rhetorical devices you find in the following from the previous section of the text (euphemisms, dysphemisms, weaselers, downplayers). Not every example may contain such a device.

Exercise 5-1

▲   1. You say you are in love with Oscar, but are you sure he's right for you? Isn't he a little too . . . uh, mature for you?

2. He was at the bar for two hours, officer, but I know he had only four drinks during that time.

▲   3. "The key principle is 'responsible energy exploration.' And remember, it's NOT drilling for oil. It's responsible energy exploration."

—Republican pollster Frank Luntz

4. Of course, it may be that Roethlisberger didn't even commit the assaults he was accused of.

▲

5. Try the Neutron Diet for just four weeks, and you can lose as many as twenty pounds!

6. Republicans stand on principle against the irresponsible plans put forth by environmental extremists to wreck the economy.

7. "Despite what many politicians continue to say, the success of the surge strategy put in place by Generals Petraeus and Odierno is undeniable."

—*House Minority Leader John Boehner (R-Ohio)*

8. Obama and his Democrat-Communist party have bloated the already bloated federal bureaucracy by 25% in ONE YEAR.

9. Charles, be sure to tinkle before we leave!

10. Him? Oh, that's just my brother.

RHETORICAL DEVICES II

These next three slanting devices rely, in one way or another, on unwarranted assumptions. We have to depend on unstated assumptions all the time, but as you'll see, we can get into trouble when those assumptions are not trustworthy.

Stereotypes

You often hear references to "the liberals," "the right-wingers," "the Jews," "the Catholics," "the Evangelicals," and, lately, "the Tea Partiers." These terms are almost always used when the speaker or writer is making use of a stereotype. A **stereotype** is a generalization or an assumption about all the members of a group that is based on an image of those in the group. Americans are often stereotyped as being friendly and generous, but also as being impatient and domineering. Asians are often stereotyped as being reserved but clever. Some stereotypes are negative and even vicious: women are emotional, men are insensitive, lesbians hate men, southerners are bigots, gay men are effeminate, and so on. Of course, a moment's thought tells us that none of these characteristics could reasonably be applied to *all* the members of the group in question.

Some of the slanters we've already talked about can involve stereotypes. For example, if we use the dysphemism "right-wing extremist" to defame a political candidate, we are utilizing a negative stereotype. Commonly, if we link a candidate with a stereotype we like or venerate, we can create a favorable impression of the individual. "Senator McCain addressed his opponent with all the civility of a gentleman" employs a favorable stereotype, that of a gentleman, in a rhetorical comparison.

Our stereotypes come from a great many sources, many from popular literature, and are often supported by a variety of prejudices and group interests. The Native American tribes of the Great Plains were considered noble people

Mention the *strict regulations*—not protocols or rules—governing nuclear power plants.

—Republican pollster FRANK LUNTZ, in "An Energy Policy for the 21st Century," advising Republicans how to sell nuclear energy

In the Media

We Get Dumber in Company of Blondes

LONDON—From Marilyn Monroe to Paris Hilton, "blonde" has long been code for a woman who's long on looks and light on brains.

Now French researchers have found that the stereotype can actually affect mental performance.

A recent study showed that otherwise intelligent men performed below par on general knowledge tests after viewing photos of blonde women.

The real surprise? Women's performance also dipped in the tests.

The study, published in the *Journal of Experimental Social Psychology,* examined people's ability to answer Trivial Pursuit game questions after viewing photos of women with different hair colors.

Exposure to blondes resulted in the lowest scores.

Thierry Meyer, joint author of the study and professor of social psychology at the University of Paris X-Nanterre, said that the study proves a general phenomenon.

"There's a decrease in performance after an unobtrusive exposure to a stereotype about people who have the reputation to be cognitively impaired," he said.

In plainer language, blondes might make people act in a less intelligent manner because the people believe—whether they want to admit it or not—that they are in the presence of someone who's not very smart.

Previous studies also have shown how information from a person's social context can influence their behavior.

For example, when people are exposed to elderly people, they tend to walk and talk more slowly. When people sit beside someone who is fidgeting, they tend to fidget as well.

"The mere knowledge of a stereotype can influence our behavior," said Clementine Bry, another author of the study.

It's not clear how the stereotype of the dumb blonde came about, although some researchers point to the 1950s movie *Gentlemen Prefer Blondes* starring Marilyn Monroe. But through the years a wide range of blonde actresses—from Mae West to Suzanne Somers to Goldie Hawn—have perpetuated the stereotype.

Bry was quick to point out that there is "absolutely no scientific evidence" to support the stereotype of the dumb blonde.

"Stereotypes are cultural beliefs about social groups, and are not truthful pictures of who people are," she said.

—*Shelley Emling, Cox News Service*

by most whites until just before the mid-nineteenth century. But as white people grew more interested in moving them off their lands and as conflicts between the two escalated, popular literature increasingly described Native Americans as subhuman creatures. This stereotype supported the group interests of whites. Conflicts in general, but especially conflicts between nations, produce derogatory stereotypes of the opposition; it is easier to destroy enemies without pangs of conscience if we think of them as less "human" than ourselves. Stereotyping becomes even easier when there are racial differences to exploit.

Nicholas Kristof notes that it isn't just the ignorant and uneducated whose thinking runs to stereotypes:

> In times of stress, even smart and sophisticated people tend to be swept up in prejudice. Teddy Roosevelt said in 1886: "I don't go so far as to think that the only good Indians are dead Indians, but I believe nine out of ten are, and I shouldn't inquire too closely in the case of the tenth. The most vicious cowboy has more moral principle than the average Indian."*

The fact that nothing could have been further from the truth seems to be irrelevant once the blood pressure gets up. (It's also helpful to remember that the stereotypical cowboy of the movies was hardly realistic. After all, it was not the pillars of society who moved West and became cowboys during the nineteenth century.)

Innuendo

The next batch of slanting devices doesn't depend as much on emotional associations as on the manipulation of other features of language. When we communicate with one another, we automatically have certain expectations and make certain assumptions. (For example, when your instructor says, "Everybody passed the exam," she doesn't mean that everybody *in the world* passed the exam. We assume that the scope of the pronoun extends to include only those who took the exam.) These expectations and assumptions help fill in the gaps in our conversations so that we don't have to explain everything we say in minute detail. Because providing such details would be a tedious and probably impossible chore, these underlying conversational factors are crucial to the success of communication.

Consider this statement:

> Ladies and gentlemen, I am proof that there is at least one candidate in this race who does not have a drinking problem.

Notice that this remark does *not* say that any opponent of the speaker *does* have a drinking problem. In fact, the speaker is even allowing for the fact that other candidates may have no such problem by using the words "at least one candidate." But because we assume there would be no need to make this remark unless there *were* a candidate who had a drinking problem, the speaker

The city voluntarily assumed the costs of cleaning up the landfill to make it safe for developers.

—Opponents of a local housing development

The opponents neglected to mention that the law *required* the city to assume the costs. This bit of innuendo on the part of the opponents suggested, of course, that the city was in bed with the developers.

---

*Nicholas D. Kristof, "Bigotry in Islam—and Here," *New York Times*, <www.nytimes.com>, op-ed section.

casts suspicion on his opponent. This is sometimes referred to as **significant mention** or **paralipsis.** It is one form of **innuendo,** which includes many ways of getting a point across without explicitly committing oneself to it.

Another example, maybe our all-time favorite, is this remark:

> I didn't say the meat was tough. I said I didn't see the horse that is usually outside.
>
> —*W. C. Fields*

As you can see, the use of innuendo enables us to insinuate something deprecatory about something or someone without actually saying it. For example, if someone asks you whether Ralph is telling the truth, you may reply, "Yes, this time," which would suggest that maybe Ralph doesn't *usually* tell the truth. Or you might say of someone, "She is competent—in many regards," which would insinuate that in some ways she is *not* competent.

Sometimes we condemn somebody with faint praise—that is, by praising a person a small amount when grander praise might be expected, we hint that praise may not really be due at all. This is a kind of innuendo. Imagine, for example, reading a letter of recommendation that says, "Ms. Flotsam has done good work for us, I suppose." Such a letter does not inspire one to want to hire Ms. Flotsam on the spot. Likewise, "She's proved to be useful so far" and "Surprisingly, she seems very astute" manage to speak more evil than good of Ms. Flotsam. Notice, though, that the literal information contained in these remarks is not negative in the least. Innuendo lies between the lines, so to speak.

As discussed later in the text, the power of photographs and other images to convey emotions is somewhat analogous to the rhetorical force of language. For example, what emotion is elicited by this image?

Loaded Questions

Another form of innuendo, one distinctive enough to warrant its own heading, is the loaded question. If you overheard someone ask, "Have you always loved to gamble?" you would naturally assume that the person being questioned did in fact love to gamble. This assumption is independent of whether the person answered yes or no, for it underlies the question itself. Every question rests on assumptions. Even an innocent question like "What time is it?" depends on the assumptions that the hearer speaks English and has some means of finding out the time, for instance. **A loaded question** is less innocent, however. It rests on one or more *unwarranted* or *unjustified* assumptions. The world's oldest example, "Have you stopped beating your wife?" rests on the assumption that the person asked has in the past beaten his wife. If there is no reason to think that this assumption is true, then the question is a loaded one.

Exercise 5-2

Identify any rhetorical devices you find in these passages that were described in the previous three sections of the text (stereotypes, innuendo, loaded questions). Not every example may contain such a device.

▲

1. An attorney questioning a witness: "So, if you were awake when you crossed the bridge, just when did you go to sleep at the wheel?"

2. No, I'm sure you'll enjoy playing tennis with Jerome. He gets around pretty well for a guy his age.

▲

3. Frankly, I believe that flash memory will make any kind of moving-part memory, such as hard drives, completely obsolete.

4. Larry Kudlow, on CNBC (in an *American Spectator* interview): "[Former Treasury secretary] Bob Rubin's a smart guy, a nice man, but he hates tax cuts. To listen to Rubin on domestic issues, you could just die. He's a free-spending left-winger."

▲

5. Has Harry been a faithful husband? Well, he's not been through a Tiger Woods phase.

6. Why is it, do you suppose, that pit bulls are all mean and vicious?

7. I wouldn't worry about the train being late. This is Germany, you know.

8. Why did Obama fail to act swiftly to end the BP oil spill?

9. It goes without saying that kid will do well in school. His kind always do.

10. The Pope does not molest children.

RHETORICAL DEVICES III

Humor and a bit of exaggeration are part of our everyday speech. But they can also be used to sway opinions if the listener is not being careful.

Ridicule/Sarcasm

Also known as the **horse laugh**, this device includes ridicule and vicious humor of all kinds. Ridicule is a powerful rhetorical tool—most of us really hate being laughed at. So it's important to remember that somebody who simply gets a laugh at the expense of another person's position has not raised any objection to that position.

One may simply laugh outright at a claim ("Send aid to Russia? Har, har, har!"), laugh at another claim that reminds us of the first ("Support the Equal Rights Amendment? Sure, when the ladies start buying the drinks! Ho, ho, ho!"), tell an unrelated joke, use sarcastic language, or simply laugh at the person who is trying to make the point.

The next time you watch a debate, remember that the person who has the funniest lines and who gets the most laughs may be the person who *seems* to win the debate, but critical thinkers should be able to see the difference between argumentation on one hand and entertainment on the other.

Notice that we are not saying there's anything *wrong* with entertainment, nor with making a valid point in a humorous way. Jon Stewart makes his living ridiculing others (as well as himself). But often there is a serious critical point alongside or underneath the humorous presentation.

Hyperbole

Hyperbole is extravagant overstatement. A claim that exaggerates for effect is on its way to becoming hyperbole, depending on the strength of its language and the point being made. To describe a hangnail as a serious injury is hyperbole; so is using the word "fascist" to describe parents who insist that their teenager be home by midnight. Not all strong or colorful language is hyperbole, of course. "Oscar Peterson is an unbelievably inventive pianist" is a strong claim, but it is not hyperbolic—it isn't really extravagant. However, "Oscar Peterson is the most inventive musician who ever lived" goes beyond emphasis and crosses over the line into hyperbole. (How could one know that Oscar Peterson is more inventive than, say, Mozart?) The test for hyperbole is basically a test for any kind of initial plausibility (see Chapter 4, p. 111). A hyperbolic claim will typically have little or none.

Dysphemisms often involve hyperbole. So do rhetorical comparisons. When we use the dysphemisms "traitorous" or "extremist" to describe the views of a member of an opposing political party, we are indulging in hyperbole. If we say that the secretary of state is less well informed than a beet, that's hyperbole in a rhetorical comparison. In similar ways, rhetorical explanations and definitions (see next two pages) can utilize hyperbole.

Hyperbole is also frequently used in ridicule. If it involves exaggeration, a piece of ridicule counts as hyperbole. The foregoing example, saying that the secretary of state is less well informed than a beet, is hyperbole in a rhetorical comparison used to ridicule that official.

A claim can be hyperbolic without containing excessively emotive words or phrases. Neither the hangnail nor the Oscar Peterson example contains such language; in fact, the word "unbelievably" is probably the most emotive word in the two claims about Peterson, and it occurs in the nonhyperbolic claim. But a claim can also be hyperbole as a result of the use of such language. "Parents who are strict about a curfew are fascists" is an example. If the word "mean" were substituted for "fascists," we might find the claim strong or somewhat exaggerated, but we would not call it hyperbole. It's when the colorfulness of language becomes *excessive*—a matter of judgment—that the claim is likely to turn into hyperbole.

Hyperbole is an obvious slanting device, but it can also have more subtle—perhaps unconscious—effects. Even if you reject the exaggeration, you may be moved in the direction of the basic claim. For example, you may reject the claim that Oscar Peterson is the most inventive musician who ever lived, but you may now believe that Oscar Peterson must certainly

■ Much sarcastic comment resulted from Sarah Palin's use of notes penned on her palm. She even got in on the act herself in a later speech.

A feminazi is a woman to whom the most important thing in life is seeing to it that as many abortions as possible are performed.

—RUSH LIMBAUGH

A rhetorical definition with hyperbole. (A straw man, too, but that's for a later chapter.)

be an extraordinary musician—otherwise, why would someone make that exaggerated claim about him? Or suppose someone says, "Charlotte Church has the most fabulous voice of any singer around today." Even if you reject the "fabulous" part of the claim, you may still end up thinking Charlotte Church must have a pretty good voice. But be careful: Without support, you have no more reason to accept the milder claims than the wilder ones. Hyperbole can add a persuasive edge to a claim that it doesn't deserve. A hyperbolic claim is pure persuasion.

RHETORICAL DEVICES IV

Definitions, explanations, analogies, and comparisons are all used in straight-forward ways most of the time. But, as we'll see, they can also be used in rhetorical fashion to slant a point one way or another.

Rhetorical Definitions and Rhetorical Explanations

We encountered rhetorical (or persuasive) definitions in Chapter 3. "Real" definitions are primarily used to clarify meaning; **rhetorical definitions** use

On Language

Legislative Misnomers

Several polls have reported that voters sometimes indicate approval of a measure when they hear its title but indicate disapproval after they've heard an explanation of what the measure actually proposes. This isn't surprising, given the misleading proposal titles assigned by members of Congress and state legislatures, and by authors of ballot measures. Here are a few examples of recent laws, initiatives, and so on, the names of which don't exactly tell the whole story:

> Healthy Forests Initiative (federal)—Reduces public involvement in decision making regarding logging, reduces environmental protection requirements, and provides timber companies greater access to national forests

> Clear Skies Act (federal)—Loosens regulation of mercury, nitrous oxide, and sulphur dioxide, and puts off required reductions of these substances for several years beyond the limits of the current Clean Air Act; allows companies to trade off "pollution credits" so that some communities would get cleaner air and others dirtier air

> Limitations on Enforcement of Unfair Business Competition Laws (California)—Makes it impossible for consumer groups of all types to sue corporations and businesses to prevent fraud, false advertising, and other deceptions before they take place

> Support Our Law Enforcement and Safe Neighborhoods Act (Arizona)—Requires law enforcement officers to determine immigration status of individuals whom they reasonably suspect to be illegal aliens

> Right to Work (many states)—Prevents unions from collecting fees from nonmembers of bargaining units

> Prohibition of Discrimination and Preferential Treatment (California)—Weakens or eliminates affirmative action programs

emotively charged language to express or elicit an attitude about something. Defining abortion as "the murder of an unborn child" does this—and stacks the deck against those who think abortion is morally defensible. Likewise, "human being" could be restricted in its meaning to an organism to which a human gives birth. Under this definition, abortion could not be classified as homicide.

In Chapter 3, we explained three forms definitions typically take. It's worth noting here that even definitions by example can slant a discussion if the examples are prejudicially chosen. Defining "conservative" by pointing to a white supremacist would be a case in point. Bill Maher once defined a conservative as one who thinks all problems can be solved by either more guns or more Jesus. If one wants to see all sides of an issue, one must avoid definitions and examples that slant a discussion.

Rhetorical explanations are the same kind of slanting device, this time clothed as explanations. "He lost the fight because he's lost his nerve." Is this different from saying that he lost because he was too cautious? Maybe, but maybe not. What isn't in doubt is that the explanation is certainly more unflattering when it's put the former way.

We recently saw a good example of a rhetorical explanation in a letter to an editor:

> I am a traditional liberal who keeps asking himself, why has there been such a seismic shift in affirmative action? It used to be affirmative action stood for equal opportunity; now it means preferences and quotas. Why the change? It's because the people behind affirmative action aren't for equal rights anymore; they're for handouts.

This isn't a dispassionate scholarly explanation but a way of expressing an opinion on, and trying to evoke anger at, affirmative action policies.

Rhetorical Analogies and Misleading Comparisons

A while back, Robert Kittle, the editorial page editor of the *San Diego Union-Tribune*, referred to the Social Security system as a Ponzi scheme. (Ponzi schemes, named for Carlo Ponzi, who was responsible for some famous examples, are pyramid schemes designed to bilk money from people who fall for them; Bernie Madoff, who made off with $65 billion of other people's money, is the most famous recent practitioner.) To compare the Social Security system to such a scheme is to make a **rhetorical analogy**—a comparison of two things or a likening of one thing to another in order to make one of them appear better or worse

Doonesbury   BY GARRY TRUDEAU

■ Stereotypes.

than it might be. Now, people use analogies for various explanatory purposes; if a friend knows nothing of rugby, for instance, you might help him understand something about it by comparing it to football. In the foregoing case, however, editor Kittle's comparison was designed not to enlighten but to persuade. "Ponzi scheme" has a strong negative connotation, and calling something a Ponzi scheme portrays it in a bad light.

Rhetorical analogies are often used as a substitute for arguments, and it is easy to see why. Facts are required to show that Social Security is financially unsustainable; it's less work and possibly just as effective to call it a Ponzi scheme. This kind of persuasion often works very well, producing conviction in the listener without the necessity of proof.

Rhetorical analogies include both metaphors and similes. "Hillary's eyes bulge just a little, like a Chihuahua's" is a simile; "Jenna is a loose cannon" is a metaphor.

Rhetorical analogies also include comparisons. "You have a better chance of being struck by lightning than of winning the lottery." Or Dave Barry's description of parenthood: "Having kids is like having a bowling alley installed in your brain." These are colorful ways of making a point, but of course they do not constitute reasons for accepting that point.

Some comparisons can be problematic, leading us into error if we're not careful. Advertising slogans often use comparisons that can mislead us because of their vagueness. "Now 25 percent larger," "New and improved formula," or "Quietest by far." We learned what problems vagueness can cause in the previous chapter; it returns to haunt these comparative claims. Larger than what? Improved how? Unless the terms of the comparison are spelled out and the manner of comparing made clear, such claims are worth very little. As we also saw in the previous chapter, claims made in advertising are not our most reliable sources of information, and that includes comparative claims.

Following are some questions that you would be wise to keep in mind when considering comparisons. They include reference to omissions and distortions, which can be among the more subtle forms of rhetorical devices.

1. *Is important information missing?* It is nice to hear that the unemployment rate has gone down, but not if you learn the reason is that a larger percent of the workforce has given up looking for work. Or, suppose someone says that 90 percent of heroin addicts once smoked marijuana. Without other information, the comparison is meaningless, since 90 percent of heroin addicts no doubt listened to the Beatles, too. Our local U.S. congressional representative Wally Herger recently warned his constituents that Social Security is in dire straits. At one time, he said, there were 42 workers to support a single retiree, and now there are only 3. This does indeed sound ominous, except Representative Herger didn't mention that the 42-to-1 ratio was at the startup of Social Security before many had retired; he also failed to mention that the 3-to-1 ratio has been around for the past 25 years, during which period Social Security accumulated a surplus.*

2. *Is the same standard of comparison used?* Are the same reporting and recording practices being used? A change in the jobless rate doesn't mean much if the government changes the way it calculates joblessness, as

---

*Statistics from our colleague, Professor (of American history) Carl Peterson.

In the Media

A Misleading Mathematical Visual

Sometimes a straightforward mathematical comparison can become misleading by the way it's presented. The bar graph below, from a CNN/USA Today/Gallup poll, compares Democrats, Republicans, and Independents with respect to their agreement with a court's judgment that the feeding tube should be removed from Terri Schiavo, a case discussed in the text, page 166. From a casual look at the bar graph, it might seem that Democrats are *much* more in favor of removing the tube than Republicans or Independents.

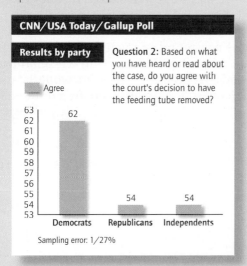

But look at the *numbers* rather than the bars themselves, and we get a different story. The first graph shows us only the *parts* of the bars, from 53 percent to 63 percent. If we display the entire bars, from 0 to 100 percent, the graph looks like this:

In this case, the Democrats look (correctly) to be only somewhat more in favor of removing the tube. The lesson here is to avoid drawing conclusions until you've had a close look at the data, including the manner in which it is displayed.

Comparison originally made by truthout.org.

sometimes happens. In 1993, the number of people in the United States with AIDS suddenly increased dramatically. Had a new form of the AIDS virus appeared? No; the federal government had expanded the definition of AIDS to include several new indicator conditions. As a result, overnight 50,000 people were considered to have AIDS who had not been so considered the day before.

Never try to wade a river just because it has an average depth of four feet.

—MARTIN FRIEDMAN

The wrong average can put you under.

3. *Are the items comparable?* It is hard to compare baseball sluggers Barry Bonds and Willie Mays if one but not the other used steroids, or if one had the benefit of improved equipment. It's hard to derive a conclusion from the fact that this April's retail business activity is way down as compared with last April's, if Easter came early this year and the weather was especially cold. That more male than female drivers are involved in traffic fatalities doesn't mean much by itself, since male drivers collectively drive more miles than do female drivers. Comparing share values of two mutual funds over the past ten years won't be useful to an investor if the comparison doesn't take into account a difference in fees.

4. *Is the comparison expressed as an average?* The average rainfall in Seattle is about the same as that in Kansas City. But you'll spend more time in the rain in Seattle because it rains there twice as often as in Kansas City. If Central Valley Components, Inc. (CVC), reports that average salaries of a majority of its employees have more than doubled over the past ten years, it sounds good, but CVC still may not be a great place to work. Perhaps the increases were due to converting the majority of employees, who worked half-time, to full-time and firing the rest. Comparisons that involve averages omit details that can be important, simply because they involve averages.

In 2003, the administration proposed a tax cut that, it was said, would give the average taxpayer $1,083.

The "average" here is the mean average. However, most taxpayers, according to the Urban Institute–Brookings Institution Tax Policy Center, would have received less than $100 under the administration's proposal.

Misleading averages

Averages are measures of central tendency, and there are different kinds of measures or averages. Consider, for instance, the average cost of a new house in your area, which may be $210,000. If that is the *mean*, it is the total of the sales prices divided by the number of houses sold, and it may be quite different from the *median*, which is an average that is the halfway figure (half the houses cost more and half cost less). The *mode*, the most common sales price, may be different yet. If there are likely to be large or dramatic variations in what is measured, one must be cautious of figures that represent an unspecific "average."

Real Life

Cause for Alarm?

According to the National Household Survey on Drug Abuse, cocaine use among Americans twelve to seventeen years of age increased by a whopping 166 percent between 1992 and 1995. Wow, right?

Except that the increase *in absolute terms* was a little less spectacular: In 1992, 0.3 percent of Americans aged twelve to seventeen had used cocaine; in 1995, the percentage was 0.8 percent of that population.

Be wary of comparisons expressed as percentage changes.

In Depth

Visual Hyperbole, Ridicule, or Just Beefcake?

Former Governor Schwarzenegger of California was the point of all manner of jokes, both verbal and visual. Most good satire and parody contain more than a kernel of truth. Schwarzenegger's fame as a bodybuilder and later as the star of such action movies as the *Terminator* series helped him get elected and also have been the source of most of the humor about him. Here, he appears in his Conan the Barbarian gear, overseeing the settling of California by whites in the nineteenth century. We think the main point here is simply to show the governor without a shirt.

Explain how rhetorical definitions, rhetorical comparisons, and rhetorical explanations differ. Find an example of each in a newspaper, magazine, or other source.

Exercise 5-3

Critique these comparisons, using the questions about comparisons discussed in the text as guides.

Exercise 5-4

Example

> You get much better service on Air Atlantic.

Answer

> Better than on what? (One term of the comparison is not clear.)
>
> In what way better? (The claim is much too vague to be of much use.)

▲ 1. New improved Morning Muffins! Now with 20 percent more real dairy butter!

2. The average concert musician makes less than a plumber.

3. Major league ballplayers are much better than they were thirty years ago.

▲ 4. What an arid place to live. Why, they had less rain here than in the desert.

5. On the whole, the mood of the country is more conservative than it was in the nineties.

6. Which is better for a person, coffee or tea?

▲ 7. The average GPA of graduating seniors at Georgia State is 3.25, as compared with 2.75 twenty years ago.

8. Women can tolerate more pain than men.

9. Try Duraglow with new sunscreening polymers. Reduces the harmful effect of sun on your car's finish by up to 50 percent.

▲ 10. What a brilliant season! Attendance was up 25 percent over last year.

PROOF SURROGATES AND REPETITION

These last two devices stand more or less alone; they don't fit comfortably into any of the other groups, so we've made a group of just the two of them.

Proof Surrogates

An expression used to suggest that there is evidence or authority for a claim without actually citing such evidence or authority is a **proof surrogate**. Sometimes we can't *prove* the claim we're asserting, but we can hint that there *is* proof available, or at least evidence or authority for the claim, without committing ourselves to what that proof, evidence, or authority is. Using "informed sources say" is a favorite way of making a claim seem more authoritative. Who are the sources? How do we know they're informed? How does the person making the claim know they're informed? "It's obvious that" sometimes precedes a claim that isn't obvious at all. But we may keep our objections to ourselves in the belief that it's obvious to everybody but us, and we don't want to appear denser than the next guy.

Proof surrogates are sometimes used as part of a more general scheme of insinuating one's way into another's confidence. Most good salespersons know that if they can establish some common personal ground with a client, they are more likely to make a sale, and the same is true in general for trying to persuade one's listeners that some claim is true. One way of making a personal connection is by establishing, or insinuating, that one is part of the same group as one's listeners. It's "just us" instead of "us and them." We generally feel more favorably toward members of groups to which we belong, and this "in-group" bias can help bring one's listeners over to one's side. It's simply true that we tend to hold our comrades—members of our own group—to a lower standard of proof than we do outsiders.

Many proof surrogates play on this presumed in-group status. When someone says, "As we know . . . ," to disagree is tantamount to admitting you are not among the in-group. Similarly, "As everybody knows . . . ," threatens to put one who disagrees among the uninformed outsiders.

The preceding considerations are fairly subtle but often more effective than we might like to admit. Other proof surrogates are rather more blunt: "Studies show" crops up a lot in advertising. Note that this phrase tells us nothing about how many studies are involved, how good they are, who did them, or any other important information. Here's a good example of a proof surrogate from the *Wall Street Journal*:

There is no other country in the Middle East except Israel that can be considered to have a stable government. . . . Is Saudi Arabia more stable? Egypt? Jordan? Kuwait? Judge for yourself!

—"Facts and Logic About the Middle East"

Proof surrogates often take the form of questions. This strategy can also be analyzed as switching the burden of proof (see Chapter 7).

We hope politicians on this side of the border are paying close attention to Canada's referendum on Quebec. . . .

Canadians turned out en masse to reject the referendum. There's every reason to believe that voters in the U.S. are just as fed up with the social engineering that lumps people together as groups rather than treating them as individuals.

There may be "every reason to believe" that U.S. voters are fed up, but nobody has yet told us what any of those reasons are. Until we hear more evidence, our best bet is to figure that the quotation mainly reflects what the writer at the *Journal* thinks is the proper attitude for U.S. voters. Without a context, such assertions are meaningless.

Remember: Proof surrogates are just that—surrogates. They are not real proof or evidence. Such proof or evidence may exist, but until it has been presented, the claim at issue remains unsupported. At best, proof surrogates suggest sloppy research; at worst, they suggest propaganda.

Repetition

"The most brilliant propagandist technique will yield no success unless one fundamental principle is borne in mind constantly—it must confine itself to a few points and repeat them over and over." (Joseph Goebbles, Nazi Minister of Propaganda)

"A lie told often enough becomes the truth." (Vladimir Lenin, Russian revolutionary)

We don't want to set Goebbles and Lenin up as models for critical thinking, but we are forced to admit that both had huge success at convincing large numbers of people to believe what they wanted them to believe. And the technique of repetition, simply making the same point over and over at every opportunity, was a main tool in their various campaigns. Similarly, in advertising and in politics today the constant repetition of a theme seems eventually to have a dulling effect on our critical faculties, and we can become lulled into believing something simply because we've become used to hearing it. A critical thinker needs to remember: it takes evidence and argument to provide believability; if a claim is not likely to be true on the first hearing, simple repetition does not make it more likely on the hundredth.

Identify any rhetorical devices you find in these passages that were described in the previous four sections of the text (ridicule/sarcasm, hyperbole, proof surrogates). Not every example may contain such a device.

Exercise 5-5

▲ 1. Medical school, huh? Right. You and your fancy 2.9 grade point are going to get into a fine medical school all right.

2. Laboratory tests have shown that Cloyon produces a sweeter taste than any other artificial sweetener.

▲ 3. I'll tell you, there's never been anybody in the entire state of Florida as blitzed as Tom and I were last night.

4. Anybody who understands how alcohol works can tell you that three drinks is enough to make that guy seriously impaired.

▲

5. According to the Department of Motor Vehicles chart, it takes only three drinks to impair somebody his size.

6. "Cable news has gone round the bend: The only thing you hear on Fox News is right-wing rants, and the only thing you hear on MSNBC are left-wing rants."

7. That the president is a Marxist simply cannot be denied by any serious observer of contemporary politics.

8. In the 1988 U.S. presidential election, campaigners for Democrat Michael Dukakis took a photograph of Dukakis in an M1 Abrams Tank. The photo was supposed to shore up Dukakis's credentials as strong on defense. Unfortunately, Dukakis had a silly grin and was wearing a helmet too large for his head, and the effect of the photograph was to make him appear diminutive and goofy. The photo was widely shown in the months preceding the election—but not by the Dukakis people. Instead, it was picked up and shown by his opponent, George H. W. Bush. After looking at the photo at the following link, state which technique was being used by the Bush campaign: <http://en.wikipedia.org/wiki/File:Michael_Dukakis_in_tank.jpg>.

9. If you want to work your way up from being a hostess to being a server at The Cheesecake Factory, plan on it taking about a thousand years.

10. The proposal isn't bad when you consider it comes from a group of knuckle-dragging morons.

PERSUASION USING VISUAL IMAGES

Before the digital age, it was much easier to take photographic evidence at face value. Even then, however, all kinds of things could be done to manipulate an image and a viewer's perception of what was taking place. But some photos and videos do not need any manipulation at all to produce a mistaken impression in the viewer. You might recall that, in 2005, a Florida woman named Terri Schiavo became the center of a controversy regarding whether she was in a "persistent vegetative state" (PVS) and could ever be expected to regain consciousness, never mind recover. Videotape made by family members sometimes appeared to show her responding to the presence of her mother. Bill Frist, himself a heart surgeon and at that time majority leader of the U.S. Senate, saw the tape and claimed that Ms. Schiavo seemed to be responding to visual stimuli. Other doctors, including her own, said that the facial expressions some took as conscious response were often exhibited by those in a PVS and were not signs of awareness. After her death, an autopsy showed that Ms. Schiavo's brain had shrunk to half its normal size, and what was left was severely damaged, including her visual cortex—she had been blind for some time before her death. The likelihood of her having anything like consciousness near the end was virtually a medical impossibility.

We describe this story to illustrate how a piece of videotape can be ambiguous—that is, it can be open to more than one interpretation. What appeared to be the case to some viewers turned out to be a mistaken impression—

leading them to make claims that turned out to be false. (Photos, videos, and other imagery technically cannot be true or false; but claims *based on* such imagery are true or false.)

As we said earlier, though, some people are not willing to let well enough alone. They perform image manipulations of various sorts to try to create mistaken impressions. Following is a list of tricks from the website <http://schools.hpcdsb.on.ca/sg/trenton/FakeImages/>.

FAKES AND MISLEADING IMAGES CAN BE THE RESULT OF . . .

* Deliberately manipulating an image (e.g., adding, deleting, combining)
* Using unaltered images but with misleading captions
* Deliberately selected camera angles that distort information
* Lack of authority (i.e., author name, credentials); inconsistency when compared to official images
* Stills taken from movies: out of context, they are given false descriptions
* Stills taken of models purported to be the real thing
* Stills that are genuine and unadulterated but "staged"
* 100% digital fabrications

In the Media

Now You See Him—Now You Don't

Hu Jintao greets Deng Xiaoping in versions of the photo, from above clockwise, featuring a blurred audience, a dark background and with Jiang Zemin.

In the Media

The Daschle Salute

This looks like a big-time "Oops!" moment for Tom Daschle, former majority leader in the U.S. Senate. In fact, as explained in the text, it is a clever attempt to influence opinion against Daschle through photo manipulation.

The photos in the box "Now You See Him—Now You Don't" on the previous page are from Hong Kong's newspaper, *The Standard*, from September 2, 2004. The original photo (lower right) showed China's then paramount leader Deng Xiaoping (in the gray jacket on the right) shaking hands with Hu Jintao (wearing the tie), who has been China's president since 2003. The person between them in the original photo is former President Jiang Zemin. We don't know what might have become of Jiang's reputation (he continued in high office for some years after the photo was made), but his image suffered a disappearing act.

In the next box, "The Daschle Salute," it looks as though Tom Daschle (the majority leader in the Senate at the time) doesn't know how to salute the flag or doesn't know his right hand from his left. In reality, he did it correctly, but someone reversed his image, flipping it right-to-left so that he appeared to be saluting with his left hand rather than his right. There are two clues to the doctoring that went on in this photo. It would take not just a critical thinker but a sharp eye to spot them. The first is that Daschle is married and wears a wedding ring. If this were really his left hand, one would see his ring. The second clue is more convincing. It's that his coat is buttoned backwards: Men's clothing always has buttons on the right side of the garment, so it's the left side that closes over the right. In the photo, the right side of Daschle's jacket closes over the left, indicating that it isn't just his hand that is on the wrong side, his clothing would have to be reversed, too!

In Depth

Don't Get Carried Away!

Once you're familiar with the ways slanting devices are used to try to influence us, you may be tempted to dismiss a claim or argument *just because it contains strongly slanted language*. But true claims as well as false ones, good reasoning as well as bad, can be couched in such language. Remember that the slanting *itself* gives us no reason to accept a position on an issue; that doesn't mean that there *are* no such reasons. Consider this example, written by someone opposed to using animals for laboratory research:

> It's morally wrong for a person to inflict awful pain on another sensitive creature, one that has done the first no harm. Therefore, the so-called scientists who perform their hideous and sadistic experiments on innocent animals are moral criminals just as were Hitler and his Nazi torturers.

Before we dismiss this passage as shrill or hysterical, it behooves us as critical thinkers to notice that it contains a piece of reasoning that may shed light on the issue.

We would not expect your typical newspaper reader or web surfer to be able to identify manipulated photos wherever they appear. *We* certainly couldn't do it, and some images are so carefully done nobody could spot the problem with them.* So, what is a critically thinking person to do? It's the same answer you've heard before in these pages: Be careful. Be aware that even though most people mean to be helpful and tell you what they actually believe, a substantial number of them are out to fool you.

*What appears to be a wonderful paint-job illusion on the truck pictured above is actually a Photoshopped illustration. You can see other examples of illustrations *on the same truck* at www.britannica.com/blogs/2009/02/optical-illusion-of-the-day-truck-art/.

Recap

Things to remember from this chapter:

■ Persuasion is the attempt to win someone to one's own point of view.

■ Rhetoric seeks to persuade through the use of the emotive power of language.

■ Although it can exert a profound psychological influence, rhetoric has no logical force; only an argument has logical force—i.e., can prove or support a claim.

■ There are a multitude of rhetorical devices in common use; they include the following:

—Euphemisms: seek to mute the disagreeable aspects of something or to emphasize its agreeable aspects

—Dysphemisms: seek to emphasize the disagreeable aspects of something

—Weaselers: words and phrases that protect a claim by weakening it

—Downplayers: techniques for toning down the importance of something

—Stereotypes: unwarranted and oversimplified generalizations about the members of a group or class

—Innuendo: using words with neutral or positive associations to insinuate something deprecatory

—Loaded questions: questions that depend on unwarranted assumptions

—Ridicule and sarcasm: widely used to put something in a bad light

—Hyperbole: overdone exaggeration

—Rhetorical definitions and explanations: used to create favorable or unfavorable attitudes about something

—Rhetorical analogies and misleading comparisons: these devices persuade by making inappropriate connections between terms.

—Proof surrogates suggest there is evidence or authority for a claim without actually saying what the evidence or authority is

—Repetition: hearing or reading a claim over and over can sometimes mistakenly encourage the belief that it is true

■ These devices can affect our thinking in subtle ways, even when we believe we are being objective.

■ Some of these devices, especially euphemisms and weaselers, have valuable, nonprejudicial uses as well as a slanting one. Only if we are speaking, writing, listening, and reading carefully can we distinguish prejudicial uses of these devices.

■ Although photographs and other images are not claims or arguments, they can enter into critical thinking by offering evidence of the truth or falsity of claims. They can also affect us psychologically in a manner analogous to that by which the emotive meaning of language affects us, and often even more powerfully.

Exercise 5-6

You will want to recognize when someone is using rhetorical slanting devices to influence your attitudes and beliefs. Let's see if you can identify some of the more common devices. Select the *best* answer.

▲ 1. "Making a former corporate CEO the head of the Securities and Exchange Commission is like putting a fox in charge of the henhouse." This is best seen as an example of

   a. rhetorical analogy
   b. rhetorical explanation
   c. innuendo
   d. dysphemism
   e. not a slanter

2. "Right. George Bush 'won' the election in 2000, didn't he?" The use of quotation marks around "won" has the effect of a

   a. weaseler
   b. dysphemism
   c. downplayer
   d. rhetorical explanation
   e. not a slanter

▲ 3. "The obvious truth is that bilingual education has been a failure." In this statement, "the obvious truth" might best be viewed as

   a. a proof surrogate
   b. a weaseler
   c. innuendo
   d. a dysphemism
   e. not a slanter

4. After George W. Bush announced he wanted to turn a substantial portion of the federal government operation over to private companies, Bobby L. Harnage Sr., president of the American Federation of Government Employees, said Bush had "declared all-out war on federal employees." Would you say that the quoted passage is

   a. a rhetorical explanation
   b. a euphemism
   c. a weaseler
   d. hyperbole/a rhetorical analogy
   e. not a slanter

5. "Harry and his daughter had a little discussion about her outfit . . . one that left her in tears."

   a. a loaded question
   b. a euphemism
   c. both a and b
   d. neither a nor b

▲ 6. "Before any more of my tax dollars go to the military, I'd like answers to some questions, such as why are we spending billions of dollars on weapons programs that don't work?" This statement contains an example of

   a. a downplayer
   b. a dysphemism
   c. a proof surrogate
   d. a loaded question
   e. hyperbole and a loaded question

7. "Can Governor Evans be believed when he says he will fight for the death penalty? You be the judge." This statement contains
   a. a dysphemism
   b. a proof surrogate
   c. innuendo
   d. hyperbole
   e. no slanters

8. President Obama promised change, but he has continued to turn government operations over to private companies, especially in Iraq and Afghanistan, just like his predecessor did.
   a. hyperbole
   b. a dysphemism
   c. a loaded question
   d. a proof surrogate
   e. no slanter

9. "Studies confirm what everyone knows: smaller classes make kids better learners."

   —Bill Clinton

   This statement contains:
   a. a proof surrogate
   b. a weaseler
   c. hyperbole
   d. an innuendo
   e. no slanter

10. MAN SELLING HIS CAR: "True, it has a few dents, but that's just normal wear and tear." This statement contains what might best be called
   a. a loaded question
   b. innuendo
   c. a dysphemism
   d. a euphemism

Exercise 5-7

Determine which of the numbered, italicized words and phrases are used as rhetorical devices in the following passage. If the item fits one of the text's categories of rhetorical devices, identify it as such.

The National Rifle Association's campaign *to arm every man, woman, and child in America*[1] received a setback when the president signed the Brady Bill. But the *gun-pushers*[2] know that the bill was only *a small skirmish in a big war*[3] over guns in America. They can give up some of their more *fanatical*[4] positions on such things as *assault weapons*[5] and *cop-killer bullets*[6] and still win on the one that counts: regulation of manufacture and sale of handguns.

Exercise 5-8

▲ Follow the directions for Exercise 5-7.

The *big money guys*[1] who have *smuggled*[2] the Rancho Vecino development onto the November ballot *will stop at nothing to have this town run just exactly as they want.*[3] *It is possible*[4] that Rancho Vecino will cause traffic congestion on the east side of town, and *it's perfectly clear that*[5] the number of houses that will be built will overload the sewer system. *But*[6] a small number of individuals have taken up the fight. *Can the developers be stopped in their desire to wreck our town?*[7]

Exercise 5-9

Follow the directions for Exercise 5-7.

The U.S. Congress has cut off funds for the superconducting supercollider that the *scientific establishment*[1] wanted to build in Texas. The *alleged*[2] virtues of the supercollider proved no match for the *huge*[3] *cost overruns*[4] that had piled up *like a mountain alongside a sea of red ink.*[5] Despite original estimates of five to six billion dollars, the latest figure was over eleven billion and *growing faster than weeds.*[6]

Exercise 5-10

Read the passage below and answer the questions that follow it. Your instructor may have further directions.

Another quality that makes [Texas Republican Tom] DeLay an un-Texas pol is that he's mean. By and large, Texas pols are an agreeable set of less-than-perfect humans and quite often well intentioned. As Carl Parker of Port Arthur used to observe, if you took all the fools out of the [legislature], it would not be a representative body any longer. The old sense of collegiality was strong, and vindictive behavior—punishing pols for partisan reasons—was simply not done. But those are Tom DeLay's specialties, his trademarks. The Hammer is not only genuinely feared in Washington, he is, I'm sorry to say, hated.

—*Excerpt from a column by Molly Ivins*, Ft. Worth Star-Telegram

1. What issue is the author addressing?
2. What position does the author take on that issue?
3. If the author supports this position with an argument, state that argument in your own words.
4. Does the author use rhetorical devices discussed in this chapter? If so, classify any that fall into the categories described in this chapter.

Exercise 5-11

Follow the directions for Exercise 5-10, using the same list of questions.

> Schools are not a microcosm of society, any more than an eye is a microcosm of the body. The eye is a specialized organ which does something that no other part of the body does. That is its whole significance. You don't use your eyes to lift packages or steer automobiles. Specialized organs have important things to do in their own specialties. So schools, which need to stick to their special work as well, should not become social or political gadflies.
>
> —*Thomas Sowell*

Exercise 5-12

Follow the directions for Exercise 5-10, using the same list of questions.

> Here is what I believe: The country has just witnessed an interlude of religious hysteria, encouraged and exploited by political quackery. The political cynicism of Republicans shocked the nation. But even more alarming is the enthusiasm of self-described "pro-life" forces for using the power of the state to impose their obtuse moral distinctions on the rest of us. The Catholic Church and many Protestant evangelicals are acting as partisan political players in a very dangerous manner. Once they have mobilized zealots to their moral causes, they can expect others to fight back in the same blind, intolerant manner.
>
> —*William Greider, "Pro-Death Politics," the* Nation, *April 2, 2005*

Exercise 5-13

Follow the directions for Exercise 5-10, using the same list of questions.

> Asked whether he would be resigning, [U.N. Secretary General Kofi] Annan replied, "Hell, no. I've got lots of work to do, and I'm going to go ahead and do it." That's doubtful. His term is up at the end of 2006, and few—after the mess he's caused—take him seriously. He may have a lot of "work" he'd like to do, but he won't be permitted to do it. All around Annan is the wreckage of the U.N.'s spirit of high-level cronyism.
>
> —*Editorial in the* National Review Online, *April 1, 2005*

Exercise 5-14

Follow the directions for Exercise 5-10, using the same list of questions.

> "It is not the job of the state, and it is certainly not the job of the school, to tell parents when to put their children to bed," declared David Hart of the National Association of Head Teachers, responding to David Blunkett's idea that parents and teachers should draw up "contracts"

(which you could be fined for breaching) about their children's behavior, time-keeping, homework and bedtime. Teachers are apparently concerned that their five-to-eight-year-old charges are staying up too late and becoming listless truants the next day.

While I sympathize with Mr. Hart's concern about this neo-Stalinist nannying, I wonder whether it goes far enough. Is it not high time that such concepts as Bathtime, Storytime and Drinks of Water were subject to regulation as well? I for one would value some governmental guidance as to the number of humorous swimming toys (especially Hungry Hippo) allowable per gallon of water. Adopting silly voices while reading *Spot's Birthday* or *Little Rabbit Foo-Foo* aloud is something crying out for regulatory guidelines, while the right of children to demand and receive wholly unnecessary glasses of liquid after lights-out needs a Statutory Minimum Allowance.

—*John Walsh, the* Independent

Exercise 5-15

Choose which answer is best from among the alternatives provided.

1. "Yes, there may be instances of abuse connected with the new immigration law. But on the whole it will help Arizona deal with a serious problem." This contains:
   a. a downplayer
   b. a proof surrogate
   c. hyperbole

2. "Liberals need to understand the global health argument for abortion is deeply offensive. It is like fighting disease by killing everyone who has a disease." This contains:
   a. a euphemism
   b. a dysphemism
   c. a rhetorical definition
   d. none of the above

3. "Why does Senator Schmidt collect child pornography? Only the Senator can answer that." This contains:
   a. a loaded question
   b. a euphemism
   c. a dysphemism
   d. none of the above

4. "Does Senator Schmidt collect child pornography? Only the Senator can answer that." This contains:
   a. innuendo
   b. a downplayer
   c. a euphemism
   d. a stereotype

5. "Better lock up your whisky before Patrick gets here. Didn't you know he is Irish?" This contains:
   a. a loaded question

     b. a rhetorical definition

     c. a stereotype

     d. a euphemism.

     e. none of the above

6. "Ecology? I will tell you what ecology is. Ecology is the Marxist 'science' that tries to shove bogus facts about global warming down everyone's throat." This contains:

     a. a rhetorical definition

     b. a rhetorical explanation

     c. a rhetorical analogy

▲ 7. "Ecology? I will tell you what ecology is. Ecology is the Marxist 'science' that tries to shove bogus facts about global warming down everyone's throat." The quotation marks around "science" are

     a. hyperbole

     b. a proof surrogate

     c. a downplayer

     d. a stereotype

8. "Ecology? I will tell you what ecology is. Ecology is the Marxist 'science' that tries to shove bogus facts about global warming down everyone's throat." "Marxist" and "bogus" are

     a. proof surrogates

     b. euphemisms

     c. hyperbole

     d. rhetorical comparisons

     e. none of these

9. "The reason Republicans oppose health care is they don't care about anyone except their friends in the insurance industry." "Don't care about anyone except" is

     a. a rhetorical definition

     b. a rhetorical explanation

     c. a rhetorical analogy

     d. none of these

▲ 10. "Rush Limbaugh doesn't make things up? C'mon, you know as well as I do he makes things up." This contains:

     a. a stereotype

     b. hyperbole

     c. ridicule

     d. a proof surrogate

Exercise 5-16

Identify any rhetorical devices you find in the following selections, and classify those that fit the categories described in the text. For each, explain its function in the passage.

▲ 1. I trust you have seen Janet's file and have noticed the "university" she graduated from.

2. The original goal of the Milosevic government in Belgrade was ethnic cleansing in Kosovo.

3. Obamacare: The compassion of the IRS and the efficiency of the post office, all at Pentagon prices.

▲ 4. Although it has always had a bad name in the United States, socialism is nothing more or less than democracy in the realm of economics.

5. We'll have to work harder to get Representative Burger reelected because of his little run-in with the law.

▲ 6. It's fair to say that, compared with most people his age, Mr. Beechler is pretty much bald.

7. During World War II, the U.S. government resettled many people of Japanese ancestry in internment camps.

▲ 8. "Overall, I think the gaming industry would be a good thing for our state."

—*From a letter to the editor*, Plains Weekly Record

9. Capitalism, after all, is nothing more or less than freedom in the realm of economics.

10. I'll tell you what capitalism is: Capitalism is Charlie Manson sitting in Folsom Prison for all those murders and still making a bunch of bucks off T-shirts.

▲ 11. Clearly, Antonin Scalia is the most corrupt Supreme Court justice in the history of the country.

12. If MaxiMotors gave you a good price on that car, you can bet there's only one reason they did it: It's a piece of serious junk.

13. It may well be that many faculty members deserve some sort of pay increase. Nevertheless, it is clearly true that others are already amply compensated.

▲ 14. "The only people without [cable or satellite TV] are Luddites and people too old to appreciate it."

—*Todd Mitchell, industry analyst*

15. I love some of the bulleting and indenting features of Microsoft Word. I think it would have been a nice feature, however, if they had made it easy to turn some of them off when you don't need them.

Exercise 5-17

Identify any rhetorical devices you find in the following passage, and classify any that fit into the categories described in this chapter.

On March 11, the U.S. Senate passed the bankruptcy bill that will fill the coffers of the credit card companies while bleeding consumers dry.

The bill passed by a whopping 74 to 25 margin, with eighteen Democratic Senators going over to the dark side.

Here are the spineless 18: [There follows a list of senators.]

"This is not where we as Democrats ought to be, for crying out loud," as Senator Tom Harkin noted. "We are making a terrible mistake by thinking that we can have it both ways. We have to remember where our base is."

This bill is a fantasy come true for credit card companies, which have been pushing it for years. But it's not as though they're suffering. The made $30 billion in profits last year.

The bill severely limits the ability of consumers to wipe away some of their debts and get a fresh start.

Half the people who file for bankruptcy do so because of sky-high medical bills, and another 40 percent do so because of disability, job loss, family death, or divorce, according to the National Consumer Law Center. If you make more than the median income in your state, no matter how high your bills are, you can't wipe the debts clean.

As a result, debtors will be at much greater risk of losing their cars or their homes.

And even if your debts are the consequence of identity theft, of someone stealing your credit card and running up charges, you still are on the hook for them, as the Senate amazingly voted down an amendment to shelter victims of identity theft.

—*Matthew Rothschild, "Democratic Senators Cave on Bankruptcy Bill,"*
The Progressive, *March 12, 2005*

Exercise 5-18

Identify any rhetorical devices you find in the following passages, and explain their purposes. Note: Some items may contain *no* rhetorical devices.

▲ 1. "If the United States is to meet the technological challenge posed by Japan, Inc., we must rethink the way we do everything from design to manufacture to education to employee relations."

—Harper's

2. According to UNICEF reports, several thousand Iraqi children died each month because of the U.N. sanctions.

3. Maybe Professor Daguerre's research hasn't appeared in the first-class journals as recently as that of some of the other professors in his department; that doesn't necessarily mean his work is going downhill. He's still a terrific teacher, if the students I've talked to are to be believed.

▲ 4. "Let's put it this way: People who make contributions to my campaign fund get access. But there's nothing wrong with constituents having access to their representatives, is there?"

—*Loosely paraphrased from an interview with a California state senator*

5. In the 2000 presidential debates, Al Gore consistently referred to his own tax proposal as a "tax plan" and to George W. Bush's tax proposal as a "tax scheme."

▲ 6. [Note: Dr. Jack Kevorkian was instrumental in assisting a number of terminally ill people in committing suicide during the 1990s.] "We're opening the door to Pandora's Box if we claim that doctors can decide if it's proper for someone to die. We can't have Kevorkians running wild, dealing death to people."

—Larry Bunting, assistant prosecutor, Oakland County, Michigan

7. "LOS ANGELES—Marriott Corp. struck out with patriotic food workers at Dodger Stadium when the concession-holder ordered them to keep working instead of standing respectfully during the National Anthem. . . . Concession stand manager Nick Kavadas . . . immediately objected to a Marriott representative.

"Marriott subsequently issued a second memo on the policy. It read: 'Stop all activities while the National Anthem is being played.'

"Mel Clemens, Marriott's general manager at the stadium, said the second memo clarified the first memo."

—Associated Press

8. These so-called forfeiture laws are a serious abridgment of a person's constitutional rights. In some states, district attorneys' offices have only to claim that a person has committed a drug-related crime to seize the person's assets. So fat-cat DAs can get rich without ever getting around to proving that anybody is guilty of a crime.

9. "A few years ago, the deficit got so horrendous that even Congress was embarrassed. Faced with this problem, the lawmakers did what they do best. They passed another law."

—Abe Mellinkoff, in the San Francisco Chronicle

10. "[U]mpires are baseball's designated grown-ups and, like air-traffic controllers, are paid to handle pressure."

—George Will

11. "Last season should have made it clear to the moguls of baseball that something still isn't right with the game—something that transcends residual fan anger from the players' strike. Abundant evidence suggests that baseball still has a long way to go."

—Stedman Graham, Inside Sports

12. "As you know, resolutions [in the California State Assembly] are about as meaningful as getting a Publishers' Clearinghouse letter saying you're a winner."

—Greg Lucas, in the San Francisco Chronicle

13. The entire gain in the stock market in the first four months of the year was due to a mere fifty stocks.

14. Thinkers who entertain the possibility that there are lots of universes have invented a new term for the entire ensemble: "the multiverse." Why believe in the multiverse? The "pro" camp has essentially two kinds of arguments.

—Jim Holt, Slate *online magazine*

15. "[Supreme Court Justice Antonin] Scalia's ideology is a bald and naked concept called 'Majoritarianism.' Only the rights of the majority are protected."

—Letter to the editor of the San Luis Obispo Telegram-Tribune

16. "Mimi Rumpp stopped praying for a winning lottery ticket years ago. . . . But after a doctor told her sister Miki last year that she needed a kidney transplant, the family began praying for a donor. . . . Less than a year later, Miki has a new kidney, courtesy of a bank teller in Napa, Calif., to whom she had told her story. The teller was the donor; she was so moved by Miki's plight she had herself tested and discovered she was a perfect match. Coincidence? Luck? Divine intervention? Rumpp is sure: 'It was a miracle.'"

—Newsweek

▲ 17. "We are about to witness an orgy of self-congratulation as the self-appointed environmental experts come out of their yurts, teepees, and grant-maintained academic groves to lecture us over the impending doom of the planet and agree with each other about how it is evil humanity and greedy 'big business' that is responsible for it all."

—*Tim Worstall, in* New Times

18. "In the 1980s, Central America was awash in violence. Tens of thousands of people fled El Salvador and Guatemala as authoritarian governments seeking to stamp out leftist rebels turned to widespread arrests and death squads."

—USA Today

Exercise 5-19

Discuss the following stereotypes in class. Do they invoke the same kind of images for everyone? Which are negative and which are positive? How do you think they came to be stereotypes? Is there any "truth" behind them?

1. soccer mom
2. Religious Right
3. dumb blonde
4. tax-and-spend liberal
5. homosexual agenda
6. redneck
7. radical feminist
8. contented housewife
9. computer nerd
10. Tea Partier
11. interior decorator
12. Washington insider
13. Earth mother
14. frat rat
15. Deadhead
16. trailer trash

Exercise 5-20

Your instructor will give you three minutes to write down as many positive and negative stereotypes as you can. Are there more positive stereotypes on your list or more negative ones? Why do you suppose that is?

Exercise 5-21

Write two brief paragraphs describing the same person, event, or situation—that is, both paragraphs should have the same informative content. The first paragraph should be written in a *purely* informative way, using language that is as neutral as possible; the second paragraph should be slanted as much as possible either positively or negatively (your choice).

Exercise 5-22

Explain the difference between a weaseler and a downplayer. Find a clear example of each in a newspaper, magazine, or other source. Next find an example of a phrase that is sometimes used as a weaseler or downplayer but that is used appropriately or neutrally in the context of your example.

Exercise 5-23

Critique these comparisons, using the questions discussed in the text as guides.

▲ 1. You've got to be kidding. Paltrow is much superior to Blanchett as an actor.

2. Blondes have more fun.

3. The average chimp is smarter than the average monkey.

▲ 4. The average grade given by Professor Smith is a C. So is the average grade given by Professor Algers.

5. Crime is on the increase. It's up by 160 percent over last year.

6. Classical musicians, on the average, are far more talented than rock musicians.

▲ 7. Long-distance swimming requires much more endurance than long-distance running.

8. "During the monitoring period, the amount of profanity on the networks increased by 45–47 percent over a comparable period from the preceding year. A clear trend toward hard profanity is evident."

   —*Don Wildmon, founder of the National Federation for Decency*

9. "Organizations such as EMILY's List and the Women's Campaign Fund encourage thousands of small contributors to participate, helping to offset the economic power of the special interests. The political system works better when individuals are encouraged to give to campaigns."

   —*Adapted from the* Los Angeles Times

▲ 10. Which is more popular, the movie *Gone With the Wind* or Bing Crosby's version of the song "White Christmas"?

Exercise 5-24

In groups, or individually if your instructor prefers, critique these comparisons, using the questions discussed in the text as guides.

▲ 1. If you worry about the stock market, you have reason. The average stock now has a price-to-earnings ratio of around 25:1.

2. Students are much less motivated than they were when I first began teaching at this university.

3. Offhand, I would say the country is considerably more religious than it was twenty years ago.

▲ 4. In addition, for the first time since 1960, a majority of Americans now attend church regularly.

5. You really should switch to a high-fiber diet.

6. Hire Ricardo. He's more knowledgeable than Annette.

▲ 7. Why did I give you a lower grade than your roommate? Her paper contained more insights than yours, that's why.

8. Golf is a considerably more demanding sport than tennis.

9. Yes, our prices are higher than they were last year, but you get more value for your dollar.

▲ 10. So, tell me, which do you like more, fried chicken or Volkswagens?

Exercise 5-25

Individually or in a group effort, find a YouTube commentary that makes use of a selection of rhetorical devices. Identify as many as you can and compare your analysis with those of your classmates.

Exercise 5-26

Look through an issue of *Time, Newsweek,* or another newsmagazine, and find a photograph that portrays its subject in an especially good or bad light—that is, one that does a nonverbal job of creating slant regarding the subject.

Exercise 5-27

In groups, write captions that seem to fit the photo on page 155. Discussion should be about which caption fits best and why.

Exercise 5-28

After removing the slanting devices, diagram the argument in the box on page 169.

Writing Exercises

1. The illustration on the next page is for an article on banks and bankers in *Rolling Stone Magazine* online. After seeing the illustration but before reading the article, how sympathetic to bankers would you expect it to be? Try to come up with a couple of sentences that you think the image illustrates—you'll probably need some forceful language.

2. Your instructor will select an essay from those in Appendix 1 and ask you to identify as many rhetorical devices as you can find. (Your instructor may narrow the scope of the assignment to just certain paragraphs.)

3. Over the past decade, reportedly more than 2,000 illegal immigrants have died trying to cross the border into the southwestern United States. Many deaths have resulted from dehydration in the desert heat and from freezing to death on cold winter nights. A San Diego–based nonprofit

humanitarian organization now leaves blankets, clothes, and water at stations throughout the desert and mountain regions for the immigrants. Should the organization do this? Its members say they are providing simple humanitarian aid, but critics accuse them of encouraging illegal activity. Take a stand on the issue and defend your position in writing. Then identify each rhetorical device you used.

4. Until recently, tiny Stratton, Ohio, had an ordinance requiring all door-to-door "canvassers" to obtain a permit from the mayor. Presumably, the ordinance was intended to protect the many senior citizens of the town from harm by criminals who might try to gain entry by claiming to be conducting a survey. The ordinance was attacked by the Jehovah's Witnesses, who thought it violated their First Amendment right to free speech. The Supreme Court agreed and struck down the law in 2002. Should it have? Defend your position in a brief essay without using rhetoric. Alternatively, defend your position and use rhetorical devices, but identify each device you use.

More Rhetorical Devices

Psychological and Related Fallacies

F 267 74

Students will learn to . . .

1. Recognize and name fallacies that appeal directly to emotion

2. Recognize and name fallacies that appeal to psychological elements other than emotion

Recently, we've watched the country's leaders and lawmakers slog through some pretty heavy rhetoric as they dealt with health care reform, reform of the financial system, and the midterm elections of federal and state officials. We've also heard some pretty good arguments and seen some pretty good evidence—mainly in the form of studies we believe were done in a professional manner by trustworthy people—that such reforms are needed. But determining which information is "good"—something we, of course, must do to participate successfully in a democracy—can be difficult amidst the clatter and bang of warring political parties, adversarial media personalities, rantings (and sometimes unreliable information) from the blogosphere, and shouting in the streets. In fact, the emotional tone of public discussion and debate has lately reached levels we haven't seen since the 1960s, and the rhetoric often seems more gratuitously misleading now than it did in those days. (It may be that your authors were simply too young to recognize it back then, of course. Ahem.)

As it becomes more difficult to find serious discussions of important issues, it gets easier and easier to find examples of rhetorical devices designed to provoke emotional, knee-jerk reactions. Unfortunately (for us as individuals as well as for public policy), it can be altogether too easy to allow emotional responses to take the place of sound judgment and careful thinking. In this chapter, we'll target some specific devices designed to prompt ill-considered reactions rather than sound judgment—devices that go beyond the rhetorical coloration we talked about in the last chapter. The stratagems we'll discuss sometimes masquerade as arguments, complete with premises and conclusions and language that would suggest argumentation. But while they may be made to *look* or *sound* like arguments, they don't provide legitimate grounds for accepting a conclusion. In place of good reasons for a conclusion, most of the schemes we'll look at in this chapter offer us considerations that are emotionally or psychologically linked to the issue in question. The support they may appear to offer is only pretended support; you might think of them as pieces of pretend reasoning, or **pseudoreasoning.**

The devices in this chapter thus all count as fallacies (a fallacy is a mistake in reasoning). The rhetorical devices we discussed in the last chapter—euphemisms, innuendo, and so forth—aren't fallacies. Of course, *we* commit a fallacy if we think a claim has been supported when the "support" is nothing more than rhetorically persuasive language.

People constantly accept fallacies as legitimate arguments; but the reverse mistake can also happen. We must be careful not to dismiss *legitimate* arguments as fallacies just because they *remind* us of a fallacy. Often, beginning students in logic have this problem. They read about fallacies like the ones we cover here and then think they see them everywhere. These fallacies are common, but they are not everywhere; and you sometimes must consider a specimen carefully before accepting or rejecting it. The exercises we'll supply will help you learn to do this, because they contain a few reasonable arguments mixed in with the fallacies.

All the fallacies in this chapter have in common the fact that what pretends to be a premise is actually irrelevant to the conclusion. That is, even if the premise is true, it does not provide any reason for believing that the conclusion is true.

FALLACIES THAT INVOLVE APPEALS TO EMOTION

One can arrange fallacies into groups in a number of ways: fallacies of relevance, of ambiguity, of presumption, of distraction, and so on. We've chosen in this chapter to talk first about fallacies that involve appeals to emotion, followed by fallacies that depend in part on psychological impact but that do not appeal directly to one emotion or another. Incidentally, we don't want to give the idea that all appeals to emotion are fallacious, misleading, or bad in some other way. Often we accomplish our greatest good works as a result of such appeals. One burden of the next section is to help you distinguish between relevant and irrelevant calls on our emotions.

The Argument from Outrage

A while back, an article in the *Washington Post* by Ceci Connolly summarized a *New England Journal of Medicine* report that gave credit to new medical technology for lowered battlefield death rates in the wars in Iraq and Afghanistan. Many fewer casualties were dying than had ever been the case in wartime before. The most widely heard radio talk show host in America,

Rush Limbaugh, made use of this report to express his outrage at liberal critics of the war.

They're just livid—the press, the leftists in this country—are just upset there are not enough deaths to get people outraged and protesting in the streets against the war. They're mad these doctors are saving lives. They want deaths!

His voice was tense with disbelief and indignation that "the Left" wanted more soldiers to die.* This technique of expressing outrage—anybody who doesn't see *this* point must be a fool or a traitor!—is one we've identified with Limbaugh because he was one of the early masters of the method; we've even considered referring to the use of outrage to persuade people as "the Limbaugh fallacy." But the technique is not unique to Limbaugh, of course; it's typical of today's hard-line talk show people. And apparently it works, if the people who call in to the programs are any indication, since they tend to be as outraged at the goings-on as the hosts of the programs. That's the idea, of course. If a person gets angry enough about something, if one is in the throes of righteous indignation, then it's all too easy to throw reason and good sense out the window and accept whatever alternative is being offered by the speaker just from indignation alone.

Now, does this mean that we never have a right to be angry? Of course not. Anger is not a fallacy, and there are times when it's entirely appropriate. However, when we are angry—and the angrier or more outraged we are, the more true this becomes—it's easy to become illogical, and it can happen in two ways. *First, we may think we have been given a reason for being angry when in fact we have not.* It is a mistake to think that something is wrong just because it makes somebody angry, even if it's us whom it seems to anger. It's easy to mistake a feeling of outrage for evidence of something, but it isn't evidence of anything, really, except our anger.

Second, we may let the anger we feel as the result of one thing influence our evaluations of an unrelated thing. If we're angry over what we take to be the motives of somebody's detractors, we must remember that their motives are a separate matter from whether their criticisms are accurate; they might still be right. Similarly, if a person does something that makes us mad, that doesn't provide us a reason for downgrading him on some other matter, nor would it be a reason for upgrading our opinion of someone else.

The **argument from outrage,** ** then, consists of inflammatory words (or thoughts) followed by a "conclusion" of some sort. It substitutes anger for reason and judgment in considering an issue. It is a favorite strategy of dema-

---

* We should say that our own investigation could not turn up anyone, from the Left or anywhere else, who wanted more Americans to die. We did find, however, that one result of the new technology was a much higher number of soldiers who were returning alive but seriously wounded, including great numbers of amputees. (The 6 percent amputee rate for wounded soldiers is about double that of previous wars, due primarily to the widespread use of roadside bombs.)

** Although we use the phrase "argument from outrage" here, we should make it clear that evoking a person's sense of outrage does not count as making an argument, although as indicated, this emotional appeal is very often a substitute for an argument.

In the Media

Wishful Thinking

Fashion magazines are chock full of ads that are designed to associate a product with beautiful images (as discussed in Chapter 4). But even if using a product might make you smell like the guy in the photo, it isn't likely to change anything else—to believe otherwise is to engage in wishful thinking, discussed later in this chapter.

gogues. In fact, it is *the* favorite strategy of demagogues. Let's say the issue is whether gay marriages should be legal. Left-of-center demagogues may wax indignantly about "narrow-minded fundamentalist bigots dictating what people can do in their bedrooms"—talk calculated to get us steamed although it really has nothing to do with the issue. On the other side, conservative demagogues may allude to gays' demanding "special rights." Nobody wants someone else to get special rights, and when we hear about somebody "demanding" them, our blood pressure goes up. But wanting a right other people have is not wanting a special right; it's wanting an equal right.

A particularly dangerous type of "argument" from outrage is known as **scapegoating**—blaming a certain group of people, or even a single person (like George W. Bush or Barack Obama), for all of life's troubles. George Wallace, the former governor of Alabama who ran for president in 1968 on a "states' rights platform" (which then was a code word for white supremacy) said he could get good old Southern boys to do anything by "whupping" them into a frenzy over Northern civil rights workers.

"Arguments" based on outrage are so common that the fallacy ranks high on our list of the top ten fallacies of all time, which can be found inside the front cover. It's unfortunate they are so common—history demonstrates constantly that anger is a poor lens through which to view the world. Policies adopted in

The idea behind [talk radio] is to keep the base riled up.

—Republican political advisor BRENT LAUDER, explaining what talk radio is for.

Real Life

Prudential Grounds Versus Rational Grounds

A scary or threatening situation can provide us with a prudential reason for acting on a claim, even though, outside the immediate circumstances, we would not accept it. For example, a person or organization might agree to pay a settlement to a person who claims his back was injured on their property, even though they believe, with good reason, that he is faking the injury. The fear of losing an even bigger sum in court provides prudential grounds for paying, even though they would never accept the claim that they should pay except for the threatening circumstances.

anger are seldom wise, as any parent will tell you who has laid down the law in a fit of anger.

Scare Tactics

George Wallace didn't just try to anger the crowds when he told them what Northern civil rights workers were up to; he tried to *scare* them. When people become angry or afraid, they don't think clearly. They follow blindly. Demagogues like Wallace like to dangle scary scenarios in front of people.

Trying to scare people into doing something or accepting a position is using **scare tactics.** One way this might be done is the George Wallace method—dangling a frightening picture in front of someone. A simpler method might be to threaten the person, a special case of scare tactics known as **argument by force.** Either way, if the idea is to get people to substitute fear for reason and judgment when taking a position on an issue, it is a fallacy. Likewise, it is a fallacy to succumb to such techniques when others use them on us. (This does *not* mean you shouldn't give up your wallet to the guy with the gun aimed at your head. See the box "Prudential Grounds Versus Rational Grounds," above.)

Fear can befuddle us as easily as can anger, and the mistakes that happen are similar in both instances. Wallace's listeners may not have noticed (or may not have cared) that Wallace didn't actually give them *evidence* that civil rights workers were doing whatever it was he portrayed them as doing; the portrayal was its own evidence, you might say. When we are befuddled with fear, we may not notice we lack evidence that the scary scenario is real. Imagine someone talking about global warming: The speaker may paint a picture so alarming we don't notice that he or she doesn't provide evidence that global warming is actually happening. Or take gay marriages again. Someone might warn us of presumably dire consequences if gay people are allowed to marry—we'll be opening "Pandora's box"; marriage will become meaningless; homosexuality will become rampant; society will collapse—but he or she may issue these warnings without providing details as to why (or how) the consequences might actually come about. The consequences are so frightening they apparently don't need proof.

Fear of one thing, X, may also affect evaluation of an unrelated thing, Y. You have your eye on a nice house and are considering buying it, and then the real estate agent frightens you by telling you the seller has received other offers and will sell soon. Some people in this situation might overestimate what they really can afford to pay.

To avoid translating fear of one thing into an evaluation of some unrelated thing, we need to be clear on what issues our fears are relevant to. Legitimate warnings do not involve irrelevancies and do not qualify as scare tactics. "You should be careful of that snake—it's deadly poisonous" might be a scary thing to say to someone, but we don't make a mistake in reasoning when we say it, and neither does the other person if he or she turns and runs into the house. Suppose, however, that the Michelin tire people show an ad featuring a sweet (and vulnerable) baby in a ring of automobile tires. Showing pictures of car tires around infants will produce disquieting associations in any observer, and it wouldn't be unreasonable to check our tires when we see this ad. But the issue raised by the Michelin people is whether to buy *Michelin* tires, and the fear of injuring or killing a child by driving on unsafe tires does not bear on the question of *which* tires to buy. The Michelin ad isn't a legitimate warning; it's scare tactics.

Other Fallacies Based on Emotions

Other emotions work much like anger and fear as sources of mistakes in reasoning. *Compassion*, for example, is a fine thing to have. There is absolutely nothing wrong with feeling sorry for someone. But when feeling sorry for someone drives us to a position on an unrelated matter, the result is the fallacy known as **argument from pity.** We have a job that needs doing; Helen can barely support her starving children and needs work desperately. But does Helen have the skills we need? We may not care if she does; and if we don't, nobody can fault us for hiring her out of compassion. But feeling sorry for Helen may lead us to misjudge her skills or overestimate her abilities, and that is a mistake in reasoning. Her skills are what they are, regardless of her need. Or, suppose you need a better grade in this course to get into law school or to avoid academic disqualification or whatever. If you think you *deserve* or have *earned* a better grade because you need a better grade, or you try to get your instructor to think you deserve a better grade by trying to make him or her feel sorry for you, that's the argument from pity. Or, if you think someone *else*

Real Life

Knee Operation Judged Useless
Fake Surgery Worked Just as Well in Cases of Osteoarthritis.

> Here we are doing all this surgery on people and it's all a sham.
>
> —Dr. Baruch Brody, Baylor College of Medicine

Wishful thinking—allowing our desires and hopes to color our beliefs and influence our judgment—is common indeed. A powerful illustration of wishful thinking is the placebo effect, where subjects perceive improvement in a medical condition when they receive what they think is a medication but in fact is an inactive substance. Even surgical procedures, apparently, are subject to a placebo effect, judging from a study of a popular and expensive knee operation for arthritis. People who have had this procedure swear by it as significantly reducing pain. But researchers at the Houston Veterans Affairs Medical Center and Baylor College of Medicine discovered that subjects who underwent placebo (fake) surgery said exactly the same thing. Furthermore, when they tested knee functions two years after the surgery, the researchers discovered that the operation doesn't improve knee functions at all.

Source: *Sacramento Bee*, from New York Times News Service.

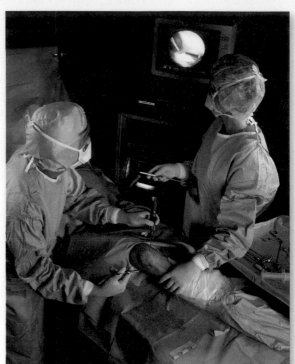

deserves a better grade because of the hardships he or she (or his or her parents) suffered, that's also the "argument" from pity.

Envy and *jealousy* can also confuse our thinking. Compassion, a desirable emotion, may tempt us to emphasize a person's good points; envy and jealousy tempt us to exaggerate someone's bad points. When we find fault with a person because of envy, we are guilty of the fallacy known as **argument from envy.** "Well, he may have a lot of money, but he certainly has bad manners" would be an example of this if it is envy that prompts us to criticize him.

Pride, on the other hand, can lead us to exaggerate *our own* accomplishments and abilities and can lead to our making other irrelevant judgments as well. It especially makes us vulnerable to **apple polishing**, by which we mean old-fashioned flattery. Moore recently sat on a jury in a criminal case involving alleged prostitution and pandering at a strip club; the defendant's attorney told the members of the jury it would take *"an unusually discerning jury"* to see that the law, despite its wording, wasn't really intended to apply to someone like his client. Ultimately, the jury members did find with the defense, but let us hope it wasn't because the attorney flattered their ability to discern things. Allowing praise of oneself to substitute for judgment about the truth

Real Life

Patriotic Passion

The 2010 health proposals brought fierce emotional responses from opponents.

of a claim, or trying to get others to do this, as the lawyer did, is the apple-polishing fallacy.

Feelings of *guilt* work similarly. "How could you not invite Jennifer to your wedding? She would never do that to you, and you know she must be very hurt." The remark is intended to make someone feel sorry for Jennifer, but even more fundamentally, it is supposed to induce a sense of guilt. Eliciting feelings of guilt to get others to do or not to do something, or to accept the view that they should or should not do it, is popularly known as putting a **guilt trip** on someone, which is to commit a fallacy. Parents sometimes use this tactic with children when they (the parents) won't (or can't) offer a clear explanation of why something should or shouldn't be done. Certainly, if the child knowingly does something wrong, he or she should feel guilty; but whatever has been done isn't wrong *because* he or she feels guilty.

Hopes, desires, and aversions can also lead us astray logically. The fallacy known as **wishful thinking** happens when we accept or urge acceptance (or rejection) of a claim simply because it would be pleasant (or unpleasant) if it were true. Some people, for example, may believe in God simply on the basis of wishful thinking or desire for an afterlife. A smoker may refuse to acknowledge the health hazards of smoking. We've had students who are in

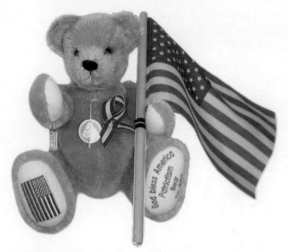

This "Patriotism Bear" is all decked out with flags, medals, and patches. He sells for $119.99 from Dollsville on the Web. Whether motivated by patriotism or profits, there are plenty of people ready to cash in on the patriotism bandwagon.

Patriotism is the last refuge of a scoundrel.

—SAMUEL JOHNSON, 1775

Boswell, Johnson's biographer, does not indicate what the context is here, but he does say that it is *false* patriotism to which Johnson referred.

denial about the consequences of cutting classes. The wishful-thinking fallacy also underlies much of the empty rhetoric of "positive thinking"—rhetoric that claims "you are what you want to be" and other such slogans. As obvious (and as obviously fallacious) as it may appear when you read about it here, wishful thinking can be a powerful influence and can sometimes defeat all but our most committed efforts to do the rational thing.

Most people desire to be liked or accepted by some circle of other people and are averse to having the acceptance withdrawn. A *desire for acceptance* can motivate us to accept a claim not because of its merits but because we will gain someone's approval (or will avoid having approval withdrawn). When we do this or try to get someone else to do it, the fallacy is the **peer pressure "argument."** Now, obviously nobody ever said anything quite so blatant as "Ralph, this claim is true because we won't like you anymore if you don't accept it." Peer pressure is often disguised or unstated, but anyone going through an American high school, where you can lose social standing merely by being seen with someone who isn't "in," knows it is a real force. Kids who feel ostracized sometimes take guns to school.

It doesn't have to be one's associates who exert peer pressure, either. In scientific experiments, people will actually revise what they say they saw if a group of strangers in the same room deny having seen the same thing.

One very common fallacy that is closely related to the peer pressure "argument" involves one's sense of *group identification,* which people experience when they are part of a group—a team, a club, a school, a gang, a state, a nation, the Elks, the Tea Party movement, the U.S.A., Mauritius, you name it. Let's define the **groupthink fallacy** as substituting pride of membership in a group for reason and deliberation in arriving at a position on an issue; and let's include the fallacy in our list of the top ten fallacies of all time, because it is exceedingly common. One obvious form of this fallacy involves national pride, or **nationalism**—a powerful and fierce emotion that can lead to blind endorsement of a country's policies and practices. ("My country right or wrong" explicitly discourages critical thinking and encourages blind patriotism.) Nationalism is also invoked to reject, condemn, or silence criticism of one's country as unpatriotic or treasonable (and may or may not involve an element of peer pressure). If a letter writer expresses a criticism of America on the opinion page of your local newspaper on Monday, you can bet that by the end of the week there will be a response dismissing the criticism with the "argument" that if so-and-so doesn't like it here, he or she ought to move to Russia (or Cuba or Iraq or Iran).

Groupthink does not play cultural or political favorites, either. On the opposite side of the political spectrum are what some people call the "blame America first" folks. The groupthink ethic of this club includes, most importantly, automatically assuming that whatever is wrong in the world is the result of some U.S. policy. The club has no formal meetings or rules for membership, but flying an American flag would be grounds for derision and instant dismissal.

Groupthink "reasoning" is certainly not limited to political groups, either. It occurs whenever one's affiliations are of utmost psychological importance.

Remember, these various emotional fallacies, from the "argument" from outrage to the groupthink fallacy, all share certain properties. They often (though not always) contain assertions you might call "premises" and other assertions that you might call a "conclusion." But the "premises" don't actually *support* the "conclusion"; rather, they evoke emotions that make us want to accept the conclusion without support. So, although they can wear the clothing of arguments, they are really pieces of *persuasion* (Chapter 5). Whenever language is used to arouse emotions, it is wise to consider carefully whether any "conclusions" that come to mind have been supported by evidence.

In the passages that follow identify any fallacies that were discussed in the previous section of the text. There may be examples in which no fallacy occurs—don't find them where they don't exist!

Exercise 6-1

▲ 1. The tax system in this country is unfair and ridiculous! Just ask anyone!

2. Overheard:
"Hmmmm. Nice day. Think I'll go catch some rays."
"Says here in this magazine that doing that sort of thing is guaranteed to get you a case of skin cancer."
"Yeah, I've heard that, too. I think it's a bunch of baloney, personally. If that were true, you wouldn't be able to do anything—no tubing, skiing, nothing. You wouldn't even be able to just plain lie out in the sun. Ugh!"

3. I've come before you to ask that you rehire Professor Johnson. I realize that Mr. Johnson does not have a Ph.D., and I am aware that he has yet to publish his first article. But Mr. Johnson is over forty now, and he has a wife and two high-school-aged children to support. It will be very difficult for him to find another teaching job at his age, I'm sure you will agree.

▲ 4. JUAN: But, Dad, I like Horace. Why shouldn't I room with him, anyway?
JUAN'S DAD: Because I'll cut off your allowance, that's why!

5. That snake has markings like a coral snake. Coral snakes are deadly poisonous, so you'd better leave it alone!

6. HE: Tell you what. Let's get some ice cream for a change. Sunrise Creamery has the best—let's go there.

SHE: Not that old dump! What makes you think their ice cream is so good, anyway?

HE: Because it is. Besides, that old guy who owns it never gets any business anymore. Every time I go by the place, I see him in there all alone, just staring out the window, waiting for a customer. He can't help it that he's in such an awful location. I'm sure he couldn't afford to move.

▲ 7. "Listen, Ruth, we've been together three years, now, and you can't just decide to break up with me just like that. Why do you say you don't care for me anymore? After all, you're the only decent thing in my life, and if you leave, I'll just be absolutely miserable; I've cried until I don't have any tears left."

8. "Jim, I'm very disappointed you felt it necessary to talk to the media about the problems here in the department. When you join the FBI, you join a family, and you shouldn't want to embarrass your family."

9. "Listen, Steve lives in a huge house, drives an expensive car, and makes twice the money you do. You're never going to live like he does unless you cut some corners."

▲ 10. A fictitious western governor: "Yes, I have indeed accepted $550,000 in campaign contributions from power companies. But as I stand here before you, I can guarantee you that not one dime of that money has affected any decision I've made. I make decisions based on data, not on donors."

SOME NON-EMOTION-BASED FALLACIES

The next three fallacy families—(1) red herrings, (2) appeals to popularity and tradition and such, and (3) rationalizing—all have psychological elements, but they do not make the same kind of direct emotional appeal that we find in the preceding fallacies.

Red Herring/Smoke Screen

When a person brings a topic into a conversation that distracts from the original point, especially if the new topic is introduced in order to distract, the person is said to have introduced a **red herring.** (It is so called because dragging a herring across a trail will cause a dog to leave the original trail and follow

In Depth

The "True For . . ." Cop-Out

Sometimes, especially when a controversial subject is under discussion, you'll hear someone say, "Well, that may be true for you, but it isn't true for me."

If you stop to think about it, this is a peculiar thing to say. Certainly if the issue is about an objective fact—whether there is water on the moon, for example—then if it's "true for" anybody, it's true for everybody. As somebody recently said, you can choose your own opinions, but you can't choose your own facts; the facts are just what they are, and they're the same for everybody.

Of course, one person can *believe* something is true while another *believes* it isn't true, but that's a different matter entirely. If that is what the speaker means, he should simply say so clearly instead of using the paradoxical version we're calling a cop-out.

When we say the expression is a cop-out, we mean it's simply a way of saying "I don't want to talk about this anymore." It's a discussion ender. And it certainly does not do anything to resolve whatever the original issue was. We see this expression used most often, perhaps, in matters of religion, where many people hold strong beliefs, but for one reason or another, they do not want to engage in discussions about them.

The only place where our "true for . . . " expression is *not* a cop-out is when the claim in question is subjective. For example, "Zinfandel tastes better than merlot." This remark really *can* be true for one person and false for another, because they may really have two different tastes. Remember, whenever you hear the "true for..." expression about an objective factual matter, it's just a way of saying "I'm done talking."

In the Media

A Red Herring in a Letter to *Time*

Time's coverage of the medical marijuana controversy was thoughtful and scrupulously researched. But what argues most persuasively for a ban on marijuana is the extraordinary threat the drug poses for adolescents. Marijuana impairs short-term memory, depletes energy and impedes acquisition of psychosocial skills. Perhaps the most chilling effect is that it retards maturation for young people. A significant number of kids who use lots of pot simply don't grow up. So it is hardly surprising that marijuana is the primary drug for more than half the youngsters in the long-term residential substance-abuse programs that Phoenix House operates throughout the country.

       —MITCHELL S. ROSENTHAL, M.D., president, Phoenix House, New York City

The issue is legalization of marijuana for *adults;* the question of what it would do to children, who presumably would be prohibited from its use, is a red herring.

Source: *Time*, November 28, 2002.

---

the path of the herring.) In the strip-joint jury trial we mentioned earlier, the defendant was charged with pandering; but the prosecuting attorney introduced evidence that the defendant had also sold liquor to minors. That was a red herring that had nothing to do with pandering.

The difference between red herrings and their close relatives, **smoke screens,** is subtle (and really not a matter of crucial importance). Generally speaking, red herrings distract by pulling one's attention away from one topic and toward another; smoke screens tend to pile issues on or to make them extremely complicated until the original is lost in the (verbal) "smoke." Sometimes, the red herring or smoke screen involves an appeal to emotion, but often it does not. When Bill Clinton had missiles fired at terrorists in Sudan, he was accused of creating a red herring to deflect public scrutiny from the Monica Lewinsky business. When George W. Bush talked about Iraq having missiles capable of threatening the United States, about that country's potential of having a nuclear weapon "within six months," and about similar possible Iraqi threats, he was accused of putting up a smoke screen to hide his real reasons for wanting to attack Iraq, which were said to be oil interests and his own personal desire to complete his father's unfinished business.

Let's take another example, this one made up but typical of what often happens. Suppose that Felipe Calderón, the president of Mexico, holds a press conference, and a reporter asks him whether his use of federal troops in Juárez has made the city any safer from drug-related murders. Mr. Calderón answers, "I can guarantee you that everything the federal government can do to pacify the situation in Juárez is now being done."

Calderón has avoided the reporter's original question, possibly because he is not interested in admitting that the city is *not* any safer. He has changed the issue to one of what kind of effort the government is making. In so doing, he has dragged a red herring across the trail, so to speak. The government may or may not be doing all it can to keep the peace in Juárez, but in either case

We admit that this measure is popular. But we also urge you to note that there are so many bond issues on this ballot that the whole concept is getting ridiculous.

—A generic red herring (unclassifiable irrelevance) from a California ballot pamphlet that is a separate matter from whether citizens are safer in Juárez since federal troops arrived.*

Let's imagine that the conversation continues like this:

> REPORTER: "Mr. Calderón, polls say that most of the country believes that the government has failed to make the situation safer. How do you answer your critics?"
>
> FELIPE CALDERÓN: We are making progress toward reassuring people, but quite frankly our efforts have been hampered by the tendency of the press to concentrate on the negative side of the issue."

Once again (in our fictional news conference), Calderón brings in a red herring to sidestep the issue raised by the reporter.

Whether a distraction or an obfuscation is a plain red herring or a smoke screen is often difficult to tell in real life, and it's better to spend your energy getting a discussion back on track rather than worrying which type you have before you.

Many of the other fallacies we have been discussing in this chapter (and will be discussing in the next chapter) qualify, in some version or other, as red herrings/smoke screens. For example, a defense attorney might talk about a defendant's miserable upbringing to steer a jury's attention away from the charges against the person; doing this would qualify as an appeal to pity as well as a smoke screen/red herring. Likewise, a prosecuting attorney may try to get a jury so angry about a crime it doesn't notice the weakness of the evidence pointing to the defendant. This would be an argument from outrage—and a red herring.

To simplify things, your instructor may reserve the red herring/smoke screen categories for irrelevancies that don't qualify as one of the other fallacies mentioned in this or the next chapter. In other words, he or she may tell you that if something qualifies as, say, an argument from outrage, you should call it that rather than a red herring or a smoke screen.

Everyone Knows . . .

In Chapter 5, we examined such proof surrogates as "Everyone knows . . ." and "It's only common sense that . . .". Phrases like this are often used when a speaker or writer doesn't really have an argument.

Such phrases often appear in peer pressure "arguments" ("Pardner, in these parts everyone thinks . . ."). They also are used in the groupthink fallacy ("As any red-blooded American patriot knows, . . .). There is, however, a third way these phrases can be used. An example would be when Robert Novak said on CNN's *Crossfire*, "Liberals are finally admitting what everyone knows, that airline safety demands compromise." Novak wasn't applying or evoking peer pressure or groupthink; he was offering "proof" that airline safety demands compromise. His proof is the fact that everyone knows it.

---

*Unfortunately, the number of homicides in Ciudad Juárez went from 317 in 2007 to 1,623 in 2008 and to 2,754 in 2009, according to government reports. That would make it the most dangerous city in the world during the latter two years.

Could somebody please show me one hospital built by a dolphin? Could somebody show me one highway built by a dolphin? Could someone show me one automobile invented by a dolphin?

—RUSH LIMBAUGH, responding to the *New York Times*' claim that dolphins' "behavior and enormous brains suggest an intelligence approaching that of human beings"

Good point. Anyone know of a hospital or highway built by Rush Limbaugh or an automobile invented by him?

Real Life

Is It Still a Lie If Everybody Does It?

"Shell [Oil Company] was charged with misleading advertising in its Platformate advertisements. A Shell spokesman said: 'The same comment could be made about most good advertising of most products.'"

—SAMM S. BAKER, *The Permissible Lie*

A perfect example of the common-practice fallacy.

When we do this, when we urge someone to accept a claim (or fall prey to someone's doing it to us) simply on the grounds that all or most or some substantial number of people (other than authorities or experts, of course) believe it, we commit the fallacy known as the **appeal to popularity.**

That most people believe something is a fact is not evidence that it is a fact—most people believe in God, for example, but that isn't evidence that God exists. Likewise, if most people didn't believe in God, that wouldn't be evidence that God didn't exist.

Most people seem to assume that bus driving and similar jobs are somehow less desirable than white-collar jobs. The widespread acceptance of this assumption creates its own momentum—that is, we tend to accept it because everybody else does, and we don't stop to think about whether it actually has anything to recommend it. For a lot of people, a job driving a bus might make for a much happier life than a job as a manager.

In *some* instances, we should point out, what people think actually *determines* what is true. The meanings of most words, for example, are determined by popular usage. In addition, it would not be fallacious to conclude that the word "ain't" is out of place in formal speech because most speakers of English believe that it is out of place in formal speech.

There are other cases where what people think is an *indication* of what is true, even if it cannot *determine* truth. If several Bostonians of your acquaintance think that it is illegal to drink beer in their public parks, then you have some reason for thinking that it's true. And if you are told by several Europeans that it is not gauche to eat with your fork in your left hand in Europe, then it is not fallacious to conclude that European manners allow eating with your fork in your left hand. The situation here is one of credibility, which we discussed in Chapter 4. Natives of Boston in the first case and Europeans in the second case can be expected to know more about the two claims in question, respectively, than others know. In a watered-down sense, they are "experts" on the subjects, at least in ways that many of us are not. In general, when the "everyone" who thinks that X is true includes experts about X, then what they think is indeed a good reason to accept X.

Thus, it would be incorrect to automatically label as a fallacy any instance in which a person cites people's beliefs to establish a point. (No "argument" fitting a pattern in this chapter should be dismissed *unthinkingly*.) But it is important to view such references to people's beliefs as red alerts. These are cautionary signals that warn you to look closely for genuine reasons in support of the claim asserted.

Two variations of the appeal to popularity deserve mention: **Appeal to common practice** consists in trying to justify or defend an *action* or *practice* (as distinguished from an assertion or claim) on the grounds that it is common. "I shouldn't get a speeding ticket because everyone drives over the limit" is an example. "Everyone cheats on their taxes, so I don't see why I shouldn't" is another. Now, there is something to watch out for here: When a person defends an action by saying that other people do the same thing, he or she might just be requesting fair play. He or she might be saying, in effect, "Okay, okay, I know it's wrong, but nobody else gets punished, and it would be unfair to single me out." That person isn't trying to justify the action; he or she is asking for equal treatment.

The other variant of the popularity fallacy is the **appeal to tradition,** a name that is self-explanatory. People do things because that's the way things have always been done, and they believe things because that's what people have always believed. But, logically speaking, you don't prove a claim or prove a practice is legitimate on the basis of tradition; when you try to do so, you are guilty of the appeal to tradition fallacy. The fact that it's a tradition among most American children to believe in Santa Claus, for instance, doesn't prove Santa Claus exists; and the fact that it's also a tradition for most American parents to deceive their kids about Santa Claus doesn't necessarily mean it is okay for them to do so. Where we teach, there has been a long tradition of fraternity hazing, and over the years several unfortunate hazing incidents have happened. We have yet to hear a defense of hazing that amounted to anything other than an appeal to tradition, which is equivalent to saying we haven't heard a defense at all.

Rationalizing

Let's say Mr. Smith decides to do something really nice for his wife on her birthday and buys her a new table saw. "This saw wasn't cheap," he tells her. "But you're going to be glad we have it, because it will keep me out in the garage and out of your way when you're working here in the house."

The fallacy in the reasoning in this made-up example is pretty obvious. Mr. Smith is confusing his wife's desires with his own.

When we do this, when we use a false pretext to satisfy our own desires or interests, we're guilty of **rationalizing,** a very common fallacy. It almost made our list of the top ten fallacies of all time.

Now, there is nothing wrong with satisfying one's desires, at least if they don't harm someone or aren't illegal. But in this book, we're talking logic, not morals. Rationalizing involves a confusion in thinking, and to the extent we wish to avoid being confused in our thinking, we should try to avoid rationalizing.

"But," you may be saying, "it is good to do nice things for other people. If you do something that helps them, or that they like, or that benefits the world, what difference does motivation make? If, for whatever reason, the table saw makes Mr. Smith's wife happy, that's what counts."

Now, there is something to be said for this argument, because it is good to make people happy. But whether Mr. Smith's wife is happy or not, there has been a confusion in his thinking, a fallacy. And it is a common fallacy indeed. Obviously, most instances of rationalizing are not as blatant as Mr. Smith's, but people frequently deceive themselves as to their true motives.

Rationalizing need not be selfish, either. Let's say a former oilman is elected governor of a state that produces oil. He may act in what at some level he thinks are the best interests of his state—when in fact he is motivated by a desire to help the oil industry. (Incidentally, you can't just assume he would do this.) To the extent that he is deceiving himself about his true motivation, he is rationalizing. But this isn't *selfish* rationalizing; his actions don't benefit him personally.

Rationalizing, then, involves an element of self-deception, but otherwise it isn't necessarily devious. However, some people encourage others to rationalize because they themselves stand to benefit in some way. "Hey, Smith," his buddy Jones says to him. "That's a fine idea! Really creative. Your wife will really like a saw. Maybe you could build a boat for her, and you and I could go fishing." Jones may or may not say this innocently: If he does, he, too, is guilty of rationalizing; if he doesn't, he's just cynical.

In the following passages, identify any fallacies discussed in the preceding section of the text (red herring/smoke screen; appeals to popularity, tradition, common practice; rationalizing). There may be passages that contain no fallacy.

Exercise 6-2

▲ 1. DEMOCRAT: What do you think of your party's new plan for Social Security?
REPUBLICAN: I think it is pretty good, as a matter of fact.
DEMOCRAT: Oh? And why is that?
REPUBLICAN: Because you Democrats haven't even offered a plan, that's why!

2. FRED: I think we should just buy the new truck and call it a business expense so we can write it off on our taxes.
   ETHEL: I don't know, Fred. That sounds like cheating to me. We wouldn't really use the truck very much in the business, you know.
   FRED: Oh, don't worry about it. This kind of thing is done all the time.

3. A fictitious western governor: "Yes, I have indeed accepted $550,000 in campaign contributions from power companies. But as I stand here before you, I can guarantee you that not one dime of that money has affected any decision I've made. I make decisions based on data, not on donors."

▲ 4. They finally passed the immigration law. Did you see the latest poll? It says that over two-thirds of Americans believe it's going to solve the immigration problem once and for all. It's about time they did the right thing in Congress.

5. REPORTER COKIE ROBERTS: Mr. Cheney, aside from the legal issues that stem from the various United Nations resolutions, isn't there an overriding moral dimension to the suffering of so many Kurdish people in Iraq?
   DICK CHENEY: Well, we recognize that's a tragic situation, Cokie, but there are tragic situations occurring all over the world.

   —*Adapted from an interview on National Public Radio's* Morning Edition

6. I'm going to use the textbook that's on reserve in the library. I'll have to spend more time on the campus, but it's sure better than shelling out over a hundred bucks for one book.

▲ 7. The animal rights people shouldn't pick on rodeos about animal treatment. If they'd come out and see the clowns put smiles on kids' faces and see horses buck off the cowboys and hear the crowd go "ooh" and "ahh" at the bull riding, why, then, they'd change their minds.

8. You know, Selina, I've been thinking lately that we've been putting away money for our retirement for quite a while now, and since the economy seems to be recovering from the recession, I think we're going to be in pretty good shape when we're ready to retire—we'll at least have enough to get by. Meanwhile, I've been looking at these new Ford trucks, and they really come with everything these days, even GPS and satellite radio. And if we put a portion of our income toward purchase of a new truck, it would be a sort of investment in the future itself, you know?

9. What's wrong with socialism? I'll tell you what's wrong with socialism. Americans don't like it, is what's wrong with socialism.

10. Should I spend time doing more of these logic exercises when I could be outside playing golf? Well, one thing is for sure. Doing one or two more exercises won't make a difference to my grade, but playing golf will make a difference to my health.

TWO WRONGS MAKE A RIGHT

Let's say you get tired of the people upstairs stomping around late at night, and so, to retaliate, you rent a tow truck and deposit their car in the river. From an emotional standpoint, you're getting even. From a reasoning standpoint, you're committing the fallacy known as **"two wrongs make a right."** It's a fallacy because wrongful behavior on someone else's part doesn't convert wrongful behavior on your part into rightful behavior any more than illegal behavior on someone else's part converts your illegal activity into legal activity. If an act is wrong, it is wrong. Wrong acts don't cross-pollinate such that one comes out shorn of wrongfulness.

However, there is a well-known and somewhat widely held theory known as *retributivism,* according to which it is acceptable to harm someone in return for a harm he or she has done to you. But we must distinguish legitimate punishment from illegitimate retaliation. A fallacy clearly occurs when we consider a wrong to be justification for *any* retaliatory action, as would be the case if you destroyed your neighbors' car because they made too much noise at night. It is also a fallacy when the second wrong is directed at someone who didn't do the wrong in the first place—a brother or a child of the wrongdoer, for example. And it is a fallacy to defend doing harm to another on the grounds that that individual *would* or *might* do the same to us. This would happen, for example, if we didn't return excess change to a salesclerk on the grounds that "if the situation were reversed," the clerk wouldn't have given us back the money.

On the other hand, it isn't a fallacy to defend an action on the grounds that it was necessary to prevent harm from befalling oneself; bopping a mugger to prevent him from hurting you would be an instance. To take another example, near the end of World War II, the United States dropped two atomic bombs on Japanese cities, killing tens of thousands of civilians. Politicians, historians, and others have argued that the bombing was justified because it helped end the war and thus prevented more casualties from the fighting, including the deaths of more Americans. People have long disagreed on whether the argument provides *sufficient* justification for the bombings, but there is no disagreement about its being a real argument and not empty rhetoric.

Argument Diagram

(1) The people upstairs keep making noise late at night and (2) it bothers me so (3) I have the right to rent a tow truck and deposit their car in the river.

    (1) The people upstairs keep making noise late at night.
    (2) It bothers me.
    **(3) Therefore I have the right to rent a tow truck and deposit
        their car in the river.**

Recap

Fallacies run the gamut from attempts to stir up emotion to attempts to distract us from a subject entirely. In this chapter we've covered a selection of fallacies that are based on appeals to our emotions as well as several others that, while they have a psychological aspect, are less emotion-based.

Fallacies that appeal to emotion:

- Argument from outrage
- Scare tactics
- Argument by force
- Argument from pity
- Argument from envy
- Apple polishing
- Guilt trip
- Wishful thinking
- Peer pressure "argument"
- Groupthink fallacy
- Nationalism

Other fallacies discussed in this chapter don't invoke emotions directly but are closely related to emotional appeals. These include

- Red herring/smoke screen
- Appeal to popularity
- Appeal to common practice
- Appeal to tradition
- Rationalization
- Two wrongs make a right

In all these specimens, there is something one might call a "premise" and something one might call a "conclusion," but the "premise" either fails to support the conclusion or "supports" some tangential claim. In any case, a mistake in reasoning has been made; a fallacy has been committed.

Additional Exercises

In the exercises that follow, we ask you to name fallacies, and your instructor may do the same on an exam. (At the end of Chapter 7, there are more exercises that refer back to the fallacies in this chapter.)

Exercise 6-3

Working in groups, invent a simple, original, and clear illustration of each type of fallacy covered in this chapter. Then, in the class as a whole, select the illustrations that are clearest and most straightforward. Go over these illustrations before doing the remaining exercises in this chapter, and review them before you take a test on this material.

Exercise 6-4

Answer the following questions and explain your answers.

▲   1. A brand of toothpaste is advertised as best selling. How relevant is that to whether to buy the brand?

2. A brand of toothpaste is best selling. How relevant is that to whether to buy that brand?

▲ 3. An automobile is a best-seller in its class. How relevant is that to whether to buy that kind of automobile?

4. A movie is a smash hit. Would that influence your opinion of it? Should it?

5. Your friends are all Republicans. Would that influence your decision about which party to register with? Should it?

6. Your friends are all Democrats. Would that influence what you say about Democrats to them? Should it?

▲ 7. Your friend's father wrote a novel. How relevant is that to whether you should say nice things about the book to your friend?

8. Your friend's mother is running for office. How relevant is that to whether you should vote for her?

9. Your own mother is running for office. How relevant is that to whether she will do a good job? To whether you should vote for her?

▲ 10. Movie critic Roger Ebert gives a movie a "thumbs-up" and calls it one of the best of the year. How relevant is this to whether you should go see the movie?

Exercise 6-5

Which of the following do you believe? Which of the following do you *really* have evidence for? Which of the following do you believe on an "everyone knows" basis? Discuss your answers with other members of your class.

1. Small dogs tend to live longer than large dogs.

2. Coffee has a dehydrating effect.

3. Most people should drink at least eight glasses of water a day.

4. If you are thirsty, it means you are already dehydrated.

5. Rape is not about sex; it's about aggression.

6. Marijuana use leads to addiction to harder drugs.

7. The news media are biased.

8. You get just as much ultraviolet radiation on a cloudy day as on a sunny day.

9. If you don't let yourself get angry every now and then, your anger will build up to the exploding point.

10. Carrots make you see better.

11. Reading in poor light is bad for your eyes.

12. Sitting too close to the TV is bad for your eyes.

13. Warm milk makes you sleepy.

14. Covering your head is the most effective way of staying warm in cold weather.

15. Smoking a cigarette takes seven minutes off your life.

16. Government-run health care management is more (or less—choose one) expensive than private-run health care management.

Exercise 6-6

For each of the passages that follow, determine whether fallacies are present and, if so, whether they fit the categories described in this chapter.

▲ 1. Boss to employee: "I'll be happy to tell you why this report needs to be finished by Friday. If it isn't ready by then, you'll be looking for another job. How's that for a reason?"

2. Mother: "I think he has earned an increase in his allowance. He doesn't have any spending money at all, and he's always having to make excuses about not being able to go out with the rest of his friends because of that."

3. Mother to father: "You know, I really believe that our third grader's friend Joe comes from an impoverished family. He looks to me as though he doesn't get enough to eat. I think I'm going to start inviting him to have dinner at our house once or twice a week."

▲ 4. Statistics show that flying is much safer than driving. So why put your family at risk? This summer, travel the safe way: Fly Fracaso Airlines!

5. One political newcomer to another: "I tell you, Sam, you'd better change those liberal views of yours. The general slant toward conservatism is obvious. You'll be left behind unless you change your mind about some things."

6. If you ask me, I think breaking up with Anton is a big mistake. Have you forgotten how he stuck by you last year when you really needed somebody? Is this how you repay that kind of devotion?

▲ 7. ONE FAN: The field goal has become too big a part of the game. I think it would be more reasonable to change it from a 3-point play to a 2-point play. That would make advancing the ball more important, which is as it should be.
   ANOTHER FAN: Oh, come on. Field goals have always been three points; it's just silly to think of changing a part of the game that's been around for so long.

8. Student speaker: "Why, student fees have jumped by more than 300 percent in just two years! This is outrageous! The governor is working for a balanced budget, but it'll be on the backs of us students, the people who have the very least to spend! It seems pretty clear that these increased student fees are undermining higher education in this state. Anybody who isn't mad about this just doesn't understand the situation."

9. "What? You aren't a Cornhuskers fan? Listen, around here everybody is for the Huskers! This is Nebraska!"

▲ 10. They need to understand that it's okay for the good guys to have nuclear weapons and it's not okay for the bad guys to have them. And the U.S.A. is one of the good guys, you see. The U.S. is always going to do the right thing by these weapons, and we can't trust most of the rest of the world to do that. There's your nuclear arms policy in a nutshell.

Exercise 6-7

For each of the following, determine whether one of the lettered rhetorical devices or fallacies covered in Chapters 5 and 6 occurs in the passage. There may be items that do not contain such devices or fallacies, so be careful!

1. Letter to the editor: "Your food section frequently features recipes with veal, and your ads say veal is a wholesome, nutritious food. Well, I have a different opinion of veal. Do you know how it comes to be on your plate? At birth, a newborn calf is separated from its mother, placed in a dark enclosure, and chained by its neck so it cannot move freely. This limits muscular development so that the animal is tender. It is kept in the dark pen until the day it is cruelly slaughtered."

   a. scare tactics
   b. argument from pity
   c. common practice
   d. wishful thinking
   e. no device or fallacy

2. Listen, Bob. I've met with the rest of our neighbors on the block, and we all agree that your yard really looks terrible. It's embarrassing to all of us. Our conclusion is that you ought to do something about it.

   a. common practice
   b. use of euphemism
   c. use of dysphemism
   d. rationalizing
   e. no device or fallacy

3. Former presidential chief of staff John Sununu was charged with using Air Force executive jets for frequent trips to vacation spots. In a letter to a newsmagazine, a writer observed, "What's all the fuss about? If everybody is doing it, why get excited about Sununu?"

   a. loaded question
   b. stereotyping
   c. argument from outrage
   d. common practice
   e. no device or fallacy

4. I was thinking: Our newspaper boy has not missed a day all year, and he always throws our paper right up here near the front door. I think I'm going to leave him an extra-large tip this Christmas. I know people who do that kind of work don't make a lot of money, and I'm sure he can use it.

   a. downplayer
   b. stereotyping
   c. innuendo
   d. argument from pity
   e. no device or fallacy

5. Hey, watch what you say about my car. You won't see many that old around anymore; it's a real classic.

   a. rhetorical explanation
   b. hyperbole
   c. argument from pity
   d. use of euphemism
   e. no device or fallacy

6. Despite all the fancy technology that went into Sam's new car, it still gets a mere 29 miles per gallon.

   a. use of dysphemism
   b. weaseler
   c. rationalizing
   d. downplayer
   e. no device or fallacy

7. Text messaging teaches people to misspell and adopt the crudest style of writing possible. It's like an advanced degree in Bonehead English.

    a. rationalizing
    b. rhetorical analogy
    c. rhetorical explanation
    d. argument from outrage
    e. no device or fallacy

8. Imagine yourself alone beside your broken-down car at the side of a country road in the middle of the night. Few pass by, and no one stops to help. Don't get caught like that. You need a No-Tel cellular telephone!
    Which of the following best characterizes this passage?

    a. The passage gives someone no reason for buying anything at all.
    b. The passage gives someone no reason for buying a cell phone.
    c. The passage gives someone no reason for buying a No-Tel cell phone.
    d. The passage gives someone a reason for buying a sawed-off shotgun for the car.

Exercise 6-8

For each of the passages that follow, determine whether fallacies are present and, if so, whether they fit the categories described in this chapter.

▲ 1. "Grocers are concerned about *sanitation problems* from beverage residue that Proposition 11 could create. Filthy returned cans and bottles—*over 11 billion a year*—don't belong in grocery stores, where our food is stored and sold. . . . Sanitation problems in other states with similar laws have caused increased use of *chemical sprays* in grocery stores to combat rodents and insects. Vote no on 11."

    —*Argument against Proposition 11, California ballot pamphlet*

2. C'mon, George, the river's waiting and everyone's going to be there. You want me to tell 'em you're gonna worry on Saturday about a test you don't take 'til Tuesday? What're people going to think?

3. ATTENDANT: I'm sorry, sir, but we don't allow people to top off their gas tanks here in Kansas. There's a state law against it, you know.
    RICHARD: What? You've got to be kidding! I've never heard of a place that stopped people from doing that!

▲ 4. One roommate to another: "I'm telling you, Ahmed, you shouldn't take Highway 50 this weekend. In this weather, it's going to be icy and dangerous. Somebody slides off that road and gets killed nearly every winter. And you don't even have any chains for your car!"

5. That, in sum, is my proposal, ladies and gentlemen. You know that I trust and value your judgment, and I am aware I could not find a more astute panel of experts to evaluate my suggestion. Thank you.

6. JARED: In Sweden, atheists and agnostics outnumber believers 2 to 1, and in Germany, less than half the population believes in God. Here in the United States, though, over 80 percent believe in God. I wonder what makes the United States so different.
    ALICE: You've answered your own question. If I didn't believe in God, I'd feel like I stuck out like a sore thumb.

7. One local to another: "I tell you, it's disgusting. These idiot college students come up here and live for four years—and ruin the town—and then vote on issues that affect us long after they've gone. This has got to stop! I say, let only those who have a real stake in the future of this town vote here! Transient kids shouldn't determine what's going to happen to local residents. Most of these kids come from Philadelphia . . . let them vote there."

8. Chair, Department of Rhetoric (to department faculty): "If you think about it, I'm certain you'll agree with me that Mary Smith is the best candidate for department secretary. I urge you to join with me in recommending her to the administration. Concerning another matter, I'm now setting up next semester's schedule, and I hope that I'll be able to give you all the classes you have requested."

9. NELLIE: I really don't see anything special about Sunquist grapefruit. They taste the same as any other grapefruit to me.
NELLIE'S MOM: Hardly! Don't forget that your Uncle Henry owns Sunquist. If everyone buys his fruit, you may inherit a lot of money some day!

10. *"Don't risk letting a fatal accident rob your family of the home they love—on the average, more than 250 Americans die each day because of accidents.* What would happen to your family's home if you were one of them?

"Your home is so much more than just a place to live. It's a community you've chosen carefully . . . a neighborhood . . . a school district . . . the way of life you and your family have come to know. And you'd want your family to continue sharing its familiar comforts, even if suddenly you were no longer there. . . . Now, as a Great Western mortgage customer, you can protect the home you love. . . . Just complete the Enrollment Form enclosed for you."

—Insurance company brochure

11. "You've made your mark and your scotch says it all."

—Glen Haven Reserve

12. Dear Senator Jenkins,
I am writing to urge your support for higher salaries for state correctional facility guards. I am a clerical worker at Kingsford Prison, and I know whereof I speak. Guards work long hours, often giving up weekends, at a dangerous job. They cannot afford expensive houses or even nice clothes. Things that other state employees take for granted, like orthodontia for their children and a second car, are not possibilities on their salaries, which, incidentally, have not been raised in five years. Their dedication deserves better.
Very truly yours, . . .

13. HER: Listen, honey, we've been dating for how long now? Years! I think it's time we thought seriously about getting married.
HIM: Right, ummm, you know what? I think it's time we went shopping for a new car! What do you say to that?

14. There are very good reasons for the death penalty. First, it serves as a deterrent to those who would commit capital offenses. Second, it is just

and fair punishment for the crime committed. Third, reliable opinion polls show that over 70 percent of all Americans favor it. If so many people favor it, it has to be right.

▲ 15. FIRST IDAHOAN: I'll tell you, I think Senator Creighton has done a fine job of representing our state. He's brought a lot of federal money here, and he's on the right side of most of the social issues we care about here.
SECOND IDAHOAN: Aw, come on, man. They caught the guy trying to pick up another man in an airport restroom. Throw him out on the street where he belongs!

16. Frankly, I think the Salvation Army, the Red Cross, and the Wildlife Fund will put my money to better use than my niece Alison and her husband would. They've wasted most of the money I've given them. So I think I'm going to leave a substantial portion of my estate to those organizations instead of leaving it all to my spendthrift relatives.

17. "The president's prosecution of the War on Terror is being handled exactly right. He wasn't elected to do nothing!"

18. Student to teacher: "I've had to miss several classes and some quizzes because of some personal matters back home. I know you have a no-make-up policy, but there was really no way I could avoid having to be out of town; it really was not my fault."

▲ 19. BUD: So, here's the deal. I'll arrange to have your car "stolen," and we'll split the proceeds from selling it to a disposer. Then you file a claim with your insurance company and collect from it.
LOU: Gee, this sounds seriously illegal and dangerous.
BUD: Illegal, yeah, but do you think this is the first time an insurance company ever had this happen? Why, they actually expect it—they even budget money for exactly this sort of thing.

20. Kibitzer, discussing the job Lamar Alexander did as secretary of education: "It was absolutely clear to me that Alexander was not going to do any good for American education. He was way too involved in money-making schemes to give any attention to the job *we* were paying him for. Do you know that back before he was appointed, he and his wife invested five thousand dollars in some stock deal, and four years later that stock was worth over eight hundred thousand dollars? Tell me there's nothing fishy about a deal like that!"

21. My opponent, the evolutionist, offers you a different history and a different self-image from the one I suggest. While I believe that you and I are made in the image of God and are only one step out of the Garden of Eden, he believes that you are made in the image of a monkey and are only one step out of the zoo.

▲ 22. Recently, two Colorado lawmakers got into a shouting match when one of them marched into a news conference the other was holding in opposition to same-sex marriage. Rep. Jim Welker had called the news conference to solicit support for a constitutional amendment to bar gays and lesbians from marrying. Rep. Angie Paccione objected, saying, "We have over 700,000 Coloradans without health care; how could we possibly say gay marriage is more important than health care?"
    Welker then responded, "Gay marriage will open a Pandora's box. Where do you draw the line? A year and a half ago a lady in India married

her dog!" Welker was referring to the marriage of a 9-year-old girl to a stray dog as part of a ritual to ward off an evil spell.

"Oh, for heaven's sake," Paccione said. "Come on, Jim."

"That is true. That's a fact," Welker said.

Paccione replied, "It's not the same to have somebody marry a dog as it is to have two loving people get married. Come on."

23. What makes you think I should put a note on this guy's car? Do you think for a minute he'd have left a note on mine if he'd put a dent in it?

Writing Exercises

1. Find an example of a fallacy in a newspaper editorial or opinion magazine (substitute an example from an advertisement or a letter to the editor only as a last resort and only if your instructor permits it). Identify the issue and what side of the issue the writer supports. Explain why the passage you've chosen does not really support that position—that is, why it involves a fallacy. If the writer's claims do support some other position (possibly on a different, related issue), describe what position they do support.

2. In 1998, the police in Harris County, Texas, responded to a false report about an armed man who was going crazy. They did not find such an individual; but when they entered the home of John Geddes Lawrence, they found him and another man, Tyron Garner, having sex. Both men were arrested and found guilty of violating a Texas law that criminalizes homosexual sex acts. The men challenged their conviction, and the case went to the U.S. Supreme Court in March 2003. A district attorney from the county argued, "Texas has the right to set moral standards of its people."

   Do you agree or disagree with the district attorney's statement? Defend your answer in a one-page essay written in class. Your instructor will have other members of the class read your essay to see if they can find your basic argument in the midst of any rhetoric you may have used. They also will note any fallacies that you may have employed.

3. Should there be an amendment to the U.S. Constitution prohibiting desecration of the U.S. flag? In a one-page essay, defend a "yes" or "no" answer to the question. Your instructor will have other members of the class read your essay, following the instructions in Writing Exercise 2.

4. Listen to a talk radio program and make a note of any fallacies discussed in this chapter that you notice. Try to write down the exact words used in the program as well as the name of the fallacy you think was employed.

More Fallacies

Students will learn to . . .

1. Recognize several types of fallacies that confuse the qualities of a person making a claim with the qualities of the claim

2. Recognize the fallacy involved in thinking that a claim is refuted because of its origin

3. Recognize fallacies that misrepresent an opponent's position

4. Recognize fallacies that erroneously limit considerations to only two options

5. Recognize fallacious claims that one action or event will inevitability lead to another

6. Recognize arguments that place the burden of proof on the wrong party

7. Recognize the problem in arguments that rely on a claim that is itself at issue

What is the most common (and most seductive) error in reasoning on the planet? You are about to find out. In this chapter, we examine the infamous *argumentum ad hominem*, as well as other common fallacies.

To remind you of the overall picture, in Chapter 5 we explored ways the rhetorical content of words and phrases can be used to affect belief and attitude. In Chapter 6, we considered emotional appeals and related fallacies. The fallacies we turn to now, like the devices in the preceding chapters, can tempt us to believe something without giving us a legitimate reason for doing so.

THE AD HOMINEM FALLACY

The ad hominem fallacy (*argumentum ad hominem*) is the most common of all mistakes in reasoning. The fallacy rests on a confusion between the qualities of the person making a claim and the qualities of the claim itself. ("Claim" is to be understood broadly here, as including beliefs, opinions, positions, arguments, proposals and so forth.)

Parker is an ingenious fellow. It follows that Parker's opinion on some subject, whatever it is, is the opinion of an ingenious person. But it does not follow that Parker's *opinion itself* is ingenious. To think that it is would be to confuse the content of Parker's claim with Parker himself. Or let's suppose you are listening to somebody, your teacher perhaps, whom you regard as a bit strange or maybe even weird. Would it follow that the *car* your teacher drives is strange or weird? Obviously not. Likewise, it would not follow that some specific proposal that the teacher has put forth is strange or weird. A proposal made by an oddball is an oddball's proposal, but it does not follow that it is an oddball proposal. We must not confuse the qualities of the person making a claim with the qualities of the claim itself.

We commit the **ad hominem** fallacy when we think that considerations about a person "refute" his or her assertions. *Ad hominem* is Latin for "to the man," indicating that it is not really the subject matter that's being addressed, but the person. The most common varieties of the ad hominem fallacy are as follows.

The Personal Attack Ad Hominem

"Johnson has such-and-such a negative feature; therefore, his claim (belief, opinion, theory, proposal, etc.) stands refuted." This is the formula for the **personal attack ad hominem** fallacy. The name "personal attack" is self-explanatory, because attributing a negative feature to Johnson is attacking him personally.

Now, there are many negative features that we might attribute to a person: Perhaps Johnson is said to be ignorant or stupid. Maybe he is charged with being self-serving or feathering his own nest. Perhaps he is accused of being a racist or a sexist or a fascist or a cheat or of being cruel or uncaring or soft on communism or taking pleasure in strangling songbirds. The point to remember is that shortcomings in *a person* are not equivalent to shortcomings in that person's ideas, proposals, theories, opinions, claims, or arguments. This is not inconsistent with what was said about credibility. Indeed, facts about the source of a claim can correctly make us *skeptical* about the claim. But we should not ordinarily conclude that it is *false* on this account.

Now, it is true that there are exceptional circumstances we can imagine in which some feature of a person might logically imply that what that person says is false; but these circumstances tend to be far-fetched. "Johnson's claim is false because he has been paid to lie about the matter" might qualify as an example. "Johnson's claim is false because he has been given a drug that makes him say only false things" would qualify, too. But such situations are rare. True, when we have doubts about the credibility of a source, we must be careful before we accept a claim from that source. But the doubts are rarely sufficient grounds for outright rejection of the claim. No matter what claim Johnson might make and no matter what his faults might be, we are rarely justified in rejecting the claim as false simply because he has those faults.

The Inconsistency Ad Hominem

"Moore's claim is inconsistent with something else Moore has said or done; therefore, his claim (belief, opinion, theory, proposal, etc.) stands refuted." This is the formula for the **inconsistency ad hominem,** and you encounter versions of this fallacy all the time. An example: In 2008 Hillary Clinton and Barack Obama were both vying for the Democratic nomination for the presidency. After Obama was quoted as saying he had "no intention of taking away

They believe the Boy Scouts' position on homosexuality was objectionable, but they gave no heed to people's objections about using state money to fund displays about sodomy in the people's Capitol.

—California assemblyman BILL LEONARD (R-San Bernardino), criticizing the legislature for funding a gay pride display in the state's Capitol

Man! As if sodomy in the people's Capitol isn't bad enough, they have to go and fund displays about it!

Leonard's remark is an example of an inconsistency ad hominem. (It also contains a wild syntactical ambiguity, as noted above.)

In Depth

Ad Hominem

The idea behind the ad hominem fallacy is to point to the person making a claim and accuse him or her of some flaw, evil deed, or other negative feature. By indicting the person behind the claim, the accuser hopes to refute the claim. But while some fact about the author of a claim may affect his or her credibility, it cannot by itself demonstrate that the claim is false.

folks' guns," the Clinton campaign pointed out that on a 1996 questionnaire Obama had said he "supported banning the manufacture, sale and possession of handguns," and that this showed that his new claim about not intending to "take away folks' guns" was not really true. Again, the fact that one opinion was expressed in 1996 and a different one in 2008 is not grounds for rejecting the latter as false. Although accusations of doing a "flip-flop" are standard in political campaigns, it's important to look beneath the surface to see how different the two positions really are and whether there might be a good reason for changing one's mind. The fact that people change their minds has no bearing on the truth of what they say either before or after.

Sometimes a person's claim seems inconsistent, not with previous statements but with that person's behavior. For example, Johnson might tell us to be more generous, when we know Johnson himself is as stingy as can be. Well, Johnson may well be a hypocrite, but we would be guilty of the inconsistency ad hominem fallacy if we regarded Johnson's stinginess or hypocrisy as grounds for rejecting what he says. This type of reasoning, where we reject what somebody says because what he or she says seems inconsistent with what he or she does, even has a Latin name: *tu quoque*, meaning "you, too." This version of the inconsistency ad hominem often boils down to nothing more than saying "You, too" or "You do it, too!" If a smoker urges another smoker to give up the habit, the second smoker commits the inconsistency ad hominem if she says, "Well, you do it, too!"

The Circumstantial Ad Hominem

"Parker's circumstances are such and such; therefore, his claim (belief, opinion, theory, proposal, etc.) stands refuted." This is the formula for the **circumstantial ad hominem.** An example would be "Well, you can forget about what Father Hennesy says about the dangers of abortion, because Father Hennesy's a priest, and priests are required to hold such views." The speaker in this example is citing Father Hennesy's circumstances (being a priest) to "refute" Father Hennesy's opinion. This example isn't a personal attack ad hominem because the speaker may think very highly of priests in general and of Father Hennesy in particular. Clearly, though, a person could intend to issue a personal attack by mentioning circumstances that (in the opinion of the speaker) constituted a defect on the part of the person attacked. For example, consider "You can forget about what Father Hennesy says about the dangers of abortion because he is a priest and priests all have sexual hang-ups." That would qualify as both a circumstantial ad hominem (he's a priest) and a personal attack ad hominem (priests have sexual hang-ups).

Poisoning the Well

Poisoning the well can be thought of as an ad hominem in advance. If someone dumps poison down your well, you don't drink from it. Similarly, when A poisons your mind about B by relating unfavorable information about B, you may be inclined to reject what B says to you.

Well-poisoning is easier to arrange than you might think. You might suppose that to poison someone's thinking about Mrs. Jones, you would have to say or at least insinuate something deprecatory or derogatory about her. In fact, recent psycholinguistic research suggests you can poison someone's thinking about Mrs. Jones by doing just the opposite! If we don't know Mrs. Jones, even a sentence that expresses an outright denial of a connection between her and something unsavory is apt to make us form an unfavorable impression of her. Psychological studies indicate that people are more apt to form an unfavorable impression of Mrs. Jones from a sentence like "Mrs. Jones is not an ax murderer" than from a sentence like "Mrs. Jones has a sister."

Moral: Because it might be easy for others to arrange for us to have a negative impression of someone, we must be extra careful not to reject what a person says *just because* we have an unfavorable impression of the individual.

I get calls from nutso environmentalists who are filled with compassion for every snail darter that is threatened by some dam somewhere. Yet, they have no interest in the 1.5 million fetuses that are aborted every year in the United States. I love to argue with them and challenge their double standard.

—RUSH LIMBAUGH

Often an inconsistency ad hominem will accuse someone of having a double standard. Notice how this example is combined with ridicule (See Chapter 5).

Hey, maybe you have no better sense, but I personally would not accept anything as news coming from that fat drug-addicted loudmouth.

—Comment on a media blog

An ad hominem used against Limbaugh.

"Positive Ad Hominem Fallacies"

An ad hominem fallacy, then, is committed if we rebut a person on the basis of considerations that, logically, apply to the person rather than to his or her claims. Strictly speaking, if we automatically transfer the positive or favorable attributes of a person to what he or she says, that's a mistake in reasoning, as well. The fact that you think Moore is clever does not logically entitle you to conclude that any specific opinion of Moore's is clever. The fact that, in your view, the NRA represents all that is good and proper does not enable you to infer that any specific proposal from the NRA is good and proper. Logicians did not always limit the ad hominem fallacy to cases of rebuttal, but that seems to be the usage now, and we shall follow that policy in this book. You should just remember that a parallel mistake in reasoning happens if you confuse the favorable qualities of a person with the qualities of his or her assertion.

THE GENETIC FALLACY

The **genetic fallacy** occurs when we try to "refute" a claim (or urge others to do so) on the basis of its origin or its history. If this sounds like what we've been talking about in the ad hominem section, it's no surprise. The genetic fallacy is often considered to be a blanket category for all fallacies that mistake an attack on a source for an attack on the claim in question. Taken this way, all versions of ad hominem, poisoning the well, and so forth, are also examples of the genetic fallacy.

In our treatment, we reserve the use of the term "genetic fallacy" for cases where it isn't a person that is disparaged as the source of a claim but some other kind of entity—a club, a political party, an industrial group, or even an entire epoch. An example of the latter would be attempting to refute a belief in God because that belief first rose in superstitious times when we had few natural explanations for events like storms, earthquakes, and so on. We have heard people declare the U.S. Constitution "invalid" because it was (allegedly) drafted to protect the interests of property owners. This is another example of the genetic fallacy.

If we "refute" a proposal (or urge someone else to reject it) on the grounds that it was part of the Republican (or Democratic) party platform, we commit the genetic fallacy. If we "refute" a policy (or try to get others to reject it) on the grounds that a slave-holding state in the nineteenth century originated the policy, that qualifies. If we "rebut" (or urge others to reject) a ballot initiative on the grounds that the insurance industry or the association of trial lawyers or the American Civil Liberties Union or "Big Tobacco" or "Big Oil" or multinational corporations or the National Education Association or the National Rifle Association or the National Organization for Women proposed it or back it, we commit the fallacy. Knowing that the NRA or the NEA or NOW proposed or backs or endorses a piece of legislation may give one reason (depending on one's politics) to be suspicious of it or to have a careful look at it; but a perceived lack of merit on the part of the organization that proposed or backs or endorses a proposal is not equivalent to a lack of merit in the proposal itself. Knowing the NRA is behind a particular ballot initiative is not the same as knowing about a specific defect in the initiative itself, even if you detest the NRA.

Whom are they kidding? Where are NOW's constitutional objections to the billions of dollars (including about $1 million to NOW itself) that women's groups receive under the Violence Against Women Act?

—Armin Brott, issuing an ad hominem response to opposition by the National Organization for Women to a proposal to provide poor fathers with parenting and marital-skills training and classes on money management

Gender-based inconsistency ad hominem

Classify each of the following cases of ad hominem as personal attack ad hominem, circumstantial ad hominem, inconsistency ad hominem, poisoning the well, or genetic fallacy. Identify the cases, if any, in which it might be difficult or futile to assign the item to any single one of these categories, as well as those cases, if any, where the item doesn't fit comfortably into any of these categories at all.

Exercise 7-1

▲   1. The proponents of this spend-now–pay-later boondoggle would like you to believe that this measure will cost you only one billion dollars. That's NOT TRUE. In the last general election, some of these very same people argued against unneeded rail projects because they would cost taxpayers millions more in interest payments. Now they have changed their minds and are willing to encourage irresponsible borrowing. Connecticut is already awash in red ink. Vote NO.

2. Rush Limbaugh argues that the establishment clause of the First Amendment should not be stretched beyond its intended dimensions by precluding voluntary prayer in public schools. This is a peculiar argument, when you consider that Limbaugh is quite willing to stretch the Second Amendment to include the right to own assault rifles and Saturday night specials.

3. I think you can safely assume that Justice Scalia's opinions on the cases before the Supreme Court this term will be every bit as flaky as his past opinions.

▲   4. Harvard now takes the position that its investment in urban redevelopment projects will be limited to projects that are environmentally friendly. Before you conclude that that is such a swell idea, stop and think. For a long time, Harvard was one of the biggest slumlords in the country.

5. Capital punishment was invented during barbaric times. No civilized society ought to tolerate it.

6. Dear Editor—
   I read with amusement the letter by Leslie Burr titled "It's time to get tough." Did anyone else notice a little problem in her views? It seems a little odd that somebody who claims that she "loathes violence" could also say that "criminals should pay with their life." I guess consistency isn't Ms. Burr's greatest concern.

▲   7. YOU: Look at this. It says here that white males still earn a lot more than minorities and women for doing the same job.
   YOUR FRIEND: Yeah, right. Written by some woman, no doubt.

8. "Steve Thompson of the California Medical Association said document-checking might even take place in emergency rooms. That's because, while undocumented immigrants would be given emergency care, not all cases that come into emergency rooms fall under the federal definition of an emergency.
   "To all those arguments initiative proponents say hogwash. They say the education and health groups opposing the initiative are

interested in protecting funding they receive for providing services to the undocumented."

—Article in Sacramento Bee

9. Ugh. Fred Smith. FedEx Founder and CEO. Presented as an "American Leader." Hard for me to get past what an ineffective father he is. [Smith is the father of Richard Wallace Smith, who pled guilty to assault and battery charges after he and two accomplices beat up a freshman student on the University of Virginia campus.]

—Jason Linkins, The Huffington Post, *December 2, 2007*

10. Are Moore and Parker guilty of the ad hominem fallacy or poisoning the well in their discussion of Rush Limbaugh on page 186?

▲ 11. "Creationism cannot possibly be true. People who believe in a literal interpretation of the Bible just never outgrew the need to believe in Santa Claus."

—Melinda Zerkle

12. "Americans spend between $28 billion and $61 billion a year in medical costs for treatment of hypertension, heart disease, cancer and other illnesses attributed to consumption of meat, says a report out today from a pro-vegetarian doctor's group.

"Dr. Neal D. Barnard, lead author of the report in the *Journal of Preventive Medicine,* and colleagues looked at studies comparing the health of vegetarians and meat eaters, then figured the cost of treating illnesses suffered by meat eaters in excess of those suffered by vegetarians. Only studies that controlled for the health effects of smoking, exercise and alcohol consumption were considered.

"The American Medical Association, in a statement from Dr. M. Roy Schwarz, charged that Barnard's group is an 'animal rights front organization' whose agenda 'definitely taints whatever unsubstantiated findings it may claim.'"

—USA Today

STRAW MAN

A man made of straw is easier to knock over than a real one. And that's the reason this fallacy has its name. We get a **straw man fallacy** when a speaker or writer distorts, exaggerates, or otherwise misrepresents an opponent's position. In such a case, the position attributed to the opponent isn't a real one; it's a position made of straw and thus more easily criticized and rejected. Here's a simple example: Imagine that our editor's wife says to him, "Mark, it's time you got busy and cleaned out the garage." He protests, "What? Again? Do I have to clean out the garage every blasted day?" In saying this, he is attributing to his wife a much less defensible position than her real one, since nobody would agree that he should have to clean out the garage every day.

Here's a real-life example from a newspaper column by George Will:

[Senator Lindsey] Graham believes that some borrowing is appropriate to make stakeholders of future generations, which will be the

In the Media

Sieg Heil? . . . or Shut Up?

In November 2006, Andrés Manuel López Obrador was a candidate for the presidency of Mexico after a bitterly contested national election. He is shown here before a speech in Mexico City. It certainly appears that López Obrador is giving a facist salute in this photo (it may be that his party makes use of such a gesture; we are not sufficiently informed to say), but we've also been told that he was just trying to quiet the crowd at the moment the shot was taken. In any case, it's another example of a photo that can be used to mislead, whichever interpretation you choose.

biggest beneficiaries of personal accounts. But substantially reducing the borrowing would deny Democrats the ability to disguise as fiscal responsibility their opposition to personal accounts, *which really is rooted in reluctance to enable people to become less dependent on government.*

It's the final portion, which we've put in italics, that's the straw man, and a wonderful example it is. Will describes the Democrats' position as being reluctant to enable people to become less dependent on government. We're pretty sure you could question every Democrat in Washington, D.C., and maybe every Democrat in the United States, and you could not find *even one* who is reluctant "to enable people to become less dependent on government." To be in favor of government programs to help people who need them is a far cry from being in favor of *keeping people on those programs as long as possible.*

A second point regarding this example, and one that is often a part of a straw man fallacy, is that the writer is presuming to read the minds of an entire group of people—how could he possibly know the "real" reason Democrats

In the Media

Straw Man in the Elder Competition

In 2005, the political group USA NEXT ran an ad attacking the AARP, a nationwide organization of retired persons. The ad made it appear that the AARP stood for gay marriage when in fact the organization had never taken a stand on the subject. Charlie Jarvis, chairman of USA Next, defended the ad by saying that an AARP affiliate in Ohio had come out against a same-sex marriage ban in that state. To claim that this is the same as saying the AARP endorses gay marriage is a good example of a straw man fallacy.

I'm a very controversial figure to the animal rights movement. They no doubt view me with some measure of hostility because I am constantly challenging their fundamental premise that animals are superior to human beings.

—RUSH LIMBAUGH, setting up a straw man for the kill

oppose personal accounts if they're claiming something entirely different? (This is sometimes called "reliance on an unknown fact.")

The straw man fallacy is so common that it ranks next to the top on our list of the top ten fallacies of all time (see inside front cover). One person will say he wants to eliminate the words "under God" from the Pledge of Allegiance, and his opponent will act as if he wants to eliminate the entire pledge. A conservative will oppose tightening emission standards for sulfur dioxide, and a liberal will accuse him of wanting to relax the standards. A Democratic congresswoman will say she opposes cutting taxes, and her Republican opponent will accuse her of wanting to raise taxes.

The ad hominem fallacy attempts to "refute" a claim on the basis of considerations that logically apply to its source. The straw man fallacy attempts to "refute" a claim by altering it so that it seems patently false or even ridiculous.

FALSE DILEMMA

Suppose our editor's wife, in the example earlier, says to him, "Look, Mark, either we clean out the garage, or all this junk will run us out of house and home. Would you prefer that?" Now she is offering him a "choice": either clean out the garage or let the junk run them out of house and home. But the choice she offers is limited to just two alternatives, and there are alternatives that deserve consideration, such as doing it later or not acquiring additional junk.

The **false dilemma** fallacy occurs when you limit considerations to only two alternatives although other alternatives may be available. Like the straw man fallacy, it is encountered all the time. You say you don't want to drill for oil in the Alaskan National Wildlife Reserve? Would you prefer letting the Iranians dictate the price of oil?

Or take a look at this example:

CONGRESSMAN CLAGHORN: Guess we're going to have to cut back expenditures on social programs again this year.

YOU: Why's that?

CLAGHORN: Well, we either do that or live with this high deficit, and that's something we can't allow.

Here, Claghorn maintains that either we live with the high deficit, or we cut social programs, and that therefore, because we can't live with the high deficit, we have to cut social programs. But this reasoning works only if cutting social programs is the *only* alternative to a high deficit. Of course, that is not the case (taxes might be raised or military spending cut, for example). Another example:

DANIEL: Theresa and I both endorse this idea of allowing prayer in public schools, don't we, Theresa?

THERESA: I never said any such thing!

DANIEL: Hey, I didn't know you were an atheist!

Here, Daniel's "argument" amounts to this: Either you endorse prayer in public schools, or you are an atheist; therefore, because you do not endorse school prayer, you must be an atheist. But a person does not have to be an atheist in order to feel unfavorable toward prayer in public schools. The alternatives Daniel presents, in other words, could both be false. Theresa might not be an atheist and still might not endorse school prayer.

The example Daniel provides shows how this type of fallacy and the preceding one can work together: A straw man is often used as part of a false dilemma. A person who wants us to accept X may not only ignore other alternatives besides Y but also exaggerate or distort Y. In other words, this person leaves only *one* "reasonable" alternative because the only other one provided is really a straw man. You can also think of a false dilemma as a false dichotomy.

Here's an example of a false dilemma by President Obama from an interview on March 17, 2010, with Bret Baier of Fox News:

OBAMA: "What I can tell you is that the vote that's taken in the House will be a vote for health care reform. And if people vote yes, whatever form that takes, that is going to be a vote for health care reform."

[Baier breaks in for a moment.]

OBAMA: Bret, let me finish. If they don't, if they vote against, then they're going to be voting against health care reform and they're going to be voting in favor of the status quo.

Reduced to bare bones, Obama is saying that either the House will vote for the health care bill before it or they'll be voting for the status quo. In fact, many members of the House were unsatisfied with the status quo but did not like the bill in question either; those members would rather have been voting against the status quo but for a different health care bill.

One might defend the president's remark by saying that, in fact, no other health care bill was going to be available to vote on; therefore, members of the House really had only two alternatives: this health care bill or no health care bill. However, without this being made clear, the remark is a false dilemma as it stands.

It might help in understanding false dilemmas to look quickly at a *real* dilemma. Consider: You know that the Smiths must heat their house in the

Real Life

Which Is It Going to Be, Springfield?

This   or   **THIS!**

This was the message on a flyer urging a "no" vote on a proposed zoning law change in a western city. Since the photos depict only two (fairly extreme) alternatives, and given that there are surely many other reasonable ones, the flyer presents an excellent example of a false dilemma.

winter. You also know that the only heating options available in their location are gas and electricity. Under these circumstances, if you find out that they do *not* have electric heat, it must indeed be true that they must use gas heat because that's the only alternative remaining. False dilemma occurs only when reasonable alternatives are ignored. In such cases, both X and Y may be false, and some other alternative may be true.

Therefore, before you accept X because some alternative, Y, is false, make certain that X and Y cannot *both* be false. Look especially for some third alternative, some way of rejecting Y without having to accept X. Example:

> MOORE: Look, Parker, you've been worrying about whether
> you could afford that bigger house on the corner
> for over a year. You need to grit your teeth and
> buy it or just get used to staying where you are
> and doing without the extra space.

Parker could reject both of Moore's alternatives (buying the house on the corner or staying where he is) because of some obvious but unmentioned alternatives. Parker might find another house to buy, bigger than his present one but less expensive than the one on the corner; or he might remodel his current house, making it bigger at less expense than buying the corner house.

Before moving on, we should point out that there is more than one way to present a pair of alternatives. Aside from the obvious "either X or Y" version we've described so far, we can use the form "if not X, then Y."

For instance, in the example at the beginning of the section, Congressman Claghorn can say, "Either we cut back on expenditures, or we'll have a big deficit," but he can accomplish the same thing by saying, "If we don't cut back on expenditures, then we'll have a big deficit." These two ways of stating the dilemma are equivalent. Claghorn gets the same result: After denying that we can tolerate the high deficit, he concludes that we'll have to cut back expenditures. Again, it's the artificial narrowness of the alternatives—the falsity of the claim that says "if not one, then surely the other"—that makes this a fallacy.

The Perfectionist Fallacy

A particular subspecies of false dilemma and common rhetorical ploy is something we call the **perfectionist fallacy.** It comes up when a plan or policy is under consideration, and it goes like this:

> If policy X will not meet our goals as well as we'd like them met (i.e., "perfectly"), then policy X should be rejected.

This principle downgrades policy X simply because it isn't perfection. It's a version of false dilemma because it says, in effect, "Either the policy is perfect, or else we must reject it."

An excellent example of the perfectionist fallacy comes from the National Football League's experience with the instant replay rule, which allows an off-field official to review video recordings of a play to determine whether the on-field official's ruling was correct. To help the replay official, recordings from several angles can be viewed, and the play runs in slow motion.

When it was first proposed, the argument most frequently heard against the replay policy went like this: "It's a mistake to use replays to make calls because no matter how many cameras you have following the action on the field, you're still going to miss some calls. There's no way to see everything that's going on."

According to this type of reasoning, we should not have police unless they can prevent *every* crime or apprehend *every* criminal. You can probably think of other examples that show perfectionist reasoning to be very unreliable indeed.

The Line-Drawing Fallacy

Another version of the false dilemma is called the line-drawing fallacy. An example comes from the much-publicized Rodney King case, in which four Los Angeles police officers were acquitted of charges of using excessive force when they beat King during his arrest. After the trial, one of the jurors indicated that an argument like the following finally convinced her and at least one other juror to vote "not guilty":

> Everybody agrees that the first time one of the officers struck King with a nightstick it did not constitute excessive force. Therefore, if we are to conclude that excessive force was indeed used, then sometime during the course of the beating (during which King was hit about fifty times) there must have been a moment—a particular blow—at which the force *became* excessive. Since there is no point at which we can determine that the use of force changed from warranted to excessive, we are forced

to conclude that it did not become excessive at any time during the beating; and so the officers did not use excessive force.

These jurors accepted the **line-drawing fallacy,** the fallacy of insisting that a line must be drawn at some precise point when in fact it is not necessary that such a precise line be drawn.

To see how this works, consider another example: Clearly, it is impossible for a person who is not rich to become rich by our giving her one dollar. But, equally clearly, if we give our lucky person fifty million dollars, one at a time (very quickly, obviously—maybe we have a machine to deal them out), she will be rich. According to the line-drawing argument, however, *if we cannot point to the precise dollar that makes her rich, then she can never get rich, no matter how much money she is given.*

The problem, of course, is that the concepts referred to by "rich" and "excessive force" (and many others) are vague concepts. (Remember our discussion in Chapter 3.) We can find cases where the concepts clearly apply and cases where they clearly do not apply. But it is not at all clear exactly where the borderlines are.

Many logicians interpret line drawing as a variety of slippery slope (discussed next). The King case might be seen this way: If the first blow struck against King did not amount to excessive violence, then there's nothing in the series of blows to change that fact. So there's no excessive violence at the end of the series, either.

Our own preference is to see the line-drawing fallacy as a version of false dilemma. It presents the following alternatives: Either there is a precise place where we draw the line, or else there is no line to be drawn (no difference) between one end of the scale and the other. Either there is a certain blow at which the force used against King became excessive, or else the force never became excessive.

Again, remember that our categories of fallacy sometimes overlap. When that happens, it doesn't matter as much which way we classify a case as that we see that an error is being made.

SLIPPERY SLOPE

We've all heard people make claims of this sort: "If we let X happen, the first thing you know, Y will be happening." This is one form of the **slippery slope.** Such claims are fallacious when in fact there is no reason to think that X will lead to Y. Sometimes X and Y can be the same kind of thing or can bear some kind of similarity to one another, but that doesn't mean that one will inevitably lead to the other.

Opponents of handgun control sometimes use a slippery slope argument, saying that if laws to register handguns are passed, this will eventually lead to making ownership of any kind of gun illegal. This is fallacious if there is no reason to think that the first kind of law will lead eventually to the second kind. It's up to the person who offers the slippery slope claim to show *why* the first action will lead to the second.

It is also argued that one should not experiment with certain drugs because experimentation is apt to lead to serious addiction or dependence. In the case of drugs that are known to be addictive, there is no fallacy present— the likelihood of the progression is clear.

Real Life

$8 Billion Down the Tube!

Eight billion dollars in utility ratepayers' money and 20 years of effort will be squandered if this resolution is defeated.

> —SENATOR FRANK MURKOWSKI, R-Alaska, using a slippery slope fallacy
> to argue for going forward with government plans to bury
> radioactive waste in Yucca Mountain, Nevada

The fact that we've spent money on it already doesn't make it a good idea.

The other version of slippery slope occurs when someone claims we must continue a certain course of action simply because we have already begun that course. It was said during the Vietnam War that, because the United States had already sent troops to Vietnam, it was necessary to send more troops to support the first ones. Unless there is some reason supplied to show that the first step *must* lead to the others, this is a fallacy. (Notice that it's easy to make a false dilemma out of this case as well; do you see how to do it?) Although there are other factors that make the Iraq War somewhat different, many believe the fallacy applies there as well.

Sometimes we take the first step in a series, and then we realize that it was a mistake. To insist on taking the remainder when we could admit our mistake and retreat is to fall prey to the slippery slope fallacy. This is illustrated by the example from Senator Murkowski in the box above. (If you're the sort who insists on following one bad move with another one, we'd like to tell you about our friendly Thursday night poker game.)

The slippery slope fallacy has considerable force because *psychologically* one item does often lead to another, even though *logically* it does no such thing. When we think of X, say, we may be led immediately to think of Y. But this certainly does not mean that X itself is necessarily followed by Y. Once again, to think that Y has to follow X is to engage in slippery slope thinking; to do so when there is no particular reason to think Y must follow X is to commit a slippery slope fallacy.

We should note in conclusion that the slope is sometimes a longer one: If we do X, it will lead to Y, and Y will lead to Z, and Z will lead to . . . eventually to some disaster. To avoid the fallacy, it must be shown that each step is likely to follow from the preceding step.

MISPLACING THE BURDEN OF PROOF

Moore asks Parker, "Say, did you know that, if you rub red wine on your head, your gray hair will turn dark again?"

Parker, of course, will say, "Baloney."

Let's suppose Moore then says, "Baloney? Hey, how do you know it won't work?"

In the Media

A Double Slippery Slope

Next time it will be easier. It always is. The tolerance of early-term abortion made it possible to tolerate partial-birth abortion, and to give advanced thinkers a hearing when they advocate outright infanticide. Letting the courts decide such life-and-death issues made it possible for us to let them decide others, made it seem somehow wrong for anyone to stand in their way. Now they are helping to snuff out the minimally conscious. Who's next?
—Editorial, *National Review Online*, March 31, 2005

There are actually two slippery slope arguments built into this passage. One says that one type of abortion (early-term) led to another (partial-birth); the second says that letting the courts decide some issues led to allowing them to decide more issues. Both cases are fallacious because in neither is there any evidence advanced for the slipperiness of the slope. Was it tolerance of early-term abortion that led to partial-birth abortion? In fact, the slope seems not to have been slippery, since a ban on partial-birth abortion became federal law in 2003. And many issues, including many life-and-death issues, are properly within the purview of the courts from the outset; there is no reason to think that some became matters for the judiciary simply because others were.

Moore's question is odd, because the **burden of proof** rests on him, not on Parker. Moore has misplaced the burden of proof on Parker, and this is a mistake, a fallacy.

Misplacing the burden of proof occurs when the burden of proof is placed on the wrong side of an issue. This is a common rhetorical technique, and sometimes you have to be on your toes to spot it. People are frequently tricked into thinking that they have to prove their opponent's claim wrong, when in fact the opponent should be proving that the claim is right. For example, back in 2003 you often heard people trying their darnedest to prove that we shouldn't go to war with Iraq, in a context in which the burden of proof rests on those who think we should go to war.

What reasonable grounds would make us place the burden of proof more on one side of an issue than the other? There are a variety of such grounds, but they fall mainly into three categories. We can express them as a set of general rules:

1. *Initial plausibility.* In Chapter 4, we said that the more a claim coincides with our background information, the greater its initial plausibility. The general rule that most often governs the placement of the burden of proof is simply this: The less initial plausibility a claim has, the greater the burden of proof we place on someone who asserts that claim. This is just good sense, of course. We are quite naturally less skeptical about the claim that Charlie's now-famous eighty-seven-year-old grandmother drove a boat across Lake Michigan than we are about the claim that she *swam* across Lake Michigan. Unfortunately, this rule is a general rule, not a rule that can be applied precisely. We are unable to assess the specific degree of a claim's plausibility and then determine with precision just exactly how much evidence its advocates

■ Paleological misplacement of the burden of proof!

(© Dan Piraro. Reprinted with special permission of King Features Syndicate.)

need to produce to make us willing to accept the claim. But, as a general rule, the initial-plausibility rule can keep us from setting the requirements unreasonably high for some claims and allowing others to slide by unchallenged when they don't deserve to.

2. *Affirmative/negative.* Other things being equal, the burden of proof falls automatically on those supporting the affirmative side of an issue rather than on those supporting the negative side. In other words, we generally want to hear reasons why something *is* the case before we require reasons why it is *not* the case. Consider this conversation:

> MOORE: The car won't start.
>
> PARKER: Yeah, I know. It's a problem with the ignition.
>
> MOORE: What makes you think that?
>
> PARKER: What makes you think it isn't?

Parker's last remark seems strange because we generally require the affirmative side to assume the burden of proof; it is Parker's job to give reasons for thinking that the problem *is* in the ignition.

This rule applies to cases of existence versus nonexistence, too. Most often, the burden of proof should fall on those who claim something exists rather than on those who claim it doesn't. There are people who believe in ghosts, not because of any evidence that there *are* ghosts, but because nobody has shown there are no such things. (When someone claims that we should believe in such-and-such because nobody has proved that it *isn't* so, we have a version of burden of proof known as **appeal to ignorance.**) This is a burden-of-proof fallacy because it mistakenly places the requirement of proving their position on those who do not believe in ghosts. (Of course, the first rule applies here, too, because ghosts are not part of background knowledge for most of us.)

In Depth

Innocent Until Proved Guilty

We must point out that sometimes there are specific reasons why the burden of proof is placed entirely on one side. The obvious case in point is in criminal court, where it is the prosecution's job to prove guilt. The defense is not required to prove innocence; it must only try to keep the prosecution from succeeding in its attempt to prove guilt. We are, as we say, "innocent until proved guilty." As a matter of fact, it's possible that more trials might come to a correct conclusion (i.e., the guilty get convicted and the innocent acquitted) if the burden of proof were equally shared between prosecution and defense. But we have wisely decided that if we are to make a mistake, we would rather it be one of letting a guilty person go free than one of convicting an innocent person. Rather than being a fallacy, then, this lopsided placement of the burden of proof is how we guarantee a fundamental right: the presumption of innocence.

In general, the affirmative side gets the burden of proof because it tends to be much more difficult—or at least much more inconvenient—to prove the negative side of an issue. Imagine a student who walks up to the ticket window at a football game and asks for a discounted student ticket. "Can you prove you're a student?" he is asked. "No," the student replies, "Can you prove I'm not?" Well, it may be possible to prove he's not a student, but it's no easy chore, and it would be unreasonable to require it.

Incidentally, some people say it's *impossible* to "prove a negative." But difficult is not the same as impossible. And some "negatives" are even easy to prove. For example, "There are no elephants in this classroom."

3. *Special circumstances.* Sometimes getting at the truth is not the only thing we want to accomplish, and on such occasions we may purposely place the burden of proof on a particular side. Courts of law provide us with the most obvious example. (See the box "Innocent Until Proved Guilty.") Specific agreements can also move the burden of proof from where it would ordinarily fall. A contract might specify, "It will be presumed that you receive the information by the tenth of each month unless you show otherwise." In such cases, the rule governing the special circumstances should be clear and acceptable to all parties involved.

In the Media

So Much for Presumed Innocence . . .

I would rather have an innocent man executed than a guilty murderer go free.

—Caller on *Talk Back Live* (CNN)

This not uncommon thought is a bizarre false dilemma, since if the innocent man is executed, the guilty murderer *does* go free.

One important variety of special circumstances occurs when the stakes are especially high. For example, if you're thinking of investing your life savings in a company, you'll want to put a heavy burden of proof on the person who advocates making the investment. However, if the investment is small, one you can afford to lose, you might be willing to lay out the money even though it has not been thoroughly proved that the investment is safe. In short, it is reasonable to place a higher burden of proof on someone who advocates a policy that could be dangerous or costly if he or she is mistaken.

These three rules cover most of the ground in placing the burden of proof properly. Be careful about situations where people put the burden of proof on the side other than where our rules indicate it should fall. Take this example:

PARKER: I think we should invest more money in expanding the interstate highway system.

MOORE: I think that would be a big mistake.

PARKER: How could anybody object to more highways?

With his last remark, Parker has attempted to put the burden of proof on Moore. Such tactics can put one's opponent in a defensive position; if he takes the bait, Moore now has to show why we should *not* spend more on roads rather than Parker having to show why we *should* spend more. This is an inappropriate burden of proof.

You should always be suspicious when someone tells you that your inability to disprove his claim shows that his claim is true. Take note of where the burden of proof falls in such situations; your speaker may be trying to erroneously place that burden on you. We should also point out that if repeated attempts to prove something end in failure, that may be a reason for doubting it. Psychics' repeated failure to prove that ESP exists is a reason to be skeptical of ESP.

BEGGING THE QUESTION

Here's a version of a simple example of begging the question, a fairly silly one but one that makes the point clearly (we'll return to it later):

Two gold miners roll a boulder away from its resting place and find three huge gold nuggets underneath. One says to the other, "Great!

That's one nugget for you and two for me," handing one nugget to his associate.

"Wait a minute!" says the second miner. "Why do you get two and I get just one?"

"Because I'm the leader of this operation," says the first.

"What makes you the leader?" asks miner number two.

"I've got twice the gold you do," answers miner number one.

This next example is as famous as the first one was silly: Some people say they can prove God exists. When asked how, they reply, "Well, the Scriptures say very clearly that God must exist." Then, when asked why we should believe the Scriptures, they answer, "The Scriptures are divinely inspired by God himself, so they must be true."

The problem with such reasoning is that the claim at issue—whether God exists—turns out to be one of the very assumptions the argument is based on. If we can't trust the Scriptures, then the argument isn't any good, but the reason given for trusting the Scriptures requires the existence of God, the very thing we were questioning in the first place! Examples like this are sometimes called circular reasoning or arguing in a circle because they start from much the same place as they end up.

Gay marriages should not be legal because if there wasn't anything wrong with them they would already be legal, which they aren't.

—From a student essay

If you examine this "reasoning" closely, it says that gay marriages shouldn't be legal because they aren't legal. This is not quite "X is true just because X is true," but it's close. The issue is whether the law should be changed. So, giving the existence of the law as a "reason" for its *not* being changed can carry no weight, logically.

Real Life

Getting Really Worked Up over Ideas

Not long ago, the editor of *Freethought Today* magazine won a court case upholding the constitutional separation of church and state. Following are a few samples of the mail she received as a result (there was much more), as they were printed in the magazine. We present them to remind you of how worked up people can get over ideas.

Satan worshipping scum . . .

If you don't like this country and what it was founded on & for *get the f— out of it* and go straight to hell.

F— you, you communist wh–.

If you think that mathematical precision that governs the universe was established by random events then you truly are that class of IDIOT that cannot be aptly defined.

These remarks illustrate extreme versions of more than one rhetorical device mentioned in this part of the book. They serve as a reminder that some people become defensive and emotional when it comes to their religion. (As Richard Dawkins, professor of Public Understanding of Science at Oxford University, was prompted to remark, "A philosophical opinion about the nature of the universe, which is held by the great majority of America's top scientists and probably the elite intelligentsia generally, is so abhorrent to the American electorate that no candidate for popular election dare affirm it in public.")

Adapted from *Free Inquiry*, Summer 2002.

On Language

Begging . . . or Begging *For*?

We should point out that the phrase "beg the question" is frequently used incorrectly these days, presumably by people who do not know its actual meaning (after reading this book and taking your class, this does not include you). Here's an example:

> Brett Favre has now started in 250 consecutive games. That begs the question, "Can any other quarterback ever hope to approach that record?"

No, it doesn't beg the question; it begs *for* the question, or it *calls* for the question, or it *brings up* the question about other quarterbacks approaching Favre's record.

One of your authors first saw this misuse of the phrase in a television ad for Volvo automobiles in about 2001. Since then, it has begun to turn up everywhere. It may be that common usage will eventually sanction this new usage; in the meantime, we recommend that you not use it. You can also feel a bit smug about knowing better when you hear it or see it in print.

Rhetorical definitions can beg questions. Consider an example from an earlier chapter: If we define abortion as "the murder of innocent children," then it's obvious that abortion is morally wrong. But, of course, anyone who doubts that abortion is morally wrong is certainly not going to accept this definition. That person will most likely refuse to recognize an embryo or early-stage fetus as a "child" at all and will certainly not accept the word "murder" in the definition.

And this brings us to the real problem in cases of question begging: a misunderstanding of what premises (and definitions) it is reasonable for one's audience to accept. We are guilty of **begging the question** when we ask our audience to accept premises that are as controversial as the conclusion we're arguing for and that are controversial on the same grounds. The sort of grounds on which people would disagree about the morality of abortion are much the same as those on which they would disagree about the definition of abortion above. The person making the argument has not "gone back far enough," as it were, to find common ground with the audience whom he or she wishes to convince.

Let's return to our feuding gold miners to illustrate what we're talking about. Clearly, the two disagree about who gets the gold, and, given what being the leader of the operation means, they're going to disagree just as much about that. But what if the first miner says, "Look, I picked this spot, didn't I? And we wouldn't have found anything if we'd worked where you wanted to work." If the second miner agrees, they'll have found a bit of common ground. Maybe—*maybe*—the first miner can then convince the second that this point, on which they agree, is worth considering when it comes to splitting the gold. At least there's a chance of moving the discussion forward when they proceed this way.

In fact, if you are ever to hope for any measure of success in trying to convince somebody of a claim, you should always try to argue for it based on whatever common ground you can find between the two of you. Indeed, the attempt to find common ground from which to start is what underlies the entire enterprise of rational debate.

Recap

The fallacies in this chapter, like those in Chapter 6, may resemble legitimate arguments, but none gives a reason for accepting (or rejecting) a claim. The discussions in this part of the book should help make you sensitive to the difference between relevant considerations and emotional appeals, factual irrelevancies, and other dubious argumentative tactics.

In this chapter, we examined:

- Personal attack ad hominem—thinking a person's defects refute his or her beliefs
- Inconsistency ad hominem—thinking a person's inconsistencies refute his or her beliefs
- Circumstantial ad hominem—thinking a person's circumstances refute his or her beliefs
- Poisoning the well—encouraging others to dismiss what someone will say, by citing the speaker's defects, inconsistencies, circumstances, or other personal attributes
- Genetic fallacy—thinking that the origin or history of a belief refutes it
- Straw man—"rebutting" a position held or presumed to be held by others by offering a distorted or exaggerated version of that position
- False dilemma—an erroneous narrowing down of the range of alternatives; saying we have to accept X or Y (and omitting that we might accept Z)
- Perfectionist fallacy—arguing that if a solution does not solve a problem completely and perfectly, it should not be adopted at all
- Line-drawing fallacy—requiring that a precise line be drawn someplace on a scale or continuum when no such precise line can be drawn; usually occurs when a vague concept is treated like a precise one
- Slippery slope—refusing to take the first step in a progression on unwarranted grounds that doing so will make taking the remaining steps inevitable, or insisting erroneously on taking the remainder of the steps simply because the first one was taken
- Misplacing the burden of proof—requiring the wrong side of an issue to make its case
- Begging the question—assuming as true the claim that is at issue and doing this as if you were giving an argument

Additional Exercises

Exercise 7-2

Working in groups, invent a simple, original, and clear example of each fallacy covered in this chapter. Then, in the class as a whole, select the illustrations that are clearest and most straightforward. Go over these illustrations before doing the remaining exercises in this chapter, and review them before you take a test on this material.

Exercise 7-3

Identify any examples of fallacies in the following passages. Tell why you think they are present, and identify which category they belong in, if they fit any category we've described.

▲ 1. Of course, Chinese green tea is good for your health. If it weren't, how could it be so beneficial to drink it?

2. Overheard: "No, I'm against this health plan business. None of the proposals are gonna fix everything, you can bet on that."

3. You have a choice: Either you let 'em out to murder and rape again and again, or you put up with a little prison overcrowding. I know what I'd choose.

▲ 4. "The legalization of drugs will not promote their use. The notion of a widespread hysteria sweeping across the nation as every man, woman, and child instantaneously becomes addicted to drugs upon their legalization is, in short, ridiculous."

—From a student essay

5. Way I figure is, giving up smoking isn't gonna make me live forever, so why bother?

6. "I tell you, Mitt Romney would *have* to favor the Mormons if he were to become president. After all Mormons are supposed to believe that theirs is the one true religion."

—From a newspaper call-in column

▲ 7. Aid to Russia? Gimme a break! Why should we care more about the Russians than about our own people?

8. Well, most of the recent Treasury secretaries have been officers of Goldman Sachs at one time or another. It's no wonder their claims about the economy always favor the company.

9. I believe Tim is telling the truth about his brother, because he just would not lie about that sort of thing.

▲ 10. I think I was treated unfairly. I got a ticket out on McCrae Road. I was doing about sixty miles an hour, and the cop charged me with "traveling at an unsafe speed." I asked him just exactly what would have been a *safe* speed on that particular occasion—fifty? forty-five?—and he couldn't tell me. Neither could the judge. I tell you, if you don't know what speeds are unsafe, you shouldn't give tickets for "unsafe speeds."

Exercise 7-4

Identify any fallacies in the following passages. Tell why you think they are present, and identify which category they belong in, if they fit any of those we've described. Instances of fallacies are all from the types found in Chapter 7.

▲ 1. Suspicious: "I would forget about whatever Moore and Parker have to say about pay for college teachers. After all, they're both professors themselves; what would you *expect* them to say?"

2. It's obvious to me that abortion is wrong—after all, everybody deserves a chance to be born.

3. Overheard: Well, I think that's too much to tip her. It's more than 15 percent. Next time it will be 20 percent, then 25 percent—where will it stop?

▲ 4. CARLOS: Four A.M.? Do we really have to start that early? Couldn't we leave a little later and get more sleep?
JEANNE: C'mon, don't hand me that! I know you! If you want to stay in bed until noon and then drag in there in the middle of the night, then go by yourself! If we want to get there at a reasonable hour, then we have to get going early and not spend the whole day sleeping.

5. I know a lot of people don't find anything wrong with voluntary euthanasia, where a patient is allowed to make a decision to die and that wish is carried out by a doctor or someone else. What will happen, though, is that if we allow voluntary euthanasia, before you know it we'll have the patient's relatives or the doctors making the decision that the patient should be "put out of his misery."

6. "Rudy Giuliani's position on terrorism has to be the best [of the candidates in 2008]. After all, when 9/11 happened, he was *there.*"

▲ 7. Whenever legislators have the power to raise taxes, they will always find problems that seem to require for their solution doing exactly that. This is an axiom, the proof of which is that the power to tax always generates the perception on the part of those who have that power that there exist various ills the remedy for which can only lie in increased governmental spending and hence higher taxes.

8. Don't tell me I should wear my seat belt, for heaven's sake. I've seen you ride a motorcycle without a helmet!

9. I'll tell you what the Congress passed. They call it health care reform, but what it really is is communism, pure and simple. It's designed to tax everybody who works so people who don't work can still have an easy life.

▲ 10. When it comes to the issue of race relations, either you're part of the solution, or you're part of the problem.

11. What! So now you're telling me we should get a new car? I don't buy that at all. Didn't you claim just last month that there was nothing wrong with the Plymouth?

12. Letter to the editor: "The Supreme Court decision outlawing a moment of silence for prayer in public schools is scandalous. Evidently the American Civil Liberties Union and the other radical groups will not be satisfied until every last man, woman and child in the country is an atheist. I'm fed up."

—Tri-County Observer

▲ 13. We should impeach the attorney general. Despite the fact that there have been many allegations of unethical conduct on his part, he has not done anything to demonstrate his innocence.

14. Amnesty International only defends criminals. This is obvious because the people they help are already in jail, and that shows they're guilty of something.

15. Overheard: "Hunting immoral? Why should I believe that, coming from you? You fish, don't you?"

16. "Will we have an expanding government, or will we balance the budget, cut government waste and eliminate unneeded programs?"

—*Newt Gingrich, in a Republican National Committee solicitation*

17. When Bill O'Reilly appeared on *The David Letterman Show*, the conversation was spirited and widely reported. At one point, O'Reilly presented Letterman with the following question: "Do you want the United States to win in Iraq?" This is a fairly clever example of one of our fallacies and a standard debating ploy. Identify the fallacy and describe the problem it presents for Letterman.

Exercise 7-5

Identify any fallacies in the following passages. Tell why you think they are present, and identify which category they belong in, if they fit in any of those we've described.

▲ 1. Despite all the studies and the public outcry, it's still true that nobody has ever actually *seen* cigarette smoking cause a cancer. All the anti-smoking people can do is talk about statistics; as long as there isn't real proof, I'm not believing it.

2. "Clinton should have been thrown in jail for immoral behavior. Just look at all the women he has had affairs with since he left the presidency."

    "Hey, wait a minute. How do you know he has had affairs since he was president?"

    "Because if he didn't, then why would he be trying to cover up the fact that he did?"

3. On *The Colbert Report*, Steven Colbert regularly asked his guests: "George W. Bush: a great president? or the greatest president?"

▲ 4. In 1996, a University of Chicago study gave evidence that letting people carry concealed guns appears to sharply reduce murders, rapes, and other violent crimes. Gun-control backer Josh Sugarman of the Violence Policy Center commented: "Anyone who argues that these laws reduce crime either doesn't understand the nature of crime or has a preset agenda."

5. Letter to the editor: "I strongly object to the proposed sale of alcoholic beverages at County Golf Course. The idea of allowing people to drink wherever and whenever they please is positively disgraceful and can only lead to more alcoholism and all the problems it produces—drunk driving, perverted parties, and who knows what else. I'm sure General Stuart, if he were alive today to see what has become of the land he deeded to the county, would disapprove strenuously."

    Tehama County Tribune

6. Letter to the editor: "I'm not against immigrants or immigration, but something has to be done soon. We've got more people already than we can provide necessary services for, and, at the current rate, we'll have people standing on top of one another by the end of the century. Either we control these immigration policies or there won't be room for any of us to sit down."

    —Lake County Recorder

▲ 7. Letter to the editor: "So now we find our local crusader-for-all-that-is-right, and I am referring to Councilman Benjamin Bostell, taking up arms against the local adult bookstore. Is this the same Mr. Bostell who owns the biggest liquor store in Chilton County? Well, maybe booze isn't the

same as pornography, but they're the same sort of thing. C'mon,
Mr. Bostell, aren't you a little like the pot calling the kettle black?"

—Chilton County Register

8. Letter to the editor: "Once again the *Courier* displays its taste for slanted journalism. Why do your editors present only one point of view?

"I am referring specifically to the editorial of May 27, regarding the death penalty. So capital punishment makes you squirm a little. What else is new? Would you prefer to have murderers and assassins wandering around scot-free? How about quoting someone who has a different point of view from your own, for a change?"

—Athens Courier

9. There is only one way to save this country from the domination by the illegal drug establishment to which Colombia has been subjected, and that's to increase tenfold the funds we spend on drug enforcement and interdiction.

▲ 10. It's practically a certainty that the government is violating the law in the arms deals with Saudi Arabians. When a reporter asked officials to describe how they were complying with the law, he was told that details about the arms sales were classified.

Exercise 7-6

Identify any examples of fallacies in the following passages. Tell why you think these are fallacies, and identify which category they belong in, if they fit any category we've described.

▲ 1. Letter to the editor: "I would like to express my feelings on the recent conflict between county supervisor Blanche Wilder and Murdock County Sheriff Al Peters over the county budget.

"I have listened to sheriffs' radio broadcasts. Many times there have been dangerous and life-threatening situations when the sheriff's deputies' quickest possible arrival time is 20 to 30 minutes. This is to me very frightening.

"Now supervisor Wilder wants to cut two officers from the Sheriff's Department. This proposal I find ridiculous. Does she really think that Sheriff Peters can run his department with no officers? How anyone can think that a county as large as Murdock can get by with no police is beyond me. I feel this proposal would be very detrimental to the safety and protection of this county's residents."

2. Letter to the editor: "Andrea Keene's selective morality is once again showing through in her July 15 letter. This time she expresses her abhorrence of abortion. But how we see only what we choose to see! I wonder if any of the anti-abortionists have considered the widespread use of fertility drugs as the moral equivalent of abortion, and, if they have, why they haven't come out against them, too. The use of these drugs frequently results in multiple births, which leads to the death of one of the infants, often after an agonizing struggle for survival. According to the rules of the pro-lifers, isn't this murder?"

—North-State Record

3. In one of her columns, Abigail Van Buren printed the letter of "I'd rather be a widow." The letter writer, a divorcée, complained about widows who said they had a hard time coping. Far better, she wrote, to be a widow than to be a divorcée, who are all "rejects" who have been "publicly dumped" and are avoided "like they have leprosy." Abby recognized the fallacy for what it was, though she did not call it by our name. What is our name for it?

▲ 4. Overheard: "Should school kids say the Pledge of Allegiance before class? Certainly. Why shouldn't they?"

5. Letter to the editor: "Once again the Park Commission is considering closing North Park Drive for the sake of a few joggers and bicyclists. These so-called fitness enthusiasts would evidently have us give up to them for their own private use every last square inch of Walnut Grove. Then anytime anyone wanted a picnic, he would have to park at the edge of the park and carry everything in—ice chests, chairs, maybe even grandma. I certainly hope the Commission keeps the entire park open for everyone to use."

6. "Some Christian—and other—groups are protesting against the placing, on federal property near the White House, of a set of plastic figurines representing a devout Jewish family in ancient Judaea. The protestors would of course deny that they are driven by any anti-Semitic motivation. Still, we wonder: Would they raise the same objections (of unconstitutionality, etc.) if the scene depicted a modern, secularized Gentile family?"

—National Review

▲ 7 "It's stupid to keep on talking about rich people not paying their fair share of taxes while the budget is so far out of balance. Why, if we raised the tax rates on the wealthy all the way back to where they were in 1980, it would not balance the federal budget."

—Radio commentary by Howard Miller

8. From a letter to the editor: "The counties of Michigan clearly need the ability to raise additional sources of revenue, not only to meet the demands of growth but also to maintain existing levels of service. For without these sources those demands will not be met, and it will be impossible to maintain services even at present levels."

9. In February 1992, a representative of the Catholic Church in Puerto Rico gave a radio interview (broadcast on National Public Radio) in which he said that the Church was against the use of condoms. Even though the rate of AIDS infection in Puerto Rico is much higher than on the U.S. mainland, the spokesman said that the Church could not support the use of condoms because they are not absolutely reliable in preventing the spread of the disease. "If you could prove that condoms were absolutely dependable in preventing a person from contracting AIDS, then the Church could support their use."

▲ 10. [California] Assemblyman Doug La Malfa said AB 45 [which bans handheld cell phone use while driving] is one more example of a "nanny government." "I'm sick and tired of being told what to do on these trivial things," he said. "Helmet laws, seat-belt laws—what's next?"

Exercise 7-7

Identify any examples of fallacies in the following passages. Tell why you think they are present, and identify which category they belong in, if they fit any category we've described.

▲   1. The U.S. Congress considered a resolution criticizing the treatment of eth-nic minorities in a Near Eastern country. When the minister of the interior was asked for his opinion of the resolution, he replied, "This is purely an internal affair in my country, and politicians in the U.S. should stay out of such affairs. If the truth be known, they should be more concerned with the plight of minority peoples in their own country. Thousands of black and Latino youngsters suffer from malnutrition in the United States. They can criticize us after they've got their own house in order."

2. It doesn't make any sense to speak of tracing an individual human life back past the moment of conception. After all, that's the beginning, and you can't go back past the beginning.

3. MOE: The death penalty is an excellent deterrent for murder.
   JOE: What makes you think so?
   MOE: Well, for one thing, there's no evidence that it's *not* a deterrent.
   JOE: Well, states with capital punishment have murder rates just as high as states that don't have it.
   MOE: Yes, but that's only because there are so many legal technicalities standing in the way of executions that convicted people hardly ever get executed. Remove those technicalities, and the rate would be lower in those states.

▲   4. Overheard: "The new sculpture in front of the municipal building by John Murrah is atrocious and unseemly, which is clear to anyone who hasn't forgotten Murrah's mouth in Vietnam right there along with Hayden and Fonda calling for the defeat of America. I say: Drill holes in it so it'll sink and throw it in Walnut Pond."

5. Overheard: "Once we let these uptight guardians of morality have their way and start censoring *Playboy* and *Penthouse*, the next thing you know they'll be dictating everything we can read. We'll be in fine shape when they decide that *Webster's* should be pulled from the shelves."

6. It seems the biggest problem the nuclear industry has to deal with is not a poor safety record but a lack of education of the public on nuclear power. Thousands of people die each year from pollution generated by coal-fired plants. Yet, to date there has been no death directly caused by radiation at a commercial nuclear power plant in the United States. We have a clear choice: an old, death-dealing source of energy or a safe, clean one. Proven through the test of time, nuclear power is clearly the safest form of energy and the least detrimental to the environment. Yet it is perceived as unsafe and an environmental hazard.

▲   7. A high school teacher once told my class that, if a police state ever arose in America, it would happen because we freely handed away our civil rights in exchange for what we perceived would be security from the government. We are looking at just that in connection with the current drug crisis.
      For almost thirty years, we've seen increasing tolerance, legally and socially, of drug use. Now we are faced with the very end of America as

we know it, if not from the drug problem, then from the proposed solutions to it.

First, it was urine tests. Officials said that the innocent have nothing to fear. Using that logic, why not allow unannounced police searches of our homes for stolen goods? After all, the innocent would have nothing to fear.

Now we're looking at the seizure of boats and other property when even traces of drugs are found. You'd better hope some drug-using guest doesn't drop the wrong thing in your home, car, or boat.

The only alternative to declaring real war on the real enemies—the Asian and South American drug families—is to wait for that knock on the door in the middle of the night.

8. The mayor's argument is that, because the developers' fee would reduce the number of building starts, ultimately the city would lose more money than it would gain through the fee. But I can't go along with that. Mayor Tower is a member of the Board of Realtors, and you know what *they* think of the fee.

9. Letter to the editor: "Next week the philosopher Tom Regan will be in town again, peddling his animal rights theory. In case you've forgotten, Regan was here about three years ago arguing against using animals in scientific experimentation. As far as I could see then and can see now, neither Regan nor anyone else has managed to come up with a good reason why animals should not be experimented on. Emotional appeals and horror stories no doubt influence many, but they shouldn't. I've always wondered what Regan would say if his children needed medical treatment that was based on animal experiments."

▲ 10. Not long before Ronald and Nancy Reagan moved out of the White House, former chief of staff Don Regan wrote a book in which he depicted a number of revealing inside stories about First Family goings-on. Among them was the disclosure that Nancy Reagan regularly sought the advice of a San Francisco astrologer. In response to the story, the White House spokesman at the time, Marlin Fitzwater, said, "Vindictiveness and revenge are not admirable qualities and are not worthy of comment."

Exercise 7-8

Elegant Country Estate

- Stunning Federal-style brick home with exquisite appointments throughout
- 20 picturesque acres with lake, pasture, and woodland
- 5 bedrooms, 4.5 baths
- 5,800 sq. ft. living space, 2,400 sq. ft. basement
- Formal living room; banquet dining with butler's pantry; luxurious foyer, gourmet kitchen, morning room
- 3 fireplaces, 12 chandeliers

Maude and Clyde are discussing whether to buy this nice little cottage. Identify as many fallacies and rhetorical devices as you can in their conversation. Many are from this chapter, but you may see something from Chapters 5 and 6 as well.

CLYDE: Maude, look at this place! This is the house for us! Let's make an offer right now. We can afford it!

MAUDE: Oh, Clyde, be serious. That house is way beyond our means.

CLYDE: Well, I think we can afford it.

MAUDE: Honey, if we can afford it, pigs can fly.

CLYDE: Look, do you want to live in a shack? Besides, I called the real estate agent. She says it's a real steal.

MAUDE: Well, what do you expect her to say? She's looking for a commission.

CLYDE: Sometimes I don't understand you. Last week you were pushing for a really upscale place.

MAUDE: Clyde, we can't make the payments on a place like that. We couldn't even afford to heat it! And what on earth are we going to do with a lake?

CLYDE: Honey, the payments would only be around $5,000 a month. How much do you think we could spend?

MAUDE: I'd say $1,800.

CLYDE: Okay, how about $2,050?

MAUDE: Oh, for heaven's sake! Yes, we could do $2,050!

CLYDE: Well, how about $3,100?

MAUDE: Oh, Clyde, what is your point?

CLYDE: So $3,100 is okay? How about $3,200? Stop me when I get to exactly where we can't afford it.

MAUDE: Clyde, I can't say exactly where it gets to be too expensive, but $5,000 a month is too much.

CLYDE: Well, I think we can afford it.

MAUDE: Why?

CLYDE: Because it's within our means!

MAUDE: Clyde, you're the one who's always saying we have to cut back on our spending!

CLYDE: Yes, but this'll be a great investment!

MAUDE: And what makes you say that?

CLYDE: Because we're bound to make money on it.

MAUDE: Clyde, honey, you are going around in circles.

CLYDE: Well, can you prove we can't afford it?

MAUDE: Once we start spending money like drunken sailors, where will it end? Next we'll have to get a riding mower, then a boat for that lake, a butler for the butler's pantry—we'll owe everybody in the state!

CLYDE: Well, we don't have to make up our minds right now. I'll call the agent and tell her we're sleeping on it.

MAUDE: Asleep and dreaming.

Exercise 7-9

In groups, vote on which option best depicts the fallacy found in each passage; then compare results with other groups in the class. *Note:* The fallacies include those found in Chapter 6 and Chapter 7.

▲   1. The health editor for *USA Today* certainly seems to know what she is talking about when she recommends we take vitamins, but I happen to know she works for Tishcon, Inc., a large manufacturer of vitamin supplements.

    a. smoke screen/red herring
    b. subjectivism
    c. appeal to popularity
    d. circumstantial ad hominem
    e. no fallacy

   2. The president is right. People who are against fighting in Afghanistan are unwilling to face up to the threat of terrorism.

    a. common practice
    b. peer pressure
    c. false dilemma
    d. straw man
    e. begging the question

   3. Well, I, for one, think the position taken by our union is correct, and I'd like to remind you before you make up your mind on the matter that around here we employees have a big say in who gets rehired.

    a. wishful thinking
    b. circumstantial ad hominem
    c. scare tactics (argument from force)
    d. apple polishing
    e. begging the question

▲   4. On the whole, I think global warming is a farce. After all, most people think winters are getting colder, if anything. How could that many people be wrong?

    a. argument from outrage
    b. appeal to popularity
    c. straw man
    d. no fallacy

   5. MARCO: I think global warming is a farce.
    CLAUDIA: Oh, gad. How can you say such a thing, when there is so much evidence behind the theory?
    MARCO: Because. Look. If it isn't a farce, then how come the world is colder now than it used to be?

    a. begging the question
    b. appeal to popularity
    c. red herring
    d. circumstantial ad hominem
    e. no fallacy

6. Of course you should buy a life insurance policy! Why shouldn't you?

   a. smoke screen/red herring
   b. wishful thinking
   c. scare tactics
   d. peer pressure argument
   e. misplacing the burden of proof

▲ 7. My opponent, Mr. London, has charged me with having cheated on my income tax. My response is, When are we going to get this campaign out of the gutter? Isn't it time we stood up and made it clear that vilification has no place in politics?

   a. smoke screen/red herring
   b. wishful thinking
   c. appeal to common practice
   d. appeal to popularity
   e. circumstantial ad hominem

8. Look, even if Bush did lie about the WMD threat, what's the surprise? Clinton lied about having sex with that intern, and Bush's own father lied about raising taxes.

   a. smoke screen/red herring
   b. straw man
   c. false dilemma
   d. inconsistency ad hominem
   e. common practice

9. If cigarettes aren't bad for you, then how come it's so hard on your health to smoke?

   a. circumstantial ad hominem
   b. genetic fallacy
   c. slippery slope
   d. begging the question

▲ 10. GARRY: I think the people who lost their livelihood because of the Gulf oil spill ought to be paid their losses in full.
    HARRY: But there are disasters all over the place. You can't compensate *everybody*.

   a. perfectionist fallacy
   b. straw man
   c. appeal to tradition
   d. appeal to common practice

Exercise 7-10

In groups, vote on which option best depicts the fallacy found in each passage, and compare results with other groups. (It is all right with us if you ask anyone who is not participating in the discussions in your group to leave.) *Note:* The fallacies include those found in Chapter 6 and Chapter 7.

▲ 1. So what if the senator accepted a little kickback money—most politicians are corrupt, after all.

   a. argument from envy
   b. argument from tradition

   c. common practice
   d. subjectivism
   e. no fallacy

2. Me? I'm going to vote with the company on this one. After all, I've been with them for fifteen years.

   a. genetic fallacy
   b. groupthink fallacy
   c. slippery slope
   d. no fallacy

3. Public opinion polls? They're rigged. Just ask anyone.

   a. appeal to common practice
   b. guilt trip
   c. begging the question
   d. appeal to popularity
   e. no fallacy

4. Hey! It can't be time for the bars to close. I'm having too much fun.

   a. false dilemma
   b. misplacing the burden of proof
   c. wishful thinking
   d. appeal to tradition
   e. no fallacy

5. A mural for the municipal building? Excuse me, but why should public money, *our* tax dollars, be used for a totally unnecessary thing like art? There are potholes that need fixing. Traffic signals that need to be put up. There are a *million* things that are more important. It is an *outrage*, spending taxpayers' money on unnecessary frills like art. Give me a break!

   a. inconsistency ad hominem
   b. argument from outrage
   c. slippery slope
   d. perfectionist fallacy
   e. no fallacy

6. Mathematics is more difficult than sociology, and I *really* need an easier term this fall. So I'm going to take a sociology class instead of a math class.

   a. circumstantial ad hominem
   b. argument from pity
   c. false dilemma
   d. begging the question
   e. no fallacy

7. Parker says Macs are better than PCs, but what would you expect him to say? He's owned Macs for years.

   a. personal attack ad hominem
   b. circumstantial ad hominem
   c. inconsistency ad hominem
   d. perfectionist fallacy
   e. no fallacy

8. The congressman thought the president's behavior was an impeachable offense. But that's nonsense, coming from the congressman. He had an adulterous affair himself, after all.

    a. inconsistency ad hominem
    b. poisoning the well
    c. personal attack ad hominem
    d. genetic fallacy
    e. no fallacy

9. Your professor wants you to read Moore and Parker? Forget it. Their book is so far to the right it's falling off the shelf.

    a. poisoning the well
    b. inconsistency ad hominem
    c. misplacing the burden of proof
    d. appeal to tradition
    e. no fallacy

▲ 10. How do I know God exists? Hey, how do you know he doesn't?

    a. perfectionist fallacy
    b. inconsistency ad hominem
    c. misplacing the burden of proof
    d. slippery slope
    e. begging the question

Exercise 7-11

In groups, vote on which option best depicts the fallacy found in each passage, and compare results with other groups. *Note:* The fallacies include those found in Chapter 6 and Chapter 7.

▲ 1. Laws against teenagers drinking?—They are a total waste of time, frankly. No matter how many laws we pass, there are always going to be some teens who drink.

    a. misplacing the burden of proof
    b. perfectionist fallacy
    c. line-drawing fallacy
    d. no fallacy

2. Even though Sidney was old enough to buy a drink at the bar, he had no identification with him, and the bartender would not serve him.

    a. perfectionist fallacy
    b. inconsistency ad hominem
    c. misplacing the burden of proof
    d. slippery slope
    e. no fallacy

3. Just how much sex has to be in a movie before you call it pornographic? Seems to me the whole concept makes no sense.

    a. perfectionist fallacy
    b. line-drawing fallacy
    c. straw man
    d. slippery slope
    e. no fallacy

▲ 4. Studies confirm what everyone already knows: Smaller classes make students better learners.

a. appeal to common practice
b. begging the question
c. misplacing the burden of proof
d. appeal to popularity
e. no fallacy

5. The trouble with impeaching the president is this: Going after every person who occupies the presidency will take up everyone's time, and the government will never get anything else done.

   a. inconsistency ad hominem
   b. straw man
   c. groupthink
   d. argument from envy
   e. red herring

6. The trouble with impeaching the president is this. If we start going after him, next we'll be going after senators, representatives, governors. Pretty soon, no elected official will be safe from partisan attack.

   a. inconsistency ad hominem
   b. slippery slope
   c. straw man
   d. false dilemma
   e. misplacing the burden of proof

▲ 7. MR. IMHOFF: That does it. I'm cutting down on your peanut butter cookies. Those things blimp me up.
   MRS. IMHOFF: Oh, Imhoff, get real. What about all the ice cream you eat?

   a. circumstantial ad hominem
   b. subjectivism
   c. straw man
   d. slippery slope
   e. inconsistency ad hominem

8. KEN: I think I'll vote for Andrews. She's the best candidate.
   ROBERT: Why do you say she's best?
   KEN: Because she's my sister-in-law. Didn't you know that?

   a. apple polishing
   b. argument from pity
   c. scare tactics
   d. peer pressure argument
   e. none of the above

9. MOE: You going to class tomorrow?
   JOE: I s'pose. Why?
   MOE: Say, don't you get tired of being a Goody Two-shoes? You must have the most perfect attendance record of anyone who ever went to this school—certainly better than the rest of us; right, guys?

   a. poisoning the well
   b. argument from pity
   c. scare tactics
   d. no fallacy
   e. none of the above

▲   10. Morgan, you're down-to-earth and I trust your judgment. That's why I know I can count on you to back me up at the meeting this afternoon.

   a. apple polishing
   b. argument from pity
   c. scare tactics
   d. guilt trip
   e. no fallacy

11. "Do you want to sign this petition to the governor?"

   "What's it about?"
   "We want him to veto that handgun registration bill that's come out of the legislature."
   "Oh. No, I don't think I want to sign that."
   "Oh, really? So are you telling me you want to get rid of the Second Amendment?"

   a. false dilemma
   b. personal attack ad hominem
   c. genetic fallacy
   d. misplacing the burden of proof
   e. no fallacy

12. Outlaw gambling? Man, that's a strange idea coming from you. Aren't you the one who plays the lottery all the time?

   a. inconsistency ad hominem
   b. circumstantial ad hominem
   c. genetic fallacy
   d. scare tactics
   e. no fallacy

Exercise 7-12

Most of the following passages contain fallacies from Chapter 6 or Chapter 7. Identify them where they occur and try to place them in one of the categories we have described.

▲   1. "People in Hegins, Pennsylvania, hold an annual pigeon shoot in order to control the pigeon population and to raise money for the town. This year, the pigeon shoot was disrupted by animal rights activists who tried to release the pigeons from their cages. I can't help but think these animal rights activists are the same people who believe in controlling the human population through the use of abortion. Yet, they recoil at a similar means of controlling pigeons. What rank hypocrisy."

   —*Rush Limbaugh*

2. Dear Mr. Swanson: I realize I'm not up for a salary increase yet, but I thought it might make my review a bit more timely if I pointed out to you that I have a copy of all the recent e-mail messages between you and Ms. Flood in the purchasing department.

3. I don't care if Nike has signed up Michael Jordan, Tiger Woods, and even Santa Claus to endorse their shoes. They're a crummy company that makes a crummy product. The proof is the fact that they pay poor

women a dollar sixty for a long day's work in their Vietnamese shoe factories. That's not even enough to buy a day's worth of decent meals!

4. I don't care if Nike has signed up Michael Jordan, Tiger Woods, and even Santa Claus to endorse their shoes. They're a crummy company, and I wouldn't buy their shoes no matter what the circumstance. You don't need any reason beyond the fact that they pay poor women a dollar sixty for a long day's work in their Vietnamese shoe factories. That's not even enough to buy a day's worth of decent meals!

5. Nike is a crummy company that makes crummy shoes. Look: they still sponsor Tiger Woods even after all the bad stuff that came to light about him.

6. POWELL FAN: Colin Powell says that diplomatic efforts to avoid war with Iraq were serious and genuine, and his word is good enough for me.
SKEPTIC: And what makes you so sure he's telling it like it is?
FAN: Because he's the one guy in the administration you can trust.

7. I know the repair guy in the service center screwed up my computer; he's the only one who's touched it since it was working fine last Monday.

8. If you give the cat your leftover asparagus, next thing you know you'll be feeding him your potatoes, maybe even your roast beef. Where will it all end? Pretty soon that wretched animal will be sitting up here on the table for dinner. He'll be eating us out of house and home.

9. Look, either we refrain from feeding the cat table scraps, or he'll be up here on the table with us. So don't go giving him your asparagus.

10. We have a simple choice. Saving Social Security is sure as hell a lot more important than giving people a tax cut. So write your representative now, and let him or her know how you feel.

11. Let gays join the military? Give me a break. God created Adam and Eve, not Adam and Steve.

12. So my professor told me if he gave me an A for getting an 89.9 on the test, next he'd have to give people an A for getting an 89.8 on the test, and pretty soon he'd have to give everyone in the class an A. How could I argue with that?

13. Those blasted Democrats! They want to increase government spending on education again. This is the same outfit that gave us $10,000 toilets and government regulations up the wazoo.

14. The way I see it, either the senator resigns, or he sends a message that no one should admit to his misdeeds.

15. Lauren did a better job than anyone else at the audition, so even though she has no experience, we've decided to give her the part in the play.

16. TERRY: I failed my test, but I gave my prof this nifty argument. I said, "Look, suppose somebody did 0.0001 percent better than I, would that be a big enough difference to give him a higher grade?" And he had to say "no," so then I said, "And if someone did 0.0001 percent better than that second person, would that be a big enough difference?" And he had to say "no" to that, too, so I just kept it up, and he never could point to the place where the difference was big enough to give the other person a higher grade. He finally saw he couldn't justify giving anyone a better grade.
HARRY: Well? What happened?
TERRY: He had to fail the whole class.

17. "Many, but not all, on the other side of the aisle lack the will to win," said Representative Charlie Norwood of Georgia. "The American people need to know precisely who they are." He said, "It is time to stand up and vote. Is it Al Qaeda, or is it America?"

—New York Times, *June 15, 2006*

18. Look, maybe you think it's okay to legalize tribal casinos, but I don't. Letting every last group of people in the country open a casino is a ridiculous idea, bound to cause trouble.

▲ 19. What, you of all people complaining about violence on TV? You, with all the pro football you watch?

20. You have three Fs and a D on your exams, and your quizzes are on the borderline between passing and failing. I'm afraid you don't deserve to pass the course.

Exercise 7-13

Where we (Moore and Parker) teach, the city council recently debated relaxing the local noise ordinance. One student (who favored relaxation) appeared before the council and stated: "If 250 people are having fun, one person shouldn't be able to stop them."

We asked our students to state whether they agreed or disagreed with that student and to support their position with an argument. Here are some of the responses.

Divide into groups, and then identify any instances of fallacious reasoning you find in any answers, drawing from the materials in the last two chapters. Compare your results with those of other students, and see what your instructor thinks.

1. I support what the person is saying. If 250 people are having fun, one person shouldn't be able to stop them. Having parties and having a good time are a way of life for Chico State students. The areas around campus have always been this way.

2. A lot of people attend Chico State because of the social aspects. If rules are too tight, the school could lose its appeal. Without the students, local businesses would go under. Students keep the town floating. It's not just bars and liquor stores, but gas stations and grocery stores and apartment houses. This town would be like Orland.

3. If students aren't allowed to party, the college will go out of business.

4. We work hard all week long studying and going to classes. We deserve to let off steam after a hard week.

5. Noise is a fact of life around most college campuses. People should know what they are getting into before they move there. If they don't like it, they should just get earplugs or leave.

6. I agree with what the person is saying. If 250 people want to have fun, what gives one person the right to stop them?

7. I am sure many of the people who complain are the same people who used to be stumbling down Ivy Street twenty years ago doing the same thing that the current students are doing.

8. Two weeks ago, I was at a party, and it was only about 9:00 P.M. There were only a few people there, and it was quiet. And then the police came and told us we had to break it up because a neighbor complained. Well, that neighbor is an elderly lady who would complain if you flushed the toilet. I think it's totally unreasonable.

9. Sometimes the noise level gets a little out of control, but there are other ways to go about addressing this problem. For example, if you are a neighbor, and you are having a problem with the noise level, why don't you call the "party house" and let them know, instead of going way too far and calling the police?

10. I'm sure that these "narcs" have nothing else better to do than to harass the "party people."

11. You can't get rid of all the noise around a college campus no matter what you do.

12. The Chico noise ordinance was put there by the duly elected officials of the city and is the law. People do not have the right to break a law that was put in place under proper legal procedures.

13. The country runs according to majority rule. If the overwhelming majority want to party and make noise, under our form of government they should be given the freedom to do so.

14. Students make a contribution to the community, and in return they should be allowed to make noise if they want.

15. Your freedom ends at my property line.

Exercise 7-14

Go back to Exercise 4-16 and determine whether the author of the article commits a fallacy in his criticism of Anthony Watts. Compare your decision with those of your classmates.

Exercise 7-15

Listen to a talk-radio program (e.g., Air America, Rush Limbaugh, Michael Reagan, Michael Savage), and see how many minutes (or seconds) go by before you hear one of the following: ad hominem, straw man, ridicule, argument from outrage, or scare tactics. Report your findings to the class, and describe the first item from the above list that you heard.

Exercise 7-16

Watch one of the news/public affairs programs on television (*NewsHour with Jim Lehrer, Nightline, Face the Nation,* and so on), and make a note of any examples of fallacies that occur. Explain in writing why you think the examples contain fallacious reasoning.

Alternatively, watch *Real Time* with Bill Maher. It usually doesn't take long to find a fallacy there, either.

Exercise 7-17

The following passages contain fallacies from both this chapter and the preceding one. Identify the category in which each item belongs.

▲   1. "I can safely say that no law, no matter how stiff the consequence is, will completely stop illegal drug use. Outlawing drugs is a waste of time."

   —From a student essay

2. "If we expand the commuter bus program, where is it going to end? Will we want to have a trolley system? Then a light rail system? Then expand Metrolink to our area? A city this size hardly needs and certainly cannot afford all these amenities."

   —From a newspaper call-in column

3. YAEKO: The character Dana Scully on *The X-Files* really provides a good role model for young women. She's a medical doctor and an FBI agent, and she's intelligent, professional, and devoted to her work.
   MICHAEL: Those shows about paranormal activities are so unrealistic. Alien abductions, government conspiracies—it's all ridiculous.

4. Overheard: "The reason I don't accept evolution is that ever since Darwin, scientists have been trying to prove that we evolved from some apelike primate ancestor. Well, they still haven't succeeded. Case closed."

▲   5. Ladies and gentlemen, as you know, I endorsed council member Morrissey's bid for reelection based on his outstanding record during his first term. Because you are the movers and shakers in this community, other people place the same high value on your opinions that I do. Jim and I would feel privileged to have your support.

6. It's totally ridiculous to suppose that creationism is true. If creationism were true, then half of what we know through science would be false, which is complete nonsense.

7. KIRSTI: I counted my CDs this weekend, and out of twenty-seven, ten of them were by U2. They are such a good band! I haven't heard anything by Bono for a long time. He has such a terrific voice!
   BEN: Is he bisexual?

8. Was Gerhard a good committee chair? Well, I for one think you have to say he was excellent, especially when you consider all the abuse he put up with. Right from the start, people went after him—they didn't even give him a chance to show what he could do. It was really vicious— people making fun of him right to his face. Yes, under the circumstances he has been quite effective.

▲   9. Medical research that involves animals is completely unnecessary and a waste of money. Just think of the poor creatures! We burn and blind and torture them, and then we kill them. They don't know what is going to happen to them, but they know something is going to happen. They are scared to death. It's really an outrage.

10. Dear Editor—
   If Christians do not participate in government, only sinners will.

   —From a letter to the Chico Enterprise Record

11. The HMO people claim that the proposal will raise the cost of doing business in the state to such a degree that insurers will be forced to leave the state and do business elsewhere. What nonsense. Just look at what we get from these HMOs. I know people who were denied decent treatment for cancer because their HMO wouldn't approve it. There are doctors who won't recommend a procedure for their patients because they

are afraid the HMO will cancel their contract. And when an HMO does cancel some doctor's contract, the patients have to find a new doctor themselves—*if* they can. Everybody has a horror story. Enough is enough.

12. From an interview by Gwen Ifill (PBS *News Hour*) with Senator Kit Bond, ranking Republican on the Senate Intelligence Committee:

IFILL: Do you think that waterboarding, as I have described it, constitutes torture?

BOND: There are different ways of doing it; it's like swimming: freestyle, backstroke. Waterboarding could be used, almost, to define some of the techniques that our trainees are put through. But that's beside the point. It's not being used. There are some who say that, in extreme circumstances, if there is a threat of an imminent major attack on the United States, it might be used.

—From the video at <talkingpointsmemo.com/archives/060899.php>

▲ 13. The opposing party is going to give its reply to the president's speech in just a few minutes. Prepare yourself for the usual misstatements of fact, exaggerated criticism, and attempts to distract from the real issues.

14. The proposal to reduce spending for the arts just doesn't make any sense. We spend a paltry $620 million for the NEA [National Endowment for the Arts], while the deficit is closing in on $200 billion. Cutting support for the arts isn't going to eliminate the deficit; that's obvious.

15. Year-round schools? I'm opposed. Once we let them do that, the next thing you know they'll be cutting into our vacation time and asking us to teach in the evenings and on the weekends, and who knows where it will end. We teachers have to stand up for our rights.

▲ 16. Romney was for abortion rights before he began running for president. Now he's anti-abortion. I think he should be ignored completely on the subject since you can't depend on what he says.

17. Even if we outlaw guns, we're still going to have crime and murder. So I really don't see much point in it.

—From a student essay

18. Do you think affirmative action programs are still necessary in the country? *Answers:*

   a. Yes, of course. I don't see how you, a woman, can ask that question. It's obvious we have a very long way to go still.
   b. No. Because of affirmative action, my brother lost his job to a minority who had a lot less experience than he did.
   c. Yes. The people who want to end affirmative action are all white males who just want to go back to the good-old-boy system. It's always the same: Look out for number one.
   d. No. The people who want it to continue know a good deal when they see one. You think I'd want to end it if I were a minority?

Exercise 7-18

Explain in a sentence or two how each of the following passages involves a type of fallacy mentioned in either this chapter or the preceding one. *Many of these examples are difficult* and should serve to illustrate how fallacies sometimes conform only loosely to the standard patterns.

▲ 1. I believe that the companies that produce passenger airliners should be more strictly supervised by the FAA. I mean, good grief, everybody knows that you can make more money by cutting corners here and there than by spending extra time and effort getting things just right, and you know there have got to be airlines that are doing exactly that.

2. From a letter to a college newspaper editor: "I really appreciated the fact that your editorial writer supports the hike in the student activity fee that has been proposed. Since the writer is a senior and won't even be here next year, he will escape having to pay the fee himself, so of course there's no downside to it as far as he's concerned. I'm against the fee, and I'll be one of those who pay it if it passes. Mine is an opinion that should count."

3. "'There's a certain sameness to the news on the Big Three [ABC, NBC, and CBS] and CNN,' says Moody, . . . who is in charge of Fox News's day-to-day editorial decisions. That's the message, Moody says, that 'America is bad, corporations are bad, animal species should be protected, and every cop is a racist killer. That's where "fair and balanced" [Fox's slogan] comes in. We don't think all corporations are bad, every forest should be saved, every government spending program is good. We're going to be more inquisitive.'"

—From an interview with John Moody, vice president for news editorial at Fox News Network, in Brill's Content *magazine*

▲ 4. During the Reagan and G. H. W. Bush administrations, Democratic members of Congress pointed to the two presidents' economic policies as causing huge deficits that could ultimately ruin the country's economy. President Bush dismissed such charges as "the politics of doom and gloom." "These people will find a dark cloud everywhere," he has said. Was this response fallacious reasoning?

▲ 5. "Louis Harris, one of the nation's most influential pollsters, readily admits he is in the polling business to 'have some impact with the movers and shakers of the world.' So poll questions are often worded to obtain answers that help legitimize the liberal Establishment's viewpoints."

—Conservative Digest

6. "At a White House meeting in February of 1983 with Washington, D.C., anchormen, Ronald Reagan was asked to comment on 'an apparent continuing perception among a number of black leaders that the White House continues to be, if not hostile, at least not welcome to black viewpoints.' President Reagan replied as follows: 'I'm aware of all that, and it's very disturbing to me, because anyone who knows my life story knows that long before there was a thing called the civil-rights movement, I was busy on that side. As a sports announcer, I didn't have any Willie Mayses or Reggie Jacksons to talk about when I was broadcasting major league baseball. The opening line of the Spalding Baseball Guide said, "Baseball is a game for Caucasian gentlemen." And as a sports announcer I was one of a very small fraternity that used that job to editorialize against that ridiculous blocking of so many fine athletes and so many fine Americans from participating in what was called the great American game.' Reagan then went on to mention that his father refused to allow him to see *Birth of a Nation* because it was based on the Ku Klux Klan and once slept in a

car during a blizzard rather than stay at a hotel that barred Jews. Reagan's 'closest teammate and buddy' was a black, he said."

—*James Nathan Miller*, The Atlantic

7. From a letter to the editor of the *Atlantic Monthly:* "In all my reading and experience so far, I have found nothing presented by science and technology that precludes there being a spiritual element to the human being. . . . The bottom line is this: Maybe there are no angels, afterlife, UFOs, or even a God. Certainly their existence has not yet been scientifically proved. But just as certainly, their *nonexistence* remains unproved. Any reasonable person would therefore have to reserve judgment."

8. Stop blaming the developers for the fact that our town is growing! If you want someone to blame, blame the university. It brings the new people here, not the developers. Kids come here from God knows where, and lots of them like what they find and stick around. All the developers do is put roofs over those former students' heads.

▲ 9. Two favorite scientists of the Council for Tobacco Research were Carl Seltzer and Theodore Sterling. Seltzer, a biological anthropologist, believes smoking has no role in heart disease and has alleged in print that data in the huge 45-year, 10,000-person Framingham Heart Study—which found otherwise—have been distorted by anti-tobacco researchers. Framingham Director William Castelli scoffs at Seltzer's critique but says it "has had some impact in keeping the debate alive."

    Sterling, a statistician, disputes the validity of population studies linking smoking to illness, arguing that their narrow focus on smoking obscures the more likely cause—occupational exposure to toxic fumes.

    For both men, defying conventional wisdom has been rewarding. Seltzer says he has received "well over $1 million" from the Council for research. Sterling got $1.1 million for his Special Projects work in 1977–82, court records show.

—*From "How Tobacco Firms Keep Health Questions 'Open' Year After Year,"*
Alix Freedman and Laurie Cohen. The article originally appeared in the
Wall Street Journal *and was reprinted in the* Sacramento Bee.

10. We have had economic sanctions in effect against China ever since the Tienanmen Square massacre. Clearly, they haven't turned the Chinese leadership in Beijing into a bunch of good guys. All they've done, in fact, is cost American business a lot of money. We should get rid of the sanctions and find some other way to make them improve their human rights record.

Writing Exercises

1. Your instructor will assign one or more of the Essays for Analysis in Appendix 1 for you to scan for fallacies and rhetorical devices.

2. In the spring of 2010, the Texas State Board of Education voted to "put a conservative stamp on history and economics textbooks, questioning the Founding Fathers' commitment to a purely secular government and presenting Republican political philosophies in a more positive light." The majority of the board, a 10-vote bloc (of 15 total), "question Darwin's theory of evolution and believe the Founding Fathers were guided by

Christian principles." On the other side are "a handful of Democrats and moderate Republicans who have fought to preserve the teaching of Darwinism and the separation of church and state."

Which side do you think has the better case? Should Texas schools teach Darwin's theory of evolution? Should they teach that the United States was consciously founded on Christian principles? Write a two-page essay in which you describe and defend your position. When the class has finished, read the essays in groups, looking for fallacies and other rhetorical devices. (Your instructor may have further or alternative instructions.)

3. A Schedule I drug, as defined by the Controlled Substances Act of 1970, is one that (a) has a high potential for abuse, (b) has no currently accepted medical use in treatment in the United States, and (c) has a lack of accepted safety for use of the drug under medical supervision. Should marijuana be classified as a Schedule I drug? Defend a position on the issue following the same instructions as for Writing Exercise 2.

4. Choose two of the examples in Exercise 7-17 and diagram them according to the procedure described in Chapter 2.

Deductive Arguments I

Categorical Logic

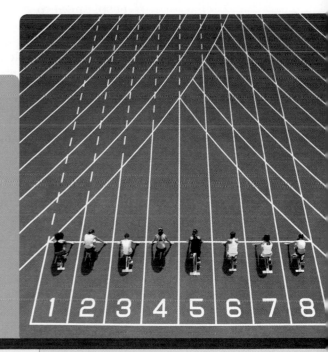

... The Science of Deduction and Analysis is one which can only be acquired by long and patient study, nor is life long enough to allow any mortal to attain the highest possible perfection in it.

*—From an article by Sherlock Holmes,
in* A Study in Scarlet *by Sir Arthur Conan Doyle*

Fortunately, the greatest detective was doing some serious exaggerating in this quotation. While it may be that few of us mortals will attain "the highest possible perfection" in "the Science of Deduction," most of us can learn quite a bit in a fairly short time if we put our minds to it. In fact, you already have an understanding of the basics from Chapter 2.* In this chapter and the next, you'll learn two kinds of techniques for making and evaluating deductive inferences—in other words, arguments.

If you flip through the pages of these two chapters, you'll see diagrams with circles and Xs, and in Chapter 9, page after page of weird symbols that remind some people of

---

*An understanding that's somewhat better than Sir Arthur's, as a matter of fact. Many instances of what he has Sherlock Holmes referring to as "deduction" turn out to be *inductive* arguments, not deductive ones, as was mentioned in Chapter 2. We mean no disrespect, of course; one of your authors is a dyed-in-the-wool Holmes fanatic.

Students will learn to . . .

1. Recognize the four types of categorical claims and the Venn diagrams that represent them

2. Translate a claim into standard form

3. Use the square of opposition to identify logical relationships between corresponding categorical claims

4. Use conversion, obversion, and contraposition with standard form to make valid arguments

5. Recognize and evaluate the validity of categorical syllogisms

mathematics. These pages may look intimidating. But there's nothing all that complicated about them if you approach them in the right way. Nearly anybody can catch on *if* they take one of Sherlock Holmes's points seriously: Most people need to apply themselves conscientiously to understand this material. The reason is that, both here and in Chapter 9, almost everything builds on what goes before; if you don't understand what happens at the beginning of the chapter, most of what happens later won't make much sense. So take our advice (and you'll probably hear this from your instructor, too): Keep up! Don't get behind. This stuff is not easy to learn the night before an exam. But if you apply yourself regularly, it really isn't all that hard. In fact, many of our students find this part of the book the most fun, because practicing the subject matter is like playing a game. So, be prepared to put in a little time on a regular basis, pay close attention to the text and your instructor's remarks, and just maybe you'll have a good time with this.

The first technique we'll discuss is **categorical logic.** Categorical logic is logic based on the relations of inclusion and exclusion among classes (or "categories") as stated in categorical claims. Its methods date back to the time of Aristotle, and it was the principal form that logic took among most knowledgeable people for more than two thousand years. During that time, all kinds of bells and whistles were added to the basic theory, especially by monks and other scholars during the medieval period. So as not to weigh you down with unnecessary baggage, we'll just set forth the basics of the subject in what follows.

Like truth-functional logic, the subject of the next chapter, categorical logic is useful in clarifying and analyzing deductive arguments. But there is another reason for studying the subject: There is no better way to understand

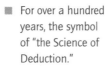

For over a hundred years, the symbol of "the Science of Deduction."

the underlying logical structure of our everyday language than to learn how to put it into the kinds of formal terms we'll introduce in these chapters.

To test your analytical ability, take a look at these claims. Just exactly what is the difference between them?

(1) Everybody who is ineligible for Physics 1A must take Physical Science 1.
(2) No students who are required to take Physical Science 1 are eligible for Physics 1A.

Here's another pair of claims:

(3) Harold won't attend the meeting unless Vanessa decides to go.
(4) If Vanessa decides to go, then Harold will attend the meeting.

You might be surprised at how many college students have a hard time trying to determine whether the claims in each pair mean the same thing or something different. In this chapter and the next, you'll learn a foolproof method for determining how to unravel the logical implications of such claims and for seeing how any two such claims relate to each other. (Incidentally, claims 1 and 2 do not mean the same thing at all, and neither do 3 and 4.) If you're signing a lease or entering into a contract of any kind, it pays to be able to figure out just what is said in it and what is not; those who have trouble with claims like the ones above risk being left in the dark.

Studying categorical and truth-functional logic can teach us to become more careful and precise in our own thinking. Getting comfortable with this type of thinking can be helpful in general, but for those who will someday apply to law school, medical school, or graduate school, it has the added advantage that many admission exams for such programs deal with the kinds of reasoning discussed in this chapter.

Let's start by looking at the four basic kinds of claims on which categorical logic is based.

CATEGORICAL CLAIMS

A **categorical claim** says something about classes (or "categories") of things. Our interest lies in categorical claims of certain standard forms. A **standard-form categorical claim** is a claim that results from putting names or descriptions of classes into the blanks of the following structures:

A: All _____ are _____.
   (*Example:* All Presbyterians are Christians.)

E: No _____ are _____.
   (*Example:* No Muslims are Christians.)

I: Some _____ are _____.
   (*Example:* Some Christians are Arabs.)

O: Some _____ are not _____.
   (*Example:* Some Muslims are not Sunnis.)

The phrases that go in the blanks are **terms;** the one that goes into the first blank is the **subject term** of the claim, and the one that goes into the second blank is the **predicate term.** Thus, "Christians" is the predicate term of the first example above and the subject term of the third example. In many of the examples and explanations that follow, we'll use the letters *S* and *P* (for "subject" and "predicate") to stand for terms in categorical claims. And we'll talk about the subject and predicate *classes,* which are just the classes that the terms refer to.

But first, a caution: Only nouns and noun phrases will work as terms. An adjective alone, such as "red," won't do. "All fire engines are red" does *not* produce a standard-form categorical claim, because "red" is not a noun or noun phrase. To see that it is not, try switching the places of the terms: "All red are fire engines." This doesn't make sense, right? But "red vehicles" (or even "red things") will do because "All red vehicles are fire engines" makes sense (even though it's false).

Looking back at the standard-form structures just given, notice that each one has a letter to its left. These are the traditional names of the four types of standard-form categorical claims. The claim "All Presbyterians are Christians" is an A-claim, and so are "All idolators are heathens," "All people born between 1946 and 1964 are baby boomers," and any other claim of the form "All S are P." The same is true for the other three letters, E, I, and O, and the other three kinds of claims.

Venn Diagrams

Each of the standard forms has its own graphic illustration in a **Venn diagram,** as shown in Figures 1 through 4. Named after British logician John Venn, these diagrams exactly represent the four standard-form categorical claim types. In the diagrams, the circles represent the classes named by the terms, colored areas represent areas that are empty, and areas containing Xs represent areas

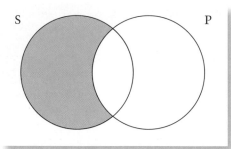

FIGURE 1   A-claim: All S are P.

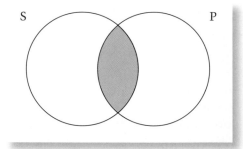

FIGURE 2   E-claim: No S are P.

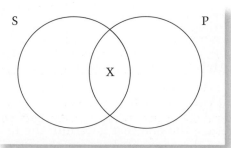

FIGURE 3   I-claim: Some S are P.

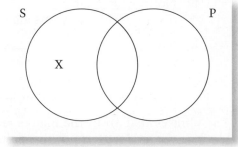

FIGURE 4   O-claim: Some S are not P.

that are not empty—that contain at least one item. An area that is blank is one that the claim says nothing about; it may be occupied, or it may be empty.*

Notice that in the diagram for the A-claim, the area that would contain any members of the S class that were *not* members of the P class is colored—that is, it is empty. Thus, that diagram represents the claim "All S are P," since there is no S left that isn't P. Similarly, in the diagram for the E-claim, the area where S and P overlap is empty; any S that is also a P has been eliminated. Hence: "No S are P."

For our purposes in this chapter, the word "some" means "at least one." So, the third diagram represents the fact that at least one S is a P, and the X in the area where the two classes overlap shows that at least one thing inhabits this area. Finally, the last diagram shows an X in the area of the S circle that is outside the P circle, representing the existence of at least one S that is not a P.

We'll try to keep technical jargon to a minimum, but here's some terminology we'll need: The two claim types that *include* one class or part of one class within another, the A-claims and I-claims, are **affirmative claims;** the two that *exclude* one class or part of one class from another, the E-claims and O-claims, are **negative claims.**

Although there are only four standard-form claim types, it's remarkable how versatile they are. A large portion of what we want to say can be rewritten, or "translated," into one or another of them. Because this task is sometimes easier said than done, we'd best spend a little while making sure we understand how to do it. And we warn you in advance: A lot of standard-form translations are not very pretty—but it's accuracy we seek here, not style.

Translation into Standard Form

The main idea is to take an ordinary claim and turn it into a standard-form categorical claim that is exactly equivalent. We'll say that two claims are **equivalent claims** if, and only if, they would be true in all and exactly the same circumstances—that is, under no circumstances could one of them be true and the other false. (You can think of such claims as "saying the same thing" more or less.)

Lots of ordinary claims in English are easy to translate into standard form. A claim of the sort "Every X is a Y," for example, more or less automatically turns into the standard-form A-claim "All Xs are Ys." And it's easy to produce the proper term to turn "Minors are not eligible" into the E-claim "No minors are eligible people."

All standard-form claims are in the present tense, but even so, we can use them to talk about the past. For example, we can translate "There were creatures weighing more than four tons that lived in North America" as "Some creatures that lived in North America are creatures that weighed more than four tons."

What about a claim like "Only sophomores are eligible candidates"? It's good to have a strategy for attacking such translation problems. First, identify the terms. In this case, the two classes in question are "sophomores" and "eligible candidates." Now, which do we have on our hands, an A-, E-, I-, or O-claim? Generally speaking, nothing but a careful reading can serve to answer this question. So, you'll need to think hard about just what relation between

---

*There is one exception to this, but we needn't worry about it for a few pages yet.

classes is being expressed and then decide how that relation is best turned into a standard form. Fortunately, we can provide some general rules that help in certain frequently encountered problems, including one that applies to our current example. If you're like most people, you don't have too much trouble seeing that our claim is an A-claim, but *which* A-claim? There are two possibilities:

All sophomores are eligible candidates.

and

All eligible candidates are sophomores.

If we make the wrong choice, we can change the meaning of the claim significantly. (Notice that "All sophomores are students" is very different from "All students are sophomores.") In the present case, notice that we are saying something about *every* eligible candidate—namely, that he or she must be a sophomore. (*Only* sophomores are eligible—i.e., no one else is eligible.) In an A-claim, the class so restricted is always the subject class. So, this claim should be translated into

All eligible candidates are sophomores.

In fact, *all claims of the sort "Only Xs are Ys" should be translated as "All Ys are Xs."*

But there are other claims in which the word "only" plays a crucial role and which have to be treated differently. Consider, for example, this claim: "The only people admitted are people over twenty-one." In this case, a restriction is being put on the class of people admitted; we're saying that *nobody else is admitted* except those over twenty-one. Therefore, "people admitted" is the subject class: "All people admitted are people over twenty-one." And, in fact, *all claims of the sort "The only Xs are Ys" should be translated as "All Xs are Ys."*

The two general rules that govern most translations of claims that hinge on the word "only" are these:

The word "only," used by itself, introduces the *predicate* term of an A-claim.

The phrase "the only" introduces the *subject* term of an A-claim.

Note that, in accordance with these rules, we would translate both of these claims

Only matinees are half-price shows

and

Matinees are the only half-price shows

as

All half-price shows are matinees.

The kind of thing a claim directly concerns is not always obvious. For example, if you think for a moment about the claim "I always get nervous when I take logic exams," you'll see that it's a claim about *times*. It's about

On Language

The Most Versatile Word in English

Question:

There's only one word that can be placed successfully in any of the 10 numbered positions in this sentence to produce 10 sentences of different meaning (each sentence has 10 words): (1) *I* (2) *helped* (3) *my* (4) *dog* (5) *carry* (6) *my* (7) *husband's* (8) *slippers* (9) *yesterday* (10).

What is that word?

—GLORIA J., Salt Lake City, Utah

Answer:

The word is "only," which makes the following 10 sentences:

1. Only *I* helped my dog carry my husband's slippers yesterday.
   (Usually the cat helps too, but she was busy with a mouse.)
2. I only *helped* my dog carry my husband's slippers yesterday.
   (The dog wanted me to carry them all by myself, but I refused.)
3. I helped only *my* dog carry my husband's slippers yesterday.
   (I was too busy to help my neighbor's dog when he carried them.)
4. I helped my only *dog* carry my husband's slippers yesterday
   (I considered getting another dog, but the cat disapproved.)
5. I helped my dog only *carry* my husband's slippers yesterday.
   (I didn't help the dog eat them; I usually let the cat do that.)
6. I helped my dog carry only *my* husband's slippers yesterday.
   (My dog and I didn't have time to help my neighbor's husband.)
7. I helped my dog carry my only *husband's* slippers yesterday.
   (I considered getting another husband, but one is enough.)
8. I helped my dog carry my husband's only *slippers* yesterday.
   (My husband had two pairs of slippers, but the cat ate one pair.)
9. I helped my dog carry my husband's slippers only *yesterday*.
   (And now the dog wants help again; I wish he'd ask the cat.)
10. I helped my dog carry my husband's slippers yesterday only.
    (And believe me, once was enough—the slippers tasted *terrible*.)

—MARILYN VOS SAVANT, author of the "Ask Marilyn" column (Reprinted with permission from *Parade* and Marilyn vos Savant. Copyright © 1994, 1996.)

getting nervous and about logic exams indirectly, of course, but it pertains directly to times or occasions. The proper translation of the example is "All times I take logic exams are times I get nervous." Notice that the word "whenever" is often a clue that you're talking about times or occasions, as well as an indication that you're going to have an A-claim or an E-claim. "Wherever" works the same way for places: "He makes trouble wherever he goes" should be translated as "All places he goes are places he makes trouble."

There are two other sorts of claims that are a bit tricky to translate into standard form. The first is a claim about a single individual, such as "Aristotle is a logician." It's clear that this claim specifies a class, "logicians," and places Aristotle as a member of that class. The problem is that categorical claims are always about *two* classes, and Aristotle isn't a class. (We certainly don't talk about *some* of Aristotle being a logician.) What we want to do is treat such claims as if they were about classes with exactly one member—in this case, Aristotle. One way to do this is to use the term "people who are identical with Aristotle," which of course has only Aristotle as a member. (Everybody is identical with himself or herself, and nobody else is.) The important thing to remember about such claims can be summarized in the following rule:

Claims about single individuals should be treated as A-claims or E-claims.

"Aristotle is a logician" can therefore be translated "All people identical with Aristotle are logicians," an A-claim. Similarly, "Aristotle is not left-handed" becomes the E-claim "No people identical with Aristotle are left-handed people." (Your instructor may prefer to leave the claim in its original form and simply *treat* it as an A-claim or an E-claim. This avoids the awkward "people identical with Aristotle" wording and is certainly okay with us.)

It isn't just people that crop up in individual claims. Often, this kind of treatment is called for when we're talking about objects, occasions, places, and other kinds of things. For example, the preferred translation of "St. Louis is on the Mississippi" is "All cities identical with St. Louis are cities on the Mississippi."

Other claims that cause translation difficulty contain what are called *mass nouns*. Consider this example: "Boiled okra is too ugly to eat." This claim is about a *kind of stuff*. The best way to deal with it is to treat it as a claim about *examples* of this kind of stuff. The present example translates into an A-claim about *all* examples of the stuff in question: "All examples of boiled okra are things that are too ugly to eat." An example such as "Most boiled okra

In Depth

More on Individual Claims

We treat claims about individuals as A- and E-claims for purposes of diagramming. But they are not the same as A- and E-claims. This is clear from the fact that a false individual claim implies the truth of its negation. This will be clear from an example. If the claim "Socrates is Italian" is false, then, providing there is such a person as Socrates,* the claim "Socrates is not Italian" is true. So, a false A implies a true E and vice versa, but *only* when the claims are individual claims being treated as A- and E-claims.

---

*The assumption that the subject class is not empty is always necessary for this inference, just as it is for all inferences between contraries; we'll explain this point a few pages later.

is too ugly to eat" translates into the I-claim "Some examples of boiled okra are things that are too ugly to eat."

As we noted, it's not possible to give rules or hints about every kind of problem you might run into when translating claims into standard-form categorical versions. Only practice and discussion can bring you to the point where you can handle this part of the material with confidence. The best thing to do now is to turn to some exercises.

Translate each of the following into a standard-form claim. Make sure that each answer follows the exact form of an A-, E-, I-, or O-claim and that each term you use is a noun or noun phrase that refers to a class of things. Remember that you're trying to produce a claim that's equivalent to the one given; it doesn't matter whether the given claim is actually true.

Exercise 8-1

▲   1. Every salamander is a lizard.
   2. Not every lizard is a salamander.
   3. Only reptiles can be lizards.
▲   4. Snakes are the only members of the suborder Ophidia.
   5. The only members of the suborder Ophidia are snakes.
   6. None of the burrowing snakes are poisonous.
▲   7. Anything that's an alligator is a reptile.
   8. Anything that qualifies as a frog qualifies as an amphibian.
   9. There are frogs wherever there are snakes.
▲ 10. Wherever there are snakes, there are frogs.
   11. Whenever the frog population decreases, the snake population decreases.
   12. Nobody arrived except the cheerleaders.
▲ 13. Except for vice presidents, nobody got raises.
   14. Unless people arrived early, they couldn't get seats.
▲ 15. Most home movies are as boring as dirt.
▲ 16. Socrates is a Greek.
   17. The bank robber is not Jane's fiancé.
   18. If an automobile was built before 1950, it's an antique.
▲ 19. Salt is a meat preservative.
   20. Most corn does not make good popcorn.

Follow the instructions given in the preceding exercise.

Exercise 8-2

▲   1. Students who wrote poor exams didn't get admitted to the program.
   2. None of my students are failing.
   3. If you live in the dorms, you can't own a car.
▲   4. There are a few right-handed first basemen.
   5. People make faces every time Joan sings.

6. The only tests George fails are the ones he takes.
▲ 7. Nobody passed who didn't make at least 50 percent.
8. You can't be a member unless you're over fifty.
9. Nobody catches on without studying.
▲ 10. I've had days like this before.
11. Roofers aren't millionaires.
12. Not one part of Michael Jackson's face was original equipment.
▲ 13. A few holidays fall on Saturday.
14. Only outlaws own guns.
15. You have nothing to lose but your chains.
▲ 16. Unless you pass this test you won't pass the course.
17. If you cheat, your prof will make you sorry.
18. If you cheat, your friends couldn't care less.
▲ 19. Only when you've paid the fee will they let you enroll.
20. Nobody plays who isn't in full uniform.

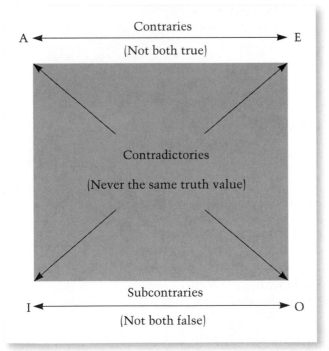

FIGURE 5 The square of opposition.

The Square of Opposition

Two categorical claims *correspond* to each other if they have the same subject term and the same predicate term. So, "All Methodists are Christians" corresponds to "Some Methodists are Christians": In both claims, "Methodists" is the subject term, and "Christians" is the predicate term. Notice, though, that "Some Christians are not Methodists" does *not* correspond to either of the other two; it has the same terms but in different places.

We can now exhibit the logical relationships between corresponding A-, E-, I-, and O-claims. The **square of opposition,** in Figure 5, does this very concisely. The A- and E-claims, across the top of the square from each other, are **contrary claims**—they can both be false, but they cannot both be true. The I- and O-claims, across the bottom of the square from each other, are **subcontrary claims**—they can both be true, but they cannot both be false. The A- and O-claims and the E- and I-claims, which are at opposite diagonal corners from each other, respectively, are **contradictory claims**—they never have the same truth values.

Notice that these logical relationships are reflected on the Venn diagrams for the claims (see Figures 1 through 4). The diagrams for corresponding A- and O-claims say exactly opposite things about the left-hand area of the diagram, namely, that the area *has* something in it and that it *doesn't*; those for corresponding E- and I-claims do the same about the center area. Clearly, exactly one claim of each pair is true no matter what—either the relevant area is empty, or it isn't.

The diagrams show clearly how both subcontraries can be true: There's no conflict in putting Xs in both left and center areas. Now, if you're paying close attention, you may have noticed that it's possible to diagram an A-claim and the corresponding E-claim on the same diagram; we just have to color the entire subject class circle. This amounts to saying that *both* an A-claim and its corresponding E-claim can be true *as long as there are no members of the subject class*. We get an analogous result for subcontraries: They can both be false as long as the subject class is empty.* We can easily avoid this result by making an assumption: *When making inferences from one contrary (or subcontrary) to another, we'll assume that the classes we're talking about are not entirely empty—that is, that each has at least one member.* On this assumption, the A-claim or the corresponding E-claim (or both) must be false, and the I-claim or the corresponding O-claim (or both) must be true.

If we have the truth value of one categorical claim, we can often deduce the truth values of the three corresponding claims by using the square of opposition. For instance, if it's true that "All serious remarks by Paris Hilton are hopeless clichés," then we can immediately infer that its contradictory claim, "Some serious remarks by Paris Hilton are not hopeless clichés," is false; the corresponding E-claim, "No serious remarks by Paris Hilton are hopeless clichés," is also false because it is the contrary claim of the original A-claim and cannot be true if the A-claim is true. The corresponding I-claim, "Some serious remarks by Paris Hilton are hopeless clichés," must be true because we just determined that *its* contradictory claim, the E-claim, is false.

However, we cannot *always* determine the truth values of the remaining three standard-form categorical claims. For example, if we know only that the A-claim is false, all we can infer is the truth value (true) of the corresponding O-claim. Nothing follows about either the E- or the I-claim. Because the A- and the E-claim can both be false, knowing that the A-claim is false does not tell us anything about the E-claim—it can still be either true or false. And if the E-claim remains undetermined, then so must its contradictory, the I-claim.

So, here are the limits on what can be inferred from the square of opposition: Beginning with a *true* claim at the top of the square (either A or E), we can infer the truth values of all three of the remaining claims. The same is true if we begin with a *false* claim at the bottom of the square (either I or O): We can still deduce the truth values of the other three. But if we begin with a false claim at the top of the square or a true claim at the bottom, all we can determine is the truth value of the contradictory of the claim in hand.

Translate the following into standard-form claims, and determine the three corresponding standard-form claims. Then, assuming the truth value in parentheses for the given claim, determine the truth values of as many of the other three as you can.

Exercise 8-3

---

*It is quite possible to interpret categorical claims this way. Allowing both the A- and the E-claims to be true and both the I- and the O-claims to be false reduces the square to contradiction alone. We're going to interpret the claims differently, however; at the level at which we're operating, it seems much more natural to see "All Cs are Ds" as conflicting with "No Cs are Ds."

Example

Most snakes are harmless. (True)

Translation (I-claim): Some snakes are harmless creatures. (True)

Corresponding A-claim: All snakes are harmless creatures. (Undetermined)

Corresponding E-claim: No snakes are harmless creatures. (False)

Corresponding O-claim: Some snakes are not harmless creatures. (Undetermined)

▲   1. Not all anniversaries are happy occasions. (True)
2. There's no such thing as a completely harmless drug. (True)
3. There have been such things as just wars. (True)
▲   4. There are allergies that can kill you. (True)
5. Woodpeckers sing really well. (False)
6. Mockingbirds can't sing. (False)
7. Some herbs are medicinal. (False)
8. Logic exercises are easy. (False)

THREE CATEGORICAL OPERATIONS

The square of opposition allows us to make inferences from one claim to another, as you were doing in the last exercise. We can think of these inferences as simple valid arguments, because that's exactly what they are. We'll turn next to three operations that can be performed on standard-form categorical claims. They, too, will allow us to make simple valid arguments and, in combination with the square, some not-quite-so-simple valid arguments.

Conversion

You find the **converse** of a standard-form claim by switching the positions of the subject and predicate terms. The E- and I-claims, but not the A- and O-claims, contain just the same information as their converses; that is,

All E- and I-claims, but not A- and O-claims, are equivalent to their converses.

Each member of the following pairs is the converse of the other:

E: No Norwegians are Slavs.
No Slavs are Norwegians.

I: Some state capitals are large cities.
Some large cities are state capitals.

Notice that the claims that are equivalent to their converses are those with symmetrical Venn diagrams.

Obversion

To discuss the next two operations, we need a couple of auxiliary notions. First, there's the notion of a *universe of discourse*. With rare exceptions, we make claims within contexts that limit the scope of the terms we use. For example, if your instructor walks into class and says, "Everybody passed the last exam," the word "everybody" does not include everybody in the world. Your instructor is not claiming, for example, that your mother and the Queen of England passed the exam. There is an unstated but obvious restriction to a smaller universe of people—in this case, the people in your class who *took* the exam. Now, for every class within a universe of discourse, there is a *complementary class* that contains everything in the universe of discourse that is *not* in the first class. Terms that name complementary classes are complementary terms. So "students" and "nonstudents" are **complementary terms.** Indeed, putting the prefix "non" in front of a term is often the easiest way to produce its complement. Some terms require different treatment, though. The complement of "people who took the exam" is probably best stated as "people who did not take the exam" because the universe is pretty clearly restricted to people in such a case. (We wouldn't expect, for example, the complement of "people who took the exam" to include *everything* that didn't take the exam, including your Uncle Bob's hairpiece.)

Now, we can get on with it: To find the **obverse** of a claim, (a) change it from affirmative to negative, or vice versa (i.e., go horizontally across the square—an A-claim becomes an E-claim; an O-claim becomes an I-claim; and so on); then (b) replace the predicate term with its complementary term.

All categorical claims of all four types, A, E, I, and O, are equivalent to their obverses.

Here are some examples; each claim is the obverse of the other member of the pair:

> A: All Presbyterians are Christians.
> No Presbyterians are non-Christians.

> E: No fish are mammals.
> All fish are nonmammals.

> I: Some citizens are voters.
> Some citizens are not nonvoters.

> O: Some contestants are not winners.
> Some contestants are nonwinners.

Contraposition

You find the **contrapositive** of a categorical claim by (a) switching the places of the subject and predicate terms, just as in conversion, and (b) replacing both terms with complementary terms. Each of the following is the contrapositive of the other member of the pair:

> A: All Mongolians are Muslims.
> All non-Muslims are non-Mongolians.

"You should say what you mean," the March Hare went on.

"I do," Alice hastily replied; "at least—at least I mean what I say—that's the same thing, you know."

"Not the same thing a bit!" said the Hatter. "Why, you might just as well say that 'I see what I eat' is the same thing as 'I eat what I see!'"

—LEWIS CARROLL, *Alice's Adventures in Wonderland*

The Mad Hatter is teaching Alice *not* to convert A-claims.

Lewis Carroll, incidentally, was an accomplished logician.

In Depth

Venn Diagrams for the Three Operations

Conversion: One way to see which operations work for which types of claim is to put them on Venn diagrams. Here's a two-circle diagram, which is all we need to explain *conversion:*

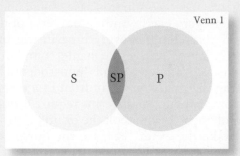

Venn 1

Imagine an I-claim, "Some S are P," diagrammed on the above. It would have an X in the central (green) area labeled SP, where S and P overlap. But its converse, "Some P are S," would also have an X in that area, since that's where P and S overlap. So, the symmetry of the diagram shows that conversion works for I-claims. The same situation holds for E-claims, except we're coloring the central area in both cases rather than placing Xs.

Now, let's imagine an A-claim, "All S are P," the diagram for which requires us to color all the subject term that's not included in the predicate term—i.e., the yellow area above. But its converse, "All P are S," would require that we color the blue area of the diagram, since the subject term is now over there on the right. So, the claims with asymmetrical diagrams cannot be validly converted.

We need a somewhat more complicated diagram to explain the other two operations. Let's use a rectangular box to represent the universe of discourse (see page 265 for an explanation of the universe of discourse) within which our classes and their complements fall. In addition to the S and P labels, we'll add $\overline{S}$ anywhere we would *not* find S, and $\overline{P}$ anywhere we would *not* find P. Here's the result (make sure you understand what's going on here—it's not all that complicated):

O: Some citizens are not voters.
    Some nonvoters are not noncitizens.

All A- and O-claims, but not E- and I-claims, are equivalent to their contrapositives.

The operations of conversion, obversion, and contraposition are important to much of what comes later, so make sure you can do them correctly and that you know which claims are equivalent to the results.

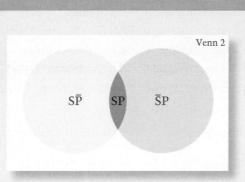

Venn 2

Obversion: Now let's look at *obversion*. Imagine an A-claim, "All S are P," diagrammed on the above. We'd color in the area labeled S$\bar{P}$ (the yellow area), wouldn't we? (All the subject class that's not part of the predicate class.) Now consider its obverse, "No S are $\bar{P}$." Since it's an E-claim, we color where the subject and predicate overlap (the green area). And that turns out to be exactly the same area we colored for its obverse! So these two are equivalent: They produce the same diagram. If you check, you'll find you get the same result for each of the other three types of claim, since obversion is valid for all four types.

Contraposition: Finally, we'll see how *contraposition* works out on the diagram. The A-claim "All S are P" once again is made true by coloring in the S$\bar{P}$ (yellow) area of the diagram. But now consider this claim's contrapositive, "All $\bar{P}$ are $\bar{S}$." Coloring in all the subject class that's outside the predicate class produces the same diagram as the original, thus showing that they are equivalent. Try diagramming an O-claim and its contrapositive, and you'll find yourself putting an X in exactly the same area for each.

But if you diagram an I-claim, "Some S are P," putting an X in the central SP area, and then diagram its contrapositive, "Some $\bar{P}$ are $\bar{S}$", you'll find that the X would have to go entirely outside both circles, since that's the only place $\bar{P}$ and $\bar{S}$ overlap! Clearly, this says something different from the original I-claim. You'll find a similarly weird result if you consider an E-claim, since contraposition does *not* work for either I- or E-claims.

Find the claim described, and determine whether it is equivalent to the claim you began with.   Exercise 8-4

1. Find the contrapositive of "No Sunnis are Christians."
2. Find the obverse of "Some Arabs are Christians."
3. Find the obverse of "All Sunnis are Muslims."

▲   4. Find the converse of "Some Kurds are not Christians."

5. Find the converse of "No Hindus are Muslims."

6. Find the contrapositive of "Some Indians are not Hindus."

▲   7. Find the converse of "All Shiites are Muslims."

8. Find the contrapositive of "All Catholics are Christians."

9. Find the converse of "All Protestants are Christians."

▲   10. Find the obverse of "No Muslims are Christians."

Exercise 8-5

Follow the directions given in the preceding exercise.

▲   1. Find the obverse of "Some students who scored well on the exam are students who wrote poor essays."

2. Find the obverse of "No students who wrote poor essays are students who were admitted to the program."

3. Find the contrapositive of "Some students who were admitted to the program are not students who scored well on the exam."

▲   4. Find the contrapositive of "No students who did not score well on the exam are students who were admitted to the program."

5. Find the contrapositive of "All students who were admitted to the program are students who wrote good essays."

6. Find the obverse of "No students of mine are unregistered students."

▲   7. Find the contrapositive of "All people who live in the dorms are people whose automobile ownership is restricted."

8. Find the contrapositive of "All commuters are people whose automobile ownership is unrestricted."

9. Find the contrapositive of "Some students with short-term memory problems are students who do poorly in history classes."

▲   10. Find the obverse of "No first basemen are right-handed people."

Exercise 8-6

For each of the following, find the claim that is described.

Example

Find the contrary of the contrapositive of "All Greeks are Europeans." First, find the contrapositive of the original claim. It is "All non-Europeans are non-Greeks." Now, find the contrary of that. Going across the top of the square (from an A-claim to an E-claim), you get "No non-Europeans are non-Greeks."

1. Find the contradictory of the converse of "No clarinets are percussion instruments."

▲   2. Find the contradictory of the obverse of "Some encyclopedias are definitive works."

3. Find the contrapositive of the subcontrary of "Some English people are Celts."

▲   4. Find the contrary of the contradictory of "Some sailboats are not sloops."

5. Find the obverse of the converse of "No sharks are freshwater fish."

For each of the numbered claims below, determine which of the lettered claims that follow are equivalent. You may use letters more than once if necessary. (Hint: This is a lot easier to do after all the claims are translated, a fact that indicates at least one advantage of putting claims into standard form.)

Exercise 8-7

1. Some people who have not been tested can give blood.
▲ 2. People who have not been tested cannot give blood.
▲ 3. Nobody who has been tested can give blood.
▲ 4. Nobody can give blood except those who have been tested.

    a. Some people who have been tested cannot give blood.
    b. Not everybody who can give blood has been tested.
    c. Only people who have been tested can give blood.
    d. Some people who cannot give blood are people who have been tested.
    e. If a person has been tested, then he or she cannot give blood.

Try to make the claims in the following pairs correspond to each other—that is, arrange them so that they have the same subject and the same predicate terms. Use only those operations that produce equivalent claims; for example, don't convert A- or O-claims in the process of trying to make the claims correspond. You can work on either member of the pair or both. (The main reason for practicing on these is to make the problems in the next two exercises easier to do.)

Exercise 8-8

Example

    a. Some students are not unemployed people.
    b. All employed people are students.

    These two claims can be made to correspond by obverting claim (a) and then converting the result (which is legitimate because the claim has been turned into an I-claim before conversion). We wind up with "Some employed people are students," which corresponds to (b).

▲ 1. a. Some Slavs are non-Europeans.
    b. No Slavs are Europeans.

2. a. All Europeans are Westerners.
    b. Some non-Westerners are non-Europeans.

3. a. All Greeks are Europeans.
    b. Some non-Europeans are Greeks.

▲ 4. a. No members of the club are people who took the exam.
    b. Some people who did not take the exam are members of the club.

5. a. All people who are not members of the club are people who took the exam.
    b. Some people who did not take the exam are members of the club.

6. a. Some cheeses are not products high in cholesterol.
    b. No cheeses are products that are not high in cholesterol.

▲ 7. a. All people who arrived late are people who will be allowed to perform.
    b. Some of the people who did not arrive late will not be allowed to perform.

8. a. No nonparticipants are people with name tags.
   b. Some of the people with name tags are participants.

9. a. Some perennials are plants that grow from tubers.
   b. Some plants that do not grow from tubers are perennials.

▲ 10. a. Some decks that play digital tape are not devices equipped for radical oversampling.
   b. All devices that are equipped for radical oversampling are decks that will not play digital tape.

Exercise 8-9

Which of the following arguments is valid? (Remember, an argument is valid when the truth of its premises guarantees the truth of its conclusion.)

▲ 1. Whenever the battery is dead, the screen goes blank; that means, of course, that whenever the screen goes blank, the battery is dead.

2. For a while there, some students were desperate for good grades, which meant some weren't, right?

3. Some players in the last election weren't members of the Reform Party. Obviously, therefore, some members of the Reform Party weren't players in the last election.

▲ 4. Since some of the students who failed the exam were students who didn't attend the review session, it must be that some students who weren't at the session failed the exam.

5. None of the people who arrived late were people who got good seats, so none of the good seats were occupied by latecomers.

6. Everybody who arrived on time was given a box lunch, so the people who did not get a box lunch were those who didn't get there on time.

▲ 7. None of the people who gave blood are people who were tested, so everybody who gave blood must have been untested.

8. Some of the people who were not tested are people who were allowed to give blood, from which it follows that some of the people who were *not* allowed to give blood must have been people who were tested.

9. Everybody who was in uniform was able to play, so nobody who was out of uniform must have been able to play.

▲ 10. Not everybody in uniform was allowed to play, so some people who were not allowed to play must not have been people in uniform.

Exercise 8-10

For each pair of claims, assume that the first has the truth value given in parentheses. Using the operations of conversion, obversion, and contraposition along with the square of opposition, decide whether the second claim is true, is false, or remains undetermined.

Example

a. No aardvarks are nonmammals. (True)
b. Some aardvarks are not mammals.

Claim (a) can be obverted to "All aardvarks are mammals." Because all categorical claims are equivalent to their obverses, the truth of this claim follows from that of (a). Because this claim is the contradictory of claim (b), it follows that claim (b) must be false.

Note: If we had been unable to make the two claims correspond without performing an illegitimate operation (such as converting an A-claim), then the answer is automatically *undetermined*.

▲ 1. a. No mosquitoes are poisonous creatures. (True)
   b. Some poisonous creatures are mosquitoes.

2. a. Some students are not ineligible candidates. (True)
   b. No eligible candidates are students.

▲ 3. a. Some sound arguments are not invalid arguments. (True)
   b. All valid arguments are unsound arguments.

4. a. Some residents are nonvoters. (False)
   b. No voters are residents.

▲ 5. a. Some automobile plants are not productive factories. (True)
   b. All unproductive factories are automobile plants.

Many of the following will have to be rewritten as standard-form categorical claims before they can be answered.

6. a. Most opera singers take voice lessons their whole lives. (True)
   b. Some opera singers do not take voice lessons their whole lives.

7. a. The hero gets killed in some of Gary Brodnax's novels. (False)
   b. The hero does not get killed in some of Gary Brodnax's novels.

8. a. None of the boxes in the last shipment are unopened. (True)
   b. Some of the opened boxes are not boxes in the last shipment.

▲ 9. a. Not everybody who is enrolled in the class will get a grade. (True)
   b. Some people who will not get a grade are enrolled in the class.

10. a. Persimmons are always astringent when they have not been left to ripen. (True)
    b. Some persimmons that have been left to ripen are not astringent.

CATEGORICAL SYLLOGISMS

A **syllogism** is a two-premise deductive argument. A **categorical syllogism** (in standard form) is a syllogism whose every claim is a standard-form categorical claim and in which three terms each occur exactly twice in exactly two of the claims. Study the following example:

> All Americans are consumers.
> Some consumers are not Democrats.
> Therefore, some Americans are not Democrats.

Notice how each of the three terms "Americans," "consumers," and "Democrats" occurs exactly twice in exactly two different claims. The *terms of a syllogism* are sometimes given the following labels:

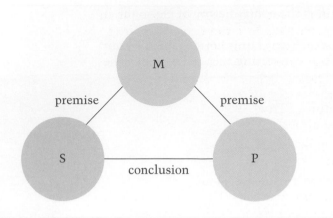

FIGURE 6   Relationship of terms in categorical syllogisms.

Major term: the term that occurs as the predicate term of the syllogism's conclusion

Minor term: the term that occurs as the subject term of the syllogism's conclusion

Middle term: the term that occurs in both of the premises but not at all in the conclusion

The most frequently used symbols for these three terms are *P* for major term, *S* for minor term, and *M* for middle term. We use these symbols throughout to simplify the discussion.

In a categorical syllogism, each of the premises states a relationship between the middle term and one of the other terms, as shown in Figure 6. If both premises do their jobs correctly—that is, if the proper connections between S and P are established via the middle term, M—then the relationship between S and P stated by the conclusion will have to follow—that is, the argument is valid.

In case you're not clear about the concept of validity, remember: An argument is valid if, and only if, it is not possible for its premises to be true while its conclusion is false. This is just another way of saying that, *were the*

Real Life

Some Do; Therefore, Some Don't

Some mosquitoes carry West Nile virus. So it must be that there are some that don't.

The conclusion of this type of argument ("Some don't"), while it may be *true*, does *not* follow from the premise, because it could just as easily be false.

You sometimes hear arguments like this worked in reverse: "Some mosquitoes don't carry West Nile; therefore, some do." Equally invalid. The only way to get an I-claim from an O-claim is by obverting the O-claim.

premises of a valid argument true (whether or not they are in fact true), then the truth of the conclusion would be guaranteed. In a moment, we'll begin developing the first of two methods for assessing the validity of syllogisms.

First, though, let's look at some candidates for syllogisms. In fact, only one of the following qualifies as a categorical syllogism. Can you identify which one? What is wrong with the other two?

1. All cats are mammals.
   Not all cats are domestic.
   Therefore, not all mammals are domestic.

2. All valid arguments are good arguments.
   Some valid arguments are boring arguments.
   Therefore, some good arguments are boring arguments.

3. Some people on the committee are not students.
   All people on the committee are local people.
   Therefore, some local people are nonstudents.

We hope it was fairly obvious that the second argument is the only proper syllogism. The first example has a couple of things wrong with it: Neither the second premise nor the conclusion is in standard form—no standard-form categorical claim begins with the word "not"—and the predicate term must be a noun or noun phrase. The second premise can be translated into "Some cats are not domestic creatures" and the conclusion into "Some mammals are not domestic creatures," and the result is a syllogism. The third argument is okay up to the conclusion, which contains a term that does not occur anywhere in the premises: "nonstudents." However, because "nonstudents" is the complement of "students," this argument can be turned into a proper syllogism by obverting the conclusion, producing "Some local people are not students."

Once you're able to recognize syllogisms, it's time to learn how to determine their validity. We'll turn now to our first method, the Venn diagram test.

The Venn Diagram Method of Testing for Validity

Diagramming a syllogism requires three overlapping circles, one representing each class named by a term in the argument. To be systematic, in our diagrams we put the minor term on the left, the major term on the right, and the middle term in the middle but lowered a bit. We will diagram the following syllogism step by step:

No Republicans are collectivists.
All socialists are collectivists.
Therefore, no socialists are Republicans.

In this example, "socialists" is the minor term, "Republicans" is the major term, and "collectivists" is the middle term. See Figure 7 for the three circles required, labeled appropriately.

We fill in this diagram by diagramming the premises of the argument just as we diagrammed the A-, E-, I-,

"Syllogisms won't do you any good here, Mr. Aristotle."

and O-claims earlier. The premises in the foregoing example are diagrammed like this: First: No Republicans are collectivists (Figure 8). Notice that in this figure we have colored the entire area where the Republican and collectivist circles overlap.

Second: All socialists are collectivists (Figure 9). Because diagramming the premises resulted in the coloring of the entire area where the socialist and Republican circles overlap, and because that is exactly what we would do to diagram the syllogism's conclusion, we can conclude that the syllogism is valid. In general, a syllogism is valid if and only if diagramming the premises automatically produces a correct diagram of the conclusion.* (The one exception is discussed later.)

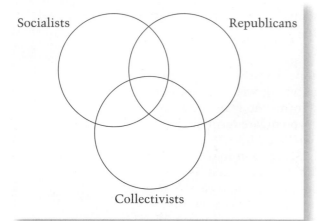

FIGURE 7   Before either premise has been diagrammed.

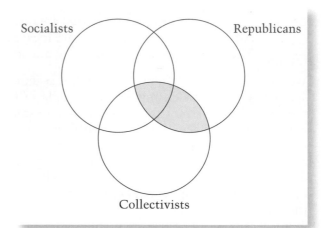

FIGURE 8   One premise diagrammed.

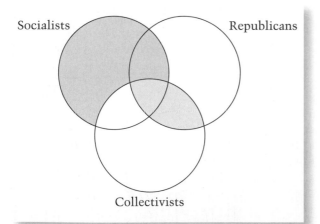

FIGURE 9   Both premises diagrammed.

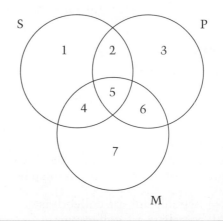

FIGURE 10

---

*It might be helpful for some students to produce two diagrams, one for the premises of the argument and one for the conclusion. The two can then be compared: Any area of the conclusion diagram that is colored must also be colored in the premises diagram, and any area of the conclusion diagram that has an X must also have one in the premises diagram. If both of these conditions are met, the argument is valid. (Thanks to Professor Ellery Eells of the University of Wisconsin, Madison, for the suggestion.)

When one of the premises of a syllogism is an I- or O-premise, there can be a problem about where to put the required X. The following example presents such a problem (see Figure 10 for the diagram). Note in the diagram that we have numbered the different areas in order to refer to them easily.

Some S are not M.
<u>All P are M.</u>
Some S are not P.

(The horizontal line separates the premises from the conclusion.)

An X in either area 1 or area 2 of Figure 10 makes the claim "Some S are not M" true, because an inhabitant of either area is an S but not an M. How do we determine which area should get the X? In some cases, the decision can be made for us: *When one premise is an A- or E-premise and the other is an I- or O-premise, diagram the A- or E-premise first.* (Always color areas in before putting in Xs.) Refer to Figure 11 to see what happens with the current example when we follow this rule.

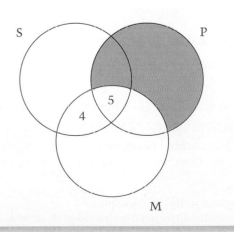

FIGURE 11

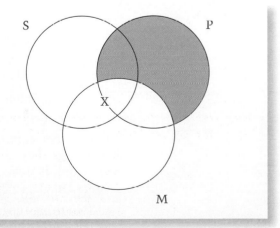

FIGURE 12

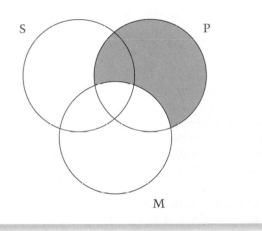

FIGURE 13

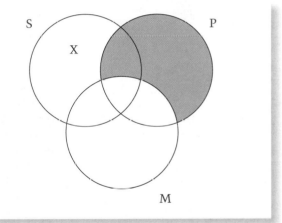

FIGURE 14

Once the A-claim has been diagrammed, there is no longer a choice about where to put the X—it has to go in area 1. Hence, the completed diagram for this argument looks like Figure 12. And from this diagram, we can read the conclusion "Some S are not P," which tells us that the argument is valid.

In some syllogisms, the rule just explained does not help. For example,

All P are M.
Some S are M.
Some S are P.

A syllogism like this one still leaves us in doubt about where to put the X, even after we have diagrammed the A-premise (Figure 13): Should the X go in area 4 or 5? When such a question remains unresolved, here is the rule to follow: *An X that can go in either of two areas goes on the line separating the areas*, as in Figure 14.

In essence, an X on a line indicates that the X belongs in one or the other of the two areas, maybe both, but we don't know which. When the time comes to see whether the diagram yields the conclusion, we look to see whether there is an X *entirely* within the appropriate area. In the current example, we would need an X entirely within the area where S and P overlap; because there is no such X, the argument is invalid. An X *partly* within the appropriate area fails to establish the conclusion.

Please notice this about Venn diagrams: When both premises of a syllogism are A- or E-claims and the conclusion is an I- or O-claim, diagramming the premises cannot possibly yield a diagram of the conclusion (because A- and E-claims produce only coloring of areas, and I- and O-claims require an X to be read from the diagram). In such a case, remember our assumption that every class we are dealing with has at least one member. This assumption justifies our looking at the diagram and determining whether any circle has all but one of its areas colored. *If any circle has only one area remaining uncolored, an X should be put in that area.* This is the case because any member of that class has to be in that remaining area. Sometimes placing the X in this way will enable us to read the conclusion, in which case the argument is valid (on the assumption that the relevant class is not empty); sometimes placing the X will not enable us to read the conclusion, in which case the argument is invalid, with or without any assumptions about the existence of a member within the class.

Categorical Syllogisms with Unstated Premises

Many "real-life" categorical syllogisms have unstated premises. For example, suppose somebody says,

You shouldn't give chicken bones to dogs. They could choke on them.

The speaker's argument rests on the unstated premise that you shouldn't give dogs things they could choke on. In other words, the argument, when fully spelled out, is this:

All chicken bones are things dogs could choke on.
[No things dogs could choke on are things you should give dogs.]
Therefore, no chicken bones are things you should give dogs.

The unstated premise appears in brackets.

To take another example:

> Driving around in an old car is dumb, since it might break down in a dangerous place.

Here, the speaker's argument rests on the unstated premise that it's dumb to risk a dangerous breakdown. In other words, when fully spelled out, the argument is this:

> All examples of driving around in an old car are examples of risking dangerous breakdown.
> [All examples of risking dangerous breakdown are examples of being dumb.]
> Therefore, all examples of driving around in an old car are examples of being dumb.

When you hear (or give) an argument that looks like a categorical syllogism that has only one stated premise, usually a second premise has been assumed and not stated. Ordinarily, this unstated premise remains unstated because the speaker thinks it is too obvious to bother stating. The unstated premises in the arguments above are good examples: "You shouldn't give dogs things they could choke on," and "It is dumb to risk a dangerous breakdown."

When you encounter (or give) what looks like a categorical syllogism that is missing a premise, ask: Is there a reasonable assumption I could make that would make this argument valid? We covered this question of unstated premises in more detail in Chapter 2, and you might want to look there for more information on the subject.

At the end of this chapter, we have included a few exercises that involve missing premises.

Real-Life Syllogisms

We'll end this section with a word of advice. Before you use a Venn diagram (or the rules method described below) to determine the validity of real-life arguments, it helps to use a letter to abbreviate each category mentioned in the argument. This is mainly just a matter of convenience: It is easier to write down letters than to write down long phrases.

Take the first categorical syllogisms given on page 275:

> You shouldn't give chicken bones to dogs because they could choke on them.

The argument spelled out, once again, is this:

> All chicken bones are things dogs could choke on.
> [No things dogs could choke on are things you should give dogs.]
> Therefore, no chicken bones are things you should give dogs.

Abbreviating each of the three categories with a letter, we get

> C = chicken bones; D = things dogs could choke on; and S = things you should give dogs.

Real Life

The World's Most Common Syllogism

We're pretty sure the syllogism you'll run across most frequently is of this form:

All As are Bs.
All Bs are Cs.
All As are Cs.

Some real-life versions are easier to spot than others. Here's an example: "The chords in that song are all minor chords because every one of them has a flatted third, and that automatically makes them minor chords." Here's another: "Jim will be on a diet every day next week, so you can expect him to be grumpy the whole time. He's *always* grumpy when he's on a diet."

Real Life

The World's Second Most Common Syllogism

If a real, live syllogism turns out not to have the form described in the previous box, there's a very good chance it has this form:

All As are Bs.
No Bs are Cs.
No As are Cs.

Here's an example: "Eggs and milk are obviously animal products, and since real vegans don't eat any kind of animal product at all, they surely don't eat eggs or milk."

Then, the argument is

All C are D
[No D are S]
Therefore, no C are S.

Likewise, the second argument was this:

Driving around in an old car is dumb, since it might break down in a dangerous place.

When fully spelled out, the argument is

All examples of driving around in an old car are examples of risking dangerous breakdown.
[All examples of risking dangerous breakdown are examples of being dumb.]
Therefore, all examples of driving around in an old car are examples of being dumb.

■ We're not certain exactly what the AT&T people had in mind here, but it *looks* like a syllogism with the conclusion unstated. With the conclusion "Your world is AT&T," is the argument valid? What if the conclusion were "AT&T is your world"?

Abbreviating each of the three categories, we get

> D = examples of driving around in an old car; R = examples of risking dangerous breakdown; S = examples of being dumb.

Then, the argument is

> All D are R
> [All R are S]
> Therefore, all D are S.

A final tip: Take the time to write down your abbreviation key clearly.

Use the diagram method to determine which of the following syllogisms are valid and which are invalid.

Exercise 8-11

▲ 1. All paperbacks are books that use glue in their spines.
No books that use glue in their spines are books that are sewn in signatures.
_____
No books that are sewn in signatures are paperbacks.

2. All sound arguments are valid arguments.
Some valid arguments are not interesting arguments.
_____
Some sound arguments are not interesting arguments.

3. All topologists are mathematicians.
Some topologists are not statisticians.
_____
Some mathematicians are not statisticians.

▲ 4. Every time Louis is tired, he's edgy. He's edgy today, so he must be tired today.

5. Every voter is a citizen, but some citizens are not residents. Therefore, some voters are not residents.

6. All the dominant seventh chords are in the mixolydian mode, and no mixolydian chords use the major scale. So no chords that use the major scale are dominant sevenths.

▲ 7. All halyards are lines that attach to sails. Painters do not attach to sails, so they must not be halyards.

8. Only systems with no moving parts can give you instant access. Standard hard drives have moving parts, so they can't give you instant access.

9. All citizens are residents. So, since no noncitizens are voters, all voters must be residents.

▲ 10. No citizens are nonresidents, and all voters are citizens. So, all residents must be nonvoters.

Exercise 8-12

Put the following arguments in standard form (you may have to use the obversion, conversion, or contraposition operations to accomplish this); then determine whether the arguments are valid by means of diagrams.

▲ 1. No blank disks contain any data, although some blank disks are formatted. Therefore, some formatted disks do not contain any data.

2. All ears of corn with white tassels are unripe, but some ears are ripe even though their kernels are not full-sized. Therefore, some ears with full-sized kernels are not ears with white tassels.

3. Prescription drugs should never be taken without a doctor's order. So no over-the-counter drugs are prescription drugs, because all over-the-counter drugs can be taken without a doctor's order.

▲ 4. All tobacco products are damaging to people's health, but some of them are addictive substances. Some addictive substances, therefore, are damaging to people's health.

5. A few CD players use 24× sampling, so some of them must cost at least twenty dollars, because you can't buy any machine with 24× sampling for less than twenty dollars.

6. Everything that Pete won at the carnival must be junk. I know that Pete won everything that Bob won, and all the stuff that Bob won is junk.

▲ 7. Only people who hold stock in the company may vote, so Mr. Hansen must not hold any stock in the company, because I know he was not allowed to vote.

8. No off-road vehicles are allowed in the unimproved portion of the park, but some off-road vehicles are not four-wheel-drive. So some four-wheel-drive vehicles are allowed in the unimproved part of the park.

9. Some of the people affected by the new drainage tax are residents of the county, and many residents of the county are already paying the sewer tax. So, it must be that some people paying the sewer tax are affected by the new drainage tax, too.

▲ 10. No argument with false premises is sound, but some of them are valid. So, some unsound arguments must be valid.

Real Life

Brodie!

"Otterhounds are friendly, are fond of other dogs, bark a lot, and like to chase cats."
"That describes Brodie exactly! He must be an otterhound."

Not so fast, dog lover. The argument seems to be

All otterhounds are friendly, fond of other dogs, and like to chase cats.
Brodie is friendly, fond of other dogs, and likes to chase cats.
Therefore, Brodie is an otterhound.

This argument has the form

All As are X.
All Bs are X.
Therefore, all Bs are As.

If you use techniques described in this chapter, you will see that arguments with this form are invalid. If you just stumbled on this box, or if your instructor referred you to it, common sense should tell you the same. It's like arguing, "All graduates of Harvard are warm-blooded, and Brodie is warm-blooded; therefore, Brodie is a graduate of Harvard."

In Depth

Additional Common Invalid Argument Forms

Other common invalid argument forms (see the box about Brodie) include these:

All As are X.
No As are Y.
Therefore, no Xs are Ys.

All Xs are Ys; therefore, all Ys are Xs.

Some Xs are not Ys. Therefore, some Ys are not Xs.

Some Xs are Ys. Therefore, some Xs are not Ys.

Some Xs are not Ys. Therefore, some Xs are Ys.

So you don't get lost in all the Xs and Ys, and to help you remember them, we recommend you make up examples of each of these forms and share them with a classmate.

The Rules Method of Testing for Validity

The diagram method of testing syllogisms for validity is intuitive, but there is a faster method that makes use of three simple rules. These rules are based on two ideas, the first of which has been mentioned already: affirmative and negative categorical claims. (Remember, the A- and I-claims are affirmative;

A-claim:	All $\text{\small Ⓢare P.}$
E-claim:	No $\text{\small Ⓢ are Ⓟ.}$
I-claim:	Some S are P.
O-claim:	Some S are not $\text{\small Ⓟ}$

FIGURE 15   Distributed terms.

the E- and O-claims are negative.) The other idea is that of *distribution*. Terms that occur in categorical claims are either distributed or undistributed: Either the claim says something about every member of the class the term names, or it does not.* Three of the standard-form claims distribute one or more of their terms. In Figure 15, the circled letters stand for distributed terms, and the uncircled ones stand for undistributed terms. As the figure shows, the A-claim distributes its subject term, the O-claim distributes its predicate term, the E-claim distributes both, and the I-claim distributes neither.

We can now state the three *rules of the syllogism*. A syllogism is valid if, and only if, all of these conditions are met:

1. **The number of negative claims in the premises must be the same as the number of negative claims in the conclusion.** (Because the conclusion is always one claim, this implies that no valid syllogism has two negative premises.)
2. **At least one premise must distribute the middle term.**
3. **Any term that is distributed in the conclusion of the syllogism must be distributed in its premises.**

These rules are easy to remember, and with a bit of practice, you can use them to determine quickly whether a syllogism is valid.

Which of the rules is broken in this example?

> All pianists are keyboard players.
> Some keyboard players are not percussionists.
> Some pianists are not percussionists.

The term "keyboard players" is the middle term, and it is undistributed in both premises. The first premise, an A-claim, does not distribute its predicate term; the second premise, an O-claim, does not distribute its subject term. So this syllogism breaks rule 2.

Another example:

> No dogs up for adoption at the animal shelter are pedigreed dogs.
> Some pedigreed dogs are expensive dogs.
> Some dogs up for adoption at the animal shelter are expensive dogs.

This syllogism breaks rule 1 because it has a negative premise but no negative conclusion.

A last example:

> No mercantilists are large landowners.
> All mercantilists are creditors.
> No creditors are large landowners.

---

*The above is a rough-and-ready definition of distribution. If you'd like a more technical version, here's one: A term is *distributed* in a claim if, and only if, on the assumption that the claim is true, the class named by the term can be replaced by *any* subset of that class without producing a false claim. Example: In the claim "All senators are politicians," the term "senators" is distributed because, assuming the claim is true, you can substitute *any* subset of senators (Democratic ones, Republican ones, tall ones, short ones) and the result must also be true. "Politicians" is not distributed: The original claim could be true while "All senators are honest politicians" was false.

Real Life

A Guide to Dweebs, Dorks, Geeks, and Nerds

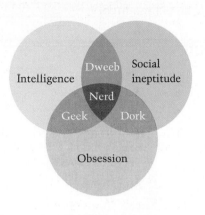

We found this Venn diagram floating around on the web. It gives us a tongue-in-cheek (we think) sorting of various categories of people based on three characteristics: intelligence, social ineptitude, and obsession. You can interpret this in the same way we interpreted such diagrams in this chapter (e.g., a dweeb is a member of the class of intelligent people and of the class of the socially inept, but not a member of the class of the obsessed).

The minor term, "creditors," is distributed in the conclusion (because it's the subject term of an E-claim) but not in the premises (where it's the predicate term of an A-claim). So this syllogism breaks rule 3.

The following list of topics covers the basics of categorical logic as discussed in this chapter:

Recap

- ■ The four types of categorical claims include A, E, I, and O.
- ■ There are Venn diagrams for the four types of claims.
- ■ Ordinary English claims can be translated into standard-form categorical claims. Some rules of thumb for such translations are as follows:
  - —"only" introduces predicate term of A-claim
  - —"the only" introduces subject term of A-claim
  - —"whenever" means times or occasions
  - —"wherever" means places or locations
  - —claims about individuals are treated as A- or E-claims
- ■ The square of opposition displays contradiction, contrariety, and subcontrariety among corresponding standard-form claims.

■ Conversion, obversion, and contraposition are three operations that can be performed on standard-form claims; some are equivalent to the original, and some are not.

■ Categorical syllogisms are standardized deductive arguments; we can test them for validity by the Venn diagram method or by the rules method—the latter relies on the notions of distribution and the affirmative and negative qualities of the claims involved.

Additional Exercises

Exercise 8-13

In each of the following items, identify whether A, B, or C is the middle term.

▲   1. All A are B.
       All A are C.
       All B are C.

   2. All B are C.
       No C are D.
       No B are D.

   3. Some C are not D.
       All C are A.
       Some D are not A.

▲   4. Some A are not B.
       Some B are C.
       Some C are not A.

   5. No C are A.
       Some B are A.
       Some C are not B.

Exercise 8-14

Which terms are distributed in each of the following?

▲   1. All A are B.
       a. A only
       b. B only
       c. Both A and B
       d. Neither A nor B

   2. No A are B.
       a. A only
       b. B only
       c. Both A and B
       d. Neither A nor B

   3. Some A are B.
       a. A only
       b. B only
       c. Both A and B
       d. Neither A nor B

▲ 4. Some A are not B.

    a. A only
    b. B only
    c. Both A and B
    d. Neither A nor B

Exercise 8-15

How many negative claims appear in the premises of each of the following arguments? (In other words, how many of the premises are negative?) Your options are 0, 1, or 2.

▲ 1. All A are B.
    All A are C.
    Therefore, all B are C.

2. All B are C.
    No C are D.
    Therefore, no B are D.

3. Some C are not D.
    All C are A.
    Therefore, some D are not A.

▲ 4. Some A are not B.
    Some B are C.
    Therefore, some C are not A.

5. No A are B.
    Some B are not C.
    Some A are C.

Exercise 8-16

Which rules (if any) are broken in each of the following? Select from these options:

    a. Breaks rule 1 only
    b. Breaks rule 2 only
    c. Breaks rule 3 only
    d. Breaks more than one rule
    e. Breaks no rule

▲ 1. All A are B.
    All A are C.
    Therefore, all B are C.

2. All B are C.
    No C are D.
    Therefore, no B are D.

3. Some C are not D.
    All C are A.
    Therefore, some D are A.

▲ 4. Some A are not B.
Some B are C.
Therefore, some C are not A.

5. Some A are C.
Some C are B.
Therefore, some A are B.

6. Some carbostats are framistans.
No framistans are arbuckles.
Some arbuckles are not carbostats.

▲ 7. All framistans are veeblefetzers.
Some veeblefetzers are carbostats.
Some framistans are carbostats.

8. No arbuckles are framistans.
All arbuckles are carbostats.
No framistans are carbostats.

9. All members of the class are registered students.
Some registered students are not people taking fifteen units.
Some members of the class are not people taking fifteen units.

▲ 10. All qualified mechanics are people familiar with hydraulics.
No unschooled people are people familiar with hydraulics.
No qualified mechanics are unschooled people.

Exercise 8-17

Which rules (if any) are broken in each of the following?

Note: If an argument breaks a rule, *which* rule is broken depends on how you translate the claims in the argument. For example, the claim "Dogs shouldn't be given chicken bones" could be translated as an *E-claim:* "No dogs are animals that should be given chicken bones." But it also could be translated as an *A-claim:* "All dogs are animals that shouldn't be given chicken bones." If the original claim appeared in an invalid argument, one rule would be broken if you translated it as the E-claim. A different rule would be broken if you translated it as the A-claim.

▲ 1. All tigers are ferocious creatures. Some ferocious creatures are zoo animals. Therefore, some zoo animals are tigers. (For this and the following items, it will help if you abbreviate each category with a letter. For example, let T = tigers, F = ferocious creatures, and Z = zoo animals.)

2. Some pedestrians are not jaywalkers. Therefore, some jaywalkers are not gardeners, since no gardeners are pedestrians.

3. Because all shrubs are ornamental plants, it follows that no ornamental plants are cacti, since no cacti qualify as shrubs.

▲ 4. Weightlifters aren't really athletes. Athletics requires the use of motor skills; and few, if any, weightlifters use motor skills.

5. The trick to finding syllogisms is to think categorically, as well as to focus on the key argument in a passage. For example, some passages contain a good bit of rhetoric, and some passages that do this make it hard to spot syllogisms, with the result that it is hard to spot syllogisms in some passages.

6. Every broadcast network has seen its share of the television audience decline during the past six years. But not every broadcast network that has a decline in television audience share has lost money. So, not every broadcast network has lost money.

▲ 7. Many students lift papers off the Internet, and this fact is discouraging to teachers. However, it must be noted that students who do this are only cheating themselves, and anyone who cheats himself or herself loses in the long run. Therefore, lifting papers off the Internet is a losing proposition in the long run.

8. When he was Speaker of the House, Mr. Newt Gingrich could be counted on to advance Republican causes. At the time, nobody who would do that could be accused of being soft on crime, which explains why, at the time, Gingrich could hardly be accused of being soft on crime.

9. It would be in everyone's interest to amend the Constitution to permit school prayer. And it is obviously in everyone's interest to promote religious freedom. It should be no surprise, then, that amending the Constitution to permit school prayer will promote religious freedom.

▲ 10. If you want to stay out all night dancing, it is fine with me. Just don't cry about it if you don't get good grades. Dancing isn't a total waste of time, but dancing the whole night certainly is. There are only so many hours in a day, and wasting time is bound to affect your grades negatively. So, fine, stay out dancing all night. It's your choice. But you have to expect your grades to suffer.

Exercise 8-18

▲ Refer back to Exercises 8-11 and 8-12 (pages 279–280), and check the arguments for validity using the rules. We recommend abbreviating each category with a letter.

Once again, remember: If an argument breaks a rule, *which* rule is broken depends on how you translate the claims in the argument. For example, the claim "Dogs shouldn't be given chicken bones" could be translated as an E-claim: "No dogs are animals that should be given chicken bones." But it also could be translated as an A-claim (the obverse of the other version): "All dogs are animals that shouldn't be given chicken bones." If the original claim appeared in an invalid argument, one rule would be broken if you translated it as an E-claim. A different rule would be broken if you translated it as an A-claim.

Answers to 2, 5, 7, and 8 of both exercises are given in the answer section.

Exercise 8-19

For each of the following items: Abbreviate each category with a letter, then translate the argument into standard form using the abbreviations. Then test the argument for validity using either the diagram method or the rules method.

Note: For many of these items, it can be difficult to translate the arguments into standard form.

▲ 1. Some athletes are not baseball players, and some baseball players are not basketball players. Therefore, some athletes are not basketball players.

2. Rats are disease-carrying pests and, as such, should be eradicated, because such pests should all be eradicated.

3. All creationists are religious, and all fundamentalists are religious, so all creationists are fundamentalists.

4. Every sportscaster is an athlete, and no athlete is a college professor. Therefore, no sportscasters are college professors.

5. Anyone who voted for the Democrats favors expansion of medical services for the needy. So, the people who voted for the Democrats all favor higher taxes, since anyone who wants to expand medical services must favor higher taxes.

6. All cave dwellers lived before the invention of the radio, and no one alive today is a cave dweller. Thus, no person who lived before the invention of the radio is alive today.

7. Conservationists don't vote for Republicans, and all environmentalists are conservationists. Thus, environmentalists don't vote for Republicans.

8. Since all philosophers are skeptics, it follows that no theologian is a skeptic, since no philosophers are theologians.

9. Each philosopher is a skeptic, and no philosopher is a theologian. Therefore, no skeptic is a theologian.

10. Peddlers are salesmen, and confidence men are, too. So, peddlers are confidence men.

11. Should drug addicts be treated as criminals? Well, addicts are all excluded from the class of decent people, yet all criminals belong to that class. Accordingly, no addicts are criminals.

12. Critical thinkers recognize invalid syllogisms; therefore, critical thinkers are logicians, since logicians can spot invalid syllogisms, too.

13. The Mohawk Indians are Algonquin, and so are the Cheyenne. So, the Mohawks are really just Cheyenne.

14. Idiots would support the measure, but no one else would. Whatever else you may think of the school board, you can't say they are idiots. [Therefore . . .]

▲ 15. This is not the best of all possible worlds, because the best of all possible worlds would not contain mosquitoes, and *this* world contains plenty of mosquitoes!

16. From time to time, the police have to break up parties here on campus, since some campus parties get out of control, and when a party gets out of control, well, you know what the police have to do.

17. I know that all fundamentalist Christians are evangelicals, and I'm pretty sure that all revivalists are also evangelicals. So, if I'm right, at least some fundamentalist Christians must be revivalists.

▲ 18. "Their new lawn furniture certainly looks cheap to me," she said. "It's made of plastic, and plastic furniture just looks cheap."

19. None of our intramural sports are sports played in the Olympics, and some of the intercollegiate sports are not Olympic sports, either. So, some of the intercollegiate sports are also intramural sports.

20. The moas were all Dinornithidae, and no moas exist anymore. So, there aren't any more Dinornithidae.

▲   21. Everybody on the district tax roll is a citizen, and all eligible voters are also citizens. So, everybody on the district tax roll is an eligible voter.

22. Any piece of software that is in the public domain may be copied without permission or fee. But that cannot be done in the case of software under copyright. So, software under copyright must not be in the public domain.

23. None of the countries that have been living under dictatorships for these past few decades are familiar with the social requirements of a strong democracy—things like widespread education and a willingness to abide by majority vote. Consequently, none of these countries will make a successful quick transition to democracy, since countries where the aforementioned requirements are unfamiliar simply can't make such a transition.

▲   24. Trust Senator Cobweb to vote with the governor on the new tax legislation. Cobweb is a liberal, and liberals just cannot pass up an opportunity to raise taxes.

25. Investor-held utilities should not be allowed to raise rates, since all public utilities should be allowed to raise rates, and public utilities are not investor held.

26. Masterpieces are no longer recorded on cassettes. This is because masterpieces belong to the classical repertoire, and classical music is no longer recorded on cassettes.

27. It isn't important to learn chemistry, since it isn't very useful, and there isn't much point in learning something that isn't useful.

28. Stockholders' information about a company's worth must come from the managers of that company, but in a buy-out, the managers of the company are the very ones who are trying to buy the stock from the stockholders. So, ironically, in a buyout situation, stockholders must get their information about how much a company is worth from the very people who are trying to buy their stock.

▲   29. All the networks devoted considerable attention to reporting poll results during the last election, but many of those poll results were not especially newsworthy. So, the networks have to admit that some unnewsworthy items received quite a bit of their attention.

▲   30. If a person doesn't understand that the earth goes around the sun once a year, then that person can't understand what causes winter and summer. Strange as it may seem, then, there are many American adults who don't know what causes winter and summer, because a survey a year or so ago showed that many such adults don't know that the earth goes around the sun.

31. Congress seems ready to impose trade sanctions on China, and perhaps it should. China's leaders cruelly cling to power. They flout American interests in their actions in Tibet, in their human-rights violations, in their weapons sales, and in their questionable trade practices. Any country with a record like this deserves sanctions.

▲   32. Since 1973, when the U.S. Supreme Court decided *Miller v. California*, no work can be banned as obscene unless it contains sexual depictions that are "patently offensive" to "contemporary community standards" and unless the work as a whole possesses no "serious literary, artistic, political or scientific value." As loose as this standard may seem when compared with earlier tests of obscenity, the pornographic novels of "Madame Toulouse" (a pseudonym, of course) can still be banned. They would offend the contemporary standards of *any* community, and to claim any literary, artistic, political, or scientific value for them would be a real joke.

Exercise 8-20

This exercise is a little different, and you may need to work one or more such items in class in order to get the hang of them. Your job is to try to prove each of the following claims about syllogisms true or false. You may need to produce a general argument—that is, show that *every* syllogism that does *this* must also do *that*—or you may need to produce a counterexample, that is, an example that proves the claim in question false. The definition of categorical syllogism and the rules of the syllogism are of crucial importance in working these examples.

▲   1. Every valid syllogism must have at least one A- or E-claim for a premise.
     2. Every valid syllogism with an E-claim for a premise must have an E-claim for a conclusion.
     3. Every valid syllogism with an E-claim for a conclusion must have an E-claim for a premise.
▲   4. It's possible for a syllogism to break two of the rules of the syllogism.
     5. No syllogism can break all three of the rules of the syllogism.

Exercise 8-21

For each of these, identify a premise (or conclusion) that makes the item a valid, standard-form categorical syllogism. If this cannot be done, say so.

▲   1. All A are B.
        ???
        Therefore, all A are C.
     2. All B are C.
        ???
        Therefore, no B are D.
     3. Some C are D.
        ???
        Therefore, some D are not A.
▲   4. All A are B.
        Some B are not C.
        Therefore, ???
     5. Some A are B.
        Some B are C.
        Therefore, ???
     6. Some A are not C.
        Some A are not D.
        Therefore, ???

▲   7. All A are B.
        No A are C.
        Therefore, ????

    8. No A are B.
        ???
        Therefore, some B are not C.

    9. No B are A.
        ???
        Therefore, no B are C.

   10. Some A are B.
        Some B are not C.
        Therefore, ???

Exercise 8-22

Follow the instructions for each item.

▲   1. "All business executives have accounting experience, and some business
        executives are not economists."
        Which of the following statements follows validly from these
        premises?

        a. Some economists do not have accounting experience.
        b. Some people with accounting experience are not economists.
        c. All people with accounting experience are business executives.
        d. More than one of these.
        e. None of these.

    2. "Coffee is a stimulant, since coffee contains caffeine."
        What statement must be added to this syllogism to make it valid?

        a. All substances that contain caffeine are stimulants.
        b. All stimulants are substances that contain caffeine.
        c. Neither of the above makes it valid.
        d. Both of the above make it valid.

    3. "All musicians can read music; plus, all Washington University music
        majors can read music."
        Which of the following statements follows validly from these
        premises?

        a. Anyone who can read music is a musician.
        b. All Washington University music majors
            are musicians.
        c. Neither of the above.
        d. Both of the above.

▲   4. "All CEOs are college grads. Therefore, some college grads are
        not economists."
        What statement must be added to this syllogism to make
        it valid?

        a. Some CEOs are not economists.
        b. Some economists are not CEOs.
        c. Neither of the above makes it valid.
        d. Both of the above make it valid.

5. "Some economists are historians; therefore, some radicals are not historians."

   What statement must be added to this syllogism to make it valid?

   a. No economists are radicals.
   b. Some economists are not radicals.
   c. Some radicals are not economists.
   d. None of the above make it valid.

6. "All online businesses are modern businesses, from which an obvious conclusion follows, since modern businesses don't include any brick-and-mortar businesses." What conclusion, if any, makes this a valid categorical syllogism?

▲ 7. "Political radicals never become Navy SEALS, from which it follows that some patriots are not Navy Seals." What premise must be added to make this a valid categorical syllogism?

8. "A few NASCAR drivers are NASCAR fans, but no Minnesotans are NASCAR fans." What conclusion, if any, makes this a valid categorical syllogism?

9. "All physicians own mutual funds, from which it follows that no professors are physicians." What premise must be added to make this a valid categorical syllogism?

▲ 10. "Some private investigators carry sidearms, and some people who carry sidearms are not licensed to do so." What conclusion, if any, makes this a valid categorical syllogism?

Exercise 8-23

The following is an anonymous statement of opinion that appeared in a newspaper call-in column.

> This is in response to the person who called in that we should provide a shelter for the homeless, because I think that is wrong. These people make the downtown area unsafe because they have nothing to lose by robbing, mugging, etc. The young boy killed by the horseshoe pits was attacked by some of these bums, assuming that witnesses really saw people who were homeless, which no doubt they did, since the so-called homeless all wear that old worn-out hippie gear, just like the people they saw. They also lower property values. And don't tell me they are down and out because they can't find work. The work is there if they look for it. They choose for themselves how to live, since if they didn't choose, who did?

A lot of things might be said in criticism of this tirade, but what we want you to notice is the breakdown of logic. The piece contains, in fact, a gross logic error, which we ask you to make the focus of a critical essay. Your audience is the other members of your class; that is, you are writing for an audience of critical thinkers.

Exercise 8-24

> Pornography violates women's rights. It carries a demeaning message about a woman's worth and purpose and promotes genuine violence. This is indeed a violation of women's civil rights and justifies the Minneapolis City Council in attempting to ban pornography.

This letter to the editor is, in effect, two syllogisms. The conclusion of the first is that pornography violates women's rights. This conclusion also functions as a premise in the second syllogism, which has as its own conclusion the claim that the Minneapolis City Council is justified in attempting to ban pornography. Both syllogisms have unstated premises. Translate the entire argument into standard-form syllogisms, supplying missing premises, and determine whether the reasoning is valid.

Exercise 8-25

Each of the following arguments contains an unstated premise, which, together with the stated premise, makes the argument in question valid. Your job is to identify this unstated premise, abbreviate each category with a letter, and put the argument in standard form.

▲ 1. Ladybugs eat aphids; therefore, they are good to have in your garden.
2. CEOs have lots of responsibility; therefore, they should be paid a lot.
3. Anyone who understands how a computer program works knows how important logic is. Therefore, anyone who understands how a computer program works understands how important unambiguous writing is.
▲ 4. Self-tapping screws are a boon to the construction industry. They make it possible to screw things together without drilling pilot holes.
5. No baseball player smokes anymore. Baseball players all know that smoking hampers athletic performance.
6. You really ought to give up jogging. It is harmful to your health.
7. Camping isn't much fun. It requires sleeping on the hard ground and getting lots of bug bites.
8. Having too much coffee makes you sleep poorly. That's why you shouldn't do it.
9. Do you have writer's block? No problem. You can always hire a secretary.
10. "You think those marks were left by a—snake? That's totally crazy. Snakes don't leave footprints."

Exercise 8-26

Diagram the argument found in the passage in Exercise 8-24 using the methods described in Chapter 2.

Writing Exercises

1. Should dogs be used in medical experiments, given that they seem to have the capacity to experience fear and feel pain? Write a short paper defending a negative answer to this question, taking about five minutes to do so. When you have finished, exchange arguments with a friend and rewrite each other's argument as a categorical syllogism or a combination of categorical syllogisms. Remember that people often leave premises unstated.

2. Follow the instructions for Writing Exercise 1, but this time defend the position that it is not wrong to use dogs in medical experiments.

3. Turn to Selection 15A, 15B, 16A, or 16B in the Appendix and follow the second alternative assignment.

9

Deductive Arguments II

Truth-Functional Logic

The earliest development of truth-functional logic took place among the Stoics, who flourished from about the third century B.C.E. until the second century C.E. But it was in the late nineteenth and twentieth centuries that the real power of **truth-functional logic** (known also as *propositional* or *sentential logic*) became apparent.

The "logic of sentences" is one of the bases on which modern symbolic logic rests, and as such it is important in such intellectual areas as set theory and the foundations of mathematics. It is also the model for electrical circuits of the sort that are the basis of digital computing. But truth-functional logic is also a useful tool in the analysis of language, and, in particular, of arguments.

The study of truth-functional logic can benefit you in several ways. For one thing, you'll learn something about the structure of language that you wouldn't learn any other way. For another, you'll get a sense of what it's like to work with a very precise, nonmathematical system of symbols that is nevertheless very accessible to nearly any student willing to invest a modest effort. The model of precision and clarity that such systems provide can serve you well when you communicate with others in ordinary language.

Students will learn to . . .

1. Understand the basics of truth tables and truth-functional symbols

2. Symbolize normal English sentences with claim letters and truth-functional symbols

3. Build truth tables for symbolizations with several letters

4. Evaluate truth-functional arguments using common argument forms

5. Use the truth-table and short truth-table methods to determine whether an argument is truth-functionally valid

6. Use elementary valid argument forms and equivalences to determine the validity of arguments

7. Use deductions to demonstrate the validity of truth-functional arguments

If you're not comfortable working with symbols, the upcoming sections on truth-functional arguments and deductions might look intimidating. But they are not as forbidding as they may appear. We presume that the whole matter of a symbolic system is unfamiliar to you, so we'll start from absolute scratch. Keep in mind, though, that everything builds on what goes before. It's important to master each concept as it's explained and not fall behind. Catching up can be very difficult. If you find yourself having difficulty with a section or a concept, put in a bit of extra effort to master it before moving ahead. It will be worth it in the end.

TRUTH TABLES AND THE TRUTH-FUNCTIONAL SYMBOLS

Our "logical vocabulary" will consist of claim variables and truth-functional symbols. Before we consider the real heart of the subject, truth tables and the symbols that represent them, let's first clarify the use of letters of the alphabet to symbolize terms and claims.

Claim Variables

In Chapter 8, we used uppercase letters to stand for terms in categorical claims. Here, we use uppercase letters to stand for claims. Our main interest is now in the way that words such as "not," "and," "or," and so on affect claims and link them together to produce compound claims out of simpler ones. So, don't confuse the Ps and Qs, called **claim variables,** that appear in this chapter with the variables used for terms in Chapter 8.*

Truth Tables

Let's now consider truth tables and symbols. In truth-functional logic, any given claim, P, is either true or false. The following little table, called a **truth table,** displays both possible truth values for P:

P
T
F

*Whichever truth value the claim P might have, its negation or contradictory, which we'll symbolize ~P, will have the other. Here, then, is the truth table for **negation:***

P	~P
T	F
F	T

---

*It is customary to use one kind of symbol, usually lowercase letters or Greek letters, as *claim variables* and plain or italicized uppercase letters for *specific claims*. Although this use has some technical advantages and makes possible a certain theoretical neatness, beginning students can find it confusing. Therefore, we'll use uppercase letters for both variables and specific claims and simply make it clear which way we're using the letters.

■ The word "and," when used in questions, can produce some interesting and amusing results. In this case, Brutus means to ask, "How many of them are boys, and how many of them are girls?" But Jack thinks he asks, "How many of them are girls or boys?" There's even a third version: "How many of them are *both* girls and boys?" Presumably, none.

The left-hand column of this table sets out both possible truth values for P, and the right-hand column sets out the truth values for ~P based on P's values. This is a way of defining the negation sign, ~, in front of the P. The symbol means "change the truth value from T to F or from F to T, depending on P's values." Because it's handy to have a name for negations that you can say aloud, we read ~P as "not-P." So, if P were "Parker is at home," then ~P would be "It is not the case that Parker is at home," or, more simply, "Parker is not at home." In a moment we'll define other symbols by means of truth tables, so make sure you understand how this one works.

Because any given claim is either true or false, two claims, P and Q, must both be true, both be false, or have opposite truth values, for a total of four possible combinations. Here are the possibilities in truth-table form:

P	Q
T	T
T	F
F	T
F	F

A **conjunction** is a compound claim made from two simpler claims, called *conjuncts. A conjunction is true if and only if both of the simpler claims that make it up (its conjuncts) are true.* An example of a conjunction is the claim "Parker is at home and Moore is at work." We'll express the conjunction of P and Q by connecting them with an ampersand (&). The truth table for conjunctions looks like this:

P	Q	P & Q
T	T	T
T	F	F
F	T	F
F	F	F

P & Q is true in the first row only, where both P and Q are true. Notice that the "truth conditions" in this row match those required in the italicized statement above the truth table.*

Here's another way to remember how conjunctions work: If either part of a conjunction is false, the conjunction itself is false. Notice finally that, although the word "and" is the closest representative in English to our ampersand symbol, there are other words that are correctly symbolized by the ampersand: "but" and "while," for instance, as well as such phrases as "even though." So, if we let P stand for "Parsons is in class" and let Q stand for "Quincy is absent," then we should represent "Parsons is in class even though Quincy is absent" by P & Q. The reason is that the compound claim is true only in one case: where both parts are true. And that's all it takes to require an ampersand to represent the connecting word or phrase.

A **disjunction** is another compound claim made up of two simpler claims, called *disjuncts. A disjunction is false if and only if both of its disjuncts are false.* Here's an example of a disjunction: "Either Parker is at home, or Moore is at work." We'll use the symbol ∨ ("wedge") to represent disjunction when we symbolize claims—as indicated in the example, the closest word in English to this symbol is "or." The truth table for disjunctions is this:

P	Q	P ∨ Q
T	T	T
T	F	T
F	T	T
F	F	F

Notice here that a disjunction is false only in the last row, where both of its disjuncts are false. In all other cases, a disjunction is true.

The third kind of compound claim made from two simpler claims is the **conditional claim.** In ordinary English, the most common way of stating conditionals is by means of the words "if . . . then . . . ," as in the example "If Parker is at home, then Moore is at work."

We'll use an arrow to symbolize conditionals: P → Q. The first claim in a conditional, the P in the symbolization, is the **antecedent,** and the second—Q in this case—is the **consequent.** *A conditional claim is false if and only if its antecedent is true and its consequent is false.* The truth table for conditionals looks like this:

P	Q	P → Q
T	T	T
T	F	F
F	T	T
F	F	T

---

*Some of the words that have truth-functional meaning have other kinds of meanings as well. For example, "and" can signify not only that two things happened but that one happened earlier than the other. An example: "Melinda got on the train and bought her ticket" is quite different from "Melinda bought her ticket and got on the train." In this case, "and" operates as if it were "and then."

Only in the second row, where the antecedent P is true and the consequent Q is false, does the conditional turn out to be false. In all other cases, it is true.*

Of the four types of truth-functional claims—negation, conjunction, disjunction, and conditional—the conditional typically gives students the most trouble. Let's have a closer look at it by considering an example that may shed light on how and why conditionals work. Let's say that Moore promises you that, if his paycheck arrives this morning, he'll buy lunch. So, now we can consider the conditional

> If Moore's paycheck arrives this morning, then Moore will buy lunch.

We can symbolize this using P (for the claim about the paycheck) and L (for the claim about lunch): $P \rightarrow L$. Now let's try to see why the truth table above fits this claim.

The easiest way to see this is by asking yourself what it would take for Moore to break his promise. A moment's thought should make this clear: Two things have to happen before we can say that Moore has fibbed to you. The first is that his paycheck must arrive this morning. (After all, he didn't say what he was going to do if his paycheck *didn't* arrive, did he?) Then, it being true that his paycheck arrives, he must then *not* buy you lunch. Together, these two items make it clear that Moore's original promise was false. Notice: Under no other circumstances would we say that Moore broke his promise. And *that* is why the truth table has a conditional false in one and only one case, namely, where the antecedent is true and the consequent is false. Basic information about all four symbols is summarized in Figure 1.

Our truth-functional symbols can work in combination. Consider, for example, the claim "If Paula doesn't go to work, then Quincy will have to work a double shift." We'll represent the two simple claims in the obvious way, as follows:

P = Paula goes to work.
Q = Quincy has to work a double shift.

And we can symbolize the entire claim like this:

$\sim P \rightarrow Q$

Here is a truth table for this symbolization:

P	Q	~P	~P → Q
T	T	F	T
T	F	F	T
F	T	T	T
F	F	T	F

---

*Like the conjunction, conditionals in ordinary language can have more than the meaning we assign to the arrow. The arrow represents what is often called the "material conditional," conditionals that are true except when the antecedent is true and the consequent false.

Differences between material conditionals and the conditionals used in ordinary language have held the attention of logicians and philosophers for a long time and are still controversial. See, for example, Richard Bradley, "A Defence of the Ramsey Test," in the January 2007 issue of the philosophical journal *Mind* (Vol. 116, Number 461, pp. 1–21).

FIGURE 1 The Four Basic
Truth-Functional Symbols

Negation (~)			Conjunction (&)		
Truth table:			Truth table:		
P	~P		P	Q	(P & Q)
T	F		T	T	T
F	T		T	F	F
			F	T	F
			F	F	F

Closest English counterparts:
"not," or "it is not the case that" (Negation)

Closest English counterparts:
"and," "but," "while" (Conjunction)

Disjunction (∨)			Conditional (→)		
Truth table:			Truth table:		
P	Q	(P ∨ Q)	P	Q	(P → Q)
T	T	T	T	T	T
T	F	T	T	F	F
F	T	T	F	T	T
F	F	F	F	F	T

Closest English counterparts: "or," "unless" (Disjunction)

Closest English counterparts: "if . . . then," "provided that" (Conditional)

Notice that the symbolized claim ~P → Q is false in the *last* row of this table. That's because, here and only here, the antecedent, ~P, is true and its consequent, Q, is false. Notice that we work from the simplest parts to the most complex: The truth value of P in a given row determines the truth value of ~P, and that truth value in turn, along with the one for Q, determines the truth value of ~P → Q.

Consider another combination: "If Paula goes to work, then Quincy and Rogers will get a day off." This claim is symbolized this way:

P → (Q & R)

This symbolization requires parentheses in order to prevent confusion with (P → Q) & R, which symbolizes a different claim and has a different truth table. Our claim is a conditional with a conjunction for a consequent, whereas (P → Q) & R is a conjunction with a conditional as one of the conjuncts. The parentheses are what make this clear.

You need to know a few principles to produce the truth table for the symbolized claim P → (Q & R). First, you have to know how to set up all the possible combinations of true and false for the three simple claims P, Q, and R. In claims with only one letter, there were two possibilities, T and F. In claims with two letters, there were four possibilities. *Every time we add another letter, the number of possible combinations of T and F doubles, and so, therefore, does the number of rows in our truth table.* The formula for determining the number of rows in a truth table for a compound claim is $r = 2^n$, where r is the number of rows in the table and n is the number of letters in the symbolization. Because the claim we are interested in has three letters, our truth table will have eight rows, one for each possible combination of T and F for P, Q, and R. Here's how we do it:

P	Q	R
T	T	T
T	T	F
T	F	T
T	F	F
F	T	T
F	T	F
F	F	T
F	F	F

The systematic way to construct such a table is to alternate Ts and Fs in the right-hand column, then alternate *pairs* of Ts and *pairs* of Fs in the next column to the left, then sets of *four* Ts and sets of *four* Fs in the next, and so forth. The leftmost column will always wind up being half Ts and half Fs.

The second thing we have to know is that the truth value of a compound claim in any particular case (i.e., any row of its truth table) depends entirely upon the truth values of its parts; and if these parts are themselves compound, their truth values depend upon those of their parts; and so on, until we get down to letters standing alone. The columns under the letters, which you have just learned to construct, will then tell us what we need to know. Let's build a truth table for P → (Q & R) and see how this works.

In Depth

Test Yourself

These cards are from a deck that has letters on one side and numbers on the other. They are supposed to obey the following rule: "If there is a vowel on one side, then the card has an even number on the other side."

Question: To see that the rule has been kept, which card(s) must be turned over and checked? (Most university students flunk this simple test of critical thinking.)

P	Q	R	Q & R	P → (Q & R)
T	T	T	T	T
T	T	F	F	F
T	F	T	F	F
T	F	F	F	F
F	T	T	T	T
F	T	F	F	T
F	F	T	F	T
F	F	F	F	T

The three columns at the left, under P, Q, and R, are our *reference columns*, set up just as we discussed previously. They determine what goes on in the rest of the table. From the second and third columns, under the Q and the R, we can fill in the column under Q & R. Notice that this column contains a T only in the first and fifth rows, where both Q and R are true. Next, from the column under the P and the one under Q & R, we can fill in the last column, which is the one for the entire symbolized claim. It contains Fs only in rows two, three, and four, which are the only ones where its antecedent is true and its consequent is false.

What our table gives us is a *truth-functional analysis* of our original claim. Such an analysis displays the compound claim's truth value, based on the truth values of its simpler parts.

If you've followed everything so far without problems, that's great. If you've not yet understood the basic truth table idea, however, as well as the truth tables for the truth-functional symbols, then by all means stop now and go back over this material. You should also understand how to build a truth table for symbolizations consisting of three or more letters. What comes later builds on this foundation, and as with any construction project, without a strong foundation the whole thing collapses.

A final note before we move on: Two claims are **truth-functionally equivalent** if they have exactly the same truth table—that is, if the Ts and Fs in the column under one claim are in the same arrangement as those in the column under the other. Generally speaking, when two claims are equivalent, one can be used in place of another—truth-functionally, they each imply the other.

Okay. It's time now to consider some tips for symbolizing truth-functional claims.

SYMBOLIZING COMPOUND CLAIMS

Most of the things we can do with symbolized claims are pretty straightforward; that is, if you learn the techniques, you can apply them in a relatively clear-cut way. What's less clear-cut is how to symbolize a claim in the first place. We'll cover a few tips for symbolization in this section and then give you a chance to practice with some exercises.

Remember, when you symbolize a claim, you're displaying its truth-functional structure. The idea is to produce a version that will be truth-functionally equivalent to the original informal claim—that is, one that will

In Depth

Truth-Functional Logic and Electrical Circuits

We mentioned at the beginning of the chapter that truth-functional logic is the basis of digital computing. This is because, translated into hardware systems, "true" and "false" become "on" and "off." Although there's a lot more to it than this, we can illustrate in a crude way a little of how this works.

Let's construct a simple electrical circuit from an electrical source to a ground and put a lightbulb in it somewhere, like this:

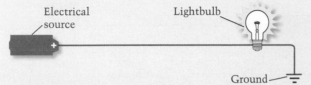

In this situation, the light burns all the time. Now, let's add a switch and give it a name, "P," like so:

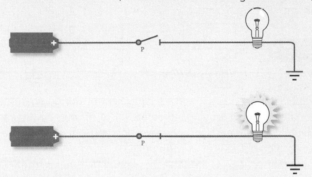

(Switch P represents a sentence that can be true or false, just as the switch can be open or closed.) When the switch is open (corresponding to false), in the second drawing, the light doesn't come on, but when it's closed (corresponding to true) in the third drawing the light comes on. Now, let's add another switch in the same line and call it "Q":

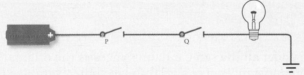

This simple circuit is analogous to a simple conjunction, "P & Q," because *both* switches must be closed for the bulb to come on, just as both conjuncts have to be true in order for the conjunction to be true. So, although there are four possible combinations for the switches (open + open, open + closed, closed + open, closed + closed), only one of them causes the bulb to burn, just as there is only one T in the truth table for conjunction.

We can represent disjunction with a different circuit, one with the switches wired in parallel rather than in series:

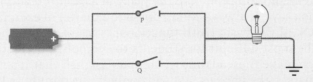

In this case, if *either* the P switch or the Q switch is on, the bulb will light up. So, it lights up in three of the four possible combinations of open/closed for the two switches, just as the disjunction "P ∨ Q" is true in three of the rows in its truth table.

We complicate our circuit-making chores somewhat when we bring in negation. If we have a switch labeled "~P," for example, we just treat it the same as if it were "P": It's either open or closed. But if our circuit contains a switch, P, and another switch, ~P, then we have to connect them (we'll do it with a dotted line), indicating that these switches are always opposite; when one closes, the other automatically opens. Now we get two interesting results: When two switches that are "negations" of each other are wired in series like this:

we have a dysfunctional circuit: The light can never come on! But we get the opposite result when we wire the two negation switches in parallel:

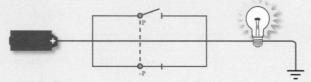

Here, the light can never go off! (This circuit is the exact equivalent of our original one, in which there were no switches at all.) In truth-functional logic, what is being represented here, of course, is that a contradiction is never true (bulb never comes on), and a tautology is never false (bulb never goes off). ("Tautology" is a traditional and somewhat fancy word for a sentence with nothing but "T"s in its truth table.)

This gives you nothing more than a peek at the subject (among other things, truth-functional logic can help us design circuits that are the simplest possible for doing a certain job—i.e., for being on and off under exactly the right circumstances); unfortunately, we don't have room to go further into the subject here. An Introduction to Computer Science class would be the best next step.

be true under all the same circumstances as the original and false under all the same circumstances. Let's go through some examples that illustrate a few of the most frequently encountered symbolization problems.

"If" and "Only If"

In symbolizing truth-functional claims, as in translating categorical claims in Chapter 8, nothing can take the place of a careful reading of what the claim in question says. It always comes down to a matter of exercising careful judgment.

Of all the basic truth-functional types of claim, the conditional is probably the most difficult for students to symbolize correctly. There are so many ways to make these claims in ordinary English that it's not easy to keep track. Fortunately, the phrases "if" and "only if" account for a large number of conditionals, so you'll have a head start if you understand their uses. Here are some general rules to remember:

Real Life

Truth-Functional Trickery

Using what you know about truth-functional logic, can you identify how the sender of this encouraging-looking notice can defend the claim (because it *is* true), even though the receiver is not really going to win one nickel?

You Have Absolutely Won
$1,000,000.00

If you follow the instructions inside
and return the winning number!

Answer: Because there is not going to be any winning number inside (there are usually several *losing* numbers, in case that makes you feel better), the conjunction "You follow the instructions inside and [you] return the winning number" is going to be false, even if you do follow the instructions inside. Therefore, because this conjunction is the antecedent of the whole conditional claim, the conditional claim turns out to be true.

Of course, uncritical readers will take the antecedent to be saying something like "If you follow the instructions inside *by returning the winning number inside* (as if there were a winning number inside). These are the people who may wind up sending their own money to the mailer.

The word "if," used alone, introduces the antecedent of a conditional. The phrase "only if" introduces the consequent of a conditional.

To put it another way: It's not the location of the part in a conditional that tells us whether it is the antecedent or the consequent; it's the logical words that identify it. Consider this example:

Moore will get wet *if* Parker capsizes the boat.

The "Parker" part of the claim is the antecedent, even though it comes *after* the "Moore" part. It's as though the claim had said,

If Parker capsizes the boat, Moore will get wet.

We would symbolize this claim as $P \rightarrow M$. Once again, it's the word "if" that tells us what the antecedent is.

Parker will pay up *only if* Moore sinks the nine ball.

This claim is different. In this case, the "Parker" part is the antecedent because "only if" introduces the consequent of a conditional. This is truth-functionally the same as

---

Real Life

Damned If You Do, But If You Don't . . .

The fearful, and unbelieving, and the abominable, and murderers, and whoremongers, and sorcerers, and idolators, and all liars, shall have their part in the lake which burneth with fire and brimstone.

—Revelation 21:8

This came to us in a brochure from a religious sect offering salvation for the believer. Notice, though, that the passage from the Bible doesn't say that, if you believe, you *won't* go to hell. It says, if you don't believe, you *will* go to hell.

If Parker pays up (P), then Moore sunk (or must have sunk) the nine ball (M).

Using the letters indicated in parentheses, we'd symbolize this as

P → M

Don't worry about the grammatical tenses; we'll adjust those so that the claims make sense. We can use "if" in front of a conditional's antecedent, or we can use "only if" in front of its consequent; we produce exactly equivalent claims in the two cases. As is the case with "if," it doesn't matter where the "only if" part of the claim occurs. The part of this claim that's about Moore is the consequent, even though it occurs at the beginning of this version:

Only if Moore sinks the nine ball will Parker pay up.

Once again: P → M.

Exercise 9-1

Symbolize the following using the claim variables P and Q. (You can ignore differences in past, present, and future tense.)

▲ 1. If Quincy learns to symbolize, Paula will be amazed.
▲ 2. Paula will teach him if Quincy pays her a big fee.
▲ 3. Paula will teach him only if Quincy pays her a big fee.
▲ 4. Only if Paula helps him will Quincy pass the course.
▲ 5. Quincy will pass if and only if Paula helps him.

Claim 5 in the preceding exercise introduces a new wrinkle, the phrase "if and only if." Remembering our general rules about how "if" and "only if" operate separately, it shouldn't surprise us that "if and only if" makes both antecedent and consequent out of the claim it introduces. We can make P both antecedent and consequent this way:*

(P → Q) & (Q → P)

There are other ways to produce conditionals, of course. In one of its senses, the word "provided" (and the phrase "provided that") works like the word "if" in introducing the antecedent of a conditional. "Moore will buy the car, provided the seller throws in a ton of spare parts" is equivalent to the same expression with the word "if" in place of "provided."

Necessary and Sufficient Conditions

Conditional claims are sometimes spelled out in terms of necessary and sufficient conditions. Consider this example:

The presence of oxygen is a necessary condition for combustion.

This tells us that we can't have combustion without oxygen, or "If we have combustion (C), then we must have oxygen (O)." Notice that *the necessary condition becomes the consequent of a conditional*: C → O.

A sufficient condition *guarantees* whatever it is a sufficient condition for. Being born in the United States is a sufficient condition for U.S. citizenship— that's *all* one needs to be a U.S. citizen. *Sufficient conditions are expressed as the antecedents of conditional claims*, so we would say, "If Juan was born in the United States (B), then Juan is a U.S. citizen (C)": B → C.

Okay, Lew, the deal is, you can use the car tonight only if you wash and wax it this afternoon.

■ Comment: We often use "only if" when we mean to state both necessary and sufficient conditions, even though, literally speaking, it produces only the former. If Lew were a critical thinker, he'd check this deal more carefully before getting out the hose and bucket. See the text below.

---

*Many texts introduce a new symbol ("P ↔ Q") to represent "P if and only if Q." It works exactly like our version; i.e., it has the same truth table as "(P → Q) & (O → P)." Under some circumstances, the extra symbol provides some efficiencies, but for us it is unnecessary and would be merely something else to learn and remember.

On Language

Another "If" and "Only If" Confusion

Do you want to install and run Flasher 3.0 distributed by SE Digital Arts? Caution: SE Digital Arts claims that this content is safe. You should install or view this content if you trust SE Digital Arts to make that assertion.

—A typical download caution

Presumably, they mean not "if" but "only if." Do you see why? In any case, this caution contains one heck of a weaseler (Chapter 5).

You should also notice the connection between "if" and "only if" on the one hand and necessary and sufficient conditions on the other. The word "if," by itself, introduces a sufficient condition; the phrase "only if" introduces a necessary condition. So the claim "X is a necessary condition for Y" would be symbolized "Y → X."

From time to time, one thing will be both a necessary and a sufficient condition for something else. For example, if Jean's payment of her dues to the National Truth-Functional Logic Society (NTFLS) guaranteed her continued membership (making such payment a sufficient condition) and there were no way for her to continue membership *without* paying her dues (making payment a necessary condition as well), then we could express such a situation as "Jean will remain a member of the NTFLS (M) if and only if she pays her dues (D)": (M → D) & (D → M).

We often play fast and loose with how we state necessary and sufficient conditions. A parent tells his daughter, "You can watch television only if you clean your room." Now, the youngster would ordinarily take cleaning her room as both a necessary and a sufficient condition for being allowed to watch television, and probably that's what a parent would intend by those words. But notice that the parent actually stated only a necessary condition; technically, he would not be going back on what he said if room cleaning turned out not to be sufficient for television privileges. Of course, he'd better be prepared for more than a logic lesson from his daughter in such a case, and most of us would be on her side in the dispute. But, literally, it's the necessary condition that the phrase "only if" introduces, not the sufficient condition.

"Unless"

Consider the claim "Paula will foreclose unless Quincy pays up." Asked to symbolize this, we might come up with ~Q → P because the original claim is equivalent to "If Quincy doesn't pay up, then Paula will foreclose." But there's an even simpler way to do it. Ask yourself, What is the truth table for ~Q → P? If you've gained familiarity with the basic truth tables by this time, you realize that it's the same as the table for P ∨ Q. And, as a matter of fact, you can treat the word "unless" exactly like the word "or" and symbolize it with a "∨".

"Either . . . Or"

Sometimes we need to know exactly where a disjunction begins; it's the job of the word "either" to show us. Compare the claims

> Either P and Q or R

and

> P and either Q or R.

These two claims say different things and have different truth tables, but the only difference between them is the location of the word "either"; without that word, the claim would be completely ambiguous. "Either" tells us that the disjunction begins with P in the first claim and Q in the second claim. So, we would symbolize the first (P & Q) ∨ R and the second P & (Q ∨ R).

The word "if" does much the same job for conditionals that "either" does for disjunctions. Notice the difference between

> P and if Q then R

and

> If P and Q then R.

"If" tells us that the antecedent begins with Q in the first example and with P in the second. Hence, the second must have P & Q for the antecedent of its symbolization.

In general, the trick to symbolizing a claim correctly is to pay careful attention to exactly what the claim says—and this often means asking yourself just exactly what would make this claim false (or true). Then, try to come up with a symbolization that says the same thing—that is false (or true) in exactly the same circumstances. There's no substitute for practice, so here's an exercise to work on.

When we symbolize a claim, we're displaying its truth-functional structure. Show that you can figure out the structures of the following claims by symbolizing them. Use these letters for the first ten items:

Exercise 9-2

> P = Parsons signs the papers.
> Q = Quincy goes (or will go) to jail.
> R = Rachel files (or will file) an appeal.

Use the symbols ~, &, ∨, and →. We suggest that, at least at first, you make symbolization a two-stage process: First, replace simple parts of claims with letters; then, replace logical words with logical symbols, and add parentheses as required. We'll do an example in two stages to show you what we mean.

Example

If Parsons signs the papers, then Quincy will go to jail but Rachel will not file an appeal.

Stage 1: If P, then Q but ~R.
Stage 2: P → (Q & ~R)

▲   1. If Parsons signs the papers then Quincy will go to jail, and Rachel will file an appeal.

▲   2. If Parsons signs the papers, then Quincy will go to jail and Rachel will file an appeal.

   3. If Parsons signs the papers and Quincy goes to jail then Rachel will file an appeal.

   4. Parsons signs the papers and if Quincy goes to jail Rachel will file an appeal.

▲   5. If Parsons signs the papers then if Quincy goes to jail Rachel will file an appeal.

   6. If Parsons signs the papers Quincy goes to jail, and if Rachel files an appeal Quincy goes to jail.

   7. Quincy goes to jail if either Parsons signs papers or Rachel files an appeal.

   8. Either Parsons signs the papers or, if Quincy goes to jail, then Rachel will file an appeal.

   9. If either Parsons signs the papers or Quincy goes to jail then Rachel will file an appeal.

 10. If Parsons signs the papers then either Quincy will go to jail or Rachel will file an appeal.

For the next ten items, use the following letters:

   C = My car runs well.
   S = I will sell my car.
   F = I will have my car fixed.

▲ 11. If my car doesn't run well, then I will sell it.

▲ 12. It's not true that, if my car runs well, then I will sell it.

 13. I will sell my car only if it doesn't run well.

 14. I won't sell my car unless it doesn't run well.

 15. I will have my car fixed unless it runs well.

▲ 16. I will sell my car but only if it doesn't run well.

 17. Provided my car runs well, I won't sell it.

 18. My car's running well is a sufficient condition for my not having it fixed.

 19. My car's not running well is a necessary condition for my having it fixed.

▲ 20. I will neither have my car fixed nor sell it.

▲ Construct truth tables for the symbolizations you produced for Exercise 9-2.
Determine whether any of them are truth-functionally equivalent to any others. (Answers to the items with triangles are provided in the answer section at
the end of the book.)   Exercise 9-3

TRUTH-FUNCTIONAL ARGUMENT PATTERNS (BRIEF VERSION)

This section is an alternative to the two sections that follow ("Truth-
Functional Arguments" and "Deductions"). Those instructors who want to
go into the subject of truth-functional logic in some depth should skip this
section and cover the next two instead; they constitute a fairly thorough treatment and a concise introduction to symbolic logic.

For those who want briefer and more practical coverage of the subject,
this section should suffice.

Three Common Valid Argument Patterns

Three forms of truth-functional argument are almost ubiquitous; they appear
so frequently, and we are so accustomed to them, that we often make use
of them almost without thinking. But it is important to understand and be
able to recognize them because there are imposters that, because of superficial
similarities, may look like valid argument patterns but are not.

First, we should recall what it means for an argument to be *valid*. To be
valid, the truth of the argument's premises must guarantee the truth of its
conclusion. Another way to say this is that it is impossible for the premises to
be true while the conclusion is false. If it is even possible for the premises
to be true without the conclusion being true, the argument is *invalid*.

Modus ponens ("in the affirmative mode," more or less) is a two-premise valid
argument form, one premise of which is a conditional and the other of which
is the antecedent of that conditional. The conclusion of the argument is the
consequent of the conditional. (See page 298 if you need refreshing on the
meanings of these terms.) So all cases of modus ponens fit this pattern:

Modus Ponens

> If P then Q.
> P.
> ―――――――
> Therefore Q.

You can see that one premise is the conditional: "If P then Q," and the
other premise is the antecedent of that conditional: "P." The conclusion, "Q,"
is the consequent of the conditional. Every argument that has this form is
valid. For example,

Example 1:

> If the referee scored the fight in favor of Madderly, then Madderly wins the
> decision.
> The referee did score the fight in favor of Madderly.
> ―――――――
> Therefore, Madderly wins the decision.

Remember from the previous section that there are other ways of stating conditional claims besides using "if . . . then. . . ." For example, this is another way to state the foregoing argument:

Example 2:

> Madderly wins the decision provided the referee scored the fight in his favor.
>
> The referee did score the fight in favor of Madderly.
>
> Therefore, Madderly wins the decision.

Here are some other examples of arguments that fit the modus ponens form, accompanied by some remarks about why they do. Make sure you understand each one. (We'll continue to separate premises from the conclusion with the horizontal line; it works the same as "therefore" in introducing the conclusion.)

Example 3:

> The generator works.
>
> The generator works only if the polarity of the circuit has been reversed.
>
> The polarity of the circuit has been reversed.

The second premise is the required conditional, with "only if" introducing the consequent (see page 298). It does not matter which of the two premises is stated first. The full conditional is stated second in this example.

Example 4:

> Failure to melt at 2,600 degrees is sufficient for determining that this item is not made of steel.
>
> The item failed to melt at 2,600 degrees.
>
> The item is not made of steel.

The first premise is a conditional stated in terms of a sufficient condition (see page 301).

Modus Tollens

Modus tollens ("in the denial mode," approximately) is also a two-premise argument with one of the premises a conditional and the other premise the *negation* of that conditional's consequent. The conclusion is the negation of the antecedent. It looks like this:

> If P then Q.
>
> Not-Q.
>
> Not-P.

It is crucially important to notice that the nonconditional premise is the negation of the consequent of the other premise, not its antecedent. It isn't valid the other way, as you'll see in the following examples. Every argument that fits the form above, however, is valid. You'll sometimes hear someone use modus tollens in this way: "Hey, if X had happened, then Y would have had to happen, but it (Y) didn't happen. So X must not have happened."

Here are some examples of modus tollens. Make sure you understand why they fit the modus tollens form.

Example 1:

> If the new generator will work, then the polarity of the circuit has been reversed.
>
> But the polarity of the circuit has not been reversed.
>
> The new generator will not work.

Example 2:

> If the song is in A-minor, there are no black keys in its scale.
>
> However, there are black keys in its scale.
>
> The song is not in A-minor.

Example 3:

> If he got his forms in on time, he's automatically accepted. But he wasn't automatically accepted; consequently, he must not have gotten his forms in on time.

Example 4:

> Bill was not with AT&T; but he'd have to have been with AT&T if he'd had an early iPhone. So he clearly did not have an early iPhone.

A last point about modus tollens: This argument form is the logical structure underlying the technique known as *"reductio ad absurdum"*—literally, to reduce to an absurdity. This technique, widely used in science and mathematics (where it's sometimes known as "indirect proof"), attempts to show that a given claim clearly leads to (implies) a second claim, and that the second claim cannot be true. Thus, by modus tollens, the first claim cannot be true either.

A chain argument comprises two conditionals for premises and another for the conclusion. Here's the form:

Chain Argument

> If P then Q.
>
> If Q then R.
>
> If P then R.

The important thing is the arrangement of the simple sentences, P, Q, and R. It's crucial that the consequent of one premise be the same as the antecedent of the other premise. The remaining antecedent and consequent get hooked up in the conclusion. This way of laying it out may help:

> If P . . . then Q.
>
>   If Q . . . then R.
>
>   If P . . . then R.

Here, Q is the consequent of the first premise and the antecedent of the second. This makes possible the conclusion with P as antecedent and R as consequent. Here are further examples of the chain argument:

Example 1:

> If Casey goes to the meeting, then Simone will go.
> If Simone goes, then Chris will go.
> If Casey goes to the meeting, then Chris will go.

Example 2:

> If the stock is lightweight, then it's aluminum; but if it's aluminum, then it will be hard to weld. So, if the stock is lightweight, it will be hard to weld.

Example 3:

> If the picture is a daguerreotype, then it has to have been made after 1837; and the man in the picture can't be Hegel if it was made after 1837. So it isn't Hegel in the picture if it's a daguerreotype.

Example 4:

> If the oil gusher in the gulf of Mexico continues until August, it will be ten times bigger than the Exxon Valdez spill. And if it's that much bigger than the Exxon Valdez, it'll be the biggest man-made environmental disaster ever. You draw the conclusion.

Three Mistakes: Invalid Argument Forms

Each of the three foregoing argument forms has an invalid imposter that resembles it fairly closely. We'll have a brief look at each and see why they fail the test of validity.

Affirming the
Consequent

This fallacy masquerades as modus ponens, because one of its premises is a conditional and the other premise is a part of that conditional, while the conclusion is the other part of the conditional. But modus ponens, you'll recall, has the *antecedent* of the conditional as its other premise and its *consequent* as conclusion. The fallacious version has the consequent as the other premise and the antecedent of the conditional as conclusion. Thus the title, since the second premise "affirms" or states the consequent of the conditional rather than its antecedent. This is easy to see when we lay it out like this:

> If P then Q.
> Q.
> Therefore, P.

You might take a moment to compare this argument form to the one for modus ponens on page 311. In this case, it is entirely possible for the premises to both be true and the conclusion false. If Q is true and P is false, then both premises are true* and the conclusion false—exactly the thing that cannot happen with

---

* Since a conditional with false antecedent and true consequent is true; remember the truth table for the conditional on page 298.

a valid argument. So remember, a conditional with its *antecedent* as the other premise can validly give the consequent as a conclusion. However, a conditional with its *consequent* as the other premise cannot validly produce the antecedent as conclusion.

Example 1:

> If Shelley has read the *Republic*, then she's bound to know who Thrasymachus is. And, since she clearly *does* know who Thrasymachus is, we can conclude that she must have read the *Republic*.

Example 2:

> This zinfandel would have a smooth finish if it came from very old vines. In fact, it does have a smooth finish, so it must have come from very old vines.

Here, the fallacy impersonates modus tollens. In modus tollens, a conditional and the negation of its consequent validly give us the negation of its antecedent. But the fallacious version has us trying to draw a conclusion from a conditional and the negation of its *antecedent*, and this does not produce a valid argument.

Denying the Antecedent

Here's the way it looks:

> If P then Q.
> Not-P.
> _____
> Therefore, not-Q.

Now, if P is false and Q is true, the premises of the argument are true and the conclusion is false; thus the argument is invalid. A couple of examples:

Example 1:

> If Jared studies really hard for the final, he will pass the course. [Later:] Well, Jared didn't study for the final, so it's a sure thing that he won't pass.

Example 2:

> Joel will automatically be accepted provided he got his forms in on time. Unfortunately, he did not get his forms in on time; so he won't be automatically accepted.

Our final invalid form mimics the chain argument. It differs from that argument, though, by having the same consequent for each of its conditional premises:

Undistributed Middle (truth-functional version)

> If P then Q.
> If R then Q.
> _____
> Therefore, if P then R.

If we allow P and Q to be true and R to be false, we'll see that both premises turn out to be true and the conclusion false. So this is clearly not a valid form of argument. Here's what it can look like:

Example 1:

> If Robinson had had some great success in business, he'd be well-known. Furthermore, if he were extremely rich, he'd be well-known. So, of course, if Robinson had had some great success in business, he'd be extremely rich.

Example 2:

> If you eat fish, you're a carnivore; and if you're an omnivore, you must be a carnivore. So, if you eat fish, that would make you an omnivore.

Exercise 9-4

Go through the eighteen examples in this section and symbolize each. Alternatively, use "if . . . then . . ." and "not- . . ." in place of the special symbols.

Exercise 9-5

For each of the last six examples (of the invalid forms), explain why each is invalid. For each, try to imagine and describe circumstances in which the premises are true and the conclusion is false.

Exercise 9-6

Determine which of the argument forms mentioned in this section is found in each of the following passages. Which contain valid arguments and which do not?

▲ 1. There are Taliban in North Waziristan; and if there are Taliban there, you can be sure they're in South Waziristan, too. So we have to believe there are Taliban in South Waziristan.

2. If the Saints win the Super Bowl again, it will be poetic justice for New Orleans, the country's most bad-luck city in recent years. Unfortunately, the Saints have no chance to repeat the win, so there'll be no poetic justice this year for "N'awlins."

3. If you read Ayn Rand, you'll be a libertarian. And, of course, if you're an anarchist, you're already a libertarian. Hmm. It looks like if you read Ayn Rand, you'll be an anarchist!

▲ 4. If Sheila were ever to become a successful trader, she would have to develop a ruthless personality. But you know her: she could never be ruthless, even for a minute. So it's not going to be in her future to be a successful trader.

5. It's true, Ms. Zerkle will be accepted into law school only if she has excellent grades. But I'm telling you, you should see her transcript; she's made straight A's for the past two years. So don't worry about her getting into law school. She'll be accepted without a doubt.

6. If the Lambda Xi's continue to throw those open parties, they're going to get cited by the police. So if they continue the parties, they'll get decertified by the university because the university will certainly decertify them if they're cited by the police.

▲   7. Jamal is a devout Muslim only if he follows the Sharia law, and I know for a fact that he follows it to the letter. So he is a devout Muslim.

8. If the carburetor is clogged, the engine will run lean, and running lean will lead to overheating. So overheating can result if the carburetor is clogged up.

More exercises related to this section can be found in Exercise 9-19, near the end of the chapter.

TRUTH-FUNCTIONAL ARGUMENTS

Categorical syllogisms (discussed in Chapter 8) have a total of 256 forms. A truth-functional argument, by contrast, can take any of an infinite number of forms. Nevertheless, we have methods for testing for validity that are flexible enough to encompass every truth-functional argument. In the remainder of this chapter, we'll look at three of them: the truth-table method, the short truth-table method, and the method of deduction.

Before doing anything else, though, let's quickly review the concept of validity. An argument is *valid,* you'll recall, if and only if the truth of the premises guarantees the truth of the conclusion—that is, if the premises were true, the conclusion could not then be false. (Where validity is concerned, remember, it doesn't matter whether the premises are *actually* true.)

The Truth-Table Method

The *truth-table test for validity* requires familiarity with the truth tables for the four truth-functional symbols, so go back and check yourself on those if you think you may not understand them clearly. Here's how the method works: We present all of the possible circumstances for an argument by building a truth table for it; then we simply look to see if there are any circumstances in which the premises are all true and the conclusion false. If there are such circumstances—one row of the truth table is all that's required—then the argument is invalid.

Let's look at a simple example. Let P and Q represent any two claims. Now, look at the following symbolized argument:

$P \rightarrow Q$
$\underline{\sim P}$
Therefore, $\sim Q$

We can construct a truth table for this argument by including a column for each premise and one for the conclusion:

1	2	3	4	5
P	Q	~P	P → Q	~Q
T	T	F	T	F
T	F	F	F	T
F	T	T	T	F
F	F	T	T	T

The first two columns are reference columns; they list truth values for the letters that appear in the argument. The reference columns should be constructed in accordance with the method described on page 301. The third and fourth columns appear under the two premises of the argument, and the fifth column is for the conclusion. The truth values in these columns are determined by those in the appropriate rows of the reference columns. Note that in the third row of the table, both premises are true and the conclusion is false. This tells us that it is possible for the premises of this argument to be true while the conclusion is false; thus, the argument is invalid. Because it doesn't matter what claims P and Q might stand for, the same is true for *every* argument of this pattern. Here's an example of such an argument:

> If the Saints beat the Forty-Niners, then the Giants will make the playoffs. But the Saints won't beat the Forty-Niners. So the Giants won't make the playoffs.

Using S for "The Saints beat (or will beat) the Forty-Niners" and G for "The Giants make (or will make) the playoffs," we can symbolize the argument like this:

$$S \rightarrow G$$
$$\underline{{\sim}S}$$
$${\sim}G$$

The first premise is a conditional, and the other premise is the negation of the antecedent of that conditional. The conclusion is the negation of the conditional's consequent. It has exactly the same structure as the argument for which we just did the truth table; accordingly, it, too, is invalid.

Let's do another simple one:

> We're going to have large masses of arctic air (A) flowing into the Midwest unless the jet stream (J) moves south. Unfortunately, there's no chance of the jet stream's moving south. So you can bet there'll be arctic air flowing into the Midwest.

Symbolization gives us

$$A \vee J$$
$$\underline{{\sim}J}$$
$$A$$

Here's a truth table for the argument:

1 **A**	2 **J**	3 **A $\vee$ J**	4 **~J**
T	T	T	F
T	F	T	T
F	T	T	F
F	F	F	T

Note that the first premise is represented in column 3 of the table, the second premise in column 4, and the conclusion in one of the reference columns, column 1. Now, let's recall what we're up to. We want to know whether this argument is valid—that is to say, is it possible for the premises to be true and the conclusion false? If there is such a possibility, it will turn up in the truth table because, remember, the truth table represents every possible situation with respect to the claims A and J. We find that the premises are both true in only one row, the second, and when we check the conclusion, A, we find it is true in that row. Thus, there is *no* row in which the premises are true and the conclusion false. So, the argument is valid.

Here's an example of a rather more complicated argument:

> If Scarlet is guilty of the crime, then Ms. White must have left the back door unlocked and the colonel must have retired before ten o'clock. However, either Ms. White did not leave the back door unlocked, or the colonel did not retire before ten. Therefore, Scarlet is not guilty of the crime.

Let's assign some letters to the simple claims so that we can show this argument's pattern.

S = Scarlet is guilty of the crime.

W = Ms. White left the back door unlocked.

C = The colonel retired before ten o'clock.

Now we symbolize the argument to display this pattern:

$$S \rightarrow (W \mathbin{\&} C)$$
$$\underline{\sim W \vee \sim C}$$
$$\sim S$$

Let's think our way through this argument. As you read, refer back to the symbolized version above. Notice that the first premise is a conditional, with "Scarlet is guilty of the crime" as antecedent and a conjunction as consequent. In order for that conjunction to be true, both "Ms. White left the back door unlocked" and "The colonel retired before ten o'clock" have to be true, as you'll recall from the truth table for conjunctions. Now look at the second premise. It is a disjunction that tells us *either* Ms. White did not leave the back door unlocked *or* the colonel did not retire before ten. But if either or both of those disjuncts are true, at least one of the claims in our earlier conjunction is false. So it cannot be that *both* parts of the conjunction are true. This means the conjunction symbolized by W & C must be false. And so the consequent of the first premise is false. How can the entire premise be true, in that case? The only way is for the antecedent to be false as well. And that means that the conclusion, "Scarlet is not guilty of the crime," must be true.

All of this reasoning (and considerably more that we don't require) is implicit in the following truth table for the argument:

Real Life

An Al Gore Chain Argument

If governments (which have not indicated they are willing to act) do not act soon, carbon emissions will cause a serious increase in global temperatures. And if that happens, there will be a series of planetary catastrophes. Finally, if these catastrophes take place, the world will become uninhabitable. So, unfortunately, our ability to live on this planet depends on the timely actions of governments that so far have shown little inclination to act.

—Our exaggeration of an Al Gore thesis

Notice that this passage is simply two chain arguments linked together.

1	2	3	4	5	6	7	8	9
S	W	C	~W	~C	W & C	S → (W & C)	~W ∨ ~C	~S
T	T	T	F	F	T	T	F	F
T	T	F	F	T	F	F	T	F
T	F	T	T	F	F	F	T	F
T	F	F	T	T	F	F	T	F
F	T	T	F	F	T	T	F	T
F	T	F	F	T	F	T	T	T
F	F	T	T	F	F	T	T	T
F	F	F	T	T	F	T	T	T

The first three columns are our reference columns, columns 7 and 8 are for the premises of the argument, and column 9 is for the argument's conclusion. The remainder—4, 5, and 6—are for parts of some of the other symbolized claims; they could be left out if we desired, but they make filling in columns 7 and 8 a bit easier.

Once the table is filled in, evaluating the argument is easy. Just look to see whether there is any row in which the premises are true and the conclusion is false. One such row is enough to demonstrate the invalidity of the argument.

In the present case, we find that both premises are true only in the last three rows of the table. And in those rows, the conclusion is also true. So there is no set of circumstances—no row of the table—in which both premises are true and the conclusion is false. Therefore, the argument is valid.

The Short Truth-Table Method

Although filling out a complete truth table always produces the correct answer regarding a truth-functional argument's validity, it can be quite a tedious chore—in fact, life is much too short to spend much of it filling in truth tables. Fortunately, there are shorter and more manageable ways of finding such an answer. The easiest systematic way to determine the validity or invalidity of truth-functional arguments is the *short truth-table method.* Here's the idea behind it: *If an argument is invalid, there has to be at least one row in the argument's truth table where the premises are true and the conclusion is false.* With the short truth-table method, we simply focus on finding such a row. Consider this symbolized argument:

$P \rightarrow Q$
$\underline{\sim Q \rightarrow R}$
$\sim P \rightarrow R$

We begin by looking at the conclusion. Because it's a conditional, it can be made false only one way, by making its antecedent true and its consequent false. So, we do that by making P false and R false.

Can we now make both premises true? Yes, as it turns out, by making Q true. This case,

P	Q	R
F	T	F

makes both premises true and the conclusion false and thus proves the argument invalid. What we've done is produce the relevant row of the truth table without bothering to produce all the rest. Had the argument been valid, we would not have been able to produce such a row.

Here's how the method works with a valid argument. Consider this example:

$(P \lor Q) \rightarrow R$
$\underline{S \rightarrow Q}$
$S \rightarrow R$

The only way to make the conclusion false is to make S true and R false. So, we do that:

P	Q	R	S
		F	T

Now, with S true, the only way we can make the second premise true is by making Q true. So, we do that next:

P	Q	R	S
	T	F	T

But now, there is no way at all to make the first premise true, because P ∨ Q is going to be true (because Q is true), and R is already false. Because there is no other way to make the conclusion false and the second premise true, and because this way fails to make the first premise true, we can conclude that the argument is *valid*.

In many cases, there will be more than one way to make the conclusion false. Here's a symbolized example:

$$\left.\begin{array}{l} \text{P \& (Q ∨ R)} \\ \text{R → S} \\ \text{P → T} \end{array}\right\} \text{trying to make these true}$$
$$\left.\begin{array}{l} \text{S \& T} \end{array}\right\} \text{trying to make this false}$$

Because the conclusion is a conjunction, it is false if either or both of its conjuncts are false, which means we could begin by making S true and T false, S false and T true, or both S and T false. This is trouble we'd like to avoid if possible, so let's see if there's someplace else we can begin making our assignment. (Remember: The idea is to try to assign true and false to the letters so as to make the premises true and the conclusion false. If we can do it, the argument is invalid.)

In this example, to make the first premise true, we *must* assign true to the letter P. Why? Because the premise is a conjunction, and both of its parts must be true for the whole thing to be true. That's what we're looking for: places where we are *forced* to make an assignment of true or false to one or more letters. Then we make those assignments and see where they lead us. In this case, once we've made P true, we see that, to make the third premise true, we are forced to make T true (because a true antecedent and a false consequent would make the premise false, and we're trying to make our premises true).

After making T true, we see that, to make the conclusion false, S must be false. So we make that assignment. At this point we're nearly done, needing only assignments for Q and R.

P	Q	R	S	T
T			F	T

Are there any other assignments that we're forced to make? Yes: We must make R false to make the second premise true. Once we've done that, we see that Q must be true to preserve the truth of the first premise. And that completes the assignment:

P	Q	R	S	T
T	T	F	F	T

This is one row in the truth table for this argument—the only row, as it turned out—in which all the premises are true and the conclusion is false; thus, it is the row that proves the argument invalid.

In the preceding example, there was a premise that forced us to begin with a particular assignment to a letter. Sometimes, neither the conclusion nor any of the premises forces an assignment on us. In that case, we must use trial and error: Begin with one assignment that makes the conclusion false (or some premise true) and see if it will work. If not, try another assignment. If all fail, then the argument is valid.

Often, several rows of a truth table will make the premises true and the conclusion false; any one of them is all it takes to prove invalidity. Don't get the mistaken idea that, just because the premises are all true in one row and so is the conclusion, the conclusion follows from the premises—that is, that the argument must be valid. To be valid, the conclusion must be true in *every* row in which all the premises are true.

To review: Try to assign Ts and Fs to the letters in the symbolization so that all premises come out true and the conclusion comes out false. There may be more than one way to do it; any of them will do to prove the argument invalid. If it is impossible to make the premises and conclusion come out this way, the argument is valid.

Construct full truth tables or use the short truth-table method to determine which of the following arguments are valid.

Exercise 9-7

1. P ∨ ~Q
    ~Q
    ―――
    ~P

2. P → Q
    ~Q
    ―――
    ~P

3. ~(P ∨ Q)
    R → P
    ―――――
    ~R

4. P → (Q → R)
    ~(P → Q)
    ―――――――
    R

5. P ∨ (Q → R)
    Q & ~R
    ―――――
    ~P

6. (P → Q) ∨ (R → Q)
    P & (~P → ~~R)
    ―――――――――
    Q

▲ 7. (P & R) → Q

$$\frac{\sim Q}{\sim P}$$

8. P & (~Q → ~P)

$$\frac{R \rightarrow \sim Q}{\sim R}$$

9. L ∨ ~J

$$\frac{R \rightarrow J}{L \rightarrow \sim R}$$

10. ~F ∨ (G & H)

$$\frac{P \rightarrow F}{\sim H \rightarrow \sim P}$$

Exercise 9-8

Use either the long or short truth-table method to determine which of the following arguments are valid.

▲ 1. K → (L & G)

M → (J & K)

$$\frac{B \, \& \, M}{B \, \& \, G}$$

▲ 2. L ∨ (W → S)

P ∨ ~S

$$\frac{\sim L \rightarrow W}{P}$$

▲ 3. M & P

R → ~P

F ∨ R

$$\frac{G \rightarrow M}{G \, \& \, F}$$

▲ 4. (D & G) → H

M & (H → P)

$$\frac{M \rightarrow G}{D \, \& \, P}$$

▲ 5. R → S

(S & B) → T

$$\frac{T \rightarrow E}{(R \vee B) \rightarrow E}$$

DEDUCTIONS

The next method we'll look at is less useful for proving an argument *invalid* than the truth-table methods, but it has some advantages in proving that an argument is valid. The method is that of **deduction.**

When we use this method, we actually deduce (or "derive") the conclusion from the premises by means of a series of basic, truth-functionally valid argument patterns. This is a lot like "thinking through" the argument, taking one step at a time to see how, once we've assumed the truth of the premises, we eventually arrive at the conclusion. (We do this for an example on page 319.) We'll consider some extended examples showing how the method works as we explain the first few basic argument patterns. We'll refer to these patterns as truth-functional rules because they govern what steps we're allowed to take in getting from the premises to the conclusion. (Your instructor may ask that you learn some or all of the basic valid argument patterns. It's a good idea to be able to identify these patterns whether you go on to construct deductions from them or not.)

Group I Rules: Elementary Valid Argument Patterns

This first group of rules should be learned before you go on to the Group II rules. Study them until you can work Exercise 9-9 with confidence.

Any argument of the pattern

$$P \rightarrow Q$$
$$\frac{P}{Q}$$

Rule 1: Modus ponens (MP), also known as *affirming the antecedent*

is valid. If you have a conditional among the premises, and if the antecedent of that conditional occurs as another premise, then by **modus ponens** the consequent of the conditional follows from those two premises. The claims involved do not have to be simple letters standing alone—it would have made no difference if, in place of P, we had had something more complicated, such as (P ∨ R), as long as that compound claim appeared everywhere that P appears in the pattern above. For example:

1. (P ∨ R) → Q   Premise
2. P ∨ R   Premise
3. Q   From the premises, by modus ponens

The idea, once again, is that if you have *any conditional whatsoever* on a line of your deduction, and if you have the antecedent of that conditional on some other line, you can write down the consequent of the conditional on your new line.

If the consequent of the conditional is the conclusion of the argument, then the deduction is finished—the conclusion has been established. If it is not the conclusion of the argument you're working on, the consequent of the conditional can be listed just as if it were another premise to use in deducing the conclusion you're after. An example:

1. P → R
2. R → S
3. P   Therefore, S

We've numbered the three premises of the argument and set its conclusion off to the side. (Hereafter we'll use a slash and three dots [/∴] in place of "therefore" to indicate the conclusion.) Now, notice that line 1 is a conditional, and line 3 is its antecedent. Modus ponens allows us to write down the consequent of line 1 as a new line in our deduction:

4. R   1, 3, MP

At the right, we've noted the abbreviation for the rule we used and the lines the rule required. These notes are called the *annotation* for the deduction. We can now make use of this new line in the deduction to get the conclusion we were originally after, namely, S.

5. S   2, 4, MP

Again, we used modus ponens, this time on lines 2 and 4. The same explanation as that for deriving line 4 from lines 1 and 3 applies here.

Notice that the modus ponens rule and all other Group I rules can be used only on whole lines. This means that you can't find the items you need for MP as *parts* of a line, as in the following:

$$(P \to Q) \vee R$$
$$\underline{P}$$
$$Q \vee R \qquad \text{(erroneous!)}$$

This is *not* a legitimate use of MP. We do have a conditional as *part* of the first line, and the second line is indeed the antecedent of that conditional. But the rule cannot be applied to parts of lines. The conditional required by rule MP must take up the entire line, as in the following:

$$P \to (Q \vee R)$$
$$\underline{P}$$
$$Q \vee R$$

Rule 2: Modus tollens (MT), also known as *denying the consequent*

The **modus tollens** pattern is this:

$$P \to Q$$
$$\underline{\sim Q}$$
$$\sim P$$

If you have a conditional claim as one premise and if one of your other premises is the negation of the consequent of that conditional, you can write down the negation of the conditional's antecedent as a new line in your deduction. Here's a deduction that uses both of the first two rules:

1. (P & Q) → R
2. S
3. S → ~R   /∴ ~(P & Q)
4. ~R   2, 3, MP
5. ~(P & Q)   1, 4, MT

In this deduction, we derived line 4 from lines 2 and 3 by modus ponens, and then 4 and 1 gave us line 5, which is what we were after, by modus tollens. The fact that the antecedent of line 1 is itself a compound claim, (P & Q), is not important; our line 5 is the antecedent of the conditional with a negation sign in front of it, and that's all that counts.

Real Life

If the Dollar Falls . . .

The valid argument patterns are in fact fairly common. Here's one from an article in *Time* as to why a weakening dollar is a threat to the stock market:

> Why should we care? . . . If the dollar continues to drop, investors may be tempted to move their cash to currencies on the upswing. That would drive the U.S. market lower. . . . Because foreigners hold almost 40% of U.S. Treasury securities, any pullout would risk a spike in interest rates that would ultimately slaughter the . . . market.

The chain argument here is reasonably obvious. In effect: If the dollar falls, then investors move their cash to currencies on the upswing. If investors move their cash to currencies on the upswing, then the U.S. market goes lower. If the U.S. market goes lower, then interest rates on U.S. Treasury securities rise. If interest rates on U.S. Treasury securities rise, then the . . . market dies. [Therefore, if the dollar falls, then the . . . market dies.]

$$\frac{\begin{array}{l} P \rightarrow Q \\ Q \rightarrow R \end{array}}{P \rightarrow R}$$

Rule 3: Chain argument (CA)

The **chain argument** rule allows you to derive a conditional from two you already have, provided the antecedent of one of your conditionals is the same as the consequent of the other.

$$\frac{\begin{array}{l} P \vee Q \\ \sim P \end{array}}{Q} \qquad \frac{\begin{array}{l} P \vee Q \\ \sim Q \end{array}}{P}$$

Rule 4: Disjunctive argument (DA)

From a disjunction and the negation of one disjunct, the other disjunct may be derived.

This one is obvious, but we need it for obvious reasons:

Rule 5: Simplification (SIM)

$$\frac{P \& Q}{P} \qquad \frac{P \& Q}{Q}$$

If the conjunction is true, then of course the conjuncts must all be true. You can pull out one conjunct from any conjunction and make it the new line in your deduction.

$$\frac{\begin{array}{l} P \\ Q \end{array}}{P \& Q}$$

Rule 6: Conjunction (CONJ)

This rule allows you to put any two lines of a deduction together in the form of a conjunction.

Rule 7: Addition (ADD)

$$\frac{P}{P \lor Q} \qquad \frac{Q}{P \lor Q}$$

Clearly, no matter what claims P and Q might be, if P is true then *either* P or Q must be true. The truth of one disjunct is all it takes to make the whole disjunction true.

Rule 8: Constructive dilemma (CD)

$$P \rightarrow Q$$
$$R \rightarrow S$$
$$\frac{P \lor R}{Q \lor S}$$

The disjunction of the antecedents of any two conditionals allows the derivation of the disjunction of their consequents.

Rule 9: Destructive dilemma (DD)

$$P \rightarrow Q$$
$$R \rightarrow S$$
$$\frac{\sim Q \lor \sim S}{\sim P \lor \sim R}$$

The disjunction of the negations of the consequents of two conditionals allows the derivation of the disjunction of the negations of their antecedents. (Refer to the pattern above as you read this, and it will make a lot more sense.)

Real Life

Logician at Work

No, really. Problem solving in matters like auto mechanics involves a great deal of deductive reasoning. For example, "The problem had to be either a clogged fuel filter or a defective fuel pump. But we've replaced the fuel filter, and it wasn't that, so it has to be a bad fuel pump." This is an example of one of our Group I rules.

For each of the following groups of symbolized claims, identify which Group I rule was used to derive the last line.

Exercise 9-9

▲ 1. P → (Q & R)
      (Q & R) → (S ∨ T)
      P → (S ∨ T)

▲ 2. (P & S) ∨ (T → R)
      ~(P & S)
      T → R

▲ 3. P ∨ (Q & R)
      (Q & R) → S
      P → T
      S ∨ T

▲ 4. (P ∨ R) → Q
      ~Q
      ~(P ∨ R)

▲ 5. (Q → T) → S
      ~S ∨ ~P
      R → P
      ~(Q → T) ∨ ~R

Construct deductions for each of the following, using the Group I rules. Each can be done in just a step or two (except number 10, which takes more).

Exercise 9-10

▲ 1. 1. R → P
      2. Q → R   /∴Q → P

   2. 1. P → S
      2. P ∨ Q
      3. Q → R   /∴S ∨ R

   3. 1. R & S
      2. S → P   /∴P

▲ 4. 1. P → Q
      2. ~P → S
      3. ~Q   /∴S

   5. 1. (P ∨ Q) → R
      2. Q   /∴R

   6. 1. ~P
      2. ~(R & S) ∨ Q
      3. ~P → ~Q   /∴~(R & S)

▲　7. 1. ~S
　　　2. (P & Q) → R
　　　3. R → S　　　　　　/∴~(P & Q)

　　8. 1. P → ~(Q & T)
　　　2. S → (Q & T)
　　　3. P　　　　　　　　/∴~S

　　9. 1. (P ∨ T) → S
　　　2. R → P
　　　3. R ∨ Q
　　　4. Q → T　　　　　　/∴S

▲　10. 1. (T ∨ M) → ~Q
　　　2. (P → Q) & (R → S)
　　　3. T　　　　　　　　/∴~P

Group II Rules: Truth-Functional Equivalences

These rules are different from our Group I rules in some important ways. First, they are expressed as truth-functional equivalences. This means that they each take the form of two types of symbolizations that have exactly the same truth table. We'll use a double-headed arrow, ↔, to indicate that we can move from either side to the other. (Remember that Group I rules allow us to go only one direction, from premises to conclusion.) A second major difference is that these rules can be used on *parts* of lines. So, if we have a conjunction in a deduction, and we have a Group II rule that says one of the conjuncts is equivalent to something else, we can substitute that something else for the equivalent conjunct. You'll see how this works after an example or two.

　　　Here is the overall principle that governs how Group II rules work: *A claim or part of a claim may be replaced by a claim to which it is equivalent by one of the following Group II rules.* Once again, how this works should become clear in a moment. As in the case of the first group, the Ps and Qs and so forth in the statement of the rules can stand for any symbolized claim whatever, as long as each letter stands for the same claim throughout.

Rule 10: Double negation (DN)

　　　　　P ↔ ~~P

This rule allows you to add or remove two negation signs in front of any claim, whether simple or compound. For example, this rule allows the derivation of either of the following from the other,

　　　P → (Q ∨ R)　　　　P → ~~(Q ∨ R)

because the rule guarantees that (Q ∨ R) and its double negation, ~~(Q ∨ R), are equivalent. This in turn guarantees that P → (Q ∨ R) and P → ~~(Q ∨ R) are equivalent, and hence that each implies the other.

　　　Here's an example of DN at work:

1. P ∨ ~(Q → R)
2. (Q → R)　　　　　　/∴P

3. ~~(Q → R)   2, DN
4. P   1, 3, DA

(P & Q) ↔ (Q & P)
(P ∨ Q) ↔ (Q ∨ P)

This rule allows any conjunction or disjunction to be "turned around" so that the conjuncts or disjuncts occur in reverse order. Here's an example:

P → (Q ∨ R)   P → (R ∨ Q)

Either of these symbolized claims can be deduced from the other. Notice that commutation is used on *part* of the claim—just the consequent.

This rule allows us to change a conditional into a disjunction and vice versa.

(P → Q) ↔ (~P ∨ Q)

Notice that the antecedent always becomes the negated disjunct or vice versa, depending on which way you're going. Another example:

(P ∨ Q) → R   ~(P ∨ Q) ∨ R

This rule may remind you of the categorical operation of contraposition (see Chapter 8)—this rule is its truth-functional version.

(P → Q) ↔ (~Q → ~P)

This rule allows us to exchange the places of a conditional's antecedent and consequent but only by putting on or taking off a negation sign in front of each. Here's another example:

(P & Q) → (P ∨ Q)   ~(P ∨ Q) → ~(P & Q)

Sometimes you want to perform contraposition on a symbolization that doesn't fit either side of the equivalence because it has a negation sign in front of either the antecedent or the consequent but not both. You can do what you want in such cases, but it takes two steps, one applying double negation and one applying contraposition. Here's an example:

(P ∨ Q) → ~R
~~(P ∨ Q) → ~R   Double negation
R → ~(P ∨ Q)   Contraposition

Your instructor may allow you to combine these steps (and refer to both DN and CONTR in your annotation).

~(P & Q) ↔ (~P ∨ ~Q)
~(P ∨ Q) ↔ (~P & ~Q)

Notice that, when the negation sign is "moved inside" the parentheses, the "&" changes into a "∨," or vice versa. It's important not to confuse the use of the negation sign in DeMorgan's Laws with that of the minus sign in algebra. Notice that when you take ~(P ∨ Q) and "move the negation sign in," you do *not* get (~P ∨ ~Q). The wedge must be changed to an ampersand or vice versa whenever DEM is used. You can think of ~(P ∨ Q) and (~P & ~Q) as saying "neither P nor Q," and you can think of ~(P & Q) and (~P ∨ ~Q) as saying "not both P and Q."

Rule 15: Exportation (EXP)

$$[P \rightarrow (Q \rightarrow R)] \leftrightarrow [(P \& Q) \rightarrow R]$$

Square brackets are used exactly as parentheses are. In English, the exportation rule says that "If P, then if Q, then R" is equivalent to "If both P and Q, then R." (The commas are optional in both claims.) If you look back to Exercise 9-2, items 3 and 5 (page 310), you'll notice that, according to the exportation rule, each of these can replace the other.

Rule 16: Association (ASSOC)

$$[P \& (Q \& R)] \leftrightarrow [(P \& Q) \& R]$$
$$[P \vee (Q \vee R)] \leftrightarrow [(P \vee Q) \vee R]$$

Association simply tells us that, when we have three items joined together with wedges or with ampersands, it doesn't matter which ones we group together. If we have a long disjunction with more than two disjuncts, it still requires only one of them to be true for the entire disjunction to be true; if it's a conjunction, then all the conjuncts have to be true, no matter how many of them there are, in order for the entire conjunction to be true. Your instructor may allow you to drop parentheses in such symbolizations, but if you're developing these rules as a formal system, he or she may not.

Rule 17: Distribution (DIST)

This rule allows us to "spread a conjunct across a disjunction" or to "spread a disjunct across a conjunction." In the first example below, look at the left-hand side of the equivalence. The P, which is conjoined with a disjunction, is picked up and dropped (distributed) across the disjunction by being conjoined with each part. (This is easier to understand if you see it done on a chalkboard than by trying to figure it out from the page in front of you.) The two versions of the rule, like those of DEM, allow us to do exactly with the wedge what we're allowed to do with the ampersand.

$$[P \& (Q \vee R)] \leftrightarrow [(P \& Q) \vee (P \& R)]$$
$$[P \vee (Q \& R)] \leftrightarrow [(P \vee Q) \& (P \vee R)]$$

Rule 18: Tautology (TAUT)

$$(P \vee P) \leftrightarrow P$$
$$(P \& P) \leftrightarrow P$$

This rule allows a few obvious steps; they are sometimes necessary to "clean up" a deduction.

The twelve-step and seven-step examples that follow show some deductions that use rules from both Group I and Group II. Look at them carefully, covering up the lines with a piece of paper and uncovering them one at a time as you progress. This gives you a chance to figure out what you might do before you see the answer. In any case, make sure you understand how each line was achieved before going on. If necessary, look up the rule used to make sure you understand it.

The first example is long but fairly simple. Length is not always proportional to difficulty.

1. P → (Q → R)
2. (T → P) & (S → Q)
3. T & S   /∴ R

4. T → P   2, SIM
5. S → Q   2, SIM
6. T   3, SIM
7. S   3, SIM
8. P   4, 6, MP
9. Q   5, 7, MP
10. P & Q   8, 9, CONJ
11. (P & Q) → R   1, EXP
12. R   10, 11, MP

Group I

1. Modus ponens (MP) P → Q $\underline{P}$ Q	2. Modus tollens (MT) P → Q $\underline{\sim Q}$ ~P	3. Chain argument (CA) P → Q $\underline{Q \to R}$ P → R
4. Disjunctive argument (DA) P v Q P v Q $\underline{\sim P}$ $\underline{\sim Q}$ Q P	5. Simplification (SIM) P & Q P & Q $\underline{}$ $\underline{}$ P Q	6. Conjunction (CONJ) P $\underline{Q}$ P & Q
7. Addition (ADD) $\underline{P}$ $\underline{Q}$ P v Q P v Q	8. Constructive dilemma (CD) P → Q R → S $\underline{P \lor R}$ Q v S	9. Destructive dilemma (DD) P → Q R → S $\underline{\sim Q \lor \sim S}$ ~P v ~R

Group II

10. Double negation (DN) P ↔ ~~P	11. Commutation (COM) (P & Q) ↔ (Q & P) (P v Q) ↔ (Q v P)	12. Implication (IMPL) (P → Q) ↔ (~P v Q)
13. Contraposition (CONTR) (P → Q) ↔ (~Q → ~P)	14. DeMorgan's Laws (DEM) ~(P & Q) ↔ (~P v ~Q) ~(P v Q) ↔ (~P & ~Q)	15. Exportation (EXPORT) [P → (Q → R)] ↔ [(P & Q) → R]
16. Association (ASSOC) [P & (Q & R)] ↔ [(P & Q) & R] [P v (Q v R)] ↔ [(P v Q) v R]	17. Distribution (DIST) [P & (Q v R)] ↔ [(P & Q) v (P & R)] [P v (Q & R)] ↔ [(P v Q) & (P v R)]	18. Tautology (TAUT) (P v P) ↔ P (P & P) ↔ P

FIGURE 2   Truth-Functional Rules for Deductions

It's often difficult to tell how to proceed when you first look at a deduction problem. One strategy is to work backward. Look at what you want to get, look at what you have, and see what you would need in order to get what you want. Then determine where you would get *that*, and so on. We'll explain in terms of the following problem.

1. P → (Q & R)
2. S → ~Q
3. S   /∴~P
4. ~Q   2, 3, MP
5. ~Q ∨ ~R   4, ADD
6. ~(Q & R)   5, DEM
7. ~P   1, 6, MT

We began by wanting ~P as our conclusion. If we're familiar with modus tollens, it's clear from line 1 that we can get ~P if we can get the negation of line 1's consequent, which would be ~(Q & R). That in turn is the same as ~Q ∨ ~R, which we can get if we can get either ~Q or ~R. So now we're looking for some place in the first three premises where we can get ~Q. That's easy: from lines 2 and 3, by modus ponens. A little practice and you'll be surprised how easy these strategies are to use, at least *most* of the time!

Exercise 9-11

The annotations that explain how each line was derived have been left off the following deductions. For each line, supply the rule used and the numbers of any earlier lines the rule requires.

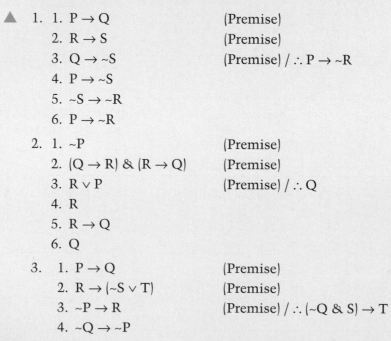

▲ 1. 1. P → Q   (Premise)
2. R → S   (Premise)
3. Q → ~S   (Premise) / ∴ P → ~R
4. P → ~S
5. ~S → ~R
6. P → ~R

2. 1. ~P   (Premise)
2. (Q → R) & (R → Q)   (Premise)
3. R ∨ P   (Premise) / ∴ Q
4. R
5. R → Q
6. Q

3. 1. P → Q   (Premise)
2. R → (~S ∨ T)   (Premise)
3. ~P → R   (Premise) / ∴ (~Q & S) → T
4. ~Q → ~P

5. ~Q → R
6. ~Q → (~S ∨ T)
7. ~Q → (S → T)
8. (~Q & S) → T

▲ 4. 1. (P & Q) → T   (Premise)
     2. P   (Premise)
     3. ~Q → ~P   (Premise) / ∴ T
     4. P → Q
     5. Q
     6. P & Q
     7. T

5. 1. ~(S ∨ R)   (Premise)
    2. P → S   (Premise)
    3. T → (P ∨ R)   (Premise) / ∴ ~T
    4. ~S & ~R
    5. ~S
    6. ~P
    7. ~R
    8. ~P & ~R
    9. ~(P ∨ R)
    10. ~T

Derive the indicated conclusions from the premises supplied.   Exercise 9-12

▲ 1. 1. P & Q
     2. P → R   / ∴ R

▲ 2. 1. R → S
     2. ~P ∨ R   / ∴ P → S

3. 1. P ∨ Q
   2. R & ~Q   / ∴ P

▲ 4. 1. ~P ∨ (~Q ∨ R)
     2. P   / ∴ Q → R

5. 1. T ∨ P
   2. P → S   / ∴ ~T → S

6. 1. Q ∨ ~S
   2. Q → P   / ∴ S → P

7. 1. ~S ∨ ~R
   2. P → (S & R)   / ∴ ~P

▲   8. 1. ~Q & (~S & ~T)
        2. P → (Q ∨ S)   / ∴ ~P

     9. 1. P ∨ (S & R)
         2. T → (~P & ~R)   / ∴ ~T

     10. 1. (S & P) → R
         2. S   /P → R

Exercise 9-13   Derive the indicated conclusions from the premises supplied.

▲   1. 1. P → R
         2. R → Q   / ∴ ~P ∨ Q

     2. 1. ~P ∨ S
         2. ~T → ~S   / ∴ P → T

     3. 1. F → R
         2. L → S
         3. ~C
         4. (R & S) → C   / ∴ ~F ∨ ~L

▲   4. 1. P ∨ (Q & R)
         2. (P ∨ Q) → S   / ∴ S

     5. 1. (S & R) → P
         2. (R → P) → W
         3. S   / ∴ W

     6. 1. ~L → (~P → M)
         2. ~(P ∨ L)   / ∴ M

▲   7. 1. (M ∨ R) & P
         2. ~S → ~P
         3. S → ~M   / ∴ R

     8. 1. Q → L
         2. P → M
         3. R ∨ P
         4. R → (Q & S)   / ∴ ~M → L

     9. 1. Q → S
         2. P → (S & L)
         3. ~P → Q
         4. S → R   / ∴ R & S

▲   10. 1. P ∨ (R & Q)
         2. R → ~P
         3. Q → T   / ∴ R → T

Conditional Proof

Conditional proof (CP) is both a rule and a strategy for constructing a deduction. It is based on the following idea: Let's say we want to produce a deduction for a conditional claim, P → Q. If we produce such a deduction, what have we proved? We've proved the equivalent of "If P were true, then Q would be true." One way to do this is simply to *assume* that P is true (that is, to add it as an additional premise) and then to prove that, on that assumption, Q has to be true. If we can do that—prove Q after assuming P—then we'll have proved that, if P then Q, or P → Q. Let's look at an example of how to do this; then we'll explain it again.

Here is the way we'll use CP as a new rule: Simply write down the antecedent of whatever conditional we want to prove, drawing a circle around the number of that step in the deduction; in the annotation, write "CP Premise" for that step. Here's what it looks like:

1. P ∨ (Q → R)   Premise
2. Q   Premise   / ∴ ~P → R
(3.) ~P   CP Premise

Then, after we've proved what we want—the consequent of the conditional—in the next step, we write the full conditional down. Then we draw a line in the margin to the left of the deduction from the premise with the circled number to the number of the line we deduced from it. (See below for an example.) In the annotation for the last line in the process, list *all the steps from the circled number to the one with the conditional's consequent,* and give CP as the rule. Drawing the line that connects our earlier CP premise with the step we derived from it indicates we've stopped making the assumption that the premise, which is now the antecedent of our conditional in our last step, is true. This is known as *discharging the premise.* Here's how the whole thing looks:

1. P ∨ (Q → R)   Premise
2. Q   Premise   / ∴ ~P → R
┌ (3.) ~P   CP Premise
│ 4. Q → R   1, 3, DA
└ 5. R   2, 4, MP
6. ~P → R   3–5, CP

Here's the promised second explanation. Look at the example. Think of the conclusion as saying that, given the two original premises, *if we had ~P, we could get R.* One way to find out if this is so is to *give ourselves ~P* and then see if we can get R. In step 3, we do exactly that: We give ourselves ~P. Now, by circling the number, we indicate that *this is a premise we've given ourselves* (our "CP premise") and therefore that it's one we'll have to get rid of before we're done. (We can't be allowed to invent, use, and keep just any old premises we like—we could prove *anything* if we could do that.) But once we've given ourselves ~P, getting R turns out to be easy! Steps 4 and 5 are pretty obvious, aren't they? (If not, you need more practice with the other rules.) In steps 3 through 5, what we've actually proved is that *if we had ~P,* then we could get R. So we're justified in writing down step 6 because that's exactly what step 6 says: If ~P, then R.

Once we've got our conditional, ~P → R, we're no longer dependent on the CP premise, so we draw our line in the left margin from the last step that depended on the CP premise back to the premise itself. We *discharge* the premise.

Here are some very important restrictions on the CP rule:

1. CP can be used only to produce a conditional claim: After we discharge a CP premise, the very next step must be a conditional with the preceding step as consequent and the CP premise as antecedent. [Remember that lots of claims are equivalent to conditional claims. For example, to get (~P ∨ Q), just prove (P → Q), and then use IMPL.]

2. If more than one use is made of CP at a time—that is, if more than one CP premise is brought in—they must be discharged in exactly the reverse order from that in which they were assumed. This means that the lines that run from different CP premises must not cross each other. See examples below.

3. Once a CP premise has been discharged, no steps derived from it—those steps encompassed by the line drawn in the left margin—may be used in the deduction. (They depend on the CP premise, you see, and it's been discharged.)

4. All CP premises must be discharged.

This sounds a lot more complicated than it actually is. Refer back to these restrictions on CP as you go through the examples, and they will make a good deal more sense.

Here's an example of CP in which two additional premises are assumed and discharged in reverse order.

1.	P → [Q ∨ (R & S)]	Premise	
2.	(~Q → S) → T	Premise	/ ∴ P → T
(3.)	P	CP Premise	
4.	Q ∨ (R & S)	1, 3, MP	
(5.)	~Q	CP Premise	
6.	R & S	4, 5, DA	
7.	S	6, SIM	
8.	~Q → S	5–7, CP	
9.	T	2, 8, MP	
10.	P → T	3–9, CP	

Notice that the additional premise added at step 5 is discharged when step 8 is completed, and the premise at step 3 is discharged when step 10 is completed. Once again: Whenever you discharge a premise, you must make that premise the antecedent of the next step in your deduction. (You might try the preceding deduction without using CP; doing so will help you appreciate having the rule, however hard to learn it may seem at the moment. Using CP makes many deductions shorter, easier, or both.)

Here are three more examples of the correct use of CP:

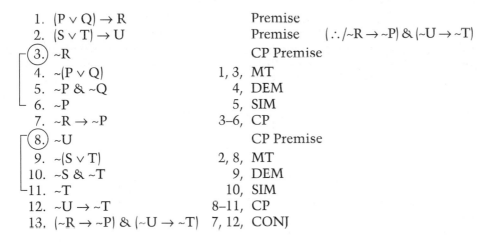

1. (R → -P) → S   Premise
2. S → (T ∨ Q)   Premise   / ∴ ~(R & P) → (T ∨ Q)
3. ~(R & P)   CP Premise
4. ~R ∨ ~P   3, DEM
5. R → ~P   4, IMPL
6. S   1, 5, MP
7. (T ∨ Q)   2, 6, MP
8. ~(R & P) → (T ∨ Q)   3–7, CP

In this case, one use of CP follows another:

1. (P ∨ Q) → R   Premise
2. (S ∨ T) → U   Premise   (∴ /~R → ~P) & (~U → ~T)
3. ~R   CP Premise
4. ~(P ∨ Q)   1, 3, MT
5. ~P & ~Q   4, DEM
6. ~P   5, SIM
7. ~R → ~P   3–6, CP
8. ~U   CP Premise
9. ~(S ∨ T)   2, 8, MT
10. ~S & ~T   9, DEM
11. ~T   10, SIM
12. ~U → ~T   8–11, CP
13. (~R → ~P) & (~U → ~T)   7, 12, CONJ

In this case, one use of CP occurs "inside" another:

1. R → (S & Q)   Premise
2. P → M   Premise
3. S → (Q → ~M)   Premise
4. (J ∨ T) → B   Premise   / ∴ R → (J → (B & ~P))
5. R   CP Premise
6. J   CP Premise
7. J ∨ T   6, ADD
8. B   4, 7, MP
9. (S & Q)   1, 5, MP
10. (S & Q) → ~M   3, EXP
11. ~M   9, 10, MP
12. ~P   2, 11, MT
13. B & ~P   8, 12, CONJ
14. J → (B & ~P)   6–13, CP
15. R → (J → (B & ~P))   5–14, CP

Before ending this section on deductions, we should point out that our system of truth-functional logic has a couple of properties that are of great theoretical interest: It is both sound and complete. To say that a logic system is sound (in the sense most important to us here) is to say that *every deduction that can be constructed using the rules of the system constitutes a valid argument.* Another way to say this is that no deduction or string of deductions allows us to begin with true sentences and wind up with false ones.

To say that our system is complete is to say that *for every truth-functionally valid argument that there is (or even could be), there is a deduction in our system of rules that allows us to deduce the conclusion of that argument from its premises.* That is, if conclusion C really does follow validly from premises P and Q, then we know for certain that it is possible to construct a deduction beginning with just P and Q and ending with C.

We could have produced a system that is both sound and complete and that had many fewer rules than our system has. However, in such systems, deductions tend to be very difficult to construct. Although our system is burdened with a fairly large number of rules, once you learn them, producing proofs is not too difficult. So, in a way, every system of logic is a trade-off of a sort. You can make the system small and elegant but difficult to use, or you can make it larger and less elegant but more efficient in actual use. (The smaller systems are more efficient for some purposes, but those purposes are quite different from ours in this book.)

Recap

The following topics were covered in Chapter 9:

■ Truth-functional symbols, their truth tables, and their English counterparts: negation, conjunction, disjunction, conditional (see Figure 1, page 300, for a summary).

■ Symbolizations of truth functions can represent electrical circuits because "true" and "false" for sentences can be made to correspond to "on" and "off" for circuits.

■ Sentences in normal English can be symbolized by claim letters and our four truth-functional symbols; care is required to make sure the result is equivalent.

■ Many truth-functional arguments can be evaluated using just a few common argument forms.

■ The truth-table method and the short truth-table method both allow us to determine whether an argument is truth-functionally valid.

■ Certain elementary valid argument forms and equivalences are helpful in determining the validity of arguments (see Figure 2, page 333, for a summary).

■ Deductions can be used to prove the validity of truth-functional arguments; they make use of the rules on the Figure 2, page 333, and the rule of conditional proof, page 337.

Exercise 9-14

Display the truth-functional structure of the following claims by symbolizing them. Use the letters indicated.

D = We do something to reduce the deficit.

B = The balance of payments gets worse.

C = There is (or will be) a financial crisis.

▲ 1. The balance of payments will not get worse if we do something to reduce the deficit.

2. There will be no financial crisis unless the balance of payments gets worse.

3. Either the balance of payments will get worse, or, if no action is taken on the deficit, there will be a financial crisis.

▲ 4. The balance of payments will get worse only if we don't do something to reduce the deficit.

5. Action cannot be taken on the deficit if there's a financial crisis.

6. I can tell you about whether we'll do something to reduce the deficit and whether our balance of payments will get worse: Neither one will happen.

▲ 7. In order for there to be a financial crisis, the balance of payments will have to get worse and there will have to be no action taken to reduce the deficit.

8. We can avoid a financial crisis only by taking action on the deficit and keeping the balance of payments from getting worse.

9. The *only* thing that can prevent a financial crisis is our doing something to reduce the deficit.

Exercise 9-15

For each of the numbered claims below, there is exactly one lettered claim that is equivalent. Identify the equivalent claim for each item. (Some lettered claims are equivalent to more than one numbered claim, so it will be necessary to use some letters more than once.)

▲ 1. Oil prices will drop if the OPEC countries increase their production.

2. Oil prices will drop only if the OPEC countries increase their production.

3. Neither will oil prices drop, nor will the OPEC countries increase their production.

▲ 4. Oil prices cannot drop unless the OPEC countries increase their production.

5. The only thing that can prevent oil prices dropping is the OPEC countries' increasing their production.

6. A drop in oil prices is necessary for the OPEC countries to increase their production.

▲   7. All it takes for the OPEC countries to increase their production is a drop in oil prices.

8. The OPEC countries will not increase their production while oil prices drop; each possibility excludes the other.

   a. It's not the case that oil prices will drop, and it's not the case that the OPEC countries will increase their production.
   b. If OPEC countries increase their production, then oil prices will drop.
   c. Only if OPEC countries increase their production will oil prices drop.
   d. Either the OPEC countries will not increase their production, or oil prices will not drop.
   e. If the OPEC countries do not increase production, then oil prices will drop.

Exercise 9-16

Construct deductions for each of the following. (Try these first without using conditional proof.)

▲   1. 1. P
       2. Q & R
       3. (Q & P) → S   / ∴ S

    2. 1. (P ∨ Q) & R
       2. (R & P) → S
       3. (Q & R) → S   / ∴ S

    3. 1. P → (Q → ~R)
       2. (~R → S) ∨ T
       3. ~T & P   / ∴ Q → S

▲   4. 1. P ∨ Q
       2. (Q ∨ U) → (P → T)
       3. ~P
       4. (~P ∨ R) → (Q → S)   / ∴ T ∨ S

    5. 1. (P → Q) & R
       2. ~S
       3. S ∨ (Q → S)   / ∴ P → T

    6. 1. P → (Q & R)
       2. R → (Q → S)   / ∴ P → S

▲   7. 1. P → Q   / ∴ P → (Q ∨ R)

    8. 1. ~P ∨ ~Q
       2. (Q → S) → R   / ∴ P → R

    9. 1. S
       2. P → (Q & R)
       3. Q → ~S   / ∴ ~P

▲ 10. 1. $(S \rightarrow Q) \rightarrow \sim R$
    2. $(P \rightarrow Q) \rightarrow R$ $/\therefore \sim Q$

Exercise 9-17

Use the rule of conditional proof to construct deductions for each of the following.

▲ 1. 1. $P \rightarrow Q$
      2. $P \rightarrow R$ $/\therefore P \rightarrow (Q \& R)$

   2. 1. $P \rightarrow Q$
      2. $R \rightarrow Q$ $/\therefore (P \vee R) \rightarrow Q$

   3. 1. $P \rightarrow (Q \rightarrow R)$ $/\therefore (P \rightarrow Q) \rightarrow (P \rightarrow R)$

▲ 4. 1. $P \rightarrow (Q \vee R)$
      2. $T \rightarrow (S \& \sim R)$ $/\therefore (P \& T) \rightarrow Q$

   5. 1. $\sim P \rightarrow (\sim Q \rightarrow \sim R)$
      2. $\sim (R \& \sim P) \rightarrow \sim S$ $/\therefore S \rightarrow Q$

   6. 1. $P \rightarrow (Q \rightarrow R)$
      2. $(T \rightarrow S) \& (R \rightarrow T)$ $/\therefore P \rightarrow (Q \rightarrow S)$

▲ 7. 1. $P \vee (Q \& R)$
      2. $T \rightarrow \sim (P \vee U)$
      3. $S \rightarrow (Q \rightarrow \sim R)$ $/\therefore \sim S \vee \sim T$

   8. 1. $(P \vee Q) \rightarrow R$
      2. $(P \rightarrow S) \rightarrow T$ $/\therefore R \vee T$

   9. 1. $P \rightarrow \sim Q$
      2. $\sim R \rightarrow (S \& Q)$ $/\therefore P \rightarrow R$

▲ 10. 1. $(P \& Q) \vee R$
      2. $\sim R \vee Q$ $/\therefore P \rightarrow Q$

Exercise 9-18

Display the truth-functional form of the following arguments by symbolizing them; then use the truth-table method, the short truth-table method, or the method of deduction to prove them valid or invalid. Use the letters provided. (We've used underscores in the example and in the first two problems to help you connect the letters with the proper claims.)

Example

If _Maria does not go to the movies, then she will _help Bob with his logic homework. Bob will _fail the course unless Maria _helps him with his logic homework. Therefore, if _Maria goes to the movies, Bob will _fail the course. (M, H, F)

Symbolization

1. ~M → H   (Premise)
2. ~H → F   (Premise)   / ∴ M → F

Truth Table

M	H	F	~M	~H	~M → H	~H → F	M → F
T	T	T	F	F	T	T	T
T	T	F	F	F	T	T	F

We need to go only as far as the second row of the table, since both premises come out true and the conclusion comes out false in that row.

▲   1. If it's <u>c</u>old, Dale's motorcycle won't <u>s</u>tart. If Dale is not <u>l</u>ate for work, then his motorcycle must have <u>s</u>tarted. Therefore, if it's <u>c</u>old, Dale is <u>l</u>ate for work. (C, S, L)

2. If profits depend on <u>u</u>nsound environmental practices, then either the <u>q</u>uality of the environment will deteriorate, or profits will <u>d</u>rop. <u>J</u>obs will be plentiful only if profits do not drop. So, either jobs will not be plentiful, or the quality of the environment will deteriorate. (U, Q, D, J)

3. The new road will not be built unless the planning commission approves the funds. But the planning commission's approval of the funds will come only if the environmental impact report is positive, and it can't be positive if the road will ruin Mill Creek. So, unless they find a way for the road not to ruin Mill Creek, it won't be built. (R, A, E, M)

▲   4. The message will not be understood unless the code is broken. The killer will not be caught if the message is not understood. Either the code will be broken, or Holmes's plan will fail. But Holmes's plan will not fail if he is given enough time. Therefore, if Holmes is given enough time, the killer will be caught. (M, C, K, H, T)

5. If the senator votes against this bill, then he is opposed to penalties against tax evaders. Also, if the senator is a tax evader himself, then he is opposed to penalties against tax evaders. Therefore, if the senator votes against this bill, he is a tax evader himself. (V, O, T)

6. If you had gone to class, taken good notes, and studied the text, you'd have done well on the exam. And if you'd done well on the exam, you'd have passed the course. Since you did not pass the course and you did go to class, you must not have taken good notes and not studied the text.

▲   7. Either John will go to class, or he'll miss the review session. If John misses the review session, he'll foul up the exam. If he goes to class, however, he'll miss his ride home for the weekend. So John's either going to miss his ride home or foul up the exam.

8. If the government's position on fighting crime is correct, then if more people are locked up, then the crime rate should drop. But the crime rate has not dropped, despite the fact that we've been locking up record numbers of people. It follows that the government's position on fighting crime is not correct.

9. The creation story in the book of Genesis is compatible with the theory of evolution but only if the creation story is not taken literally. If, as most scientists think, there is plenty of evidence for the theory of evolution, the Genesis story cannot be true if it is not compatible with evolution theory. Therefore, if the Genesis story is taken literally, it cannot be true.

▲ 10. The creation story in the book of Genesis is compatible with the theory of evolution but only if the creation story is not taken literally. If there is plenty of evidence for the theory of evolution, which there is, the Genesis story cannot be true if it is not compatible with evolution theory. Therefore, if the Genesis story is taken literally, it cannot be true.

11. If there was no murder committed, then the victim must have been killed by the horse. But the victim could have been killed by the horse only if he, the victim, was trying to injure the horse before the race; and, in that case, there certainly was a crime committed. So, if there was no murder, there was still a crime committed.

12. Holmes cannot catch the train unless he gets to Charing Cross Station by noon; and if he misses the train, Watson will be in danger. Because Moriarty has thugs watching the station, Holmes can get there by noon only if he goes in disguise. So, unless Holmes goes in disguise, Watson will be in danger.

▲ 13. It's not fair to smoke around nonsmokers if secondhand cigarette smoke really is harmful. If secondhand smoke were not harmful, the American Lung Association would not be telling us that it is. But they are telling us that it's harmful. That's enough to conclude that it's not fair to smoke around nonsmokers.

14. If Jane does any of the following, she's got an eating disorder: if she goes on eating binges for no apparent reason, if she looks forward to times when she can eat alone, or if she eats sensibly in front of others and makes up for it when she's alone. Jane does in fact go on eating binges for no apparent reason. So it's clear that she has an eating disorder.

15. The number of business majors increased markedly during the past decade; and if you see that happening, you know that younger people have developed a greater interest in money. Such an interest, unfortunately, means that greed has become a significant motivating force in our society; and if greed has become such a force, charity will have become insignificant. We can predict that charity will not be seen as a significant feature of this past decade.

Exercise 9-19

Determine which of these contain valid arguments. The section titled "Truth-Functional Argument Patterns" (page 311) is sufficient to answer these. Otherwise, either truth-tables or deductions may be used.

1. If Bobo is smart, then he can do tricks. However, Bobo is not smart. So he cannot do tricks.

2. If God is always on America's side, then America wouldn't have lost any wars. America has lost wars. Therefore, God is not always on America's side.

3. If your theory is correct, then light passing Jupiter will be bent. Light passing Jupiter is bent. Therefore, your theory is correct.

4. Moore eats carrots and broccoli for lunch, and if he does that, he probably is very hungry by dinnertime. Conclusion: Moore is very hungry by dinnertime.

5. If you value your feet, you won't mow the lawn in your bare feet. Therefore, since you do mow the lawn in your bare feet, we can conclude that you don't value your feet.

6. If Bobo is smart, then he can do tricks; and he can do tricks. Therefore, he is smart.

7. If Charles had walked through the rose garden, then he would have mud on his shoes. We can deduce, therefore, that he did walk through the rose garden, because he has mud on his shoes.

8. If it rained earlier, then the sidewalks will still be wet. We can deduce, therefore, that it did rain earlier, because the sidewalks are still wet.

9. If you are pregnant, then you are a woman. We can deduce, therefore, that you are pregnant, because you are a woman.

10. If this stuff is on the final, I will get an A in the class because I really understand it! Further, the teacher told me that this stuff will be on the final, so I know it will be there. Therefore, I know I will get an A in the class.

11. If side A has an even number, then side B has an odd number, but side A does not have an even number. Therefore, side B does not have an odd number.

12. If side A has an even number, then side B has an odd number, and side B does have an odd number. Therefore, side A has an even number.

13. If the theory is correct, then we will have observed squigglyitis in the specimen. However, we know the theory is not correct. Therefore, we did not observe squigglyitis in the specimen.

14. If the theory is correct, then we will have observed dilation in the specimen. Therefore, since we did not observe dilation in the specimen, we know the theory is not correct.

15. If we observe dilation in the specimen, then we know the theory is correct. We observed dilation—so the theory is correct.

16. If the comet approached within 1 billion miles of the earth, there would have been numerous sightings of it. There weren't numerous sightings. So it did not approach within 1 billion miles.

17. If Baffin Island is larger than Sumatra, then two of the five largest islands in the world are in the Arctic Ocean. And Baffin Island, as it turns out, is about 2 percent larger than Sumatra. Therefore, the Arctic Ocean contains two of the world's largest islands.

18. If the danger of range fires is greater this year than last, then state and federal officials will hire a greater number of firefighters to cope with the danger. Since more firefighters are already being hired this year than were

hired all last year, we can be sure that the danger of fires has increased this year.

19. If Jack Davis robbed the Central Pacific Express in 1870, then the authorities imprisoned the right person. But the authorities did not imprison the right person. Therefore, it must have not been Jack Davis who robbed the Central Pacific Express in 1870.

20. If the recent tax cuts had been self-financing, then there would have been no substantial increase in the federal deficit. But they turned out not to be self-financing. Therefore, there will be a substantial increase in the federal deficit.

21. The public did not react favorably to the majority of policies recommended by President Ronald Reagan during his second term. But if his electoral landslide in 1984 had been a mandate for more conservative policies, the public would have reacted favorably to most of those he recommended after the election. Therefore, the 1984 vote was not considered a mandate for more conservative policies.

22. Alexander will finish his book by tomorrow afternoon only if he is an accomplished speed reader. Fortunately for him, he is quite accomplished at speed reading. Therefore, he will get his book finished by tomorrow afternoon.

23. If higher education were living up to its responsibilities, the five best-selling magazines on American campuses would not be *Cosmopolitan*, *People*, *Playboy*, *Glamour*, and *Vogue*. But those are exactly the magazines that sell best in the nation's college bookstores. Higher education, we can conclude, is failing in at least some of its responsibilities.

24. Broc Glover was considered sure to win if he had no bad luck in the early part of the race. But we've learned that he has had the bad luck to be involved in a crash right after the start, so we're expecting another driver to be the winner.

25. If Boris is really a spy for the KGB, then he has been lying through his teeth about his business in this country. But we can expose his true occupation if he's been lying like that. So, I'm confident that if we can expose his true occupation, we can show that he's really a KGB spy.

26. The alternator is not working properly if the ammeter shows a negative reading. The current reading of the ammeter is negative. So, the alternator is not working properly.

27. Fewer than 2 percent of the employees of New York City's Transit Authority are accountable to management. If such a small number of employees are accountable to the management of the organization, no improvement in the system's efficiency can be expected in the near future. So, we cannot expect any such improvements any time soon.

28. If Charles did not pay his taxes, then he did not receive a refund. Thus, he did not pay his taxes, since he did not receive a refund.

29. If they wanted to go to the party, then they would have called by now. But they haven't, so they didn't.

30. "You'll get an A in the class," she predicted.
"What makes you say that?" he asked.
"Because," she said, "if you get an A, then you're smart, and you *are* smart."

31. If Florin arrived home by eight, she received the call from her attorney. But she did not get home by eight, so she must have missed her attorney's call.

32. The off-shore drilling problem will be solved, but only if the administration stops talking and starts acting. So far, however, all we've had from the president is words. Words are cheap. Action is what counts. The problem will not be remedied, at least not while this administration is in office.

Exercise 9-20

Using the method described in Chapter 2, diagram five of the items in the previous exercise.

Writing Exercises

1. a. In a one-page essay evaluate the soundness of the argument in the box on page 320. Write your name on the back of your paper.

   b. When everyone is finished, your instructor will collect the papers and redistribute them to the class. In groups of four or five, read the papers that have been given to your group and select the best one. The instructor will select one group's top-rated paper to read to the class for discussion.

2. Take about fifteen minutes to write an essay responding to the paper the instructor has read to the class in Writing Exercise 1. When everyone is finished, the members of each group will read each other's responses and select the best one to share with the class.

Thinking Critically About Inductive Reasoning

In this chapter we explain how to think critically about inductive reasoning. You may recall from Chapter 2 that inductive reasoning is used to support rather than to demonstrate a conclusion, and that we evaluate an inductive argument as relatively strong or weak depending on how much its premise increases the probability of the conclusion. As we use these terms, "strong" and "weak" are not absolutes. One argument for a conclusion is stronger than another argument for that conclusion if its premise increases the probability of the conclusion by a greater amount.

Now, the key to understanding inductive reasoning—and the material in this chapter—is to keep in mind always that we are concerned with the strength of arguments, not with the probability of claims in and of themselves. Here comes an acquaintance, Mr. York. Is York a Democrat? Estimating the probability that he is a Democrat is one thing; gauging the strength of this or that argument that he is a Democrat is another thing. Accurately gauging the probability that Mr. York is a Democrat requires employing what logicians refer to as the **Principle of Total Evidence**, which means simply that you must take into account all the information you have. But gauging the strength of this or that argument that Mr. York is a Democrat is a separate order of business and does not require us to employ the Principle of Total Evidence.

Students will learn to . . .

1. Identify and differentiate statistical syllogisms, inductive generalizations from samples, and inductive arguments from analogy

2. Explain the Principle of Total Evidence in inductive reasoning

3. Define and explain the key terms related to samples and sampling

4. Differentiate between scientific generalizing from samples and everyday generalizing from samples

5. Apply the two principles of evaluating everyday generalizations from samples

6. Analyze analogies and analogues

7. Identify informal indicators of confidence levels and error margins

8. Understand and identify various fallacies related to induction

Take the argument, "York is a teacher; therefore he is a Democrat." The strength of that argument depends on how being a teacher affects the probability that York is a Democrat. This is separate from the question, "How likely is it that York is a Democrat?" which requires us to consider all the evidence. Everything else being equal, the fact York is a teacher raises the probability he is a Democrat more than does the fact he wears glasses. So, without consulting the Principle of Total Evidence we can say that argument (A):

(A) York is a teacher; therefore he is a Democrat

is stronger than argument (B):

(B) York wears glasses; therefore he is a Democrat.

Of course, we can't say (A) is stronger than (B) without knowing that the proportion of teachers who are Democrats is higher than the proportion

In Depth

Everyday Statistical Syllogisms

Avalanche probability is rated on an avalanche hazard scale of 1 to 5. Hazard level 5, in which the snow pack is "generally poorly bonded and largely unstable" assesses the probability as this: "Many large spontaneous avalanches can be expected, even in moderately steep areas." Avalanche assessments are conclusions of inductive generalizations and follow the principles discussed in this chapter. Precise probability calculations are not always possible, even in matters of life and death.

of glasses-wearers who are Democrats. But we could know these proportions without consulting the Principle of Total Evidence.

Again, to repeat, you will find inductive reasoning—and this chapter—much easier to comprehend if you always keep in mind the difference between gauging the probability of a claim when everything is considered, and gauging the strength of this or that argument used to support the claim.

REASONING FROM THE GENERAL TO THE SPECIFIC (STATISTICAL SYLLOGISMS)

If you meet Mr. York, a teacher, then everything else being equal, it's a good bet he is a Democrat. Why? Because most teachers are Democrats. How might one establish that most teachers are Democrats? We will get to that in the next section; for the moment let's just assume that is the case.

Here is your reasoning:

Most teachers are Democrats.
York is a teacher.
Therefore York is a Democrat.

You would be right if you thought the strength of this argument, which is known as a statistical syllogism, depends on the general statement, "Most teachers are Democrats." The higher the proportion of teachers said to be Democrats, the stronger the argument, assuming what is said is true.

However, many other considerations bear on the *overall* probability that York is a Democrat. If, for example, York has told you he is a Democrat, that makes it all but certain he is one, everything else being equal. But our purpose here is not to quantify the *overall probability* that York is a Democrat. Our purpose is to gauge the strength of this particular argument. The strength of this argument remains what it is, regardless of what York has told you. Regardless of what he has said, the argument on the right is stronger than the argument on the left:

Around 60 percent of teachers   **Around 90 percent of teachers**
are Democrats.   **are Democrats.**
York is a teacher.   **York is a teacher.**
Therefore York is a Democrat   **Therefore York is a Democrat.**

To summarize, a **statistical syllogism** has this form:

Such-and-such proportion of Xs are Ys.
This is an X.
Therefore this is a Y.

The strength of these arguments depends on the proportion of Xs that are Ys: the greater the proportion, the stronger the argument. (Later in the chapter we will see that conclusions of this and other inductive arguments should be expressed at an appropriate "confidence level," but more about that in a moment.)

■ Inductive reasoning is at the heart of conclusions we reach about things around us. Take this truck. Reasoning from our past encounters with people who drive vehicles like this, we'd consider each of the following conclusions likely: The owner of this vehicle: (1) is a male, (2) doesn't worry about global warming, any other environmental problem, or his cholesterol level, and (3) doesn't play chess.

REASONING FROM THE SPECIFIC TO THE GENERAL (INDUCTIVE GENERALIZING FROM A SAMPLE)

Generalizing from a sample is something we all do every day. Is the soup seasoned right? We sample it. Is the coffee too strong? We take a sip. Should we buy the grapes at Kroger? When nobody's looking we pop one into our mouth and find out how they taste. Do students at our university want a new recreation center? We poll them.

Statisticians refer to any identifiable group of things as a population. It's what in Chapter 8 is called a category. It takes getting used to, to think of a pot of coffee as a population, but you can view it as a population of sips. Populations have various characteristics—some are small; others are large; some, like "crimes committed in New York City this year," are extremely diverse; and others, like the sips in our coffee pot, not so much.

Our experience sometimes leads us to conjecture about the properties of populations that interest us. There seem to be a lot of Priuses in the faculty parking lot; are university professors as a group especially fond of them? Well—there are a lot of university professors; to answer our question scientifically, we need a better sample than the professors who park in our faculty parking lot. Those professors might not be typical.

Already you can see room for critical thinking. Who counts as a "university professor," and when can someone be described as "fond of Priuses"? To begin answering the question, we would devise what statisticians call a sampling frame. A **sampling frame** is a precise definition of a population and of the attribute in which we are interested, a definition that enables us to tell for any individual whether he, she, or it is in the population and whether he, she, or it has the attribute of interest. A sampling frame for our question, for example, might be professors who are current members of the American Association of University Professors (AAUP) and are registered owners of a Prius. This sampling frame removes the vagueness from the question, "What proportion of university professors are fond of Priuses?"*

From the sampling frame, a sample would be selected for examination, a sample that, one hopes, would represent the population accurately. A sample represents a population accurately, or is said to be **representative**, if variables linked to the attribute of interest are present in the sample in the same proportion as in the population. For example, the kind of car someone drives is linked to his or her income; you'd want the same proportion of high-income individuals in the AAUP sample as in the general AAUP population. To the extent a variable is not present in the sample in the same proportion as in the population, the sample is **biased** with respect to that variable.

---

*From the standpoint of scientific sampling, a sampling frame must be chosen with care, to make sure that among other things it doesn't include duplicate entries or extraneous items or leave out members of the population we'd want included.

Because we don't know what all the important variables are—for example, we don't know what proportion of AAUP professors are at a given income level—the sample must be selected by a procedure that ensures that every member of the population has an equal chance of being included. A sample selected by such a method is a **random sample**. But even random samples will not be totally free from bias, because the variables present in a sample are subject to random variation from sample to sample. The range of this random variation is known as the sample's **error margin**, and the larger the sample the more probable it is that the random variation will fall within a given range. Or, to put exactly the same point in different terms, at a given level of probability, the larger the sample the smaller the error margin for that sample. The level of probability is referred to as the **confidence level**.

This can be terribly confusing, and an example will help. Proceed slowly.

Let's assume that, in fact, 20 percent of AAUP members own a Prius. Suppose now we take many random samples of 1,000 AAUP members. The proportion of AAUP members in the samples who own a Prius will vary randomly from sample to sample. What is the limit of this variation? There is a 95 percent probability that the random variation, for a random sample of 1,000, will be within 3 percentage points on either side of the true proportion (20 percent). In other words, for a random sample of 1,000, *at the 95 percent confidence level the error margin is ± 3 percentage points*. This means that in 95 out of every 100 random samples of this size, between 17 and 23 percent of the AAUP members will own a Prius. If the samples were larger, the error margin would be smaller at a given confidence level.

We won't discuss the mathematics that lie behind the calculations just described, but they are among the most basic mathematics in this field; you can trust them. They guarantee the details you'll find in Table 10-1, which applies to very large populations, and which you should look at now. You will see that the confidence level of the table is 95 percent, which is the level scientific polling organizations have settled on. In a reputable scientific poll, if the confidence level is not mentioned, assume it is 95 percent. Though we are illustrating things by talking about populations consisting of people, what we say applies to generalizing from a sample of any kind of identifiable entity.

The leftmost column of the table represents a series of increasing sample sizes. In the second column is the error margin corresponding to each sample size—expressed as plus or minus so many percentage points. These error margins are approximate; they've been rounded off for convenience. The third column is the entire range of those percentage points.

Notice three things. First, as the sample size increases, the error margin decreases. Second, a small sample has a huge error margin; with a sample of 10, the error margin is plus or minus 30 points (at the 95 percent confidence level). You can see that if you generalize from a small sample to a very large population, you'd want to give yourself a large margin of error if you wanted to be confident about the generalization.

Third, when you look at the table, the error margin narrows quickly as the size of the sample increases from 10 to 25; but then the narrowing effect slows down rapidly. By the time we get to a sample size of 500, which has an error margin of plus or minus 4 percentage points, you would have to double the sample size to narrow the error margin by only a single percentage point.

Table 10-1

Approximate Error Margins for Various Random Samples from Large Populations

Confidence level of 95 percent in all cases.

Sample Size	Error Margin (%)	Corresponding Range (Percentage Points)
10	±30	60
25	±22	44
50	±14	28
100	±10	20
250	±6	12
500	±4	8
1,000	±3	6
1,500	±2	4

The error margin decreases rapidly as the sample size begins to increase, but this decrease slows markedly as the sample gets larger. It is usually pointless to increase the sample beyond 1,500 unless there are special requirements of precision or confidence level.

(We assume, both here and in the text, that the population is large—that is, 10,000 or larger. When the population is small, a correction factor can be applied to determine the appropriate error margin. But most reported polls have large enough populations that we need not concern ourselves with the calculation methods for correcting the error margin here.)

Now that you see this, you won't be surprised to learn that, no matter what a reputable public opinion survey is about, it usually involves between 1,000 and 1,500 in the sample. Trying to further reduce the error margin generally isn't worth the extra expense.

With this information about scientific generalizing from samples in mind, let's look at the kind of generalizing from samples we do in everyday life.

Everyday Inductive Generalizing from a Sample

Everyday inductive generalizing from samples differs from the scientific variety in two important respects. First, it doesn't involve carefully selected samples. Second, as a result, one cannot calculate probabilities with anything like the precision of Table 10-1. However, the underlying principles of scientific inductive generalizing apply to reasoning of the everyday variety.

Let's begin here: A **variable**, as is obvious, is something that varies. As we mentioned, and as is clear anyway, some variables are associated with the attribute in which one is interested. Driving a Prius, for example, is associated with the level of one's income. If a sample is to represent a population, such variables must be present in the sample in the same proportion as in the population. To repeat what we said earlier, if that happens, the sample *represents* the population well. If it doesn't, it is *biased* with respect to whatever variable it over- or under-represents.

At the heart of scientific inductive generalizing are procedures for sampling that help minimize bias in samples that help ensure that samples are "representative" and not atypical or skewed. Thus, if we were statisticians critically examining (for instance) a public opinion poll, we might be especially interested in how the sample was selected. Unfortunately, samples used in everyday inductive generalizing are not selected scientifically. As a result, critical thinking about everyday reasoning from samples focuses on factors other than the procedure used to select a sample. Instead, *one focuses on the sample itself*, considering two things carefully.

First, one looks for important *differences* between the sample and the population it supposedly represents, differences that could bias the sample. Second, one considers whether the sample is *large and diversified* enough to be representative. For example, the title page of this book is the same from copy to copy. If you wanted to know what percentage of the title pages contain spelling mistakes, you would not need a very large sample; the population is so uniform that a small sample (even a sample of one) would contain all the diversification you require.

■ For the purposes of inductive generalizing, the diversification of a population should be replicated in the sample.

We can distill these considerations into two basic principles for thinking critically about everyday generalizing from samples.

Principles for thinking critically about an inductive generalization from a sample:

1. If a difference between the sample and the population it supposedly represents biases the sample, that difference weakens the argument.
2. Samples that are too small or too undiversified to represent the population well weaken the argument.

Examples of thinking critically about everyday generalizing from samples:

First example:

"There aren't any fleas in this motel room; therefore, there aren't fleas anywhere here in Lodi."

The argument is so intuitively weak it is hard to imagine anyone saying such a thing. Still, let's just think about why it is weak. A presence of fleas is related to multiple variables that might well not be found in a sample consisting of a single motel room. Also, a motel room is more apt to have been treated for pests in the first place. So this sample differs from the population it supposedly represents, is not diversified in the least, and is small. Compare this example with the following one.

Second example:

"Dave's Lawn Care does shoddy work maintaining the neighbor's lawn; they probably do shoddy work generally."

The population here consists of lawns maintained by Dave's. Yes, the sample in this example is no larger or more diversified than the one in the first example. But a motel room is apt to be atypical in that it may well have been treated for fleas, whereas there is no special reason for thinking the neighbor's lawn is atypical. So as it stands, this is a stronger argument for its conclusion than the first argument is for its conclusion.

Third example:

"Most of my teachers are Democrats, so I think most teachers are Democrats."

Let's just assume this speaker is thinking of a population of American university teachers and has in mind by "Democrats" something like the people who voted for Barack Obama in the last presidential election. Now the population "Democrats" is far larger and more multifaceted (diversified) than the populations in the previous two examples. The speaker's sample is not only too small and too undiversified, but relative to the population it represents, it is *way* too small and *way* too undiversified.

Fourth example:

"I don't like Jane; others probably feel the same."

Let's say the first statement is offered as support for the second statement. Then once again the speaker is generalizing from a single thing, in this case himself or herself, to the "population" of people who are in a position to like or dislike Jane. Many factors could affect whether Jane (or anyone) is likeable; the sample is insufficiently diversified with respect to such variables.

Fifth example:

"OMG! Look at this rash I got from that plant! I'll steer clear of it next time."

The speaker means that in the future he or she will stay away from plants of this species. Again, someone is generalizing from a sample of one. But here the "population" is relatively undiversified, and the potential differences between the sample and the population aren't many. (Variables that might be important include age of plant and dormancy.) It is true that a more diversified sample would have produced a stronger argument. But even as it stands, this is the strongest of the five examples so far.

Sixth example:

"Eight of the ten people in this class think the midterm was too hard, and we don't know about the other two, but it is safe to say everyone thinks the midterm was too hard."

Here the sample is small, but it is 80 percent of the population, so the argument is relatively very strong.

The following exercise sets will help you further explore the difference between statistical syllogisms and inductive reasoning from samples.

Divide the following statements into two categories, based on a distinction implicit in the material discussed so far in this chapter. Identify the distinction.

Exercise 10-1

▲   1. Danielle is older than Christina.
    2. Annual ryegrass dies out in the summer.
    3. Feral donkeys cause considerable damage to the ecology of Death Valley.
▲   4. A significant proportion of small-business owners oppose raising the minimum wage.
    5. The president of the senior class didn't wear a tux to the prom, if you can believe it.
    6. It costs $55 a year to subscribe to *Consumer Reports*.
▲   7. Glasses purchased online may not be satisfactory for your purposes.
    8. Tony the Shark works for No Doz Escobar.
    9. The most common seeing-eye dog is the German shepherd.
▲ 10. The Toledo museum isn't open this evening.

Five of the following items are inductive generalizations from samples and five are statistical syllogisms. Determine which are which.

Exercise 10-2

▲   1. Rainbird sprinklers don't last long, judging from my experience.
    2. That sprinkler won't last long: it's a Rainbird.
    3. Don't worry about your tree losing its leaves; it's a camphor tree.
▲   4. I don't think camphor trees are deciduous; at any rate ours isn't.
    5. Blu-ray disks aren't any better than regular old DVDs; so don't expect this disk to be better than what you are used to.
    6. Target gives refunds no questions asked. I found that out when I returned a shirt without a receipt.
▲   7. It's difficult to find a grocery store in Fresno; the time I was there I looked all over the place and only found car parts places and liquor stores.
    8. Marsha will be on time; she usually is.
    9. Jorge and Susan are both really bright; apparently most music majors are.
▲ 10. Jorge and Susan are both really bright; after all, they are music majors.

For each of the following, mark:

Exercise 10-3

    A = statistical syllogism
    B = inductive generalization from a sample
    C = neither

▲   1. Here, try this one. It'll stop your cough. It's a Breezer.

2. Costco charges less than Walmart for comparable items. I've shopped at both for years.

3. Alvid likes the president; after all, he's a Democrat.

▲   4. The local Kia dealership is thriving, which suggests that Kia is doing well nationally.

5. Professor Stooler is a tough grader; he teaches physics.

6. Almost every Shih Tzu I've run into is smart; there probably aren't any anywhere that aren't.

▲   7. A majority of Republicans favor immigration reform, and Horace is a Republican. Connect the dots.

8. Sally is apt to be cranky; she usually is when she skips breakfast.

9. Comcast service has improved a lot over the past year judging from what has happened around here.

▲   10. It will still be cool there in June; the elevation at Denver is over 5,000 feet.

Exercise 10-4

Complete each of these statistical syllogisms by supplying an appropriate premise or conclusion.

Example:

Marilyn is a florist; I bet she's a nice person.
Premise: Most florists are nice people.

▲   1. Don't waste your time trying to teach that dog to fetch. Otterhounds don't do that.

2. I don't see how you could have high blood pressure; you jog, what, ten miles a day?

3. Most people who drive that kind of car have money to burn, so I imagine he has money to burn.

▲   4. Dr. Walker belongs to the ACLU; and most people who belong to the ACLU are liberals.

5. Sharon shops online; I bet she doesn't pay sales tax.

6. York belongs to the NRA; he's probably a Republican.

▲   7. Most members of the NRA are Republicans; therefore, probably York is a Republican.

8. Most smokers drink; I imagine, therefore, that Sally drinks.

9. Melody will be upset; who wouldn't if her husband did that?

▲   10. Verizon provides service to most small towns; so you'll probably get service in Chabot Gap.

Exercise 10-5

Complete each of these statistical syllogisms by supplying an appropriate premise or conclusion.

▲ 1. Christine's probably pretty athletic; she's a professional dancer.

2. I doubt Lays have preservatives; most chips these days don't.

3. Aubrey is fibbing; nine times out of ten, when somebody says she doesn't care what people think, she's fibbing.

▲ 4. Kids around here generally don't drop out of school, so Jim won't drop out.

5. I don't think their band will be popular; they play jazz.

6. Deanna isn't likely to help; she's too concerned about herself.

▲ 7. I expect it's going to rain; it usually does when it's hot.

8. Probably they have a key; most members do.

9. We might have trouble parking; it's New Year's Eve, don't forget.

▲ 10. Most governors haven't been very good presidents, and Mitt is a governor.

Identify the sample, the population, and the attribute of interest in each of the following inductive generalizations from a sample.

Exercise 10-6

▲ 1. I've seen at least ten Disney movies and not one of them has been violent. Apparently Disney doesn't make violent movies.

2. Most of my professors wear glasses; it's a good bet most professors everywhere wear glasses.

3. Conservatives I know don't like Huckabee. Based on that, I'd say most conservatives don't like him.

▲ 4. Judging from what I saw, Columbus State is a fun place to be.

5. Seven of the last ten El Niños were associated with below-average rainfall across southern Canada. Therefore 70 percent of all El Niños will be associated with below-average rainfall across southern Canada.

6. MRS. BRUDER: Bruder! Bruder! Can you believe it? The Music Department is selling two grand pianos!
MR. BRUDER: Well, let's check it out. But remember, the last pianos they sold were overpriced. Probably all their pianos are overpriced.

▲ 7. Costco's store-brand coffee tastes as good as any name brand; I'll bet any store brand product from Costco is as good as the name brand.

8. A 55 percent approval rating? Them polls is rigged! Most people I know think he's a Marxist.

9. The young people around here sure are crazy! Did you see those two dudes drag racing?

▲ 10. The fries at McDonald's are too salty, judging from these.

Identify the sample, the population, and the attribute of interest in each of the following:

Exercise 10-7

▲ 1. Whoa, is this joint overpriced or what! Look at what they want for quart of milk!

2. Carmel? People there are snobs, judging from what I've seen.

3. PCs are way faster than Macs! Just compare these two puppies!

▲   4. Life insurance salespeople are always trying to sell you stuff you don't need; anyway, the ones I know do.

5. Did you see that? The drivers in this town are crazy!

6. I get lots of dropped calls with AT&T where I live; it's probably the same everywhere.

▲   7. After the first test, I knew I'd do well in this class.

8. The doorbell doesn't ring and the hot water heater is busted. Doesn't anything work in this house?

9. I never saw a frost after March. I don't think it can happen this close to the coast.

▲   10. English classes are boring, judging from the one I took.

Exercise 10-8   ▲   Rank order the following populations from least diversified to most diversified.

1. Television sitcoms
2. Movies
3. Episodes of Survivor
4. Movies rated PG
5. Movies starring Meryl Streep

Exercise 10-9   ▲   Rank order the following populations from least diversified to most diversified.

1. Professional athletes
2. National Football League referees
3. Physically fit people
4. Major League baseball players
5. Olympic shot-putters

Exercise 10-10   ▲   Rank order the following populations from least diversified to most diversified.

1. People
2. Cowboys
3. Democrats
4. Teachers
5. Cowboys who are teachers

Exercise 10-11

Think of as many variables as you can that are linked to each of the following attributes. For example, height and jumping ability are linked to being a professional basketball player: the more professional basketball players there are in a population the more tall people who are good at jumping there are apt to be.

Your instructor may make this a timed competition, giving the person who wins an opportunity to go home after class.

▲   1. Driving a Lexus
      2. Owning a pet
      3. Having no cavities
▲   4. Being susceptible to poison oak or ivy
      5. Owning a hand gun
      6. Being afraid of the dark
▲   7. Being nearsighted
      8. Reading romance novels
      9. Drinking Budweiser
▲   10. Watching reality shows
     11. Owning an iPad
     12. Seeing a psychotherapist
     13. Attending church once a week

Rate how well each sample represents its population on a scale of 1 to 5, where   Exercise 10-12

     1 = the sample represents its population very well.
     5 = the sample represents its population very poorly.

▲   1. The coffee in that pot is lousy; I just had a cup.
      2. The coffee at that restaurant is lousy; I just had a cup.
      3. Starbuck's coffee is bitter, judging from this cup.
▲   4. Sherry doesn't write well, based on how poorly she did on this 5-page paper.
      5. Sherry writes very well, based on how well she did on this 5-page paper.
      6. Terrence will treat her like a queen, to judge from how well he treated her on their first date.
▲   7. Acura transmissions fail before 100,000 miles, judging from what happened to my car.
      8. I've been to one ballet and I've never been so bored in my life. I'm sure they will all be the same.
      9. I love ballet! I've only been to one, but I fell in love instantly.
▲   10. Lupe's sister and father both have high blood pressure. It probably runs in the family.
     11. SALESPERSON: As you can see from these two pictures, HDTV is much sharper than regular TV.
     12. Yes. Blue Cross will cover that procedure. They covered it for me.
     13. Cockers eat like pigs, judging from the cocker I had as a kid.

Exercise 10-13

"Most Ohio State students I've met believe in God. Therefore, most Ohio State students believe in God."

How should each of the following suppositions affect the speaker's confidence in his or her conclusion?

1. Suppose the students in the sample were interviewed as they left a local church after Sunday services. (Ohio State has no admission requirements pertaining to religious beliefs.)

2. Suppose the students in the sample were first-year students.

3. Suppose the students in the sample were on the university football team.

▲ 4. Suppose the students in the sample were selected by picking every tenth name on an alphabetical list of students' names.

5. Suppose the students in the sample were respondents to a questionnaire published in the campus newspaper titled "Survey of Student Religious Beliefs."

6. Suppose the students in the sample were randomly selected from a list of registered automobile owners.

Exercise 10-14

Read the passage below, and answer the questions that follow.

In the Georgia State University History Department, students are invited to submit written evaluations of their instructors to the department's personnel committee, which uses those evaluations to determine whether history instructors should be recommended for retention and promotions. In his three history classes, Professor Ludlum has a total of one hundred students. Six students turned in written evaluations of Ludlum; two of these evaluations were favorable and four were negative. Professor Hitchcock, who sits on the History Department Personnel Committee, argued against recommending Ludlum for promotion. "If a majority of the students who bothered to evaluate Ludlum find him lacking," he stated, "then it's clear a majority of all his students find him lacking."

▲ 1. What is the sample in Hitchcock's reasoning?

2. What is the population?

3. What is the attribute of interest?

▲ 4. Are there differences between the sample and the population that should reduce our confidence in Hitchcock's conclusion?

5. Is the sample random?

6. Is the sample large enough?

▲ 7. Based on these considerations, how strong is Hitchcock's reasoning?

REASONING FROM THE SPECIFIC TO THE SPECIFIC: INDUCTIVE ARGUMENTS FROM ANALOGY

If you have heard of arguments from analogy, you may be surprised to learn that strictly speaking, there aren't any. Strictly speaking, an analogy is a metaphor or a simile, a nonpropositional entity that is neither true nor false. Metaphors and similes may be described as useful, enlightening, apt, accurate, startling, and in other ways; but they aren't literally true, and they aren't literally false. Consequently, an analogy cannot be the premise of an argument because a premise must be either true or false. What is commonly called an inductive argument from analogy is, in fact, an argument from a claim that two (or more) things share one or more attributes.

Let's begin by looking at the way these arguments work. Then we'll consider other uses of analogy.

The Way Inductive Arguments from Analogy Work

The fact that two things share some attributes increases the probability they will share others. For example, the fact that two cell phones are made by the same manufacturer increases the probability that they are of the same quality. Because of this, the fact that one cell phone doesn't work well is a reason for thinking the other cell phone won't either. That is how the premises of an inductive argument from analogy can support—increase the probability of—the conclusion.

Schematically, an argument from analogy has this form:

X and Y both share attributes p, q, r (and so forth).
X also has the attribute of interest to us—attribute I.
Therefore Y has attribute I.

An example in English can't hurt:

Cheryl and Denise are teenage sisters who go to the same school and watch the same TV programs.
Cheryl liked *The Chronicles of Narnia*.
Therefore, Denise will like *The Chronicles of Narnia*.

The things that are said to have similar attributes are called **analogues.** Here the analogues are Cheryl and Denise. Although our example has only two analogues, there can be more. There might be more sisters, for example.

When we think critically about arguments of this type, it helps to keep in mind that we are *not* trying to gauge the probability of the conclusion, everything considered. We are *not* trying to determine the *overall* probability that Denise will like *The Chronicles of Narnia*. To make *that* determination we would need to adhere to the Principle of Total Evidence. Our task is more limited. We are simply trying to determine the relative strength of a specific argument from analogy. This is something we can do without paying attention to the Principle of Total Evidence.

If you doubt this, consider these two arguments for the same conclusion:

A. Cheryl and Denise are teenage sisters, attend the same school, and watch the same TV shows. Cheryl liked *The Chronicles of Narnia*. Therefore Denise will like *The Chronicles of Narnia*.

B. Cheryl and Denise both wear glasses. Cheryl likes *The Chronicles of Narnia*. Therefore Denise will like *The Chronicles of Narnia*.

We do not need to invoke the Principle of Total Evidence to know that (A) is the stronger argument.

When we evaluate an inductive argument from analogy, forgetting that we are *not* called upon to gauge the overall probability of the conclusion will almost inevitably lead to confused estimates of the relative strength of the argument.

This being said, the relative strength of an inductive argument from analogy comes down largely to the question of how similar and dissimilar the analogues are. The more similar Cheryl and Denise are to each other, the more apt they are to be like each other in other ways. The less similar they are, the more apt are they not to be alike in other ways. In our example, Cheryl and Denise are teenage sisters, attend the same school, and watch the same TV programs. The more similarities like that they have, the more likely Denise will also like *The Chronicles of Narnia*, given that Cheryl does. And the more differences they have, the less apt they are to like the same movies.

Of course, the similarities and differences that count must be related to the attribute of interest. Are Cheryl's and Denise's big toes the same size? It doesn't matter. As far as we know, the size of a person's big toe doesn't have anything to do with his or her taste in movies.

Note as well that the more *diversified* the similarities are between Cheryl and Denise, the more likely it is that the two sisters have similar tastes in movies. Likewise, the more diversified are the *dissimilarities*, the less likely it is. For instance, if Cheryl and Denise have the same tastes across a diversified spectrum of books, web pages, TV programs, hobbies, friends, and so forth, they are more likely to agree about a movie. Of course, having different tastes across such a diversified spectrum makes it more likely they will have different tastes in movies.

Here, however, we encounter a complication. Some similarities are more closely related than are others to the similarity we are concerned with. The fact Denise and Cheryl attend *the same school* may slightly increase the probability they have the same taste in movies; the fact they watch *the same TV programs* increases it more. Having similar tastes in TV programs is a better predictor of having similar tastes in movies, than is going to the same school. Roughly, how closely related one similarity is to another depends on how strong the association is between the two similarities—on how reliable the presence of one similarity is as a predictor of the presence of the other similarity.

One thing more needs to be said. Let's pretend Denise has another teenage sister, Barbara, who goes to the same school and watches the same TV programs, but did *not* like *The Chronicles of Narnia*. That fact diminishes the probability that Denise will share Cheryl's fondness for *The Chronicles of Narnia*. Barbara is a **contrary analogue**—an analogue that shares some of the attributes of the other analogues but does *not* share the attribute of interest. Clearly, the existence of contrary analogues makes the claim stated in the conclusion of an analogical argument less likely. A contrary analogue, if known, is a reason for having less confidence in the conclusion of the original argument.

---

(1) Cheryl and Denise are teenage sisters who go to the same school and watch the same TV programs.
(2) Cheryl liked *The Chronicles of Narnia*.
(3) Therefore, Denise will like *The Chronicles of Narnia*.

Evaluation of an inductive argument from an analogy is far from an exact science and requires us mainly to rely on our experience about what similarities are associated with other similarities, and how tight the association is. Thinking critically about such arguments is basically just *comparing and contrasting* the analogues, the same thing you practiced in high school English. However, as critical thinkers we do want to pay special attention to the ways the analogues are *dissimilar*. **Attacking the analogy** is the time-honored strategy for rebutting an argument from analogy—showing that the analogues are not as similar as stated or implied. This could mean showing there are fewer similarities between them, or more dissimilarities, or both. Often it means calling attention to a single, glaring dissimilarity between the analogues that undermines the argument. For example, one might point out that Denise has been living in Spain the past several months on a student exchange program.

Guidelines for Thinking Critically About an Argument from Analogy

■ The more numerous and diversified the similarities are between the analogues, the stronger the argument, and the more numerous and diversified the differences, the weaker the argument.

■ It must be kept in mind that some similarities and differences are more relevant than are others to the similarity we are interested in.

■ The fewer "contrary analogues," the stronger the argument, the more contrary analogues, the weaker the argument.

Examples of Thinking Critically About Arguments from Analogy

First example:

"The federal budget is like a household budget; bad things result from not balancing a household budget; therefore bad things will result from not balancing the federal budget."

Yes, whether the federal budget is like a household budget is rather a subjective question. Still, the federal budget is more like a household budget than it is like, say, a snowshoe; but the dissimilarities between the analogues are striking. Among them: the federal government, unlike a household, can raise taxes and print money. Given those dissimilarities, the argument does not seem strong.

Second example:

"Last year Kris Allen won *American Idol*. Two years ago David Cook won. Therefore Lee Dewyze will probably win this year, because he looks and sounds like the other two."

Here, too, whether someone looks and sounds like someone else is a judgment call; but most people who watch *American Idol* would agree these three singers look and sound more like each other than any of them looks or sounds like Barbara Streisand or Pavarotti. No doubt they would also agree they look and sound more like each other than they look or sound like the other contestant going into the current finals round, Crystal Bowersox. Are there dissimilarities that weaken the argument? Is Bowersox a better singer? Is she especially likeable? Does she have a compelling story? Have the judges praised her more? If one could not think of such dissimilarities, Dewyze would be the better bet.

Third example:

"Harvey mistreats his dog. He wouldn't make a good babysitter."

The analogues in this argument (Harvey's treatment of his dog and his treatment of someone's child) are so similar you wouldn't want Harvey to babysit your child.

Fourth example:

"Harvey mistreats his child. He wouldn't make a good dog sitter."

The analogues in this example are the same as in the previous one. Likewise, the similarities and dissimilarities between the analogues (whatever they may be) are the same in both examples. However, the fourth example is a stronger argument for its conclusion. A person who could mistreat a dog might draw the line there; after all, more people eat meat than eat children. But, we think, most (though perhaps not all) people who would mistreat a child wouldn't hesitate to mistreat an animal.

Again, appraisal of arguments from analogy is not an exact science. Analyzing them blindly according to some formula isn't the best idea.

Other Uses of Analogies

As you've seen, our primary interest in analogies has been their use in analogical arguments. But analogies are also used—and are also useful—in explanations, as rhetorical devices, and in other capacities. Here's an example of an analogy that might look like an argument but isn't:

> Bears, as everybody (especially Stephen Colbert) knows, are dangerous. If you get too close, you can lose it all. The same holds true of bear markets. In the presence of a bear market, the thing to do is the same as when in the presence of a real bear: Keep your distance!

Now, it may be that staying out of the stock market during a bear market is a wise move. But this passage certainly gives us no reason for believing it. No fact whatsoever about real bears is relevant to the stock market (except, maybe, for stocks in bear-hunting companies, if such things existed). Here, the analogy supplies a psychological connection and nothing more; the only thing the terms of the analogy share is the word "bear." Neither term tells us anything about the other, but you might be surprised at how many people fall for this kind of "reasoning."

On the other hand, analogies figure into moral and legal arguments in an important way. As you'll see in Chapter 12, a basic moral principle is based on the comparison of different cases, the principle that we should treat like cases alike. If we have two analogous cases, two people performing similar

Real Life

Bears!

The fact that bears are dangerous doesn't mean that bear markets are dangerous. See text above.

Real Life

Whom Do You Trust?

■ When it comes to deciding which kind of car to buy, which do you trust more—the reports of a few friends or the results of a survey based on a large sample?

■ When it comes to deciding whether an over-the-counter cold remedy (e.g., vitamin C) works, which do you trust more—a large clinical study or the reports of a few friends?

Many people trust the reports of friends over more reliable statistical information. We hope you aren't among 'em. (According to R. E. Nisbett and L. Ross, *Human Inference: Strategies and Shortcomings of Human Social Judgment* [Englewood Cliffs, N.J.: Prentice Hall, 1980], people tend to be insensitive to sample size when evaluating some product, being swayed more by the judgments of a few friends than by the results of a survey based on a large sample.)

actions in similar circumstances, for example, it would be morally suspect to praise one of them and blame the other. Similarly, the legal principle of *stare decisis* (to stand by things decided) is based on making analogies between present cases and cases that have been settled in the past. More on this, as well, in Chapter 12.

Analogies also come into play in explanations. Some explanations would be made more difficult or even impossible if we could not make use of analogous cases. For instance, back in Chapter 5 we mentioned that an analogy could be very helpful in explaining rugby to a person who knew nothing about the game. If the person did know something about American football, one could begin with that game and point out differences between football and rugby. This would be a great time-saver, since the points the two games have in common would not have to be listed as features of rugby.

Historical analogies are used both to explain and to argue for a point of view. For example, the history of the Roman Empire is often compared to that of the British Empire as historians look for similar themes in the hope of drawing conclusions about the way empires rise and fall. Lately, analogies between the Vietnam and Iraq conflicts have been used, especially by antiwar advocates, to try to show that the course of the second conflict will follow that of the first unless there is a drastic change in approach.

Finally, we should mention the use of **logical analogies** in the refutation of arguments. You can often show someone that an argument is invalid by providing another argument that is just like the first but obviously invalid. The important phrase here is "just like the first." What this means is that the second argument *must have the same form* as the first. You'll see what we mean as you follow this example, in which Gary presents an argument and Melinda refutes Gary's argument by logical analogy. Gary says, "All your liberal friends believe there should be universal health care, and anyone who wants socialized medicine also believes there should be universal health care. So, all your liberal friends want socialized medicine." Melinda points out that this conclusion doesn't follow. She uses an analogy: "Gary, that's invalid. That's just like saying because all your friends breathe air and all terrorists breathe air, all your friends are terrorists."

With her example, Melinda has shown that, if Gary's argument were valid, her argument would also be valid. Since her argument obviously isn't valid, Gary's isn't either.

The following exercises will help you understand reasoning from analogy and how to evaluate it.

Identify whether each of these is

Exercise 10-15

A = argument from analogy

B = an analogy that isn't an argument *No*

▲ 1. These shrubs have shiny green leaves, and so does privet. I bet these shrubs keep their leaves in the winter, too.

2. Working in this office is like driving around Florida without AC.

3. Between you and me, Huck has less personality than a pincushion.

▲ 4. You don't like picnicking? Well, you won't like camping, either. You can't do either without getting eaten by mosquitoes.

5. As soon as I saw all these formulas and stuff, I knew I'd like symbolic logic. It's just like math, which I love.

6. I love washing dishes like I love cleaning the bathroom.

▲ 7. Driving fast is playing with fire.

8. Too much sun will make your face leathery. I suppose it will have that effect on your hands, too.

9. Here, use that screwdriver like a chisel. Just give it a good whack with the hammer.

▲ 10. She's no good at tennis. No way she's good at racquetball.

11. "Religion . . . is the opium of the people. To abolish religion as the illusory happiness of the people is to demand their real happiness."

—*Karl Marx*

12. "Publishing is to thinking as the maternity ward is to the first kiss."

—*Friedrich von Schlegel*

13. "A book is like a mirror. If an ape looks in, a saint won't look out."

—*Ludwig Wittgenstein*

14. Historically, the market goes up when the employment situation worsens and goes down when it gets better. Right now, there is bad news on employment, and the latest statistics show unemployment is getting worse. This could be a good time to buy stocks.

15. Yamaha makes great motorcycles. I'll bet their pianos are pretty good, too.

16. "Life is a roll of toilet paper. The closer you get to the end, the faster it goes."

—*Anonymous*

Exercise 10-16

In each item, identify the analogues and the attribute of interest. State which analogue is said to have that attribute, and which is predicted to have it.

▲   1. Saccharin causes cancer in rats, and rats are like humans, biologically speaking. So saccharin will cause cancer in humans, too.

2. Doug Gray is a successful businessman; he'd make a fine mayor.

3. Jeb Bush is very popular in Georgia. He'd be just as popular in Alabama, since most voters in both states are southern conservatives.

▲   4. Tell you what, this ant poison looks like Windex. I bet we can clean the windows with it.

5. You need strong, quick fingers if you're going to play a violin or a viola. Angus is great on the violin; he'd probably be great on the viola, too.

6. I liked Will Smith's last movie, so I'll probably like this one too, especially since they have the same story line.

▲   7. January's heating bill will be high, given that December's was outrageous and January is supposed to be even colder.

8. Expect Hawes to speak his mind at the meeting. He always speaks up in class.

9. Appeasement didn't work with Hitler; why should it work with Kim Jong Il?

▲   10. Abortion means killing a live person. If abortion is wrong, then so is capital punishment, since it also involves killing a live person.

Exercise 10-17

In each item, identify the analogues and the attribute of interest. State which analogue is said to have that attribute, and which is predicted to have it.

▲   1. It's easy to use an iPod; it's got to be easy to use an iPad. Apple makes them both.

2. Almonds upset my stomach; I'd bet hazel nuts do, too.

3. The bagels at Safeway are great; the sourdough's probably fine.

▲   4. Odwalla carrot juice tastes moldy; I'd bet their orange juice tastes that way as well.

5. My PC slowed way down after a couple of years; it'll happen to yours, too.

6. L.L. Bean makes great sheets; I bet they make great bedspreads.

▲   7. It's a good thing auto insurance is mandatory; why would it be different with health insurance?

8. The Greek economy collapsed because of all the government pensions. If it happened there, it can happen here.

9. I can't play a baritone; I doubt I could play a Sousaphone.

▲   10. What, you don't like *Dancing with the Stars?* Well, don't bother watching *So You Think You Can Dance.*

11. Let's get a Whirlpool washing machine. Their dishwashers are great!

▲ Rank these analogues from most similar to most dissimilar.   Exercise 10-18

    a. football and bowling
    b. football and rugby
    c. football and golf
    d. football and basketball
    e. football and chess
    f. football and tennis

Rank these analogues from most similar to most dissimilar.   Exercise 10-19

    a. going to a rock concert and going to a bluegrass concert
    b. watching Lady Gaga on YouTube and seeing her in concert
    c. going to a ballet and going to a classical concert
    d. going to a ballet and watching Lady Gaga on YouTube
    e. listening to classical music and reading poetry
    f. seeing Lady Gaga in concert or going to a July Fourth fireworks show

Based on the similarities and differences between the analogues, evaluate   Exercise 10-20
each of the following arguments from analogy as relatively strong or relatively
weak. To a certain extent this will be a judgment call, but the class as a whole
should reach approximate consensus on many items.

▲   1. Earth is like Mars. Since Earth can support life, so can Mars.
    2. Tucker wasn't any good when he managed Big Five Sports; I doubt he'd be
      good at managing an auto parts store.
    3. Hey, work for Harris if you can. She leaves big tips; she probably pays her
      employees well, too.
▲   4. Saddam was another Hitler. Obviously we had to take him out.
    5. Julia is good at bowling; I bet she'd be great at poker.
    6. Julia is good at croquet; I bet she'd be great at bowling.
▲   7. Ann takes care of her dog; she'd make a great babysitter.
    8. Hey, Carl? When you don't return something you borrowed, that's like
      stealing. Give Tony back his wheelbarrow.
    9. Warren shows up to work on time; I bet he pays his rent on time.
▲ 10. Norway is like Sweden. There's no crime in Norway, so there won't be
      any in Sweden, either.

What kind of argument is this? Is it as good as the writer thinks it is?   Exercise 10-21

    The proponents of [school] vouchers say, in essence, that if competition
    produces excellences in other fields—consumer products, athletics, and
    higher education, to name but three—it would be healthy for the schools
    as well. Their logic is difficult to refute.

                                             —*Dan Walters, political columnist*

Exercise 10-22   For the past four years, Cliff has attempted the 100-mile bike ride on the Fourth of July. He has never had the stamina to finish. He decides to attempt the ride again, but is pessimistic about his chances of finishing. How should each of the following suppositions affect his confidence that once again he *won't* finish? Use the principles discussed on page 365.

▲   1. Suppose past attempts were done in a variety of weather conditions.

2. Suppose Cliff will ride the same bike this year as on all previous attempts.

3. Suppose past attempts were on the same bike, but that is not the bike Cliff will ride this year.

▲   4. Suppose Cliff hasn't yet decided what kind of bike to ride this year.

5. Suppose past attempts were all on flat ground, and this year's ride will also be on flat ground.

6. Suppose past attempts were all on flat ground, and this year's ride will be in hilly terrain.

▲   7. Suppose past attempts were all in hilly terrain, and this year's ride will be on flat ground.

▲   8. In answering question 7, did you consider only the stated information, or did you consider other things you know about bike riding?

▲   9. Suppose some of past attempts were on flat ground and others were in hilly terrain, but where this year's ride will be hasn't been announced yet.

Exercise 10-23   During three earlier years, Kirk has tried to grow artichokes in his backyard garden, and each time, his crop has been ruined by mildew. Billie prods him to try one more time, and he agrees to do so, though he secretly thinks, "This is probably a waste of time. Mildew is likely to ruin this crop, too." How should each of the following suppositions affect his confidence that mildew will ruin this crop, too?

▲   1. Suppose this year Kirk plants the artichokes in a new location.

2. Suppose on the past three occasions Kirk planted his artichokes at different times of the growing season.

3. Suppose this year Billie plants marigolds near the artichokes.

▲   4. Suppose the past three years were unusually cool.

5. Suppose only two of the three earlier crops were ruined by mildew.

6. Suppose one of the earlier crops grew during a dry year, one during a wet year, and one during an average year.

▲   7. Suppose this year, unlike the preceding three, there is a solar eclipse.

8. Suppose this year Kirk fertilizes with lawn clippings for the first time.

9. Suppose this year Billie and Kirk acquire a large dog.

▲   10. Suppose this year Kirk installs a drip irrigation system.

REASONING FROM GENERAL TO GENERAL

Let's summarize: So far we've discussed the following:

- Reasoning from the general to the specific: *statistical syllogisms*
- Reasoning from the specific to the general: *inductive generalizing from samples*
- Reasoning from the specific to the specific: *arguments from analogy*

What remains is this:

- Reasoning from the general to the general.

You *can* inductively support a conclusion about the attributes of one population by considering the attributes of another population. You do this by viewing the two populations as analogues, and by reasoning analogically.

Example:

Major league baseball players widely use performance-enhancing drugs. ML baseball players and NFL football players are under comparable pressure to perform well; and performance-enhancing drugs are as available to NFL football players as to ML baseball players. Further, the methods used for preventing and detecting the use of performance-enhancing drugs are the same for both NFL and ML players, and the penalties for using the drugs are similar for both sets of individuals.

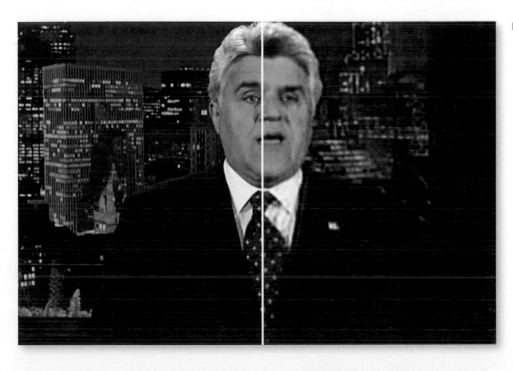

- HDTV vs. SDTV images. The "populations" of such images are highly uniform; so a single comparison image may suffice to let you know which populations you'd be happier with.

Therefore, National Football League players probably widely use performance-enhancing drugs, too.

Using the guidelines mentioned on page 365 leads to the finding that this argument from analogy is relatively strong. However, it is not strong enough to warrant conclusions about specific individuals. That kind of conclusion would require hard evidence in the form, perhaps, of tests. But it is strong enough to raise concern on the part of those who think that professional football players should not use performance-enhancing drugs.

An argument like this one, based on an analogy between two populations, is a legitimate inductive argument.* However, there is another way people attempt to come to a conclusion about the attributes of one population by considering the attributes of another population. Sometimes people think that information about the proportion of Xs that are Ys automatically supports conclusions about the proportion of Ys that are Xs. It is a mistake to think this.

Example of Mistaken Reasoning

Most men with prostate cancer have an elevated PSA level.

Therefore most men with an elevated PSA level have prostate cancer.

Without additional information, you *cannot* derive a conclusion about the proportion of Xs that are Ys from information about the proportion of Ys that are Xs. The fact that few mammals are aardvarks does not support the conclusion that few aardvarks are mammals. The fact that only a small fraction of this year's college graduates will be seniors from your university does not mean that only a small fraction of the seniors from your university will graduate. This mistake we shall call an **illicit inductive conversion**; here are four additional examples:

First example:

Most people who have lung cancer are smokers; therefore most smokers have lung cancer.

Second example:

Few members of the National Rifle Association are Marxists; therefore few Marxists are members of the National Rifle Association.

Third example:

Only a tiny percentage of traffic accidents involve stoned 90-year-old drivers. Therefore, stoned 90-year-old drivers have little chance of getting into a traffic accident.

Fourth example:

Most meth addicts are former marijuana users; therefore most former marijuana users are meth addicts.

---

*In fact, you could view all inductive generalizations from samples as arguments from analogy, in which one analogue is the sample and the other analogue is the population it supposedly represents.

INFORMAL ERROR-MARGIN AND CONFIDENCE-LEVEL INDICATORS

Confidence level (explained earlier in the chapter) is a technical concept from statistics; a confidence level is a quantitative statement of the probability that random variation among samples of a given size falls within certain limits known as the error margin. We have, however, everyday expressions that convey our level of confidence that a statement is true. We might speak, for example, of a proposition as being *almost certainly true* or as *true beyond any reasonable doubt.* If someone were to say, "I'd bet my shirt that blahblahblah," you would know he or she is very confident of that assertion.

In everyday discourse, we use phrases like the following to express how much confidence we have in a proposition:

Informal "confidence level" indicating phrases:
- Undoubtedly
- I'd bet anything
- Almost certainly
- Very probably
- It's likely
- There's a good chance
- The chances are 50/50
- There's a chance
- Maybe
- There's not much chance
- It's utterly impossible

And so forth.

Error margins too may be expressed informally. To give oneself an "error margin" when asserting a proportion, one might use terms like the following:

Informal "error margin" indicating words:
- around
- about
- approximately
- roughly
- most
- many

And so on.

Everyday "error margins" and "confidence levels" are also expressed by implication. Recently we encountered a man with a dog whose name—judging from what the man kept shouting—was "Getoverhere." He assured us Getoverhere wasn't dangerous—bared fangs notwithstanding. "Dad-gum dog won't bite," he said. "I've raised lots of pits and the breed don't bite." The man expressed this without caveat, indicating he placed great confidence in the probability that pit bulls don't bite.

Definition of Statistics: The science of producing unreliable facts from reliable figures.
—Evan Esar

Conclusions of statistical syllogisms and arguments from analogy are also expressed with levels of confidence, though not with "error margins," since they are about individuals rather than populations. The argument the dog owner made about Getoverhere was both generalizing from a sample and a statistical syllogism:

> *Generalizing from a sample:*
>   The pits I've raised don't bite.
>   Therefore pits don't bite.
> *Statistical syllogism:*
>   Pits don't bite.
>   This dog is a pit.
>   Therefore this dog "don't bite."

Informal error-margin and confidence-level indicators (and other expressions that do the same job) enable us to express an estimation of the probability of claims. Thinking critically about everyday inductive reasoning from samples means matching error-margin and confidence-level indicators to the size and representativeness of a sample. For example, generalizing from a small, atypical sample isn't a mistake in reasoning—unless we overestimate the probability of the conclusion relative to the size of our sample and the error margin we allow ourselves.

Example of Inflated Confidence Level and Unduly Narrow Error Margin

I bought two apples at Kroger and one tasted awful. Therefore, it is dead certain that exactly 50 percent of all the apples at Kroger taste awful.

Example of a More Appropriate Confidence Level and a More Appropriate Error Margin

I bought two apples at Kroger and one tasted awful. Therefore, it's possible that a rather significant proportion of all apples at Kroger taste awful.

FALLACIES IN INDUCTIVE REASONING, AND RELATED PROBLEMS

Thinking critically means, perhaps above everything else, eliminating fallacies from your thinking. Several fallacies associated with inductive reasoning bear keeping in mind.

Hasty Generalization

Sometimes "hasty generalizing" is depicted simply as reasoning from a sample that is too small relative to the size of the population it is said to represent. But there is no mistake in reasoning from a small sample even if the population it is said to represent is very large. The mistake lies in being overly confident of how likely the small sample makes the conclusion.

Example of Hasty Generalization

This pit bites. Therefore all pits bite.

Example That Is Not Hasty Generalization

This pit bites. Therefore some pits bite.

The latter example isn't "hasty generalization" because the word "some" conveys a wide error-margin.

Anecdotal Evidence

One version of hasty generalizing deserves special mention. You sometimes hear statisticians, psychologists, and social scientists dismiss an argument as "merely anecdotal." An anecdote is a story, and the **fallacy of anecdotal evidence** is a version of hasty generalizing where the sample is presented as a narrative.

Example of the Fallacy of Anecdotal Evidence

These reports about pits being mean—there's nothing to them. You should see ol' Getoverhere playing with the grandkids. Dad-gum dog lets them eat out of his bowl.

Often, as with this example, generalizing from an anecdote is used to rebut a general statement. It's still generalizing from a sample of one or two, and if one overestimates the probability of the conclusion given the evidence (as the speaker does above), he or she commits the fallacy of anecdotal evidence.

One of the most important things you can learn from this book is to be on guard against this fallacy. "Evidence" that consists only of an anecdote is psychologically almost ravishing in its power to persuade. Whenever you hear someone supporting a general statement, or a rebuttal of a general statement, with nothing more than a story, remind yourself that a story is a sample of one.

Biased Generalization

The fallacy known as biased generalization happens when one is overly confident of how likely a biased sample makes a conclusion. (Again, a biased sample over- or under-represents one or more important variables found in its population.)

Now, a very small sample of a large and highly diversified population just *can't* be representative; the sample wouldn't be large enough to incorporate the important variables. Because such cases are automatically biased, it is customary to apply the **biased generalization** label to reasoning based on a relatively large sample that nevertheless is biased.

Example of the Fallacy Biased Generalization

Apparently nearly half of college students use Adderall, judging from a study of 1,000 seniors at Arizona State University. Nearly 50 percent of those surveyed said they use Adderall to prepare for final exams.*

Studies indicate that more brunettes than blondes or redheads have high-paying corporate jobs.

—From a letter in the *San Francisco Chronicle*

Is this evidence of discrimination against blondes and redheads, as the writer of the letter thought?

Nope; there are more brunettes to begin with. We'd be suspicious if *fewer* brunettes had high-paying corporate jobs.

---

*A made-up statistic.

The Self-Selection Fallacy

On any given night, a thousand people may register an opinion online about a question posed on a CNN or FOX News program. That's as many people as you'd find in the sample of a professional opinion poll. But the informal cable news poll sample has not been scientifically selected to make sure every viewpoint has an equal chance of being included. What should reduce our confidence in conclusions about public opinion derived from such samples isn't necessarily that the samples are too small, but that they are self-selected.

A self-selected sample is one whose members are included by their own decision. A famous example would be a large poll conducted in 1993 by the political organization of H. Ross Perot, a wealthy businessman who ran for president. The poll was conducted by means of the magazine *TV Guide*; people were asked to answer questions posed in the magazine, then tear out or reproduce the pages and send them in for processing. You've already heard all you need to know to discount any results it produced. It, and all self-selected samples, over-represent people who want to be in the sample and under-represent people who don't have strong enough feelings on the issues to respond or who don't have the time to go to the trouble. Such a situation almost guarantees the sample will have views that are significantly different from those of its purported population.

Real Life

The Great Slip-Up of 1948

Because of a strike, the *Chicago Daily Tribune* had to go to press earlier than usual the night of the 1948 presidential election. So, they relied on some early returns, some "expert" opinion, and public opinion polls to decide on the famous "Dewey Defeats Truman" headline. But the polls were not sufficiently accurate, as Truman edged Dewey in a narrow upset victory.

When we overestimate the probability of a conclusion derived from a relatively large but self-selected sample, we commit the **self-selection fallacy**. As should be clear, this fallacy is merely a subcategory of the biased generalization fallacy, when the reasoning is founded on a large but self-selected sample. Common examples include online public opinion polls and person-on-the-street interviews.

Example of the Self-Selection Fallacy

Over sixty percent of people who responded to an online survey on CNN say they like President Obama as a person; clearly, most Americans like President Obama as a person.

Slanted Questions

A major source of unreliability in polling practices is the wording of the questions. It is possible to ask nearly any question of importance in many different ways. Consider this pair of questions:

- Do you think the school board should agree to teachers' demands for higher pay?
- Do you think it is reasonable for local public school teachers to seek pay raises?

These questions ask essentially the same thing, but you would be smart to expect more negative answers to the first version than to the second. The context in which a question is asked can be important, too. Imagine a question asking about approval of pay raises for public school teachers, but imagine it coming after one or the other of the following questions.

- Are you aware that teachers in this district have not had a salary increase for the past six years?
- Are you aware that the school district is facing a budget shortfall for the coming fiscal year?

We'd expect the approval of raises to fare better when asked after the first of these questions than after the second.

We might add that the inclusion of slanted questions is not always accidental. Often, a group or an organization will want to produce results that are slanted in their direction, and so they will include questions that are designed to do exactly that. This is an exercise in deception, of course, but unfortunately it is more widespread than we'd wish.

Have a look at the box "Ask Us No (Loaded) Questions . . ." (page 380), and you'll see how one large, very expensive poll can contain most of the errors we've been discussing.

Weak Analogy

When we overestimate the probability of a conclusion derived from an argument from analogy, we commit the fallacy called **weak analogy**. As in the preceding cases, the mistake will be apparent through phrases or other features that disclose one's confidence level.

On Language

Ask Us No (Loaded) Questions; We'll Tell You No Lies

In the spring of 1993, H. Ross Perot did a nationwide survey that received a lot of publicity. But a survey is only as good as the questions it asks, and loaded questions can produce a biased result. *Time* and CNN hired the Yankelovich Partners survey research firm to ask a split random sample of Americans two versions of the questions; the first was Perot's original version, the second was a rewritten version produced by the Yankelovich firm. Here is what happened for three of the topics covered.

Question 1

PEROT VERSION: "Do you believe that for every dollar of tax increase there should be two dollars in spending cuts with the savings earmarked for deficit and debt reduction?"

YANKELOVICH VERSION: "Would you favor or oppose a proposal to cut spending by two dollars for every dollar in new taxes, with the savings earmarked for deficit reduction, even if that meant cuts in domestic programs like Medicare and education?"

RESULTS: Perot version: 67 percent yes; 18 percent no
Yankelovich version: 33 percent in favor; 61 percent opposed

Question 2

PEROT VERSION: "Should the President have the Line Item Veto to eliminate waste?"

YANKELOVICH VERSION: "Should the President have the Line Item Veto, or not?"

RESULTS: Perot version: 71 percent in favor; 16 percent opposed
Yankelovich version: 57 percent in favor; 21 percent opposed

Question 3

PEROT VERSION: "Should laws be passed to eliminate all possibilities of special interests giving huge sums of money to candidates?"

YANKELOVICH VERSION: "Should laws be passed to prohibit interest groups from contributing to campaigns, or do groups have a right to contribute to the candidate they support?"

RESULTS: Perot version: 80 percent yes; 17 percent no
Yankelovich version: 40 percent for prohibition; 55 percent for right to contribute

Example of Weak Analogy

"My neighbor's pit bull is aggressive, so the one you're thinking of getting will also be aggressive."

The argument lists just one similarity between the analogues: both are pit bulls. Pit bulls, of course, share important genetic similarities that are related to aggressiveness. The conclusion of this argument, however, is expressed unconditionally. The speaker has overestimated how likely the premise makes the conclusion. If he had said, "My neighbor's pit bull is aggressive, so the one you're thinking of getting might have that problem, too," the argument would have been expressed with an appropriate confidence-level indicator. Expressed that way, no fallacy would have been committed. Likewise, there would be no fallacy if the speaker had said, "That pit you're thinking of getting could well be aggressive; its litter mate certainly is."

Vague Generalities

If someone told you that successful people think outside the box, you *might* ask him or her for evidence. But don't. A more pertinent question—though a bit rude—would be, "What are you talking about?" Until you know what counts as a successful person and thinking outside the box, you don't really know what it is you want evidence for.

A **vague generality** is a general statement too vague to be meaningful for practical purposes. This happens when a group is so vaguely named we don't know exactly who or what is in the group, or when an attribute is so obscure we can't tell if a given person or thing has it. "Environmentalists are the real enemy" and "Kids are too into themselves these days" will serve as examples.

A smart move in the critical thinking game is to watch for vague generalities in our own thinking and in the statements of others. If we have a genuine interest in checking to see if a general statement is true, we should be able to specify a sampling frame, a concept mentioned earlier. A sampling frame is essentially a precising definition, a definition that enables us to determine unambiguously whether someone or something is a member of a population and has an attribute of interest. Recently, someone told us that people with long necks make good listeners. That assertion contains a couple of pretty subjective concepts, but one could specify reasonably precisely (even though arbitrarily) how long a long neck is and could establish (arbitrarily) a standard for good listening. We doubt, however, that you could secure a grant from the National Science Foundation for testing even a precise version of the claim.

When a vague generality is couched in words and phrases with strongly positive associations, words like "freedom," "hard working," "principled," "courage," "change," and "taking back," the result is a **glowing generality**. Political ads and speeches are filled with examples.

"The people are taking back their government."

—Sarah Palin

"We owe our children more than we have been giving them."

—Hillary Clinton

The opposite of a glowing generality has no widely accepted name, but it obviously includes negative stereotypes and other dysphemisms (Chapter 5). Democrats generalize about Republicans using words like "rigid" and "inflexible," and refer to them as "right-wing extremists"; Republicans accuse Democrats of being "Marxists" and "secular socialists." Generalities of either variety amount to nothing more than name-calling; we express our attitudes when we use them, but we do not convey further substantive information.

Almost no one in Las Vegas believes the gambler's fallacy is in fact a fallacy.

—From an anonymous reviewer of this book

How does he or she know this?

Recap

Before we recap, we want to point something out. You should not get the idea from this chapter that informal reasoning from analogies or from nonscientific samples should be dismissed or avoided or that conclusions based on such reasoning should be routinely rejected. Everyday reasoning of this sort often has little confirmatory power, but it has considerable utility in suggesting ideas for more systematic, scientific exploration and confirmation. Smoking's linkage to various medical conditions would probably not have been investigated scientifically if it had not occurred to people that health problems seem greater among smokers. The moral of this chapter is not that you should never generalize or reason analogically, but only that, when you do, you should think critically and not overestimate the strength of your arguments.

The following list summarizes topics and concepts from this chapter.

- Inductive reasoning is used to support a conclusion rather than to demonstrate or prove it.

- Inductive arguments can be depicted as relatively strong or relatively weak, depending on how much their premises increase the probability of the conclusion.

- The strength of an argument is distinct from the overall probability of the conclusion. You can have a relatively strong argument for a conclusion whose overall probability is very low, and a relatively weak argument for a conclusion whose overall probability is quite high.

- Statistical syllogisms have the form: Most Xs are Ys; this is an X; therefore this is a Y.

- The strength of a statistical syllogism is distinct from the probability of its conclusion everything considered. The latter depends on The Principle of Total Evidence. The former depends on the proportion of Xs that are Ys.

- Everyday inductive generalizations from samples differ from scientific inductive generalizations from samples in that everyday samples are not scientifically selected to eliminate bias, and probabilities in everyday generalizing cannot be calculated precisely.

- Thinking critically about everyday generalizations from samples involves the two principles stated on page 355.

- Inductive reasoning from analogy is based on the idea that things alike in some respects will be alike in further respects.

- Thinking critically about inductive arguments from analogy involves the principles stated on page 365.

- The time-honored strategy for rebutting an argument from analogy is to "attack the analogy" by calling attention to important dissimilarities between the analogues.

- Arguments from analogy are especially important in ethics, history, and law, and to refute other arguments.

- We can support a conclusion about one population by reasoning analogically from a second population that has similar attributes.

- An overestimation of the strength of an argument based on a small sample is "hasty generalization."

■ An overestimation of the strength of an argument based on a biased but not-so-small sample is "biased generalization."

■ The fallacy of "anecdotal evidence" is a version of hasty generalization in which the sample is presented as a narrative.

■ Generalizations based on anecdotes are often persuasive psychologically, even though they are based on a sample of one.

■ The self-selection fallacy is a version of biased generalization in which the sample is self-selected.

■ When we overestimate the probability of a conclusion derived from an argument from analogy, we commit the fallacy called weak analogy.

■ Vague generalizations suffer not so much from lack of support as from lack of substantive meaning.

These exercises will help you identify slanted questions, informal confidence-level and error-margin indicators, vague generalizations, and fallacies in inductive reasoning.

Additional Exercises

Exercise 10-24

Explain how each of the following public opinion poll questions is slanted, if it is.

▲ 1. Some say Republican plans to reduce environmental safeguards will lead to more ecological disasters. Do you favor or oppose these plans?

2. Was British Petroleum slow to respond to the gulf oil spill because they didn't care or because they hadn't adequately prepared for drilling in deep water?

3. Do you agree or disagree that immigration laws should be more vigorously enforced?

▲ 4. Some say that the high cost of medicine is due to frivolous lawsuits. Do you favor or oppose ceilings on the amount doctors can be sued for?

5. Polls indicate that most Americans are satisfied with their health care. Do you agree or disagree that health care reform is needed?

6. To reduce the federal deficit, do you favor raising taxes on working families or reducing excessive government spending?

▲ 7. To reduce the federal deficit, do you favor raising taxes on the super wealthy or slashing services for the needy?

8. Should a doctor be able to withhold medical care from a baby who has survived an abortion?

9. When framing new laws, should legislators be guided by Judeo-Christian values or only by secular considerations?

▲ 10. Would you favor or oppose reasonable background checks on people who want to purchase deadly assault weapons?

Exercise 10-25

Find a confidence-level indicator or an error-margin indicator in each of the following arguments. Then, create a new argument with a more appropriate indicator.

Example

Original argument:

> It rained yesterday. Therefore, it absolutely, positively will rain again today.

New argument with a more appropriate confidence-level indicator:

> It rained yesterday. Therefore, it could well rain again today.

▲ 1. Paulette, Georgette, Babette, and Brigitte are all Miami University students, and they all are members of Webkinz. Therefore, all Miami University students are members of Webkinz.

2. Paulette, Georgette, Babette, and Brigitte are all Miami University students and the first three are members of Webkinz. Therefore, exactly three out of every four Miami University students is a member of Webkinz.

3. Gustavo likes all the business courses he has taken at Foothill College. Therefore, he is bound to like the next business course he takes at Foothill.

▲ 4. Gustavo liked two of the four business profs he has had at Foothill College. Therefore, he will like 50 percent of all his business profs at Foothill.

5. Gustavo likes all the business courses he has had at Foothill. No doubt his brother Sergio will like all his Foothill business courses, too.

6. Twenty percent of York's 8:00 A.M. class watch PBS. Therefore, 20 percent of York's 9:00 A.M. class watch PBS.

▲ 7. Twenty percent of York's 8:00 A.M. class watch PBS. Therefore, it is certain that exactly 20 percent of all the students at York's community college watch PBS.

8. Bill Clinton lied about his relationship with Monica Lewinsky; therefore, he lied about Jennifer Flowers as well.

9. Seventy percent of Wal-Mart shoppers own cars. Therefore, the same percentage of Target customers own cars.

▲ 10. Susan likes Thanksgiving. We can be very certain, therefore, that she likes Christmas too.

Exercise 10-26

Arrange the alternative conclusions of the following arguments in order of decreasing confidence level. Some options are pretty close to tied; don't get into feuds with classmates over close calls.

▲ 1. Not once this century has this city gone Republican in a presidential election. Therefore,

a. I wouldn't count on it happening this time
b. it won't happen this time
c. in all likelihood, it won't happen this time
d. there's no chance whatsoever that it will happen this time
e. it would be surprising if it happened this time
f. I'll be a donkey's uncle if it happens this time

2. Byron doesn't know how to play poker, so,

a. he sure as heck doesn't know how to play blackjack
b. it's doubtful he knows how to play blackjack
c. there's a possibility he doesn't know how to play blackjack
d. don't bet on him knowing how to play blackjack
e. you're nuts if you think he knows how to play blackjack

3. Every time I've used the Beltway, the traffic has been heavy, so I figure that

a. the traffic is almost always heavy on the Beltway
b. frequently the traffic on the Beltway is heavy
c. as a rule, the traffic on the Beltway is heavy
d. the traffic on the Beltway can be heavy at times
e. the traffic on the Beltway is invariably heavy
f. typically, the traffic on the Beltway is heavy
g. the traffic on the Beltway is likely to be heavy most of the time

Exercise 10-27

In which of the following arguments is the implied confidence level too high or low, given the premises? After you have decided, compare your results with those of three or four classmates.

▲ 1. We spent a day on the Farallon Islands last June, and was it ever foggy and cold! So, dress warmly when you go there this June. Based on our experience, it is 100 percent certain to be foggy and cold.

2. We've visited the Farallon Islands on five different days, two during the summer and one each during fall, winter, and spring. It's been foggy and cold every time we've been there. So, dress warmly when you go there. Based on our experience, there is an excellent chance it will be foggy and cold whenever you go.

3. We've visited the Farallon Islands on five different days, all in June. It's been foggy and cold every time we've been there. So, dress warmly when you go there in June. Based on our experience, it could well be foggy and cold.

▲ 4. We've visited the Farallon Islands on five different days, all in June. It's been foggy and cold every time we've been there. So, dress warmly when you go there in June. Based on our experience, there is a small chance it will be foggy and cold.

5. We've visited the Farallon Islands on five different days, all in January. It's been foggy and cold every time we've been there. So, dress warmly when you go there in June. Based on our experience, it almost certainly will be foggy and cold.

Exercise 10-28

In each of the following, determine whether the sample, the population, or the attribute of interest is excessively vague.

▲ 1. The tests in the class are going to be hard, judging from the first midterm.

   2. The transmissions in Chrysler minivans tend to fail prematurely, if my Voyager is an indication.

   3. Judging from my experience, technical people are exceedingly difficult to communicate with sometimes.

▲ 4. Men cannot tolerate stress. My husband even freaks if the newspaper is a little late.

   5. Movies are too graphic these days. Just go to one—you'll see.

   6. Violence in movies carries a message that degrades women. The movies playing right now prove the point.

▲ 7. You need to get cooler clothing than that if you're going to Minneapolis in the summer. I've been there.

   8. Entertainment is much too expensive these days. Just look at what they charge for movies.

   9. Art majors sure are weird! I roomed with one once. Man.

▲ 10. The French just don't like Americans. I couldn't find anyone in Paris who would speak English to me.

 11. All the research suggests introverts are likely to be well versed in computer skills.

 12. Suspicious people tend to be quite unhappy, from what I've observed.

 13. Everyone marries someone who looks like him/her. Just check out the married people you know.

Exercise 10-29

If you can, specify a sampling frame for each of the following populations and attributes. In other words, define them so one could determine whether a person or thing is a member of the population and has the attribute.

▲ 1. The proportion of Denver residents who watch *The Bachelorette*.

   2. The proportion of religious people in your city who are conservatives.

   3. The proportion of blondes at your university.

▲ 4. The proportion of country songs about lost love.

   5. The proportion of plumbers in Chicago who play the Illinois Lotto.

   6. The proportion of people with long necks who make good listeners.

Exercise 10-30

Identify any fallacies or other problems in each of the following arguments or statements. Some items may be relatively free of problems.

▲ 1. My cousin uses a Dodge truck on his ranch; it has over 300,000 miles on the original engine. Obviously, Dodge really does build tough trucks.

2. Things are getting better all the time.

3. I ordered a packet of California watermelon seeds from Hansen Seed Company last year, and they germinated like crazy. I expect the seeds I ordered this year to sprout, too. Of course it's a little colder up here in Canada than it was in El Paso.

▲ 4. Poker? Nah, I don't like card games.

5. Drug abuse among pro athletes is unquestionably a serious and wide-spread problem. Why, last week three players from just one team said they used HGH!

6. Orange cats are easy to train. I had one once—Gross Kitty we called him—and you could teach that cat to ski if you wanted to.

▲ 7. You're gonna take a course from Toadstool? Two guys I know think he's terrible! He flunked both of them!

8. Most Americans favor a national lottery to reduce the federal debt, judging from a poll taken in Las Vegas where about 80 percent said they liked the idea.

9. Young people these days are too easily distracted by things. Just look at the kids in this class.

▲ 10. Most Ohio residents are worried about air quality. In a survey taken in Cleveland, more than half the respondents identified air pollution as the most significant environmental hazard.

Exercise 10-31

Identify any fallacies or other problems in each of the following arguments or statements. Some items may be relatively free of problems.

▲ 1. The IRS isn't interested in the big corporations, just middle-class taxpayers like you and me. I was audited last year—you ever hear of Exxon-Mobile getting nailed?

2. The weatherman on Channel 12 sure knows his stuff. I bet he knows a lot about global warming, too.

3. It's time to take back our government. Most Americans agree with that.

▲ 4. I wouldn't buy anything from Ace. The lawn mower I got there didn't work worth beans.

5. Border collies are way smarter than Rottweilers. I know: I've owned both.

6. Daniel showed me a photo of his sister yesterday; that girl is photogenic!

▲ 7. My Zenon plasma TV broke down three times in the first six month. It's a bad brand.

8. The dinner we had in Paris was great. I bet the food's great in London, too.

9. I liked watching *American Idol* last year; chances are I'll like it again this year.

▲   10. Did you know there's no Starbuck's in Pincus, Nebraska? I guess Starbuck's doesn't like the state.

11. Southwest doesn't assign seats. Leastwise they didn't on the flights I've taken.

12. You get what you pay for.

13. Charles cheated on his income tax. I bet he cheats on his wife.

Writing Exercises

1. Select one of the following general claims and explain how you might find out if it is true. Begin by making the generalization more precise by specifying a sampling frame, and then explain how you might select a sample from the frame. Alternatively, if you think you already have evidence the claim is true, produce an argument that supports it.

   Politicians can't be trusted.

   Government intrudes in our private lives/business affairs too much.

   Many welfare recipients take advantage of the system.

   Anyone who really wants a job can find one.

   College teachers are liberals.

   The super-wealthy don't pay much in taxes.

   The media are biased.

2. When everyone is finished, the instructor will redistribute everyone's paper to another member of the class. In groups of four or five, read the papers and select the best one to share with everyone in the class. Be prepared to explain why it is the best.

11

Causal Explanation

So far in this book, we have been talking mainly about arguments. Now it is time to say something about explanations.

Explanations and arguments are different things. You use arguments to support or demonstrate statements; you use explanations to elucidate something in one way or another. "In one way or another" can mean many things, including why something happened, how it happened, how it works, what it does, what will happen to it, what became of it, what can be done about it, why something isn't done about it, and many other things—really, the list is almost endless.

Although explanations and arguments are different things and serve different purposes, one source of confusion is that a sentence that can be used to explain something can also be used *in* an argument, either as a premise or as a conclusion. The statement "The puddle was caused by the leak in the toilet" might be the conclusion of an argument whose premise is "There wasn't a puddle until the toilet started leaking." Alternatively, it might be a premise in an argument that has the conclusion "Therefore, let's fix the toilet."

Students will learn to . . .

1. Differentiate between arguments and explanations

2. Recognize two important types of explanations

3. Apply standards for evaluating explanations

4. Apply methods for forming causal hypotheses

5. Learn methods for confirming causal hypotheses

6. Recognize mistakes in causal reasoning

7. Distinguish the concept of cause as it applies to law

Premise: There wasn't a puddle until the toilet started leaking.

Conclusion: Therefore the puddle was caused by the leak in the toilet.

Premise: The puddle was caused by the leak in the toilet.

Conclusion: Therefore let's fix the toilet.

TWO KINDS OF EXPLANATIONS

Many kinds of things need explaining, and it isn't surprising that many kinds of explanations exist. Here, we briefly explain two important and common types of explanations to help you recognize and understand an explanation when you see one.

Physical Causal Explanations

How did we get this flat tire?

What caused the puddle on the floor?

Why did the rocket explode?

How come I have high blood pressure?

Why is there so much snow this year?

What caused global warming?

Why did the dinosaurs die out?

Each of these questions asks for a causal explanation of an event or phenomenon that refers to its *physical* background. "Physical" here is used in the broad sense, which includes not only the domain of the discipline of physics but also those of chemistry, geology, biology, neuroscience, and the other natural sciences.

The physical background includes the general conditions under which the event occurred—in the case of the question about the rocket, for example, the physical background includes such meteorological facts as ambient temperature, atmospheric pressure, relative humidity, and so forth. However, these general conditions are usually left unstated in an explanation if they are normal for the situation; we simply take them for granted. It's when they are unusual that they might be worth noting. For example, if we have been driving on a blisteringly hot day, we might note that as a part of our explanation of the cause of our flat tire.

More important, the physical background of an event includes whatever events we determine to be the direct or immediate cause of the phenomenon in question. But there is a complication: More than one chain of causes contributes to an event's occurrence. For example, the home run clears the right-field fence; depending on our interests and knowledge, we might focus on the chain of causation that accounts for the *bat's* arrival at the point of impact; or, if we are students of pitching, we might focus on the causal chain that accounts for the *ball's* arrival. Our interests and knowledge also determine which link in a causal chain we identify as *the* cause of an event. Whether we say the home run's direct cause was a good swing, a bad pitch, or both depends on our interests; each way of putting it can be useful for different purposes.

Likewise, under many circumstances, a short explanation of the cause of an event may suffice. How did Moore get a flat tire? "There was a nail in it" would be enough of an explanation for many purposes. But under different circumstances, a more complete explanation may be required. If the tire had been in Moore's garage rather than on his van, he might require another link in the causal chain, one that explains how the nail got into the tire.

In short, what counts as an adequate physical causal explanation depends on our circumstances and needs, as we set forth in more detail following.

Behavioral Causal Explanations

Why did the union vote to approve the contract?

Why did Borkmiser veto the bill?

Why doesn't Schwarzenegger try to balance the budget?

Why are all southern states red states?

Why are butlers paid more if they have English accents?

Why does Adrian let his kids walk all over him?

What explains the popularity of text messaging?

Why does Britney Spears get so much attention?

What causes people to fight?

These are requests for behavioral causal explanations, explanations that attempt to elucidate the causes of behavior in terms of psychology, political science, sociology, history, economics, and other behavioral and social sciences. Also included as behavioral causal explanations are explanations for behavior in terms of "commonsense psychology," that is, in terms of reasons or motives. (In some contexts, it would be appropriate to distinguish reasons from motives, and both from causes, but for this discussion we need not do so.)

Like physical causal explanations, many behavioral causal explanations provide the relevant background information and, in addition, attempt to identify the immediate or direct cause of the behavior in question. In this case, however, the causal background is of a historical nature and includes political, economic, social, or psychological factors. Which factors are important depends on our interests and knowledge; one and the same event may have different explanations at the hands of psychologists, economists, historians, and sociologists. Why was Arnold Schwarzenegger elected governor of California? An explanation might talk about voters' reaction to his predecessor's policies, his popularity as an actor, or his persona. It makes little sense to suppose there is a single correct explanation of any instance of voluntary behavior.

Because behavior is less than fully predictable—at least given current knowledge—we should expect more exceptions to generalizations about behavior than to statements about regular occurrences in nature. We should similarly anticipate that theories of the behavioral and social sciences and history will be less rigid, more qualified, more probabilistic, and sometimes more philosophical than many physical theories. It would be incorrect to automatically regard this looseness as a shortcoming of a behavioral explanation.

Unlike physical causal explanations and other behavioral explanations, explanations of behavior in terms of an agent's motives or reasons make

Real Life

Behavioral Causal Explanations

Associated Press file, 2003

North Korea's march toward acquiring nuclear weapons could instigate an arms race in the Asia-Pacific region. Japan and South Korea have the capability to enter the nuclear-weapons club but have not done so because they have had confidence in the U.S. nuclear umbrella.

This photo's caption is a behavioral causal explanation, explained in this chapter.

reference not to the past but to the future. Why did Peter leave class early? He wanted to get home in time to watch *American Idol*. Why did the union vote not to approve the contract? The contract contained provisions that members thought diminished benefits. Why is the governor asking the legislature to approve a state lottery? Because she thinks it will decrease the need for new taxes. Explanations in terms of reasons and motives are forward looking, not backward looking.

One mistake is peculiar to this type of explanation—namely, failing to see the difference between *a reason* for doing something and *a particular person's reason* for doing it. Let's take a simple example: There might be a reason for aiding homeless people, but that reason might not be any particular person's reason for helping them. We have to be clear about whether we are requesting (or giving) reasons for doing something, or whether we are requesting (or giving) some individual person's reasons for doing it. When we give a reason for doing something, we are presenting an *argument* for doing it. When we cite an individual person's reason for doing it, we are *explaining* why she or he did it.

EXPLANATORY ADEQUACY: A RELATIVE CONCEPT

When is an explanation "adequate" or "satisfactory"? When does it get the job done? Obviously, this depends *entirely* on what one is looking for. If you want to know how to set up your computer, an explanation that leaves you wondering what to do next isn't satisfactory. An explanation of what happened to a missing acquaintance might be adequate for *your* interests but not for that person's parents. Even a simple phenomenon, like a puddle of water on the bathroom floor, can be explained in various ways, and which explanation is satisfactory depends on what you are looking for. Discovering that the puddle came from a leaking toilet would be enough for you to call a plumber, but if you wanted to fix the problem yourself, you'd want to know specifically where the toilet was leaking. Learning that the leak was caused by the wax sealing ring might be all you need to know to fix the problem, but maybe not. If you are interested in preventing future problems, you might want to know what caused the ring to leak in the first place. And there are various answers to the question of what caused the ring to leak, the "explanatory adequacy" of which again depends on your needs. "It leaked because it wasn't installed right" might be adequate if your interest is whether to submit the bill to the landlord. In an unusual circumstance, you might need an explanation that drilled down to the physical properties of wax. "Explanatory adequacy" is a relative concept that depends entirely on one's needs. Other phrases used to describe explanations, such as "complete," "useful," and "satisfactory," are also relative.

Nevertheless, certain minimal conditions must be met by every explanation if it is to be useful to someone. That an explanation cannot be *self-contradictory, vague, ambiguous,* or *incompatible with established fact or theory* perhaps goes without saying. That it cannot lead to *false predictions* is almost as obvious but raises a conceptual point worth examining more closely.

The Importance of Testability

A physical causal explanation generates expectations. If a leaking toilet explains the puddle, you expect the water to be cold. You expect the floor to remain dry if you fix the leak. If the reason your head cold didn't develop was that you took Zicam, you expect head colds not to develop in the future when you take Zicam. Such expectations are really predictions about the future. If an explanation generates predictions that turn out to be false, you reject it. If in the future there is no discernible improvement in your cold symptoms upon taking Zicam, you conclude that it doesn't work. If you fix the leak in the toilet and a few days later there is another puddle on the bathroom floor, you think that your first explanation probably wasn't correct or wasn't the whole story—or that you didn't do a good job fixing the problem. We test an explanation for correctness by seeing if the predictions it generates turn out to be true.

Nontestable Explanations

It's obvious that something is wrong with an explanation that leads to false predictions. Sometimes, however, an explanation generates meaningless predictions or (and this is not quite the same thing) no predictions at all. Such an explanation is said to be nontestable. Generating meaningless predictions or none is almost as bad as generating false predictions.

For example, suppose someone says that the reason butlers who speak with English accents get paid more is that "they give off good vibes." If this explanation were correct, then we would expect there to be more good vibes in a group of butlers with English accents than in a comparison group. Alternatively, one might expect to find a higher percentage of butlers with English accents in a group of butlers with good vibes. Unfortunately, we have no idea how to measure or even identify "good vibes." So it's not that our expectations aren't borne out, but rather that we have no way of telling if they are borne out. The problem with the explanation isn't that it is incorrect but that it is meaningless.

An explanation's correctness makes a difference in how the world is. If it is correct, then the world is one way; if it isn't, then the world is different. When you hear an explanation of the cause of something, you have to ask yourself the difference between the explanation's being correct and not being correct. Imagine that Uncle Charlie blames his heart problems on a sedentary life. If it is correct to say that a sedentary life causes heart problems, you would expect more heart problems among sedentary people than among active people. You would also expect to find a disproportionate number of sedentary people among those who have heart problems. If these predictions are borne out, you conclude that the explanation could well be correct; if they are not borne out, then you arrive at the opposite conclusion. Suppose, however, that Aunt Clara thinks that Uncle Charlie's heart problems are due to sins Uncle Charlie committed in a previous life. It would be unusual for Aunt Clara to think this, but not terribly so. We do occasionally hear people explaining misfortunes by attributing them to misdeeds in earlier incarnations. What predictions are generated by Aunt Clara's theory? Well, if it is true that past-life sins cause heart problems, we would expect to find more heart problems among past-life sinners than among people who did not sin in their past lives. We would also expect to find a disproportionate number of past-life sinners among people with heart problems. Immediately, we see a problem: Who is a past-life sinner? We cannot identify them. In fact, we cannot even identify people who have *had* past lives—regardless of whether they sinned. Since more people are alive now than at any time in the past, not everyone has had a past life in human form, and there is no way of distinguishing those who did from those who did not. This problem is somewhat different from the "good vibes" problem in that "good vibes" suffers from vagueness in the way in which "has had a past life" doesn't. We aren't sure exactly what counts as a "good vibe." We understand, or think we understand, what it would be to have had a past life and in it to have sinned, but we can't tell which people fall into these categories. The problem with the past life theory is that we can't tell whether it is true, whereas the problem with the "good vibes" theory is that we don't know what its being true would look like. Neither explanation, however, generates testable predictions.

Some predictions, of course, are difficult or even impossible to test due to practical limitations. Present instruments may not be sensitive enough to make certain kinds of measurements, for example. While it may be disappointing that a hypothesis isn't testable due to practical limitations, it isn't a mark against the correctness of the hypothesis. It's when a hypothesis is untestable in principle that we should abandon it.

In the Media

Scientists: Warming Could Kill Two-Thirds of World's Polar Bears

"Global warming" refers to increases in average temperatures in global temperature databases over the past one hundred years. In figuring out the causes of observed global warming, among other methods scientists use computer models of the climate. They compare observed changes in the climate to changes projected from various causes by the computer models; the possible causes whose projections best match the observations provide the likeliest explanation of the observation. Think of the various possible causes (increased concentration of greenhouse gases in the atmosphere and solar variation, among others) as hypotheses that generate alternative predictions; if one hypothesis generates more accurate predictions than another, it is a likelier hypothesis.

Most predictions we read about in the newspaper—rising sea levels, melting polar ice caps, altered rainfall patterns, more violent hurricanes, and so forth—are a different kind of prediction. They are what computer models project will happen to climate in the future under various scenarios. The prediction that warming will kill the polar bears is an inference from projected reductions in sea ice and livable habitat.

The two kinds of predictions—those generated by possible explanations of a phenomenon and those generated by the phenomenon itself—are logically distinct. The hypothesis that the puddle on the bathroom floor was caused by a leaking toilet generates predictions such as that the puddle will be cold and won't recur if the toilet is fixed. Not doing something about the puddle generates a different sort of prediction, such as that the vinyl will be stained or the subflooring damaged.

A mother polar bear and her cub sleep near the ice outside Churchill, Canada, Nov. 4, 2006. Computer predictions of a dramatic decline of sea ice in regions of the Arctic are confirmed by actual observations, according to scientists for the National Oceanic and Atmospheric Administration.

Circular Explanations

A circular explanation is one that simply restates itself. "Why do butlers who speak with English accents get paid more? Because they earn more money." "Why is the floor wet? Because there is water on it." Because these explanations simply repeat that which they are supposed to be explaining, they don't generate meaningful predictions.

Unnecessary Complexity

For good reason, unnecessary complexity is considered undesirable in an explanation. It is easy to see why, if we forget about causal explanations for the moment and think of two explanations of how to do something, such as, say, build a fence. If one explanation instructs you to randomly pound nails into a piece of wood that has nothing to do with the fence, you'd be better off going with the other explanation—assuming both explanations are just as good in other respects.

In a similar way, if two *causal* explanations do an equally good job of explaining something, the least complicated explanation is preferable. An explanation that is unnecessarily complex contains elements in which there is no reason to believe. It makes assumptions that aren't really necessary. Here is an example:

> Why is there a puddle on the floor? Because both the toilet and the roof leaked.

This explanation is unnecessarily complicated.

It is *possible* that the roof and toilet both leak (in which case the example is a case of necessary complexity rather than the opposite). However, unless there is reason to suppose the leaking toilet doesn't entirely explain the puddle, it isn't necessary to assume the roof also leaks.

Explaining Uncle Charlie's health as punishment for something he did in a prior life also qualifies as unnecessarily complex. It raises difficult and entirely unnecessary questions: How did he get from the previous life to this one? Who or what is punishing Uncle Charlie? There are simpler ways of explaining Uncle Charlie's health issues.

In summary, what qualifies as an adequate explanation depends on one's needs, but at a minimum an explanation should

- be consistent
- not conflict with established fact or theory
- be testable
- not be circular
- avoid unnecessary assumptions or other unnecessary complexities

The following exercises will help you to distinguish explanations from arguments, identify physical causal explanations and behavioral causal explanations, and give you practice looking for breakdowns in explanatory adequacy.

Exercise 11-1

Which of the following state or imply cause/effect?

1. Smith's being healthy is probably what made Philadelphia more competitive this year.
2. Dress warmly! It's windy out there.
3. Gilbert's disposition has deteriorated since he and his wife separated; it isn't coincidence.

▲   4. Senator Craig's behavior forced conservatives to call for his resignation.

5. Getting a new trumpet player certainly improved the brass sections.

6. When men wear swimsuits, they have difficulty doing math problems.

▲   7. Despite the injuries, the Dolphins kept winning. It must have something to do with their positive attitude.

8. Too little sleep slows down your reaction time.

9. Women are worse drivers than men.

▲ 10. Why does Chaz remove the paper towels from the kitchen before his mother-in-law visits? He's a creep.

11. Randomized clinical trials produced unbiased data on the benefits of drugs.

12. The batteries in this dang flashlight are completely dead!

▲ 13. This flashlight won't work because the batteries are completely dead.

14. Believe me, the batteries in that flashlight are dead. Try it. You'll see.

15. Aunt Clara thinks her prayers cured Uncle Pete. [Caution!]

▲ 16. The risk of having a heart attack is 33 percent higher in the winter than in the summer in Philadelphia.

What is the cause and what is the effect in each of the following?   **Exercise 11-2**

▲   1. The cat won't eat, so Mrs. Quibblebuck searches her mind for a reason. "Now, could it be," she muses, "that I haven't heard mice scratching around in the attic lately?" "That's the explanation," she concludes.

2. Each time one of the burglaries occurred, observers noticed a red Mustang in the vicinity. The police, of course, suspect the occupants are responsible.

3. Violette is a strong Cowboys fan. Because of her work schedule, however, she has been able to watch their games only twice this season, and they lost both times. She resolves not to watch any more. "It's bad luck," she decides.

▲   4. Giving the little guy more water could have prevented him from getting dehydrated, said Ms. Delacruz.

5. OAXACA, Mexico (AP)—Considered by many to be Mexico's culinary capital, this city took on McDonald's and won, keeping the hamburger giant out of its colonial plaza by passing around tamales in protest.

6. Eating fish or seafood at least once a week lowers the risk of developing dementia, researchers have found.

▲   7. It has long puzzled researchers why people cannot detect their own bad breath. One theory is that people get used to the odor.

8. Researchers based at McDuff University put thirty young male smokers on a three-month program of vigorous exercise. One year later, only 14 percent of them still smoked. An equivalent number of young male smokers who did not go through the exercise program were also checked after a year, and it was found that 60 percent still smoked. The experiment is regarded as supporting the theory that exercise helps chronic male smokers kick the habit.

9. The stronger the muscles, the greater the load they take off the joint, thus limiting damage to the cartilage, which explains why leg exercise helps prevent osteoarthritis.

▲ 10. Many judges in Oregon will not process shoplifting, trespassing, and small-claims charges. This saves the state a lot of money in court expenses.

Exercise 11-3

Divide these statements into two groups of five each, based on a distinction mentioned in this chapter.

▲ 1. The air is smoky because that house is on fire.

2. That house is on fire because the air is smoky.

3. She had a great workout because she is sweating.

▲ 4. She is sweating because she had a good workout.

5. He has indigestion because he ate something harmful.

6. He ate something harmful because he has indigestion.

▲ 7. She is late because she had car trouble.

8. She had car trouble because she is late.

9. It is late because the bars are closed.

▲ 10. The bars are closed because it is late.

Exercise 11-4

Some of the following items would normally be seen as arguments others as explanations. Sort the items into the proper categories.

▲ 1. Why am I crying? I am crying because you never remember my birthday.

2. If I were you, I wouldn't wear an outfit like that. It makes you look too old.

3. The Eagles will never make a comeback. They just don't appeal to today's younger crowd.

▲ 4. Steph won't wear outfits like that because she thinks they are tacky.

5. My toe hurts because I stubbed it.

6. The board has lost faith in the president. Why else would they ask her to resign?

▲ 7. If I were you, I wouldn't open a furniture store here, because students give away furniture every spring.

8. Most people like freestone peaches more than clingstone because they are easier to eat.

9. Around here, people don't take no for an answer. Just ask anyone.

▲ 10. Dr. York flunks people because he is a crank.

Exercise 11-5

Some of the following items would normally be seen as arguments and others as explanations. Sort the items into the proper categories.

▲ 1. Collins will probably be absent again today. She seemed pretty sick when I saw her.

2. Yes, I know Collins is sick, and I know why: She ate raw seafood.

3. Did Bobbie have a good time last night? Are you kidding? She had a great time! She stayed up all night, she had such a great time.

▲ 4. You don't think the toilet leaks? Why, just look at the water on the floor. What else could have caused it?

5. You know, it occurs to me the reason the band sounded so bad is the new director. They haven't had time to get used to her.

6. What a winter! And to think it's all just because there's a bunch of warm water off the Oregon coast.

▲ 7. Hmmm. I'm pretty sure you have the flu. If you had a cold, you wouldn't have aches and a fever. Aches and fever are a sign you have the flu.

8. Secretary Clinton goes up and down in the opinion polls. That's 'cause sometimes she makes sense, and other times she sounds crazy.

9. VIKKI: Remember the California Raisins? What happened to them?
   NIKKI: They faded. I guess people got tired of them or something.

▲ 10. Believe it or not, for a while there, a lot of young women were shaving their heads. It was probably the Britney Spears influence.

11. Couples that regard each other as equal are more likely to suffer from high blood pressure than are couples in which one perceives the other as dominant. This is an excellent reason for marrying someone you think is beneath you.

12. Couples that regard each other as equal are more likely to suffer from high blood pressure than are couples in which one perceives the other as dominant. This is apparently because couples who see their partners as an equal argue more, and that raises their blood pressure.

Divide the following ten items into two groups, based on a distinction covered early in this chapter.   **Exercise 11-6**

▲ 1. The reason we're so late? The car wouldn't start.

2. The reason we're so late? We wanted to visit the Simpsons.

3. The Meisters bought a new dishwasher because the old one stopped working.

▲ 4. Their dishwasher stopped working because the drain was clogged.

5. Her health problems resulted from exposure to secondhand smoke.

6. She was exposed to secondhand smoke because her parents weren't aware of the danger.

▲ 7. The planning commission approved the new subdivision because the developers enlarged lot sizes.

8. The developers enlarged lot sizes because they wanted their plans approved.

9. The tree damaged the roof by falling on it.

▲ 10. Thanks to the strong winds, the tree fell on the roof.

Exercise 11-7   Which of the following are physical causal explanations and which are behavioral causal explanations?

▲ 1. The reason the car won't start? Bad battery, I expect.

2. Why doesn't Sue like Joe anymore? She doesn't think much of his new friends.

3. We are in a recession because consumers aren't spending as much as they used to.

▲ 4. The reason consumers aren't spending as much as they used to is they are afraid the economy is getting worse.

5. Professor Snark gave a test on Friday because he wanted to surprise everyone.

6. People worship God because they are afraid of dying.

▲ 7. The hot weather we've been having is due to global warming.

8. Lightning started the fire.

9. Backpacking isn't popular these days, because people want more action in their sports.

▲ 10. The reason you can't sleep is all the coffee you drink.

Exercise 11-8   For each of the following, identify the presumed cause and the presumed effect. Then identify which items contain or imply a causal claim, hypothesis, or explanation that isn't testable. If an item falls into that category, decide whether the problem is due to vagueness, circularity, or some other problem.

▲ 1. What causes your engine to miss? Perhaps a fouled spark plug?

2. Antonio had a run of hard luck, but that's to be expected if you throw a chain letter away.

3. Petunia is grouchy because she doesn't sleep well.

▲ 4. Divine intervention can cure cancer.

5. The CIA destroyed the files because they didn't want agents identified.

6. Having someone pray for you can cure cancer.

▲ 7. Having your mother pray for you brings good luck.

8. Oatmeal lowers cholesterol.

9. Why did Claudius get the flu? Because he's susceptible to it, obviously.

▲ 10. Federer won the match mainly because Roddick couldn't return his serve.

11. Federer won the match because he wanted to win more than Roddick did.

12. The reason Tuck can play high notes so well is that he has command of the upper register.

13. Professor York's French is improving, thanks to his trips to Paris.

▲ 14. "Men are biologically weaker than women and that's why they don't live as long."

—attributed to "a leading expert" by the Weekly World News

15. Smoking marijuana can cause lung cancer.

For each of the following, identify the presumed cause and the presumed effect. Then identify which items contain or imply a causal claim, hypothesis, or explanation that isn't testable. If an item falls into that category, decide whether the problem is due to vagueness, circularity, or some other problem. If you see some other problem, raise your hand and tell everybody what it is.

Exercise 11-9

▲ 1. He has blue eyes because he had them in a previous incarnation.

   2. The Pacers did much better in the second half. That's because they gained momentum.

   3. Alcoholics can't give up drinking, because they are addicted to liquor.

▲ 4. *Gone with the Wind* was a big hit only because reviewers praised it.

   5. Monfort, you want to know why you have so much bad luck? It's because you want to have bad luck. You have a subconscious desire for bad luck.

   6. Why do I like Budweiser? Maybe I was subjected to subliminal advertising.

▲ 7. This part of the coast is subject to mudslides because there's a lack of mature vegetation.

   8. As Internet use grew, insurance costs fell. The Internet apparently drove insurance prices down.

   9. Within eleven months of September 11, 2001, eleven men connected to bioterror and germ warfare died in strange and violent circumstances. Don't tell me that's coincidence!

▲ 10. When his dog died, Hennley was so upset he could hardly eat. In my opinion, he was transferring his grief from his mother's death to his dog's.

   11. Why does she sleep so late? Obviously, she's just one of those people who have a hard time waking up in the morning.

   12. When parapsychologist Susan Blackmore failed to find evidence of ESP in numerous experiments, *Fate* magazine's consulting editor D. Scott Rogo explained her negative results as due to subconscious resistance to the idea that psychic phenomena exist.

   —reported in The Skeptical Inquirer

   13. According to a report in *Weekly World News*, when tourists defied an ancient curse and took rocks home from Hawaii's Volcanoes National Park, they paid the consequences. According to the report, the curse caused a Michigan man to tumble to his death falling downstairs, a Massachusetts woman to lose her savings in the stock market, and a Canadian tourist to die in a head-on car accident.

   14. Why is there so much violence these days? Rap music, that's why.

   15. The reason I got into so much trouble as a kid was that my father was a heavy drinker.

   16. According to Martin Gardner, in Shivpuri, a village in India, there is a large stone ball weighing about 140 pounds. It is possible for five men to stand around the ball and touch the lower half with a forefinger; if they recite a prayer while doing so, the ball rises. Some believe this is a miracle of Allah.

FORMING HYPOTHESES

A statement to the effect that X causes or caused Y can be offered as a *hypothesis* rather than as a claim. A **hypothesis** is a causal explanation offered for further investigation or testing. When you hypothesize, you aren't yet stating an explanation; you are offering what you think is a likely explanation.

Often, when we are concerned with the cause of something, our reasoning falls into two parts: (1) forming a hypothesis and (2) testing the hypothesis. These are separate and distinct activities (though they involve overlapping principles). If the car won't start, we first think of possible causes; those that seem most likely we offer as hypotheses. We then test them if we can. In real life, when a car won't start, it's usually either because the battery is dead or because the cables are loose; if we find a loose cable, it seems the most likely cause, and we test this hypothesis by tightening the cable and trying to start the car.

The general strategy for arriving at the most likely hypothesis is sometimes called **Inference to the Best Explanation.** As an example, the puddle on the bathroom floor might be explained by a leaking roof, by a leaking toilet, or by somebody's having left a block of ice on the floor. But the leaking roof and melted ice theories don't explain the fact that the side of the toilet is damp; plus, perhaps, we can't see how ice could have gotten into the bathroom in the first place. In light of these considerations, we infer that the best explanation is that a leaking toilet caused the water on the floor. We then test the hypothesis by fixing the toilet and seeing what happens.

Sometimes it is difficult to find a hypothesis that explains all the facts. In the infamous O. J. Simpson murder trial, many facts seemed best explained by the hypothesis that Simpson's ex-wife, Nicole Brown Simpson, and her friend Ronald Goldman were murdered by Simpson. At the same time, a few facts seemed incompatible with this explanation and suggested an alternative hypothesis, that Simpson had been framed. The jury apparently did not think the Simpson-did-it hypothesis explained all the recalcitrant facts, and they acquitted Simpson.

Sometimes, due to practical considerations, it is difficult or impossible to definitively test a hypothesis; in such cases, we are forced to accept the hypothesis just because it is the best explanation we have. However, it is probably better to think of inference to the best explanation as a method of forming hypotheses rather than a method for confirming them.

In what follows, we shall explain four common methods used in forming hypotheses. As we shall eventually see, a rigorous application of a combination of two of them (the Method of Difference and the Method of Agreement) is used to confirm hypotheses.

The Method of Difference

Coming up with causal hypotheses requires ingenuity and clear thinking. If something unusual happens and we want to know what caused it, and if we then find that something else unusual has happened, we should suspect that as the possible cause. If you suddenly get sick after eating sushi for the first time, a reasonable hypothesis is that the sushi caused you to get sick. If the car won't start after you have been working on it, a reasonable hypothesis is that you did something that caused it not to start.

In Depth

Global Warming and Hypothesis Forming

The most widely accepted explanation of the rise in global temperatures is that it is primarily due to an increase in the concentration of greenhouse gases resulting from human activity. The greenhouse gas explanation illustrates the methodology we have been talking about in this chapter.

Speaking very generally and omitting much detail, the story goes like this. Something happens (global temperatures increase) that requires explanation. Scientists employ the Method of Difference and ask, What else is different? The greenhouse effect is well established in science and confirmed in everyday experience. Guided by this background knowledge, scientists hypothesize that the warming is due to an increase in the concentration of greenhouse-effect-producing gases. The hypothesis generates predictions, such as what data from ice cores and computer models of climate will show. These predictions do not show a perfect match with observations, but they show a better match than do projections from alternative explanations. Using the Best Diagnosis method (see page 406), that global warming is primarily due to increased concentrations of greenhouse gases becomes the best explanation of the phenomenon in question.

Following John Stuart Mill, a famous nineteenth-century English philosopher and logician, we might call this way of coming up with a causal hypothesis the **Method of Difference.** If something happens that hasn't happened in similar situations, look for some other difference between the two situations and consider whether it might not be the cause. If you wake up one morning with a splitting headache, and you remember doing something different the night before, such as reading in poor light, you should suspect it had something to do with the headache.

As mentioned above, a rigorous application of the Method of Difference in combination with the next method is used not merely to suggest a causal hypothesis but to confirm it—as you shall see in a bit.

The Method of Agreement

A correlation between two phenomena provides another good starting point for causal hypothesizing. One type of correlation is that in which occurrences of one event are accompanied by occurrences of another: The two events are said to be *associated*. If from time to time you get migraine headaches, naturally you look for something else that always precedes them. If you noticed that, say, each time you had a headache, you had eaten a bacon sandwich a few hours earlier, you'd consider the possibility that the bacon sandwich caused the headaches.

If the azaleas bloom prolifically in some years, and in other years they don't, you look for an association between the good-bloom years (or the poor-bloom years) and another phenomenon. If the good-bloom years are associated with a particular pruning technique, you suspect that as a possible cause.

One summer, every Saturday evening mosquitoes swarmed in the backyard of one author, making it unpleasant to be out there. What was it about Saturday evenings? What did they have in common, the author wondered? It dawned on him that he also mowed the grass late on Saturday afternoons; the association between the grass mowing and the mosquito problem suggested the hypothesis that mowing the grass stirred up the mosquitoes.

As we write this, scientists are trying to explain "colony collapse disorder"—an affliction of honeybee colonies in which bees simply fly off from their colonies and disappear forever. Are the afflicted colonies all near cell-phone towers? Is the same type of pesticide used around the hives? Are the colonies near genetically altered plants? So far, no associations between abandoned hives and other possible factors have been found; but if one is, it will be plausible to suspect it as a possible cause of colony collapse. In general, when we want to find the cause of some phenomenon that has multiple occurrences, an association with some other phenomenon is a reasonable starting point for causal hypothesizing.

Another type of correlation also provides a good jumping-off point for causal hypothesizing. **Covariation** is the term for when variation in one phenomenon is accompanied by variation in another. The covariation between atmospheric CO_2 and global warming suggests a causal linkage between the two. When tobacco companies spend more money on cigarette ads, smoking rates increase. The covariation suggests that causation may be present.

We can refer to this method of generating causal hypotheses as the **Method of Agreement:** If an effect present in multiple situations is associated with or covaries with some other phenomenon, there may be a causal link between the two phenomena.*

It should be clear that causal links suggested by correlation are only *possible* links: a boy's hair gets longer as he learns the multiplication table, but there is no causal link between them. Skiing accidents increase as Christmas sales pick up, but there is no causal connection. At best, association and covariation only suggest a causal hypothesis; they don't confirm it.

In fact, thinking that a correlation or covariation between two variables *proves* that one causes the other is a mistake in logic, a fallacy that even has a Latin name: ***cum hoc, ergo propter hoc*** ("with that, therefore because of that").

Another infamous Latin phrase used to depict a logical fallacy is ***post hoc, ergo propter hoc*** ("after that, therefore because of that"). This mistake occurs when one thinks that the mere fact that one event *preceded* another event proves that the earlier event caused the later one. Suppose, for example, you get a headache, and the only other thing you can remember that was out of the ordinary is that you ate sushi beforehand: It is reasonable to *hypothesize* that the sushi caused the headache. But thinking that the circumstance *confirms* that the sushi caused the headache is reasoning incorrectly: *post hoc, ergo propter hoc*.

According to a report in the *Journal of the American Medical Association,* infants who are breastfed have higher IQs later in life.

Maybe parents with higher IQs are more aware of the health advantages of breastfeeding and as a result are more likely to breastfeed their children.

The moment that declaration was made, oil prices jumped over $18 a barrel.

—*Post hoc, ergo propter hoc* from SENATOR JOSEPH BIDEN, criticizing a U.S. Senate resolution declaring the IRG (Iranian Revolutionary Guard) a terrorist organization.

---

*Mill thought of the Method of Agreement as using an association between two phenomena as an indicator of causation. He spoke of the Method of Concomitant Variation as using covariation between two phenomena as an indicator of causation. We refer to both as the Method of Agreement.

Causal Mechanisms and Background Knowledge

To utilize the Method of Difference and the Method of Agreement for developing causal hypotheses, you have to use common sense and your background knowledge of what causes what and how things work. Eating sushi probably wasn't the only unusual thing that happened before you acquired a headache: On your way to the restaurant, for example, a raccoon might have crossed your path. Now, it isn't plausible to think that a raccoon crossing your path could cause a headache. Why isn't it plausible? Because, given normal experience, one cannot see *how* a raccoon crossing your path *could* cause a headache. One cannot conceive of a "causal mechanism."

The concept of a causal mechanism derives from the philosophy of science and research methodology in the social sciences, but we can describe a **causal mechanism** metaphorically as an interface between a cause and an effect—an apparatus, if you want to think of it that way—that has the property of making the effect happen, given the cause. Where there is no causal mechanism between X and Y, if Y happens after X, it is due to coincidence rather than causation.

Famously, the hemlines on women's skirts are said to covary with the stock market: As hemlines get longer, the stock market declines. Equally famously, as nonemployment decreases, the stock market declines. The idea that decreasing nonemployment could cause the stock market to *decline* is surprising but not as implausible as the idea that lengthening hemlines could cause it to decline. The latter idea is not plausible, because one cannot see how the length of hemlines *could* affect stock prices: One cannot picture a causal interface between the two things. The first hypothesis—that increasing employment causes the stock market to decline—is more plausible because one can at least imagine how this could work: Increasing employment has an inflationary effect, which in turn causes the Federal Reserve to tighten credit, which depresses the value of stocks.

In the Media

Working at Night to Be Listed as "Probable" Cause of Cancer

According to a report by Maria Cheng of the Associated Press, the World Health Organization will soon add working on overnight shifts as a probable carcinogen. That the night shift could be right there along with UV radiation and diesel exhaust fumes as a probable cause of cancer is pretty surprising. But when we think up explanatory hypotheses, we should be *guided* by our background knowledge of what causes what and how things work, not *chained* by it. (Actually, the idea that the night shift can cause cancer isn't so terribly surprising: the hormone melatonin, which can suppress tumors, is normally produced at night.)

In real life, we probably do not even begin to look for correlations as suggesting causation, except where a causal mechanism can be conceived. From our background knowledge, we can see how pesticides or cell-phone radiation might harm a bee colony; consequently, we look first for that kind of correlation rather than just any old correlation. Research indicates that people do indeed look first for plausible causal mechanisms rather than for correlations when hypothesizing about possible causes.*

What this boils down to is this: In forming causal hypotheses, in order to reduce the field of possible causes to a manageable size, one must rely on one's background knowledge about what sorts of things could cause other things. This is the way science, too, works. It builds on past understandings and doesn't start off from square one on each new occasion.

The Best Diagnosis Method

Often, finding a hypothesis is likened to assembling the pieces of a puzzle so as to create an overall picture, or solving a crime by considering clues, or—and this is our favorite analogy—diagnosing symptoms of a medical condition. You go to a physician about numbness in a leg. The doctor asks a series of questions: Exactly where in the leg is the numbness? When did it begin? Did it begin suddenly? Is it worse at some times of the day? Do you experience it in the other leg? Does it depend on your activities or the position of the leg? Have you been injured? Do you smoke? Do you have a history of high blood pressure? Are you experiencing other unusual symptoms? The doctor also considers such factors as your age, lifestyle, medical history, and the medical history of your family. The investigation discloses various symptoms (or their absence): Some of them might possibly be associated with a neurological condition, another with an orthopedic condition, perhaps another with a psychiatric condition, and so forth. The physician tries to ascertain the strongest associations and then diagnoses the patient's condition accordingly. The diagnosis is the physician's causal hypothesis. It represents the physician's idea of the best explanation of the various symptoms and other information.

Let's call this approach to forming causal hypotheses the **Best Diagnosis Method** of forming causal hypotheses, to distinguish it from the Method of Difference and the Method of Agreement. A murder has been committed, and investigators have narrowed the field to three possible suspects. Bullets from Adams's gun killed the victim, and Adams turns out to have lied about his whereabouts at the time of the murder. But Adams was a good friend of the victim, and investigators cannot discern a motive. Brady, on the other hand, owed the victim money, was known to have threatened him, and had access to Adams's gun; but he has an alibi. Cox was seen in the vicinity of the murder at the time it happened, knew the victim, and also might have had access to Adams's gun; but he has no apparent motive. As in the medical case, the investigators try to come up with the best "diagnosis" for a series of "symptoms": the diagnosis, as in the medical case described earlier, rests heavily on known or suspected associations between "symptoms" and "disease." The "disease" here is murder, and the "symptoms" are such things as being linked to the murder weapon, knowing the victim, having been seen at the crime scene, having a reason to kill the victim, lying about one's whereabouts, and so forth.

---

*See, for example, <http://www.ncbi.nlm.nih.gov/sites/entrez?db=pubmed&uid=7720361&cmd=showdetailview&indexed=google>.

Adams exhibits some of these "symptoms," Cox and Brady exhibit others. And, when Brady's alibi collapses, the investigators move Brady's name to the top of their list of suspects.

Which diagnosis is the best? There is no abstract answer to that, except "the one that gets confirmed" (see the next section, "General Causal Claims"). But you can see that the best diagnosis is not necessarily the one that explains the most "symptoms." Symptoms vary in their importance. In forming a "diagnosis" (hypothesis) about a murder, fingerprints on the murder weapon cannot be overlooked, but lying to a policeman might be. In the murder of Nicole Brown Simpson and Ronald Goldman, a limousine driver, Allan Park, told investigators he could not contact anyone on the intercom at O. J. Simpson's gate around the time Brown and Goldman were murdered. This fact, though important, was (we assume) less important to investigators than that there was a glove outside Brown's condo with Simpson's and both victims' blood mixed on it.

As you can also see, one relies on one's background knowledge to guide one when using this method for developing causal hypotheses. Physicians will be better than most at finding the causes of medical conditions, police investigators better than most at solving crimes, and historians better than most at explaining historical events. And our own causal hypothesizing will be best in whatever areas we end up knowing best.

As a final point about the Best Diagnosis Method, you might note how it is used for developing hypotheses about everything from the cause of the universe to why the car won't start. Many of those who believe in God, for example, do so because the existence of God seems to them the best "diagnosis" for such things as love and morality, the emergence of life, the complexity and vastness of the cosmos, the seeming presence of overall design, the wording of sacred texts, apparent miracles, and so forth. At the other extreme, the car won't start, and your shift at McDonald's starts in twenty minutes. Using the Method of Difference, you look for something else that is different about the car besides the fact that it won't start. Unfortunately, as invariably happens, there is more than one "difference," more than one thing out of the norm: The car won't start, plus you heard funny clickity-click sounds when you started the car the night before, it is unusually cold out, the lights are dim, you just filled up with

On Language

The Wrong Initials Can Shorten Your Life

Researchers at the University of California, San Diego, looking at twenty-seven years of California death certificates, found that men with "indisputably positive" initials like JOY and WOW and ACE and GOD and WIN and VIP lived 4.48 years longer than a control group of men with neutral initials and ambiguous initials, like DAM and WET and RAY and SUN, that had both positive and negative interpretations. Further, men with "plainly negative" initials like ASS or DUD died on average 2.8 years earlier than did the men in the control group.

As an exercise, propose an explanation for these findings that isn't defective in terms of the criteria discussed in this chapter. Explain how you would test the explanation.

a new brand of gas, you noted a strange odor when you tried starting the car, you just installed a new battery, you started trying to charge your cell phone in the car (and it wasn't charging very well), a radio was installed the week before, and so forth. Using your understanding of how things work and what sorts of things can cause other things, you look for the correct diagnosis of the various facts: What "disease" is associated with these "symptoms"? The obvious diagnosis, of course, is that the battery is weak. Notice that some of the symptoms don't fit that diagnosis, may even conflict with it, just as some of the evidence in the Brown-Goldman murders didn't mesh with the Simpson diagnosis and just as, perhaps, some of your numbness symptoms did not quite square with the diagnosis your doctor thought was best.

Once upon a time, the authors' good friend Maureen* experienced various mysterious occurrences in her household. One morning, Maureen found an empty milk bottle on her living room floor; the next night, eerie clanging came from her garage; shortly thereafter, one of her children went into the bathroom in the middle of the night and found the bathtub mysteriously filled with water and—pillows. The eeriest occurrence was the night Maureen was awakened by the phone ringing on the nightstand. When she checked the caller ID, she found that the call had originated from her own cell phone, which was also lying on the nightstand.

Maureen thought she might need an exorcist; what she really needed was a "diagnosis" for these various "symptoms," a hypothesis that would make sense of them. Fortunately, she found one.**

The following exercises will help you recognize the Method of Difference and Method of Agreement, will give you practice understanding causal mechanisms and using your causal background knowledge, and will provide you with an opportunity to form a causal hypothesis.

Exercise 11-10

Identify each reasoning pattern as (a) the Method of Difference or (b) the Method of Agreement.

1. Pat never had trouble playing that passage before. I wonder what the problem is. It must have something to do with the piano she just bought.

2. Sometimes the fishing is pretty good here; sometimes it isn't. When I try to pin down why, it seems like the only variable is the wind. For some reason, wind keeps the fish from biting.

3. Gas prices have gone up by 40 cents a gallon in the past three weeks. It all started when they had that refinery fire down there in Texas. Must have depleted the supplies.

4. Whenever we have great roses like this, it's always been after a long period of cloudy weather. Must be they don't like direct sun.

5. All of a sudden, he's all "Let's go to Beano's for a change." Right. Am I supposed to think it's just coincidence his old girlfriend started working there?

---

*Not her real name.
**Maureen had been sleepwalking.

6. You really want to know what gets me and makes me be so angry? It's you! You and your stupid habit of never closing your closet door.

▲ 7. Why in heck am I so tired today? Must be all the studying I did last night. Thinking takes energy.

8. The computer isn't working again. Every time it happens, the dang kids have been playing with it. Why can't they just use the computers they have down at school?

9. What makes your dog run away from time to time? I bet it has to do with that garbage you feed him. You want him to stay home? Feed him better dog food.

▲ 10. I'll tell you what caused all these kids to take guns to school and shoot people. Every single one of them liked to play violent videogames; that's what caused it.

11. Gag! What did you do to this coffee, anyway—put Ajax in it?

12. Can you beat that? I set this battery on the garage floor last night, and this morning it was dead. I guess the old saying about cement draining a battery is still true.

▲ 13. Clinton was impeached. Then his standing went up in the opinion polls. Just goes to show: No publicity is bad publicity.

14. Why did the dog yelp? Are you serious? You'd yelp, too, if someone stomped on your foot.

15. Freddy certainly seems more at peace with himself these days. I guess psychotherapy worked for him.

16. Whenever we have people over, the next morning the bird is all squawky and grumpy. The only thing I can figure is it must not get enough sleep when we have company.

17. The mower worked fine last week, and now it won't even start. Could letting it stand out in the rain have something to do with that?

18. Every time Greg plays soccer, his foot starts hurting. It also hurts when he jogs. But when he rides his bike, he doesn't have a problem. It must be the pounding that causes the problem.

19. You know, all of a sudden she started acting cold? She didn't like it when I told her I was going to play poker with you guys.

20. Your Suburban is hard to start. Mine starts right up. You always use Chevron; I use Texaco. You'd better switch to Texaco.

Use your understanding of what causes what and how things work to answer the following questions. There is not necessarily a correct answer, but interesting controversies may be suitable for class discussion.

Exercise 11-11

▲ 1. Do any of these explanations or any combination of them seem better or worse as an explanation of why more people come down with flu in the winter? Can you think of a better explanation?

   a. In winter, people wear warmer clothes.
   b. Flu viruses survive longer in cold air.
   c. More hot chocolate is consumed in winter.
   d. People stay indoors more and are in closer proximity to one another.

2. Reportedly, obesity among American children is increasing. Do any of these explanations seem better or worse?

   a. Children are eating more.
   b. Children are eating more fast food.
   c. Text messaging takes up so much time, kids have no time left for exercise.
   d. It's getting too hot to exercise, thanks to global warming.

3. In a recent study of more than 40,000 Japanese adults, it was found that those who drank lots of green tea were less likely to die from cardiovascular disease than were those who drank only a little. Do any of these explanations of that result seem better or worse?

   a. Green tea may be more popular than black tea.
   b. Green tea is better for your health than black tea is.
   c. Green tea is known to contain more antioxidants than black tea.
   d. Green-tea drinkers may be more likely to eat fruits and vegetables.

▲ 4. Japanese are less likely than Americans to die of stroke. Do any of these explanations seem better or worse?

   a. Japanese people drink more green tea.
   b. Japanese people eat more sushi.
   c. NASCAR racing is more popular in America than in Japan.
   d. Americans spend more time mowing lawns.

5. There is a strong association between lack of sleep and depression. Do any of these explanations seem better or worse?

   a. Sleeplessness causes depression.
   b. Depression causes sleeplessness.
   c. Sleeplessness and depression may both result from some underlying cause.

6. When Horace thinks of doing a dusty job like vacuuming his car or sweeping out the garage, he almost always sneezes. Do any of these explanations seem better or worse?

   a. Thinking of dust causes Horace to sneeze.
   b. A sneeze coming on makes Horace think of dust.
   c. It is probably just coincidence.

▲ 7. Every spring and summer, increased snow-cone consumption is correlated with each of the following. Which correlations may involve cause and effect?

   a. Increased number of drownings
   b. Increased sales of swimsuits
   c. Increased sales of beer
   d. Increased number of lightning strikes
   e. Increased numbers of mosquitoes

8. The early 2000s saw a downturn in armed robbery, which coincided with increased cell phone ownership. Do any of these explanations seem better or worse?

   a. Robbers backed off because they knew more people could call for help.
   b. It's probably just coincidence.

c. Criminals were becoming too busy talking on cell phones to rob anyone.

d. Robbers know most cell phones can take photos; they worried about having their pictures taken.

9. In 2007, the homicide rate was higher than in 2006. To which of the following is that fact possibly related by cause or effect?

a. In 2007, fewer hurricanes hit Florida.

b. During the preceding two years, the war in Iraq went badly.

c. Several years earlier, Bill Clinton had sex with an intern and lied about it.

d. In 2007, the price of houses declined sharply.

10. The junior high basketball team played exceptionally well against a tough opponent. The coach rewarded the players with lavish praise and ice cream. In the next game, the team didn't play as well. Select the best responses:

a. "Obviously, rewarding the team backfired."

b. "The coach should have given them a better reward."

c. "The coach should have rewarded only the best players."

d. "The team probably still wouldn't have played as well, even if the coach hadn't rewarded the players."

11. Can mere reading of articles about dieting cause teenage girls to resort to extreme weight-loss measures? According to a study published in the journal *Pediatrics* (reported by Carla K. Johnson of the Associated Press in January 2007), the answer might well be yes. In the study, female middle school students were interviewed in 1999 and again in 2004 and their heights and weights were measured. Those in the first interview who said they frequently read magazine articles about dieting were more likely than those who said they never read such articles to report in the second survey that they indulged in extreme weight-loss measures like vomiting and taking laxatives. The effect was present whether or not the girls were overweight or considered their weight important when they started reading the articles, the researchers said.

Propose two explanations for the findings that seem likely or possible.

Go to Church and Live Longer

Exercise 11-12

According to Bill Scanlon, a reporter for the Scripps Howard News Service, researchers from the University of Colorado, the University of Texas, and Florida State University determined that twenty-year-olds who attend church at least once a week for a lifetime live on the average seven years longer than twenty-year-olds who never attend. The data came from a 1987 National Health Interview Survey that asked 28,000 people their income, age, church-attendance patterns, and other questions. The research focused on 2,000 of those surveyed who subsequently died between 1987 and 1995.

a. Propose two different causal hypotheses to explain these findings.

b. What data would you need to have greater confidence in these hypotheses?

GENERAL CAUSAL CLAIMS

Recently, one of us experienced a scratchy throat of the sort that is the indisputable harbinger of an oncoming cold. On the recommendation of a friend, this author tried Zicam. He never did get a cold. Was this due to the Zicam? Well, maybe. But from the mere fact that a cold didn't develop after he took Zicam, we cannot conclude that the Zicam *caused* this result. That would be *post hoc, ergo propter hoc*. We can say, "I took Zicam, *and* the cold didn't develop." We can't say, "I took Zicam, and that *prevented* the cold from developing."

It is an interesting fact about human psychology that, if we were to read about a "clinical trial" that consisted of a single cold sufferer taking Zicam, we would laugh out loud. However, if a friend tells us that Zicam worked for him, we might very well take it ourselves. Logically, though, there is no difference between a "clinical trial" consisting of a single subject and a report from a friend.

The trouble with a report from a friend or a clinical trial with only one subject is that, generally, you can't control for all the variables, and as a result, you can't calculate the probability that the outcome was not just chance or due to some unrelated cause that was present coincidentally.

Scientists resolve this problem by concerning themselves with general causal claims, such as "Zicam reduces the frequency of colds." A statement like "Zicam kept me from getting a cold" is a claim about a specific cause-and-effect event; as such, it can be difficult to establish. "My uncle got lung cancer from smoking" is a statement about a specific cause-effect event, whereas "Smoking causes lung cancer" is a general causal claim. Science is mainly concerned with general causal hypotheses.

A general causal claim can be understood somewhat differently than a claim about a specific cause-effect event.* At least some general causal claims can be given a statistical interpretation that lends itself to scientific confirmation. For example, "Zicam prevents colds" can be interpreted as meaning not that Zicam will prevent every single cold but that, for humans, there is an association between taking Zicam and a reduced frequency of colds that cannot be attributed to chance. Given this interpretation, it could be true that Zicam prevents colds and also true that taking Zicam didn't prevent you from getting a cold.

CONFIRMING CAUSAL HYPOTHESES

This brings us at long last to the question of confirming a causal hypothesis.

When we apply heat to a pot of water, the water boils. We repeat the experiment, and we see that the water again boils. The Method of Agreement suggests a hypothesis: The heat caused the water to boil. Now we have to eliminate other possibilities: It could just be *coincidence* that the water boiled when we applied heat. But if we repeat the experiment many times, it would be a miraculous coincidence, since the water boils every time we apply heat. Could the aluminum pan we heated the water in have caused the water to boil? Unlikely; we can boil water in other pans as well. Unlike the heat, the

---

*For the following analysis, we follow Ronald N. Giere, *Understanding Scientific Reasoning*, 3rd ed. (Fort Worth: Holt, Rinehart, and Winston, 1991).

aluminum doesn't always accompany the boiling water, so we can eliminate it as the cause. Using the Method of Difference, we see that the only difference between the water boiling and not is the presence or absence of heat.

Let's apply the same ideas to a more complicated hypothesis, that Zicam prevents colds. How might you confirm this hypothesis?

Controlled Cause-to-Effect Experiments

One obvious way would be a controlled experiment: Infect willing subjects with a cold virus; randomly divide them into two groups, giving only the subjects in one group Zicam. To attach real numbers to this, let's say there are 100 subjects in the Zicam group ("experimental group") and 100 in the other ("control group"). Let's then suppose that 46 percent of the Zicam group came down with colds versus 60 percent of the control group. This is a **difference (d) in the frequency** of colds of 14 percentage points. Could such a difference be because the subjects in the Zicam group had mysterious cold-blocking properties? Probably not; subjects were randomly assigned to one of the two groups, so subjects with mysterious cold-blocking properties probably would have been evenly distributed between the two groups.

Could the difference in cold frequency (d) be due to chance? Well, you can't eliminate chance completely, but the probability that it wasn't due to chance can be quantified. As it turns out, with 100 subjects each in the Zicam group and the control group, there is a 95 percent probability that a d greater than 13 percentage points isn't due to chance. Another way of phrasing this is to say that, at the 95 percent level of confidence, d must exceed 13 percentage points to be **statistically significant**. If there were 250 subjects in each of the two groups (rather than 100), then any d greater than 8 percentage points would be statistically significant at the 95 percent level. Obviously, the larger the two groups of subjects, the smaller d needs to be to be statistically significant, that is, due to something other than chance (see Table 11-1).

Clearly, it isn't always feasible to conduct a controlled cause-to-effect experiment. Nevertheless, such experiments involve the same principles as testing the hypothesis that heat causes water to boil. In some situations, the

Table 11-1

Approximate Statistically Significant d's at .05 Level

Number in Experimental Group *(with Similarly Sized Control Group)*	Approximate Figure That d Must Exceed to Be Statistically Significant *(in Percentage Points)*
10	40
25	27
50	19
100	13
250	8
500	6
1,000	4
1,500	3

In the Media

Here's to Wine and Cheese

Substance in Red Grapes Extends Mice Lives

WASHINGTON—A substance found in red wine protected mice from the ill effects of obesity, raising the tantalizing prospect the compound could do the same for humans and might also help people live longer, healthier lives, researchers reported Wednesday.

The substance, called resveratrol, enabled mice that were fed a high-calorie, high-fat diet to live normal, active lives despite becoming obese—the first time any compound has been shown to do that. Tests found the agent activated a host of genes that protect against the effects of aging, essentially neutralizing the adverse effects of a bad diet on the animals' health and life span.

Although much more work is needed to explore the benefits and safety of the substance, which is sold over the counter as a nutritional supplement, the findings could lead to the long-sought goal of extending the healthy human life span, experts said.

The researchers cautioned that the findings should not encourage people to eat badly, think-

ing resveratrol could make gluttony completely safe. They also noted that a person would have to drink at least 100 bottles of red wine a day or take mega doses of the commercially available supplements to get the levels given to the mice, which may not be safe in humans.

Preliminary tests in people are already under way.

"We've been looking for something like this . . . and maybe it's right around the corner—a molecule that could be taken in a single pill to delay the diseases of aging and keep you healthier as you grow old," said David A. Sinclair, a Harvard University molecular biologist who led the study. "The potential impact would be huge."

➤ RED WINE, Page A14
Mice photo, Associated Press/National Institutes of Health, Doug Hansen
—Rob Stein, *Washington Post*

effect we are interested in (boiling water, reduced frequency of colds) is present; in others, it isn't. Unless the effect is a random event, the cause also is present if and only if the effect is present. Something that has nothing to do with the effect may be present coincidentally when and only when the effect is present. But by repeating the experiment (using multiple subjects randomly divided into two groups, or heating water on multiple occasions), we reduce the possibility of coincidence.

At bottom, hypothesis confirmation is really just careful application of the Method of Difference combined with the Method of Agreement. The water boils when it is heated (and, up to a point, boils more vigorously as the heat increases)—that's the Method of Agreement. And the only difference between its boiling and not boiling is the application of heat—that's the Method of Difference. Similarly, every subject in the experimental group has Zicam—that's the Method of Agreement. And the only difference, apart from the fact that the Zicam group shows the effect (reduced frequency of colds), is the Zicam they took—that's the Method of Difference.

For various reasons, researchers prefer to experiment on laboratory animals rather than on humans. Here, for example, the resveratrol that was given to the mice was equivalent to that found in more than 100 bottles of red wine.

BENEFITS FROM RED GRAPES

High concentrations of the antioxidant resveratrol are found in red wine and the skin of red grapes.

RESVERATROL'S EFFECTS

- Decreases stickiness of blood's platelet cells, reduces risk of heart disease
- Anti-cancer agent
- Anti-inflammatory

Sources. Functional Food for Health, *Science* magazine U.S. National Library of Medicine, MCT graphics.

Alternative Methods of Testing Causal Hypotheses in Human Populations

Experimenting on humans isn't always practical or ethically desirable. However, researchers have alternatives.

One alternative is to match a group of people who have subjected themselves to a suspected causal agent with a control group—supposedly similar people who haven't done so—in order to see if the frequency of a possible effect is greater in the first group. For example, to find out if obesity contributes to heart disease, you wouldn't want deliberately to try to make people obese. Instead, you'd match a group of people who have become obese for other reasons with a similar group of non-obese people, to see it there is more heart disease in the first group. Such cause-to-effect studies aren't nearly as conclusive in their findings as controlled experiments, because one cannot be sure that factors other than the hypothesized cause that contribute to heart disease are equally distributed in the two groups.

Nonexperimental Cause-to-Effect Studies

Nonexperimental Effect-to-Cause Studies

Another method of testing a causal hypothesis that avoids direct experimentation on subjects is to compare a group of subjects who have the *effect* (rather than the suspected cause) with a group of subjects who don't, in order to see whether the hypothesized cause is more prevalent in the former group. For example, a researcher might compare a group of people who have heart problems with a matched group of people who do not, to see if there is more obesity in the first group. The problem here is that other factors besides obesity that are linked to heart disease cannot be known to have been equally distributed among both groups.

Experiments on Animals

Another method of testing causal hypotheses that avoids experimenting on humans is to conduct the experiments on animals. Apart from ethical considerations, findings from such experiments apply to humans by analogical reasoning, which we discussed in Chapter 10.

The following exercise sets will help you tell the difference between general and specific causal claims and will give you practice analyzing experiments and studies aimed at testing causal hypotheses.

Exercise 11-13

Identify each of the following as (a) a claim about a specific case of cause and effect, (b) a general causal claim, or (c) neither of these.

▲ 1. The hibiscus died while we were away. There must have been a frost.

2. Carlos isn't as fast as he used to be; that's what old age will do.

3. Kent's college education helped him get a high-paying job.

▲ 4. The most frequently stolen utility vehicle is a 2007 Honda Civic.

5. Vitamin C prevents colds.

6. The woman he returned to be with is Deborah.

▲ 7. The high reading on the thermometer resulted from two causes: This thermometer was located lower to the ground than at other stations, and its shelter was too small, so the ventilation was inadequate.

8. Oily smoke in the exhaust is caused by worn rings.

9. The initial tests indicate that caffeine has toxic effects in humans.

▲ 10. Neonatal sepsis is usually fatal among newborns.

11. WIN 51,711 halts development of paralysis in mice that have been infected with polio-2.

12. A stuck hatch cover on *Spacelab* blocked a French ultraviolet camera from conducting a sky survey of celestial objects.

13. An experimental drug has shown broad antiviral effects on a large number of the picornaviruses against which it has been tested.

▲ 14. Investigation revealed the problem was a short-circuited power supply.

15. Arteriovenous malformations—distortions of the capillaries connecting an arteriole and a small vein in the brain—can bleed, causing severe headaches, seizures, and even death.

16. Because of all the guns that its citizens own, the United States has never been invaded.

▲ 17. According to two reports in the *New England Journal of Medicine*, oil from fish can prevent heart disease.

18. The most important cause in the growing problem of illiteracy is television.

19. "Raymond the Wolf passed away in his sleep one night from natural causes; his heart stopped beating when the three men who slipped into his bedroom stuck knives in it."

— *Jimmy Breslin*, The Gang That Couldn't Shoot Straight

▲ 20. The dramatic increases in atmospheric CO_2, produced by the burning of fossil fuels, are warming the planet and will eventually alter the climate.

> There is no single event, activity, decision, law, judgment, in this period of time that I call the "three strikes" era—other than "three strikes"— that could explain the tremendous acceleration in the drop in crime.
>
> — *Dan Lungren, former California attorney general, who helped draft California's Three Strikes law*

Exercise 11-14

Under this law, conviction for a third felony carried with it a mandatory sentence of twenty-five years to life. Although the crime rate in California had been falling before the law took effect in 1994, it reportedly fell even faster after the law was enacted, and California's crime rate dropped to levels not seen since the 1960s.

Provide two reasonable alternative hypotheses to explain the acceleration of the drop in the crime rate in California. What data would you need to be convinced that Lungren's hypothesis is the best?

Exercise 11-15

Suppose a university teacher wants to know whether or not requiring attendance improves student learning. How could she find out? In groups (or individually if the instructor prefers), describe an experiment that an instructor might actually use. Groups may then compare proposals to see who has the best idea.

Exercise 11-16

For each of the following investigations:

    a. Identify the causal hypothesis at issue.
    b. Identify what kind of investigation it is.
    c. Describe the control and experimental groups.
    d. State the difference in effect (or cause) between control and experimental groups.
    e. Identify any problems in either the investigation or the report of it, including but not necessarily limited to uncontrolled variables.
    f. State the conclusion you think is warranted by the report.

▲ 1. Scientists have learned that people who drink wine weekly or monthly are less likely to develop dementia, including Alzheimer's disease. (Daily wine drinking, however, seems to produce no protective effect.) The lead researcher was Dr. Thomas Truelsen, of the Institute of Preventive Medicine at Kommunehospitalet in Copenhagen. The researchers identified the drinking patterns of 1,709 people in Copenhagen in the 1970s and then assessed them for dementia in the 1990s, when they were aged 65 or older. When they were assessed two decades later, 83 of the participants had developed dementia. People who drank beer regularly were at an increased risk of developing dementia.

—adapted from BBC News *(online)*

2. Learning music can help children do better at math. Gordon Shaw of the University of California, Irvine, and Frances Rauscher at the University of Wisconsin compared three groups of second graders: 26 received piano instruction plus practice with a math videogame, 29 received extra English lessons plus the game, and 28 got no special lessons. After four months, the piano kids scored 15 to 41 percent higher on a test of ratios and fractions than the other participants.

—adapted from Sharon Begley, Newsweek

3. The Carolina Abecedarian Project [A-B-C-D, get it?] selected participants from families thought to be at risk for producing mildly retarded children. These families were all on welfare, and most were headed by a single mother who had scored well below average on a standardized IQ test (obtaining IQs of 70 to 85). The project began when the participating children were 6 to 12 weeks old and continued for the next 5 years. Half of the participants were randomly assigned to take part in a special day-care program designed to promote intellectual development. The program ran from 7:15 to 5:15 for 5 days a week for 50 weeks each year until the child entered school. The other children received the same dietary supplements, social services, and pediatric care but did not attend day care. Over the next 21 years, the two groups were given IQ tests and tests of academic achievement. The day-care program participants began to outperform their counterparts on IQ tests starting at 18 months and maintained this IQ advantage through age 21. They also outperformed the others in all areas of academic achievement from the third year of school onward.

—adapted from Developmental Psychology, *6th ed., David R. Schaffer*

▲ 4. Research at the University of Pennsylvania and the Children's Hospital of Philadelphia indicates that children who sleep in a dimly lighted room until age two may be up to five times more likely to develop myopia (nearsightedness) when they grow up.

The researchers asked the parents of children who had been patients at the researchers' eye clinic to recall the lighting conditions in the children's bedroom from birth to age two.

Of a total of 172 children who slept in darkness, 10 percent were nearsighted. Of a total of 232 who slept with a night light, 34 percent were nearsighted. Of a total of 75 who slept with a lamp on, 55 percent were nearsighted.

The lead ophthalmologist, Dr. Graham E. Quinn, said that "just as the body needs to rest, this suggests that the eyes need a period of darkness."

—adapted from an AP report by Joseph B. Verrengia

5. You want to find out if the coffee grounds that remain suspended as sediment in French press, espresso, and Turkish and Greek coffee can cause headaches.

   You divide fifty volunteers into two groups and feed both groups a pudding at the same time every day. However, one group mixes eight grams of finely pulverized used coffee grounds into the pudding before eating it (that's equivalent to the sediment in about one and a half liters of Turkish coffee). Within three weeks, you find that 50 percent of the group that has eaten grounds have had headaches; only 27 percent of the other group have experienced a headache. You conclude that coffee grounds may indeed cause headaches and try to get a grant for further studies. (This is a fictitious experiment.)

6. Do you enjoy spicy Indian and Asian curries? That bright yellow-orange color is due to curcumin, an ingredient in the spice turmeric. An experiment conducted by Bandaru S. Reddy of the American Health Foundation in Valhalla, New York, and reported in *Cancer Research* suggests that curcumin might suppress the development of colon cancer.

   Places where turmeric is widely used have a low incidence of colon cancer, so the research team decided to investigate. They administered a powerful colon carcinogen to sixty-six rats and then added curcumin at the rate of 2,000 parts per million to the diet of thirty of them. At the end of a year, 81 percent of the rats eating regular rat food had developed cancerous tumors, compared with only 47 percent of those that dined on the curcumin-enhanced diet. In addition, 38 percent of the tumors in rats eating regular food were invasive, and that was almost twice the rate in rodents eating curcumin-treated chow.

   —*adapted from* Science News

▲ 7. Does jogging keep you healthy? Two independent researchers interested in whether exercise prevents colds interviewed twenty volunteers about the frequency with which they caught colds. The volunteers, none of whom exercised regularly, were then divided into two groups of ten, and one group participated in a six-month regimen of jogging three miles every other day. At the end of the six months, the frequency of colds among the joggers was compared both with that of the nonjoggers and with that of the joggers prior to the experiment. It was found that, compared with the nonjoggers, the joggers had 25 percent fewer colds. The record of colds among the joggers also declined in comparison with their own record prior to the exercise program.

8. "In the fifty-seven-month study, whose participants were all male physicians, 104 of those who took aspirin had heart attacks, as compared with 189 heart attacks in those who took only a sugar pill. This means ordinary aspirin reduced the heart attack risk for healthy men by 47 percent. At least seven long-term studies of more than 11,000 heart attack victims have shown that one-half or one aspirin per day can reduce the risk of a second attack by up to 20 percent."

   —*adapted from the* Los Angeles Times

9. "Although cigarette ads sometimes suggest that smoking is 'macho,' new studies indicate that smoking can increase the risk of impotence. In a study of 116 men with impotence caused by vascular problems, done at the University of Pretoria, South Africa, 108 were smokers. Two independent studies, one done by the Centre d'Etudes et de Recherches di l'Impuissance in Paris, and reported in the British medical journal *Lancet*, and the other done by Queen's University and Kingston General Hospital in Ontario, found that almost two-thirds of impotent men smoked.

"To test whether smoking has an immediate effect on sexual response, a group of researchers from Southern Illinois and Florida State universities fitted 42 male smokers with a device that measures the speed of arousal. The men were divided into three groups, one group given high-nicotine cigarettes, one group cigarettes low in nicotine, and one group mints. After smoking one cigarette or eating a mint, each man was placed in a private room and shown a two-minute erotic film while his sexual response was monitored. Then he waited ten minutes, smoked two more cigarettes or ate another mint, and watched a different erotic film, again being monitored.

"The results: Men who smoked high-nicotine cigarettes had slower arousal than those who smoked low-nicotine cigarettes or ate mints."

—*adapted from* Reader's Digest

10. "A study published in the July 27 *Journal of the American Medical Association* indicates that taking androgen (a male sex hormone) in high doses for four weeks can have important effects on the high density lipoproteins (HDLs) in the blood, which are believed to protect against the clogging of vessels that supply the heart. Ben F. Hurley, an exercise physiologist from the University of Maryland in College Park who conducted the study at Washington University, monitored the levels of HDL in the blood of sixteen healthy, well-conditioned men in their early thirties who were taking androgens as part of their training program with heavy weights. Prior to use of the hormone, all had normal levels of HDLs. After four weeks of self-prescribed and self-administered use of these steroids the levels dropped by about 60 percent.

"Hurley is cautious in interpreting the data. 'You can't say that low HDL levels mean that a specified person is going to have a heart attack at an earlier age. All you can say is that it increases their risk for heart disease.'"

—*D. Franklin*, Science News

11. "New studies reported in the *Journal of the American Medical Association* indicate that vasectomy is safe. A group headed by Frank Massey of UCLA paired 10,500 vasectomized men with a like number of men who had not had the operation. The average follow-up time was 7.9 years, and 2,300 pairs were followed for more than a decade. The researchers reported that, aside from inflammation in the testes, the incidence of diseases for vasectomized men was similar to that in their paired controls.

"A second study done under federal sponsorship at the Battelle Human Affairs Research Centers in Seattle compared heart disease in 1,400 vasectomized men and 3,600 men who had not had the operation.

Over an average follow-up time of fifteen years, the incidence of heart diseases was the same among men in both groups."

—*Edward Edelson*, New York Daily News; *reprinted in* Reader's Digest

12. "A new study shows that the incidence of cancer tumors in rats exposed to high doses of X-rays dropped dramatically when the food intake of the rats was cut by more than half. Dr. Ludwik Gross of the Veterans Administration Medical Center noted that this study is the first to demonstrate that radiation-induced tumors can be prevented by restricting diet.

"The experimenters exposed a strain of laboratory rats to a dose of X-rays that produced tumors in 100 percent of the rats allowed to eat their fill—about five or six pellets of rat food a day.

"When the same dose of X-rays was given to rats limited to two pellets of food a day, only nine of 29 females and one of 15 males developed tumors, the researchers reported.

"The weight of the rats on the reduced diet fell by about one-half, but they remained healthy and outlived their counterparts who died of cancer, Gross said. He noted that the restricted diet also reduced the occurrence of benign tumors. There is no evidence that restriction of food intake will slow the growth of tumors that have already formed in animals, he said."

—*Paul Raeburn*, Sacramento Bee

13. "Encephalitis, or sleeping sickness, has declined greatly in California during the past thirty years because more people are staying inside during prime mosquito-biting hours—7:00 P.M. to 10:00 P.M., researchers said. Paul M. Gahlinger of San Jose State University and William C. Reeves of the School of Public Health at UC Berkeley conducted the study. 'People who watch television on warm summer evenings with their air conditioners on are less likely to be exposed during the peak biting period of mosquitoes that carry encephalitis,' Reeves said.

"The researchers found that those counties in California's Central Valley with the highest television ownership had the lowest encephalitis rates for census years. Of 379 Kern County residents interviewed by telephone, 79 percent said they used their air conditioners every evening and 63 percent said they watched television four or more evenings a week during the summer.

"The percentage of residents who spend more time indoors now because of air conditioning than in 1950 more than doubled, from 26 percent to 54 percent, the researchers said."

—*Associated Press*, Enterprise-Record *(Chico, California)*

▲ 14. "A study released last week indicated that Type A individuals, who are characteristically impatient, competitive, insecure and short-tempered, can halve their chances of having a heart attack by changing their behavior with the help of psychological counseling.

"In 1978, scientists at Mt. Zion Hospital and Medical Center in San Francisco and Stanford University School of Education began their study of 862 predominantly male heart attack victims. Of this number, 592 received group counseling to ease their Type A behavior and improve their self-esteem. After three years, only 7 percent had another heart attack, compared with 13 percent of a matched group of 270 subjects who received only cardiological advice. Among 328 men who continued with the counseling for the full three years, 79 percent reduced their Type A behavior. About half of the comparison group was similarly able to slow down and cope better with stress.

"This is the first evidence 'that a modification program aimed at Type A behavior actually helps to reduce coronary disease,' says Redford Williams of Duke University, an investigator of Type A behavior."

—Science News

Exercise 11-17

Researchers from Tenon Hospital in Paris reported to the American Urological Association that dogs can be trained to detect the odor of chemicals released into urine by prostate cancer. The researchers first trained a Belgian Malinois to identify urine samples from patients with prostate cancer and to differentiate them from urine samples from healthy subjects. They then determined whether the dog could select a urine sample from a prostate cancer victim when four urine samples from healthy people were present. The dog was correct in 63 out of 66 tests—more accurate than the PSA test now used to detect prostate cancer. The researchers currently are training other dogs.*

1. Do you think the dog's success rate was coincidental? Why or why not?
2. Do you see any weakness in the experiment?
3. If you were testing the ability of this dog to detect urine from victims of prostate cancer, would you do anything differently?

Exercise 11-18

Let's say you randomly divide 700 men in the early stages of prostate cancer into two groups. The men in one group have their prostates removed surgically; those in the other group are simply watched to let the disease take its course. Researchers did this to 700 Scandinavian men and reported the results in the *New England Journal of Medicine* in fall 2002. As it turns out, 16 of those who underwent surgery died from prostate cancer, as compared with 31 of those who did not undergo surgery. On the face of it, these figures suggest your chances of not dying from prostate cancer are better if you have surgery. But put on your thinking caps and answer the following questions.

1. Suppose that, despite these findings, there was no statistically significant difference in how long the men in each group lived. What would that suggest?
2. The follow-up comparison lasted six years. Suppose that, after ten years, the death rates from prostate cancer were the same for the two groups. What would that suggest?
3. Suppose Scandinavian men are not screened for prostate cancer as aggressively as American men and tend to be older when they get the first diagnosis.

---

* Reported by Thomas H. Maugh II, *Los Angeles Times*, June 3, 2010.

4. Suppose Scandinavian men are screened more aggressively for prostate cancer than American men and tend to be younger when they get the first diagnosis.

Here, as elsewhere, you need to know the whole picture to make a judgment. How old were the men to begin with? If they were relatively young men, how long did the study last? Was there a difference in how long the men in the two groups lived? (Note that prostate removal has risks and sometimes produces important negative side effects.)

MISTAKES IN CAUSAL REASONING

We've already discussed how thinking critically means rejecting causal explanations that are

- unduly complicated
- incompatible with known facts or theories
- vague, ambiguous, or circular
- for other reasons inherently untestable

In addition, we noted that causal explanations involving either of the following two fallacies should be rejected:

- *Post hoc, ergo propter hoc* (thinking the fact that one thing immediately precedes another thing proves that the first thing caused or causes the second thing)
- *Cum hoc, ergo propter hoc* (thinking that correlation between two things proves that one caused or causes the other)

Let's represent these two fallacies schematically:

Cum hoc, ergo propter hoc:

A's are correlated with B's.
_____
Therefore, it has been proved that A's cause B's (or that this particular A caused this particular B).

Post hoc, ergo propter hoc:

A's immediately precede B's (or this particular A immediately preceded this particular B)
_____
Therefore, it has been proved that A's cause B's (or that this particular A caused this particular B).

- Jeff Fulcher, a former student of ours, read this book and then flew airplanes in Alaska. See what an exciting career can come from reading this book? (This is an example of *post hoc, ergo propter hoc.*)

Why are these mistakes in reasoning? Because they do not establish the improbability of the following three possibilities:

1. <u>That the connection between A and B is coincidental.</u> *Illustration 1:* You took Zicam and a cold didn't develop; does that prove that Zicam was the cause? No; that result might be just coincidence. *Illustration 2:* The cancer rate is notably higher in the vicinity of a dry-cleaning business. Does that prove that the dry-cleaning business was a causal factor in the high cancer rate? No; the elevated cancer rate might be due to chance (cancer cases aren't distributed evenly throughout a region).

2. <u>A and B both result from a third thing (an "underlying cause").</u> *Illustration 1:* Suppose you notice that, whenever you go to bed without brushing your teeth, you wake up with a headache. Does this prove that not brushing caused the headaches? No; the headache and the not brushing might both be the result of an underlying cause, such as going to bed too late or drinking too much. *Illustration 2:* Chimney fires increase just as purchases of long underwear increase. Does this mean that one causes the other? No; there is an underlying cause of the covariation: People increase their use of warm clothes and fireplaces as the result of an underlying cause, the weather turning colder.

3. <u>B caused A, rather than the other way around ("confusing effect with cause").</u> *Illustration:* Having a positive attitude is associated with good health. Does this prove that having a positive attitude contributes to good health? No; it could be the other way around: Being healthy might give you a positive attitude.

Notice that, if B came *after* A, then it cannot be said to have caused A. So, *post hoc, ergo propter hoc* reasoning is not guilty of confusing effect with cause.

■ *The Golden Compass.* Just as it was supposed to, this picture makes us want to see this movie. We don't know why it has that effect, but we do not need an argument to know that it does have that effect.

Confusing Conditional Probabilities in Medical Tests

The probability of X given Y is distinct from the probability of Y given X. The probability the toilet is leaking given there is water on the floor is distinct from the probability there is water on the floor given the toilet is leaking. The probability Priglet has fleas given she itches is distinct from the probability she itches given she has fleas. The probability you are drunk if you get into a car accident is distinct from the probability you will get in a car accident if you are drunk.

These points seem plain enough, but they are easy to forget when it comes to medical tests. People sometimes assume that the probability they have a medical condition is high if they score high on a test for that condition. For example, suppose you are a male and you get a positive result on a test for male bladder cancer. The test is reported to be 90 percent accurate. Do you have a 90 percent chance of having bladder cancer? You might think so, but read on.

Testing positive for a medical condition (or for any other condition) is the *effect* of having that condition. If a test for male bladder cancer is 90 percent accurate, that means that 90 percent of those who have the cause—bladder cancer—will have the effect, meaning a positive test result. If you are a male, and you test positive, to determine your chances of having bladder cancer, you need to know two additional things: (1) what percentage of males who *don't* have bladder cancer test positive ("false positives"), and (2) what percentage of males have bladder cancer in the first place ("base rate").

To continue with this example, if 10 percent of males who do not have bladder cancer test positive, and the base rate for male bladder cancer is, for example, 1 percent, then out of every 1,000 males:

■ 10 males will have bladder cancer

■ 9 of them will test positive

■ 990 will not have bladder cancer

■ 99 of them will test positive

Hence: out of every 1,000 males, 108 (99 + 9) will test positive; and out of the 108, only 9 will actually have bladder cancer. So, given these data, if a male tests positive on this test, his chances of having this condition are not 90 percent but 8 percent (9/108).*

People make this mistake not only when it comes to medical tests but also with other known symptoms of medical conditions. But symptoms are *effects* of a condition, not causes, and remembering this may save you unnecessary grief. That 90 percent of heart attack victims experience symptom X does not mean that 90 percent of people who experience X are having a heart attack.

Overlooking Statistical Regression

"Statistical regression" and "regression to the mean" refer to a statistical property of measurements of mean values of populations. Let's say (to use

If you look at the new cases of death from AIDS, the fastest-growing category could be ladies over the age of 70. If last year one woman over 70 died from AIDS and this year two do, you get a 100 percent increase in AIDS deaths for that category.

—John Allen Paulos

Percentage increases from a small baseline can be misleading.

---

*This is a modified example of "frequency" calculations of probability in medical tests, given by Gerd Gigerenzer, *Calculated Risks: How to Know When Numbers Deceive You* (New York: Simon & Schuster, 2002). See, for example, Chapter 4.

the classic example) that the average (mean) height of a forty-year-old male is 5 feet 10 inches. Suppose you measure the average height of the children of forty-year-old male fathers whose average height is over 6 feet 4 inches. The average height of the children will be closer to 5 feet 10 inches. In other words, the children of unusually tall fathers are apt to be closer than their fathers to average height. One might wonder why the children of tall fathers are apt to be shorter than their dads. The explanation, however, does not involve cause and effect. The fathers of unusually tall *children* are also apt to be shorter than their kids, a fact that, obviously, cannot be explained by cause and effect.

Likewise, suppose you give a true/false test to the freshmen at your university and have them guess at the answers. Some test-takers will score above 50 percent and some will score below 50 percent, but the average of all the scores will be around 50 percent. If those who scored above 60 percent took another true/false test and guessed at the answers, their average on the second test would be closer to 50 percent. If you compare these two examples, you will see that they illustrate the same principle, statistical regression.

With these examples in mind, you might ponder why it so often happens that, say, a basketball player who has an unusually great game and shoots well above his average usually won't repeat the performance the next game. Or why the major league baseball Rookie of the Year, who has an unusually high batting average, usually doesn't do as well in his second season. Frequently, people propose explanations of these regressions: Did success destroy his concentration? Did other players start keying on him? Was there a coaching change? However, the regression could simply be statistical.

From time to time, the sexual activity of a large sample of young people is measured, in terms of, say, reported frequency of sex and number of partners over a period of time, say, six weeks. Suppose you then ask those whose reported sexual activity was in the top 10 percent to attend church more frequently and report their sexual activity during the following six weeks. Chances are that their reported sexual activity will be lower, closer to the mean for the original study. Did going to church explain the reduction? You might think so, until you remember the examples cited earlier. Chances are that their reported sexual activity would be lower if you had had them adopt a pet or drink extra water or do nothing at all.

Regression to the mean can happen whenever you encounter a phenomenon like either of those just mentioned. Two examples: Was the average daily total of American soldiers killed in Iraq in July 2007 exceptionally high? August's daily average will probably be lower—with or without a "surge" or another particular intervention. From a group of heart patients, select those whose average of blood pressure readings is atypically high. Administer a medication to these individuals, and retake their blood pressure. The second average will probably be lower, that is, closer to the mean for the entire group. (This example should explain why, in the Zicam experiment previously discussed, potential cold sufferers are randomly selected into experimental and control groups.)

This is not to say that attending church, troop surges, or heart medications cannot be known to be working. In the heart medication case, for example, subjects will be randomly selected into experimental and control groups, which means that those patients with atypically high blood pressure readings will be more or less evenly divided between the two groups. Without such

In the Media

Decoding Your Handwriting Style

M's and N's

How you mind your M's and N's is a reflection of your temperament and how you relate to others, experts say. They have four terms for your style:

- **Garland.** The garland looks like a bowl and is ready to receive. This means you have a willingness to please, and are kind and compassionate. The home and hearth is very important to you.

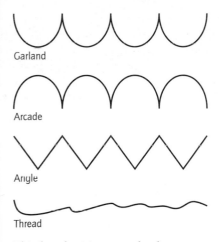

Garland

Arcade

Angle

Thread

This handwriting sample shows former President John F. Kennedy's "visionary" t's.

- **Arcade.** The arcade closes off everything underneath, symbolizing your emotional impenetrability—you are an emotional person but don't want anybody to know.

- **Angle.** Like the jarring shape of your M's and N's, you are combative with little room for flexibility. If things are going too smoothly, you feel unsettled and will make waves. But when you use your power for good, you can be incredibly effective.

- **Thread.** With your M's and N's flat and wavy, you think and act fast. You're adaptable and can fit in wherever you are, like a chameleon.

T's

There are two parts of the T that represent your work and your goals. The stem is a reflection of your self-image as it relates to your work, and the crossbar represents your ability to set goals.

citizen of the world—ask not or other what America will do for you—

A regular stem like you are taught in school shows you are conventional and happy to go along with the crowd. A looped stem means you're emotional and sensitive, especially to criticism of your work. A very tall stem means you are proud of your accomplishments, while a short one means your own

➤ HANDWRITING, Page L3

Handwriting analysts (graphologists) think of handwriting the same way cardiologists think of heart symptoms: as the effect of a cause. However, the skeptics that we are, we'd bet the associations between handwriting "symptoms" and their supposed causes (personality traits) are not as well established as the associations between cardiac symptoms and causes. Among other problems, we find it difficult (though perhaps not impossible) to imagine how a personality trait *could* cause a particular handwriting style.

Real Life

See What Happens When You Watch the Tube?

Recent research indicates that people who watch several hours of TV each day, as compared with those who don't watch very much, express more racially prejudiced attitudes, perceive women as having more limited abilities and interests than men, overestimate the prevalence of violence in society, and underestimate the number of old people. Does this suggest to you that these attitudes and  misconceptions are the *result* of watching a lot of TV, that TV *causes* people to have these attitudes and misconceptions? If so, that's fine. But remembering not to overlook possible underlying common causes should lead you to contemplate another idea. It's possible that what accounts for these attitudes and misconceptions isn't too much TV but rather *ignorance*, and that ignorance is also what makes some people happy spending hours in front of the tube. An underlying common cause?

safeguards, one cannot conclude from the fact that a "remedy" was followed by an improvement in something, that the remedy caused the improvement. The improvement could be simple regression.

Proof by Absence of Disproof

Sometimes you will hear a person say something like this:

> "Well, nobody's proved that Zicam doesn't prevent colds. . . ."

Sometimes, what the person has in mind when he or she says something like this is that the absence of disproof of a causal hypothesis increases the likelihood of the hypothesis. Is it true that the absence of disproof of a causal hypothesis increases the likelihood of the hypothesis?

Cases do arise in which one attempts to disprove a causal claim. For example, if a teacher has good reason to think a student's high score was the result of cheating, the student may attempt to disprove the hypothesis. The most famous argument in the history of philosophy is the Argument from Evil, which attempts to disprove that a good and all-powerful God created our universe, on the grounds that our universe contains evil within it.

However, in general, a failure to disprove a causal hypothesis only leaves intact whatever reasons there already were for thinking the hypothesis is true: The absence does not create a new and additional reason for thinking the hypothesis is true.

Appeal to Anecdote

In Chapter 10, we discussed the mistake of trying to generalize on the basis of an anecdote or story. Anecdotes are sometimes also used to prove or disprove causal hypotheses. Thinking that port prevents colds because Uncle Charlie drinks it and rarely catches cold would be an instance of this type of reasoning. Someone who submits that smoking pot doesn't hurt your lungs because she has a friend who smokes pot who has never had a lung problem employs similar reasoning. One could, of course, counter these arguments simply by pointing out that one knows someone who drinks port or smokes pot who does catch colds or have lung problems. So, the arguments don't really show anything and are really just hasty generalizations or *post hoc* reasoning.

Confusing Explanations with Excuses

After the September 11 suicide attacks on the World Trade Center, a speaker at our university attempted to explain the causes of the attacks. Some assumed him to be excusing or justifying the attacks; Rush Limbaugh invited him to move to Afghanistan.

If you assume without thinking about it that anyone who tries to explain the causes of bad behavior is trying to excuse it, you commit the fallacy we might call **confusing explanations with excuses.** For example, someone may try to explain why many Germans adopted the views of the Nazi Party during the 1930s. The speaker may point out that the German economy was in a mess, that the country still suffered from terms imposed on it at the end of World War I, and so forth. To assume without further reason that the speaker must be trying to excuse or muster sympathy for Nazi supporters would be to make this mistake. One can propose an explanation in order to excuse bad behavior, but one isn't necessarily trying to do so.

CAUSATION IN THE LAW

In concluding this chapter, we direct your attention to an arena in which a great deal of money and sometimes even human life depend on establishing causation. In the law, causation is the connection between action and harm. Only if your action causes harm (or contributes to its cause) can you be said to be responsible for that harm. In civil law, it is a necessary condition of tort liability that a person's action caused the harm in question. It is also a necessary condition for some, but not all, kinds of criminal liability. (Not all crimes involve harm—attempted crimes, for example.) It may seem simple to say that X caused Y, but, as we'll see, there is almost always a lot more to be said than that.

The broadest sense of the word "cause" is that of ***conditio sine qua non*** ("a condition without which nothing"). Such causes are often called "but for" causes. Y would not have happened but for X's having happened. If the gun had not fired, Ernest would not have been killed. Clearly, *sine qua non* causes are relevant. It would be silly to punish a person for causing harm Y by doing X when Y would have happened even if X had not been done.

But a cause, in this sense, can have effects that go on indefinitely. We might say, for example, that a physician's having written a prescription in 1925 caused the assassination of John F. Kennedy in 1963. This is because that prescription led to a man's going into a drugstore in 1925, where he met the woman he was to marry and with whom he was to have a child, Lee Harvey

On Language

The Great 9/11 Mystery

How could all these facts be mere coincidence?

- The day was 9/11 (9 plus 1 plus 1 equals 11).
- American Airlines Flight 11 was the first to hit the World Trade Center.
- 92 people were on board (9 plus 2 equals 11).
- September 11 is the 254th day of the year (2 plus 5 plus 4 equals 11).
- "New York City" has 11 letters in it.
- "The Pentagon" has 11 letters in it.
- "Saudi Arabia" (where most of the 9/11 terrorists were from) has 11 letters in it.
- "Afghanistan" has 11 letters in it.
- And get this: Within 11 months of September 11, 2001, 11 men, all connected to bioterror and germ warfare, died in strange and violent circumstances: One suffocated; another was stabbed; another was hit by a car; another was shot dead by a fake pizza delivery boy; one was killed in an airplane crash; one died from a stroke while being mugged; and the rest met similar ends.

Could this possibly be coincidence? What are the odds against all these things happening and being connected by the number 11?

Well, if you think these events must somehow be causally interconnected, you have a lot of company. But it doesn't include mathematicians—or us. Why not? In a world where so many things happen, strange and seemingly improbable coincidences are bound to happen every second of every day.

Not convinced? Ask each of your classmates to think of as many events or things connected with the 9/11 attack that involve the number 11 as possible. Give each person a week to work on this. We'll bet the collected list of "suspicious" coincidences is very long. There are even websites devoted to 9/11 coincidences.

As for the men connected with bioterrorism and germ warfare, you might be interested to know that the American Society for Microbiology alone has 41,000 members, and the total number of people "connected" in some way or another with bioterrorism and germ warfare would be indefinitely larger than that. We'd bet our royalties that in the eleven months following September 11, a lot more than just eleven people connected with bioterrorism and germ warfare died mysteriously and/or violently.

Lisa Belkin of the *New York Times Magazine* wrote an article on this subject (August 18, 2002), from which we learned about the coincidences mentioned above.

Incidentally, "Moore/Parker" has eleven letters.

Oswald, who would in November 1963 shoot John Kennedy from the School Book Depository Building in Dallas, Texas.

Clearly, we don't want to trace causes back this far in order to assign liability for a harm. In order to identify a **legal cause** (or a "proximate cause," as it is sometimes known) of an event, we need to put severe restrictions on the notion of cause *sine qua non*.

On Language

AC and IBE

> If the surge had been successful, we would have seen a reduction
> in violence in Baghdad.
> A reduction in violence in Baghdad was seen.
> _____
> Therefore, the troop surge was successful.

This looks very much like Affirming the Consequent (AC), which is listed inside the back cover (and in Chapter 9) as a mistake in logic. (We say "very much like" because the second premise isn't 100 percent identical to the second part of the first premise.)

However, it would be more charitable to interpret the argument as an IBE, an Inference to the Best Explanation:

> Violence was reduced.
> The most likely explanation of that is that it was due to the surge.
> _____
> Therefore, it was due to the surge.

Often, reputed real-life examples of AC can more charitably be interpreted as examples of IBE, where the second premise is accepted on the basis of a comparison of assumed (or calculated) probabilities of alternative explanations.

Whereas a *sine qua non* or "but for" cause is a matter of fact, a legal or proximate cause is generally said to be a combination of fact and decision or fact and policy. This is because deciding what is "important" or "significant" requires that we make a decision of some sort or that we have a policy that indicates what is important. In a famous essay on the subject,* H. L. A. Hart and A.M. Honoré try to show that common sense can guide the necessary decisions. They argue that, in order for a person to be legally responsible for a harm, we must be able to trace the harm caused back to that person's action. Let's say Smith throws a lighted cigarette into some roadside brush. The brush catches fire, a breeze causes the fire to spread, and eventually much of San Diego County burns up. We do not excuse Smith because of the intervention of the breeze, because that is a "common recurrent feature," a part of what we might call the "causal background," something like the presence of oxygen in the air. Such features are not seen as intervening forces that mitigate Smith's responsibility.

But say that Jones comes along and pours gasoline on the fire, which might have gone out otherwise. Here, because Jones's intervention is voluntary, it contravenes Smith's causal role. Here, we are content to say that Jones caused the destruction.

Sometimes coincidence intervenes: Moore punches Merton, who falls to the ground. At that moment, a tree falls over in the wind and strikes Merton, killing him. Because the tree's falling is pure coincidence, not foreseen by Moore, we cannot hold Moore responsible for Merton's death. We can

_____

*H. L. A. Hart and A. M. Honoré, *Causation and the Law* (Oxford, 1959), esp. pp. 59–78.

say that Moore caused his bruises, but not his death. The idea here is that we do not hold a person responsible when coincidence intervenes in this way.

Obviously, there is more to say about this subject, but at least here you have seen some of the directions that the discussion on causation in the law takes.

Recap

- Explanations are different from arguments. They are used to elucidate a phenomenon. Arguments are used to support or prove a claim.
- Sentences that can be used as explanations can also be used to state the conclusion or a premise of an argument.
- Explanations serve a variety of purposes. Two important purposes are (1) to provide physical causal explanations of something and (2) to provide behavioral causal explanations of something.
- What counts as an adequate explanation is relative to one's purposes and needs.
- Nevertheless, an adequate explanation shouldn't be unnecessarily complicated, inconsistent, incompatible with known fact or theory, or untestable due to vagueness, circularity, or other reasons.
- Arriving at a causal hypothesis involves an Inference to the Best Explanation.
- Methods of arriving at causal hypotheses (IBE methods) are the Method of Difference, the Method of Agreement, and the Best Diagnosis Method.
- These methods are guided by one's background knowledge of causal mechanisms, what causes what, and how things work.
- Confirming a causal hypothesis consists primarily in rigorously applying a combination of the Methods of Difference and Agreement.
- Two important mistakes in causal reasoning are *post hoc, ergo propter hoc*, and *cum hoc, ergo propter hoc*.
- These are mistakes because they do not eliminate the possibility of coincidence, an underlying cause, or confusion between effect and cause.
- An important case of confusing effect and cause is forgetting that symptoms are effects.
- Changes due to statistical regression are sometimes mistakenly assumed to be due to causation.
- Absence of disproof of causation is not equivalent to proof of causation.
- Using an anecdote to establish causation or to refute a general causal claim involves hasty generalizing.
- Explanations of bad behavior are not always intended to excuse the behavior.
- In the law, in its broadest sense, a "cause" is that "but for" which an effect would not have happened, but the legal cause of an effect often requires a judgment regarding what causal agent is most relevant.

Additional Exercises

Here are additional exercises to help you tell when an explanation is part of an argument, and when an explanation overlooks the possibility of coincidence or other problems. Another exercise gives you an opportunity to propose a causal hypothesis.

Exercise 11-19

Match each item to a concept on this list:

A = Confusing conditional probabilities
B = Overlooking statistical regression
C = Proof by Absence of Disproof
D = Appeal to Anecdote
E = *conditio sine qua non*
F = Confusing explanations with excuses

Every concept is used at least once.

▲ 1. The Amazing Vikings had an off night. Their shooting was poor, their defense uninspired. Everything was reflected in the lopsided score. "Laps," Coach Snort said after the loss. "Nobody showers before he does ten laps!" When the guys won their next game, the coach knew he had done the right thing. "You just gotta motivate them," he thought.

2. If your eyes are extremely sensitive to light, there is better than a 50-50 chance you have bacterial meningitis, since light sensitivity almost always accompanies the disease.

3. Wood smoke a health hazard? You kidding? We been using wood our entire lives to heat with. You gonna tell me we wouldn't know about it if it had hurt us?

▲ 4. Eat plenty of carbohydrates before an intense workout. Nobody has ever shown that carbo-loading doesn't enhance athletic performance.

5. The research team administered Deconolate to the men whose recent PSA readings were highly elevated, and then rested them. The average PSA reading for the group had declined markedly, suggesting that Deconolate may be useful in the fight against prostate cancer.

6. It is ridiculous for the FDA to ban ephedrine. I used the stuff for years to help with allergies, and I am as healthy as a horse.

▲ 7. SPOKESPERSON FOR BRITISH PETROLEUM: Halliburton cemented the drill in place, not BP.
CONGRESSMAN: Don't try to put the blame on someone else.

8. "It's your fault!"
"What? I didn't run over the sprinkler! You did!!"
"Yeah, but if you had remembered the milk, I wouldn't even be going to the store."

9. After an evening when the mosquitoes were particularly bad, Tony rushed out to Ace and bought a Mosquito Magnet. That evening the mosquitoes didn't seem as bad. "It works," Tony told his wife.

▲ 10. If the HDL reading of a male over 50 is low, the odds are he has heart disease, since most men over 50 with heart disease have low HDL readings.

Exercise 11-20

Into which category do each of the following items fall? Keep your wits about you. This exercise set and the next one are challenging.

A = An explanation appears as a premise.

B = An explanation appears as a conclusion.

C = An explanation stands by itself as an unsupported claim.

▲ 1. Awww, don't get on her, Mom. She didn't rake the leaves because her stomach was hurting and she had to lie down.

2. The garage gets cluttered because we never throw anything away. So, if we want a neat garage, we'd better change our habits.

3. Mr. Snork is taking French so he can speak the language when he goes to Europe in the spring.

▲ 4. The reason the door keeps banging is that the windows are open on the south side of the house, and there is a strong breeze.

5. We eliminated the other possibilities. The puddle was caused by a leaking wax ring.

6. I am sure Professor York will end on time this evening. He always ends on time because he likes to watch the 11:00 news.

▲ 7. You think the mower won't start because it's old? That's not why. You let gas sit in the carburetor all winter, and it gums up the works. That's why it won't start. It has nothing to do with its being old.

8. All eleven Taco Bells implicated in an *E. coli* outbreak in New York and New Jersey used the same food distributor. It seems likely the source of the bacteria was the distributor.

9. The coffee I drink in the evening must explain why I can't sleep. The only other things it could be are sweet desserts and anxiety, and I don't eat dessert, and I'm not worried about anything.

▲ 10. I believe God exists. That's the best explanation for why there is life.

Exercise 11-21

Into which category does each of the following items fall?

A = An explanation appears as a premise.

B = An explanation appears as a conclusion.

C = An explanation stands by itself as an unsupported claim.

▲ 1. Yes, I know Emily doesn't go out much, but you can hardly blame her. She doesn't go out because she wants to study.

2. The zucchini grows better than the eggplant because it gets more fertilizer.

3. Why didn't the tomatoes do better? I don't think we were fertilizing them enough. Right after I gave them Miracle-Gro, they did fine.

▲ 4. You don't believe me when I say sometimes you can see Pluto with the naked eye? Just think of how the solar system works. The planets all orbit the Sun, and at a certain point, Pluto's orbit gets close to ours.

5. Just look at the cat hair on this keyboard! Where do you let your cat sleep? No wonder your computer doesn't work right.

6. Given your symptoms, Charles, I'd say your pain is due to a sprain, not a break. Plus, your X-rays don't show a broken bone.

▲ 7. Maria can tell what note you are playing because she has perfect pitch.

8. Give 'em a break. That kind of work makes noise, and they gotta start work early to get it done.

9. Why did Dr. York give a test on Friday? He wanted to surprise us.

▲ 10. Harold didn't return the book on time, but he couldn't help it. Someone broke into his car and stole his backpack.

11. TV watching leads to violent behavior. Studies show that adolescents who watch more television are more prone to act violently.

Exercise 11-22

Using your background knowledge of how things work and what causes what, classify each of the following as probably

A = coincidence

B = confusing effect with cause

C = a case in which an implied cause and an implied effect are really the effects of an underlying cause

D = legitimate cause and effect

▲ 1. Whenever I mow the lawn, I end up sneezing a lot more than usual. Must be gas fumes from the mower.

2. Maybe the reason he's sick is all the aspirin he's taking.

3. The only thing that could possibly account for Clark and his two brothers all having winning lottery tickets is that all three had been blessed by the Reverend Dim Dome just the day before. I'm signing up for the Reverend's brotherhood.

▲ 4. What else could cause the leaves to turn yellow in the fall? It's got to be the cold weather!

5. Perhaps Jason is nearsighted because he reads so many books.

6. First, Rodrigo gets a large inheritance. Then Charles meets the girl of his dreams. And Amanda gets the job she was hoping for. What did they all have in common? They all thought positively. It can work for you, too.

▲ 7. It's common knowledge that osteoarthritis of the knee causes weakness in the quadriceps.

8. Ever since the country lost its moral direction, the crime rate has gone through the ceiling. What more proof do you need that the cause of skyrocketing crime is the breakdown in traditional family values?

9. Wow! Is Johnson hot or what? After that rocky start, he has struck out the last nine batters to face him. That's what happens when ol' Randy gets his confidence up.

▲ 10. Research demonstrates that people who eat fish are smarter. I'm going to increase my intake.

11. What a night! All those dogs barking made the coyotes yap, and nobody could get any sleep.

12. Isn't it amazing how, when the leaves drop off in the winter, it makes the branches brittle?

▲ 13. What explains all the violence in society today? TV. Just look at all the violence they show these days.

14. On Monday, Mr. O'Toole came down with a cold. That afternoon, Mrs. O'Toole caught it. Later that evening, their daughter caught it, too.

15. Retail sales are down this year. That's because unemployment is so high.

▲ 16. Yes, they're saying electric blankets aren't really a health threat, but I know better. A friend had cancer, and know what? He slept with an electric blanket.

17. At finals time, the bearded man on the front campus offers prayers in return for food. Donald is thinking, "Sure. Why not?—can't hurt anything." He approaches the bearded man with a tidbit. Later: The bearded man prays. Donald passes his finals. To skeptical friends: "Hey, you never know. I'll take all the help I can get."

18. It is an unusually warm evening, and the birds are singing with exceptional vigor. "Hot weather does make a bird sing," Uncle Irv observes.

▲ 19. Why did Uncle Ted live such a long time? A good attitude, that's why.

20. Studies demonstrate that people who are insecure about their relationships with their partners have a notable lack of ability to empathize with others. That's why we recommend that partners receive empathy training before they get married.

21. Lack of self-confidence can be difficult to explain, but common sense suggests that stuttering is among the causes, judging from how often the two things go together.

▲ 22. When I went to Munich last summer, I went to this movie, and who was there? This guy I went to school with and hadn't seen in fifteen years! No way that could be coincidence!

23. It's odd. I've seen a huge number of snails this year, and the roses have mildew. Don't know which caused which, but one of them obviously caused the other.

24. Her boyfriend is in a bad mood, you say? I'll bet it's because she's trying too hard to please him. Probably gets on his nerves.

▲ 25. Many people note that top executives wear expensive clothes and drive nice cars. They do the same, thinking these things must be a key to success.

26. ". . . and let's not underestimate the importance of that home field advantage, guys."

    "Right, Dan. Six of the last seven teams that had the home field advantage went on to win the Super Bowl."

27. On your trip across the country, you note that the traffic is awful at the first intersection you come to in New Jersey. "They certainly didn't do anyone a favor by putting a traffic light at this place," you reflect. "Look at all the congestion it caused."

Exercise 11-23

Here's a news report on the costs of drug abuse that appeared during the administration of George II. W. Bush. See if you can find any flaws in the reasoning by which the figures were reached.

> J. Michael Walsh, an officer of the National Institute on Drug Abuse, has testified that the "cost of drug abuse to U.S. industry" was nearly $50 billion a year, according to "conservative estimates." President Bush has rounded this figure upward to "anywhere from $60 billion to $100 billion." This figure would seem to be a difficult one to determine. Here's how Walsh arrived at it. After a survey of 3,700 households, a NIDA contractor analyzed the data and found that the household income of adults who had *ever* smoked marijuana daily for a month [or at least twenty out of thirty days] was 28 percent less than the income of those who hadn't. The analysts called this difference "reduced productivity due to daily marijuana use." They calculated the total "loss," when extrapolated to the general population, at $26 billion. Adding the estimated costs of drug-related crimes, accidents, and medical care produced a grand total of $47 billion for "costs to society of drug abuse."

Exercise 11-24

Men are involved in far more fatal automobile crashes than are women. List as many plausible explanations for this as you can.

Writing Exercises

1. Construct a brief essay in which you (a) support the claim that cheating is widespread in high school (or was widespread in your high school), (b) offer an explanation of why it is widespread, and (c) show why your explanation is a good one.

2. Are women less competitive than men? In a brief essay, (a) explain what you think the investigations in the box on the following page show, if anything; or (b) set forth alternative explanations for the results; or (c) describe what implications you think these investigations have.

3. Which of the following causal hypotheses do you accept? Select one that you accept and, using the Internet or other sources, marshal evidence that supports your position. Limit yourself to one page unless instructed otherwise.

   > Marijuana use is a gateway to hard drug use.
   >
   > The death penalty is/isn't a deterrent to murder.
   >
   > Welfare makes people lazy.
   >
   > Beer is better/not better/worse for you after a workout than water.
   >
   > Rap music/TV/movies/pornography promotes violent crime.

Real Life

Are Women Less Competitive?

Studies Uncover a Striking Pattern

Although women have made huge strides in catching up with men in the workplace, a gender gap persists both in wages and levels of advancement. Commonly cited explanations for this gap range from charges of sex discrimination to claims that women are more sensitive than men to work-family conflicts and thus less inclined to make sacrifices for their careers.

Now, however, two new studies by economists Uri Gneezy of the University of Chicago and Aldo Rustichini of the University of Minnesota suggest that another factor may be at work: a deeply in-grained difference in the way men and women react to competition that manifests itself even at an early age.

The first study focused on short races run by some 140 9- and 10-year-old boys and girls in a physical education class. At that age, there was no significant difference between the average speeds of boys and girls when each child ran the course alone. But when pairs of chil-

dren with similar initial speeds ran the race again, things changed. Boys' speeds increased appreciably when running against either a boy or a girl, but more so when paired with a girl. Girls showed no increase when running against a boy and even ran a bit more slowly when paired with a girl.

The second study, by Gneezy, Rustichini, and Muriel Niederle of Stanford University, involved several hundred students at an elite Israeli technical university. Groups of six students were paid to solve simple maze problems on a computer. In some groups, subjects were paid 50¢ for each problem they solved during the experiment. In others, only the person solving the most problems got rewarded—but at the rate of $3 for each maze solved.

Regardless of the sexual makeup of the groups, men and women, on average, did equally well when students were paid for their own performance. But when only the top student was paid, average male performance rose sharply—by about 50%—while female performance remained the same.

The authors conclude that females tend to be far less responsive to competition than males—a tendency with important implications for women and business. It may hurt women in highly competitive labor markets, for example, and hamper efficient job placement—especially for positions in which competitiveness is not a useful trait.

That's something companies with highly competitive atmospheres may need to consider, says Rustichini. If they don't, the results could be "both a subtle bias against women and, in many cases, foregone worker productivity."

—*Gene Koretz*

Let's race: Boys' speeds went up.

Source: Business Week, December 9, 2002.

12

Moral, Legal, and Aesthetic Reasoning

H er fiancé had been in Iraq for eleven months, and his tour of duty had been extended for four more. While he was away, she met someone else. Should she tell her fiancé immediately, or wait until he returned? "Feeling Guilty" asked Dear Abby what to do.

Abby* didn't mince words. "Grow up and think about someone other than yourself," she began (somewhat harshly, we thought). Feeling Guilty's number one duty, Abby said, is making sure not to distract her fiancé. "Under no circumstances should you write him a 'Dear John' letter or tell him anything that could unnerve or depress him."

Was "Dear Abby" correct about this?

From time to time, we all face tough moral decisions. A mother must decide whether her daughter's softball game has a higher priority than her professional responsibility. A president may have to decide whether to take a nation to war. When he was governor of Texas, George W. Bush had to decide whether to bestow clemency on Karla Faye Tucker, an ax murderer who became a likable born-again Christian in prison and whose execution some said would be hugely wrong.

When people think abstractly, sometimes they believe that moral issues are subjective. You hear them say such

*Actually, Jeanne Phillips, the original Abby's daughter, writes the column. This column was printed September 6, 2006.

Students will learn to . . .

1. Distinguish moral value judgments from value judgments

2. Apply the principles of moral reasoning

3. Recognize the problem of inconsistency in moral judgment

4. Explain the most influential frameworks for moral reasoning in Western thought

5. Recognize the place of perspectives in moral deliberations

6. Recognize principles that underlie legal reasoning and argument

7. Explain various definitions of aesthetic value and judgment

Advice given in Dear Abby and similar columns often employs moral reasoning, which is discussed in this chapter.

things as "When it comes to what you should do, the right thing is what seems right to you. End of story." However, we asked a class how many thought Abby should just have told Feeling Guilty, "Hey, do whatever you feel like"—not a single hand was raised. When people hear about a real moral dilemma, not to mention confront one for themselves, they usually *don't* think it's merely a matter of personal opinion. They discuss the issue with others, seek advice, consider options, and weigh consequences. When they do this, they find that some considerations and arguments carry more weight and are better than others. (You may remember our brief treatment of this topic in Chapter 1, page 6.)

In the first part of this chapter, we look at what actually is involved in moral reasoning and deliberation. Then we will do the same for aspects of legal reasoning and for aesthetic reasoning.

VALUE JUDGMENTS

Let's begin by fine-tuning what we mean when we talk about moral reasoning. Recently, our colleague Becky White debated what to do about a student who had copied parts of someone else's term paper and was silly enough to think Professor White wouldn't notice. Many things could be said about the student; what Professor White said was, "He deserves an F." And that's what she gave him—for the entire course.

Professor White's statement is what people call a "value judgment."* A **value judgment** assesses the merit, desirability, or praiseworthiness of someone or something. When our colleague said the student deserved an F, she wasn't describing him; she was *judging* him. She thought he had done something *wrong*.

Moral reasoning differs from other kinds of reasoning in that it consists mainly in trying to establish moral value judgments. Because moral reasoning is all about moral value judgments, you need to be able to identify one when you run into it.

A difficulty is that not every value judgment expresses a *moral* value judgment. When you say a movie is pretty good, you are judging the movie, but not morally. When you say Pepsi is better than Coke, you are making a taste value judgment, not a moral value judgment.

To help solidify your grasp of the important concept of a moral value judgment, the claims in the left column are all moral value judgments; those in the right are value judgments, but not of the moral variety. Exercises on moral reasoning are at the end of the section titled "Moral Deliberation" in this chapter.

Moral Value Judgments	**Nonmoral Value Judgments**
1. It was wrong for the senator to withhold information.	1. The senator dresses well.
2. The senator ought not to claim residence in one district when he actually lives in another.	2. *Avatar* has some of the best special effects of any movie ever made.

---

*Value judgments are also known as "normative" or "prescriptive" statements. We'll stick with "value judgments" because the term is largely self-explanatory and we want to avoid terminological clutter.

3. Abortion is immoral.
4. Children should be taught to respect their elders.
5. I don't deserve to be flunked for an honest mistake.

3. As an actress, Paris Hilton is a nice clothes rack.
4. Frank Zappa was an excellent guitarist.
5. Keith Lewis must be a total flake.

Typically, moral value judgments employ such words as "good," "bad," "right," "wrong," "ought," "should," "proper," and "justified," "fair," and so forth, and their opposites. But you need to bear in mind that, although these words often signal a moral evaluation, they do not always do so. Telling someone she should keep her promise is making a moral value judgment; telling her she should keep her knees bent when skiing is assigning a positive value to keeping bent knees, but not a moral value.

It's also worth noticing that implicit value judgments can be made inside claims that are not themselves value judgments. For example, "David Axelrod, a good man, engineered President Obama's election" is not a value judgment, but the part about Axelrod being a good man is.

Moral Versus Nonmoral

A source of confusion in discussions that involve moral reasoning is the word "moral." The word has two separate and distinct meanings. First, "moral" may be used as the opposite of "nonmoral." This is the sense in which we have been using the term. The claim "Karl Rove weighs more than 200 pounds" is a nonmoral claim, meaning it has nothing to do with morality. "Karl Rove is an evil man," by contrast, has a lot to do with morality: It is a moral value judgment, a claim that expresses a moral value. The same is true of the claim, "Karl Rove is a good man."

The second meaning of "moral" is the opposite not of "nonmoral" but of "immoral." Kicking a cat for the heck of it would be immoral; taking care of it would be moral. In this sense of the word, "moral" is used to mean "good," "right," "proper," and so forth.

To avoid confusion, when we use the word "moral" in this chapter, we always mean moral as opposed to nonmoral; that is, as having to do with morality. Thus, the statements "It was wrong to kick the cat" and "It wasn't wrong to kick the cat" are both moral judgments.

Two Principles of Moral Reasoning

Suppose Moore announces on the first day of class that the final exam will be optional. "Except," he says, pointing at some person at random, "for the young woman there in the third row. For you," he says, "the final is mandatory."

The problem here is that this student is no different from everyone else, yet Moore is treating her differently. And this brings us to the first principle of moral reasoning.

Moral Reasoning Principle 1

If separate cases aren't different in any relevant way, then they should be treated the same way, and if separate cases are treated the same way, they should not be different in any relevant way.

For convenience, let's call this the **consistency principle.** If Moore gives two students the same grade despite the fact that one student did much better than the other, Moore has violated the principle.

It is important to see that this is a principle of *moral reasoning,* not a moral principle. It's not like saying, "You should be kind to animals." It's like saying, "If all Xs are Ys, then if this thing is an X, then it is a Y"—"If all students are entitled to an optional final, then if the young woman in the third row is a student, then she is entitled to an optional final."

The second principle of moral reasoning is procedural rather than logical:

Moral Reasoning Principle 2

If someone appears to be violating the consistency principle, then the burden of proof is on that person to show that he or she is in fact not violating the principle.

For example, if Parker says, "Blue-eyed students can take tests with books open, but nobody else can," he needs to show that he is not violating the consistency principle. He must show that there is something about having blue eyes that should entitle such individuals to take their tests with their books open.

When do separate cases count as the same or different? Fortunately, Principle 2 enables us to sidestep having to answer this question in the abstract. If Harlan approves of the war in Iraq but opposed the war in Vietnam, and the cases seem to us not to differ in any relevant way, then, if Harlan cannot point to a difference that seems satisfactory to us, then we are justified in regarding him as inconsistent. If Carol treats black customers and white customers differently and cannot identify for us some relevant difference between the two, then we are justified in regarding her as inconsistent.

Suppose, however, that Carol thinks that skin color itself is a difference between blacks and whites relevant to how people should be treated, and she charges us with failing to make relevant discriminations. Here, it would be easy for us to point out to Carol that skin color is an immutable characteristic of birth like height or eye color; does Carol adjust her civility to people depending on those characteristics?

It isn't difficult to perceive the inconsistency on the part of a salesperson who is more polite to customers of one group; but other cases are far tougher, and many are such that reasonable people will disagree about their proper assessment. Is a person inconsistent who approves of abortion but not capital punishment? Is a person inconsistent who, on the one hand, believes that the states should be free to reduce spending on welfare but, on the other, does not think that the states should be able to eliminate ceilings on punitive damages in tort cases? No harm is done in asking, "What's the difference?" and because much headway can be made in a discussion by doing so, it seems wise to ask.

In Chapter 7, we talked about the inconsistency ad hominem, a fallacy we commit when we think we rebut the content of what someone says by pointing out inconsistency on his or her part. Now, let's say Ramesh tells us it is wrong to hunt, and then we find out Ramesh likes to fish. And let's say that, when we press Ramesh, he cannot think of any relevant moral difference between the two activities. Then he is being inconsistent. But that does not mean that it is right to hunt, nor does it mean that it is wrong to fish. An inconsistency ad hominem occurs if we say something like "Ramesh, you are mistaken when you say it is wrong to hunt, because you yourself fish." It is not an inconsistency ad hominem to say, "Ramesh, you are being inconsistent. You must change your position on either hunting or fishing."

Similarly, let's suppose Professor Moore gives Howard an A and gives James a C but cannot think of any differences between their performance in his course. It would be committing the inconsistency ad hominem if we said, "Moore, James does not deserve a C, because you gave Howard an A." Likewise, it would be committing the inconsistency ad hominem if we said, "Moore, Howard does not deserve an A, because you gave James a C." But it is *not* illogical to say, "Moore, you are being inconsistent. You have misgraded one of these students."

Moral Principles

Because separate moral cases, if similar, must be given similar treatment, a moral principle is a value judgment that is general in nature. That is, a moral principle refers to what should be done (or is right, proper, etc.) not just in a single case but in all similar cases. "Stealing is wrong" is a moral principle. "It is wrong to steal from Billy Bob" is just a true moral value judgment about a specific case. Likewise, "It is wrong for Billy Bob to steal" is a specific moral value judgment and not a moral principle. To qualify as a moral principle, a moral value judgment must be general in scope. Actually, this follows from the consistency principle. The largest part of everyday moral reasoning takes the form of deducing specific moral value judgments from general moral principles. We'll look next at how this works.

In Depth

Deducing the Right Thing to Do

Nearly any kind of reasoning can appear in a discussion of moral matters. For example, we might need to generalize from a sample in order to support a utilitarian claim about how many people would be made happy by some action. However, we've come to the conclusion that the great majority of arguments people make in this context are deductive ones. Whenever an issue arises about what one should do, the claim "You (or she or he or I) should do X" is almost always the conclusion of a categorical syllogism or a chain argument. (The first of these is discussed in Chapter 8, the second in Chapter 9.) Something like this would be typical:

> Everybody who benefited from the program should contribute to its continuance.
> Denzil certainly benefited from the program.
> Therefore, Denzil should contribute to its continuance.

The fact that such arguments are so frequently part of a discussion about what one should do is not surprising, since they seem to reflect our powerful reliance on the consistency principle—that like cases be treated alike. This principle is embedded in the general claim in the premises regarding Denzil, as it groups together everybody who benefited from the program as *prima facie* similar cases.

More about how this works is found in the section "Deriving Specific Moral Value Judgments."

Deriving Specific Moral Value Judgments

From the standpoint of logic, there is something puzzling about deriving a specific moral value judgment from a premise that is not a value judgment. For example, consider this argument:

> 1a. Elliott's father depends on Elliott. Therefore, Elliott should take care of him.

We hear such arguments in everyday life and tend to think nothing of them; they certainly do not seem illogical. If facts and statistics are not grounds for making moral decisions, what is? Nevertheless, logically, arguments like this—the basic kind of argument of moral reasoning—are puzzling, because the premise ("Elliott's father depends on Elliott") is not a value judgment, whereas the conclusion ("Elliott should take care of him") is. How, logically, can we get from the "is" premise to the "should" conclusion? How does the "should" get in there?

The answer is that the conclusion of this argument follows logically from the stated premise, only if a *general* moral principle is assumed. In this case, a principle that would work is: Adult children should take care of parents who are dependent on them. Here is the argument with its conclusion:

> 1b. Premise: Elliott's father depends on Elliott.
> [Unstated general moral principle: Adult children should take care of their parents who are dependent on them.]
> Conclusion: Therefore, Elliott should take care of his father.

The result is a valid deductive argument. Likewise, any chain of moral reasoning that starts from a claim about facts and ends up with a moral value judgment assumes a general principle that ties the fact-stating "is" premise to the value-stating "should" conclusion.

So far, this is just a point about the logic of moral reasoning. But there is a practical point to be made here as well. It helps clarify matters to consider our general moral principles when we advance moral arguments. If we agree with the premise that Elliott's father depends on Elliott but disagree with the conclusion that Elliott should take care of his father, then our quarrel must be with the unstated general principle that adult children should take care of their parents who are dependent on them. For example, should an adult take care of parents even if it means sacrificing the welfare of his or her spouse? Considering the assumed general moral principle that ties the fact-stating premise with the value-judging conclusion can go a long way toward clarifying the issues involved in a moral decision.

For another example, you sometimes hear this said:

> Homosexuality is unnatural. Therefore, it ought not to be practiced.

A general moral principle assumed here might be: Whatever is unnatural ought not to be done. Bringing that principle to light sets the stage for fruitful discussion. What counts as unnatural? Is it unnatural to fly? To wear clothing? To live to 100? To have sex beyond one's reproductive years? And is it true that unnatural things never should be done? In the natural world, severely disabled offspring are left to fend for themselves; are we wrong to care for our own severely disabled children? Scratching oneself in public certainly qualifies as natural, but in our culture not to do so is considered the proper thing to do.

Earlier, we mentioned our colleague Becky White, who failed a student for copying parts of another student's paper. As it so happens, Professor White also considered whether to penalize the student who allowed his paper to be read by a classmate. Was it wrong for Charles (whose name we have changed) to show his work to a classmate who then copied parts of it? Thinking that it was wrong would require a general principle, and one that would work would be: It is wrong to show your work to classmates before they have turned in their own work. This principle would yield a deductively valid argument, and there is something to be said for the principle. For example, showing your exam answers to the classmate sitting next to you is grounds for dismissal in many universities. At the same time, showing a term paper to a classmate to get constructive feedback is a good thing. Careful consideration of the principle above might lead to the conclusion that, in fact, Charles did nothing wrong.

Now let's look at the most general and fundamental moral principles assumed in most moral reasoning.

Which of the following claims are value judgments?   Exercise 12-1

▲   1. Lizards make fine pets.
     2. You can get a clothes rack at True Value for less than $15.00.
     3. The last haircut I got at Supercuts was just totally awful.
▲   4. It was a great year for regional politics.
     5. Key officials of the Department of Defense are producing their own unverified intelligence reports about an arms buildup.
     6. Texas leads the nation in accidental deaths caused by police chases.
▲   7. Napoleon Bonaparte was the greatest military leader of modern times.
     8. Racial segregation is immoral anytime, anywhere.
     9. President Bush deployed a "missile defense" that wasn't adequately tested.
▲   10. Air consists mainly of nitrogen and oxygen.

Which of the following claims are value judgments?   Exercise 12-2

▲   1. T-shirts made by Fruit of the Loom are soft and luxurious.
     2. Rumsfeld was nearly as detailed as Rice in reports to the press.
     3. The Pentagon was not nearly as supportive of a war as it should have been.
▲   4. Tens of billions of dollars have been wasted on worthless public transportation schemes.
     5. Atlanta is sultry in the summer.
     6. Religious school teachers are stricter than their nonreligious counterparts.
▲   7. Six Flags has the scariest rides in the state.

8. The politician with the best sense of humor? That would have to be Al Sharpton.

9. Eugene is not nearly as happy as his wife, Polly.

10. Polly is more selfish than she should be.

Exercise 12-3

Which of the following are moral value judgments?

▲ 1. Marina's car puts out horrible smoke; for the sake of us all, she should get it tuned up.

2. After the surgery, Nicky's eyesight improved considerably.

3. Ms. Beeson ought not to have embezzled money from the bank.

▲ 4. Violence is always wrong.

5. Matthew ought to wear that sweater more often; it looks great on him.

6. Sandy, you are one of the laziest people I know!

▲ 7. My computer software is really good; it even corrects my grammar.

8. Lisa has been very good tonight, according to the babysitter.

9. Judge Ramesh is quite well-informed.

▲ 10. Judge Ramesh's decision gave each party exactly what it deserved.

11. The editor couldn't use my illustrations; she said they were not particularly interesting.

12. Wow. That was a tasty meal!

13. The last set of essays was much better than the first set.

14. Do unto others as you would have them do unto you.

15. People who live in glass houses shouldn't throw stones.

16. You really shouldn't make so much noise when the people upstairs are trying to sleep.

17. It is unfair the way Professor Smith asks questions no normal person can answer.

18. "Allegro" means fast, but not that fast!

19. Being in touch with God gives your life meaning and value.

20. Thou shalt not kill.

MAJOR PERSPECTIVES IN MORAL REASONING

Moral reasoning usually takes place within one or more frameworks or perspectives. Here, we consider perspectives that have been especially influential in Western thought.

Consequentialism

The perspective known as **consequentialism** is the view that the *consequences* of a decision, deed, or policy determine its moral value. If an action produces better consequences than the alternatives, then it is the better action, morally speaking. One of the most important versions of this view is **utilitarianism,** which says that, if an act will produce more happiness than will alternatives, it is the right thing to do, and if it will produce less happiness, it would be wrong to do it in place of an alternative that would produce more happiness.

Many of us use a pro/con list of consequences as a guideline when considering what course of action to take. Your parents are divorced; should you spend Thanksgiving with your father's side of the family or with your mother's? Someone will be disappointed, but there may be more people disappointed on one side. Or the disappointment may be more deeply felt on one side. As a utilitarian, you calculate as best you can how your decision will affect the happiness of people on both sides of the equation. Plus, (using inductive reasoning) you have to factor in how *certain* the outcomes of each alternative are with respect to happiness, assigning more weight to relatively more certain positive outcomes. Because you can generally be more certain of the effect of an act on your own happiness and on the happiness of others you know well, it is often morally proper to favor the act that best promotes your own or their happiness. Of course, you must not use this as an excuse to be entirely self-serving: Your own happiness isn't more important morally than another's. The best course of action morally is not always the one that best promotes your own happiness.

In sum, utilitarians weigh the consequences of the alternatives, pro and con, and then choose the alternative that maximizes happiness. One of the original and most profound intellects behind utilitarianism, Jeremy Bentham (1748–1832), even went so far as to devise a *hedonistic calculus* a method of assigning actual numerical values to pleasures and pains based on their intensity, certainty, duration, and so forth. Other utilitarians think that some pleasures are of a higher quality (e.g., reading Shakespeare is of a higher quality than watching SpongeBob). Although there are other important issues in utilitarianism, the basic idea involves weighing the consequences of possible actions in terms of happiness. Utilitarianism has considerable popular appeal, and real-life moral reasoning is often utilitarian to a considerable extent.

Nevertheless, some aspects of the theory are problematic. Typically, when we deliberate whether or not to do something, we don't always take into consideration only the effect of the action on happiness. For example, other people have *rights* that we sometimes take into account. We would not make someone in our family a slave, even if the happiness produced for the family by doing so outweighed the unhappiness it created for the slave. We also consider our *duties* and *obligations*. We think it is our duty to return a loan to someone, even if we are still short of cash and the other person doesn't need the money and doesn't even remember having loaned it to us. If we make a date and then want to break it because we've met the love of our life, we think twice about standing up our original date, even if we believe that our overall happiness will far outweigh the temporary unhappiness of our date. To many, the moral obligation of a promise cannot be ignored for the sake of the overall happiness that might result from breaking it.

In estimating the moral worth of what people do, utilitarianism also seems to discount people's *intentions*. Suppose a mugger attacks somebody just as a huge flower pot falls from a balcony above. The mugger happens to push the individual the instant before the flower pot lands on the exact spot where the victim had been standing. The mugger has saved the victim's life, as it turns out. But would we say that the mugger did a morally good deed just because his action had a happy result? According to utilitarianism, we would—assuming the net result of the action was more happiness than would

In Depth

Acts and Rules

Thinking of cheating on a test? Maybe the sum total of happiness in the world would be increased by this single *act* of cheating. But it isn't inconceivable that, if the *principle* involved were adopted widely, the sum total of happiness would be decreased.

This raises the question: When calculating happiness outcomes, should we contemplate happiness outcomes of the particular *act* in question? Or should we contemplate happiness outcomes of adoption of the *principle* involved in the act?

Accordingly, some philosophers make a distinction between "act utilitarianism," which evaluates the moral worth of an act on the happiness it would produce, and "rule utilitarianism," which evaluates the moral worth of an act on the happiness that would be produced by adoption of the principle it exemplifies. (A possible middle ground might be to attempt to factor in, as a part of the happiness outcomes of a particular act, the likelihood that doing it will contribute to a general adoption of the principle involved. This is often what we do when we ask, "But what if everyone did this?")

otherwise have been the case. So, utilitarianism doesn't seem to be the complete story in moral reasoning.

Another important consequentialist theory is **ethical egoism,** the idea that, if an act produces more happiness for oneself than will the alternatives, then it is the right thing to do, and if it produces less happiness for oneself than the alternatives, it is wrong to do it. Clearly, any well-thought-out theory of ethical egoism does not prescribe acting purely selfishly, for selfish behavior is not likely to produce the most happiness for oneself in the long run. Still, there is a difference between saying that the reason for doing something is to bring yourself happiness and saying that the reason for doing something is to bring others happiness. The latter doctrine is **ethical altruism,** which discounts one's own happiness as of lesser value than the happiness of others. From this perspective, utilitarianism is the middle ground, in which one's own happiness and others' happiness are treated as equally important.

Duty Theory/Deontologism

Immanuel Kant (1724–1804), who witnessed the beginning phases of the utilitarian philosophy, found utilitarianism deficient because of its neglect, among other things, of moral duty. Kant's theory is a version of what is called **duty theory,** or **deontologism.**

Kant acknowledged that our lives are full of imperatives based on our own situations and our objectives. If we want to advance at work, then it is imperative that we keep our promises; if we are concerned about our friends' happiness, then it is imperative that we not talk about them behind their backs. But this type of **hypothetical imperative,** which tells us we ought to do (or ought not to do) something in order to achieve such and such a result, is not a *moral* imperative, Kant argued. Keeping a promise so we'll get a solid reputation is neither morally praiseworthy nor morally blameworthy, he said. For our act to be *morally* praiseworthy, it must be done, not for the sake of some objective, but simply because *it is right*. Our action of keeping our promise is morally praise-worthy, he said, only if we do it simply because it is right to keep our promises. A moral imperative is unconditional or **categorical;** it prescribes an action, not for the sake of some result, but simply because that action is our moral duty.

It follows from this philosophy that, when it comes to evaluating an action morally, what counts is not the result or consequences of the action, as utilitarianism maintains, but the intention from which it is done. And the morally best intention—indeed, in Kant's opinion the *only* truly morally praiseworthy intention—is that according to which you do something just because it is your moral duty.

But what makes something our moral duty? Some deontologists ground duty in human nature; others ground it in reason; in Western culture, of course, many believe moral duty is set by God. How can we tell what our duty is? Some believe our duty is to be found by consulting conscience; others believe that it is just self-evident or is clear to moral intuition. Those who maintain that human moral duties are established by God usually derive their specific understanding of these duties through interpretations of religious texts such as the Bible, though there is disagreement over what the correct interpretation is and even over who should do the interpreting.

Kant answered the question, How can we tell what our moral duty is? as follows: Suppose you are considering some course of action—say, whether to borrow some money you need very badly. But suppose you know you can't pay back the loan. Is it morally permissible for you to borrow money under such circumstances? Kant said to do this: First, find the *maxim* (principle of action) involved in what you want to do. In the case in question, the maxim is "When I'm in need of money, I'll go to my friends and promise I'll pay it back, even if I know I can't." Next, ask yourself, "Could I want this maxim to be a *universal* law or rule, one that everyone should follow?" This process of *universalization* is the feature that lets you judge whether something would work as a moral law, according to Kant. Could you make it a universal law that it is okay for every-body to lie about paying back loans? Hardly: If everyone adopted this principle, then there would be no such thing as loan making. In short, the universalization of your principle undermines the very principle that is universalized. If everyone adopted the principle, then nobody could possibly follow it. The universaliza-tion of your principle is illogical, so it is your duty to pay back loans.

As you can see, the results of acting according to Kant's theory can be radically different from the results of acting according to utilitarianism. Utili-tarianism would condone borrowing money with no intention of repaying it, assuming that doing so would produce more happiness than would be pro-duced by not doing so. But Kant's theory would not condone it.

Kant also noted that, if you were to borrow a friend's money with no intention of repaying it, you would be treating your friend merely as a means to an end. If you examine cases like this, in which you use other people as mere tools for your own objectives, then, Kant said, you will find in each case a transgression of moral duty, a principle of action that cannot be universal-ized. Thus, he warned us, it is our moral duty never to treat someone else *merely* as a tool, as means to an end. Of course, Kant did not mean that Moore cannot ask Parker for help on some project; doing so would not be a case of Moore's using Parker *merely* as a tool.

Kant's theory of the moral necessity of never treating other people as mere tools can be modified to support the ideas that people have rights and that treatment of others must always involve fair play. Regardless of whether

Real Life

Inmate Who Got New Heart While Still in Prison Dies

A California prison inmate believed to be the first in the nation to receive a heart transplant while incarcerated has died, officials said Tuesday.

Department of Corrections spokesman Russ Heimerich said the inmate, whose identity has been withheld, died late Monday at Stanford University Medical Center.

Heimerich said the exact cause of death was still undetermined, "but it looks like his body was rejecting the heart" he received in an expensive and controversial taxpayer-financed operation in January.

Officials estimated the surgery and subsequent care—including the $12,500 a day it cost to keep him in the Stanford facility after he was admitted Nov. 23—have cost more than $1.25 million. Heimerich said that figure does not include transportation, medication or providing round-the-clock security while the inmate was in the hospital.

"It could easily reach $2 million when it's all added in," Heimerich said.

The prisoner was a 32-year-old two-time felon serving a 14-year sentence for robbing a Los Angeles convenience store in 1996. He was eligible for parole in October 2008.

He became the center of a national controversy after *The Bee* disclosed the surgery, which also took place at Stanford.

The operation raised questions about whether there should be limits on the kinds of medical care to which prison inmates are entitled.

At the time of the transplant, prison officials said they were required under numerous court orders, including a 1976 U.S. Supreme Court decision, to provide necessary health care to all inmates.

The decision to provide the inmate, who had longtime heart problems caused by a viral infection, with a new heart was made by a medical panel at Stanford. The surgery was performed on a day when at least 500 other Californians were waiting for similar operations.

But medical professionals and organ transplant centers said they can make decisions about who gets organs and who doesn't based only on medical protocols and not social factors.

While the first of its kind, the transplant is not likely to be the last. As California's prison population ages, authorities are concerned the cost of inmate health care will soar far above last fiscal year's $663 million.

Compounding the problem, Heimerich said, is that many inmate patients don't follow doctor's orders. He said the heart recipient apparently did not follow all of the medical recommendations, although it wasn't clear his failure to do so played a role in his death.

"We can treat them," Heimerich said, "but we can't baby-sit them."

—*Steve Wiegand,*
Bee *staffwriter*

Comment: Such cases involve legal reasoning (see next section of this chapter) as well as moral reasoning. The position taken here by medical professionals is duty theory; they are explicitly ruling out utilitarian considerations in deciding to whom to give transplants.

Source: The *Sacramento Bee.*

you subscribe to Kant's version of duty theory, the chances are that your own moral deliberations are more than just strictly utilitarian and may well involve considerations of what you take to be other moral requirements, including your duties and the rights of others.

Moral Relativism

One popular view of ethics, especially perhaps among undergraduates taking a first course in philosophy, is **moral relativism,** the idea that what is right and wrong depends on and is determined by one's group or culture.

A mistake sometimes made in moral reasoning is to confuse the following two claims:

1. What is *believed* to be right and wrong may differ from group to group, society to society, or culture to culture.

2. What *is* right and wrong may differ from group to group, society to society, or culture to culture.

The second claim, but not the first, is moral relativism. Please go back and read the two claims carefully. They are so similar that it takes a moment to see they are actually quite different. But they are different. The first claim is incontestable; the second claim is controversial and problematic. It may well have been the majority belief in ancient Greece that there was nothing wrong with slavery. But that does not mean that at that time there was nothing wrong with slavery.

It is worth noting that moral relativism suffers from three potential difficulties. First, exactly what counts as a group, society, or culture, and what are the criteria for membership in one? How many groups, societies, or cultures do you belong to? You probably find it hard to say. This makes it difficult to specify which set of general principles apply to a person.

The second difficulty is that conflicting views about moral principles are to be found within all but the very smallest groups. For example, even within small communities, people may disagree about gay marriage.

A third difficulty is perhaps less obvious. To understand the problem, if someone belongs to a society that believes it is permissible to kill Americans, then you, as a moral relativist, must concede it is permissible for that person to kill Americans. But if Americans in general agree on anything, it is that nobody should kill another person simply because of his or her national status. Therefore, if you are an American, you must also say it is *not* permissible for that person to kill Americans. Subscribing to moral relativism has placed you in a self-contradictory position.

Another popular moral perspective is **moral subjectivism,** the idea that what is right and wrong is merely a matter of subjective opinion, that thinking that something is right or wrong makes it right or wrong for that individual. We considered subjectivism in Chapter 1 and saw there the mistake in thinking that all value judgments are subjective.

Religious Relativism

As you might expect, **religious relativism** is the belief that what is right and wrong is whatever one's religious culture or society deems. The problems attending this view are the same as those for other versions of relativism. First,

I'm not guilty of murder. I'm guilty of obeying the laws of the Creator.

—BENJAMIN MATTHEW WILLIAMS, who committed suicide while awaiting sentencing for having murdered a gay couple

The Ten Commandments represent the perspective of religious absolutism.

what counts as a religious culture or society and as membership within one? Are Baptists and Catholics part of the same culture? Are you a Christian even if you never attend church? Second, even within a single culture, conflicting moral views are likely to be found. The United Church of Christ, for example, currently is conflicted about gay marriage.

Third, those who belong to one religion might well consider practices of other religions to be sinful. For example, members of the first religion may think it is sinful to worship a false god. Thus, according to religious relativism, if you belong to the first religion, then you must say that those who worship the other god are doing something sinful, because that is the view of your religion. But as a religious relativist, you must also say that those who worship the other god are *not* doing something sinful.

Religious Absolutism

One way out of this difficulty might be to subscribe to **religious absolutism,** which maintains that the correct moral principles are those accepted by the "correct" religion. A problem, of course, is that opinions vary as to what the correct religion is, and there seems to be no good reason for thinking that one is more correct—more likely to be true— than another.

Virtue Ethics

Up to this point, the ethical perspectives discussed have focused on the question of what is the right or proper act, decision, practice, or policy. For that reason, these perspectives are referred to as "ethics of conduct." However, another approach, one predominant in classical Greek thinking, has regained popularity among some contemporary moral philosophers. This approach, known as **virtue ethics,** focuses not on what to do but on how to be.

To find an excellent example of virtue ethics, one need look no further than the Boy Scout pledge. A Boy Scout doesn't pledge to do or to refrain from doing this or that particular action; instead, he pledges to *be* a certain kind of person. He pledges to *be* trustworthy, loyal, helpful, friendly, courteous, kind, brave, and so forth. This is a list of "virtues," or traits of character. A person who has them is disposed by habit to act in certain ways and not to act in others.

The ancient Greeks believed it was supremely important for a person to achieve psychological and physical balance; and to do that, the person needed to develop a consistently good character. A person out of balance will not be able to assess a situation properly and will tend to overreact or to not react strongly enough; moreover, such a person will not know his or her proper limits. People who recognize their own qualifications and limitations and who are capable of reacting to the right degree, at the right time, toward the right person, and for the right reason are virtuous persons. They understand the value of the idea of moderation: not too much and not too little, but in each case a response that is just right.

Aristotle (384–322 B.C.E.) regarded virtue as a trait, like wisdom, justice, or courage, that we acquire when we use our capacity to reason to moderate our impulses and appetites. The largest part of Aristotle's major ethical writing, the *Nicomachean Ethics*, is devoted to analysis of specific moral virtues as means between extremes (for example, courage is the mean between fearing everything and fearing nothing). He also emphasized that virtue is a matter of habit; it is a trait, a way of living.

Virtue ethics is not an abstruse ethical theory. Many of us (fortunately) wish to be (or to become) persons of good character. And as a practical matter, when we are deliberating a course of action, our approach often is to consider what someone whose character we admire would do in the circumstances.

Still, it is possible that virtue theory alone cannot answer all moral questions. Each of us may face moral dilemmas of such a nature that it simply isn't clear what course of action is required by someone of good character.

Determine which ethical perspective is primarily reflected in each of the following statements. Choose from

Exercise 12-4

    A = consequentialism

    B = duty ethics/deontology

    C = virtue ethics

    D = moral relativism

    E = religious absolutism

1. Yes, innocent civilians have been killed in Iraq. But in the long run, the world will be a safer place if Iraq becomes a democracy.

2. Although many cultures have practiced human sacrifice, within the culture it was not thought to be wrong. So, human sacrifice within those cultures wasn't really immoral.

3. *(Note: "Preferential treatment" refers to the practice of some universities and professional schools of lowering entrance requirements for women and ethnic minorities.)* Preferential treatment is wrong, period. You shouldn't discriminate against anyone, no matter how much society benefits from it.

4. Sure, we might benefit from expanding Highway 99. But seizing a person's property against his or her wishes is just wrong, period.

5. Sure, we might benefit from expanding Highway 99. But it's wrong to seize someone's property, at least in this country. In our society, property rights are fundamental.

6. Sure, we might benefit from expanding Highway 99. But it's wrong to seize someone's property! You have a God-given right to own property.

▲ 7. If a company doesn't want to hire a woman, nobody should force it to. A company has a right to hire whomever it wants!

8. You have to balance a person's rights against the common good. Pornography isn't good for a society, and we should get rid of it.

9. Gay marriage? I think it is only fair! The right to happiness is a basic human right.

▲ 10. Gay marriage? I am against it. Once gays start marrying, the next thing you know, brothers and sisters will get married. Then moms and sons. Society will come apart at the seams.

Exercise 12-5

In each of the following passages, a general moral principle must be added as an extra premise to make the argument valid. Supply such a principle.

Example

> Mrs. Montez's new refrigerator was delivered yesterday, and it stopped working altogether. She has followed the directions carefully but still can't make it work. The people she bought it from should either come out and make it work or replace it with another one.

Principle

> People should make certain the things they sell work.

1. After borrowing Morey's car, Leo had an accident and crumpled a fender. So, Leo ought to pay whatever expenses were involved in getting Morey's car fixed.

▲ 2. When Sarah bought the lawn mower from Jean, she promised to pay another fifty dollars on the first of the month. Since it is now the first, Sarah should pay Jean the money.

3. Kevin worked on his sister's car all weekend. The least she could do is let him borrow the car for his job interview next Thursday.

4. Harold is obligated to supply ten cords of firewood to the lodge by the beginning of October, since he signed a contract guaranteeing delivery of the wood by that date.

▲ 5. Since it was revealed yesterday on the 11:00 news that Mayor Ahearn has been taking bribes, he should step down any day now.

6. As a political candidate, Havenhurst promised to put an end to crime in the inner city. Now that she is in office, we'd like to see results.

▲ 7. Since he has committed his third felony, he should automatically go to prison for twenty-five years.

▲ 8. Laura's priest has advised Laura and her husband not to sign up for the in vitro fertilization program at the hospital, because such treatments are unnatural.

9. Ali has been working overtime a lot lately, so he should receive a bonus.
10. It is true there are more voters in the northern part of the state. But that shouldn't allow the north to dictate to the south.

MORAL DELIBERATION

Before you began this chapter, you may have assumed that moral discussion is merely an exchange of personal opinion or feeling, one that reserves no place for reason or critical thinking. But moral discussion usually assumes some sort of perspective like those we have mentioned here. Actually, in real life, moral reasoning is often a mixture of perspectives, a blend of utilitarian considerations weighted somewhat toward one's own happiness, modified by ideas about duties, rights, and obligations, and mixed often with a thought, perhaps guilty, about what the ideally virtuous person (a parent, a teacher) would do in similar circumstances. It also sometimes involves mistakes—value judgments may be confused with other types of claims, inconsistencies may occur, inductive arguments may be weak or deductive arguments invalid, fallacious reasoning may be present, and so forth.

In Depth

Why Moral Problems Seem Unresolvable

Differences of opinion over ethical issues sometimes seem irreconcilable. Yet this fact often strikes thoughtful people as amazing, because ethical opponents often share a great deal of common ground. For example, pro-life and pro-choice adherents agree on the sanctity of human life. So why in the world can't they resolve their differences? Likewise, those who favor affirmative action and those who agree that racism and sexism still exist and are wrong and need to be eradicated—why can't they resolve their differences?

The answer, in some cases, comes down to a difference in moral perspective. Take affirmative action. Those who favor affirmative action often operate within a utilitarian perspective: They assume that whether a policy should be adopted depends on whether adopting the policy will produce more happiness than will not adopting it. From this perspective, if policies of affirmative action produce more happiness over the long run, then they should be adopted—end of discussion. But those who oppose affirmative action (on grounds other than blatant racism) do so because they believe deontologism trumps utilitarianism. From the deontologist perspective, even if affirmative action policies would produce more happiness in the long run, if they involve even temporarily using some people as a means to that objective, then they are wrong—end of discussion.

In other disputes, the root difference lies elsewhere. Pro-life and pro-choice adherents often both are deontologists and agree, for example, that in the absence of a powerful justification, it is wrong to take a human life. They may disagree, however, either as to what counts as a human life or as to what counts as a powerful justification. This difference, then, comes down to a difference in basic definitions—which fact, incidentally, illustrates how silly it can be to dismiss a discussion as "mere semantics."

We can make headway in our own thinking about moral issues by trying to get clear on what perspective, if any, we are assuming. For example, suppose we are thinking about the death penalty. Our first thought might be that society is much better off if murderers are executed. Are we then assuming a utilitarian perspective? Asking ourselves this question might lead us to consider whether there are *limits* to what we would do for the common good—for example, would we be willing to risk sacrificing an innocent person? It might also lead us to consider how we might *establish* whether society is better off if murderers are executed—if we are utilitarians, then ultimately we will have to establish this if our reasoning is to be compelling.

Or suppose we have seen a friend cheating on an exam. Should we report it to the teacher? Whatever our inclination, it may be wise to consider our perspective. Are we viewing things from a utilitarian perspective? That is, are we assuming that it would promote the most happiness overall to report our friend? Or do we simply believe that it is our duty to report him or her, come what may? Would a virtuous person report his or her friend? Each of these questions will tend to focus our attention on a particular set of considerations—those that are the most relevant to our way of thinking.

It may occur to you to wonder at this point if there is any reason for choosing among perspectives. The answer to this question is yes: Adherents of these positions, philosophers such as those we mentioned, offer grounding or support for their perspectives in theories about human nature, the natural universe, the nature of morality, and other things. In other words, they have *arguments* to support their views. If you are interested, we recommend a course in ethics.

Additional Exercises on Moral Reasoning

Exercise 12-6

Identify each of the following questions as A, B, or C.

   A = moral value judgment
   B = nonmoral value judgment
   C = not a value judgment

▲ 1. You should avoid making such a large down payment.
   2. You can't go wrong taking Professor Anderson's class.
   3. Misdemeanors are punished less severely than felonies.
▲ 4. Anyone who would do a thing like that to another human being is a scumbag.
   5. He thought about homeschooling his kids.
   6. He should have thought about homeschooling his kids.
▲ 7. He thought about whether he should homeschool his kids.
   8. Did he think about homeschooling his kids? Apparently.
▲ 9. It was a darn good thing he thought about homeschooling his kids.

Exercise 12-7

Identify each of the following statements as A, B, or C.

   A = moral value judgment
   B = nonmoral value judgment
   C = not a value judgment

▲   1. The employees deserve health care benefits.

    2. Last year, the employees may have deserved health care benefits, but they don't now.

    3. The employees' health care benefits consumed 40 percent of our operating costs.

▲   4. The health care benefits we gave the employees last year were excessive.

    5. The health care benefits we gave the employees were generous, but not excessive.

    6. Susan is the best photographer in the department.

▲   7. Susan should not have used a filter when she made those photographs.

    8. Susan upset that man when she photographed him; she shouldn't have done that.

    9. Susan's photographs are exquisite in their realism and detail.

▲   10. Be more careful mowing the lawn! You could hurt yourself.

    11. Be more tactful dealing with people! You could hurt them.

    12. Use more fertilizer! You'll get better plants.

    13. Use more deodorant! Your kids will thank you for it.

Answer the question or respond to the statement that concludes each item.   **Exercise 12-8**

▲   1. Tory thinks women should have the same rights as men. However, he also thinks that, although a man should have the right to marry a woman, a woman should not have the right to marry a woman. Is Tory being consistent in his views?

▲   2. At Shelley's university, the minimum GPA requirement for admission is relaxed for 6 percent of incoming students. Half of those admitted under this program are women and minorities, and the other half are athletes, children of alumni, and talented art and music students. Shelley is opposed to special admissions programs for women and minority students; she is not opposed to special admission programs for art and music students, athletes, or children of alumni. Is she consistent?

▲   3. Marin does not approve of abortion because the Bible says explicitly, "Thou shalt not kill." "'Thou shalt not kill' means thou shalt not kill," he says. Marin does, however, approve of capital punishment. Is Marin consistent?

    4. Koko believes that adults should have the unrestricted right to read whatever material they want to read, but she does not believe that her seventeen-year-old daughter Gina should have the unrestricted right to read whatever she wants to read. Is Koko consistent?

    5. Jack maintains that the purpose of marriage is procreation. On these grounds, he opposes same-sex marriages. "Gays can't create children," he explains. However, he does not oppose marriages between heterosexual partners who cannot have children due to age or medical reasons. "It's not the same," he says. Is Jack being consistent?

    6. Alisha thinks the idea of outlawing cigarettes is ridiculous. "Give me a break," she says. "If you want to screw up your health with cigarettes, that's your own business." However, Alisha does not approve of the

legalization of marijuana. "Hel-loh-o," she says. "Marijuana is a *drug*, and the last thing we need is more druggies." Is Alisha being consistent?

7. California's Proposition 209 amends the California state constitution to prohibit "discrimination or preferential treatment" in state hiring based on race, gender, or ethnicity. Opponents say that Proposition 209 singles out women and members of racial and ethnic minorities for unequal treatment. Their argument is that Proposition 209 makes it impossible for members of these groups to obtain redress for past discrimination through preferential treatment, whereas members of other groups who may have suffered past discrimination (gays, for example, or members of religious groups) are not similarly restricted from seeking redress. Evaluate this argument.

▲ 8. Harold prides himself on being a liberal. He is delighted when a federal court issues a preliminary ruling that California's Proposition 209 (see previous item) is unconstitutional. "It makes no difference that a majority of California voters approved the measure," Harold argues. "If it is unconstitutional, then it is unconstitutional." However, California voters also recently passed an initiative that permits physicians to prescribe marijuana, and Harold is livid when the U.S. attorney general says that the federal government will ignore the California statute and will use federal law to prosecute any physician who prescribes marijuana. Is Harold consistent?

9. Graybosch is of the opinion that we should not perform medical experiments on people against their will, but he has no problem with medical experiments being done on dogs. His wife disagrees. She sees no relevant difference between the two cases.

    "What, no difference between people and dogs?" Graybosch asks.

    "There are differences, but no differences that are relevant to the issue," Graybosch's wife responds. "Dogs feel pain and experience fear just as much as people."

    Is Graybosch's wife correct?

10. Mr. Bork is startled when a friend tells him he should contribute to the welfare of others' children as much as to his own.

    "Why on earth should I do that?" Mr. Bork asks his friend.

    "Because," his friend responds, "there is no relevant difference between the two cases. The fact that your children are yours does not mean that there is something different about them that gives them a greater entitlement to happiness than anyone else's children."

    How should Mr. Bork respond?

11. The university wants to raise the requirements for tenure. Professor Peterson, who doesn't have tenure, says that doing so is unfair to her. She argues that those who received tenure before she did weren't required to meet such exacting standards; therefore, neither should she. Is she correct?

12. Reverend Heinz has no objection to same-sex marriages but is opposed to polygamous marriages. Is there a relevant difference between the two cases, or is Reverend Heinz being inconsistent?

Exercise 12-9

1. Roy needs to sell his car, but he doesn't have money to spend on repairs. He plans to sell the vehicle to a private party without mentioning that

the rear brakes are worn. Evaluate Roy's plan of action from a deontological perspective—that is, can the maxim of Roy's plan be universalized?

2. Defend affirmative action from a utilitarian perspective.

3. Criticize affirmative action from a deontological perspective. (Hint: Consider Kant's theory that people must never be treated as means only.)

4. Criticize or defend medical experimentation on animals from a utilitarian perspective.

5. Criticize or defend medical experimentation on animals from a religious absolutist perspective.

6. A company has the policy of not promoting women to be vice presidents. What might be said about this policy from the perspective of virtue ethics?

7. What might be said about the policy mentioned in item 6 from the perspective of utilitarianism?

8. Evaluate embryonic stem cell research from a utilitarian perspective.

9. In your opinion, would the virtuous person, the person of the best moral character, condemn, approve, or be indifferent to bisexuality?

10. "We can't condemn the founding fathers for owning slaves; people didn't think there was anything wrong with it at the time." Comment on this remark from the standpoint of deontologism.

11. "Let's have some fun and see how your parrot looks without feathers." (The example is from philosopher Joseph Grcic.) Which of the following perspectives seems best equipped to condemn this suggestion?

    a. utilitarianism
    b. deontologism
    c. religious absolutism
    d. virtue ethics
    e. moral relativism

12. "Might makes right." Could a utilitarian accept this? Could a virtue ethicist? Could Kant? Could a moral relativist? Could someone who subscribes to divine command theory?

> This is Darwin's natural selection at its very best. The highest bidder gets youth and beauty.

Exercise 12-10

These are the words of fashion photographer Ron Harris, who auctioned the ova of fashion models via the Internet. The model got the full bid price, and the website took a commission of an additional 20 percent. The bid price included no medical costs, though it listed specialists who were willing to perform the procedure. Harris, who created the video "The 20 Minute Workout," said the egg auction gave people the chance to reproduce beautiful children who would have an advantage in society. Critics, however, were numerous. "It screams of unethical behavior," one said. "It is acceptable for an infertile couple to choose an egg donor and compensate her for her time, inconvenience and discomfort," he said. "But this is something else entirely. Among other things, what happens to the child if he or she turns out to be unattractive?"

Discuss the (moral) pros and cons of this issue for five or ten minutes in groups. Then take a written stand on the question "Should human eggs be auctioned to the highest bidder?" When you are finished, discuss which moral perspective seems to be the one in which you are operating.

LEGAL REASONING

When we think about arguments and disputes, the first image to come to most minds is probably that of an attorney arguing a case in a court of law. Although it's true that lawyers require a solid understanding of factual matters related to their cases and of psychological considerations as well, especially where juries are involved, it is still safe to say that a lawyer's stock-in-trade is argument. Lawyers are successful—in large part—to the extent that they can produce evidence in support of the conclusion that most benefits their clients—in other words, their success depends on how well they can put premises and conclusions together into convincing arguments.

When one thinks of the many varieties of law—administrative law, commercial law, criminal law, international law, tax law, and so on—one is apt to think that there may be no distinctive common ground that one might call "uniquely legal reasoning." This conclusion is absolutely correct. Still, we can distinguish broadly between questions of *interpreting and applying the law in specific instances* and questions related to *what the law should be.* Typically, jurists and practicing attorneys are more interested in the former type of question and legal philosophers in the latter.

Reasoning used by jurists and attorneys in applying the law is both deductive and inductive; if deductive, the reasoning can be sound, valid, or invalid; and if inductive, it can range from strong to weak. Deductive reasoning, of course, includes categorical and hypothetical reasoning; and inductive reasoning includes generalizing, reasoning by analogy, and reasoning about cause and effect. Reasoning by analogy and reasoning about cause and effect deserve special mention in connection with applying the law.

One kind of argument occupies a special place in applying the law: the **appeal to precedent.** This is the practice of using a case that has already been decided as an authoritative guide in deciding a new case that is similar. The appeal to precedent is none other than an argument by analogy, in which the current case is argued to be sufficiently like the previous case to warrant deciding it in the same way. Appeal to precedent also assumes the consistency principle that is found in moral reasoning: Cases that aren't relevantly different must be treated the same way. To treat similar cases differently would be illogical; it would also be unjust.

The Latin name for the principle of appeal to precedent is **stare decisis** ("Don't change settled decisions," more or less). In the terminology of Chapter 10, the "analogues" are the earlier, settled cases on one hand and the current case on the other. The important question is whether

John Roberts, Chief Justice of the U.S. Supreme Court, which decides the constitutionality of legislation, actions of public officials, lower court decisions, and other public matters. This power, known as "judicial review," is not explicit in the U.S. Constitution but was established in *Marbury v. Madison* (1803), a landmark decision of the Supreme Court.

the analogues are so similar that treating them differently would violate *stare decisis*. Apart from their significance to the parties involved, legal reasoning by analogy is not different in principle from reasoning by analogy in any other context.

Also especially important when it comes to applying the law is reasoning about cause and effect. Causation is the foundation of legal liability. In some contexts, that a party is legally liable for something may mean more than simply that he or she caused it; but having caused it is normally a necessary condition for being legally liable for it. In Chapter 11, we discussed causation in the law.

Justifying Laws: Four Perspectives

The reasoning employed to justify or defend specific laws is similar to moral reasoning, discussed in the previous section. Both types of reasoning involve applying general principles to specific cases, and both refer ultimately to one or more of a handful of basic perspectives within which the reasoning takes place. Indeed, the moral perspectives already discussed can and are used to justify and defend specific laws. For example, the utilitarian idea that it is desirable to increase the sum total of happiness is used to defend eminent domain (by which a state seizes a person's property without his/her consent). And the deontological principle that others should not be used as the means to some end is used to argue against it. The harm principle, discussed below, which holds that only what harms others should be legally forbidden, is an extension of deontological ethics (although its most eloquent exponent was the utilitarian John Stuart Mill).

Of course, we are often most interested in the justification of laws that would forbid us to do something we might otherwise want to do or would require us to do something we would prefer not to do. Consider, then, whether a law that forbids doing X should be enacted by your state legislature.* Typically, there are four main grounds, or "perspectives," on which a supporter of a law can base his or her justification. The first is simply that doing X is immoral. The claim that the law should make illegal anything that is immoral is the basis of the position known as **legal moralism.** One might use such a basis to justify laws forbidding murder, assault, or unorthodox sexual practices. For a legal moralist, the kinds of arguments designed to show that an action is immoral are directly relevant to the question of whether the action should be illegal.

The next ground on which a law can be justified is probably the one that most people think of first. It is very closely associated with John Stuart Mill (1806–1873) and is known as the **harm principle:** The only legitimate basis for forbidding X is that doing X causes harm to others. Notice that the harm principle states not just that harm to others is a good ground for forbidding an activity but that it is the *only* ground. (In terms of the way we formulated such claims in Chapter 9, on truth-functional logic, the principle would be stated, "It is legitimate to forbid doing X *if and only if* doing X causes harm to others.") A person who defends this principle and who wants to enact a law

---

*The example here is of a criminal law—part of a penal code designed to require and forbid certain behaviors and to punish offenders. The situation is a little different in civil law, a main goal of which is to shift the burden of a wrongful harm (a "tort") from the person on whom it fell to another, more suitable person usually the one who caused the harm.

forbidding X will present evidence that doing X does indeed cause harm to others. Her arguments could resemble any of the types covered in earlier chapters.

A third ground on which our hypothetical law might be based is legal paternalism. **Legal paternalism** is the view that laws can be justified if they prevent a person from doing harm to him- or herself; that is, they forbid or make it impossible to do X, *for a person's own good.* Examples include laws that require that seat belts be worn while riding in automobiles and that helmets be worn while riding on motorcycles.

The last of the usual bases for justifying criminal laws is that some behavior is generally found offensive. The **offense principle** says that a law forbidding X can be justifiable if X causes great offense to others. Laws forbidding burning of the flag are often justified on this ground.

What is the law, and how should it be applied? These questions are perhaps somewhat easier than the question, What should the law be? But they are still complicated. An example will provide an indication. Back in Chapter 3, we discussed vague concepts, and we found that it is impossible to rid our talk entirely of vagueness. Here's an example from the law. Let's suppose that a city ordinance forbids vehicles on the paths in the city park. Clearly, a person violates the law if he or she drives a truck or a car down the paths. But what about a motorbike? A bicycle? A go-cart? A child's pedal car? Just what counts as a vehicle and what does not? This is the kind of issue that must often be decided in court because—not surprisingly—the governing body writing the law could not foresee all the possible items that might, in somebody's mind, count as a vehicle.

The process of narrowing down when a law applies and when it does not, then, is another kind of reasoning problem that occurs in connection with the law.

Exercise 12-11

For each of the following kinds of laws, pick at least one of the four grounds for justification discussed in the text—legal moralism, the harm principle, legal paternalism, and the offense principle—and construct an argument designed to justify the law. You may not agree either with the law or with the argument; the exercise is to see if you can connect the law to the (allegedly) justifying principle. For many laws, more than one kind of justification is possible, so there can be more than one good answer for many of these.

▲   1. Laws against shoplifting

▲   2. Laws against forgery

    3. Laws against suicide

▲   4. Laws against spitting on the sidewalk

    5. Laws against driving under the influence of drugs or alcohol

▲   6. Laws against adultery

    7. Laws against marriage between two people of the same sex

    8. Laws that require people to have licenses before they practice medicine

    9. Laws that require drivers of cars to have driver's licenses

▲ 10. Laws against desecrating a corpse

11. Laws against trespassing

12. Laws against torturing your pet (even though it may be legal to kill your pet, if it is done humanely)

Exercise 12-12

This exercise is for class discussion or a short writing assignment. In the text, "Vehicles are prohibited on the paths in the park" was used as an example of a law that might require clarification. Decide whether the law should be interpreted to forbid motorcycles, bicycles, children's pedal cars, and battery-powered remote-control cars. On what grounds are you deciding each of these cases?

Exercise 12-13

The U.S. Supreme Court came to a decision not long ago about the proper application of the word "use." Briefly, the case in point was about a man named John Angus Smith, who traded a handgun for cocaine. The law under which Smith was charged provided for a much more severe penalty—known as an enhanced penalty—if a gun was used in a drug-related crime than if no gun was involved. (In this case, the enhanced penalty was a mandatory thirty-year sentence; the "unenhanced" penalty was five years.) Justice Antonin Scalia argued that Smith's penalty should not be enhanced because he did not use the gun in the way the writers of the law had in mind; he did not use it *as a gun.* Justice Sandra Day O'Connor argued that the law requires only the *use* of a gun, not any particular *kind* of use. If you were a judge, would you vote with Scalia or with O'Connor? Construct an argument in support of your position. (The decision of the Court is given in the answer section at the back of the book.)

AESTHETIC REASONING

Like moral and legal thinking, aesthetic thinking relies on a conceptual framework that integrates fact and value. Judgments about beauty and art—even judgments about whether something is a work of art or just an everyday object—appeal to principles that identify sources of aesthetic or artistic value. So, when you make such a judgment, you are invoking aesthetic concepts, even if you have not made them explicit to yourself or to others.

Eight Aesthetic Principles

Here are some of the aesthetic principles that most commonly support or influence artistic creation and critical judgment about art. The first three identify value in art with an object's ability to fulfill certain cultural or social functions.

1. *Objects are aesthetically valuable if they are meaningful or teach us truths.* For example, Aristotle says that tragic plays teach us general truths about the human condition in a dramatic way that cannot be matched by real-life experience. Many people believe art shows us truths that are usually hidden from us by the practical concerns of daily life.

2. *Objects are aesthetically valuable if they have the capacity to convey values or beliefs that are central to the cultures or traditions in which they*

■ Christo, The Gates.

originate or that are important to the artists who made them. For example, John Milton's poem *Paradise Lost* expresses the seventeenth-century Puritan view of the relationship between human beings and God.

3. *Objects are aesthetically valuable if they have the capacity to help bring about social or political change.* For instance, Abraham Lincoln commented that Harriet Beecher Stowe's *Uncle Tom's Cabin* contributed to the antislavery movement.

Another group of principles identifies aesthetic value with objects' capacities to produce certain subjective—that is, psychological—states in persons who experience or appreciate them. Here are some of the most common or influential principles of the second group:

4. *Objects are aesthetically valuable if they have the capacity to produce pleasure in those who experience or appreciate them.* For instance, the nineteenth-century German philosopher Friedrich Nietzsche identifies one kind of aesthetic value with the capacity to create a feeling of ecstatic bonding in audiences.

5. *Objects are aesthetically valuable if they have the capacity to produce certain emotions we value, at least when the emotion is brought about*

This watercolor by Alicia Alvarez and pen and ink by Rachel Steiner both evoke humorous responses, although they do it in entirely different ways.

by art rather than life. In the *Poetics*, Aristotle observes that we welcome the feelings of fear created in us by frightening dramas, whereas in everyday life fear is an experience we would rather avoid. The psychoanalyst Sigmund Freud offers another version of this principle: While we enjoy art, we permit ourselves to have feelings so subversive that we have to repress them to function in everyday life.

6. *Objects are aesthetically valuable if they have the capacity to produce special nonemotional experiences, such as a feeling of autonomy or the willing suspension of disbelief.* This principle is the proposal of the nineteenth-century English poet Samuel Taylor Coleridge. One of art's values, he believes, is its ability to stimulate our power to exercise our imaginations and consequently to free ourselves from thinking that is too narrowly practical.

Notice that principles 4 through 6 resemble the first three in that they identify aesthetic value with the capacity to fulfill a function. According to these last three, the specified function is to create some kind of subjective or inner state in audiences; according to the first three, however, art's function is to achieve such objective outcomes as conveying information or knowledge or preserving or changing culture or society. But there are yet other influential aesthetic principles that do not characterize art in terms of capacities for performing functions. According to one commonly held principle, art objects attain aesthetic value by virtue of their possessing a certain special aesthetic property or certain special formal configurations.

7. *Objects are aesthetically valuable if they possess a special aesthetic property or exhibit a special aesthetic form.* Sometimes this aesthetic property is called "beauty," and sometimes it is given another name. For instance, the early-twentieth-century art critic Clive Bell insists that good art is valuable for its own sake, not because it fulfills any function. To know whether a work is good aesthetically, he urges, one need only look at it or listen to it to see or hear whether it has "significant form." "Significant form" is valuable for itself, not for any function it performs.

Finally, one familiar principle insists that no reasons can be given to support judgments about art. Properly speaking, those who adhere to this principle think that to approve or disapprove of art is to express an unreasoned preference rather than to render judgment. This principle may be stated as follows:

8. *No reasoned argument can conclude that objects are aesthetically valuable or valueless.* This principle is expressed in the Latin saying *"De gustibus non est disputandum,"* or *"Tastes can't be disputed."*

The principles summarized here by no means exhaust the important views about aesthetic value, nor are they complete expositions of the views they represent. Historically, views about the nature of art have proven relatively fluid, for they must be responsive to the dynamics of technological and cultural change. Moreover, even though the number of familiar conceptions of aesthetic value is limited, there are many alternative ways of stating these that combine the thoughts behind them in somewhat different ways.

Consequently, to attempt to label each principle with a name invites confusion. For example, let's consider whether any of the principles might be designated *formalism*, which is an important school or style of art. Although the seventh principle explicitly ascribes aesthetic value to a work's form as opposed to its function, the formal properties of artworks also figure as valuable, although only as means to more valuable ends, in certain formulations of the first six principles. For instance, some scholars, critics, and artists think certain formal patterns in works of art can evoke corresponding emotions, social patterns, or pleasures in audiences—for example, slow music full of minor chords is commonly said to make people feel sad.

You should understand that all of the principles presented here merely serve as a basic framework within which you can explore critical thinking about art. If you are interested in the arts, you will very likely want to develop a more complex and sophisticated conceptual framework to enrich your thinking about this subject.

Using Aesthetic Principles to Judge Aesthetic Value

The first thing to notice about the aesthetic principles we've just discussed is that some are compatible with each other. Thus, a reasonable thinker can

The story is told of the American tourist in Paris who told Pablo Picasso that he didn't like modern paintings because they weren't realistic. Picasso made no immediate reply. A few minutes later the tourist showed him a snapshot of his house.

"My goodness," said Picasso, "is it really *as small as that?*"

—Jacob Braude

appeal to more than one in reaching a verdict about the aesthetic value of an object. For instance, a consistent thinker can use both the first and the fifth principle in evaluating a tragic drama. Aristotle does just this in his *Poetics*. He tells us that tragedies are good art when they both convey general truths about the human condition and help their audiences purge themselves of the pity and fear they feel when they face the truth about human limitations. A play that presents a general truth without eliciting the proper catharsis (release of emotion) in the audience or a play that provokes tragic emotions unaccompanied by recognition of a general truth is not as valuable as a play that does both.

However, some of these principles cannot be used together consistently to judge aesthetic value. These bear the same relationship to each other as do contrary claims (recall the square of opposition in Chapter 8). They cannot both be true, although both might be false. For instance, the principle that art is valuable in itself by virtue of its form or formal configuration (not because it serves some function), and the principle that art is valuable because it serves a social or political function cannot be used consistently together. You might have noticed, also, that the eighth principle contradicts the others; that is, the first seven principles all specify kinds of reasons for guiding and supporting our appreciation of art, but the last principle denies that there can be any such good reasons.

Finally, it is important to understand that the same principle can generate both positive and negative evaluations, depending on whether the work in question meets or fails to meet the standard expressed in the principle. For example, the fourth principle, which we might call "aesthetic hedonism," generates positive evaluations of works that produce pleasure but negative evaluations of works that leave their audiences in pain or displeased.

Suppose that the two statements in each of the following pairs both appear in a review of the same work of art. Identify which of the eight aesthetic principles each statement in the pair appeals to. Then state whether the principles are compatible (that is, they are not contrary to each other) and thus form the basis for a consistent critical review.

Exercise 12-14

1. a. Last weekend's performance of the Wagnerian operatic cycle was superb; the music surged through the audience, forging a joyous communal bond.
    b. Smith's forceful singing and acting in the role of Siegfried left no doubt why Wagner's vision of heroic morality was attractive to his Teutonic contemporaries.

2. a. Leni Riefenstahl's film *Triumph of the Will* proved to be effective art because it convinced its audiences that the Nazi Party would improve the German way of life.
    b. Despite its overtly racist message, *Triumph of the Will* is great art, for films should be judged on the basis of their visual coherence and not in terms of their moral impact.

3. a. All lovers of art should condemn Jackson Pollock's meaningless abstract expressionist splatter paintings.
    b. These paintings create neither sadness nor joy; those who view them feel nothing, neither love nor hate nor any of the other passions that great art evokes.

▲ 4. a. Laurence Olivier's film production of *Hamlet* has merit because he allows us to experience the impact of the incestuous love that a son can feel for his mother.

   b. Nevertheless, Olivier's *Hamlet* is flawed because it introduces a dimension inconceivable to an Elizabethan playwright.

5. a. There is no point arguing about or giving reasons for verdicts about art, because each person's tastes or responses are so personal.

   b. Those who condemn sexually explicit performance art do not recognize that art is valuable to the extent it permits us to feel liberated and free of convention.

Evaluating Aesthetic Criticism: Relevance and Truth

Is any evaluation of a work of art as good as any other in creating a critical treatment of that work? The answer is no, for two reasons: (1) the principles of art that one adopts function as a conceptual framework that distinguishes relevant from irrelevant reasons; (2) even a relevant reason is useless if it is not true of the work to which it is applied.

Let's consider the first reason. What would convince you of the value of a work if you accepted principles 4 through 6—all of which maintain that aesthetic value resides in the subjective responses art evokes in its audiences? In this case, you are likely to be drawn to see Picasso's *Guernica* if you are told that it has the power to make its viewers experience the horrors of war; but you would not be attracted by learning, instead, that *Guernica* explores the relationship of two- and three-dimensional spatial concepts. Suppose you reject principles 1 through 3, which conceive of aesthetic value in terms of the work's capacity to perform an objective, cognitive, moral, social, or political function. The fact that Picasso was a communist will strike you as irrelevant to appreciating *Guernica* unless you accept one or more of the first three principles.

To illustrate the second reason, look at the nearby reproduction of *Guernica*. Suppose a critic writes, "By giving his figures fishlike appearances and

> The aim of art is to represent not the outward appearance of things, but their inward significance.
>
> —ARISTOTLE

■ Pablo Picasso, *Guernica*.

showing them serenely floating through a watery environment, Picasso makes us feel that humans will survive under any conditions." But no figures in *Guernica* look anything like fish; moreover, they are surrounded by fire, not water, and they are twisted with anguish rather than serene. So, this critic's reasons are no good. Because they are not true of the work, they cannot guide us in perceiving features that enhance our appreciation. A similar problem occurs if reasons are implausible. For instance, an interpretation of *Guernica* as a depiction of the Last Supper is implausible, because we cannot recognize the usual signs of this theme, the twelve disciples and Jesus at a table (or at least at a meal), in the far fewer figures of the painting.

State whether each of the reasons below is relevant according to any one of the aesthetic principles. If the reason is relevant, identify the principle that makes it so. If no principle makes the reason relevant, state that it is irrelevant.

Exercise 12-15

▲ 1. Raphael's carefully balanced pyramidal compositions give his paintings of the Madonna such beautiful form that they have aesthetic value for Christian and atheist alike.

2. By grouping his figures so that they compose a triangle or pyramid, Raphael directs the viewer's eye upward to heaven and thereby teaches us about the close connection between motherhood and God.

3. The melody from the chorus "For unto Us a Child Is Born" in Handel's *Messiah* was originally composed by Handel for an erotic love song. Consequently, it evokes erotic responses that distract and detract from the devotional feeling audiences are supposed to experience when they hear *Messiah* performed.

▲ 4. Vincent van Gogh tells us that he uses clashing reds and greens in *The Night Café* to help us see his vision of "the terrible passions of humanity"; it is the intensity with which he conveys his views of the ugliness of human life that makes his work so illuminating.

5. The critics who ignored Van Gogh's painting during his lifetime were seriously mistaken; by damaging his self-esteem, they drove him to suicide.

6. Moreover, these critics misjudged the aesthetic value of his art, as evidenced by the fact that his paintings now sell for as much as $80 million.

▲ 7. By showing a naked woman picnicking with fully clothed men in *Déjeuner sur l'herbe*, Édouard Manet treats women as objects and impedes their efforts to throw off patriarchal domination.

▲ Asuka, a three-year-old chimpanzee in Japan, was sad and lonely, so the zoo director gave her paper, paints, and brushes to keep her busy. Look at the photograph of Asuka and her painting on page 470. Does the painting have aesthetic value? Use each of the eight aesthetic principles to formulate one reason for or against the aesthetic value of Asuka's work. You should end up with eight reasons, one appealing to each principle.

Exercise 12-16

Asuka the chimpanzee.

Why Reason Aesthetically?

The various aesthetic principles we've introduced are among those most commonly found, either explicitly or implicitly, in discussions about art. Moreover, they have influenced both the creation of art and the selection of art for both private and public enjoyment. But where do these principles come from? There is much debate about this; to understand it, we can draw on notions about definition (introduced in Chapter 3) as well as the discussion of generalizations (Chapter 10).

Some people think that aesthetic principles are simply elaborate definitions of our concepts of art or aesthetic value. Let's explain this point. We use definitions to identify things; for example, by definition we look for three sides and three angles to identify a geometric figure as a triangle. Similarly, we can say that aesthetic principles are definitions; that is, these principles provide an aesthetic vocabulary to direct us in recognizing an object's aesthetic value.

If aesthetic principles are true by definition, then learning to judge art is learning the language of art. But because artists strive for originality, we are constantly faced with talking about innovative objects to which the critic's familiar vocabulary does not quite do justice. This aspect of art challenges even the most sophisticated critic to continually extend the aesthetic vocabulary.

Others think that aesthetic principles are generalizations that summarize what is true of objects treated as valuable art. Here, the argument is by analogy from a sample class to a target population. Thus, someone might hold that all or most of the tragic plays we know that are aesthetically valuable have had something important to say about the human condition; for this reason, we can expect this to be true of any member of the class of tragic plays we have not yet evaluated. Or, also by inductive analogy, musical compositions that are valued so highly that they continue to be performed throughout the centuries all make us feel some specific emotion, such as joy or sadness; so we can predict that a newly composed piece will be similarly highly valued if it also evokes a strong, clear emotion. Of course, such arguments are weakened to the extent that the target object differs from the objects in the sample class. Because there is a drive for originality in art, newly created works may diverge so sharply from previous samples that arguments by analogy sometimes prove too weak.

It is sometimes suggested that these two accounts of the source of aesthetic principles really reinforce each other: Our definitions reflect to some extent our past experience of the properties or capacities typical of valuable art, and our past experience is constrained to some extent by our definitions. But if art changes, of what use are principles, whether analytic or inductive, in guiding us to make aesthetic judgments and—even more difficult—in fostering agreement about these judgments?

At the very least, these principles have an emotive force that guides us in perceiving art. You will remember that emotive force (discussed briefly in Chapter 3) is a dimension of language that permits the words we use to do something more than convey information. In discussion about art, the words that constitute reasons can have an emotive force directing our attention to particular aspects of a work. If the critic can describe these aspects accurately and persuasively, it is thought, the audience will focus on these aspects and experience a favorable (or unfavorable) response similar to the critic's. If a critic's reasons are too vague or are not true of the work to which they are applied, they are unlikely to bring the audience into agreement with the critic.

The principles of art, then, serve as guides for identifying appropriate categories of favorable or unfavorable response, but the reasons falling into these categories are what bring about agreement. They are useful both in developing our own appreciation of a work of art and in persuading others. The reasons must be accurately and informatively descriptive of the objects to which they are applied. The reasons enable us (1) to select a particular way of viewing, listening, reading, or otherwise perceiving the object and (2) to recommend, guide, or prescribe that the object be viewed, heard, or read in this way.

So, aesthetic reasons contain descriptions that prompt ways of perceiving aspects of an object. These prescribed ways of seeing evoke favorable (or unfavorable) responses or experiences. For instance, suppose a critic states that Van Gogh's brush strokes in *Starry Night* are dynamic and his colors intense. This positive critical reason prescribes that people focus on these features when they look at the painting. The expectation is that persons whose vision is swept into the movement of Van Gogh's painted sky and pierced by the presence of his painted stars will, by virtue of focusing on these formal properties, enjoy a positive response to the painting.

To learn to give reasons and form assessments about art, practice applying these principles as you look, listen, or read. Consider what aspects of a painting, musical performance, poem, or other work each principle directs you to contemplate. It is also important to expand your aesthetic vocabulary so that you have words to describe what you see, hear, or otherwise sense in a work. As you do so, you will be developing your own aesthetic expertise. And, because your reasons will be structured by aesthetic principles others also accept, you will find that rational reflection on art tends to expand both the scope and volume of your agreement with others about aesthetic judgments.

Recap

The key points in this chapter are as follows:

- Value judgments are claims that express values.
- Moral value judgments express moral values.
- Certain words, especially "ought," "should," "right," "wrong," and their opposites, are used in moral value judgments, though they can also be used in a nonmoral sense.

▇ Reasoning about morality is distinguished from other types of reasoning in that the conclusions it tries to establish are moral value judgments.

▇ Conclusions containing a value judgment cannot be reached solely from premises that do not contain a value judgment ("you cannot get an 'ought' from an 'is'"). A general moral principle must be supplied to tie together the fact-stating premise and the value-judgment conclusion.

▇ In a case in which we disagree with a value-judgment conclusion but not with the fact-stating premise, we can point to this general moral principle as the source of disagreement.

▇ People are sometimes inconsistent in their moral views: They treat similar cases as if they were different, even when they cannot tell us what is importantly different about them.

▇ When two or more cases that are being treated differently seem similar, the burden of proof is on the person who is treating them differently to explain what is different about them.

▇ Moral reasoning is usually conducted within a perspective or framework. Influential Western perspectives include consequentialism, utilitarianism, ethical egoism, deontologism, moral relativism, religious absolutism, religious relativism, and virtue ethics.

▇ Often, different perspectives converge to produce similar solutions to a moral issue.

▇ Keeping in mind our own perspective can help focus our own moral deliberations on relevant considerations.

▇ Legal reasoning, like moral reasoning, is often prescriptive.

▇ Legal studies are devoted to such problems as justifying laws that prescribe conduct.

▇ Legal moralism, the harm principle, legal paternalism, and the offense principle are grounds for justifying laws that prescribe conduct.

▇ Determining just when and where a law applies often requires making vague claims specific.

▇ Precedent is a kind of analogical argument by means of which current cases are settled in accordance with guidelines set by cases decided previously.

▇ Whether a precedent governs in a given case is decided on grounds similar to those of any other analogical argument.

▇ To reason aesthetically is to make judgments within a conceptual framework that integrates facts and values.

▇ Aesthetic value is often identified as the capacity to fulfill a function, such as to create pleasure or promote social change.

▇ Alternatively, aesthetic value is defined in terms of a special aesthetic property or form found in works of art.

▇ Still another view treats aesthetic judgments as expressions of tastes.

▇ Reasoned argument about aesthetic value helps us to see, hear, or otherwise perceive art in changed or expanded ways and to enhance our appreciation of art.

A critic who gives reasons in support of an aesthetic verdict forges agreement by getting others to share perceptions of the work. The greater the extent to which we share such aesthetic perceptions, the more we can reach agreement about aesthetic value.

Exercise 12-17

State whether the following reasons are (a) helpful in focusing perception to elicit a favorable response, (b) helpful in focusing perception to elicit an unfavorable response, (c) too vague to focus perception, (d) false or implausible and therefore unable to focus perception, or (e) irrelevant to focusing perception. The information you need is contained in the reasons, so try to visualize or imagine what the work is like from what is said. All of these are paraphrases of testimony given at a hearing in 1985 about a proposal to remove *Tilted Arc*, an immense abstract sculpture, from a plaza in front of a federal office building.

1. Richard Serra's *Tilted Arc* is a curved slab of welded steel 12 feet high, 120 feet long, weighing over 73 tons, and covered completely with a natural oxide coating. The sculpture arcs through the plaza. By coming to terms with its harshly intrusive disruption of space, we can learn much about how the nature of the spaces we inhabit affects our social relations.

2. Richard Serra is one of our leading artists, and his work commands very high prices. The government has a responsibility to the financial community. It is bad business to destroy this work because you would be destroying property.

3. *Tilted Arc*'s very tilt and rust remind us that the gleaming and heartless steel and glass structures of the state apparatus can one day pass away. It therefore creates an unconscious sense of freedom and hope.

Richard Serra's *Tilted Arc*.

▲ 4. *Tilted Arc* looks like a discarded piece of crooked or bent metal; there's no more meaning in having it in the middle of the plaza than in putting an old bicycle that got run over by a car there.

5. *Tilted Arc* launches through space in a thrilling and powerful acutely arched curve.

6. *Tilted Arc* is big and rusty.

▲ 7. Because of its size, thrusting shape, and implacably uniform rusting surface, *Tilted Arc* makes us feel hopeless, trapped, and sad. This sculpture would be interesting if we could visit it when we had time to explore these feelings, but it is too depressing to face every day on our way to work.

8. Serra's erotically realistic, precise rendering of the female figure in *Tilted Arc* exhibits how appealingly he can portray the soft circularity of a woman's breast.

9. *Tilted Arc* is sort of red; it probably isn't blue.

Exercise 12-18

The artist Artemisia Gentileschi (ca. 1597–after 1651) was very successful in her own time. Success came despite the trauma of her early life, when she figured as the victim in a notorious rape trial. But after she died, her work fell into obscurity; it was neither shown in major museums nor written about in art history books. Recently, feminist scholars have revived interest in her work by connecting the style and/or theme of such paintings as her *Judith* with her rape and with feelings or issues of importance to women. But other scholars have pointed out that both her subject matter and her treatment of it are conventionally found as well in the work of male painters of the Caravaggist school, with which she is identified. Based on this information, and using one or more of the aesthetic principles described in this chapter, write an essay arguing either that the painting *Judith* has aesthetic value worthy of our attention or that it should continue to be ignored.

Writing Exercises

1. In the movie *Priest,* the father of a young girl admits to the local priest—in the confessional—that he has molested his daughter. However, the man lacks remorse and gives every indication that he will continue to abuse the girl. For the priest to inform the girl's mother or the authorities would be to violate the sanctity of the confessional, but to not inform anyone would subject the girl to further abuse. What should the priest do? Take about fifteen minutes to do the following:

   a. List the probable consequences of the courses of action available to the priest.

   b. List any duties or rights or other considerations that bear on the issue.

   When fifteen minutes are up, share your ideas with the class.

   Now, take about twenty minutes to write an essay in which you do the following:

a. State the issue.
b. Take a stand on the issue.
c. Defend your stand.
d. Rebut counterarguments to your position.

When you are finished, write down on a separate piece of paper a number between 1 and 10 that indicates how strong you think your argument is (1 = very weak; 10 = very strong). Write your name on the back of your paper.

When everyone is finished, the instructor will collect the papers and redistribute them to the class. In groups of four or five, read the papers and assign a number from 1 to 10 to each one (1 = very weak; 10 = very strong). When all groups are finished, return the papers to their authors. When you get your paper back, compare the number you assigned to your work with the number the group assigned it. The instructor may ask volunteers to defend their own judgment of their work against the judgment of the group. Do you think there is as much evidence for your position as you did at the beginning of the period?

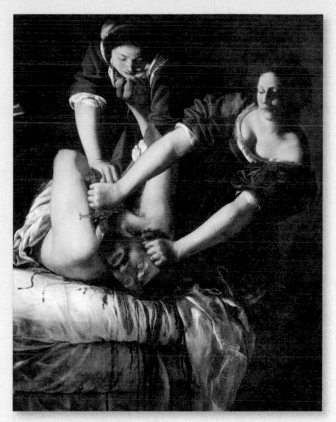

■ Artemisia Gentileschi's *Judith.*

2. Follow the same procedure as above to address one of the following issues:

   a. A friend cheats in the classes he has with you. You know he'd just laugh if you voiced any concern. Should you mention it to your instructor?
   b. You see a friend stealing something valuable. Even though you tell your friend that you don't approve, she keeps the item. What should you do?
   c. Your best friend's fiancé has just propositioned you for sex. Should you tell your friend?
   d. Your parents think you should major in marketing or some other practical field. You want to major in literature. Your parents pay the bills. What should you do?

Appendix

Nineteen Topics for Analysis

Selection 1

Three Strikes and the Whole Enchilada

In this first selection, we've taken a real-life case of some importance and identified how various sections of the book bear on the issue and on various aspects of the controversy that surround it. As we said at the beginning, this material is not designed to operate just in the classroom.

1. As you no doubt know, several states have "three strikes" laws, which call for life terms for a criminal convicted of any felony—if the criminal already has two prior felony convictions that resulted from serious or violent crime.

2. Have such laws helped to reduce crime in the states that have them? This is an objective question, a question of causation (Chapter 11). How might the issue be resolved?

3. In California, Frank Zimring, a University of California, Berkeley, law professor, analyzed the records of 3,500 criminal defendants in Los Angeles, San Diego, and San Francisco before and after California's law was enacted. Zimring found no evidence that the law deterred crime. For our purposes, we do not need to go into the details of the study.

4. People Against Crime, an organization that favors tougher penalties for criminals, denounced the study as "so much more left-wing propaganda coming out of a notoriously liberal university."

5. This charge is an ad hominem fallacy (Chapter 7). But is it nevertheless a reasonable challenge to Zimring's credibility that warrants not outright rejection of the study but suspension of judgment about its findings (Chapter 4)? The answer is no. Stripped of its rhetoric (Chapter 5), the charge is only that the author of the study is a professor at Berkeley, and that charge gives no reason to suspect bias on his part.

6. Other criticisms of the study were reported in the news. A spokesperson for the California secretary of state said, "When you see the crime rate going down 38 percent since three strikes, you can't say it doesn't work."

7. This remark is an example of the fallacy *post hoc, ergo propter hoc*, discussed in Chapter 11. In fact, that's being charitable. According to Zimring's research, the crime rate had been declining at the same rate before the law was passed.

8. The same spokesperson also criticized the Zimring study for ignoring the number of parolees leaving the state (to avoid getting a third strike, presumably). This is a red herring (Chapter 6). If the decline in the crime rate was unaffected after the law passed, as the Zimring study reportedly learned, then the law had no effect regardless of what parolees did or did not do.

9. The spokesperson also said, "Clearly when people are committing 20 to 25 crimes a year, the year they are taken off the street, that's 20 to 25 crimes that aren't going to happen." This, too, is a red herring (Chapter 6): If the decline in the crime rate remained the same before and after the "three strikes" law,

then that's the end of the story. The criticism assumes criminals will continue to commit crimes at the same rate if there is no mandatory life sentence for a third felony. It therefore also begs the question (Chapter 7)—it assumes the law works in order to prove the law works. You will also have noticed the proof surrogate "clearly" (Chapter 5) in the criticism.

10 One might, of course, maintain that, without the law, the crime rate would have *stopped* declining, which would mean that the law had an effect after all. But the burden of proof (Chapter 7) is not on Zimring to *disprove* the possibility that the crime rate would have stopped declining if the law had not been passed.

11 A critic might also say that Zimring's study was conducted too soon after the law for the effects of the law to show up. This is another red herring (Chapter 6). It is not a weakness in the study that it failed to find an effect that might show up at a *later* time.

Selection 2

This is not a selection to evaluate but a challenge to produce an argumentative paragraph or two yourself.

1 In a moment we'll offer a question about the probable effects of "three-strikes" laws, which are laws that mandate harsh sentences for a person who commits a violent felony and who already has two previous felony convictions. Imagine this scenario: You are drawing near to your car in the back corner of an isolated parking lot when a man suddenly appears and approaches you. He has one hand in his coat pocket, and you suspect he may be armed.

2 Now, here is the issue: Is it better for you if this event happens in a state with a three-strikes law or in a state without such a law?

3 Using your critical thinking skills, construct at least one argument supporting one side of the issue or the other. Then compare your work with that of other students to see if one side has come up with stronger arguments.

Selection 3

Controlling Irrational Fears After 9/11*

We present this selection as an example of a fairly well-reasoned argumentative essay. There is more here than arguments—there's some window dressing, and you'll probably find some slanters here and there as well. You should go through the selection and identify the issues, the positions taken on those issues, and the arguments offered in support of those arguments. Are any arguments from opposing points of view considered? What is your final assessment of the essay?

. . .

1 The terrorist attacks of September 11, 2001, produced a response among American officials, the media, and the public that is probably matched only by the attack on Pearl Harbor in 1941. Since it is the very nature of terrorism not only to cause immediate damage but also to strike fear in the hearts of the

---

*Note: This essay borrows very heavily from "A Skeptical Look at September 11th," an article in the *Skeptical Inquirer* of September/October 2002 by Clark R. Chapman and Alan W. Harris. Rather than clutter the essay with numerous references, we simply refer the reader to the original, longer piece.

population under attack, one might say that the terrorists were extraordinarily successful, not just as a result of their own efforts but also in consequence of the American reaction. In this essay, I shall argue that this reaction was irrational to a great extent and that to that extent Americans unwittingly cooperated with the terrorists in achieving a major goal: spreading fear and thus disrupting lives. In other words, we could have reacted more rationally and as a result produced less disruption in the lives of our citizens.

2   There are several reasons why one might say that a huge reaction to the 9/11 attacks was justified. The first is simply the large number of lives that were lost. In the absence of a shooting war, that 2,800 Americans should die from the same cause strikes us as extraordinary indeed. But does the sheer size of the loss of life warrant the reaction we saw? Clearly sheer numbers do not always impress us. It is unlikely, for example, that many Americans remember that, earlier in 2001, an earthquake in Gujarat, India, killed approximately 20,000 people. One might explain the difference in reaction by saying that we naturally respond more strongly to the deaths of Americans closer to home than to those of others halfway around the world. But then consider the fact that, every *month* during 2001 more Americans were killed in automobile crashes than were killed on 9/11 (and it has continued every month since as well). Since the victims of car accidents come from every geographical area and every social stratum, one can say that those deaths are even "closer to home" than the deaths that occurred in New York, Washington, and Pennsylvania. It may be harder to identify with an earthquake victim in Asia than with a 9/11 victim, but this cannot be said for the victims of fatal automobile accidents.

3   One might say that it was the *malice* of the perpetrators that makes the 9/11 deaths so noteworthy, but surely there is plenty of malice present in the 15,000 homicides that occur every year in the United States. And while we have passed strict laws favoring prosecution of murderers, we do not see the huge and expensive shift in priorities that has followed the 9/11 attacks.

4   It seems clear, at least, that sheer numbers cannot explain the response to 9/11. If more reasons were needed, we might consider that the *actual total* of the number of 9/11 deaths seemed of little consequence in post-attack reports. Immediately after the attacks, the estimated death toll was about 6,500. Several weeks later it was clear that fewer than half that many had actually died, but was there a great sigh of relief when it was learned that over 3,000 people who were believed to have died were still alive? Not at all. In fact, well after it was confirmed that no more than 3,000 people had died, Secretary of Defense Donald Rumsfeld still talked about "over 5,000" deaths on 9/11. So the actual number seems to be of less consequence than one might have believed.

5   We should remember that fear and outrage at the attacks are only the beginning of the country's response to 9/11. We now have a new cabinet-level Department of Homeland Security; billions have been spent on beefing up security and in tracking terrorists and potential terrorists; billions more have been spent supporting airlines whose revenues took a nosedive after the attacks; the Congress was pulled away from other important business; the National Guard was called out to patrol the nation's airports; air travelers have been subjected to time-consuming and expensive security measures; you can probably think of a half-dozen other items to add to this list.

6   It is probable that a great lot of this trouble and expense is unwarranted. We think that random searches of luggage of elderly ladies getting on airplanes in

Laramie, Wyoming, for example, is more effective as a way of annoying elderly ladies than of stopping terrorism.

7   We might have accomplished something if we had been able to treat the terrorist attacks of 9/11 in a way similar to how we treat the carnage on the nation's highways—by implementing practices and requirements that are directly related to results (as in the case of speed limits, safety belts, and the like, which took decades to accomplish in the cause of auto safety)— rather than by throwing the nation into a near panic and using the resulting fears to justify expensive but not necessarily effective or even relevant measures.

8   But we focused on 9/11 because of its terrorist nature and because of the spectacular film that was shown over and over on television, imprinting forever the horrific images of the airliners' collision with the World Trade Center and the subsequent collapse of the two towers. The media's instant obsession with the case is understandable, even if it is out of proportion to the actual damage, as awful as it was, when we compare the actual loss to the loss from automobile accidents.

9   Finally, our point is that marginal or even completely ineffective expenditures and disruptive practices have taken our time, attention, and national treasure away from other matters with more promise of making the country a better place. We seem to have all begun to think of ourselves as terrorist targets, but, in fact, reason tells us we are in much greater danger from our friends and neighbors behind the wheels of their cars.

. . .

The remainder of the essays in this section are here for analysis and evaluation. Your instructor will probably have specific directions if he or she assigns them, but at a minimum, they offer an opportunity to identify issues, separate arguments from other elements, identify premises and conclusions, evaluate the likely truth of the premises and the strength of the arguments, look for unstated assumptions or omitted premises, and lots of other stuff besides. We offer sample directions for many of the pieces.

Selection 4

Excerpts from Federal Court Ruling on the Pledge of Allegiance

The following are excerpts from the ruling by a three-judge federal appeals court panel in San Francisco that reciting the Pledge of Allegiance in public schools is unconstitutional because it includes the phrase "one nation, under God." The vote was 2 to 1. Judge Alfred T. Goodwin wrote the majority opinion, in which Judge Stephen Reinhardt joined. Judge Ferdinand F. Fernandez wrote a dissent.

From the Opinion by Judge Goodwin

1   In the context of the pledge, the statement that the United States is a nation "under God" is an endorsement of religion. It is a profession of a religious belief, namely, a belief in monotheism. The recitation that ours is a nation "under God" is not a mere acknowledgment that many Americans believe in a deity. Nor is it merely descriptive of the undeniable historical significance of religion in the founding of the republic. Rather, the phrase "one nation under God" in the context of the pledge is normative. To recite the pledge is not to describe the United States; instead, it is to swear allegiance to the values for

which the flag stands: unity, indivisibility, liberty, justice, and—since 1954—monotheism. The text of the official pledge, codified in federal law, impermissibly takes a position with respect to the purely religious question of the existence and identity of god. A profession that we are a nation "under God" is identical, for Establishment Clause purposes, to a profession that we are a nation "under Jesus," a nation "under Vishnu," a nation "under Zeus," or a nation "under no god," because none of these professions can be neutral with respect to religion. "The government must pursue a course of complete neutrality toward religion." Furthermore, the school district's practice of teacher-led recitation of the pledge aims to inculcate in students a respect for the ideals set forth in the pledge, and thus amounts to state endorsements of these ideals. Although students cannot be forced to participate in recitation of the pledge, the school district is nonetheless conveying a message of state endorsement of a religious belief when it requires public school teachers to recite, and lead the recitation, of the current form of the pledge. . . .

2 The pledge, as currently codified, is an impermissible government endorsement of religion because it sends a message to unbelievers "that they are outsiders, not full members of the political community, and an accompanying message to adherents that they are insiders, favored members of the political community."

From the Dissent by Judge Fernandez

3 We are asked to hold that inclusion of the phrase "under God" in this nation's Pledge of Allegiance violates the religion clauses of the Constitution of the United States. We should do no such thing. We should, instead, recognize that those clauses were not designed to drive religious expression out of public thought; they were written to avoid discrimination. We can run through the litany of tests and concepts which have floated to the surface from time to time. Were we to do so, the one that appeals most to me, the one I think to be correct, is the concept that what the religion clauses of the First Amendment require is neutrality; that those clauses are, in effect, an early kind of equal protection provision and assure that government will neither discriminate for nor discriminate against religion or religions. But, legal world abstractions and ruminations aside, when all is said and done, the danger that "under God" in our Pledge of Allegiance will tend to bring about a theocracy or suppress somebody's belief is so minuscule as to be *de minimis.* The danger that phrase presents to our First Amendment freedoms is picayune at most.

Selection 5

The Threat from Same-Sex Marriage

By Jeff Jacoby
The Boston Globe
August 6, 2001

1 IT WAS A YEAR AGO LAST MONTH that the Vermont law authorizing same-sex civil unions—marriage by another name—took effect, and *The New York Times* marked the anniversary with a story on July 25. "Quiet Anniversary for Civil Unions," the double headline announced. "Ceremonies for Gay

Couples Have Blended Into Vermont Life." It was an upbeat report, and its message was clear: Civil unions are working just fine.

2 The story noted in passing that most Vermonters oppose the new law, and that many support a constitutional amendment confirming that marriage is the union of a man and a woman. Presumably they have reasons for not wanting legal recognition conferred on homosexual couples, but the *Times* had no room to mention them. It did have room, though, to dismiss those reasons—whatever they might be—as meritless:

3 "The sky has not fallen," Governor Howard Dean said, "and the institution of marriage has not collapsed. None of the dire predictions have come true. . . . There was a big rhubarb, a lot of fear-mongering, and now people realize there was nothing to be afraid of.'"

4 In *The Wall Street Journal* two days later, much the same point was made by Jonathan Rauch, the esteemed Washington journalist and vice president of the Independent Gay Forum.

5 Opponents of same-sex marriage, he wrote, worry "that unyoking marriage from its traditional male-female definition will destroy or severely weaken it. But this is an empirical proposition, and there is reason to doubt it. Opponents of same-sex marriage have done a poor job of explaining why the health of heterosexual marriage depends on the exclusion of a small number of homosexuals."

6 The assertion that same-sex marriage will not damage traditional family life is rarely challenged, a fact seized on by U.S. Representative Barney Frank during the 1996 congressional debate over the Defense of Marriage Act.

7 "I have asked and I have asked and I have asked and I guess I will die . . . unanswered," Frank taunted. "How does the fact that I love another man and live in a committed relationship with him threaten your marriage? Are your relations with your spouses of such fragility that the fact that I have a committed, loving relationship with another man jeopardizes them? . . . Whose marriage does it threaten?" When another congressman replied that legitimizing gay unions "threatens the institution of marriage," Frank was scornful:

8 "That argument ought to be made by someone in an institution because it has no logical basis whatsoever."

9 But Frank's sarcasm, Rauch's doubts, and Dean's reassurances notwithstanding, the threat posed by same-sex unions to traditional marriage and family life is all too real. Marriage is harmed by anything that diminishes its privileged status. It is weakened by anything that erodes the social sanctions that Judeo-Christian culture developed over the centuries for channeling men's naturally unruly sexuality into a monogamous, lasting, and domestic relationship with one woman. For proof, just look around.

10 Over the last 40 years, marriage has suffered one blow after another. The sexual revolution and the Pill made it much easier for men to enjoy women sexually without having to marry them. The legalization of abortion reduced the pressure on men to marry women they impregnated, and reduced the pressure on women to be sexually responsible, or to wait for lasting love. The widespread acceptance of unmarried cohabitation—an arrangement that used to be disdained as "shacking up"—diminished marriage even further. Why get married if intimate companionship can be had without public vows and ceremony?

11 The rise of the welfare state with its subsidies for single mothers subverted marriage by sending the unmistakable message that husbands were no longer essential for family life. And the rapid spread of no-fault divorce detached

marriage from any presumption of permanence. Where couples were once expected to stay married "for as long as you both shall live"—and therefore to put effort into making their marriage work—the expectation today is that they will remain together only "for as long as you both shall love."

12 If we now redefine marriage so it includes the union of two men or two women, we will be taking this bad situation and making it even worse.

13 No doubt the acceptance of same-sex marriage would remove whatever stigma homosexuality still bears, a goal many people would welcome. But it would do so at a severe cost to the most basic institution of our society. For all the assaults marriage has taken, its fundamental purpose endures: to uphold and encourage the union of a man and a woman, the framework that is the healthiest and safest for the rearing of children. If marriage stops meaning even that, it will stop meaning anything at all.

Selection 6

Death Penalty Has No Place in U.S.

Cynthia Tucker

1 Many Americans will applaud the decision of a Jasper, Texas, jury to condemn John William King to die. They will argue that the death penalty is exactly what King deserves for chaining James Byrd Jr. to the back of a pickup truck and dragging him until his body was torn apart—his head and right arm here, his torso there.

2 If there is to be capital punishment in this country, isn't this just the sort of case that demands it? King is the epitome of cold-blooded evil, a man who bragged about his noxious racism and attempted to win converts to his views. He believed he would be a hero after Byrd's death. He has proved himself capable of the sort of stomach-churning cruelty that most of us would like to believe is outside the realm of human behavior.

3 Besides, there is the matter of balancing the books. King is a white man who (with the help of accomplices, apparently) killed a black man. For centuries, the criminal justice system saw black lives as so slight, so insignificant, that those who took a black life rarely got the death penalty. Isn't it a matter of fairness, of equity, of progress, that King should be put to death?

4 No. Even though King is evil. Even though he is utterly without remorse. Even though he is clearly guilty. (After the prosecution mounted a case for five days, King's lawyers mounted a defense of only one hour. The jury of 11 whites and one black then deliberated only two and half hours to determine King's guilt.)

5 This is no brief for King, who would probably chain me to the back of a pickup truck as quickly as he did Byrd. This is a plea for America, which is strong enough, just enough and merciful enough to have put aside, by now, the thirst for vengeance.

6 The question is not, Does John William King deserve the death penalty? The question is, Does America deserve the death penalty?

7 Capital punishment serves no good purpose. It does not deter crime. If it did, this country would be blessedly crime-free. It does not apply equally to all. King notwithstanding, the denizens of death row are disproportionately blacks and Latinos who have killed whites. It remains true that the lives of

blacks and Latinos count for less, that their killers are less likely to be sentenced to die.

8   Death row also counts among its inmates a high quotient of those who are poor, dumb and marginalized. Those criminals blessed with education, status and connections can usually escape capital punishment:

9   Last Tuesday, William Lumpkin, an attorney in Augusta, Ga., was found guilty of capital murder in the death of real estate agent Stan White, who owned the title to Lumpkin's home and was about to evict him. Lumpkin beat White to death with a sandbag and dumped the body in the Savannah River. But Lumpkin descends from Georgia gentry; one ancestor was a state Supreme Court justice. He was sentenced to life in prison.

10 Worse than those inequities, capital punishment is sometimes visited upon the innocent. Lawrence C. Marshall, a law professor at Northwestern University, is director of the National Conference on Wrongful Convictions and the Death Penalty. Since 1972, he says, 78 innocent people have been released from death row.

11 It does not strain the imagination to think that maybe, just maybe, the system did not catch all of its errors and some of those who were wrongly convicted have already been sent to their deaths. How many? There is no way to know, but even one is too many. The execution of even one innocent man puts us law-abiding citizens uncomfortably close to the level of a John William King.

Selection 7

The following guest editorial appeared in a small town's weekly newspaper after it was announced that a tribal association had bought land nearby and was planning to build a casino. The author's name has been removed at her request.

Please, No More Gambling!

1   It was a mistake at the outset to allow Indians to open casinos. It was bad enough that anybody could go to Nevada or Atlantic City and gamble, but at least they had to go *there* to do it. Nowadays, with all the Indian casinos, nearly everybody can gamble in their own backyard—and yours. And that means they can turn your backyard into a high-crime, high-danger place with lowered property values and a lower quality of life.

2   I speak from personal experience. A close cousin was loved and appreciated by everybody and had a wonderful family with two darling little girls. But he went with friends to a casino, where he liked playing the games. Before long he was addicted to gambling and wound up with a drinking problem and an empty bank account. He is now divorced and if it weren't for the rest of his family (including me) he would be homeless.

It is said that casinos are good for the states' economy. But states have cut deals with the devil for the paltry amount these casinos pay in taxes. Can the taxes they contribute pay for the misery, poverty, and broken families? Can anybody doubt the money is tainted? Surely we can pay for schools for our children without putting their parents at risk for this disease known as gambling addiction.

3   We got along in this country for two hundred years without Indian casinos. Why can't we get through the next two hundred without them? It's clear the

whole thing is a fad. Once the first ones got going, they popped up everywhere. Over 20 states now have legalized Indian gambling. Please write to the governor and ask him not to support more of this vice in our state.

4 I'll end with a quotation from an American whom everybody admires and who knew what was best for his country:

> . . . avoid Gaming. This is a vice which is productive of every possible evil, equally injurious to the morals and health of its votaries. It is the child of Avarice, the brother of iniquity, the father of Mischief. It has been the ruin of many worthey families; the loss of many a man's honor, and the cause of Suicide.

—George Washington, to his nephew, January 15, 1783

Reprinted by permission from the Tule Lake (California) *Press-Record*

Selection 8

Identify the main issue in this essay and the author's position on this issue. Then state in your own words three arguments given by the author in support of his position.

As an additional exercise, show how at least two of these arguments can be treated as categorical syllogisms (Chapter 8), as truth-functional arguments (Chapter 9), or as common deductive argument patterns (inside back cover and Chapter 9).

Hetero by Choice?

A radio commentary by Richard Parker

1 For a while there, everybody who could get near a microphone was claiming that only he or she and his or her group, party, faction, religion, or militia stood for real American family values.

2 Now, it was seldom made clear just what those values were supposed to be. I have a notion that if [my son] Alex and I were to go out and knock over a few gas stations and convenience stores, the mere fact that we did it together would make it count as somebody's family values.

3 For some, the phrase "family values" never amounted to more than a euphemism for gay-bashing. I remember a [few] years ago, during the loudest squawking about values, when a reporter asked Dan Quayle whether he believed that a gay person's homosexuality was a matter of his or her psychological makeup or whether it was a matter of choice. He answered that he believed it was mainly a matter of choice. Two weeks later, Barbara Bush was quoted as saying that sexual orientation is mainly a matter of choice. Since then, it's turned up frequently.

4 It seems to me that people who make such a remark are either being remarkably cynical (if they don't really believe it themselves) or remarkably fatuous (if they do believe it).

5 If it were *true* that a person's sexual preference were a matter of choice, then it must have happened that each of us, somewhere back along the way, *decided* what our sexual preference would be. Now, if we'd made such decisions, you'd think that somebody would remember doing it, but nobody does.

6 In my case, I just woke up one morning when I was a kid and discovered that girls were important to me in a way that boys were not. I certainly didn't

sit down and *decide* that it was girls who were going to make me anxious, excited, terror-struck, panicky, and inclined to act like an idiot.

7 Now, if the people who claim to hold the "choice" view were right, it must mean that gay people have always chosen—they've *decided*—to have the sexual orientation they have. Can you imagine a person, back in the fifties, say, who would *choose* to have to put up with all the stuff gay people had to put up with back then? It's bad enough now, but only the mad or the criminally uninformed would have *chosen* such a life back then.

8 (Actually, it seems clear to me that the whole idea of a preference rules out the notion of choice. I choose to eat chocolate rather than vanilla, but I don't choose to *prefer* chocolate to vanilla. One simply discovers what one prefers.)

9 If it's clear that people don't consciously choose their sexual preferences, why would anybody make such claims? I can think of a cynical reason: It only makes sense to condemn someone for something they choose, not for things they can't do anything about.

10 Is it just a coincidence that people who claim we choose our sexual preferences are often the same people who demonize homosexuals? No, of course not. In fact, their cart comes before their horse: They are damned sure going to condemn gay people, and so, since you can only condemn someone for voluntary actions, it *must* be that one's sexuality is a voluntary choice. Bingo! Consistent logic. Mean, vicious, and mistaken. But consistent.

Selection 9

In a brief essay, argue for whether Bonnie and Clyde should receive the same or different punishment.

Bonnie and Clyde

1 Bonnie and Clyde are both driving on roads near a mountain community in northern California. Both are driving recklessly—much faster than the posted speed limit. Each of them has a passenger in the car.

2 At a sharp and very dangerous curve, Bonnie loses control of her car and crashes into some nearby trees; only moments later, on another dangerous section of road, Clyde's car goes into a skid, leaving the road and rolling over several times down an embankment.

3 As a result of their accidents, Bonnie and Clyde are bruised and shaken but not seriously hurt. However, both of their passengers are hurt badly and require medical attention. Passersby call an ambulance from the next town, and soon it arrives, taking the injured passengers to the only medical facility in the area.

4 A neurosurgeon who is on duty examines both passengers when they arrive at the medical center. She determines that both have suffered serious head injuries and require immediate cranial surgery if they are to survive. However, she is the only person available who is competent to perform the surgery, and she cannot operate on both patients at once. Not knowing what to do, she tries to find someone to call for advice. But she can reach nobody. So she flips a coin.

5 As a result of the coin flip, the surgeon operates on Bonnie's passenger and leaves Clyde's passenger in the care of two medical technicians. The latter do the best they can, but Clyde's passenger dies. Because of the attention of the physician, Bonnie's passenger survives and, in time, makes a complete recovery.

Selection 10

Determine the author's main point. Identify any rhetorical devices present; identify and evaluate any arguments present.

Disinformation on Judges

Thomas Sowell

1 Judges who decide cases on the basis of the plain meaning of the words in the laws—like Justices Brown and Owen—may be what most of the public want but such judges are anathema to liberals.

2 The courts are the last hope for enacting the liberal agenda because liberals cannot get enough votes to control Congress or most state legislatures. Unelected judges can cut the voters out of the loop and decree liberal dogma as the law of the land.

3 Liberals don't want that stopped.

4 The damage that is done by judicial activism extends beyond the particular policies that happen to catch the fancy of judges. Judicial ad-libbing creates a large area of uncertainty, making the law a trap for honest people and a bonanza for the unscrupulous.

5 A disinformation campaign has already been launched to depict judges who believe in following the written law as being "activist" conservatives, just like liberal activists.

6 Those who play this game of verbal equivalence can seldom, if ever, come up with concrete examples where conservative judges made rulings that went directly counter to what the written law says or who made rulings for which there is no written law.

7 Meanwhile, nothing is easier to come up with than such examples among liberal judicial activists who have made decisions based on "evolving standards," "world opinion" or other such lofty hokum worthy of the Wizard of Oz.

8 "Pay no attention to that man behind the curtain," the Wizard said—and "Don't attack our judges" the liberals say.

9 Even some conservative Republicans have fallen for this line. President Bush's former Solicitor General Theodore Olson recently condemned "personal attacks" on judges by their critics, and somehow lumped those critics with criminals or crackpots who have committed violence against judges or their family members.

10 Criticizing someone's official conduct is not a "personal attack." Nor does criticism equate with violence. An independent judiciary does not mean judges independent of the law. Nor is the rule of judges the same as the rule of law. Too often it is the rule of lawlessness from the bench.

Selections 11A and 11B

Evaluate the arguments on both sides. Who has the stronger arguments, and why? Make certain your response does not rest too heavily on rhetorical devices. As an alternative assignment, determine which author relies more heavily on rhetorical devices to persuade the audience.

Equal Treatment Is Real Issue—Not Marriage

USA Today

Our view: The fact is that marriage is already a messy entanglement
of church and state.

1 With shouting about "gay marriage" headed for a new decibel level . . . chances for an amicable resolution seem bleak.

2 Traditionalists see the issue in private, religious terms, and with legislators in many states mobilizing around their cause, they're in no mood to compromise. They say marriage, by common definition, involves a man and a woman. And for most people, it's just that. In polls, two-thirds of the public supports the status quo.

3 But looking through the lenses of history and law, as judges must, marriage is far from a private religious matter. So much so that short of a constitutional amendment, compromise is inevitable.

4 Not only does the state issue marriage licenses and authorize its officers to perform a civil version of the rite, it gives married couples privileged treatment under law.

5 For example, when one spouse dies the house and other property held jointly transfer easily for the other's continued use and enjoyment. The survivor gets a share of continuing Social Security and other benefits. Joint health and property insurance continues automatically.

6 If there's no will, the law protects the bereaved's right to inherit. There's no question of who gets to make funeral arrangements and provide for the corpse.

7 It's the normal order of things, even for households that may have existed for only the briefest time, or for couples who may be long estranged though not divorced.

8 But some couples next door—even devoted couples of 20 or 30 years' standing—don't have those rights and can't get them because of their sex.

9 Support for marriage is justified as important to community stability, and it undoubtedly is. But when it translates into economic and legal discrimination against couples who may be similarly committed to each other, that should be disturbing.

10 The U.S. Constitution says every person is entitled to equal protection under law. Some state constitutions go farther, specifically prohibiting sexual discrimination. . . .

11 Ironically, people who oppose gay marriages on religious grounds would have their way but for the fact that marriage has evolved as a messy entanglement of church and state. To millions, marriage is a sacrament, and the notion that the state would license or regulate a sacrament ought to be an outrage. Imagine the uproar if a state legislature tried to license baptisms or communions, and wrote into law who could be baptized or who could receive bread and wine. Or worse yet gave tax breaks to those who followed those practices.

12 Short of getting out of the marriage business altogether, which isn't likely to happen, the state must figure a way to avoid discrimination. The hundreds of employers now extending workplace benefits to unmarried but committed couples and the handful of municipalities offering informal "domestic partner" status may be pointing in the right direction.

13　The need is not necessarily to redefine marriage but to assure equal treatment under the law.

Gay Marriage "Unnatural"

The Rev. Louis P. Sheldon

The Rev. Louis P. Sheldon is chairman of the Traditional Values Coalition, a California-based organization of some 32,000 churches.

Opposing view: Opinion polls show that nearly 80% of Americans don't accept "homosexual marriage."

1　In everything which has been written and said about . . . homosexual marriage . . ., the most fundamental but important point has been overlooked. Marriage is both culturally and physiologically compatible but so-called homosexual marriage is neither culturally nor physiologically possible.

2　Homosexuality is not generational. The family tree that starts with a homosexual union never grows beyond a sapling. Without the cooperation of a third party, the homosexual marriage is a dead-end street. In cyber language, the marriage is not programmed properly and there are hardware problems as well.

3　. . . Across America, "rights" are being created and bestowed routinely by judges indifferent to the wishes and values of their communities. This new wave of judicial tyranny confers special rights upon whichever group can cry the shrillest claim of victimhood.

4　At the core of the effort of homosexuals to legitimize their behavior is the debate over whether or not homosexuality is some genetic or inherited trait or whether it is a chosen behavior. The activists argue that they are a minority and homosexuality is an immutable characteristic.

5　But no school of medicine, medical journal or professional organization such as the American Psychological Association or the American Psychiatric Association has ever recognized the claim that homosexuality is genetic, hormonal or biological.

6　While homosexuals are few in number, activists claim they represent about 10% of the population. More reliable estimates suggest about 2% of Americans are homosexual. They also are the wealthiest, most educated and most traveled demographic group measured today. Per capita income for the average homosexual is nearly twice that for the average American. They are the most advantaged group in America.

7　Homosexuality is a behavior-based life-style. No other group of Americans have ever claimed special rights and privileges based solely on their choice of sexual behavior, and the 1986 Supreme Court decision of *Bowers vs. Hardwick* said sodomy is not a constitutionally protected right.

8　When the state enacts a new policy, it must be reflected in its public school curriculum. Textbook committees and boards of education will ensure that all of that flows into the classroom. American families do not want the "normalcy" of homosexual marriage taught to their children.

9　Churches may not be forced to perform homosexual weddings but individual churches that resist may be subjected to civil suit for sexual discrimination. Resistance may be used as a basis for denying them access to federal, state or local government programs. In the Archdiocese of New York, Catholic churches were singled out by the city and denied reimbursement given to every other church for providing emergency shelter to the city's homeless. The reason cited was Catholic opposition to homosexual "rights" ordinances.

10 Whatever the pronouncements of the . . . nation's highest court, Americans know that "homosexual marriage" is an oxymoron. Calling a homosexual relationship a marriage won't make it so. There is no use of rhetoric that can sanitize it beyond what it is: unnatural and against our country's most basic standards. Every reputable public opinion poll demonstrates that nearly 8 of every 10 Americans don't accept the pretense of "homosexual marriage."

Selection 12

Same directions as previous selection.

Liberals Love America Like O.J. Loved Nicole

Ann Coulter

1 Let's review.

2 The *New York Times* calls the U.S. "stingy" and runs letters to the editor redoubling the insult, saying: "The word 'stingy' doesn't even come close to accurately describing the administration's pathetic initial offer of aid. . . . I am embarrassed for our country."

3 Al Franken flies into a rage upon discovering that O'Reilly imagines the U.S. is the most generous nation in the world.

4 The *Washington Post* criticizes Bush for not rushing back to Washington in response to the tsunami—amid unfavorable comparisons to German Chancellor Gerhard Schroeder, who immediately cut short his vacation and returned to Berlin. (Nothing snaps a German to attention like news of mass death!).

5 The prestigious Princeton "ethicist" Peter Singer, who endorses sex with animals and killing children with birth defects, says "when it comes to foreign aid, America is the most stingy nation on Earth."

6 And has some enterprising reporter asked Sen. Patty Murray what she thinks about the U.S.'s efforts on the tsunami? How about compared to famed philanthropist Osama bin Laden?

7 In December 2002, Murray was extolling Osama bin Laden's good works in the Middle East, informing a classroom of students: "He's been out in these countries for decades building roads, building schools, building infrastructure, building day-care facilities, building health-care facilities, and the people are extremely grateful. It made their lives better." What does Murray say about bin Laden's charity toward the (mostly Muslim) tsunami victims?

8 Speaking of world leaders admired by liberals, why isn't Fidel Castro giving the tsunami victims some of that terrific care liberals tell us he has been providing the people of Cuba?

9 Stipulating that liberals love America—which apparently depends on what the meaning of "love" is—do they love America as much as they love bin Laden and Castro?

Selection 13

Determine whether this essay contains an argument and, if it does, what it is.

Alternative assignment: Identify rhetorical devices, including slanters and fallacious reasoning.

Is God Part of Integrity?

Editorial from the *Enterprise Record,* Chico, California

1   What Oroville High School was trying to do last Friday night, said Superintendent Barry Kayrell, was "maintain the integrity of the ceremony."

2   The ceremony was graduation for approximately 200 graduates.

3   The way to maintain "integrity," as it turned out, was to ban the words "God" and "Jesus Christ."

4   The result was a perfect example of out-of-control interpretation of the separation of church and state.

5   The high school's action in the name of "integrity" needlessly disrupted the entire proceeding as almost the entire graduating class streamed out of their seats in support of Chris Niemeyer, an exemplary student who had been selected co-valedictorian but was barred from speaking because he wanted to acknowledge his belief in God and Jesus Christ.

6   The speech, said Kayrell, "was more of a testimonial."

7   It was preaching, added OHS principal Larry Payne.

8   "I truly believe in the separation (of church and state)," explained Kayrell.

9   It was a complicated story that led to last Friday night.

10 Niemeyer and fellow senior Ferin Cole had prepared their speeches ahead of time and presented them to school officials. Cole, who plans to attend Moody Bible College, had been asked to deliver the invocation.

11 Both mentioned God and Jesus Christ. Both were told that was unacceptable.

12 Both filed a last-minute action in federal court, challenging the school's censorship. At a hearing Friday, just hours before graduation, a judge refused to overrule the school on such short notice. The suit, however, continues, and the judge acknowledged it will involve sorting out complex constitutional questions.

13 Defeated in court, Niemeyer and Cole met with school officials to see what could be salvaged.

14 Both agreed to remove references to the deity, but Cole wanted to mention why, in an invocation—by definition a prayer—he was not allowed to refer to God. That was nixed, and Cole simply bowed out.

15 Niemeyer was supposed to deliver his revised draft to Payne by 5 P.M.

16 He missed the deadline, but brought the draft with him to the ceremony.

17 When it was his turn to speak, Niemeyer came forward, but Payne instead skipped over the program listing for the valedictory address and announced a song. The two debated the question on stage as the audience and graduates-to-be looked on.

18 Finally turned away, Niemeyer left the stage, tears of frustration on his cheeks, and his classmates ran to his side in a dramatic show of support.

19 You might say they were inspired by integrity.

20 The object of the First Amendment to the U.S. Constitution is to bar government-enforced religion. It was not designed to obliterate belief in God.

21 To stretch that command to denying a student the right to acknowledge what has spurred him on to the honor he has won is a bitter perversion.

22 That would apply whether the student was Islamic, Buddhist or any belief—atheist included. There is room, it would seem, for diversity in valedictory speeches, too.

23 Not at Oroville High School. There God and integrity don't mix.

24 It's spectacles like that played out last Friday night that have prompted Congress to consider a constitutional amendment aimed at curbing such misguided excess.

25 Earlier in the week it drew a majority vote in House, but fell short of the two-thirds margin needed.

26 Maybe such actions as witnessed locally can push it over the top.

Selections 14A and 14B*

Identify the arguments each writer uses to support his position on the issue. Who do you think has the stronger arguments, and why?

Question: Do College and University Administration Have the Right to Establish Standards for Faculty Dress and Grooming?

Yes, a college is a business as much as any company, so dress standards should normally be expected.

By Dan Creed
Instructor in the Department of Business
Normandale Community College, Minnesota

1 The familiar phrases "dress for success" or "the clothes make the person" are as true for college faculty as they are in the corporate world.

2 First, let's address the question of why business etiquette deems a dress code proper in the business world. It is understood that dress does convey confidence, personal success and a respect to those with whom you are engaged in business. That is the philosophy behind IBM's dress code for its sales force. The leadership understands that proper dress gives their sales force an edge. Similarly. if you visited a fine dining restaurant, you might be offended if the host was dressed in worn out blue jeans.

3 I have asked students the question about faculty dress and the majority have stated they appreciate when an instructor dresses up, at least in business casual. They voiced their appreciation for the instructor going to the extra effort to show respect to the students. Students do "get" the message being conveyed—respect.

4 Appropriate dress is socially an acceptable and expected gesture as well, whether going to a wedding, church, or funeral. Many cultures consider improper dress rude and disrespectful and guests are not allowed entrance if not properly attired. Sadly, American culture seems to have lost a sense of respect when it comes to dressing for certain occasions, such as a funeral.

5 At Normandale College where I teach, many of the instructors in the business and hospitality departments emphasize dress as an important point of etiquette for our students and demonstrate how proper dress gives them an edge in the job market. It only stands to reason that we would reinforce this instruction by personally setting an example.

. . .

*Both selections from the NEA Higher Education Advocate, October 2009.

No, college faculty are professionals and should not have a dress code.

By Andy Wible
Philosophy Instructor
Muskegon Community College in Michigan

6 There are several reasons faculty should not have a dress code. First, college faculty are role models and should be teaching students that it is not what a person wears, but the content of a person's words and actions that matters.

7 Second, the professional faculty members themselves are the best ones to determine what form of dress is most suitable to their teaching style. Some teachers may decide to be formal and some may decide to be casual, the dress of each fitting the pedagogy that they desire.

8 Third, when it comes to employment, sectors differ as to what appropriate dress is. Wearing a tie when fixing a wind turbine might lead to suffocation. Even if business standards differ, some require a tie, but others such as Internet companies are notorious for encouraging Saturday casual. The companies value the input of the employee over the veneer of their clothing, and believe that better ideas come from people who are comfortable.

9 One argument might be that there should be dress codes appropriate to each discipline. Physical education faculty wear track suits, management faculty suits, and philosophy faculty togas. The problem is that there is disagreement within these areas, and once again the professional faculty member should determine what is best.

10 Some classes could properly discuss appropriate dress in certain circumstances. Political science classes might discuss the importance of wearing a black robe if you are a Supreme Court justice. But the classroom is not a court; it is a place for the mind to be cultivated and diversity encouraged.

11 Dress codes in academia should be limited to one day a year: graduation.

Selections 15A and 15B

Evaluate the arguments on both sides. Who has the stronger arguments, and why?

Alternative assignment: Identify rhetorical devices and determine which author relies more heavily on them.

Second alternative assignment: In the first essay, find as many arguments as you can that can be treated as categorical syllogisms. Set up a key, letting a letter stand for a relevant category. Be sure you identify the category in plain English. Then circle all and only the distributed terms. Then state whether each syllogism is valid, identifying rules broken by any syllogisms that are not.

Make Fast Food Smoke-Free

USA Today

Our view: The only thing smoking in fast-food restaurants should be the speed of the service.

1 Starting in June, if you go to Arby's, you may get more than a break from burgers. You could get a break from tobacco smoke, too.

2 The roast-beef-sandwich chain on Tuesday moved to the head of a stampede by fast-food restaurants to limit smoking.

3 Last year, McDonald's began experimenting with 40 smokeless restaurants. Wendy's and other fast-food chains also have restaurants that bar smoking.

4 But Arby's is the first major chain to heed a call from an 18-member state attorneys general task force for a comprehensive smoking ban in fast-food restaurants. It will bar smoking in all its 257 corporate-owned restaurants and urge its 500 franchisees to do the same in their 2,000 restaurants.

5 Other restaurants, and not just the fast-food places, should fall in line.

6 The reason is simple: Smoke in restaurants is twice as bad as in a smoker's home or most other workplaces, a recent report to the *Journal of the American Medical Association* found.

7 Fast-food restaurants have an even greater need to clear the air. A quarter of their customers and 40% of their workers are under 18.

8 Secondhand smoke is a class A carcinogen. It is blamed for killing an estimated 44,000 people a year. And its toxins especially threaten youngsters' health.

9 The Environmental Protection Agency estimates that secondhand smoke causes up to 1 million asthma attacks and 300,000 respiratory infections that lead to 15,000 hospitalizations among children each year.

10 All restaurants should protect their workers and customers. If they won't, then local and state governments should do so by banning smoking in them, as Los Angeles has.

11 A person's right to a quick cigarette ends when it threatens the health of innocent bystanders, and even more so when many of them are youngsters.

12 They deserve a real break—a meal in a smoke-free environment that doesn't threaten their health.

Don't Overreact to Smoke

Brennan M. Dawson

Opposing view: With non-smoking sections available and visits brief, what's the problem?

1 If the attorneys general from a handful of states—those charged with upholding the law—were to hold a forum in Washington, you might expect them to be tackling what polls say is the No. 1 public issue: crime.

2 Not these folks. They're worried someone might be smoking in the smoking section of a fast-food restaurant. And, there might be children in the non-smoking section. Thus, they say, fast-food chains should ban all smoking.

3 Some would argue that this raises serious questions about priorities. But it may be worth debating, since this is supposed to be about protecting children. Everyone is (and should be) concerned with children's health and well-being.

4 But what are we protecting them from—the potential that a whiff of smoke may drift from the smoking section to the non-smoking section during the average 20-minute visit for a quick burger?

5 Anyone knowledgeable would tell you that none of the available studies can reasonably be interpreted to suggest that incidental exposure of a child to smoking in public places such as restaurants is a problem. After all, with the almost universal availability of non-smoking sections, parents have the option of keeping their kids out of the smoking section.

6 A recent study published in the *American Journal of Public Health* reported that the separate smoking sections in restaurants do a good job of minimizing exposure to tobacco smoke. According to the figures cited, customers would have to spend about 800 consecutive hours in the restaurants to be exposed to the nicotine equivalent of one cigarette.

7 That would represent about 2,400 fast-food meals. Under those conditions, most parents would worry about something other than smoking.

Selections 16A and 16B

Evaluate the arguments on both sides. Who has the stronger arguments, and why?

Alternative assignment: Identify rhetorical devices and determine which author relies more heavily on them.

Second alternative assignment: In each of the two essays, find as many arguments as you can that can be treated as categorical syllogisms. Set up a key, letting a letter stand for a relevant category. Be sure you identify the category in plain English. Then circle all and only the distributed terms. Then state whether each syllogism is valid, identifying rules broken by any syllogisms that are not.

Buying Notes Makes Sense at Lost-in-Crowd Campuses

USA Today

Our view: Monster universities and phantom professors have only themselves to blame for note-selling.

1 Higher education got a message last week from a jury in Gainesville, Fla.: Its customers, the students across the nation, deserve better service.

2 The jury found entrepreneurs are free to sell notes from college professors' lectures. And Ken Brickman is an example of good, old free enterprise, even if his services encourage students to skip class.

3 Brickman is a businessman who pays students to take notes in classes at the University of Florida. From a storefront a block off campus, he resells the notes to other students with a markup.

4 Professors and deans bemoan Brickman's lack of morals. They even use the word "cheating." They'd be more credible if their complaints—and the university's legal resources—were directed equally at Brickman's competitor in the note-selling business a few blocks away.

5 The difference: The competition pays professors for their notes; Brickman pays students. Morals are absent, it seems, only when professors aren't getting their cut.

6 The deeper issue is why Brickman has found a lucrative market. It's easy to say that uninspired students would rather read someone else's notes than spend time in class, but that's not the point.

7 Why are students uninspired? Why are they required to learn in auditorium-size classes where personal attention is non-existent, taking attendance impossible, and students can "cut" an entire semester with no one noticing?

8 Why are students increasingly subjected to teaching assistants—graduate students who know little more than they—who control classes while professors are off writing articles for esoteric journals that not even their peers will read?

9 Why are there not more professors—every former student can remember one—who transmit knowledge of and enthusiasm for a subject with a fluency and flair that make students eager to show up? No one would prefer to stay away and buy that professor's notes.

10 The debate over professorial priorities—students vs. research—is old. But so long as students come in second, they'll have good reasons to go to Ken Brickman for their notes.

Buying or Selling Notes Is Wrong*

Opposing view: Note-buyers may think they're winners,
but they lose out on what learning is all about.

1 It's tough being a college student. Tuition costs and fees are skyrocketing. Classes are too large. Many professors rarely even see their students, let alone know their names or recognize their faces. The pressure for grades is intense. Competition for a job after graduation is keen.

2 But that's no excuse for buying the notes to a teacher's course. What goes around comes around. Students who buy someone else's notes are only cheating themselves—by not engaging in the learning process to the fullest extent. They aren't learning how to take notes. Or how to listen. Or how to put what someone is saying into their own words.

3 What happens if the notes are inaccurate? Will a commercial note-taker guarantee the notes? Would you want to take a test using someone else's notes?

4 Besides, what the professor says is her own property. It is the result of hard work on her part. A professor's lectures are often her principal means of livelihood. Nobody but the professor herself has the right to sell her property. Buying the notes to her lectures without her permission is just like selling a book that she wrote and keeping the money for yourself.

5 And buying the notes from someone who is selling them without the teacher's permission is the same as receiving stolen goods.

6 And that's assuming that there will be anyone out there to buy the notes in the first place. After all, most students will want to take notes for themselves because they know that is their only guarantee of accuracy. People who think they can get rich selling the notes to someone's lectures should take a course in critical thinking.

7 The pressure for good grades doesn't justify buying or selling the notes to a professor's lectures without her permission. If you can't go to class, you shouldn't even be in college in the first place. Why come to school if you don't want to learn?

Selections 17A and 17B

Evaluate the arguments on both sides. Who has the stronger arguments, and why?

---

*The author of the companion piece to the *USA Today* editorial on this subject would not give us permission to reproduce her essay in a critical thinking text, so we wrote this item ourselves.

Alternative assignment: Identify rhetorical devices and determine which author relies more heavily on them.

Next, Comprehensive Reform of Gun Laws

USA Today

Our view: Waiting periods and weapon bans are welcome controls, but they're just the start of what's needed.

1 The gun lobby got sucker-punched by the U.S. Senate last weekend. It couldn't happen to a more deserving bunch.

2 For seven years, gun advocates have thwarted the supersensible Brady bill, which calls for a national waiting period on handgun purchases. Through a mix of political intimidation, political contributions and perverse constitutional reasoning, gun lobbyists were able to convince Congress to ignore the nine out of 10 Americans who support that idea.

3 But suddenly, after two days of filibuster, the Senate abruptly adopted the Brady bill. The House has already acted, so all that remains is to do some slight tinkering in a House-Senate conference, and then it's off to the White House for President Clinton's signature.

4 That's not the end of welcome gun control news, though. As part of the anti-crime bill adopted last week, the Senate agreed to ban the manufacture and sale of 19 types of assault-style semiautomatic weapons. Although these weapons constitute fewer than 1% of all guns in private hands, they figure in nearly 10% of all crime. The bill also bans some types of ammunition and restricts gun sales to, and ownership by, juveniles.

5 These ideas are worthy, but they can't do the whole job. Waiting periods and background checks keep criminals from buying guns from legal dealers. Banning certain types of anti-personnel weapons and ammunition will keep those guns and bullets from growing more common and commonly lethal.

6 Yet the wash of guns and gun violence demands much, much more. The judicial ability to process firearm-related crimes with certainty and speed is part of the solution. But even more so is the adoption of laws that permit gun licensing, gun registration and firearm training and education.

7 After years of denying the popular mood, Congress appears ready to honor it. That merits applause. But its new laws are just a start. Without truly comprehensive controls, the nationwide slick of gun carnage is bound to continue its bloody, inexorable creep.

Gun Laws Are No Answer

Alan M. Gottlieb

Opposing view: Disarming the law-abiding populace won't stop crime. Restore gun owners' rights.

1 Every time another gun control law is passed, violent crime goes up, not down, and the gun-ban crowd starts to yelp for more anti-gun laws.

2 So it's no surprise that the gun-banners are already snapping at the heels of our Bill of Rights.

3 They turn a blind eye to the fact that California, with a 15-day waiting period, experienced a 19% increase in violent crime and a 20% increase in homicide

between 1987 and 1991. And that a 1989 ban on "assault weapons" in that state has also resulted in increased violent crime.

4   In Illinois, after a 30-day waiting period was installed, that state experienced a 31% increase in violent crime and a 36% increase in the homicide rate.

5   And, a handgun ban in Washington, D.C., has made it the murder capital of the world!

6   The results are in. Gun control makes the streets safe for violent criminals. It disarms their victims—you and me. The people's right to protect themselves should be restored, not restricted.

7   Case in point: Bonnie Elmasri of Wisconsin, who was being stalked by her estranged husband despite a court restraining order, was killed along with her two children while she waited for the handgun she purchased under that state's gun-waiting-period law.

8   Bonnie and her children are dead because of gun control laws, as are thousands of other victims each year.

9   Anybody who believes that disarming the law-abiding populace will help reduce crime has rocks in the head.

10 The next time a violent criminal attacks you, you can roll up your copy of USA TODAY and defend yourself with it. It may be all you'll have left for self-protection.

Selection 18

The following letter was sent to one of our students from the National Rifle Association. Notice the tendency—more and more common recently—to use repetition in place of argument. Are there any arguments present in the letter? Are there rhetorical devices?

Dear Friend,

1   It is critical that you accept the enclosed Black-and-Gold National Rifle Association membership card today.

2   Joining the National Rifle Association (NRA) is the single most important thing you can do to protect your Second Amendment rights and promote safe, responsible firearms ownership.

3   There has never been a more important time for America's gun owners to unite and stand up for our freedom.

4   *Anti-gun members of Congress, including Senators Hillary Clinton and Charles Schumer, Representative Patrick Kennedy and others, are aggressively pushing for more harsh anti-gun legislation.*

5   Their agenda includes *gun-owner licensing and fingerprinting, gun registration,* and *rationing, gun show bans* and *much more.*

6   Only a united effort by freedom-loving Americans can stop this assault on our rights from doing irreversible damage to our freedoms.

7   That's why the National Rifle Association needs patriotic Americans like you to join our organization and help defend our cherished freedoms.

8   Since our formation over 132 years ago, the NRA has led the effort to defend the rights of law-abiding gun owners.

9   The NRA reaches out to America's 80 million gun owners to bring them together through sponsorship of gun safety programs, hunter education

courses, self-defense training, legislative advocacy and family events like our "Friends of NRA" gatherings.

10 Remember, *the NRA is a non-partisan grassroots membership organization,* an association of millions of patriotic Americans who care about freedom and who enjoy and treasure our nation's heritage of firearms ownership and use.

11 We represent your "special-interest"—*YOUR FREEDOM!*

12 The NRA's efforts are based on the needs and concerns of our members, men and women like you from all around the country.

13 That's why we are asking you to join and help serve as *"the eyes and ears" of the NRA* to make sure grassroots gun owners in your area have their concerns addressed and your interests protected.

14 Our goal is to build a fire-wall around the Second Amendment by recruiting at least ten thousand NRA members in each Congressional district.
I know this may sound ambitious, but most Congressional elections are decided by less than 10,000 votes.

15 Each NRA member we sign up means more leverage to convince the politicians to keep their hands off the Second Amendment, or hunting lands and our other firearm freedoms—because politicians know NRA members vote!

. . .

16 *As a member of the NRA, you can have a far-reaching impact on the future of our Second Amendment right to keep and bear arms.*

. . .

17 As a *BONUS GIFT* for joining today you'll receive a NRA Black-and-Gold Shooter's Cap. This cap, like your membership card, is recognized around the world as a symbol of the organization dedicated to defending the United States Constitution, especially our Second Amendment right to keep and bear arms.

18 Of course the most important benefit of joining the NRA is knowing you are leading the fight to protect our right to keep and bear arms.

19 That's why I want you to carry your NRA Black-and-Gold membership card with pride as a reminder of all your membership does to protect your Second Amendment rights.

20 *We will never take your membership for granted and we will always remain committed to protecting your interests—your freedom—*

21 Remember, accepting your Black-and-Gold NRA membership card is the *most important step you can take to help preserve America's cherished heritage* of hunting, sport shooting, gun collecting and firearms ownership.

. . .

22 Our rights face many great challenges in Congress and throughout the country, but by working together, we can protect our freedom for today and for future Americans to enjoy.

23 Thank you in advance for accepting NRA Membership.

Sincerely,

Wayne LaPierre
Executive Vice President

P.S.   *The NRA needs the active support of patriotic Americans like you to help promote safe, responsible hunting and gun ownership.* By accepting your NRA membership today you can help us *fight back against anti-gun media bias* and educate the public about the Second Amendment's critical role in our nation.

Your membership in the NRA is critical to protecting our Second Amendment rights for future generations. Please use the enclosed reply form and postage paid envelope to send your NRA Membership dues today. Thank you.

[All emphases present in the original. —Ed.]

Selections 19A and 19B

Evaluate the arguments on both sides. Who has the stronger arguments, and why?

Alternative assignment: Identify rhetorical devices and determine which author relies more heavily on them.

How Can School Prayer Possibly Hurt? Here's How

USA Today

Our view: Mississippi case shows how people's rights can be trampled by so-called "voluntary prayer."

1 What harm is there in voluntary prayer in school?

2 That's the question . . . House Speaker Newt Gingrich and others pose in their crusade to restore prayer to the classroom. They argue that a constitutional amendment to "protect" so-called voluntary school prayer could improve morals and at worst do no harm.

3 Well, a mother's lawsuit filed Monday against Pontotoc County, Miss., schools says otherwise. It shows government-sponsored voluntary prayer in school threatens religious liberty.

4 All the mother, Lisa Herdahl, wants is that her six children get their religious instruction at home and at their Pentecostal church, not at school.

5 But their school hasn't made that easy. Prayers by students go out over the public address system every day. And a Bible study class is taught at every grade.

6 School officials argue that since no one is ordered to recite a prayer or attend the class, everything is voluntary.

7 But to Herdahl's 7-year-old son, it doesn't seem that way. She says he was nicknamed "football head" by other students after a teacher told him to wear headphones so he wouldn't have to listen to the "voluntary" prayers.

8 And she says her 11-year-old son was branded a "devil worshiper" after a teacher told students he could leave a Bible class because he didn't believe in God.

9 Indeed, Herdahl's children have suffered exactly the kind of coercion to conform that the Supreme Court found intolerable when it banned state-written prayers in 1962 and outlawed Alabama's moment of silence for meditation or voluntary prayer in 1985.

10 As the court noted in those cases, when government—including schools—strays from neutrality in religious matters, it pits one religion against another. And youngsters especially can feel pressured to submit to a majority's views.

11 That's why a constitutional amendment to protect "voluntary prayer" in school is so dangerous.

12 Students don't need an amendment to pray in school now. They have that right. And they can share their religious beliefs. They've formed more than 12,000 Bible clubs nationwide that meet in schools now, only not during class time.

13 For the Herdahls, who refused to conform to others' beliefs, state-sponsored voluntary prayer and religious studies have made school a nightmare.

14 For the nation, a constitutional amendment endorsing such ugly activities could make religious freedom a joke.

We Need More Prayer

Armstrong Williams

Armstrong Williams is a Washington, D.C.–based business executive, talk-show host, and author of The Conscience of a Black Conservative. Opposing view: The tyranny of the minority was never envisioned by the nation's Founding Fathers.

1 The furor aroused by . . . Newt Gingrich's remarks about renewing school prayer illustrates how deep cultural divisions in American society really are.

2 A few moments of prayer in schools seems a small thing—harmless enough, almost to the point of insignificance. Yet it has provoked an impassioned firestorm of debate about the dangers of imposing viewpoints and the potential for emotionally distressing non-religious children.

3 The Constitution's framers were wary of a "tyranny of the majority," and so they imposed restraints on the legislature. They never foresaw, nor would they have believed, the tyranny of the minority made possible through an activist judiciary changing legal precedents by reinterpreting the Constitution.

4 The American ideal of tolerance has been betrayed by its use in directly attacking the deeply held convictions of millions of Americans.

5 The fact that this country was once unashamedly Christian did not mean that it was necessarily intolerant of other views—at least not nearly so intolerant of them as our rigid secular orthodoxy is toward all religious expression. Through the agency of the courts, a few disgruntled malcontents have managed to impose their secular/humanist minority views on the majority.

6 But it has not always been so.

7 The confidence with which some maintain that school prayer is manifestly unconstitutional belies an ignorance of our nation's history. America was founded by religious men and women who brought their religious beliefs and expressions with them into public life.

8 It was in 1962 that an activist Supreme Court ruled that denominationally neutral school prayer was judged to violate the establishment clause of the First Amendment. Since then, the "wall of separation" between church and state has rapidly become a prison wall for religious practice.

9 The drive to protect the delicate sensibilities of American children from the ravages of prayer is particularly ironic when our public schools have become condom clearinghouses that teach explicit sex.

10 The real heart of the school prayer issue is the role of religion in our public life.

Ad hominem *See* argumentum ad hominem.

Affirmative claim A claim that includes one class or part of one class within another: A- and I-claims.

Affirming the antecedent *See* modus ponens.

Affirming the consequent An argument consisting of a conditional claim as one premise, a claim that affirms the consequent of the conditional as a second premise, and a claim that affirms the antecedent of the conditional as the conclusion.

Ambiguity Having more than one meaning. An ambiguous claim is one that can be interpreted in more than one way and whose meaning is not made clear by the context. *See also* semantic ambiguity; syntactical ambiguity.

Ambiguous pronoun reference A statement or phrase in which it is not clear to what or to whom a pronoun is supposed to refer.

Analogical argument *See* argument from analogy.

Analogues Things that have similar attributes.

Analogy A linguistic expression that treats two or more events or things as similar.

Analytic claim A claim whose truth value is known simply by understanding the claim. **Contrast with** *synthetic claim*.

Analytical definition Specification of the features a thing must possess in order for the term being defined to apply to it.

Anecdotal evidence, fallacy of A version of hasty generalization, in which the overly small sample on which the generalization is based is merely a story.

Antecedent *See* conditional claim.

Appeal to anecdote Using a story in an attempt to disprove a general claim or causal hypothesis. *See also* Fallacy of anecdotal evidence.

Appeal to common practice Justifying or defending an *action* or *practice* (as distinguished from an assertion or claim) on the grounds that it is common.

Appeal to ignorance The view that an absence of evidence *against* a claim counts as evidence *for* that claim.

Appeal to indignation *See* argument from outrage.

Appeal to pity *See* argument from pity.

Appeal to popularity Urging someone to accept a claim (or falling prey to someone's doing it to us) simply on the grounds that all or most or some substantial number of people (other than authorities or experts) believe it.

Appeal to precedent The claim (in law) that a current case is sufficiently similar to a previous case that it should be settled in the same way.

Appeal to tradition Attempting to convince someone that a claim is true or that a practice is legitimate on the basis of tradition.

Apple polishing A pattern of fallacious reasoning in which flattery is disguised as a reason for accepting a claim.

Argument An attempt to support or prove a contention by providing a reason for accepting it. The contention itself is called the *conclusion*, the statement offered as the reason for accepting the conclusion is referred to as the *premise*.

Argument by force A special case of scare tactics, threatening a person.

Argument from analogy An inductive argument in which an attribute of one or more things is concluded to be a probable attribute of a similar thing.

Argument from envy Finding fault with a person or some position the person takes because of envy.

Argument from outrage Inflammatory words or claims followed by a "conclusion" of some sort.

Argument from pity When feeling sorry for someone drives us to a position on an unrelated matter.

Argument pattern The structure of an argument. This structure is independent of the argument's content. Several arguments can have the same pattern (e.g., modus ponens) yet be about quite different subjects. Variables are used to stand for classes or claims in the display of an argument's pattern.

Argumentum ad hominem An argument that illogically conflates a person's personal qualities with those of his or her views. The most common varieties are attempts to rebut an individual's opinions by talking about his or her personal qualities.

Attacking the analogy An attempt to rebut an argument from analogy by calling attention to important dissimilarities between the analogues.

Attribute of interest The attribute ascribed to a thing or things in the conclusion of an inductive generalization, inductive argument from analogy, or statistical syllogism.

Availability heuristic Unconsciously assigning a probability to a type of event on the basis of how often one thinks of events of that type.

Background information The body of justified beliefs that consists of facts we learn from our own direct observations and facts we learn from others.

Balance of considerations reasoning Trying to determine which considerations, both for and against thinking or doing something, carries the most weight.

Bandwagon effect An unconscious tendency to modify one's views to make them consonant with those of other people.

Begging the question *See* question-begging argument.

Belief bias The tendency to evaluate an argument by how believable its conclusion is.

Best Diagnosis Method Identifying the cause of multiple effects as the condition that best explains the effects, everything considered.

Better-than-average illusion   When a majority of a group estimates they are better at something than a majority of the group, the group is said to be subject to this illusion. When the majority of a group estimates they are worse at something than a majority of group, they are said to be subject to the "worse than average illusion."

Biased generalization, fallacy of   Overestimating the strength of an argument based on a biased sample.

Biased sample   A sample is said to be biased with respect to a feature if a disproportionate number of things in the sample have or lack the variable.

Burden of proof, misplaced   A form of fallacious reasoning in which the burden of proving a point is placed on the wrong side. One version occurs when a lack of evidence on one side is taken as evidence for the other side, in cases where the burden of proving the point rests on the latter side.

Categorical claim   Any standard-form categorical claim or any claim that means the same as some standard-form categorical claim. *See* standard-form categorical claim.

Categorical imperative   Kant's term for an absolute moral rule that holds unconditionally or "categorically."

Categorical logic   A system of logic based on the relations of inclusion and exclusion among classes ("categories"). This branch of logic specifies the logical relationships among claims that can be expressed in the forms "All Xs are Ys," "No Xs are Ys," "Some Xs are Ys," and "Some Xs are not Ys." Developed by Aristotle in the fourth century B.C.E., categorical logic is also known as Aristotelian or traditional logic.

Categorical syllogism   A two-premise deductive argument in which every claim is categorical and each of three terms appears in two of the claims— for example, all soldiers are martinets and no martinets are diplomats, so no soldiers are diplomats.

Causal claim   A statement that says or implies that one thing caused or causes another.

Causal factor   A causal factor for an effect is a variable whose presence in a population raises the probability that the effect will be present as well.

Causal hypothesis   A provisional explanation of the cause or effect of something.

Causal mechanism   An interface between cause and effect that has the property of making the effect happen, given the cause.

Cause-and-effect claim   *See* causal claim.

Chain argument   An argument consisting of three Conditional claims, in which the antecedents of one premise and the conclusion are the same, the consequents of the other premise and the conclusion are the same, and the consequent of the first premise and the antecedent of the second premise are the same.

Circularity   The property of a "causal" claim where the "cause" merely restates the effect.

Circumstantial ad hominem   The illogical notion that an individual's personal circumstances somehow refute his or her views.

Claim   When a belief (judgment, opinion) is asserted in a declarative sentence, the result is a claim or statement.

Claim variable   A letter that stands for a claim.

Cognitive bias   A psychological factor that unconsciously affects belief formation.

Common practice, "argument" from   Attempts to justify or defend an action or a practice on the grounds that it is common—that "everybody," or at least lots of people, do the same thing.

Common thread   When an effect is present on multiple occasions, look for some other shared feature (common thread) as a possible cause.

Complementary term   A term is complementary to another term if and only if it refers to everything that the first term does not refer to.

Composition, fallacy of   To think that what holds true of a group of things taken individually necessarily holds true of the same things taken collectively.

Conclusion   In an argument, the claim for which a premise is supposed to give a reason.

Conclusion indicator   A word or phrase (e.g., "therefore") that ordinarily indicates the presence of the conclusion of an argument.

Conditional claim   A claim that state-of-affairs A cannot hold without state-of-affairs B holding as well—e.g., "If A, then B." The A-part of the claim is called the *antecedent*; the B-part is called the *consequent*.

Conditional proof   A deduction for a conditional claim "If P, then Q" that proceeds by assuming that P is true and then proving that, on that assumption, Q must also be true.

conditio sine qua non   A condition without which it could not be. Often referred to as a "but for" cause.

Confidence level   A quantitative expression of the probability that the random variation found from random sample to random sample will lie within the error margin.

Conflicting claims   Two claims that cannot both be correct.

Confusing explanations and excuses, fallacy of   Mistaking an explanation of something for an attempt to excuse it.

Conjunction   A compound claim made from two simpler claims. A conjunction is true if and only if both of the simpler claims that compose it are true.

Consequent   *See* conditional claim.

Consequentialism   In moral reasoning, the view that the consequences of a decision, deed, or policy determine its moral value.

Consistency principle   The first principle of moral reasoning, which states that, if separate cases aren't different in any relevant way, they should be treated the same way, and if separate cases are treated in the same way, they should not be different in any relevant way.

Contradictory claims   Two claims that are exact opposites—that is, they could not both be true at the same time and could not both be false at the same time.

Contrapositive   The claim that results from switching the places of the subject and predicate terms in a categorical claim and replacing both terms with complementary terms.

Contrary analogue   In an argument from analogy, an analogue which does not have the attribute of interest.

Contrary claims   Two claims that could not both be true at the same time but could both be false at the same time.

Control group   *See* controlled cause-to-effect experiment.

Controlled cause-to-effect experiment   An experiment designed to test whether something is a causal factor for a given effect. Basically, in such an experiment two groups are essentially alike, except that the members of one group, the *experimental group*, are exposed to the suspected causal factor, and the members of the other group, the *control group*, are not. The effect must be found to occur with significantly more frequency in the experimental group for the suspected causal agent to be considered a causal factor for the effect.

Converse   The converse of a categorical claim is the claim that results from switching the places of the subject and predicate terms.

Covariation   The accompaniment of variations in one phenomenon by variations in another phenomenon.

Critical thinking   We think critically when we rationally evaluate our own or others' thinking.

cum hoc, ergo propter hoc   The fallacy of thinking that correlation or covariation between two variables proves that one causes the other.

Deduction (proof)   A numbered sequence of truth-functional symbolizations, each member of which validly follows from earlier members by one of the truth-functional rules.

Deductive argument   An argument intended to prove or demonstrate, rather than merely support, a conclusion.

Definition by example   Pointing to, naming, or otherwise identifying one or more examples of the term being defined; also called *ostensive definition*.

Definition by synonym   Giving another word or phrase that means the same thing as the term being defined.

Denying the antecedent   An argument consisting of a conditional claim as one premise, a claim that denies the antecedent of the conditional as a second premise, and a claim that denies the consequent of the conditional as the conclusion.

Denying the consequent   *See* modus tollens.

Deontologism   *See* duty theory.

Dependent premises   Premises that depend on one another as support for their conclusion. If the assumption that a premise is false cancels the support another provides for a conclusion, the premises are dependent.

Disinterested party   A person who has no stake in our belief or disbelief in a claim. *See* interested party.

Disjunction   A compound claim made up of two simpler claims. A disjunction is false only if both of the simpler claims that make it up are false.

Divine command theory   The view that our moral duty (what's right and wrong) is dictated by God.

Division, fallacy of   To think that what holds true of a group of things taken collectively necessarily holds true of the same things taken individually.

Downplayer   An expression used to play down or diminish the importance of something.

Duty theory   The view that a person should perform an action because it is his or her moral duty to perform it, not because of any consequences that might follow from it. Also called *deontologism*.

Dysphemism   A word or phrase used to produce a negative effect on a reader's or listener's attitude about something or to minimize the positive associations the thing may have.

Emotive meaning   The positive or negative associations of a word; a word's *rhetorical force*.

Envy, "argument" from   Trying to induce acceptance of a claim by arousing feelings of envy.

Equivalent claims   Two claims are equivalent if and only if they would be true in all and exactly the same circumstances.

Error margin   Expression of the limit of random variation among random samples of a population.

Ethical altruism   The moral doctrine that discounts one's own happiness as being of lesser value than the happiness of others.

Ethical egoism   The idea that, if an act produces more happiness for oneself than will the alternatives, then it is the right thing to do.

Euphemism   An agreeable or inoffensive expression that is substituted for an expression that may offend the hearer or suggest something unpleasant.

Experimental group   *See* controlled cause-to-effect experiment.

Expert   A person who, through training, education, or experience, has special knowledge or ability in a subject.

Expertise   An unusual knowledge or ability in a given subject, most often due to specialized experience or education.

Explanation   A claim or set of claims intended to make another claim, object, event, or state of affairs intelligible.

Explanatory analogy   An analogy that is used to explain.

Explanatory definition   A definition used to explain, illustrate, or disclose important aspects of a difficult concept.

Extension   The set of things to which a term applies.

"Fact vs. opinion"   Sometimes people refer to true objective claims as "facts," and use the word "opinion" to designate any claim that is subjective.

Fallacy   An argument in which the reasons advanced for a claim fail to warrant acceptance of that claim.

Fallacy of anecdotal evidence   A version of hasty generalization in which the sample is a story. Often used in an attempt to rebut a general claim. *See also* appeal to anecdote.

Fallacy of composition   Concluding that, because each member of a group has a certain property, therefore the group as a whole must have that property.

Fallacy of division   Concluding that, because a claim about a group taken collectively is true, therefore the same claim is true about members of the group taken individually.

False consensus effect   Assuming that the views held by members of our group are held by society at large.

False dilemma   This pattern of fallacious reasoning: "X is true because either X is true or Y is true, and Y isn't," said when X and Y could both be false.

Force, "argument" by   Using a threat rather than legitimate argument to "support" a "conclusion."

Fundamental attribution error   The tendency to not appreciate that others' behavior is as much constrained by events and circumstances as our own would be if we were in their position.

Gambler's fallacy   Believing that recent past events in a series can influence the outcome of the next event in the series is fallacious when the events have a predictable ratio of results, as flipping a coin.

Generality   Lack of detail and/or specificity. The less detail a claim provides, the more general it is.

General causal claim   A statement to the effect that occurrences of one type cause occurrences of another type.

General claim   A statement that refers to multiple members of a population nonspecifically.

Generalization   This term is used to refer to a general claim or to an inductive generalization from a sample.

Genetic fallacy   Rejecting a claim on the basis of its origin or history.

Glowing generality   A vague generality couched in language with strongly positive associations.

Good deductive argument   An argument whose premises being true would mean the conclusion absolutely must be true.

Good inductive argument   An argument whose premises being true would mean the conclusion probably is true.

Grouping ambiguity   A kind of semantic ambiguity in which it is unclear whether a claim refers to a group of things taken individually or collectively.

Groupthink fallacy   Fallacy that occurs when someone lets identification with a group cloud reason and deliberation when arriving at a position on an issue.

Guilt trip   Trying to get someone to accept a claim by making him or her feel guilty for not accepting it.

Harm principle   The claim that the only way to justify a restriction on a person's freedom is to show that the restriction prevents harm to other people.

Hasty generalization, fallacy of   Overestimating the strength of an argument based on a small sample.

Heuristic   A rule of thumb employed unconsciously by people when they estimate probabilities. In psychology, the field known as "heuristics and biases" was originated by Daniel Kahneman and Amos Tversky.

Horse laugh   A pattern of fallacious reasoning in which ridicule is disguised as a reason for rejecting a claim.

Hyperbole   Extravagant overstatement.

Hypothesis   A causal explanation offered for further investigation or testing.

Hypothetical imperative   Kant's term for a command that is binding only if one is interested in a certain result.

Illicit inductive conversion   An argument of the form "Most Xs are Ys; therefore, most Ys are Xs."

Inconsistency ad hominem   The illogical idea that you rebut an opponent's position by showing that he or she didn't always subscribe to it.

Indirect proof   Proof of a claim by demonstrating that its negation is false, absurd, or self-contradictory.

Inductive analogical argument   *See* analogical argument.

Inductive argument from analogy   *See* argument from analogy.

Inductive generalization from a   Deriving a conclusion about a population from a consideration of a sample.

Inductive syllogism   *See* statistical syllogism.

Inference to the Best Explanation (IBE)   A form of inductive reasoning in which the best explanation for a phenomenon is concluded to be the proper explanation of the phenomenon.

In-group bias   A predisposition to find fault with outsiders.

Initial plausibility   One's rough assessment of how credible a claim seems.

Innuendo   An insinuation of something deprecatory.

Intension   The set of characteristics a thing must have for a term correctly to apply to it.

Interested party   A person who stands to gain from one's belief in a claim. *See* disinterested party.

Invalid argument   An argument that isn't valid.

Issue   A point that is or might be disputed, debated, or wondered about. Essentially, a question.

Knowledge   If you believe a claim, have an argument for it that is beyond reasonable doubt, and have no reason to think you are mistaken, you may be said to have knowledge that the claim is true.

Law of large numbers   A rule stating that the larger the number of chance-determined, repetitious events considered, the closer the alternatives will approach predictable ratios. Example: The more times you flip a coin, the closer the results will approach 50 percent heads and 50 percent tails.

Legal cause   That combination of fact and policy that holds a person legally responsible for harm only if the harm caused can be traced back to that person's actions. (Also referred to as *proximate cause*.)

Legal moralism   The theory that, if an activity is immoral, it should also be illegal.

Legal paternalism   The theory that a restriction on a person's freedom can sometimes be justified by showing that it is for that person's own benefit.

Lexical definition   The meaning of a word that is given in the dictionary.

Line-drawing fallacy   The fallacy of insisting that a line must be drawn at some precise point when in fact it is not necessary that such a line be drawn.

Loaded question   A question that rests on one or more unwarranted or unjustified assumptions.

Logic   The branch of philosophy concerned with whether the reasons presented for a claim, if those reasons were true, would justify accepting the claim.

Logical analogy   An analogy whose terms are arguments.

Loss aversion   Being more strongly motivated to avoid a loss than to accrue a gain.

Mean   A type of average. The arithmetic mean of a group of numbers is the number that results when their sum is divided by the number of members in the group.

Median   A type of average. In a group of numbers, as many numbers of the group are larger than the median as are smaller.

Method of Agreement   A method of generating causal hypotheses: If an effect present in multiple situations is associated with or covaries with some other phenomenon, there may be a causal link between the two phenomena.

Method of Difference   A method for arriving at a causal hypothesis. If something happens that hasn't happened in similar situations, look for some other difference between the two situations and consider that as a possible cause.

Mode   A type of average. In a group of numbers, the mode is the number occurring most frequently.

Modus ponens   An argument consisting of a conditional claim as one premise, a claim that affirms the antecedent of the conditional as a second premise, and a claim that affirms the consequent of the conditional as the conclusion.

Modus tollens   An argument consisting of a conditional claim as one premise, a claim that denies the consequent of the conditional as a second premise, and a claim that denies the antecedent of the conditional as the conclusion.

Moral relativism   The view that what is morally right and wrong depends on and is determined by one's group or culture.

Moral subjectivism   The idea that what is right and wrong is merely a matter of subjective opinion, that thinking something is right or wrong makes it right or wrong for that individual.

n   In sampling, the number of things in a sample. *See also* sample size.

Nationalism   A powerful and often fierce emotional attachment to one's country that can lead a person to blind endorsement of any policy or practice of that country. ("My country, right or wrong!") It is a subdivision of the groupthink fallacy.

Naturalistic fallacy   The assumption that one can conclude directly from a fact (what "is") what a rule or a policy should be (an "ought") without a value-premise.

Negation   The contradictory of a given claim; the negation of claim P is usually given as "not-P."

Negativity bias   An unconscious tendency to give more weight to negative evaluations than to positive evaluations.

Negative claim   A claim that excludes one class or part of one class from another: E- and O-claims.

Nonexperimental cause-to-effect study   A study designed to help determine whether something is a causal factor for a given effect. Such studies are similar to controlled cause-to-effect experiments, except that the members of the experimental group are not exposed to the suspected causal agent by the investigators; instead, exposure has resulted from the actions or circumstances of the individuals themselves.

Nonexperimental effect-to-cause study   A study designed to help determine whether something is a causal factor for a given effect. Such studies are similar to nonexperimental cause-to-effect studies, except that the members of the experimental group display the *effect*, as compared with a control group whose members do not display the effect. Finding that the suspected cause is significantly more frequent in the experimental group is reason for saying that the suspected causal agent is a causal factor in the population involved.

Non sequitur   The fallacy of irrelevant conclusion; an inference that does not follow from the premises.

Normative statement   *See* value judgment.

Obedience to authority   The tendency to comply with instructions from an authority even when they conflict with our values.

Objective claim   *See* objective statement.

Objective issue   *See* objective question.

Objective question   A question whose answer is not made true by the speaker's thinking it is true.

Objective statement   A statement which is not made true by the speaker's thinking that it is true.

Obverse   The obverse of a categorical claim is that claim that is directly across from it in the square of opposition, with the predicate term changed to its complementary term.

Offense principle   The claim that an action or activity can justifiably be made illegal if it is sufficiently offensive.

Opinion   A claim that somebody believes to be true.

Ostensive definition   *See* definition by example.

Overconfidence effect   A tendency to overestimate the percentage of correct answers we have given to questions on a subject we are not experts about.

Overestimating the strength of an argument
Assigning an inappropriately high confidence-level indicator or an inappropriately narrow error-margin indicator to the conclusion of an inductive argument.

Paralipsis   A passing over with brief mention so as to emphasize the suggestiveness of what is omitted. Also called *significant mention.*

Peer pressure "argument"   A fallacious pattern of reasoning in which you are in effect threatened with rejection by your friends, relatives, etc., if you don't accept a certain claim.

Perfectionist fallacy   Concluding that a policy or proposal should be rejected simply because it does not accomplish its goal perfectly.

Personal attack ad hominem   The illogical notion that a person's shortcomings refute his or her views.

Persuasive definition   A pseudo-definition that is designed to influence beliefs or attitudes; also called a *rhetorical definition.*

Poisoning the well   Attempting to discredit in advance what a person might claim by relating unfavorable information about the person.

Popularity, "argument" from   Accepting or urging others to accept a claim simply because all or most or some substantial number of people believe it; to do this is to commit a fallacy.

Population   In inductive reasoning, the total number of members of a given group.

***Post hoc, ergo propter hoc,* fallacy of**   Reasoning that X caused Y simply because Y occurred after X, or around the same time.

Precising definition   A definition whose purpose is to reduce vagueness or generality or to eliminate ambiguity.

Predicate term   The noun or noun phrase that refers to the second class mentioned in a standard-form categorical claim.

Predictable ratio   The ratio that results of a series of events can be expected to have, given the antecedent conditions of the series. Examples: The predictable ratio of a fair coin flip is 50 percent heads and 50 percent tails; the predictable ratio of sevens coming up when a pair of dice is rolled is 1 in 6, or just under 17 percent.

Premise   The claim or claims in an argument that provide the reasons for believing the conclusion.

Premise indicator   A word or phrase (e.g., "since it is the case that . . .") that ordinarily indicates the presence of the premise of an argument.

Principle of total evidence   The principle that, in estimating the probability a claim is true, you must take into account all available evidence.

Principle of utility   The basic principle of utilitarianism, to create as much overall happiness and/or to limit unhappiness for as many as possible.

Proof surrogate   An expression used to suggest that there is evidence or authority for a claim without actually saying what it is.

Proximate cause   *See* legal cause.

Pseudoreason   A consideration offered in support of a position that is not relevant to the truth or falsity of the issue in question.

Question-begging argument   An argument whose conclusion restates a point made in the premises or clearly assumed by the premises. Although such an argument is technically valid, anyone who doubts the conclusion of a question-begging argument would have to doubt the premises, too. *See* begging the question.

Random sample   *See* random selection process.

Random selection process   Method of drawing a sample from a population so that each member of the population has an equal chance of being selected.

Rationalizing   Using a false pretext in order to satisfy our desires or interests.

Red herring   *See* smoke screen.

Reductio ad absurdum   An attempt to show that a claim is false by demonstrating that it has false or absurd logical consequences; literally, "reducing to an absurdity."

Related variable   In sampling, a variable whose presence or absence could affect or be affected by the presence or absence of the attribute of interest. *See* attribute of interest.

Relativism   The idea that the beliefs of one society or culture are as true as those of the next, or the idea that what is true is determined by what a society/culture believes.

Relativist fallacy   Claiming a moral standard holds universally while simultaneously maintaining it doesn't hold within societies that don't accept it.

Relevant/relevance   A premise is relevant to a conclusion if it is not unreasonable to suppose that its truth has some bearing on the truth or falsity of the conclusion. *See also* relevant difference.

Relevant difference   If an effect occurs in one situation and doesn't occur in similar situations, look for something else that is different as a possible cause.

Religious absolutism   The view that the correct moral principles are those accepted by the "correct" religion.

Religious relativism   The belief that what is right and wrong is whatever one's religious culture or society deems it to be.

Representative sample   A sample that isn't biased. *See* biased sample.

Rhetoric   In our usage, "rhetoric" is language used primarily to persuade or influence beliefs or attitudes rather than to prove logically.

Rhetorical analogy   An analogy used to express or influence attitudes or affect behavior; such analogies often invoke images with positive or negative emotional associations.

Rhetorical definition   A pseudo-definition given to express our feelings or influence someone else's.

Rhetorical device   Rhetorical devices are used to influence beliefs or attitudes through the associations, connotations, and implications of words, sentences, or more extended passages. Rhetorical devices include slanters and fallacies. While rhetorical devices may be used to enhance the persuasive force of arguments, they do not add to the logical force of arguments.

Rhetorical explanation   An explanation intended to influence attitudes or affect behavior; such explanations often make use of images with positive or negative emotional associations.

Rhetorical force   *See* emotive meaning.

Sample   A subset of a population.

Sample size   Sample size can affect the size of the error margin or the confidence level of inductive generalizations from a sample.

Sampling frame   A precise definition of a sample or attribute, that makes it unambiguous whether any given thing is a member of the sample and has the attribute.

Scapegoating   Placing the blame for some bad effect on a person or group of people who are not really responsible for it but who provide an easy target for animosity.

Scare tactics   Trying to scare someone into accepting or rejecting a claim. A common form includes merely describing a frightening scenario rather than offering evidence that some activity will cause it.

Self-contradictory claim   A claim that is analytically false.

Self-selection   A situation where the members of a sample are there because they themselves chose to be there.

Self-selection fallacy   Overestimating the probability of a conclusion derived from a self-selected sample

Semantically ambiguous claim   An ambiguous claim whose ambiguity is due to the ambiguity of a word or phrase in the claim.

Semantic ambiguity   Ambiguity produced by the inclusion of an ambiguous word or phrase.

Significant mention   *See* paralipsis.

Slanter   A linguistic device used to affect opinions, attitudes, or behavior without argumentation. Slanters rely heavily on the suggestive power of words and phrases to convey and evoke favorable and unfavorable images.

Slippery slope   A form of fallacious reasoning in which it is assumed that some event must inevitably follow from some other but in which no argument is made for the inevitability.

Smoke screen   An irrelevant topic or consideration introduced into a discussion to divert attention from the original issue.

Social utility   A focus on what is good for society (usually in terms of overall happiness) when deciding on a course of action. *See also* principle of utility.

Sound argument   A valid argument whose premises are true.

Spin   A type of rhetorical device, often in the form of a red herring or complicated euphemism, to disguise a politician's statement or action that might otherwise be perceived in an unfavorable light.

Square of opposition   A table of the logical relationships between two categorical claims that have the same subject and predicate terms.

Standard-form categorical claim   Any claim that results from putting words or phrases that name classes in the blanks of one of the following structures: "All _____ are _____"; "No _____ are _____"; "Some _____ are _____"; and "Some _____ are not _____."

Stare decisis   "Letting the decision stand." Going by precedent.

"Statistically significant"   From a statistical point of view, probably not due to chance.

Statistical regression   In layman's terms statistical regression is the fact that if on one measurement the values of a variable are on average exceptionally high or low, then on a subsequent measurement the average will be closer to the norm. In other words, the exceptional average will "regress" toward the normal average on the subsequent measurement.

Statistical syllogism   A syllogism having this form:
Such-and-such proportion of Xs are Ys.
This is an X.
Therefore this is a Y.

Stereotype   An oversimplified generalization about the members of a class.

Stipulative definition   A definition (of a word) that is specific to a particular context.

Straw man   A type of fallacious reasoning in which someone ignores an opponent's actual position and presents in its place a distorted, exaggerated, or misrepresented version of that position.

Stronger/weaker arguments   The more likely the premise of an inductive argument makes the conclusion, the stronger the argument, and the less likely it makes the conclusion, the weaker the argument.

Subcontrary claims   Two claims that can both be true at the same time but cannot both be false at the same time.

Subject term   The noun or noun phrase that refers to the first class mentioned in a standard-form categorical claim.

Subjective claim   A claim not subject to meaningful dispute if the speaker thinks it is true. *See* Subjective statement.

Subjective expression   An expression you can use pretty much as you please and still be using it correctly.

Subjective issue   *See* Subjective question.

Subjective question   A question that calls for a subjective opinion for an answer.

Subjective statement   A statement which is made true by the speaker's thinking it is true.

Subjectivist fallacy   This pattern of fallacious reasoning: "Well, X may be true for you, but it isn't true for me," said with the intent of dismissing or rejecting X.

Syllogism   A deductive argument with two premises.

Syntactically ambiguous claim   An ambiguous claim whose ambiguity is due to the structure of the claim.

Synthetic claim   A claim whose truth value is not known by simply understanding the claim—an observation of some sort is also required. Contrast with *analytic claim.*

Term   A noun or noun phrase.

Tradition, "argument" from   "Arguing" that a claim is true on the grounds that it is traditional to believe it is true.

Truth   In this book we use the concept in a commonsense way: A claim is true if it is free from error.

Truth-functional equivalence   Two claims are truth-functionally equivalent if and only if they have exactly the same truth table.

Truth-functional logic   A system of logic that specifies the logical relationships among truth-functional claims—claims whose truth values depend solely upon the truth values of their simplest component parts. In particular, truth-functional logic deals with the logical functions of the terms "not," "and," "or," "if . . . then," and so on.

Truth table   A table that lists all possible combinations of truth values for the claim variables in a symbolized claim or argument and then specifies the truth value of the claim or claims for each of those possible combinations.

Two wrongs make a right   This pattern of fallacious reasoning: "It's acceptable for A to do X to B because B would do X to A," said where A's doing X to B is not necessary to prevent B's doing X to A.

Utilitarianism   The moral position that, if an act will produce more happiness than its alternatives, that act is the right thing to do, and if the act will produce less happiness than its alternatives, it would be wrong to do it in place of an alternative that would produce more happiness.

Vague claim   A claim that lacks sufficient precision to convey the information appropriate to its use.

Vague generality   A general statement too vague to be meaningful for practical purposes.

Vagueness   A word or phrase is vague if the group of things to which it applies has borderline cases.

Valid argument   An argument for which it is not possible for the premise to be true and the conclusion false. *See also* good deductive argument.

Value judgment   A claim that assesses the merit, desirability, or praiseworthiness of someone or something. Also called a *normative* or a *prescriptive statement.*

Variable   Something that varies. In deductive reasoning, the most important variables are terms, claims, and arguments. In inductive generalizing from samples, inductive arguments from analogy, and arguments for causal claims, the most important variables are attributes.

Venn diagram   A graphic means of representing a categorical claim or categorical syllogism by assigning classes to overlapping circles. Invented by English mathematician John Venn (1834–1923).

Virtue ethics   The moral position unified around the basic idea that each of us should try to perfect a virtuous character that we exhibit in all actions.

Weak analogy   Overestimating the probability of a conclusion derived from an argument from analogy, a fallacy.

Weak argument   *See* stronger/weaker arguments.

Weaseler   An expression used to protect a claim from criticism by weakening it.

Wishful thinking   Accepting a claim because you want it to be true, or rejecting it because you don't want it to be true.

Worse than average illusion   *See* better than average illusion.

Answers, Suggestions, and Tips for Triangle Exercises

Chapter 1: Critical Thinking Basics

Exercise 1-1

1. An argument consists of two parts, one of which is intended to provide a reason for accepting the other part.
4. F
7. T
10. F. As an example of an opinion that isn't subjective, we (the authors) are of the opinion there is life somewhere else in the universe. If there is life, our opinion is true. If there isn't, then it is false. We don't know whether our opinion is true or false, but we do know that it is one or the other, and we know that whether it is true or false is independent of what we think.
13. c. The first order of business is to determine what the issue is.
16. F. The only foolproof way we know of avoiding errors in thinking is to not think at all.
19. d

Exercise 1-2

1. This item belongs in one group.
4. This item belongs in the same group as item 1.
7. This belongs in a different group from 1 and 4.
10. This belongs in the same group as 1 and 4.

Exercise 1-3

1. Not objective
4. Not objective
7. Not objective
10. Objective

Exercise 1-4

1. Subjective
4. Subjective
7. Not subjective
10. Not subjective, unless the speaker intends to imply that Kerry's chin is unattractive, in which case the assertion would be subjective.

Exercise 1-5

1. Argument
4. Not an argument
7. No arguments here
10. Our conclusion is that this is an argument.

Exercise 1-6

1. Does not contain an argument.
4. Argument, whose conclusion is that computers will never be able to converse intelligently through speech.
7. Argument, whose conclusion is that chemicals in teething rings and soft plastic toys may cause cancer.
10. Does not contain an argument.

Exercise 1-7

1. a
4. c
7. b
10. b

Exercise 1-8

1. We (the authors) think we probably tend to overestimate the probability of types of events that are fresh in our minds (availability heuristic).
4. If we were in Jamela's position, we would want to get little Priglet. As a result, we would have a tendency to think that arguments in favor of our getting Priglet outweighed arguments against doing so. This is belief bias.

Exercise 1-11

1. Contains an argument whose conclusion is the stock market probably will go down.
4. Contains an argument whose conclusion is that probably more women than men are upset by pornography.
7. Does not contain an argument.
10. Subtle, but the speaker is giving a reason for thinking *AI* is the best talent show on TV. So the passage contains an argument whose conclusion is that contention.

Exercise 1-12

1. a
4. e. The issue is whether the United States should realize that reliance on imprisonment is not an effective method of reducing crime.
7. e. The issue is whether it is surprising that the winner of this year's spelling bee is a straight A student whose favorite subject is science.

10. c. But notice YOUR FRIEND hasn't given a reason for thinking the governor has been good.

Exercise 1-13

1. Whether police brutality happens often.

4. Whether we have a good reason to believe the world is independent of our minds.

7. Whether it is the case that you should sign up for lessons on how to use a synthesizer if you buy one.

10. Whether Native Americans, as true conservationists, have something to teach readers about their relationship to the earth. There are other points made in the passage, but they are subsidiary to this one.

Exercise 1-14

1. MRS. is addressing both issues raised by MR.

4. CAUTIOUS is addressing the issue raised by HEEDLESS, of whether people should complain about what we are doing in Afghanistan.

7. OLD GUY is addressing YOUNG GUY's issue of whether baseball players are better now than forty years ago.

10. SECOND NEIGHBOR is addressing the issue raised by FIRST NEIGHBOR, which is whether SECOND NEIGHBOR has a right to make so much noise at night. SECOND NEIGHBOR thinks he has the right.

13. CITIZEN TWO is addressing the issue raised by CITIZEN ONE, which is whether it will be Mitt Romney and Barack Obama for president in 2012.

16. PARKER isn't addressing MOORE's issue, which is whether Thomas Brothers or Vernon Construction does better work. Instead, he addresses whether Thomas Brothers charges too much.

19. On the surface, it may seem that both hands address the issue of whether a person such as ONE HAND can feel safe in her own home. But ONE HAND's real issue is whether the large number of handguns makes one unsafe in one's own home. OTHER HAND ignores this issue completely.

22. JENNIFER does not address the issue raised by KATIE, which is whether she (JENNIFER) should pick up more often. JENNIFER in effect changes the subject. This is different from item 10, above, where FIRST NEIGHBOR has explicitly questioned SECOND NEIGHBOR's right to make noise. KATIE has not questioned JENNIFER's right to not pick things up, though she probably thinks JENNIFER doesn't have that right.

25. INTERVIEWER is asking indirectly whether SENATOR CLINTON's fellow Democrats have a legitimate complaint when they criticize the senator for not trying to get us out of Afghanistan. SENATOR CLINTON doesn't address whether the substance of the complaint is legitimate; instead she talks about whether Democrats should even be criticizing each other about the war. In other words, she dodges the question.

Exercise 1-15

1 and 7 belong in one group. 4 and 10 belong in a different group.

Exercise 1-16

1. Pertains to moral right/wrong

4. Pertains to moral right/wrong

7. Doesn't pertain

10. Pertains to aesthetic good/bad

13. Doesn't pertain. It merely explains how to stop the decline in enrollments.

Exercise 1-17

1. b. Both make predictions based on an observation.

4. b. Both make predictions based on an observation.

7. b. Both are explanations.

10. a. Both contain two assertions, the second of which is implied to take priority.

Answer to question posed in Bear box on page 12

Can animals think critically? Animals probably think, but do they review and evaluate their thinking? We don't know, but we have our doubts.

Chapter 2: Two Kinds of Reasoning

Exercise 2-1

1. a. Premise; b. premise; c. conclusion
2. a. Premise; b. premise; c. conclusion
3. a. Conclusion; b. premise
4. a. Premise; b. premise; c. conclusion
5. a. Premise; b. conclusion; c. premise; d. premise

Exercise 2-2

1. Premise: All Communists are Marxists.
    Conclusion: All Marxists are Communists.

4. Premise: That cat is used to dogs.
    Conclusion: Probably she won't be upset if you bring home a new dog for a pet.

7. Premise: Presbyterians are not fundamentalists. Premise: All born-again Christians are fundamentalists.
Conclusion: No born-again Christians are Presbyterians.

10. Premise: The clunk comes only when I pedal.
Conclusion: The problem is in the chain, the crank, or the pedals.

Exercise 2-3

1. Conclusion: There is a difference in the octane ratings between the two grades of gasoline.

4. Conclusion: Scrub jays can be expected to be aggressive when they're breeding.

7. Conclusion: Dogs are smarter than cats.

10. Unstated conclusion: She is not still interested in me.

Exercise 2-4

1. Deductive demonstration

4. Inductive support

7. Inductive support

10. Deductive demonstration

Exercise 2-5

1. b

4. b

7. b

10. b

Exercise 2-6

1. Inductive

4. True

7. Deductive

10. Inductive

13. T

17. F

Exercise 2-7

1. Deductive demonstration

2. Inductive support

4. Inductive support

7. Two arguments here. In the first argument, if the speaker is assuming that the universe's not having arisen by chance increases the probability that God exists, then his or her argument is inductive. Likewise, in the second argument, if the speaker is assuming that an increase in the number of believing physicists increases the probability that God exists, then his or her argument is inductive.

8. Inductive support

Exercise 2-8

1. Separate arguments

6. Separate arguments

9. Separate arguments

10. Separate arguments

13. Does not contain separate arguments

Exercise 2-9

1. To explain

4. To explain

7. To explain

9. To argue

Exercise 2-10

1. a

4. a

7. a

10. a

Exercise 2-11

1. Anyone who keeps his or her word is a person of good character.

4. One cannot murder someone without being in the same room.

7. Anyone who commits murder should be executed.

10. All squeaking fans need oil.

Exercises 2-12

1. Puddles everywhere usually indicate a recent rain.

4. The next day after a week of cold weather usually is cold.

7. Having leftovers is an indication that a party wasn't successful.

10. My cold probably would not have disappeared like magic if I had not taken Zicam.

Exercise 2-13

1.

4.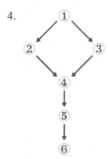

Exercise 2-14

1. ① Your distributor is the problem.
② There's no current at the spark plugs.
③ If there's no current at the plugs, then either your alternator is shot or your distributor is defective.

④ [Unstated] Either your alternator is shot, or your distributor is defective.

⑤ If the problem were in the alternator, then your dash warning light would be on.

⑥ The light isn't on.

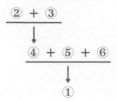

4. ① They really ought to build a new airport.

② It [a new airport] would attract more business to the area.

③ The old airport is overcrowded and dangerous.

Note: Claim ③ could be divided into two separate claims, one about overcrowding and one about danger. This would be important if the overcrowding were clearly offered as a reason for the danger.

Exercise 2-15

1. ① Cottage cheese will help you to be slender.

② Cottage cheese will help you to be youthful.

③ Cottage cheese will help you to be more beautiful.

④ Enjoy cottage cheese often.

4. ① The idea of a free press in America is a joke.

② The nation's advertisers control the media.

③ Advertisers, through fear of boycott, can dictate programming.

④ Politicians and editors shiver at the thought of a boycott.

⑤ The situation is intolerable.

⑥ I suggest we all listen to NPR and public television.

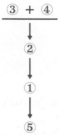

Note: The writer may see claim ① as the final conclusion and claim ⑤ as his comment upon it. Claim ⑥ is probably a comment on the results of

the argument, although it, too, could be listed as a further conclusion.

7. ① Consumers ought to be concerned about the FTC's dropping the rule requiring markets to stock advertised items.

② Shoppers don't like being lured to stores and not finding advertised products.

③ The rule costs at least $200 million and produces no more than $125 million in benefits.

④ The figures boil down to a few cents per shopper over time.

⑤ The rule requires advertised sale items to be on hand in reasonable numbers.

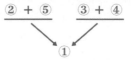

10. ① Well-located, sound real estate is the safest investment in the world.

② Real estate is not going to disappear as can dollars in savings accounts.

③ Real estate values are not lost because of inflation.

④ Property values tend to increase at a pace at least equal to the rate of inflation.

⑤ Most homes have appreciated at a rate greater than the inflation rate. . . .

12. ① About 100 million Americans are producing data on the Internet. . . .

② Each user is tracked, so private information is available in electronic form.

③ One website . . . promises, for seven dollars, to scan . . . , etc.

④ The combination of capitalism and technology poses a threat to our privacy.

14. ① Measure A is consistent with the City's General Plan and City policies. . . .

② A "yes" vote will affirm the wisdom of well-planned, orderly growth. . . .

③ Measure A substantially reduces the amount of housing previously approved for Rancho Arroyo.

④ Measure A increases the number of parks and amount of open space.

⑤ Measure A significantly enlarges and enhances Bidwell Park.

⑥ Approval of Measure A will require dedication of 130.8 acres to Bidwell Park.

⑦ Approval of Measure A will require the developer to dedicate seven park sites.

⑧ Approval of Measure A will create 53 acres of landscaped corridors and greenways.

⑨ Approval of Measure A will preserve existing arroyos and protect sensitive plant habitats. . . .

⑩ Approval of Measure A will create junior high school and church sites.

⑪ Approval of Measure A will plan villages with 2,927 dwellings.

⑫ Approval of Measure A will provide onsite job opportunities and retail services.

⑬ [Unstated conclusion:] You should vote for Measure A.

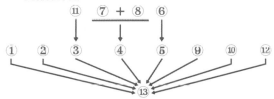

17. ① In regard to your editorial, "Crime bill wastes billions," let me set you straight. [Your position is mistaken.]

② Your paper opposes mandatory life sentences for criminals convicted of three violent crimes, and you whine about how criminals' rights might be violated.

③ Yet you also want to infringe on a citizen's rights to keep and bear arms.

④ You say you oppose life sentences for three-time losers because judges couldn't show any leniency toward the criminals no matter how trivial the crime.

⑤ What is your definition of trivial, busting an innocent child's skull with a hammer?

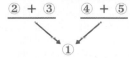

18. ① Freedom means choice.

② This is a truth antiporn activists always forget when they argue for censorship.

③ In their fervor to impose their morality, groups like Enough Is Enough cite extreme examples of pornography, such as child porn, suggesting that they are available in video stores.

④ This is not the way it is.

⑤ Most of this material portrays not actions such as this but consensual sex between adults.

⑥ The logic used by Enough Is Enough is that, if something can somehow hurt someone, it must be banned.

⑦ They don't apply this logic to more harmful substances such as alcohol or tobacco.

⑧ Women and children are more adversely affected by drunken driving and secondhand smoke than by pornography.

⑨ Few Americans would want to ban alcohol or tobacco even though these substances kill hundreds of thousands of people each year.

⑩ [Unstated conclusion] Enough Is Enough is inconsistent.

⑪ [Unstated conclusion] Enough Is Enough's antiporn position is incorrect.

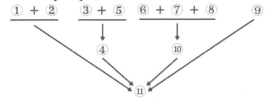

Chapter 3: Clear Thinking, Critical Thinking, and Clear Writing

Exercise 3-1

In order of decreasing vagueness:

1. d, e, b, c, f, and a. Compare (e) and (b). If Eli and Sarah made plans for the future, then they certainly discussed it. But just discussing it is more vague—they could do that with or without making plans.

4. c, d, e, a, b

Exercise 3-2

1. Answer b is more precise.

4. Answer a is more precise.

7. Answer b is more precise, but not by much.

10. a

15. b

Exercise 3-3

1. "Piano" is defined analytically.
4. "Red planet" is defined by synonym. (This one is tricky because it looks like a definition by example. But there is only one red planet, so the phrase refers to exactly the same object as the word "Mars.")
8. "Chiaroscuro" is defined by synonym.
11. "Significant other" is defined by example—several of them.

Exercise 3-4

1. Too imprecise. Sure, you can't say exactly how much longer you want it cooked, but you can provide guidelines; for example, "Cook it until it isn't pink."
4. Precise enough.
7. Precise enough.
10. For a first-timer or an inexperienced cook, this phrase is not sufficiently precise.

Exercise 3-6

"Feeding" simply means "fertilizing" and is precise enough. "Frequently" is too vague. "No more than half" is acceptable. "Label-recommended amounts" is okay, too. "New year's growth begins" and "each bloom period ends" seem a little imprecise for a novice gardener, but because pinpoint timing apparently isn't crucial, these expressions are acceptable—so it seems to us, anyhow. "Similar" is not precise enough for a novice gardener. "Immediately after bloom" suggests that precise timing is important here, and we find the phrase a bit too vague, at least for inexperienced gardeners. "When the nights begin cooling off" is too vague even if precision in timing isn't terribly important.

Exercise 3-7

1. The Raider tackle blocked the Giants linebacker.
4. How Therapy Can Help Victims of Torture
7. Chelsea's nose resembles Hillary Clinton's.
10. 6 Coyotes That Maul Girl Are Killed by Police
13. Second sentence: More than one disease can be carried and passed along to humans by a single tick.
16. We make good things happen.
19. Dunkelbrau—for those who crave the best-tasting real German beer
22. Jordan could write additional profound essays.
25. When she lay down to nap, she was disturbed by a noisy cow.
28. When Queen Elizabeth appeared before her troops, they all shouted "harrah."
31. AT&T, for as long as your business lasts.
32. This class might have had a member of the opposite sex for a teacher.
33. Married 10 times before, woman gets 9 years in prison for killing her husband.

Exercise 3-8

1. As a group
4. As a group
7. It's more likely that the claim refers to the Giants as a group, but it's possible that it refers to the play of individuals.
10. As individuals
12. Probably as individuals
15. Ambiguous. If the claim means that people are living longer than they used to, the reference is to people as individuals. If the claim means that the human race is getting older, then the reference is to people as a group. If the claim expresses the truism that to live is to age, then the reference is to people as individuals.

Exercise 3-14

7, 6, 4, 1, 3, 2, 5

Exercise 3-15

1. Students should choose their majors with considerable care.
4. If a nurse can find nothing wrong with you in a preliminary examination, a physician will be recommended to you. However, in this city physicians wish to protect themselves by having you sign a waiver.
7. Soldiers should be prepared to sacrifice their lives for their comrades.
10. Petitioners over sixty should have completed form E-7.
13. Language is nature's greatest gift to humanity.
16. The proof must be acceptable to the rational individual.
17. The country's founders believed in the equality of all.
20. Athletes who want to play for the National Football League should have a good work ethic.
24. Most U.S. senators are men. (Gender is important to the meaning of the sentence.)
27. Mr. Macleod doesn't know it, but Ms. Macleod is a feminist.
30. To be a good politician, you have to be a good salesperson.

Exercise 3-16

In case you couldn't figure it out, the friend is a woman.

All voluntary acts are done to satisfy one's own desire to do them.

↓

All voluntary acts are done for self benefit.

↓

All voluntary acts are selfish acts.

Chapter 4: Credibility

Exercise 4-2

Something like number 9 is probably true, given the huge, almost unimaginable difference in wealth between the richest and the poorest people on the planet, but we have no idea what the actual numbers are. This warning went around on the web for a while, and even Click and Clack, the car guys on NPR's "Car Talk" allowed as how there might be something to this but they didn't want to conduct the appropriate experiments to find out. As it turns out, experience has shown there is a danger of explosion due to static electricity, and cars now have warnings against the practice.

Exercise 4-7

1. Of the first five, we'd say 1, 3, and 4 are probably interested parties. Of the last three, you must presume 8 is an interested party unless you can be assured he or she will not benefit more from the sale of one brand or the other. Numbers 6 and 7 depend entirely on the level of knowledge of the individuals and their lack of brand loyalty.

Exercise 4-11

1. In terms of expertise, we'd list (d), (c), and (b) first. Given what we've got to go on, we wouldn't assign expert status to either (a) or (e). We'd list all entries as likely to be fairly unbiased except for (a), which we would expect to be very biased.

3. Expertise: First (b), then (a), then (c) and (d) about equal, and (e) last. We'd figure that (b) is most likely to be unbiased, with (c), (d), and (e) close behind; Choker would be a distant last on this scale. Her bad showing on the bias scale more than makes up for her high showing on the expertise scale.

Exercise 4-12

1. The most credible choices are either the FDA or *Consumer Reports*, both of which investigate health claims of the sort in question with reasonable objectivity. The company that makes the product is the least credible source because it is the most likely to be biased. The owner of the health food store may be very knowledgeable regarding nutrition but is not a credible source regarding drugs. Your local pharmacist can reasonably be regarded as credible, but he or she may not have access to as much information as the FDA or *CR*. (We should add here that the FDA itself has come under considerable criticism in recent years, especially for making decisions on medical issues based on political considerations. The debate over approval of Plan B, the "morning after" pill, was a case in point. [See "Morning-After Pill," *The New York Times*, August 28, 2005.])

2. It would probably be a mistake to consider any of the individuals on this list more expert than the others, although different kinds and different levels of bias are fairly predictable on the parts of the victim's father, the NRA representative, and possibly the police chief. The senator might be expected to have access to more data that are relevant to the issue, but that would not in itself make his or her credibility much greater than that of the others. The problem here is that we are dealing with a value judgment that depends very heavily upon an individual's point of view rather than his or her expertise. What is important to this question is less the credibility of the person who gives us an answer than the strength of the supporting argument, if any, that he or she provides.

3. Although problem 2 hinges on a value judgment, this one calls for an interpretation of the original intent of a constitutional amendment. Here, our choices would be either the Supreme Court justice or the constitutional historian, with a slight preference for the latter because Supreme Court justices are concerned more with constitutional issues as they have been interpreted by other courts than with original intent. (And Supreme Court Justices are not the most reliable historians of the court.) The NRA representative is paid to speak for a certain point of view and would be the least credible, in our view. The senator and the U.S. president would fall somewhere in between: Both reasonably might be expected to be knowledgeable about constitutional issues but much less so than our first two choices.

Exercise 4-13

1. Professor St. Germain would possess the greatest degree of credibility and authority on (d), (f), and (h), and, compared with someone who had not lived in both places, on (i).

Exercise 4-15

1. We'd accept this as probably true—but probably only *approximately* true. It's difficult to be precise about such matters; Campbell will most likely lay off *about* 650 workers, including *about* 175 at its headquarters.

8. We'd accept this as likely.

12. No doubt cats that live indoors do tend to live longer than cats that are subject to the perils of outdoor life. If statistics on how much longer indoor cats live on the average were available, we'd expect the manufacturer to know them. But we suspect that such statistics would be difficult to establish (and probably not worth the effort), and we therefore have little confidence in the statistic cited here.

20. Although the Defamer Blog bills itself as "the Hollywood gossip sheet," which suggests that it trades in rumor and innuendo, this claim is apparently true. It is at least partly confirmed by a Fox News report (September 7, 2007) that Hilton filed a federal lawsuit against Hallmark Cards over a $2.49 greeting card that uses her photo and "her trademarked phrase, 'That's Hot.'" Fox attributed the story to The Smoking Gun, a website that's been around for several years.

We give rather less credence to the claim (published on TheSpeciousReport.com) that Ms. Hilton also lays claim to the following assertion: "I have absolutely no talent or personality yet I'm world famous, have a hit television series, a best-selling book, and my own record label, proving beyond a shadow of a doubt that there is no God."

Solution to triangle puzzle on page 112:

If you look carefully, you'll see that the hypotenuses (the topmost, longest line) of the two triangles are different. The upper one is slightly convex and the lower is slightly concave, thus allowing for extra space inside the lower triangle. That's where the "hole" comes from!

Chapter 5: Persuasion Through Rhetoric: Common Devices and Techniques

Exercise 5-1

1. euphemism
3. euphemism
5. weaseler

Exercise 5-2

1. loaded question
3. no device
5. innuendo

Exercise 5-4

1. Twenty percent more than what? Are there products with *fake* dairy butter?

4. This is not too bad, as long as we know what is meant by "the desert." Some deserts get more rain than others.

7. This one is straightforward, but remember that grading has changed a lot in the past twenty years, and grades nearly everywhere are higher (grade inflation); this doesn't necessarily mean today's students are better.

10. This doesn't make it a brilliant season all by itself. There may have been a big change in the economy, increasing attendance proportionately. Or attendance may have been miserable last year.

Exercise 5-5

1. ridicule
3. hyperbole
5. no device

Exercise 5-6

1. a
3. a
6. d
8. e

Exercise 5-7

(1) Hyperbole (in Chapter 7 we'll also call this "straw man"), (2) dysphemism, (3) not a rhetorical device, (4) dysphemism, (5) not a rhetorical device, (6) dysphemism

Exercise 5-8

(1) Dysphemism, (2) dysphemism, (3) hyperbole, (4) weaseler, (5) proof surrogate, (6) not a downplayer in this context, (7) loaded question

Exercise 5-15

1. a
4. a
7. c
10. d

Exercise 5-16

1. The quotation marks downplay the quality of the school.

4. Rhetorical definition

6. "Pretty much" is a mild weaseler.

8. "Gaming" is a euphemism for "gambling."

11. "Clearly" is a proof surrogate; the final phrase is hyperbole.

14. "Luddites" (those opposed to technological progress) is a rhetorical analogy; the entire passage is designed to suggest that cable and satellite TV are nearly universal in acceptance and use and to characterize in a negative light those (few?) who haven't become subscribers.

Exercise 5-18

1. "Japan, Inc." is a dysphemism.

4. "Getting access" is a euphemism, and, in this context, so is "constituents." We'll bet it isn't just *any* old constituent who gets the same kind of "access" as big campaign contributors.

6. The last sentence is hyperbolic.

9. (We really like this one.) "Even," in the first sentence, is innuendo, insinuating that members of Congress are more difficult to embarrass than others. The remainder is another case of innuendo with a dash of downplaying. Although it's a first-class example, it's different from the usual ones. Mellinkoff makes you think that Congress *merely* passes a law in response to the situation. But stop and think for a moment: Aside from the odd congressional hearing or impeachment trial, *all that Congress can do is pass laws!* So Mellinkoff's charge really should not be seen as belittling Congress at all.

12. "As you know" is a variety of proof surrogate. The remainder is a rhetorical analogy, in this case a comparison.

14. Proof surrogate. A claim that there are "two kinds of arguments" in favor of a multiverse does not actually provide those reasons. (The article did not go on to give the arguments.)

17. Lots of them here! To begin, "orgy" is a dysphemism; "self-appointed" is a downplayer. The references to yurts and teepees is ridicule,

and "grant-maintained" is a downplayer. The rest of it employs a heavy dose of sarcasm.

Exercise 5-23

1. Superior? In what way? More realistic character portrayal? Better expression of emotion? Probably the claim means only "I like Paltrow more than I like Blanchett."

4. Fine, but don't infer that they both grade the same. Maybe Smith gives 10 percent A's and 10 percent F's, 20 percent B's and 20 percent D's, and 40 percent C's, whereas Jones gives everyone a C. Who do you think is the more discriminating grader, given this breakdown?

7. Well, first of all, what is "long-distance"? Second, and more important, how is endurance measured? People do debate such issues, but the best way to begin a debate on this point would be by spelling out what you mean by "requires more endurance."

10. This is like a comparison of apples and oranges. How can the popularity of a movie be compared with the popularity of a song?

Exercise 5-24

1. The price-earnings ratio is a traditional (and reasonable) measure of a stock, and the figure is precise enough. Whether this is good enough reason to worry about the stock market is another matter; such a conclusion may not be supported by the price-earnings figure.

4. "Attend church regularly" is a bit vague; a person who goes to church each and every Christmas and Easter is a regular, although infrequent, attender. We don't find "majority" too vague in this usage.

7. "Contained more insights" is much too vague. The student needs to know more specifically what was the matter with his or her paper, or at least what was better about the roommate's paper.

10. These two sorts of things are much too different to be compared in this way. If you're starving, the chicken looks better; if you need to get from here to there, it's the Volkswagen. (This is the kind of question Moore likes to ask people. Nobody can figure out why.)

Chapter 6: More Rhetorical Devices: Psychological and Related Fallacies

Exercise 6-1

1. Appeal to popularity

4. Scare tactics

7. Argument from pity; guilt trip is a strong second choice

10. No fallacy

Exercise 6-2

1. Red herring

4. Argument from popularity

7. Red herring

Exercise 6-4

1. Not very

3. Very relevant. A popular automobile may have continued support from its maker, and this can be advantageous to the owner of such a car.

7. It is a relevant consideration if you want to be polite or if you want to criticize the novel when you speak to your friend. But note that it would not be relevant if the issue had been whether the novel was well-written.

10. Relevant, especially if you have reason to think that Ebert likes or dislikes the same kinds of movies you do, or if you have opposite views (then you can avoid movies he recommends).

Exercise 6-6

1. Scare tactics

4. Scare tactics and red herring; the latter because a reason to fly is irrelevant to whether you should fly Fracaso

7. Appeal to tradition

10. Nationalism fallacy

Exercise 6-8

1. No fallacy

4. No fallacy

7. Argument from outrage

10. Scare tactics and red herring. This combination shows up frequently (e.g., in 6–6, #1; 6–7, #8).

13. Red herring

15. Red herring

19. Rationalizing, red herring, a bit of appeal to common practice

22. The most obvious fallacy present here is the scare tactics we see from Rep. Welker. He is also guilty of a slippery slope fallacy, discussed in the next chapter. Under one interpretation of the situation, one might also find Rep. Paccione guilty of a red herring, because the original point of the news conference was whether there should be a constitutional amendment barring gays and lesbians from marrying, and Rep. Paccione introduces a separate issue having to do with health care. But her claim—that as long as the health care issue remains unsolved, it is not good policy to argue about other matters such as same-sex marriage—is relevant. Whether it's true is another matter; argument would be necessary to establish that.

Chapter 7: More Fallacies

Exercise 7-1

1. Inconsistency ad hominem

4. Genetic fallacy

7. Circumstantial ad hominem

11. Personal attack ad hominem

Exercise 7-3

1. Begging the question

4. Straw man

7. Straw man

10. Line-drawing fallacy (false dilemma)

Exercise 7-4

1. Circumstantial ad hominem

4. Straw man (Jeanne responds as if Carlos wanted to sleep until noon). Can also be analyzed as false dilemma ("Either we get up right now, at 4:00 A.M., or we sleep until noon.")

7. This begs the question. The conclusion merely restates the premise.

10. False dilemma

13. Misplaced burden of proof

Exercise 7-5

1. This is an example of burden of proof. Yes, it is indeed slightly different from the varieties explained in the text, and here's what's going on. The speaker is requiring proof of a sort that *cannot be obtained*—actually *seeing* smoke cause a cancer. So, he or she is guilty of one type of "inappropriate burden of proof."

4. This is false dilemma because Sugarman's alternatives are certainly not the only ones. Notice that he is giving *no argument* against the Chicago study; he is simply using the false dilemma to deny the study's conclusion.

7. Inconsistency ad hominem

10. This is a case of misplaced burden of proof. The speaker maintains that the government is violating the law. The burden of proof therefore falls on the speaker to justify his or her opinion. Instead of doing that, he or she acts as if the fact that officials haven't disproved the claim is proof that the claim is true.

Exercise 7-6

1. Assuming that the sheriff's department has more than two officers, the speaker is misrepresenting her opponent's position. Straw man.

4. Misplaced burden of proof
7. Perfectionist fallacy (false dilemma)
10. Slippery slope, with a large dose of outrage

Exercise 7-7

1. Ad hominem: inconsistency. You hear this kind of thing a lot.
4. Ad hominem: personal attack
7. False dilemma (in the last sentence) supported by a slippery slope earlier.
10. Ad hominem: personal attack; Don Regan's motives are irrelevant to whether what he reported is true.

Exercise 7-9

1. d
4. b
7. a
10. a. This is also a case of perfectionist fallacy, but students should realize that every case of perfectionist fallacy is a case of red herring (as well as false dilemma). Red herring is a very broad category.

Exercise 7-10

1. c
4. c, to the extent this is anything beyond a complaint
7. b
10. c

Exercise 7-11

1. b
4. d, and a proof surrogate as well
7. e
10. a.

Exercise 7-12

1. Straw man, smokescreen/red herring
4. No fallacy. Notice that the passage is designed to attack the company, not the company's product. The wages it pays are relevant to the point at issue.
7. No fallacy
10. False dilemma

13. Genetic fallacy and/or red herring
16. Line drawing fallacy (false dilemma)
19. Inconsistency ad hominem

Exercise 7-17

1. Perfectionist fallacy (false dilemma)
5. Apple polishing
9. Argument from pity and argument from outrage
13. Poisoning the well
16. Ad hominem (consistency)

Exercise 7-18

1. This is an example of misplaced burden of proof. The fact that the airplane builders *might* be cutting corners is not evidence that they are *in fact* cutting corners. The speaker's contention that the manufacturers may be tempted to cut corners may be good grounds for scrutinizing their operations, but it's not good grounds for the conclusion that they really are cutting corners.
4. Yes—this is clearly fallacious. Bush's sweeping generalization would be irrelevant to the Democrats' claim even if it were true. That it isn't true makes the response a straw man. One can also see this as a smokescreen.
5. The quoted remark from Harris is not relevant to the conclusion drawn in this passage. This passage doesn't fit neatly into any of our categories, although ad hominem would not be a bad choice. Notice a possible ambiguity that may come into play: "Having an impact" might mean simply that Harris wants his work to be noticed by "movers and shakers"—or it could mean that he wishes to sway people toward a certain political view. It's likely that he intended his remark the first way, but it's being taken in the second way in this passage.
9. This is a borderline circumstantial ad hominem. It certainly does not follow that Seltzer and Sterling are making false claims from the fact that they are being paid by an interested party. But remember the cautions from Chapter 4: Expertise can be bought, and we should be very cautious about accepting claims made by experts who are paid by someone who has a vested interest in the outcome of a controversy.

Chapter 8: Deductive Arguments I: Categorical Logic

Exercise 8-1

1. All salamanders are lizards.
4. All members of the suborder Ophidia are snakes.
7. All alligators are reptiles.
10. All places there are snakes are places there are frogs.
13. All people who got raises are vice presidents.
15. Some home movies are things that are as boring as dirt.
16. All people identical with Socrates are Greeks.

19. All examples of salt are things that preserve meat.

Exercise 8-2

1. No students who wrote poor exams are students who were admitted to the program.

4. Some first-basemen are right-handed people.

7. All passers are people who made at least 50 percent.

10. Some days I've had are days like this one.

13. Some holidays are holidays that fall on Saturday.

16. All people who pass the course are people who pass this test. Or: No people who fail this test are people who pass the course.

19. All times they will let you enroll are times you've paid the fee.

Exercise 8-3

1. Translation: Some anniversaries are not happy occasions. (True)

   Corresponding A-claim: All anniversaries are happy occasions. (False)

   Corresponding E-claim: No anniversaries are happy occasions. (Undetermined)

   Corresponding I-claim: Some anniversaries are happy occasions. (Undetermined)

4. Translation: Some allergies are things that can kill you. (True)

   Corresponding A-claim: All allergies are things that can kill you. (Undetermined)

   Corresponding E-claim: No allergies are things that can kill you. (False)

   Corresponding O-claim: Some allergies are not things that can kill you. (Undetermined)

Exercise 8-4

1. No non-Christians are non-Sunnis. (Not equivalent)

4. Some Christians are not Kurds. (Not equivalent)

7. All Muslims are Shiites. (Not equivalent)

10. All Muslims are non-Christians. (Equivalent)

Exercise 8-5

1. Some students who scored well on the exam are not students who didn't write poor essays. (Equivalent)

4. No students who were not admitted to the program are students who scored well on the exam. (Not equivalent)

7. All people whose automobile ownership is not restricted are people who don't live in the dorms. (Equivalent)

10. All first basemen are people who aren't right-handed. (Equivalent)

Exercise 8-6

2. All encyclopedias are nondefinitive works.

4. No sailboats are sloops.

Exercise 8-7

Translations of the lettered claims:

a. Some people who have been tested are not people who can give blood.

b. Some people who can give blood are not people who have been tested.

c. All people who can give blood are people who have been tested.

d. Logically equivalent to: "Some people who have been tested are people who cannot give blood" [converse]. Logically equivalent to: "Some people who have been tested are not people who can give blood" [obverse of the converse].

e. Logically equivalent to: "All people who have been tested are people who cannot give blood." Logically equivalent to: "No people who have been tested are people who can give blood" [obverse].

2. Logically equivalent to: "All people who have not been tested are people who cannot give blood." Logically equivalent to: "All people who can give blood are people who have been tested" [contraposition], which is equivalent to c.

3. Logically equivalent to: "No people who have been tested are people who can give blood," which is equivalent to e.

4. Equivalent to "All people who can give blood are people who have been tested."

Exercise 8-8

1. Obvert (a) to get "some Slavs are not Europeans."

4. Obvert the conversion of (b) to get "Some members of the club are not people who took the exam."

7. Contrapose (a) to get "All people who will not be allowed to perform are people who did not arrive late." Translate (b) into "Some people who did not arrive late are people who will not be allowed to perform" and convert "Some people who will not be allowed to perform are people who did not arrive late."

10. Convert the obverse of (b) to get "No decks that will play digital tape are devices that are equipped for radical oversampling."

Exercise 8-9

1. Invalid (this would require the conversion of an A-claim).

4. Valid (the converse of an I-claim is logically equivalent to the original claim).

7. Valid (the premise is the obverse of the conclusion).

10. The premise translates to "Some people in uniform are people not allowed to play." Thus (translating the conclusion), "Some people not allowed to play are people not in uniform" does not follow and the argument is invalid.

Exercise 8-10

1. The converse of (a) is the contradictory of (b), so (b) is false.

3. The contrapositive of (a) is a true O-claim that corresponds to (b); and that means that (b), its contradictory, is false.

5. Contrapose (a) to get "Some unproductive factories are not plants not for automobiles." Then obvert (b) to get "No unproductive factories are plants not for automobiles." Because (a) is true, (b) is undetermined.

9. The translation of (a) is "Some people enrolled in the class are not people who will get a grade." The obverse of the converse of (b) is "Some people enrolled in the class are not people who will get a grade." Son of a gun: They're identical! So (b), too, is true.

Exercise 8-11

1. Valid:
All P are G.
No G are S.
No S are P.

4. Invalid:
All T are E.
All T-T are E. (T = times Louis is tired, etc.)
All T-T are T. (T-T = times identical with today)

7. Valid:
All H are S.
No P are S.
No P are H.

10. Invalid:
All C are R.
All V are C.
No R are V.

(Note: There is more than one way to turn this into standard form. Instead of turning non-residents into residents, you can do the opposite.)

Exercise 8-12

1. No blank disks are disks that contain data.
Some blank disks are formatted disks.
Some formatted disks are not disks that contain data.
Valid:

Formatted disks   Disks that contain data

Blank disks

4. All tobacco products are substances damaging to people's health.
Some tobacco products are addictive substances.
Some addictive substances are substances damaging to people's health.
Valid:

Addictive substances   Substances damaging to people's health

Tobacco products

7. All people who may vote are stockholders in the company.
No people identical with Mr. Hansen are people who may vote.
No people identical with Mr. Hansen are stockholders in the company.
Invalid:

Mr. Hansen   Stockholders in the company

People who may vote

Note: Remember that claims with individuals as subject terms are treated as A- or E-claims.

10. After converting, then obverting the conclusion:
No arguments with false premises are sound arguments.
Some arguments with false premises are valid arguments.
Some valid arguments are not sound arguments.
Valid:

Valid arguments   Sound arguments

Arguments with false premises

Exercise 8-13

1. A
4. B

Exercise 8-14

1. a
4. b

Exercise 8-15

1. 0
4. 1

Exercise 8-16

1. c
4. c
7. b
10. e

Exercise 8-17

1. All T are F.

   Some F are Z.

   Some Z are T.

   Invalid; breaks rule 2

4. There are two versions of this item, depending on whether you take the premise to say *no* weightlifters use motor skills or only some don't. We'll do it both ways:

   All A are M.

   No W are M.

   No W are A.

   Valid

   All A are M.

   Some W are not M.

   No W are A.

   Invalid; breaks rule 3

7. Using I = people who lift papers from the Internet

   C = people who are cheating themselves

   L = people who lose in the long run

   All I are C.

   All C are L.

   All I are C.

   Valid

10. D = people who dance the whole night

    W = people who waste time

    G = people whose grades will suffer

    All D are W.

    All W are G.

    All D are G.

    Valid

Exercise 8-18

(Refer to Exercise 8-11 for these first four items.)

2. (Given in standard form in the text)

   Invalid: breaks rule 2

5. All voters are citizens.

   Some citizens are not residents.

   Some voters are not residents.

   Invalid: breaks rule 2

7. All halyards are lines that attach to sails.

   No painters are lines that attach to sails.

   No painters are halyards.

   Valid

8. All systems that can give instant access are systems with no moving parts.

   All standard hard disks are systems with moving parts.

   No standard hard disks are systems that can give instant access.

   Valid; breaks no rule

(Refer to Exercise 8-12 for the next four items.)

2. After obverting both premises, we get:

   No ears with white tassels are ripe ears.

   Some ripe ears are not ears with full-sized kernels.

   Some ears with full-sized kernels are not ears with white tassels.

   Invalid: breaks rule 1

5. After obverting the second premise:

   Some CD players are machines with 24x sampling.

   All machines with 24x sampling are machines that cost at least $20.

   Some CD players are machines that cost at least $20.

   Valid

7. All people who may vote are people with stock.

   No [people identical with Mr. Hansen] are people who may vote.

   No [people identical with Mr. Hansen] are people with stock.

   Invalid: breaks rule 3 (major term)

8. No off-road vehicles are vehicles allowed in the unimproved portion of the park.

   Some off-road vehicles are not four-wheel-drive vehicles.

   Some four-wheel-drive vehicles are allowed in the unimproved portion of the park.

   Invalid: breaks rule 1

Exercise 8-19

1. A = athletes; B = baseball players;

   C = basketball players

   Some A are not B.

   Some B are not C.

   Some A are not C.

   Invalid: breaks rule 1

15. T = worlds identical to this one; B = the best of all possible worlds; M = mosquito-containing worlds

No B are M.

All T are M.

No T are B.

Valid

18. P = plastic furniture; C = cheap-looking furniture;

L = their new lawn furniture

All L are P.

All P are C.

All L are C.

Valid

21. D = people on the district tax roll; C = citizens; E = eligible voters

All D are C.

All E are C.

All D are E.

Invalid: breaks rule 2

24. C = people identical to Cobweb; L = liberals; T = officials who like to raise taxes

All C are L.

All L are T.

All C are T.

Valid

29. P = poll results; U = unnewsworthy items; I = items receiving considerable attention from the networks

All P are I.

Some P are U.

Some I are U.

Valid

30. E = people who understand that the earth goes around the sun; W = people who understand what causes winter and summer; A = American adults

All W are E.

Some A are not E.

Some A are not W.

Valid

32. N = the pornographic novels of "Madame Toulouse"; W = works with sexual depictions patently offensive to community standards and with no serious literary, artistic, political, or scientific value; O = works that can be banned as obscene since 1973

All O are W.

All N are W.

All N are O.

Invalid: breaks rule 2

Exercise 8-20

1. True. A syllogism with neither an A- nor an E-premise would have (I) two I-premises, which would violate rule 2; or (II) two O-premises, which would violate rule 1; or (III) an I-premise and an O-premise. Alternative (III) would require a negative conclusion by rule 1, and a negative conclusion would require premises that distribute at least two terms, the middle term and (by rule 3) at least one other. Because an I-premise and an O-premise collectively distribute only one term, alternative (III) won't work either.

4. True. An AIE syllogism whose middle term is the subject of the A-premise breaks exactly two rules. If the middle term is the predicate of the A premise, this syllogism breaks three rules.

Exercise 8-21

1. All B are C.

4. Cannot be done.

7. Some B are not C.

Exercise 8-22

1. b

4. a

7. Some political radicals are patriots (or the converse of this claim).

10. No conclusion validly follows.

Exercise 8-25

1. L = ladybugs; A = aphid eaters; G = good things to have in your garden

All L are A.

[All A are G.]

All L are G.

Valid

4. S = self-tapping screws; B = boons to the construction industry; P = things that make it possible to screw things together without drilling pilot holes

All S are P.

[All P are B.]

All S are B.

Valid

Chapter 9: Deductive Arguments II: Truth-Functional Logic

Test Yourself Answer

Since you've gone to the trouble to seek answers to some exercises, we'll throw in an answer to the test in the box on page 301. Two cards must be turned over, the one with the "e" and the one with the "3".

Exercise 9-1

1. Q → P
2. Q → P
3. P → Q
4. Q → P
5. (P → Q) & (Q → P)

Exercise 9-2

1. (P → Q) & R
2. P → (Q & R)
   Notice that the only difference between (1) and (2) is the location of the comma. But the symbolizations have two different truth tables, so moving the comma actually changes the meaning of the claim. And we'll bet you thought that commas were there only to tell you when to breathe when you read aloud.
5. P → (Q → R). Compare (5) with (3).
11. ~ C → S
12. ~ (C → S)
16. S → ~ C. Ordinarily, the word "but" indicates a conjunction, but in this case it is present only for emphasis—"only if" is the crucial truth-functional phrase.
20. ~ (F v S) or (~F & ~S). Notice that, when you "move the negation sign in," you have to change the wedge to an ampersand (or vice versa). Don't treat the negation sign as you would treat a minus sign in algebra class, or you'll wind up in trouble.

Exercise 9-3

1.

P	Q	R	(P → Q)	(P → Q) & R
T	T	T	T	T
T	T	F	T	F
T	F	T	F	F
T	F	F	F	F
F	T	T	T	T
F	T	F	T	F
F	F	T	T	T
F	F	F	T	F

2.

P	Q	R	(Q & R)	P → (Q & R)
T	T	T	T	T
T	T	F	F	F
T	F	T	F	F
T	F	F	F	F
F	T	T	T	T
F	T	F	F	T
F	F	T	F	T
F	F	F	F	T

5.

P	Q	R	(Q → R)	P → (Q → R)
T	T	T	T	T
T	T	F	F	F
T	F	T	T	T
T	F	F	T	T
F	T	T	T	T
F	T	F	F	T
F	F	T	T	T
F	F	F	T	T

11.

C	S	~C	~C → S
T	T	F	T
T	F	F	T
F	T	T	T
F	F	T	F

12.

C	S	C → S	~(C → S)
T	T	T	F
T	F	F	T
F	T	T	F
F	F	T	F

16.

C	S	~C	S → ~C
T	T	F	F
T	F	F	T
F	T	T	T
F	F	T	T

20.

F	S	F v S	~(F v S)
T	T	T	F
T	F	T	F
F	T	T	F
F	F	F	T

Since ~(F v S) is exactly equivalent to ~F & ~S, the latter can be substituted for the former in the preceding table and it will still be correct. Columns for ~F and for ~S would need to be added to make it complete.

Exercise 9-6

1. Modus ponens
4. Modus tollens
7. Affirming the consequent

Exercise 9-7

			(Premise)	(Premise)	(Conclusion)
1. Invalid:	P	Q	~ Q	P v ~ Q	~ P
	T	T	F	T	F
	T	F	T	T	F
	F	T	F	F	T
	F	F	T	T	T

(Row 2)

4. Invalid:

			(Conclusion)	(Premise)		(Premise)
P	**Q**	**R**	**(P → Q)**	**~(P → Q)**	**(Q → R)**	**P → (Q → R)**
T	T	T	T	F	T	T
T	T	F	T	F	F	F
T	F	T	F	T	T	T
T	F	F	F	T	T	T
F	T	T	T	F	T	T
F	T	F	T	F	F	T
F	F	T	T	F	T	T
F	F	F	T	F	T	T

(Row 4)

7. Invalid:

			(Premise)	(Premise)	(Conclusion)
P	**Q**	**R**	**~Q**	**P & R**	**(P & R) → Q**	**~P**
T	T	T	F	T	T	F
T	T	F	F	F	T	F
T	F	T	T	T	F	F
T	F	F	T	F	T	F
F	T	T	F	F	T	T
F	T	F	F	F	T	T
F	F	T	T	F	T	T
F	F	F	T	F	T	T

(Row 4)

Exercise 9-8

We've used the short truth-table method to demonstrate invalidity.

1. Valid. There is no row in the argument's table that makes the premises all T and the conclusion F.

2. Invalid. There are two rows that make the premises T and the conclusion F. (Such rows are sometimes called "counterexamples" to the argument.) Here they are:

L	**W**	**S**	**P**
T	F	F	F
T	T	F	F

(Remember: You need to come up with only *one* of these rows to prove the argument invalid.)

3. Invalid. There are two rows that make the premises T and the conclusion F:

M	**P**	**R**	**F**	**G**
T	T	F	F	T
T	T	F	T	F

4. Invalid. There are three rows that make the premises true and the conclusion F:

D	**G**	**H**	**P**	**M**
F	T	T	T	T
F	T	F	T	T
F	T	F	F	T

5. Invalid. There are two rows that make the premises T and the conclusion F:

R	**S**	**B**	**T**	**E**
T	T	F	F	F
F	F	T	F	F

Exercise 9-9

1. Chain argument
2. Disjunctive argument
3. Constructive dilemma
4. Modus tollens
5. Destructive dilemma

Exercise 9-10

1. 1. R → P   (Premise)
   2. Q → R   (Premise) /∴ Q → P
   3. Q → P   1, 2, CA

4. 1. P → Q   (Premise)
   2. ~P → S   (Premise)
   3. ~Q   (Premise) /∴ S
   4. ~P   1, 3, MT
   5. S   2, 4, MP

7. 1. ~S   (Premise)
   2. (P & Q) → R   (Premise)
   3. R → S   (Premise) /∴ ~(P & Q)
   4. ~R   1, 3, MT
   5. ~(P & Q)   4, 2, MT

10. 1. (T ∨ M) → ~Q   (Premise)
    2. (P → Q) & (R → S)   (Premise)
    3. T   (Premise) /∴ ~P
    4. T ∨ M   3, ADD
    5. ~Q   1, 4, MP
    6. P → Q   2, SIM
    7. ~P   5, 6, MT

Exercise 9-11

1. 4. 1, 3, CA
   5. 2, CONTR
   6. 4, 5, CA

4. 4. 3, CONTR
   5. 2, 4, MP
   6. 2, 5, CONJ
   7. 1, 6, MP

Exercise 9-12

There is usually more than one way to do these.

1. 1. P & R   (Premise)
   2. P → R   (Premise) / ∴ R
   3. P   1, SIM
   4. R   2, 3, MP

2. 1. R → S   (Premise)
   2. ~P ∨ R   (Premise) /∴ P → S
   3. P → R   2, IMPL
   4. P → S   1, 3, CA

4. 1. ~P ∨ (~Q ∨ R)   (Premise)
   2. P   (Premise) /∴ Q → R
   3. P → (~Q ∨ R)   1, IMPL

4.	~Q ∨ R	2, 3, MP
5.	Q → R	4, IMPL
8. 1.	~ Q & (~ S & ~ T)	(Premise)
2.	P → (Q ∨ S)	(Premise) / ∴ ~ P
3.	(~ Q & ~ S) & ~ T	1, ASSOC
4.	~ Q & ~ S	3, SIM
5.	~(Q ∨ S)	4, DEM
6.	~ P	2, 5, MT

Exercise 9-13

1. 1.	P → R	(Premise)
2.	R → Q	(Premise) / ∴ ~P ∨ Q
3.	P → Q	1, 2, CA
4.	~P ∨ Q	3, IMPL
4. 1.	P ∨ (Q & R)	(Premise)
2.	(P ∨ Q) → S	(Premise) / ∴ S
3.	(P ∨ Q) & (P ∨ R)	1, DIST
4.	P ∨ Q	3, SIM
5.	S	2, 4, MP
7. 1.	(M ∨ R) & P	(Premise)
2.	~ S → ~ P	(Premise)
3.	S → ~ M	(Premise) / ∴ R
4.	P → S	2, CONTR
5.	P	1, SIM
6.	S	4, 5, MP
7.	~ M	3, 6, MP
8.	M ∨ R	1, SIM
9.	R	7, 8, DA
10. 1.	P ∨ (R & Q)	(Premise)
2.	R → ~ P	(Premise)
3.	Q → T	(Premise) / ∴ R → T
4.	(P ∨ R) & (P ∨ Q)	1, DIST
5.	P ∨ Q	4, SIM
6.	~ P → Q	5, DN/IMPL
7.	R → Q	2, 6, CA
8.	R → T	3, 7, CA

Exercise 9-14

1. D → ~ B
4. B → ~ D
7. C → (B & ~ D)

Exercise 9-15

1. Equivalent to (b)
4. Equivalent to (c)
7. Equivalent to (c)

Exercise 9-16

1. 1.	P	(Premise)
2.	Q & R	(Premise)
3.	(Q & P) → S	(Premise) / ∴ S
4.	Q	2, SIM
5.	Q & P	1, 4, CONJ
6.	S	3, 5, MP

4. 1.	P ∨ Q	(Premise)
2.	(Q ∨ U) → (P → T)	(Premise)
3.	~ P	(Premise)
4.	(~P ∨ R) → (Q → S)	(Premise) / ∴ T ∨ S
5.	Q	1, 3, DA
6.	Q ∨ U	5, ADD
7.	P → T	2, 6, MP
8.	~P ∨ R	3, ADD
9.	Q → S	4, 8, MP
10.	T ∨ S	1, 7, 9, CD
7. 1.	P → Q	(Premise) / ∴ P → (Q ∨ R)
2.	~P ∨ Q	1, IMPL
3.	(~P ∨ Q) ∨ R	2, ADD
4.	~P ∨ (Q ∨ R)	3, ASSOC
5.	P → (Q ∨ R)	4, IMPL
10. 1.	(S → Q) → ~ R	(Premise)
2.	(P → Q) → R	(Premise) / ∴ ~ Q
3.	~ R → ~ (P → Q)	2, CONTR
4.	(S → Q) → ~ (P → Q)	1, 3, CA
5.	~ (S → Q) ∨ ~ (P → Q)	4, IMPL
6.	~ (~S ∨ Q) ∨ ~(~P ∨ Q)	5, IMPL (twice)
7.	(S & ~Q) ∨ (P & ~Q)	6, DEM/DN (twice)
8.	(~Q & S) ∨ (~Q & P)	7, COM
9.	~Q & (S ∨ P)	7, DIST
10.	~Q	8, SIM

Exercise 9-17

1. 1.	P → Q	(Premise)
2.	P → R	(Premise) / ∴ P → (Q & R)
⌐3.	P	CP Premise
4.	Q	1, 3, MP
5.	R	2, 3, MP
⌐6.	Q & R	4, 5, CONJ
7.	P → (Q & R)	3–6, CP
4. 1.	P → (Q ∨ R)	(Premise)
2.	T → (S & ~ R)	(Premise) / ∴ (P & T) → Q
⌐3.	P & T	CP Premise
4.	P	3, SIM
5.	T	3, SIM
6.	Q ∨ R	1, 4, MP
7.	S & ~ R	2, 5, MP
8.	~ R	7, SIM
⌐9.	Q	6, 8, DA
10.	(P & T) → Q	3–9, CP
7. 1.	P ∨ (Q & R)	(Premise)
2.	T → ~ (P ∨ U)	(Premise)
3.	S → (Q → ~ R)	(Premise) / ∴ ~ S ∨ ~ T
⌐4.	S	CP Premise
5.	Q → ~ R	3, 4, MP
6.	~ Q ∨ ~ R	5, IMPL
7.	~ (Q & R)	6, DEM
8.	P	1, 7, DA
9.	P ∨ U	8, ADD
10.	~~ (P ∨ U)	9, DN
⌐11.	~ T	2, 10, MT
12.	S → ~ T	4–11, CP
13.	~ S ∨ ~ T	12, IMPL

10.

1.	(P & Q) ∨ R	(Premise)
2.	~R ∨ Q	(Premise) /∴ P → Q
③	P	CP Premise
④	~ Q	CP Premise
5.	~ R	2, 4, DA
6.	P & Q	1, 5, DA
7.	Q	6, SIM
8.	~ Q → Q	4–7, CP
9.	Q ∨ Q	8, IMPL
10.	Q	9, TAUT
11.	P → Q	3–10, CP

Exercise 9-18

1. C → ~ S
    ~ L → S
    ─────────
    C → L
    Valid

4. ~ M ∨ C
    ~ M → ~ K
    C ∨ H
    T → ~ H
    ─────────
    T → K
    Invalid

7. C ∨ S
    S → E
    C → R
    ─────────
    R ∨ E
    Valid

10. C → ~L
    (E → (~C → ~T)) & E
    ─────────
    L → ~T
    Valid

13. S → ~ F
    ~S → ~ T
    T
    ─────────
    ~F
    Valid

Chapter 10: Thinking Critically About Inductive Reasoning

Exercise 10-1

1. This belongs in the same group as number 10.
4. This belongs in a different group.
7. This belongs in the same group as item 4.
10. This belongs in the same group as item 1.

Exercise 10-2

1. inductive generalization from a sample
4. inductive generalization from a sample
7. inductive generalization from a sample
10. statistical syllogism

Exercise 10-3

1. a
4. b
7. a
10. a

Exercise 10-4

1. Most (all, nearly all, etc.) Otterhounds don't fetch.
4. Therefore most likely (probably, etc.) Dr. Walker is a liberal.
7. York is a member of the NRA.
10. Chabot Gap is a small town.

Exercise 10-5

1. Most professional dancers are pretty athletic.
4. Jim is a kid from around here.
7. It's hot now.
10. Mitt probably won't be a very good president.

Exercise 10-6

1. Sample: the ten Disney movies I have seen. Population: Disney movies. Attribute of interest: being non–violent.
4. Sample: my past experience at Columbus State. Population: all my experiences at Columbus State. Attribute of interest: being fun.
7. Sample: Costco store-brand coffee. Population: Costco store-brand products. Attribute of interest: being as good as name-brand products.
10. Sample: these McDonald's fries. Population: McDonald's fries. Attribute of interest: being too salty.

Exercise 10-7

1. Sample: this quart of milk. Population: things for sale at this joint. Attribute of interest: being overpriced.

4. Sample: life insurance salespeople I know. Population: life insurance salespeople. Attribute of interest: trying to sell you stuff you don't need.

7. Sample: my performance on the first test. Population: my performance on assessments in this class. Attribute of interest: being well done.

10. Sample: the English class I took. Population: English classes. Attribute of interest: being boring.

Exercise 10-8

Movies starring Meryl Steep, episodes of *Survivor*, television sitcoms, movies rated PG, movies.

Exercise 10-9

Olympic shot–putters, National Football League referees, major league baseball players, professional athletes, physically fit people.

Exercise 10-10

Cowboys who are teachers, cowboys, teachers, Democrats, people.

Exercise 10-11

1. We'd speculate that a disproportionate number of Lexus drivers (a) own swimming pools (b) have a college degree (c) are over 40 years old, and (d) think of themselves as knowledgeable about political matters.

4. The population of people who are susceptible to poison ivy or oak might perhaps include a disproportionate number of people (a) who are fair-skinned, and (b) who are not elderly. Dog owners and hikers are more apt to have cases of poison oak or ivy, although they wouldn't necessarily be more susceptible to the plight.

7. We'd bet that a disproportionate number of nearsighted people (a) like to read (b) own more than a single pair of vision glasses (c) have family members who are nearsighted, and (d) suffer from glaucoma.

10. Those who watch reality shows, we conjecture, are more likely than the general population to (a) be under 50 (b) not have PhDs, (c) not be in the top 20% of income recipients, and (d) be impressed by expensive cars and clothes.

Exercise 10-12

1. 1
4. 1
7. 4
10. 2

Exercise 10-13

4. Given this supposition, the speaker should be more confident that most Ohio State students say they believe in God.

Exercise 10-14

1. The six students who turned in written evaluations.

4. Yes. The sample contains a disproportionate number of individuals who feel strongly enough about Ludlum to write something.

7. Poor reasoning. The sample is small and under-represents those who to not have strong enough feelings about Ludlum to write.

Exercise 10-15

1. a
4. a
7. b
10. a

Exercise 10-16

1. Analogues: rats and humans. Attribute of interest: being subject to causation of cancer by saccharin. Rats are said to have that attribute; humans are predicted to have it.

4. Analogues: Windex and this ant poison. Attribute of interest: being a window cleanser. Windex is said to have the attribute; this ant poison is predicted to have it.

7. Analogues: December and January's heating bills. Attribute of interest: being high. December's bill is said to have the attribute; January's bill is predicted to have it.

10. Analogues: abortion and capital punishment. Attribute of interest: involving the killing of a live person. Abortion is said to have this attribute; capital punishment is "predicted" to have it.

Exercise 10-17

1. Analogues: iPods and iPads. Attribute of interest: being easy to use. iPods are said to have the attribute; iPads are predicted to have it.

4. Analogues: Odwalla carrot juice and Odwalla orange juice. Attribute of interest: tasting moldy. Odwalla carrot juice is said to have the attribute; Odwalla orange juice is predicted to have it.

7. Analogues: mandatory auto insurance and mandatory health insurance. Attribute of interest: being a good thing. Mandatory auto insurance is said to have the attribute; mandatory health insurance is predicted to have it.

10. Analogues: *Dancing with the Stars* and *So You Think You Can Dance*. Attribute of interest: being something you don't like. The former is said to have the attribute; the latter is predicted to have it.

Exercise 10-18

Football and rugby; football and basketball; football and tennis; football and bowling; football and golf; football and chess.

Exercise 10-20

1. This is stronger than a parallel argument that uses "Neptune" rather than "Mars" as an analogue.

4. This is stronger than a parallel argument that uses "Muammar Gadaffi" rather than "Saddam Hussein" as an analogue.

7. This is stronger than a parallel argument that uses "Ann's rubber plant" rather than "her dog" as an analogue.

10. This is stronger than a parallel argument that employs a non-Scandinavian country as an analogue.

Exercise 10-22

1. Increasing the diversity of weather conditions in the previous rides makes it more likely that this year's weather will be similar to the weather on an occasion on which Cliff did not finish the race. This should make Cliff even more confident that this year's result will be the same as in previous years.

4. If Cliff ends up with a different bike, it would introduce a difference between the analogues, which should make him less confident this year's result will be the same as in previous years. If he ends up with the same bike, he should be more confident that this year's result will be the same as in previous years.

7. This supposition should make Cliff less confident this year will be the same as previous years, because it introduces a difference between the analogues.

8. The new supposition mentioned in 7 introduces a difference between the analogues, meaning that Cliff should be less confident this year will have the same result as previous years. He might also arrive at that finding by considering his past experience *outside* the Fourth of July ride. If his past experience is that he can go farther on flat ground, he could reason analogically that he will be more apt to finish this year's ride if it too is on flat ground.

9. The new supposition increases the diversification of of the past years' rides, making it more likely this year's ride will replicate an earlier condition in which Cliff didn't finish. This should increase his confidence this year's result will be the same as in previous years.

Exercise 10-23

1. The new supposition introduces a difference between past crops and this crop, so it weakens the argument. Kirk should be less confident the new crop will be like the previous crops.

4. The supposition here is that this year will probably be different from previous years. This makes it less likely this year's crop will be like previous crops.

7. The new supposition introduces what is probably an irrelevant difference between this year's crop and the previous crops and has no bearing on the strength of the argument.

10. The new supposition introduces a potentially relevant difference between the analogues, so it weakens the argument and makes it less likely this year's crop will be like previous crops.

Exercise 10-24

1. This is a leading question. It portrays Republicans as being against environmental safeguards, and promotes opposition to Republican plans.

4. The question suggests that the lawsuits are without merit and run up health care costs.

7. Question offers a false alternative and promotes sympathy for raising taxes.

10. Question promotes a response favoring background checks, by calling them reasonable while referring to assault weapons as deadly.

Exercise 10-25

Multiple answers to these questions are possible, because there are many ways of expressing "confidence level" and "error margin" in English. Here are suggestions for appropriate phrasing.

1. Therefore, it isn't unusual for Miami University students to be members of Webkinz.

4. Therefore, he shouldn't be too surprised if he likes some of his future business professors but not others.

7. Therefore, it wouldn't be terribly surprising if only a minority of York students watch PBS.

10. It isn't unlikely, therefore, that she likes Christmas, too.

Exercise 10-26

1. We'd say, in order of decreasing confidence level: d, f, b, c, e, a.

Exercise 10-27

1. Confidence level: "100%." Too high.

4. Confidence level: "There is a small chance." Too low; this is overly cautious.

Exercise 10-28

1. There are no difficulties involved in identifying what is in the sample or the population, and the speaker will know well enough when a test has the attribute of interest.

4. The sample is the speaker's husband; the population is men. Both of these are clear. However, the attribute of interest, "cannot tolerate stress" is excessively vague.

7. The sample consists of the speaker's past visit or visits to Minneapolis in the summer; the population is summertime visits to Minneapolis. Neither of these is vague. The attribute of interest, while subjective, isn't vague.

10. Members of the sample and population are identifiable; and whether someone possesses the attribute of interest is also easily determined.

Exercise 10-29

1. A sampling frame for "Denver residents" might be people who reside at an address within the Denver city limits. A sampling frame for people who "watch *The Bachelorette*" might be people who say they "regularly watch *The Bachelorette*."

4. A sampling frame for "country songs" might be songs listed on the Billboard "Country Songs" chart for such and such a date. A sampling frame for songs "about lost love" might be songs that a specified individual, such as a country recording artist, thinks are about lost love.

Exercise 10-30

1. The speaker overestimates the strength of the argument based on a small sample, so it is a case of hasty generalization. Since the story is presented as a story, it qualifies as committing the fallacy of anecdotal evidence.

4. No problem.

7. Unless Toadstool teaches a single small class this qualifies as "hasty generalization." It also over-represents students who have a reason to dislike Toadstool. However, we are reserving the title "biased generalization" for biased samples that are larger.

10. Assuming this is not a really small sample (which would make it hasty generalization), it qualifies as an example of a biased generalization.

Exercise 10-31

1. The speaker is generalizing from a sample of one, and presents the argument in story form so it is best categorized as committing the fallacy of anecdotal evidence.

4. Hasty generalization

7. This is generalizing from a sample of one, but the population is relatively undiversified and you don't need too many friends whose Zenon plasma TVs break down to avoid the brand. Nevertheless, "it's a bad brand" expresses a confidence level that is too high

10. Hasty generalization

Chapter 11: Causal Explanation

Exercise 11-1

1. Causal claim
4. Causal claim
7. Causal claim, although a very vague one
10. Causal claim
13. Causal claim
16. Not a causal claim

Exercise 11-2

1. Effect: cat is not eating; cause: cat is eating mice

4. Effect: the little guy's not dehydrating; cause: giving him more water

7. Effect: that people cannot detect their own bad breath; cause: becoming used to the odor

10. Effect: a savings to the state in court expenses; cause: judges' not processing shoplifting, trespassing, and small-claims charges

Exercise 11-3

1. This belongs in one group.
4. This belongs in same group as item 1.
7. This belongs in same group as items 1 and 4.
10. This belongs in same group as 1, 4, and 7, although its being late could reasonably be offered as evidence that the bars are closed.

Exercise 11-4

1. Explanation
4. Explanation
7. Argument
10. Explanation

Exercise 11-5

1. Argument
4. Argument
7. Argument
10. Explanation

Exercise 11-6

1. This belongs in one group.
4. This belongs in the same group as item 1.
7. This belongs in a different group from items 1 and 4.
10. This belongs in the same group as items 1 and 4.

Exercise 11-7

1. Physical causal explanation
4. Behavioral causal explanation
7. Physical causal explanation
10. Physical causal explanation

Exercise 12-3

1. Moral value judgment
4. Moral value judgment
7. Not a moral value judgment
10. Moral value judgment

Exercise 12-4

1. A
4. B
7. B
10. A

Exercise 12-5

2. People ought to keep their promises.
5. A mayor who takes bribes should resign.
7. Anyone who commits a third felony should automatically go to prison for twenty-five years.
8. Whatever is unnatural is wrong and should be avoided.

Exercise 12-6

1. B
4. A
7. B, the part about whether he should home-school his kids
9. B

Exercise 12-7

1. A
4. B (probably)
7. B
10. B

Exercise 12-8

1. Tory is being consistent in that what he is proposing for *both* sexes is that members of both should have the right to marry members of the *other* sex.

2. To avoid inconsistency, Shelley must be able to identify characteristics of art and music students, athletes, and children of alumni—for whom she believes the special admissions program is acceptable—and show that, aside from women and minority students who happen also to be in one of the listed categories, such students do not have these characteristics. Furthermore, the characteristics she identifies must be relevant to the issue of whether an individual should be admitted into the university. It may well be possible to identify the characteristics called for. (Remember that consistency is a necessary condition for a correct position, but not a sufficient one.)

3. Marin could be consistent only if he could show that the process of abortion involves killing and capital punishment does not. Because this is impossible—capital punishment clearly does involve killing—he is inconsistent. However, Marin's inconsistency is the result of his blanket claim that *all* killing is wrong. He could make a consistent case if he were to maintain only that the killing of *innocent* people is wrong, and that abortion involves killing innocent people but capital punishment does not. There is another approach: Marin could argue that only *state-mandated* killing (which would include capital punishment but not abortion) is permissible. (Each of these last claims would require strong arguments.)

8. To avoid inconsistency, Harold would have to identify a relevant difference between the discrimination law and the marijuana law. In fact, there is one fairly obvious one to which he can appeal: The former has been declared contrary to the state constitution; the latter has not been alleged to be contrary to any constitution. So, Harold may object to the failure to implement the latter, even if it does conflict with federal drug laws—after all, if the law has not been found unconstitutional, shouldn't the will of the voters prevail? (It is a separate matter, of course, whether he can build a strong argument in the case of the marijuana law.)

Exercise 12-11

1. The harm principle: Shoplifting harms those from whom one steals.

2. The harm principle: Forgery tends to harm others.

4. We think the offense principle is the most relevant, because the practice in question is found highly offensive by most people (at least we believe—and hope—so). But one might also include the harm principle, because spitting in public can spread disease-causing organisms.

6. Legal moralism, because many people find adultery immoral; and, to a lesser extent, both the harm principle and legal paternalism, because adultery can increase the spread of sexually transmitted diseases.

10. The offense principle

Exercise 12-13

Comment: In fact, a majority of the Supreme Court agreed with Justice O'Connor and sentenced John Angus Smith to thirty years in prison. Your authors take Justice Scalia's side and believe the Court's majority made a serious mistake.

Exercise 12-14

1. a. Principle 4
   b. Principle 2
   Compatible

4. a. Principle 5
   b. Principle 2
   Compatible

Exercise 12-15

1. Relevant on Principle 7
4. Relevant on Principle 1
7. Relevant on Principle 3

Exercise 12-16

Principle 1: Asuka's picture does not teach us anything, for no chimp can distinguish between truth and falsity; it is a curiosity rather than a work of art.

Principle 2: By looking at Asuka's very symbolic paintings, we are compelled to accept her vision of a world in which discourse is by sight rather than by sound.

Principle 3: Perhaps the most far-reaching impact of Asuka's art is its revelation of the horrors of encaging chimps; surely beings who can reach these heights of sublimely abstract expression should not see the world through iron bars.

Principle 4: Dear Zookeeper: Please encourage Asuka to keep painting, as the vibrant colors and intense brushstrokes of her canvases fill all of us with delight.

Principle 5: I never thought I would wish to feel like an ape, but Asuka's art made me appreciate how chimps enjoy perceiving us humans as chumps.

Principle 6: This is not art, for no ape's product can convey the highest, most valuable, human states of mind.

Principle 7: Whether by the hand of ape or man, that the canvases attributed to Asuka show lovely shapes and colors is indisputable.

Principle 8: What is art is simply what pleases a person's taste, and Asuka obviously finds painting tasty, as she tends to eat the paint.

Exercise 12-17

1. a
4. b
7. b

Credits

Index